VITAL RECORDS

OF

SCITUATE

MASSACHUSETTS

TO THE YEAR 1850

VOLUME I—BIRTHS

Southern Historical Press, Inc.
Greenville, South Carolina

This volume was reproduced
from a personal copy located in
the Publishers private library

All rights reserved. No part of this publication may be reproduced,
stored in a retrieval system, transmitted in any form, posted
on the web in any form or by any means without the
prior written permission of the publisher.

Please direct all correspondence and book orders to:
SOUTHERN HISTORICAL PRESS, Inc.
1071 Park West Blvd.
Greenville, SC 29611

Published 1909 by:
 The New England Historical & Genealogical Society
ISBN #978-1-63914-629-1
Printed in the United States of America

THE TOWN OF SCITUATE, Plymouth County, was established July 1, 1633, from common land.

March 7, 1643, bounds were established.

June 14, 1727, a part of Scituate was included in the new town of Hanover.

November 8, 1782, bounds between Scituate and Marshfield were established.

March 10, 1788, a part of Scituate was annexed to Marshfield.

June 14, 1823, a part of Scituate was annexed to Cohasset.

March 20, 1840, bounds between Scituate and Cohasset were established and a part of each town was annexed to the other town.

February 14, 1849, a part of Scituate was established as South Scituate.

Population by Census: 1765 (Prov.), 2488; 1776 (Prov.), 2672; 1790 (U.S.), 2856; 1800 (U.S.), 2728; 1810 (U.S.), 2969; 1820 (U.S.), 3305; 1830 (U.S.), 3468; 1840 (U.S.), 3886; 1850 (U.S.), 2149; 1855 (State), 2269; 1860 (U.S.), 2227; 1865 (State), 2269; 1870 (U.S.), 2350; 1875 (State), 2463; 1880 (U.S.), 2466; 1885 (State), 2350; 1890 (U.S.), 2318; 1895 (State), 2246; 1900 (U.S.), 2470; 1905 (State), 2597.

EXPLANATIONS

1. WHEN places other than Scituate and Massachusetts are named in the original records, they are given in the printed copy.

2. In all records the original spelling is followed.

3. The various spellings of a name should be examined, as items about the same family or individual might be found under different spellings.

4. Marriages and intentions of marriages are printed under the names of both parties. When both the marriage and intention of marriage are recorded, only the marriage record is printed; and where a marriage appears without the intention recorded, it is designated with an asterisk.

5. Additional information which does not appear in the original text of an item, i.e. any explanation, query, inference, or difference shown in other entries of the record, is bracketed. Parentheses are used to show the difference in the spelling of a name in the same entry, to indicate the maiden name of a wife, to enclose an imperfect portion of the original text, and to separate clauses in the original text — such as the birthplace of a parent in late records.

ABBREVIATIONS

a. — age
abt. — about
b. — born
ch. — child
chn. — children
Co. — county
c.r.1. — church record, First Parish, and records from Rev. John Lothrop's original manuscript
c.r.2. — church record, Second Church of Scituate, now the First Unitarian Church of Norwell
c.r.3. — church record, Trinitarian Congregational Church
c.r.4. — records of the Society of Friends of Pembroke, now in the possession of the Society at New Bedford
d. — daughter; died; day
Dea. — deacon
dup. — duplicate entry
g.r.1. — gravestone record, First Parish Cemetery, Meeting House Lane, now Prospect Street, Scituate Harbor
g.r.2. — gravestone record, Groveland Cemetery, North Scituate
g.r.3. — gravestone record, Judge Cushing's Cemetery, Greenbush
g.r.4. — gravestone record, Hatch Burying Ground, Greenbush
g.r.5. — gravestone record, James Burying Ground, Greenbush
g.r.6. — gravestone record, Union Street Cemetery, Scituate Harbor
g.r.7. — gravestone record, Fairview Cemetery, Scituate Centre
g.r.8. — gravestone record, Mt. Hope Cemetery, North Scituate
g.r.9. — gravestone record, Town Burying Ground, Scituate Centre

G.R.10. — gravestone record, Catholic Cemetery, Scituate Harbor
G.R.11. — gravestone record, Kilborn Merritt Cemetery, North Scituate
G.R.12. — gravestone record, Clapp Burying Ground, Greenbush
G.R.13. — gravestone record, Second Church Cemetery, Norwell
G.R.14. — gravestone record, South Parish Cemetery, Norwell
G.R.15. — gravestone record, Church Hill Cemetery, Norwell
G.R.16. — gravestone record, Stockbridge Cemetery, Norwell
G.R.17. — gravestone record, Bowker Street Cemetery, Norwell
G.R.18. — gravestone record, Damon Cemetery, Norwell
G.R.19. — gravestone record, Washington Street Cemetery, Norwell
G.R.20. — gravestone record, Quaker Cemetery, Norwell
G.R.21. — gravestone record, Otis Cemetery, Norwell
h. — husband
hrs. — hours
inf. — infant
int. — publishment of intention of marriage
Jr. — junior
m. — married; month
min. — minutes
P.C.R. — Plymouth County Record
P.R.1. — private record, from Little family Bible, now in the possession of Mrs. Edwin O. Stoddard of North Scituate
P.R.2. — private record, from Merritt family Bible, now in the possession of Mrs. Sarah Lewis of West Duxbury
P.R.3. — private record, from Kent Account Book, now in the possession of Frank Keene of East Pembroke
P.R.4. — private record, from Brooks-Delano Bible, now in the possession of Mrs. Arthur L. Power of Norwell

P.R.5. — private record, from Charles Foster's Register, now in the possession of Mrs. Arthur L. Power of Norwell

P.R.6. — private record, from Litchfield family Bible, now in the possession of Parker R. Litchfield of Medford

P.R.7. — private record, from Wellington family Bible, now in the possession of James E. Wellington of Medford

P.R.8. — private record, from sheet of paper of Copeland family in Eells family Bible, now in the possession of Miss Mary Smith Clark of Medford

P.R.9. — private record, from Clapp family Bible, now in the possession of Alfred Clapp of North Scituate

P.R.10. — private record, from Bailey Family Chart, now in the possession of Miss Sarah Tilden Bailey of North Scituate

P.R.11. — private record, from Bailey family Bible, now in the possession of Miss Sarah Tilden Bailey of North Scituate

P.R.12. — private record, from Barnes family Bible, now in the possession of Israel Barnes of North Scituate

P.R.13. — private record, from Clapp family Bible, now in the possession of Mrs. Mandana Morris of North Scituate

P.R.14. — private record, from a Bible, now in the possession of Mrs. Charles H. Killam of Assinippi

P.R.15. — private record, from private papers, now in the possession of Mrs. Charles H. Killam of Assinippi

P.R.16. — private record, from Glines family Bible, now in the possession of Henry H. Sylvester of North Scituate

P.R.17. — private record, from Jenkins family record, now in the possession of Mrs. Julia E. Fitts of Greenbush

P.R.18. — private record, from Litchfield family Bible, now in the possession of Henry T. Bailey

P.R.19. — private record, from Merritt family Bible, now in the possession of Mrs. David H. Stoddard of North Hanover

P.R.20. — private record, from Ripley family record, now in the possession of Miss Sarah Tilden Bailey of North Scituate

P.R.21. — private record, from Studley family Bible, now in the possession of Miss Deborah Nash Studley of North Scituate

P.R.22. — private record, from Sylvester family Bible, now in the possession of Henry H. Sylvester of North Scituate

P.R.23. — private record, from Stoddard family Bible, now in the possession of Mrs. David H. Stoddard of North Hanover

P.R.24. — private record, from Torrey family Bible, now in the possession of George Otis Torrey of Norwell

P.R.25. — private record, from Bible of Abial Turner, now in the possession of George C. Turner of Norwell

P.R.26. — private record, from Vinal family Bible, now in the possession of Mrs. Eliza (Vinal) Wade of Greenbush

P.R.27. — private record, from family records now in the possession of Mrs. Sarah Tilden Bailey of North Scituate

P.R.28. — private record, from Wade family Bible, now in the possession of Jetson Wade of Greenbush

P.R.29. — private record, from Diary of Dea. Israel Litchfield, now in the possession of the New England Historic Genealogical Society of Boston

rec. — recorded

s. — son

Sr. — senior

w. — wife; week

wid. — widow

widr. — widower

y. — year

SCITUATE BIRTHS

SCITUATE BIRTHS

To the year 1850

ADAMS (see Addams), Margaret, d. James, bp. Mar. 18, 1654. C.R.2.
Mary, d. John of Marishfield, great grandchild Widdow James, bp. Dec. 14, 1656. C.R.2.

ADDAMS (see Adams), Anne, d. James, Apr. 18, 1649. [Anna Adams, C.R.2.]
Mary, d. James, Jan. 27, 1653. [Adams, C.R.2.]
Richard, s. James, Apr. 19, 1651. [Adams, C.R.2.]
William, s. James, May 16, 1647. [Adams, C.R.2.]

ADVERD, Elizabeth, d. Henry, bp. June 29, 1651. C.R.2.
Experience, d. Henry, bp. Apr. 18, 1652. C.R.2.
Mary, d. Henry, bp. June 29, 1651. C.R.2.
Sarah, d. Henry, bp. June 29, 1651. C.R.2.

ALBEE, Dianthe, d. Amos and Judith, Sept. 14, 1803.
Judith C. [———], w. Amos, —— [1784]. G.R.2.

ALDEN (see Aldin), Isaiah, s. Isaiah and Mercy W., Sept. 1, 1819.
John, s. John and Hannah of Duxborough, bp. Dec. 10, 1710. C.R.2.
Lydia, d. Isaiah and Mercy W., Feb. 5, 1830. [w. Allen Merritt, G.R.2.]
Mercy, d. Isaiah and Mercy W., Apr. 20, 1821.
Mercy, ch. Isaiah and Mercy, bp. Oct. 7, 1832. C.R.1.
Mercy W. [———], w. Isaiah [Jan. —, 1799]. G.R.6.
Thomas, s. Isaiah and Mercy W., Aug. 17, 1827.
Thomas, ch. Isaiah and Mercy, bp. Oct. 7, 1832. C.R.1.

ALDIN (see Alden), Samuel, s. John and Hannah of Duxborouhg, bp. May 17, 1713. C.R.2.

ALLEN (see Alin), Cornelia Maria, d. George M. and Hannah E., July 10, 1832.

ALLEN, Florence T. [dup. Thomas], d. William P., merchant (b. Pembroke), and Abigail B., Dec. 4, 1848.
Geo[rge] M. [h. Hannah E.], ——, 1802. G.R.6.
George Otis, s. George M. and Hannah E., May 17, 1838.
Hannah Deane, d. George M. and Hannah E., Feb. 25, 1829.
Hannah E. [——], w. Geo[rge] M., ——, 1807. G.R.6.
James, s. W[illia]m P., merchant, and Abby [dup. Abigail] B., Apr. 7, 1845.
James O., ——, 1846. G.R.6.
John Ensign, s. George M. and Hannah E., Sep[t]. 15, 1835. [——, 1836, G.R.6.]
Joseph (see —— Allen).
Josiah Hoten, s. Josiah and Sarah N., June 11, 1825.
Mary Louisa, ch. William P. and Abigail B., Apr. —, 1841.
Sarah Byrun, ch. William P. and Abigail B., Feb. 12, 1839.
Sarah Curtis, d. Josiah and Sarah N., Feb. 8, 1828.
William Henry, ch. William P. and Abigail B., Aug. 18, 1843.
William P., ——, 1815. G.R.6.
——, s. George M. and Hannah E., Mar. 24, 1831. [Joseph, G.R.6.]

ALIN (see Allen), Jeane, d. John, May 28, 1669.

AMES, —— [——], w. Tilden, —— [1798]. C.R.1.

ANDERSON, Alexander, s. George and Jane, July 6, 1818.
Alexander Brooks, ch. Alexander and Caroline C., Dec. 10, 1843.
George, s. George and Jane, Apr. 19, 1813.
George F., s. Alexander, sailor, and Caroline L. [dup. C.], Aug. 28, 1846.
Jane Caroline, ch. Alexander and Caroline C., Apr. 30, 1840.
Jane Doane, d. George and Jane, May 19, 1815.
Mary Ball, d. George and Jane, Aug. 7, 1821.
——, ch. Alexander and Caroline C., June —, 1842.
——, s. Alexander, master mariner, and Caroline [dup. adds C.], Nov. 20, 1848.

ANNIBALL, Deborah, d. ——, bp. May 7, 1637. C.R.1.

ANTOINE, Frances M., Feb. 2, 1827. G.R.10.
Manuel, Jan. 20, 1810. G.R.10.

BADCOCKE (see Badcoke), Calub, s. Jonathan, bp. Oct. 31, 1680. C.R.2.
Mary, d. Jonathan, bp. June 26, 1681. C.R.2.

BADCOKE (see Badcocke), Mercy, d. Jonathan, bp. Sept. 5, 1680. C.R.2.

BAILEY (see Baily, Bayle, Bayley, Baylie, Bayly), Abigail, d. Amasa, bp. June 10, 1753. C.R.1.
Abigail [———], w. Israel, ——— [1767]. G.R.6.
Abigail [? m.], ———, 1810. G.R.2.
Abner, s. Abner, bp. Aug. 4, 1776. C.R.1.
Adams, s. Adams and Mary, Apr. 28, 1789.
Almira, s. Israel and Abigail, Sept. 8, 1805.
Amasa, s. Amasa, bp. Oct. 29, 1749. C.R.1.
Amasa, s. Job and Martha, May 19, 1789.
Amasa, s. Martha, bp. Dec. 15, 1793. C.R.1.
Amasa, s. Amasa and Sally F., Aug. 7, 1822.
Ann Jane, d. Whitman and Patience V., ———, 1823, in Quincy.
Anna, d. Paul, bp. Oct. 4, 1772. C.R.1.
Aseneth, twin d. Isreal and Abigail, Aug. 6, 1803.
Bathsheba, d. Amasa, bp. Aug. 11, 1759. C.R.1.
Bathsheba, d. Benja[min], bp. Oct. 21, 1759. C.R.1.
Beckey, d. Eben[eze]r and Deborah, Jan. 15, 1799.
Becky, d. Abner, bp. Oct. 25, 1789. C.R.1.
Benjamin, s. Benja[min] and Mercy, July 25, 1782.
Benjamin Franklin, s. Joseph and Sarah W., July 8, 1824.
Billings, s. Ebenezar and Deborah, Dec. 11, 1796.
Caleb, ——— [1769]. C.R.3. [[h. Deborah] G.R.2.]
Caleb, ch. Caleb and w., bp. Sept. 23, 1770. C.R.1.
Caleb, s. Job and Martha, Jan. 16, 1791.
Caleb, s. Martha, bp. Dec. 15, 1793. C.R.1.
Caleb, s. Caleb and Debby, Nov. 11, 1794. [[h. Susan N. [dup. M.]] G.R.2.]
Caleb F., s. Caleb B. Jr., ——— [1838]. C.R.3.
Catharine, d. Joseph and Lydah, May 13, 1807. [[w. Geo[rge] Tilden of Marshfield] P.R.10.]
Catharine, ch. Joseph dec'd, bp. Oct. 7, 1810. C.R.1.
Charles Edward, s. Thomas T. and Hannah, Jan. 26, 1838.
Cotton, s. Benja[min] and Mercy, June 21, 1792.
Cushing, s. Caleb and Debby, May 24, 1793.
David, s. Dr. David and Joanna, Nov. 16, 1802.
Davis Waterman, s. Waterman and Beckey, May 26, 1825.
Debby, d. Caleb and Debby, Dec. 15, 1796. [Dec. 15, 1797, P.R.9.]
Deborah [———], w. Caleb [Nov. —, 1773]. C.R.1.
Deborah, d. Ebenezar and Deborah, Mar. 1, 1793.
Deborah Tilden, d. Israel and Abigail, Apr. 13, 1796.
Desire, d. Benja[min], bp. Aug. 15, 1762. C.R.1.

BAILEY, Ebenezar, s. Ebenezar and Deborah, Aug. 1, 1791. [Ebenezer [h. Lydia], G.R.2.]
Ebenezer, ch. Caleb and w., bp. Sept. 23, 1770. C.R.1.
Ebenezer, s. Paul, bp. Sept. 11, 1774. C.R.1.
Ebenezer, s. Paul, bp. Aug. 3, 1788. C.R.1.
Ebenezer, s. Paul Jr. and Sibbel, July 21, 1830. [Ebenazar, ch. Paul and Sibel, C.R.3.]
Edwin, s. Paul Jr. and Syblel, Apr. 2, 1813.
Eleanor Curtis, d. Leonard P. and Eleanor C., Aug. 17, 1830.
Elisha, s. Benjamin, bp. Oct. 30, 1768. C.R.1.
Eliza, d. Caleb and Debby, Mar. 30, 1801.
Eliza James Harvey, d. Thomas T. and Hannah, Aug. 15, 1827. [Eliza James Hervey, P.R.11.]
Elizabeth, d. Amasa and w., bp. June 23, 1765. C.R.1.
Elizabeth, d. Amasa, bp. Oct. 18, 1772. C.R.1.
Elizabeth, d. Abner, bp. June 19, 1774. C.R.1.
Elizabeth, d. Dr. David and Joanna, June 12, 1810.
Elizabeth, d. Whitman and Patience V., Dec. 2, 1821, in Quincy.
Elizabeth Tower, d. Caleb Jr. and Ruth L., Jan. 9, 1820.
Ellen Curtis, d. Leonard P. and Eleanor C., Feb. 2, 1835.
Elvira, d. Caleb and Debby, Nov. 12, 1811.
Elvira, d. Israel, shoemaker, and Bethia, Jan. 26, 1849.
Franklin, s. Benja[min] and Mercy, Sept. 10, 1798.
George, s. Job and Lydia F., Feb. 10, 1822.
George Anson, s. Israel and Abigail, Nov. 13, 1807.
Geo[rge] Anson, ——— [1809]. G.R.6.
George Little, s. Abner, bp. Apr. 30, 1809. C.R.1.
George Whitefield, s. Job and Lydia F., Aug. 1, 1830.
Hannah W. [———], w. Thomas Tilden, ———, 1798. G.R.2.
Hannah W. [? m.], ———, 1833. G.R.2.
Hannah Wade, d. Eb[e]n[eze]r and Deborah, Dec. 24, 1801.
Hanson L., s. Amasa and Sally F., Sept. 24, 1813.
Harriet Augusta, d. Waterman and Beckey, July 19, 1830.
Harriet Elizebeth, d. Joseph Jr., carpenter, and Mary L. (b. Roxbury), July 18, 1849.
Hart, s. Eben[eze]r and Marcy, Jan. 2, 1807.
Hayward, s. Caleb and Debby, June 23, 1805.
Henry, s. Paul Jr. and Sibbel, Sept. 27, 1816.
Henry, ch. Paul Jr. and Sibel, bp. May 7, 1826. C.R.3.
Hepsibah, d. Abner, bp. Aug. 29, 1784. C.R.1.
Israel, s. Caleb and Philapha, June 19, 1773.
Israel Vinal, s. Caleb and Debby, Sept. 10, 1819.
James A., "In Civil war," Sept. 15, 1832. G.R.7.
James Thomas, s. Waterman and Beckey, Mar. 17, 1833. [[h. Sarah V.] G.R.2.]

BAILEY, Jarvis, s. Isreal and Abigail, May 16, 1801.
Jeremiah, s. Dr. David and Joanna, Aug. 11, 1822.
Joanna, d. Dr. David and Joanna, Dec. 13, 1804.
Joanna, d. Dr. David and Joanna, June 1, 1813.
Job, s. Amasa, bp. Oct. 12, 1766. C.R.1.
Job, s. Job and Martha, Sept. 26, 1792.
Job, s. Martha, wid., bp. Oct. 9, 1793. C.R.1.
Job, s. Joseph and Deborah, Feb. 4, 1794. [[h. Lydia Foster (Wade)] G.R.2.]
Job, ch. Joseph dec'd, bp. Oct. 7, 1810. C.R.1.
Job Foster, s. Job and Lydia F., Jan. 22, 1820.
Job Franklin, s. Amasa and Sally (Fletcher), Jan. 17, 1811.
John Wade, s. Job and Lydia F., Oct. 22, 1825.
Joseph, s. Caleb (Baily) and Philephe, Jan. 17, 1771. [h. Deborah (Tilden), h. Lydia (Tilden), P.R.10.]
Joseph, s. Joseph and Deborah, Mar. 22, 1796.
Joseph, ch. Joseph dec'd, bp. Oct. 7, 1810. C.R.1.
Joseph, s. Joseph and Sarah W., Sept. 10, 1822.
Joseph Foster, s. Job and Lydia F., July 11, 1816.
Joseph Franklin, s. Benj[amin] F., carpenter, and Elizebeth (b. Marblehead), Jan. 20, 1849, in Marblehead.
Joseph Tilden, s. Job and Lydia F., Feb. 1, 1818.
Joshua, s. Eben[eze]r and Marcy, Feb. 2, 1811.
Joshua, s. Eben[eze]r and Marcy, Aug. 7, 1812.
Jotham Wade, s. Thomas T. and Hannah, May 5, 1832.
Judson, s. Benja[min] and Mercy, Jan. 5, 1785.
Judson, s. Benja[min], bp. Oct. 8, 1786. C.R.1.
Kilburn, s. Caleb and Debby, July 15, 1807. [Kilborn, C.R.1.]
Leanord Peirce, s. Joseph and Lydia, June 25, 1805. [Leonard P., h. Eleanor C. (Damon), P.R.10.]
Lemuel Stetson, s. Caleb and Debby, May 3, 1814.
Leonard, s. Leonard P. and Eleanor C., Aug. 1, 1826.
Leonard Peirce (see Leanord Peirce).
Leonard Peirce, ch. Joseph dec'd, bp. Oct. 7, 1810. C.R.1.
Lucy, d. Benja[min] and Mercy, Mar. 29, 1776.
Lucy, d. Paul, bp. Apr. 24, 1785. C.R.1.
Lucy, d. Dr. David and Joanna, Sept. 11, 1818.
Luther, s. Dr. David and Joanna, Feb. 18, 1816.
Lydia, ch. Caleb and w., bp. Sept. 23, 1770. C.R.1.
Lydia, d. Joseph and Lydia, Nov. 11, 1803.
Lydia, d. Caleb and Debby, Oct. 24, 1809.
Lydia, ch. Joseph dec'd, bp. Oct. 7, 1810. C.R.1.
Lydia E., d. Leonard P. and Eleanor C., Mar. 1, 1840.
Lydia Foster, d. Job and Lydia F., Mar. 7, 1823.

BAILEY, Marcia, ch. Joseph and Deborah (Tilden), Oct. 1, 1792. P.R.10.
Marcia (see Martia).
Marcy, d. Caleb and Debby, June 28, 1803.
Margaret Tilden, ch. Thomas T. and Hannah (Wade), June 25, 1821. P.R.11.
Margaret Wade, d. Thomas T. and Hannah, Apr. 15, 1822.
Margaret Wade, d. Thomas T. and Hannah, Jan. 16, 1826.
Margaret Wade, d. Job and Lydia F., Nov. 23, 1833.
Maria Wade, d. Job and Lydia F., Feb. 14, 1828. [w. Nathaniel Vinal, G.R.8.]
Marion L. [―――], w. Tho[ma]s F. [Nov. ―, 1840]. C.R.3.
Marten, ch. Abner and w., bp. June 4, 1804. C.R.1.
Martha, ch. Caleb and w., bp. Sept. 23, 1770. C.R.1.
Martha, d. Israel and Abigail, Jan. 21, 1798.
Martha, d. Caleb Jr. and Ruth L., Feb. 3, 1816.
Martha Ann, d. Paul Jr. and Sibbel, July 18, 1809.
Martha Ann, d. Paul Jr. and Sibbel, Oct. 4, 1820.
Martha Ann, ch. Paul Jr. and Sibel, bp. May 7, 1826. C.R.3.
Martha Rowland, d. Rowland and Serissa, Sept. 8, 1828.
Martia, d. Israel and Abigail, Sept. 14, 1799.
Martin, s. Abner, bp. June 10, 1787. C.R.1.
Martin, s. Abner Jr. and Polly, Feb. 14, 1801.
Martin (see Marten).
Martin Kent, s. Amasa and Sally F., June 15, 1815.
Mary Ann [―――], w. Noah C., ―, 1808. G.R.2.
Mary Louisa, d. Joseph and Sarah W., Aug. 24, 1833, in Dorchester.
Mary Oakes, d. Caleb Jr. and Ruth L., Nov. 11, 1817.
Mary Wade, d. Thomas T. and Hannah, Jan. 29, 1835. [Dec. 29, 1834, P.R.11.]
Mercy, d. Benja[min] and Mercy, Dec. 6, 1779. [Baily, C.R.1.]
Mercy (see Marcy).
Mercy Otis, d. Noah C. and Mary Ann, Nov. 19, 1827, in Cohasset.
Mira Bates, ch. Paul and Sibel, bp. Aug. 17, 1828. C.R.3.
Molly (see Polly).
Myra Bates, d. Paul Jr. and Sibbel, May 12, 1827.
Nabba, d. Abner, bp. Mar. 14, 1779. C.R.1.
Nancy, d. Paul and Anna, Jan. 25, 1780.
Noah C., s. Eben[eze]r and Marcy, Jan. 15, 1805. [[h. Mary Ann] G.R.2.]
Otis, s. Eben[eze]r and Marcy, Oct. 4, 1808.
Patience, d. Benjamin, bp. June 7, 1767. C.R.1.

BAILEY, Paul, s. Paul and Anna, May 2, 1782. [[h. Sibyl] G.R.2.]
Paul, s. Paul Jr. and Sibbel [Sibel, C.R.3.], May 8, 1825.
Philipa, ch. Joseph dec'd, bp. Oct. 7, 1810. C.R.1.
Philipia, d. Joseph and Lydia, June 17, 1809. [Phillipia, w. Christopher Tilden, P.R.10.]
Polly, d. Paul and Anna, Mar. 16, 1777. [Molly, C.R.1.]
Polly, d. Benja[min] and Mercy, July 25, 1787.
Polly, d. Abner Jr. and Polly, Aug. 6, 1802.
Rachel, d. John, bp. Sept. 6, 1719. C.R.1.
Rebecah, d. Dr. David and Joanna, Nov. 27, 1807.
Rebecca [———], w. Waterman [Mar. —, 1796]. G.R.2.
Rebeccah, d. Amasa, bp. Oct. 2, 1768. C.R.1.
Rowland, s. Abner, bp. July 22, 1792. C.R.1.
Roxania, d. Joseph and Deborah, Mar. 25, 1791. [Roxanna, G.R.2. P.R.10.]
Rufus Clapp, s. Abner Jr. and Polly, Aug. 14, 1799.
Rufus Clapp, ch. Abner and w., bp. June 4, 1804. C.R.1.
Ruth, d. Paul and Anna, Mar. 15, 1770.
Ruth Gannett, d. Waterman and Beckey, Jan. 5, 1827.
Ruth Lothrop, d. Caleb Jr. and Ruth L., Apr. 19, 1822.
Ruthe, d. Benja[min] and Mercy, Dec. 8, 1777. [Ruth, C.R.1.]
Ruthe, d. Benja[min] and Mercy, Feb. 24, 1790.
Sally, d. Abner and w., bp. May 30, 1773. C.R.1.
Sally Bates, d. Paul Jr. and Sibbel, Nov. 26, 1818.
Sally Bates, ch. Paul Jr. and Sibel, bp. May 7, 1826. C.R.3.
Samuel, s. Paul and Sibbel, Nov. 5, 1814.
Samuel Curtis, s. Leonard P. and Eleanor C., Mar. 2, 1833.
Samuel Hach, s. Abner and Polly, Jan. 23, 1805. [Samuel Hatch, C.R.1.]
Sarah J. [? m.], ——— [1825]. G.R.2.
Sarah Minott, d. Rowland and Serissa, Feb. 5, 1827.
Sarah Tilden, d. Thomas T. and Hannah, Feb. 8, 1824.
Sarah V. [———], w. James T., Apr. 30, 1835. G.R.2.
Sarah Weld, d. Joseph and Sarah W., July 17, 1820.
Seth Kent, s. Amasa and Sally F., Mar. 28, 1817.
Sewell, twin d. Isreal and Abigail, Aug. 6, 1803.
Sibel Bates, d. Paul Jr. and Sibbel, Mar. 2, 1823.
Sibel Bates, ch. Paul Jr. and Sibel, bp. May 7, 1826. C.R.3.
Sibyl [———], w. Paul [Feb. —, 1786]. G.R.2.
Sophia Whitney, d. Caleb and Debby, Jan. 27, 1816.
Susan N. [dup. M.] [———], w. Caleb [Apr. —, 1806]. G.R.2.
Thankful, d. Benjamin, bp. Mar. 10, 1765. C.R.1.
Thomas Henry, s. Leonard P. and Eleanor C., July 9, 1828.
Thomas Otis, s. Noah C. and Mary Ann, July 25, 1830, in Cohasset.

BAILEY, Thomas Tilden, s. Joseph and Lydia, Sept. 11, 1798. [[h. Hannah W.] G.R.2.] [h. Hannah (Wade), P.R.10.]
Thomas Tilden, ch. Joseph dec'd, bp. Oct. 7, 1810. C.R.1.
Thomas Tilden, s. Thomas T. and Hannah, Feb. 21, 1830. [Thomas Tilden Jr., P.R.11.]
Thomas Weld, s. Joseph and Sarah W., May 9, 1827.
Waterman, s. Joseph and Lydia, Dec. 19, 1800. [[h. Rebecca] G.R.2.] [Warterman, h. Rebecca (Gannett), P.R.10.]
Waterman, ch. Joseph dec'd, bp. Oct. 7, 1810. C.R.1.
Whitman, s. Ebenezar and Deborah, Dec. 15, 1794.
William, s. Amasa and Sally F., Apr. 14, 1819.
William Caleb, s. Joseph and Sarah W., Jan. 13, 1835, in Dorchester.
William Francis, s. Joseph and Sarah W., Sept. 5, 1829, in Dorchester.
William Harrison, ch. David Jr. and Deborah, Mar. 20, 1835.
———, twin ch. Benja[min] and Mercy, Mar. 2, 1795.
———, twin ch. Benja[min] and Mercy, Mar. 2, 1795.
———, [twin] s. Amasa and Sally F., Mar. 3, 1821.
———, [twin] d. Amasa and Sally F., Mar. 3, 1821.
———, s. Job and Lydia F., Aug. 6, 1832.
———, ch. John W., carpenter, and Priscilla L., Nov. 5, 1849.

BAILY (see Bailey, Bayle, Bayley, Baylie, Bayly), Abigal, d. Israel and Keziah, May 2, 1738. [Abigail, C.R.1.]
Abner, s. Amasa, bp. Aug. 4, 1751. C.R.1.
Adams, s. Joseph and Jerusha, Nov. 24, 1722.
Adams, s. Adams and Sarah, Jan. 16, 1748. [Bailey, C.R.1.]
Benjamin, s. Benja[min], bp. July 27, 1740. C.R.1.
Benjamin, s. Benja[min], bp. Aug. 21, 1743. C.R.1.
Benjamin, s. Benja[min], bp. May 17, 1747. C.R.1.
Caleb, s. Jose[ph] and Jerusha, Aug. 13, 1720. [bp. Aug. 7 [sic], C.R.1.]
Caleb, s. Joseph Jr. and Eliza[beth], Dec. 11, 1738.
Caleb, s. Caleb and Philipa, Nov. 24, 1768.
Caleb, ch. Caleb, bp. June 7, 1801. C.R.1.
Cushing, ch. Caleb, bp. June 7, 1801. C.R.1.
Debbe, ch. Caleb, bp. June 7, 1801. C.R.1.
Delight, ch. Timothy and w., bp. May 20, 1733. C.R.1.
Ebenezar, s. Joseph, bp. Mar. 2, 1752. C.R.1.
Ebenezer, s. Jose[ph] and Jerusha, July 20, 1714. [Bayley, C.R.1.]
Ebenzer, s. Ebenezer and Mary, Sept. 9, 1740. [Ebenezar s. Ebenezar and w., C.R.1.]
Ebenezer, s. Caleb and Philipa, Sept. 23, 1764.

BAILY, Elijah, s. Joshua and Abigail, bp. May 21, 1758. C.R.1.
Elisha, ch. Caleb, bp. June 7, 1801. C.R.1.
Elizabeth, d. Joseph Jr. and Eliza[beth], Jan. 11, 1733.
Elizabeth, d. Capt. Israel, bp. June 22, 1746. C.R.1.
Hannah, d. Israel and Keziah, Apr. 27, 1736.
Hannah, ch. Israel and Keziah, bp. June 5, 1737. C.R.1.
Israel, s. Israel and Keziah, Feb. 3, 1732.
Israel, ch. Israel and Keziah, bp. June 5, 1737. C.R.1.
Jerusha, d. Benja[min], bp. May 9, 1736. C.R.1.
Joanna, d. Benja[min], bp. Sept. 14, 1758. C.R.1.
Job, ch. W[illia]m, bp. July 6, 1740. C.R.1.
Joseph, s. Joseph Jr., bp. Apr. 5, 1741. C.R.1.
Joseph, s. Joseph Jr., bp. July 31, 1743. C.R.1.
Joseph, s. Adams and Sarah, Jan. 21, 1749. [Bailey, C.R.1.]
Joshua, s. Joseph Jr. and Eliza[beth], June 17, 1735.
Judith, ch. W[illia]m, bp. July 6, 1740. C.R.1.
Judith, d. Amasa, bp. July 31, 1757. C.R.1. [Bailey, w. Hayward Peirce, b. Apr. 19, G.R.2.]
Keziah, d. Israel and Keziah, Sept. 24, 1734.
Keziah, ch. Israel and Keziah, bp. June 5, 1737. C.R.1.
Lusannah, ch. W[illia]m, bp. July 6, 1740. C.R.1.
Lydia, d. Caleb and Philipa, Aug. 8, 1762.
Maranda, d. Joseph, bp. June 3, 1750. C.R.1.
Martha, d. Benja[min], bp. May 7, 1738. C.R.1.
Martha, d. Benja[min], bp. June 7, 1752. C.R.1.
Martha, d. Caleb and Philipa, Aug. 12, 1766.
Mary, d. Benja[min], bp. July 30, 1749. C.R.1.
Mercy, d. W[illia]m, bp. May 7, 1743. C.R.1.
Mercy, d. Amasa, bp. Sept. 5, 1755. C.R.1.
Miranda (see Maranda).
Miranda, d. Joshua, bp. Apr. 15, 1759. C.R.1.
Nathaniel Tilden, s. Benjamin, bp. June 6, 1742. C.R.1.
Paul, s. Ebenez[e]r [Ebenezar, C.R.1.] and Mary, July 24, 1743.
Rachel, d. Israel and Keziah, Apr. 11, 1740.
Rebecca, d. Joseph Jr. and Eliza[beth], Jan. 21, 1746.
Rhoda, d. Israel and Keziah, Oct. 25, 1731.
Rhoda, d. Israel, bp. Nov. 29, 1736. C.R.1.
Rowland, s. Benjamin, bp. July 31, 1763. C.R.1.
Ruth, d. Benja[min], bp. June 2, 1745. C.R.1.
Sarah, d. Israel, bp. Mar. 10, 1744. C.R.1.
Seth, s. Joseph and Jerusha, Sept. 17, 1717. [Bayley, C.R.1.]
Seth, s. Seth, bp. Aug. 10, 1745. C.R.1.
Seth, s. Adams and Sarah, Dec. 13, 1747.
Tilden, s. Benja[min], bp. Oct. 5, 1753. C.R.1.
Ward, s. Israel and Keziah, Dec. 23, 1742.

BAITS (see Bate, Bates, Bats), John, s. James, bp. Oct. 7, 1649. C.R.2.

BAKER, Eleanor (see Elleaner).
Elizab[eth], d. Hellen, bp. July 19, 1663. C.R.2.
Elleaner, d. Samuell, bp. May 16, 1680. C.R.2.
Hannah Lincoln, d. Nath[anie]ll and Mary, Nov. 20, 1800.
Hannah Lincoln, ch. Capt. Nathaniel, bp. Nov. 3, 1805. C.R.1.
James Turner, s. Capt. Nath[anie]ll, bp. Oct. 1, 1820. C.R.1.
Kenelm, s. Helen, bp. Mar. 24, 1660. C.R.2.
Lydia, d. Hellen [of] Marishfield, bp. Mar. 24, 1660. C.R.2.
Maria, d. Nathaniell and Mary, Nov. 14, 1803.
Maria, ch. Capt. Nathaniel, bp. Nov. 3, 1805. C.R.1.
Mary T. [———], w. ———, ——— [1776]. C.R.1.
Mary Turner, d. Nath[anie]ll and Mary, July 7, 1798.
Mary Turner, ch. Capt. Nathaniel, bp. Nov. 3, 1805. C.R.1.
Mercy, d. Helene, bp. Oct. 2, 1664. C.R.2.
Nathaniel, ——— [1771]. C.R.1.
Nathaniel, s. Nath[anie]ll [Nathaniel, C.R.1.] and Mary, Sept. 15, 1808.

BALCH, Deborah, d. Benja[min], bp. July 16, 1727. C.R.1.
Elizabeth, d. Benjamin, bp. May 25, 1729. C.R.1.
Hart, s. Benja[min], bp. June 6, 1731. C.R.1.

BALDWIN, Charles L., ch. Ira and w., ——— [rec. between ch. b. June 22, 1829, and ch. b. May 17, 1834], in Wareham.
George W., ch. Ira and w., Mar. 6, 1843.
Gilbert, ch. Ira and w., Dec. 4, 1838, in Hanover.
Ira B., ch. Ira and w., May 17, 1834, in Hanover.
Laura A., ch. Ira and w., June 7, 1836, in Hingham.
Maria B., ch. Ira and w., Apr. 5, 1841, in Hanover.
Mary S., ch. Ira and w., Dec. 10, 1827, in Barnstable.
Susan S., ch. Ira and w., June 22, 1829, in Barnstable.

BARBAR, Jane, d. John, May 28, 1710.

BARCE (see Bass, Bearce, Bearse), Ebenezer Jr., ch. Ebenezer and Mary Ann, Mar. 3, 1832.
James Thomas, ch. Ebenezer and Mary Ann, Aug. 25, 1839. [h. Susan, G.R.7.]
John Henry, ch. John and Elizabeth, Dec. 3, 1831.
Mary B., ch. Ebenezer and Mary Ann, Oct. 4, 1830.
Moses, ch. John and Elizabeth, Oct. 11, 1833.
Simeon, ch. Ebenezer and Mary Ann, Oct. 25, 1837.
Susan [———], w. James T., ———, 1848. G.R.7.
Tobias C., ch. Ebenezer and Mary Ann, Oct. 23, 1834.

BARGE, Abagail C. [———], w. ——— [July —, 1769]. C.R.1. [Abigail, w. Henry, G.R.2.]

BARKER, Abigail, twin ch. Barnabas and Hannah, bp. Sept. —, 1730. C.R.2.
Abigail F., ch. Ira and Deborah, Sept. 16, 1834.
Adeline, ch. Ira and Deborah, Apr. 6, 1826.
Ann, s. Caleb and Ann, Dec. 14, 1730. C.R.4.
Ann, d. Robert and Hannah, Sept. 21, 1739. C.R.4.
Barnabas, s. Barnabas, bp. July 4, 1720. C.R.1.
Barnabas, s. Barnabas and Hannah, Apr. 13, 1723.
Barnabas, s. Bar[nabas], bp. Sept. 19, 1756. C.R.2.
Bathsheba, [ch.] Barnabas and Mary, bp. Apr. 15, 1750. C.R.2.
Bathsheba M., ch. Ira and Deborah, Sept. 18, 1836.
Benjamin, s. Samuel P. and Catharine, May 7, 1831.
Bethiah, d. Sam[ue]ll [Capt. Sam[ue]l, C.R.1.] and Patience, June 27, 1755.
Caleb, s. Caleb [s. Caleb and Ann, C.R.4.], Aug. 29, 1719.
Catharine Augusta, d. Samuel P. and Catharine, Nov. 9, 1821, in Boston.
Charles, s. Caleb and Ann, June 5, 1729. C.R.4.
Content, d. Barnabas and w., bp. Apr. 5, 1747. C.R.2.
Cordelia, ch. Ira and Deborah, Aug. 3, 1830.
David, twin ch. Barnabas and Hannah, bp. Jan. 16, 1735-6. C.R.2.
Deborah, d. Ebenezer and Deborah, Dec. 25, 1710.
Deborah, d. Sam[ue]ll [Capt. Sam[ue]l, C.R.1.] and Hannah, May 1, 1720.
Deborah, d. Sam[ue]ll [Capt. Sam[ue]l, C.R.1.] Jr. and Patience, June 14, 1747.
Deborah B. [———], w. Ira [Apr. —, 1793]. G.R.15.
Deborah B., ch. Ira and Deborah, May 15, 1816.
Desire, d. Barnabas and Hannah, Apr. 25, 1728.
Elisha, s. Ebenezer, Sept. 5, 1715.
Elizabeth, d. Ebenezer and Deborah, Feb. 9, 1712-13.
Elizabeth, d. Caleb [d. Caleb and Ann, C.R.4.], Jan. 17, 1717.
Elizabeth, d. Isaac and Elizabeth, Dec. 9, 1719. C.R.4.
Elizebeth, d. Williams, bp. July 11, 1790. C.R.1.
Elizebeth Thatcher, d. W[illia]m and Sarah, Jan. 29, 1787.
Ellen P., ch. Ira and Deborah, July 10, 1839.
Ezekiell, s. Samuell and Hannah, July 2, 1714. [Ezekiel, s. Samuel, C.R.1.]
Gideon, s. Caleb and Ann, Dec. 22, 1721. C.R.4.
Hannah, d. Samuel and Hannah, May 16, 1711.

BARKER, Hannah, d. Barnabas and Hannah, Jan. 17, 1724.
Hannah, d. Sam[ue]ll [Sam[ue]l, C.R.1.] Jr. and Patiance, July 5, 1742.
Hannah C., ch. Ira and Deborah, Dec. 20, 1827.
Ignatius, s. Samuel and Hannah, Dec. 1, 1709.
Ira [h. Deborah B.] [July —, 1791]. G.R.15.
Ira T., ch. Ira and Deborah, Feb. 21, 1813.
Isaac, s. Robert [s. Robert Jr. and Hannah, C.R.4.], Mar. 10, 1698–9.
Isaac, s. Isaac and Judath, ———. C.R.4.
Jane Eliza, d. Samuel P. and Catharine, Mar. 16, 1827.
Jeremiah, s. Sam[ue]ll [Capt. Sam[ue]l, C.R.1.] Jr. and Patiance, Mar. 31, 1752.
Jeremiah Prouty, s. Lettice, negro, Oct. 4, 1794.
John, s. Caleb [s. Caleb and Ann, C.R.4.], June 15, 1714.
John, s. Barnabas and Hannah, bp. June 27, 1731. C.R.2.
John, s. Barnabas Jr., bp. Feb. 23, 1752. C.R.2.
John S., ch. Ira and Deborah, Jan. 4, 1824.
John William, s. W[illia]m and Sarah, Oct. 7, 1782.
John Williams, s. Capt. Williams, bp. Oct. 8, 1786. C.R.1.
Joshua, s. Caleb and Ann, Dec. 22, 1721. C.R.4.
Joshua, s. Caleb and Ann, May 17, 1726. C.R.4.
Joshua, s. Barnabas and Mary, bp. Nov. 16, 1740. C.R.2.
Joshua, ch. Ira and Deborah, Aug. 6, 1820.
Laura A., d. Warters B. and Lucy, June 23, 1847.
Luce, [ch.] Barnabas and Mary, bp. June 26, 1743. C.R.2.
Luce, d. Barnabas and Mary, bp. Oct. 7, 1744. C.R.2.
Lucy A., ch. Ira and Deborah, Apr. 21, 1822.
Lucy M., ch. William and w., June 4, 1843.
Lucy S. [———], w. Waters B. [Oct. —, 1820]. G.R.15.
Lydia, [ch.] Barnabas and Hannah, bp. Apr. 21, 1734. C.R.2.
Lydia, d. Isaac and Elizabeth, ———. C.R.4.
Magret, d. Robert and Hannah, Apr. 18, 1704. C.R.4.
Mary, d. Robert and Hannah, May 13, 1701.
Mary, d. Isaac and Elisabeth, June 1, 1708. C.R.4.
Mary, d. Isaac and Elizabeth of R.I., bp. Nov. 1, 1721. C.R.2.
Mary, twin ch. Barnabas and Hannah, bp. Sept. —, 1730. C.R.2.
Mary, d. Barnbas Jr., bp. Apr. 7, 1754. C.R.2.
Mary E. [———], w. J. S. [Jan. —, 1839]. G.R.15.
Mercy, d. Barnabas, bp. May 7, 1738. C.R.2.
Patiance, d. Sam[ue]ll Jr. and Patiance, Oct. 27, 1740. [Patience, d. Sam[ue]l Jr. and Patience, C.R.1.]
Peleg, s. Isaac and Elizabeth, Feb. —, 1716–17. C.R.4.
Prince, s. Samuel P. and Catherine, May 23, 1836.

BARKER, Rebecca Partridge, d. Samuel P. and Catharine, Oct. 28, 1819, in Boston.
Robert, s. Caleb [s. Caleb and Ann, C.R.4.], Jan. 27, 1712.
Ruth Leach, d. W[illia]m and Sarah, Jan. 27, 1785.
Ruth Leach, d. Capt. Williams, bp. Oct. 8, 1786. C.R.1.
Saley, d. Capt. Wi[llia]m and Sarah, Sept. 29, 1778. [Sally, [ch.] Williams, C.R.1.]
Samuel, s. Sam[ue]ll [Capt. Sam[ue]l, C.R.1.] Jr. and Patiance, Jan. 12, 1749.
Samuel, s. Capt. Sam[ue]l, bp. Dec. 4, 1757. C.R.1.
Samuel, s. Sam[ue]ll [Samuel, C.R.1.] and Patience, Aug. 21, 1762.
Samuel Partridge, s. Samuel P. and Catharine, Dec. 4, 1824, in Boston.
Samuell, s. Samuell, Oct. 4, 1707.
Sarah, d. Barnabas and Hannah, June 2, 1721.
Sarah Elizabeth, ch. Samuel P. and Catharin, Apr. 13, 1838.
Silvester, d. Isaac and Elizabeth, May —, 1710. C.R.4.
Susan Ann, d. Samuel P. and Catharine, Apr. 3, 1826.
Susan C., ch. Ira and Deborah, Aug. 28, 1832.
Thomas, s. Barnabas and Hannah, Aug. 19, 1726.
Thomas, s. Robert and Hannah, Apr. 29, 1738. C.R.4.
Waters B., ch. Ira and Deborah, Aug. 14, 1818. [[h. Lucy S.] G.R.15.]
William, s. Barnabas and Mary, bp. May 1, 1737. C.R.2.
Williams, s. Sam[ue]ll [Capt. Samuel, C.R.1.] Jr. and Patiance, Sept. 2, 1744.
Ziporah, twin ch. Barnabas and Hannah, bp. Jan. 16, 1735-6. C.R.2.
Zipporah, d. Barnabas Sr., bp. [Oct.] 22, 1752. C.R.2.

BARLOW, Elizabeth (? Barlow), d. Elizabeth, bp. May 8, 1659. C.R.2.

BARNES (see Barns), Cushing, s. Joseph and Polly, June 16, 1808.
David, Rev., D.D. [h. Rachel (Leonard)], Mar. 24, 1731, in Marlborough. G.R.14.
Edmond Quincy, ch. Elisha J. and Harriet A., Aug. 17, 1839.
Edward Livermore, [twin] ch. Elijah V. and Lydia, Nov. 1, 1839.
Edwin Livingston, [twin] ch. Elijah V. and Lydia, Nov. 1, 1839.
Elijah Vinal, [twin] s. Joseph and Polly, Sept. 9, 1817.
Elisha James, [twin] s. Joseph and Polly, Sept. 9, 1817.
Hannah E., June 7, 1841. P.R.12.
Henry [Jan. —, 1817], in Hillsboro, N.H. G.R.14.

BARNES, Israel Merritt, s. Joseph and Polly, Sept. 22, 18[torn] [rec. after ch. b. Sept. 9, 1817]. [[h. Olive L.] Sept. 23, 1820, G.R.8.] [Sept. 23, 1820, P.R.12.]
Joseph, s. Joseph and Polly, Sept. 9, 1813.
Lydia D. S. [? m.], ———, 1816. G.R.8.
Mandana C., Oct. 18, 1843. P.R.12.
Mary, d. Joseph and Polly, June 16, 1806.
Olive L. [———], w. Israel M., Dec. 31, 1820. G.R.8.
Prissilla Vinal, d. Joseph and Polly, Feb. 23, 1811.
William, s. Joseph and Polley, Aug. 4, 1804.

BARNS (see Barnes), Anna, d. Rev. David and Rach[e]l, Sept. 26, 1765.
David Leonard, s. Rev. David and Rachel, Jan. 28, 1760.
Rachel, d. Rev. David and Rachel, July 11, 1757.

BARREL (see Barrell, Barriel), Abigail, [ch.] William and Abigail, bp. July 18, 1742. C.R.2.
Charles Henry, s. Joseph and Sarah, Jan. 15, 1835.
Colebourn, s. W[illia]m (Barrell), bp. May 7, 1738. C.R.2.
Deborah, ch. Benjamin and Eunice, Oct. 1, 1841.
Elizabeth, d. Joseph, bp. July 2[worn], 1679. C.R.2.
Ellen, ch. Benjamin and Eunice, Dec. 28, 1839.
Fanny, d. Luther and w., bp. Sept. 30, 1798. C.R.2.
Hannah, ch. William and Elizabeth, bp. Sept. 26, 1714. C.R.2.
James, s. James and Deborah, bp. June 30, 1751. C.R.2.
John, s. William and Abigail, bp. Mar. 31, 1734.
Joshua, s. William and Lydia, bp. Nov. 30, 1746. C.R.2.
Lydia, ch. William and Elizabeth, bp. Sept. 26, 1714. C.R.2.
Lydia, d. William and Lydia dec'd, bp. Dec. 16, 1748. C.R.2.
Mary, d. William and Abigail, bp. Aug. 1, 1731. C.R.2.
William, s. James and Deb[orah], bp. Oct. 14, 1753. C.R.2.
William, s. William, bp. July 1, 1804. C.R.1.
[torn]d Augustus, s. Prudence, Dec. 27, 1838.

BARRELL (see Barrel, Barriel), Abel, s. James Jr. and Martha, Jan. 28, 1784.
Abigail, ch. William and Abigail, bp. May 5, 1728. C.R.2.
Anna, d. James Jr. and Martha, June 2, 1785.
Bartlet, s. Bartlet and Relief, Aug. 16, 1799.
Bathsheba, d. William and Rebecca, June 8, 1779.
Becca, d. William and Rebecca, Nov. 25, 1777.
Benjamin, s. James Jr. and Martha, Mar. 27, 177[5].
Benj[ami]n, s. Bartlet and Relief, June 6, 1814. [[h. Eunice Leavitt] G.R.14.]

BARRELL, Betsey, d. William and Rebecca, Aug. 11, 1782.
Betsy C. [———], w. James, —— [1784]. G.R.2.
Colburn, s. James Jr. and Martha, Apr. 25, 1787.
Deborah, d. Noah and Martha, Mar. 2, 1788.
Desire, d. James Jr. and Martha, Dec. 4, 1793.
Elias, s. James Jr. and Martha, June 8, 1791.
Frederick Foster, s. Joseph and Sarah, May 3, 1821.
Hannah, d. William, Jan. 12, 1706-7.
James, s. William and w. (wid. John James Sr.), Sept. 20, 1687.
James, s. W[illia]m and Elizabeth, Dec. 29, 1727, "lived 99 years."
James, ch. William and Abigail, bp. May 5, 1728. C.R.2.
James, s. James Jr. and Martha, Aug. 5, 1773.
James Blanchard, s. Bartlet and Relief, July 27, 1804.
James Edward, s. Joseph and Sarah, June 30, 1819.
Jemima, d. James Jr. and Martha, Dec. 5, 1779.
Jenny, d. Noah and Martha, Dec. 9, 1786.
Joseph, s. Noah and Martha, Feb. 8, 1794.
Joseph Edwin, s. Joseph and Sarah, Aug. 25, 1818.
Julia, d. Benj[amin] and Eunice, Dec. 28, 1846.
Julia Ann, d. Benjamin, shoemaker, and Eunice, Apr. 5, 1844.
Lucinda, d. William and Rebecca, Jan. 11, 1784.
Lucy, d. William and Rebecca, Apr. 18, 1787.
Lucy, d. Will[ia]m and w., bp. Sept. 9, 1792. C.R.2.
Luther, s. Luther and w., bp. Jan. 13, 1793. C.R.2.
Luther, s. Luther and Abigail, Nov. 14, 1793.
Lydia, d. William and w. (wid. John James Sr.), May 25, 1684.
    [Lidia, C.R.2.]
Lydia, d. William, Dec. 15, 1709.
Lydia, d. James and Lydia, Dec. 3, 1768.
Lydia, d. James Jr. and Martha, May 18, 1789.
Martha, d. James Jr. and Martha, Oct. 3, 1777.
Mary, d. William, bp. May 22, 1681. C.R.2.
Mary, d. William and w. (wid. John James Sr.), Sept. 10, 1686.
Mary, d. Bartlet and Relief, Sept. 30, 1807.
Matilda, d. Noah and Martha, Apr. 21, 1796.
Nabby Leavitt, d. Luther and Abigail, July 25, 1795. [Nabby
    Leavet, C.R.2.]
Nelson, s. Luther and Abigail, May 4, 1800.
Noah, s. Noah and Martha, Oct. 27, 1792.
Polly, d. Noah and Martha, Aug. 15, 1785.
Prudence, d. Bartlet and Relief, Mar. 14, 1797.
Rachel, d. Noah and Martha, Feb. 15, 1790.
Relief, d. Bartlet and Relief, Nov. 11, 1794.
Ruth, d. William and Rebecca, Dec. 25, 1789.

BARRELL, Ruth, d. Will[ia]m and w., bp. Sept. 9, 1792. C.R.2.
Temperence, d. Bartlet and Relief, Jan. 10, 1802.
Thomas, s. James Jr. and Martha, Jan. 21, 1796.
William, s. William and w. (wid. John James Sr.), Mar. 28, 1683.
William, s. William and Elizabeth, June 23, 1714. [Barrel, C.R.2.]
William, s. William and Rebecca, Feb. 7, 1776.
William Dexter, s. Bartlet and Relief, Aug. 16, 1809.

BARRET (see Barrett), Ruth, w. Joseph, bp. July 2[worn], 1679. C.R.2.

BARRETT (see Barret), Hannah [———], w. Sumner F., ——— [1811]. C.R.1.

BARRIEL (see Barrel, Barrell), Elisha, s. Will[ia]m and Abigail, Sept. 15, 1735. [Barrel, C.R.2.]

BARRY, Johanna [? m.], ———, 1841. G.R.10.
Thomas, ———, 1837. G.R.10.

BARSTOW (see Bastow, Bearstow, Bersto, Berstow, Berstowe, Bestow, Bestowe), Abigail, d. John, Mar. 8, 1691–2.
Albert, ch. Elijah and Caroline, July 8, 1840.
Andrew, s. Elijah and Lucy, Dec. 30, 1813.
Barker, s. Thomas and Olive, May 12, 1793.
Charles, ch. Dea. Samuel, May 3, 1740. P.R.5.
Daniel, ch. Dea. Samuel, July 1, 1744. P.R.5.
Edwin, s. Elijah and Lucy, July 30, 1811.
Elenor, d. Thomas and Olive, Feb. 27, 1780. [Nelly, ch. Thomas and Lydia, ———, 1788, G.R.15.]
Elijah, s. Elijah and Lucy, Oct. 3, 1805.
Emma, ch. Thomas H. C. and Abby E., June 15, 1837.
Grace, ch. Dea. Samuel, May 27, 1748. P.R.5.
Grace Foster, ch. Nathaniel and Grace B., Apr. 4, 1834.
Haviland, ch. Thomas H. C. and Abby E., June 11, 1839.
Henry Briggs, ch. Elijah and Caroline, Nov. 23, 1838.
Jeremiah, s. John, Aug. 28, 1682.
Jerusha, d. John, Nov. 21, 1687.
Job, s. John, Mar. 8, 1679–80.
John, s. John, Feb. 15, 1684.
Joshua, s. Joseph and Mary, Sept. 8, 1720. [Joshuah Bestow, s. Joseph and Elizabeth, C.R.2.]
Lucanah, ch. Dea. Samuel, Oct. 9, 1732. P.R.5.
Lucy Eells, d. Elijah and Lucy, Dec. 22, 1801.
Lydia, d. John, Mar. 26, 1696.
Lydia [———], w. Tho[ma]s, ———, 1757. G.R.15.

BARSTOW, Lydia, d. Thomas and Olive, Aug. 29, 1785.
Margaret, ch. Dea. Samuel, Feb. 20, 1738. P.R.5.
Margaret, ch. Dea. Samuel, June 1, 1746. P.R.5.
Mary, d. Joseph and Mary, May 20, 1717. [Bestow, C.R.2.]
Michael, s. Samuel and Lydia, Jan. 9, 1722.
Nabby, d. Elijah and Lucy, Dec. 6, 1812.
Nathaniel, s. Elijah and Lucy, Aug. 16, 1799.
Nelly (see Elenor).
Olive S., d. Thomas and Olive, Aug. 3, 1795.
Rebekah, d. Thomas and Olive, Oct. 24, 1790.
Samuel, ch. Dea. Samuel, July 28, 1734. P.R.5.
Sarah, d. Will[ia]m and Sarah, Oct. 2, 1712.
Seth, ch. Dea. Samuel, June 15, 1742. P.R.5.
Sidney, ch. Thomas H. C. and Abby E., Apr. 14, 1842.
Sussanna, d. John, May 5, 1689.
Tho[ma]s [h. Lydia], ———, 1756. G.R.15.
Thomas, s. Thomas and Olive, "Jane" 2, 1783.
William, s. Will[ia]m and Sarah, Apr. 10, 1715.

BARTLETT, Elizabeth P., M.D. [? m.], July 9, 1823. G.R.6.
Elizabeth R., ch. Stephen and Phebe, July 6, 1830.
Lorenzo, ch. Stephen and Phebe, Nov. 9, 1828.
Mercy W., ch. Stephen and Phebe, June 26, 1843.
Phebe [———], w. Stephen, Feb. 21, 1802.
Stephen [h. Phebe], Dec. 17, 1801.

BASS (see Barce, Bearce, Bearse), Samuel B. ["or Bearce," written later], s. John, shoemaker, and Elizabeth, June 19, 1846.

BASTIANNA, Marianna [May —, 1795]. G.R.10.

BASTOW (see Barstow, Bearstow, Bersto, Berstow, Berstowe, Bestow, Bestowe), George, s. George, bp. June 12, 1653. C.R.2.
Margaret, d. George, bp. Feb. 24, 1649. C.R.2.
Martha, d. William, bp. Apr. 22, 1655. C.R.2.

BATE (see Baits, Bates, Bats), Aquilla, d. Jo[h]n, bp. May 15, 1743. C.R.1.

BATES (see Baits, Bate, Bats), Abby J., d. James Y. and Susan M., Sept. 10, 1846.
Abigail (see Nabby).
Adolphus, s. James Y., light-house keeper, and Susan M., Sept. 24, 1849.

BATES, Alexander, twin ch. Jo[h]n, bp. June 27, 1756. C.R.1.
Amanda Malvina, ch. Benjamin and Hannah, Dec. 27, 1826.
Amos, s. Joseph, Nov. 25, 1705.
Andrew Thomas, ch. Thomas C. and Clarissa G., Aug. 28, 1839.
Ann E., d. Thomas and Clarrissa G., Aug. 17, 1848.
Benjamin, [twin] s. John and Sally, Feb. 20, 1817.
Benjamin W., Feb. —, 1816. G.R.6.
Betsey Northey, d. John and Sally, Dec. 16, 1819.
Caleb, s. Jo[h]n, bp. June 12, 1749. C.R.1.
Caleb, ch. Reuben and w., bp. May 26, 1776. C.R.1.
Caleb, s. Simeon and Rachel, Aug. 18, 1795.
Caleb, [twin] s. John and Sally, Feb. 20, 1817.
Catharine, d. John and Sally, Mar. 15, 1825.
Charles, —— [1810]. G.R.2.
Charles Elliot, ch. Peter E. and Sophia, Nov. 10, 1839.
Charles Eugene, ch. Charles and Clara, Dec. 16, 1837, in Cohasset.
  ["in the 39th Regt. Mass. Vols.," G.R.2.]
Clarissa, d. Asa, shoemaker, and Clarisa, Feb. 9, 1844.
Clarissa Thomas, ch. Thomas C. and Clarissa G., Feb. 19, 1833.
Clarissa Thomas, ch. Thomas C. and Clarissa G., Mar. 26, 1837.
Clement, s. Joseph, Dec. 27, 1707.
Colman, s. John and Sally, Sept. 7, 1831.
Cyrene, d. Jaazaniah and Bulah, Feb. 10, 1819.
Decater P., ch. Ruben C. and Luzanna, Nov. 17, 1833.
Ella, d. Charles, carpenter [dup. ship joiner], and Clara, May 20, 1844.
Elvira, d. Jaazaniah and Bulah, Aug. 3, 1816.
Florett C., d. Caleb Jr., seaman, and Pamelia R., Oct. 15, 1847.
George, s. John and Sally, Aug. 1, 1822.
George, ch. Peter E. and Sophia, ——, 1841.
George H., ch. Harvey and Harriet, Aug. 7, 1837.
George Henry, ch. Benjamin and Hannah, July 24, 1832.
Guy, twin ch. Jo[h]n, bp. June 27, 1756. C.R.1.
Hannah, d. Jo[h]n, bp. Sept. 24, 1752. C.R.1.
Haret C., d. Caleb 2d and Pamelia, Nov. 10, 1845.
Harriet Ann, ch. Benjamin and Hannah, Sept. 24, 1823.
Hervey, s. Jaazaniah and Bulah, Nov. 11, 1811.
James C., ch. Thomas C. and Clarissa G., Dec. 21, 1841.
James Young, s. Simeon Jr. and Jane B., Nov. 10, 1819.
Jane, ch. Reuben and w., bp. May 26, 1776. C.R.1.
Jane, d. Simeon Jr. and Jane B., July 31, 1817.
John, s. John, bp. May 24, 1747. C.R.1.
John, s. Simeon and Rachel, Sept. 27, 1786. [Capt. John, C.R.1.]
John, s. John and Sally, June 1, 1809.

BATES, John Henry, ch. John Jr. and Sarah J., Aug. 29, 1836.
Jonathan, s. Joseph of Hingham, bp. June 5, 1720. C.R.1.
Jone, d. Simeon and Rachel, May 22, 1791.
Joseph, s. Joseph, Jan. 25, 1696–7.
Joseph, [twin] s. Simeon and Rachel, Sept. 30, 1800. [[h. Mercy V.] G.R.6.]
Joseph J., ch. Joseph and Mercy, Aug. 7, 1832.
Joseph Northey, s. John and Sally, Feb. 20, 1814.
Judah, s. Jo[h]n and Abigal, July 26, 1740.
Julia Emeline Merritt, ch. Ruben C. and Luzanna, Aug. 26, 1840.
Levi, s. Jo[h]n and Abigal, Jan. 29, 1738 [? 1738–9].
Lorenzo, ch. Harvey and Harriet, July 11, 1842.
Lorenzo, s. Thom[as] C., marriner, and Clarissa G., Apr. 14, 1847.
Louisa Ann, d. Jaazaniah and Bulah, May 15, 1810.
Martha Jane, ch. Benjamin and Hannah, Feb. 16, 1837.
Mary, d. Joseph, Mar. 13, 1700–1.
Mary, d. Simeon Jr. and Jane B., Oct. 2, 1815.
Mary Curtis, ch. Thomas C. and Clarissa G., Mar. 2, 1844.
Medora, d. James, sailor, and Susan, June 26, 1845.
Mercy, d. Joseph, Feb. 28, 1698–9.
Mercy C., d. Capt. Joseph and Mercy, Oct. 18, 1834. G.R.6.
Mercy C., ch. Ruben C. and Luzanna, Mar. 12, 1844.
Mercy V. [———], w. Joseph, Feb. 10, 1811. G.R.6.
Nabby, ch. Reuben and w., bp. May 26, 1776. C.R.1.
Nabby, d. Simeon and Rachel, Oct. 31, 1797. [Abigail, G.R.6.]
Peter Ingram, s. John and Sally, Nov. 9, 1811. [Peter J., C.R.1.]
Rachel, d. Jo[h]n, bp. May 5, 1745. C.R.1.
Rachel [———], w. Capt. Simeon, ——— [1765]. G.R.6.
Rachel, ch. Reuben and w., bp. May 26, 1776. C.R.1.
Rachel, d. Simeon and Rachel, Feb. 18, 1804.
Rachel, d. Simeon and Rachel, Oct. 13, 1805.
Rachell, d. Joseph, Feb. 22, 1710.
Rebecca, w. Abial Turner, Feb. 21, 1802. P.R.25.
Rebecca W., d. Simeon and Rachel, Aug. 25, 1793. ["A heroine of 1812," G.R.6.]
Reuben, ch. Reuben and w., bp. May 26, 1776. C.R.1.
Reuben, [twin] s. Simeon and Rachel, Sept. 30, 1800.
Reubin (see Ruben).
Rosanna, d. Jo[h]n and Abigal, Apr. 19, 1735.
Ruben, s. John and Abigal, Feb. 4, 1735[–6]. [Reubin, C.R.1.]
Ruth, d. Joseph, Apr. 9, 1695.
Samuel, s. Joseph of Cohasset, bp. June 1, 1718. C.R.1.
Semeon, ch. Reuben and w., bp. May 26, 1776. C.R.1.
Simeon, s. Jo[h]n and Abigal, Dec. 18, 1737.

BATES, Simeon, s. Reuben and Mary, July 25, 1764.
Simeon, s. Simeon and Rachel, Aug. 20, 1788.
Simeon A., s. Simeon Jr. and Jane B., Feb. 7, 1830.
Solomon, s. Joseph, Dec. 25, 1702.
Susan Cook, d. Simeon Jr. and Jane B., Apr. 8, 1814.
Susannah, ch. Reuben and w., bp. May 26, 1776. C.R.1.
Thomas, s. Simeon and Rachel, July 12, 1807.
William, s. John and Sally, Aug. 16, 1828.
———— [————], wid. Cornelius, ———— [1765]. C.R.1.
————, ch. Joseph N. and Mary N., Oct. 19, 1840.
————, s. James Y. and Susan M., Aug. 11, 1848.

BATS (see Baits, Bate, Bates), Wilber Lee, ch. John Jr. and Sarah J., Mar. 12, 1839.

BATTLES, Lydia, d. Joseph and w., bp. July 12, 1747. C.R.1.
Mabel, twin d. Joseph, bp. June 20, 1752. C.R.1.
Rachel, twin d. Joseph, bp. June 20, 1752. C.R.1.

BAYLE (see Bailey, Baily, Bayley, Baylie, Bayly), Joseph, s. Joseph, Nov. 1, 1704.

BAYLEY (see Bailey, Baily, Bayle, Baylie, Bayly), Deborah, twin d. John, bp. July 7, 1717. C.R.1.
Hannah, twin d. John, bp. July 7, 1717. C.R.1.
Israel, ch. John, bp. July 1, 1711. C.R.1.
Jacob, ch. John, bp. July 1, 1711. C.R.1.
Jane, ch. John, bp. July 1, 1711. C.R.1.
John, ch. John, bp. July 1, 1711. C.R.1.
Joshua, s. Joseph, bp. Sept. 6, 1727. C.R.1.
Naomi, d. John, bp. July 4, 1725. C.R.1.
Sarah, d. John, bp. Apr. 22, 1716. C.R.1.
Timothy, ch. John, bp. July 1, 1711. C.R.1.

BAYLIE (see Bailey, Baily, Bayle, Bayley, Bayly), Benjamin, s. John, Apr. —, 1682.
Benjamin, s. Joseph and Jerusha, Feb. 28, 1712. [Bayley, C.R.1.]
Hannah, d. John, Jan. —, 1687–8. [Bayley, C.R.2.]
Israel, s. John Jr. and Abigail, May 13, 1708.
Jacob, s. John Jr. and Abigail, Dec. 17, 1706.
Jane, d. John Jr. and Abigail, June "ye last," 1700.
John, s. John, Nov. 5, 1673.
John, s. John Jr. and Abigail, May 23, 1703.
Joseph, s. John, Oct. —, 1679.
Martha, d. Joseph and Jerusha, Apr. 1, 1707. [Bayley, C.R.1.]
Mary, d. John, Dec. —, 1677.

BAYLIE, Ruth, d. Joseph and Jerusha, Dec. 4, 1709. [Bayley, c.r.1.]
Samuel, s. John, Aug. —, 1690.
Sarah, d. John, Oct. —, 1675.
Timothy, s. John Jr. and Abigail, Mar. 20, 1709–10.
William, s. John, Feb. —, 1684–5.

BAYLY (see Bailey, Baily, Bayle, Bayley, Baylie), Abigail, d. John (Baylie) Jr. and Abigail, Feb. 4, 1712–13. [Bayley, c.r.1.]

BEACH, Julia Ann, d. Michael, basket maker, and Harriet, July 28, 1844.

BEACON, Hannah, d. Mary, bp. June 16, 1706. c.r.2.

BEAL (see Beale), Abigail Dexter, d. John and Jane T., July 4, 1835.
Catharine Kimbal, d. John and Jane T., Apr. 14, 1823.
Ensign Otis, s. John and Jane T., June 8, 1825.
George Washington, s. John and Jane T., Feb. 22, 1821. [Beale, g.r.6.]
Irene M., d. John and Lucy A. [Sept. —, 1848]. g.r.15.
Jane Elizabeth, d. John and Jane T., Feb. 14, 1830.
Jane T. [———], w. John [Nov. —, 1794]. g.r.6.
John [h. Jane T.] [Mar. —, 1792]. g.r.6.
John Brooks, s. John and Jane T., Aug. 14, 1819.
Julia Turner, d. John and Jane T., Feb. 20, 1828.
Maria Thomas, d. John and Jane T., Apr. 30, 1832.

BEALE (see Beal), Mary L. [ch. John and Jane T.], Sept. 12, 1818. g.r.6.

BEAN, Lucy Ann, ch. Lucy, wid., bp. Apr. 24, 1831. c.r.2.
Rebecca Cushing, ch. Lucy, wid., bp. Apr. 24, 1831. c.r.2.
William Harper, ch. Lucy, wid., bp. Apr. 24, 1831. c.r.2.

BEARCE (see Barce, Bass, Bearse), Evander [dup. Barce], s. John, shoemaker, and Elizebeth C. [dup. Elizabeth, omits C.], Oct. 12, 1839.
Lyman Mills [dup. Burs], s. John, shoemaker [dup. sailor], and Elizebeth [dup. Elizabeth] C., Apr. 17, 1848.
William Wallace [dup. Barce], s. John, shoemaker, and Elizebeth C. [dup. Elizabeth, omits C.], Nov. 5, 1836.

BEARSE (see Barce, Bass, Bearce), Ebenezer, —— [1813]. c.r.1.

BEARSE, Ichabod [dup. Burce], s. John, shoemaker [dup. mariner], and Elizabeth C. [dup. omits C.], July 29, 1844.

BEARSTOW (see Barstow, Bastow, Bersto, Berstow, Berstowe, Bestow, Bestowe), Benjamin, s. Benjamin and Mercy, Oct. 9, 1710.
Deborah, d. Will[iam], "begininge of" Aug., 1650. [Bastow, c.r.2.]
Deborah, d. Sam[ue]ll (Berstow) and Lydia, bp. Oct. 5, 1712. c.r.2.
Elizabeth, d. Joseph Jr., Aug. 23, 1699.
Hannah, d. William Jr. and Sarah, Aug. 10, 1710.
James, s. Joseph and Mary, Apr. 20, 1711.
Joseph, s. Joseph Jr., Sept. 6, 1701.
Joseph, s. Joseph Jr., Jan. 10, 1703-4.
Joshua, s. Joseph Jr., Sept. 8, 1706.
Martha, d. Benjamin and Mercy, Jan. 20, 1712.
Mary, d. Joseph Jr., Feb. 21, 1708-9.
Samuel, s. Samuel, Feb. 7, 1708-9. [Berstowe, s. Samuel and Lidia, c.r.2.]
William, s. Will[iam], "about the middle of" Sept., 1652. [Bastow, c.r.2.]

BECKWITH, David Barnes, s. William and Betsy, Jan. 2, 1813.
Ira Lewis, s. William and Betsy, June 24, 1811.
James Harvey, s. William and Betsy, May 16, 1809.

BELLOWS, George A., —— [1816]. g.r.2.

BEMIS, Eliza F., d. Rev. Nath[àniel] and Eliza, June 18, 1846.
Irena Miller [? m.], ——, 1808. g.r.6.

BENNET (see Bennett), Margaret, w. David Dunbar, ——, 1734. g.r.6.

BENNETT (see Bennet), Eliza, d. Barzillai and Deborah, May 27, 1800.
Jesse Sutton [dup. Bennet], s. Barzillai [dup. Bezeleel] and Deborah, Mar. 19, 1798.

BENSON, Abagil, d. Joseph and Susanna, May 2, 1795.
Artamas, s. Joseph and Susana, Oct. 19, 1778.
Gorham, s. Joseph and Susanna, Mar. 7, 1791.
Gorham, s. Joseph and w., bp. Oct. 6, 1793. c.r.2.
Hannah, d. Joseph and Susana, Sept. 6, 1787.
John, s. Joseph and Susana, Nov. 10, 1774.

BENSON, Joseph, s. Joseph Jr. and Abiel, Dec. 6, 1744.
Joseph, s. Joseph and Susana, Apr. 28, 1771.
Luica, d. Joseph and Susana, Sept. 6, 1780.
Mary P. [———], w. Stephen, —— [1827]. G.R.14.
Mercia, d. Joseph and Susana, May 22, 1785.
Nath[anie]ll, s. Joseph and Susana, Jan. 5, 1773.
Nath[anie]ll, s. Joseph and Susana, Sept. 30, 1776.
Sarah [w. Luther Tilden], —— [1795]. G.R.14.
Sarah, d. Stephen and Sarah S., Jan. 17, 1828.
Sarah Ann, ch. Stephen, bp. Nov. 16, 1828. C.R.2.
Stephen, s. Joseph and Susana, July 17, 1782.
Stephen, s. Stephen and Sarah S., May 11, 1826.

BERRY, John, s. John, bp. Nov. 24, 1678. C.R.2.
Mary, d. Richard, bp. Sept. 9, 1683. C.R.2.

BERSTO (see Barstow, Bastow, Bearstow, Berstow, Berstowe, Bestow, Bestowe), Hannah, d. William, bp. July 30, 1682. C.R.2.
Joseph, s. Joseph, bp. Oct. 3[worn], 1676. C.R.2.
William, s. William, bp. Nov. 7, 1680. C.R.2.
William, s. William, bp. Feb. 5, 1684. C.R.2.

BERSTOW (see Barstow, Bastow, Bearstow, Bersto, Berstowe, Bestow, Bestowe), Anna, d. William, June 26, 1681.
Benjamen, s. Joseph, Mar. 1, 1679–80. [Benjamin Bersto, C.R.2.]
Benjamin, s. William, July 22, 1690. [Bestow, C.R.2.]
Deborah, d. Joseph, Dec. 26, 1681. [Bersto, C.R.2.]
Joseph, s. Joseph, Jan. 22, 1675.
Lydia, d. Samuell, Apr. 1, 1717. [Lydiah Bestow, d. Samuel and Lydia, C.R.2.]
Martha, d. William, ——, 1678. [Bersto, bp. June 16, C.R.2.]
Mary, d. William, Feb. 21, 1687. [Bersto, C.R.2.]
Rebackah, d. William, Mar. 12, 1676. [Rebecca Bestow, C.R.2.]
Rebecca, d. Benjamin and w., bp. June 11, 1727. C.R.2.
Sammuell, s. Joseph, Jan. 1, 1683.
Susana, d. Joseph, June 3, 1667. [Susanna Beerstow, C.R.2.]
Susanah, d. William, Nov. 8, 1693. [Susanna Bestow, C.R.2.]
William, s. William, Nov. 23, 1684.
——, inf. d. Joseph and Mary, bp. Oct. 12, 1719. C.R.2.

BERSTOWE (see Barstow, Bastow, Bearstow, Bersto, Berstow, Bestow, Bestowe), Benjamin, s. Benjamin and Mercy, bp. June 29, 1715. C.R.2.

BESBE (see Besbee, Besbey, Besby, Besbye, Bisby), Martha, d. John, bp. Oct. 21, 1688. c.r.2.

BESBEE (see Besbe, Besbey, Besby, Besbye, Bisby), Hannah, d. Elisha, bp. Dec. 7, 1656. c.r.2.

BESBEY (see Besbe, Besbee, Besby, Besbye, Bisby), John, ch. John (Besby), bp. ——, 1696. c.r.2.

BESBY (see Besbe, Besbee, Besbey, Besbye, Bisby), Aron, ch. John, bp. ——, 1700. c.r.2.
Elijah, ch. John, bp. ——, 1696. c.r.2.
Elisha, ch. John, bp. ——, 1699. c.r.2.
Hopestil, s. John, bp. Aug. 6, 1704. c.r.2.
Hopestill, s. Elisha, bp. Sept. 7, 1645. c.r.2.
John, s. Elisha, bp. Dec. 21, 1645. c.r.2.
Mary, d. Elisha, bp. Sept. 10, 1648. c.r.2.
Mary, ch. John, bp. ——, 1696. c.r.2.
Moses, ch. John, bp. ——, 1696. c.r.2.

BESBYE (see Besbe, Besbee, Besbey, Besby, Bisby), Elisha, s. Elisha, bp. Oct. 29, 1654. c.r.1.
Martha, d. Elisha, bp. Apr. 27, 1651. c.r.2.

BESTOW (see Barstow, Bastow, Bearstow, Bersto, Berstow, Berstowe, Bestowe), Abigail, d. Joseph and Mary, bp. May 19, 1723. c.r.2.
Caleb, s. Benjamin and Mercy, bp. Mar. 20, 1719–20. c.r.2.
Elizabeth, ch. Joseph (Bestowe) and Mary, bp. Apr. 8, 1716. c.r.2.
Elizabeth, d. Sam[ue]l and Lydia, bp. July 23, 1727. c.r.2.
Job, s. Sam[ue]ll and Lydia, bp. Apr. 3, 1720. c.r.2.
Joseph, ch. Joseph (Bestowe) and Mary, bp. Apr. 8, 1716. c.r.2.
Joseph, s. Sam[ue]l and Lydia, bp. June 13, 1725. c.r.2.
Lydia, d. Sam[ue]l and Margret of Hanover, bp. Mar. 20, 1736–7, in Hanover. c.r.2. [Barstow, ch. Dea. Samuel, b. Mar. 14, 1736, p.r.5.]
Margret, d. Benj[a]m[in] and Margret, bp. June 27, 1725. c.r.2.
Mercy, d. Benj[a]m[in] and Mercy, bp. Aug. 19, 1722. c.r.2.
Micael, s. Sam[ue]ll and Lydia, bp. May 19, 1723. c.r.2.
Nathanael, s. Benj[a]m[in] and Mercy, bp. Aug. 11, 1717. c.r.2.
———, d. Benj[a]m[in] and Mercy, bp. July 10, 1728. c.r.2.

BESTOWE (see Barstow, Bastow, Bearstow, Bersto, Berstow, Berstowe, Bestow), Benjamin, s. Benj[a]m[in] and Mercy, bp. Sept. 2, 1716. c.r.2.
James, ch. Joseph and Mary, bp. Apr. 8, 1716. c.r.2.

BEVERSTOCK, Henry F. [h. Olive A. (Brown)], ———, 1849. G.R.19.

BINNEY, D. W., Oct. 11, 1847. G.R.6.

BIRCHMORE, Abigail F., ch. Francis and Abigail, July 29, 1839, in Boston.
Catharine P., ch. Francis and Abigail, Sept. 27, 1842.

BISBY (see Besbe, Besbee, Besbey, Besby, Besbye), John, s. John and Mary of Marshfield, bp. Nov. 7, 1714. C.R.2.

BISHOP (see Boshop), Abigail, ch. Hutson and Abigail, bp. July 25, 1714. C.R.2.
Ann, ch. Hutson and Abigail, bp. July 25, 1714. C.R.2.
Content, ch. Hutson and Abigail, bp. July 25, 1714. C.R.2.
Deliverance, ch. Hutson and Abigail, bp. July 25, 1714. C.R.2.
Luke, s. Hudson and w. of Pembroke, bp. Sept. 4, 1720. C.R.2.
Lusanna, d. Hutson and Abigail, bp. Nov. 17, 1717. C.R.2.
Nathanaell, s. Stutson and Abigail, bp. July 3, 1715. C.R.2.

BIXBY, Marry, w. Charles I. [?] B. Warters, June 4, 1811, in Worcester.

BLACKMER (see Blackmor), John, s. William, Dec. 16, 1669. [Blackmore, C.R.2.]
Peter, s. William, May 25, 1667. [Blackmore, C.R.2.]

BLACKMOR (see Blackmer), Phepe, d. William, Aug. 12, 1672. [Phebe Blackmoor, C.R.2.]
William, s. William, Feb. 25, 1675. [Blacmore, C.R.2.]

BLANKINSHIP, James "Alias Gordon," s. Anne, bp. ———, 1728. C.R.2.

BLOSSOM, Thomas, s. John and Thankfull, April 17, 1728.

BOO, Freeborn, s. Sam[ue]ll and Martha, July 25, 1753. [Bow, C.R.2.]
Jesse, s. Sam[ue]ll and Martha, Mar. 27, 1756.

BOOTH, Abraham, s. John, Feb. 7, 1673.
Antony, s. John Jr., Apr. 18, 1687.
Benjamen, s. John, July 4, 1667.
Benjamin, s. Benjamin, July 19, 1698.
Elisabath, d. John, May 5, 1703.
Elizabeth, d. John, Oct. 5, 1657.
Eunice (see Unice).

BOOTH, Grace, d. John, July 4, 1677.
Hannah, d. Benjamin, May 1, 1696.
Isaiah, s. Benjamin, Mar. 10, 1702–3.
John, s. John, Jan. 1, 1661.
John, s. Benjamin, Sept. 16, 1700.
Joseph, s. John, Mar. 27, 1659.
Judiffe, d. John, Mar. 13, 1680.
Judiffe, d. John Jr., Sept. 27, 1691.
Liddia, d. John, Mar. 8, 1700–1.
Mary, d. John, June 6, 1669.
Mary, d. John Jr., Apr. 11, 1698.
Naomy, d. Benjamin, July 31, 1691.
Rachell, d. Benjamin, May 5, 1693.
Unice, d. John Jr., Mar. 5, 1694–5.
Zerviah, d. John, Nov. 28, 1707.

BOSHOP (see Bishop), Abigail, d. Hudson (Boship), July 2, 0713 [sic, 1713].
Anne, d. Hudson, June 20, 1711.

BOUKER (see Bowker, Buker), Lazorus (Bauker), s. James Jr., Apr. 26, 1718.

BOURN, Abigal, d. Shearjashub and Abigal, Aug. 14, 1727. [Abigail, d. S. and Ab [second w.], c.r.1.]
Bathsheba, d. Shearjashub and Abigal, Oct. 3, 1730.
Bethiah, d. Sharejoshop and Sarah, Apr. 16, 1781.
Betty Woodworth, d. Sherej[a]s[ho]p and Sarah, Nov. 25, 1777.
Desire, d. Shearjashub and Abigal, Jan. 22, 1728.
Elizabeth, d. Rev. Shearjashub and Abigal, July 11, 1726.
Elizabeth, d. John and Abigail of Marshfield, bp. May 12, 1734. c.r.2.
John, s. John and Abigail of Marshfield, bp. Apr. 13, 1729. c.r.2.
Lydia, d. Sharejoshop and Sarah, Oct. 31, 1772.
Nabe., d. Shearjoshop and Sarah, Apr. 14, 1775.
Peter, s. John and Abigail of Marshfield, bp. June 20, 1731. c.r.2.
Roland, s. Shearjashub and Deborah, Feb. 27, 1750.
Samuel, s. Nathan and Lydia, Sept. 2, 1734.
Sarah, d. Shearjashop (Born) and Sarah, Jan. 31, 1770.
Shearjashub, s. Shearjashub and Abigal, May 8, 1732.
Shearjashub, s. Shearjashub and Sarah, Sept. 28, 1739.

BOUVE, Adeline Maria, ch. John and Lucy, Nov. 6, 1838.
Claudius, ch. Sylvanus R. and Mary, Mar. 3, 1840.

BOUVE, George Francis, ch. John and Lucy, Mar. 1, 1837.
James Henry, ch. John and Lucy, Oct. 9, 1829.
John Thomas, ch. John and Lucy, Oct. 31, 1826.
Joseph C., s. John, painter, and Lucy, Oct. 24, 1846.
Lucy Vinal, ch. John and Lucy, July 20, 1832.
Mary S., d. Sylvanus, marriner, and Mary, July 13, 1846.
Mary Thomas, ch. Sylvanus R. and Mary, June 23, 1834.
Silvanus Rich, ch. Sylvanus R. and Mary, Jan. 19, 1837.
Thomas Cummings, ch. Sylvanus R. and Mary, Aug. 27, 1835.
William I. [? J.], s. Sylvanus, sailor, and Mary, July 14 [184–].

BOWERS, Charles Lloyd, s. Henry and Mary S., July 7, 1822, in Middletown, Conn.
Henry, s. Henry and Mary S., Jan. 11, 1820, in Middletown, Conn.
Mary Stetson, d. Henry and Mary S., Oct. 1, 1816.
William Cushing, s. Henry and Mary S., Nov. 14, 1830.

BOWKER (see Bouker, Buker), Abigail, d. James, Oct. 27, 1697.
Abigail, d. James, Apr. 13, 1700.
Abigail, [ch.] Lazarus and Abigail, bp. Nov. 30, 1745. C.R.2.
Abigail, d. Lazarus Jr. and Mary, Nov. 26, 1772.
Abigail, d. Gershom and Elisabeth, Sept. 22, 1793.
Adalaide, ch. Horatio N. and Susan M., July 8, 1842.
Allen, s. Edmon and Lydia, May 1, 1775. [s. Edward and Lydia [h. Eunice O. (Vinal)], G.R.14.]
Almina F., ch. Lazarus Jr. and Margaret C. F., Sept. 16, 1841.
Andrew G., ch. Horatio N. and Susan M., Mar. 13, 1828, in Boston.
Ann Elizabeth, ch. Horatio N. and w., Oct. 18, 1832, in Boston.
Anna, d. John and Anna, Sept. 13, 1752.
Anne, d. Luke and Joanna, Sept. 13, 1753. [Anna, d. Luke and Jonna, C.R.2.]
Arabel A., ch. Lazarus Jr. and Margaret C. F., May 13, 1838.
Barshaba, d. Luke and Joanna, Mar. 20, 1755. [Bathshebah, C.R.2.]
Bartlet, s. Lazarus, bp. Sept. 12, 1748. C.R.2.
Bartlet, [ch.] John and w., bp. Dec. 25, 1748. C.R.2.
Bartlet, s. John and Anna, Jan. 22, 1749.
Benjamin, s. James and Mary, Jan. 11, 1709–10.
Benja[min], s. Benja[min] and Hannah, Feb. 14, 1738.
Benjamin, s. Benjamin and Hannah, Dec. 21, 1764.
Benjamin Cushing, s. Joshua and Ann, July 18, 1818.
Calvin, s. Luke and Joanna, Sept. 2, 1760.
Caroline, d. Warren and w., bp. Oct. 18, 1801. C.R.2.
Catharina Whiting, d. David and Eunice, Aug. 17, 1817.

BOWKER, Catharine Whiton, ch. David, bp. Aug. 6, 1820. C.R.2.
Charles, s. John and Anna, Nov. 18, 1757.
Charles, s. Elijah and Anna [Anny (Sylvester), G.R.17.], Oct. 21, 1798.
Charles H., s. David and Eunice, Oct. 21, 1830.
Charlot, d. Benja[min] and Anner, June 24, 1785.
Charlott, d. Elijah and w., bp. Oct. 18, 1801. C.R.2.
Charlotte, d. Elijah and Anna, Jan. 26, 1800. [ch. Elijah and Anny (Sylvester), ——, 1801, G.R.17.]
Chloe, d. Benja[min] Jr. and w., bp. July 1, 1792. C.R.2.
Clarissa Gardner, ch. Howard and w., Sept. 23, 1807, in Boston.
Cornelius, s. James Jr. and w., bp. Sept. 28, 1746. C.R.2.
Damson, d. John, bp. May 16, 1756. C.R.2.
David, s. Luke and Joanna, Sept. 24, 1756.
David, s. David and Eunic, June 16, 1808.
Davis Whiting, ch. Howard and Eveline T., Dec. 4, 1831.
Deborah, d. James, Aug. 13, 1693.
Deborah, d. Jam[e]s and Hanah, Nov. 4, 1730.
Deborah, d. John and Ann, bp. Oct. 4, 1747. C.R.2.
Delight, d. John and Anna, July 25, 1761.
Delight, d. Elijah and Anna [Anny (Sylvester), G.R.17.], Oct. 11, 1796.
Demmick, [ch.] Lazarus and Abigail, bp. Apr. 1, 1750. C.R.2.
Desier, d. Edmon and Lydia, May 16, 1760.
Desire, s. [*sic*] James and Hannah [d. James and Hannah, C.R.2.], Apr. 14, 1741.
Desire, d. John and Anna, Oct. 12, 1769.
Dimmick (see Demmick).
Dimmick, s. Lazarus Jr. and Mary, Dec. 10, 1769.
Dimmick Blossom, s. Dimmick and Margret, Feb. 22, 1800.
Dorcasina, ch. Elijah, bp. June 16, 1811. C.R.2.
Dorcassina, d. Elijah and Anna, Mar. 2, 1804. [ch. Elijah and Anny (Sylvester), ——, 1805, G.R.17.]
Edmon, s. Edmon and Lydia, Sept. 16, 1762.
Edmond, s. James, Aug. 15, 1704. [Edmund Buker, C.R.2.]
Edmond, s. James and Hannah, Aug. 20, 1732.
Edmond, s. Warren and w., bp. Apr. 22, 1804. C.R.2.
Edwin, s. David and Eunice, Jan. 4, 1824.
Elias, s. Dimmick and Margret, Mar. 25, 1802.
Elijah, s. John and Anna, Nov. 18, 1764. [[h. Anny (Sylvester)] G.R.17.]
Elijah, s. Elijah and Anna [Anny (Sylvester), G.R.17.], July 14, 1788.
Elisha, s. Benja[min] and Hannah, Sept. 20, 1751. [Buker, C.R.2.]

BOWKER, Elisha, s. Benjamin and Hannah, Sept. 21, 1767.
Eliza Ann, d. Homer and Tryphena, Dec. 14, 1827.
Eliza Ann, d. Homer and Tryphena, Nov. 5, 1830.
Elizabeth, d. James, May 19, 1691.
Elizabeth (Buker), ch. James, bp. May 27, 1705. C.R.2.
Elizabeth, ch. Horatio N. and Susan M., Oct. 8, 1832, in Boston.
Elvira, d. Demick and w., bp. Aug. 4, 1805. C.R.2.
Esther, d. Benjamin and Hannah, Oct. 26, 1773.
Eunic, d. David and w., bp. Oct. —, 1808. C.R.2.
Eunice (see Unice).
Eunice, d. David and Eunice, Mar. 14, 1815.
Evelina, d. Homer and Tryphena, Aug. 5, 1816.
Eveline A. [dup. Augusta], ch. Horatio N. and Susan M., Aug. 16 [dup. Aug. 18], 1838.
Eveline T., ch. Howard and Eveline T., July 21, 1821, in Boston.
George, s. David and Eunice, Sept. 30, 1826.
George, ch. David, bp. Oct. 29, 1829. C.R.2.
George F., ch. Lazarus Jr. and Margaret C. F., Mar. 28, 1836.
George R., s. Horatio N., carpenter, and Susan [dup. adds M.], Oct. 31, 1844.
Georginna, d. Parsons, farmer, and Deborah H., May 25, 1845.
Gershom, s. Lazarus and Abigail, bp. Oct. 4, 1747. C.R.2.
Gershom, s. Gershom and Elisabeth, Jan. 21, 1775.
Gustavus G., ch. Howard and w., Apr. 2, 1813, in Boston.
Hannah, d. James and Hannah, Aug. 9, 1726.
Hannah, d. Benja[min] and Hannah, Nov. 25, 1740.
Hannah, d. John and Anna, Feb. 2, 1756.
Hannah, d. Benjamin and Hannah, July 29, 1770.
Harriet Thomas, d. Homer and Tryphena, June 1, 1811.
Harris, s. Gershom, bp. July 29, 1792. C.R.2.
Harris, s. Gershom and Elisabeth, Dec. 24, 1796.
Helen Clapp, d. David and Eunice, Feb. 14, 1821.
Helen Dallas, d. Lazarus [dup. Jr.], painter, and Margaret [dup. adds C. F.], June 17 [dup. June 18], 1844.
Helena Clap, ch. David, bp. Oct. 6, 1822. C.R.2.
Henry, s. Dimmick [Dimick, C.R.2.] and Margret, July 27, 1810. [[h. Mary (Merritt)] G.R.14.]
Henry, ch. Howard and w., Jan. 16, 1811, in Boston.
Henry Warren, s. Homer and Tryphena, Oct. 6, 1819.
Homer, s. Gershom and Elisabeth, Sept. 19, 1785.
Homer [h. Tryphena (Sylvester)], ——, 1787. G.R.14.
Horatio Nelson, ch. Howard and w., Sept. 27, 1809, in Boston.
Howard, s. Lazarus Jr. and Mary, May 25, 1778.
Howard, ch. Howard and Eveline T., May 12, 1824, in Boston.

BOWKER, Huldah, d. Lazarus Jr. and Mary, Aug. 20, 1786.
Isaac Stetson, s. Gershom and Elisabeth, Mar. 1, 1778.
James, s. James, Aug. 6, 1695.
James, s. James Jr. and Hannah, Aug. 7, 1721.
James, s. Edmon and Lydia, June 9, 1765.
James, s. David and Eunice, Sept. 24, 1818.
James Clapp, ch. David, bp. Aug. 6, 1820. C.R.2.
James Silvester, s. Elijah and Anna [Anny (Sylvester), G.R.17.], Sept. 28, 1794.
Jenne, d. Lazarus Jr. and Mary, June 11, 1771.
Joel, s. Benjamin and Hannah, July 4, 1775.
John, s. James and Hannah, Oct. 3, 1724.
John, s. John and Anna, Aug. 22, 1754.
John, s. Elijah and Anna [Anny (Sylvester), G.R.17.], Sept. 11, 1792.
John Hillard, s. David and Eunice, Feb. 11, 1813.
Jonathan, s. Lazarus and Abigail, bp. Mar. 30, 1754. C.R.2.
Joseph, s. James and Hannah, Mar. 5, 1738.
Joseph W., s. Joseph, farmer, and Susanna, Dec. 18, 1847.
Joshua, s. Benja[min] and Hannah, May 1, 1747.
Joshua, s. Bemj[a]m[in] [*sic*] and Hannah, bp. May 22, 1748. C.R.2.
Joshua, s. Benja[min] and Hannah, Jan. 29, 1755.
Joshua, s. Benja[min] and Anner, Oct. 8, 1783.
Joshua, s. Joshua and Ann, Feb. 20, 1816.
Julia Ann, ch. Howard and Eveline T., June 26, 1839.
Laurinda, d. David and Eunice, July 22, 1828.
Laurinda, ch. David, bp. Oct. 22, 1829. C.R.2.
Lazarus, s. James, Nov. 3, 1686. [Bucer, C.R.2.]
Lazarus, s. James and Hannah, bp. June 28, 1719. C.R.2.
Lazarus, s. Lazarus, bp. Mar. 11, 1743-4. C.R.2.
Lazarus, s. Lazarus Jr. and Mary, May 12, 1784.
Lazrus, s. Dimmick and Margret, Nov. 13, 1817.
Lefy, d. John and Anna, Sept. 13, 1766.
Lemuel, s. Laz[arus], bp. Feb. 16, 1755. C.R.2.
Lemuel, s. Gershom and Elisabeth, Jan. 28, 1781.
Liberty, s. Luke and Joanna, May 13, 1775.
Louisa, d. Dimmick and Margret, May 10, 1805.
Lucy, d. John and Anna [Ann, C.R.2.], Mar. 7, 1751.
Lucy Cushing, d. Stephen and w., bp. Sept. 16, 1792. C.R.2.
Lydia, d. James and Hannah, Sept. 5, 1728.
Lydia, d. Edmon and Lydia, Mar. 26, 1757.
Lyman, s. David and Eunice, Dec. 7, 1833.
Margret, d. Benja[min] and Hannah, May 27, 1749.
Martha, d. James, July 8, 1684.

BOWKER, Mary (Bucer), d. James, bp. Sept. 26, 1686. C.R.2.
Mary, d. James, Feb. 20, 1688.
Mary (Buker), ch. James, bp. May 27, 1705. C.R.2.
Mary, d. James and Hanah [d. James Jr. and Hannah, C.R.2.], Aug. 10, 1719.
Mary, d. James and Hannah, Sept. 13, 1734.
Mary, d. Luke and Joanna, Nov. 8, 1758.
Mary, d. Luke and Joanna, Sept. 2, 1764.
Mary, d. Lazarus Jr. and Mary, July 12, 1782.
Mary, d. Gershom and Elisabeth, Apr. 19, 1788.
Mary Ann, d. Harriet T., Mar. 21, 1831.
Mary Ann Brooks, d. Joshua and Ann, Jan. 31, 1821.
Nabby, d. Lazarus, bp. Mar. 26, 1757. C.R.2.
Nabby, d. Stephen and w., bp. Oct. 5, 1794. C.R.2.
Nancy West, d. Homer and Tryphena, Dec. 19, 1833. [w. George Silvester, ——, 1834, G.R.14.]
Nathaniel, s. Gershom and Elisabeth, May 25, 1783.
Nathaniel Homer, s. Homer and Tryphena, June 13, 1814.
Nathaniel Homer, s. Homer and Tryphena, Oct. 5, 1824.
Parsons, s. Homer and Tryphena, May 15, 1822.
Paul, s. Edmon and Lydia, Apr. 21, 1773.
Phillup, s. Edmon and Lydia, Nov. 6, 1767.
Polly, d. Benja[min] and Anner, July 9, 1781.
Rebecca, d. John and Anna, Aug. 27, 1747.
Rebecca, d. Elijah and Anna, Feb. 26, 1802. [ch. Elijah and Anny (Sylvester), ——, 1803, G.R.17.]
Rebekah, d. James, Mar. 3, 1706-7.
R[e]bekah, d. Elijah and w., bp. Oct. 16, 1803. C.R.2.
Rhode, d. James and Mary, bp. June 17, 1744. C.R.2.
Richard, s. James, June 24, 1702.
Ruth, d. James and Hannah, Aug. 1, 1736.
Ruth, d. John and Anna, Sept. 29, 1759.
Ruth, d. Luke and Joanna, Sept. 18, 1767.
Ruth, d. Elijah and Anna, Apr. 26, 1808. [ch. Elijah and Anny (Sylvester), ——, 1809, G.R.17.]
Ruth, ch. Elijah, bp. June 16, 1811. C.R.2.
Sally, d. Lazarus Jr. and Mary, Mar. 6, 1780.
Sally, d. Elijah and Anna [Anny (Sylvester), G.R.17.], Oct. 15, 1790.
Sally, d. Elijah and Hannah, Sept. 30, 1814.
Sam[ue]ll, s. Sam[ue]ll, negro, and w., bp. Sept. 28, 1794. C.R.2.
Sarah, d. Edmon and Lydia, June 16, 1770.
Silvester, s. Benja[min] and Anner, Dec. 3, 1788.
Stephen, s. John and Anna, Feb. 17, 1763.
Stephen, s. Elijah and Hannah, Sept. 14, 1811.

BOWKER, Stephen Cushing, s. Joshua and Ann, July 25, 1826.
Susan M. [dup. Matilda], ch. Horatio N. and Susan M., July 18, 1830 [dup. 1831], in Boston.
Susanna, d. Lazarus Jr. and Mary, Jan. 21, 1776.
Theodore Persons, s. David and Eunic, Jan. 13, 1811. [Theodore Parsons, C.R.2.]
Thirza, d. Dimmick [Dimick, C.R.2.] and Margret, Jan. 16, 1813.
Unice, d. Benja[min] and Hannah, Dec. 7, 1744. [Eunice, C.R.2.]
Warren Thatcher, s. Warren and Rebekah, Nov. 24, 1799.
Worren, s. Edmon and Lydia, July 14, 1777.
———, s. Parsons, farmer, and Deborah H., Apr. 27, 1847.

BOWMAN, Hulda F. [———], w. Charles F., ——— [1836]. G.R.15.

BRADFORD, Hannah, d. Elisha and Barshua of Plymouth, bp. Sept. 18, 1720. C.R.2.
Mary Warner, d. Seth and Betsey, Mar. 20, 1831.
———, twin d. John, Dec. 9, 1849.
———, twin d. John, Dec. 9, 1849.

BRADLEY, Harris, s. Caleb S., manufacturer, and Susan, Oct. 10, 1845, in Lowell.

BRAMAN, Mary, w. W[illia]m Brooks, Jan. 12, 1718, in Norton. G.R.14.

BRIANT (see Bryan, Bryant), Abiah, d. John, bp. Aug. 23, 1755. C.R.2.
Agatha (see Egetha).
Anna, d. John Sr., Nov. 28, 1679.
Barsheba, d. David, Sept. 18, 1716. [Bryant, d. David and Hannah, C.R.2.]
Benjamen, s. John, Dec. —, 1669. [Benjamin Bryant, C.R.2.]
Deborah, d. John, Jan. 22, 1676. [Daborah Bryant, C.R.2.]
Egetha, d. John, July 16, 1712. [Agatha Bryant, d. John and Deborah, C.R.2.]
Han, [twin] d. Thomas and Mary, Nov. [22], 1724. G.R.14.
Jabish, s. John, Feb. 18, 1671. [Jabez Bryant, C.R.2.]
Jacob, s. David and Hannah, Jan. —, 1713–14. [Bryant, C.R.2.]
James, s. Peleg and Mary, bp. June 30, 1751. C.R.2.
John, s. John, Apr. 23, 1716. [Bryant, s. John and Deborah, C.R.2.]
Jonathan, s. John Jr., Jan. 1, 1679. [Bryant, C.R.2.]
Joseph, s. John, May —, 1667. [Bryant, C.R.2.]
Peleg, s. Peleg, bp. Sept. 13, 1741. C.R.1.
Rhoda, d. Peleg, bp. May 18, 1755. C.R.2.

BRIANT, Ruth, d. John, Apr. 16, 1673. [Bryant, C.R.2.]
Susanah, d. John, May 11, 1714. [Susanna Bryant, d. John and Deborah, C.R.2.]
Thomas, s. John [John Sr., C.R.2.], July 15, 1675.

BRIDGES (see Brige, Briges, Brigg, Briggs, Brigs), Joseph, s. Cornelius, bp. Apr. 20, 1679. C.R.2.
Mary, d. James, bp. June 17, 1683. C.R.2.

BRIGE (see Bridges, Briges, Brigg, Briggs, Brigs), Deborah, d. Capt. John, Oct. 8, 1685. [Briges, C.R.2.]
Hanah, d. Capt. John (Briges), May 8, 1684.

BRIGES (see Bridges, Brige, Brigg, Briggs, Brigs), Joseph, s. James, Feb. 19, 1678.
Joseph, s. James, bp. June 10, 1679. C.R.2.
Mary, d. James, May 14, 1682.

BRIGG (see Bridges, Brige, Briges, Briggs, Brigs), Nathanael, s. Joseph and Deborah, bp. Sept. 24, 1727. C.R.2.

BRIGGS (see Bridges, Brige, Briges, Brigg, Brigs), Abigail, d. John and Abigal, Feb. 11, 1753.
Abigail [———], w. Elisha, ——— [1786]. G.R.14.
Abigail Smith, d. Elisha and Abigail, Mar. 4, 1801.
Adeline [? m.], ———, 1803. G.R.14.
Adeline, ch. James P. and Adeline, Jan. 15, 1832, in Waterton.
Albert Hiram, ch. James P. and Adaline, Sept. 11, 1841.
Albert K., ch. David and Charlotte, Apr. 23, 1837, in Medford.
Alfred, s. Charles and Rhoda, May 15, 1834.
Alfred, s. Charles and Rhoda, July 18, 1838.
Alfred, s. James L., yeoman, and Adeline, May 4, 1844.
Almira, d. Charles and Rhoda, Aug. 10, 1836.
Amy Estelle, d. William, ship carpenter, and Fanny, May 24, 1848.
Ana, d. John and Abigal, Oct. 19, 1754. [Ann, C.R.2.]
Andrew J., ch. James P. and Adeline, Oct. 3, 1834, in Waterton.
Anna, d. Elisha and Abigail, June 4, 1793.
Barnabas Webb, s. Joseph and Meriam, May 25, 1805. [May 20, G.R.6.]
Bartlet, s. James Jr. and Rhodia, June 7, 1772.
Benjamin (Priggs), s. Lt. James, Jan. 20, 1695-6.
Benja[min], s. Benja[min] and Leah, Oct. 18, 1722.
Benja[min], s. Benja[min] and Rebeca, May 23, 1760.
Betsey, d. Joseph and Meriam, Feb. 10, 1802.

BRIGGS, Betty, d. James Jr. and Rhodia, Oct. 30, 1766.
Billings, s. Benja[min] Jr. and Sarah, Jan. 1, 1792.
Caroline E., d. Barnabas [dup. Barnabus] W., shipwright [dup. ship carpenter], and Deborah, Jan. 16, 1844 [dup. 1845]. [Jan. 15, 1845, G.R.6.]
Caroline Forester, ch. Otis and Caroline, Oct. 18, 1837.
Caroline Otis, d. Henry and Betsey, Aug. 23, 1813.
Caroline Otis, ch. Henry and Betsey dec'd, bp. June 6, 1834. C.R.2.
Charles, s. Benja[min] and Rebecca, Sept. 20, 1762.
Charles, s. Ezra, bp. May 29, 1763. C.R.1.
Charles, Sept. 15, 1763. G.R.14.
Charles, s. Will[ia]m and Eliza[beth], Feb. 8, 1773.
Charles, s. Thomas B. and Lucy, Oct. 12, 1791.
Charles Cushing, s. Cushing O. and Mary, Oct. 8, 1813.
Charles Cushing, ch. Cushing O. and Mercy L., bp. May 15, 1831. C.R.3.
Charles Henry, s. John and Jane, Apr. 3, 1832.
Charles Otis, s. Charles Jr. and Rhoda, Mar. 20, 1823.
Charlotte, d. Charles and Rhoda, May 10, 1832.
Church, s. Cornelu[s] and Jerusha, Dec. 6, 1768.
Clarisa, d. Joseph and Meriam, Feb. 17, 1810.
Cornelious, s. Cornelious and Mary, Dec. 10, 1680.
Cornelius, s. Joseph Sr. and Deborah (d. —— Holbrook), Sept. 26, 1705.
Cornelius, ch. Joseph and Deborah, bp. Aug. 10, 1712. C.R.2.
Cornelius, s. James and Hannah, Nov. 3, 1728.
Cornelius, s. Will[ia]m and Eliza[beth], Aug. 2, 1776.
Cornelius, "a natural son of Sarah Wade," ———.
Cornelus, s. Cornelus and Jerusha, Oct. 5, 1757.
Cushing Otis, s. Thomas B. and Lucy, Feb. 25, 1787.
Cynthia Merritt, d. John and Jane, Aug. 14, 1824.
Cynthia Miriam, d. James S. and Selina, Oct. 6, 1829.
Daniel, s. Jo[h]n, bp. Nov. 6, 1757. C.R.1.
David, s. Bartlett and Deborah, Mar. 8, 1811.
Deborah, d. Joseph and Deborah, bp. Apr. 5, 1713. C.R.2.
Deborah, d. Jo[h]n, bp. Feb. 20, 1714. C.R.1.
Deborah, d. Benja[min] and Leah, June 1, 1724.
Deborah, twin d. John, bp. Apr. 25, 1758. C.R.1.
Deborah, d. John and Abigail, Dec. 7, 1767.
Deborah [———], w. Bartlett [Oct. —, 1777]. G.R.6.
Deborah, d. Bartlett and Deborah, Dec. 27, 1806.
Deborah Clap, d. James 3d and Deborah, Apr. 10, 1782.
Deborah Clapp, d. Thomas B. and Lucy, Nov. 16, 1801.

BRIGGS, Deborah Clapp, d. Henry and Betsey, Apr. 6, 1823.
[w. Israel Nash, G.R.14.]
Deborah Otis [? m.], Sept. 12, 1806. G.R.6.
Ebenezer, s. John and Jane, Aug. 29, 1829.
Elijah, s. Will[ia]m and Eliza[beth], July 17, 1762.
Elisabeth, d. James, Dec. 20, 1715. [Elizabeth Brigs, C.R.2.]
Elisabeth, d. Elijah and w., bp. Sept. 4, 1796. C.R.2.
Elisha, s. James and Hannah, Oct. 26, 1723.
Elisha, s. John and Abigal, Aug. 10, 1761.
Elizabeth (see Elisabeth).
Elizabeth, d. Will[ia]m and Eliza[beth], July 15, 1767.
Elizabeth, d. Henry and Betsey, Apr. 25, 1820. [Elizabeth R., G.R.14.]
Elizabeth Ruggles, ch. Henry and Betsey dec'd, bp. June 6, 1834. C.R.2.
Ellen, ch. James P. and Adeline, Nov. 19, 1829, in Waterton.
Ellen Deborah, d. Barnabas W. and Deborah, Feb. 16, 1835.
Emeline, d. Charles Jr. and Rhoda, Sept. 17, 1828.
Emeline Augusta, d. Barnabas W. and Deborah, Nov. 9, 1832.
Enoch, s. Ezra, bp. June 10, 1770. C.R.1.
Enoss, s. Seth and Abigail, bp. Sept. 7, 1746. C.R.2.
Estella M., d. W[illia]m, shipwright, and Fanny, Feb. 21, 1845.
Eunice, d. Joseph and Meriam, Sept. 20, 1811.
Ezra, s. Joseph, bp. Aug. 22, 1725. C.R.1.
Ezra, s. Ezra, bp. June 1, 1760. C.R.1.
Franklin, s. Cushing O. and Mary, Jan. 7, 1833.
Franklin, ch. Cushing O. and Mercy L., bp. Apr. 6, 1834. C.R.3.
George, s. James Jr. and Rhoda, Sept. 21, 1781.
George Henry, s. Henry and Betsey, Sept. 10, 1815. [[h. Nancy L.] G.R.14.]
Geo[rge] Henry, ch. Henry and Betsey dec'd, bp. June 6, 1834. C.R.2.
Hannah, d. Joseph Jr., Feb. 8, 1714.
Hannah, d. Joseph Sr., bp. Sept. 28, 1718. C.R.1.
Hannah, d. James and Hannah, Nov. 27, 1724.
Hannah [dup. Hanah], d. James Jr. [dup. omits Jr.] and Hannah, Dec. 31, 1746. [Hannah Brigs, d. James (Briggs) and Hannah, C.R.2.]
Hannah, d. Joseph and Meriam, Nov. 24, 1803.
Hannah Barker, d. Cushing O. and Mary, June 8, 1819.
Hannah Barker, ch. Cushing O. and Mercy L., bp. May 15, 1831. C.R.3.
Hannah Stowell, d. Elisha and Abigail, Mar. 3, 1799. [Hannah Stowel, C.R.2.]

BRIGGS, Hannah Wade, d. James S. and Selina, Oct. 29, 1833.
Harriet, d. Benja[min] Jr. and Sarah, Apr. 20, 1801.
Harriet Atwood, d. Bartlett and Deborah, ——— [rec. after ch. b. Jan. 20, 1814].
Harriot, ch. Benjamin Jr., bp. Oct. 10, 1813. C.R.1.
Harrison, s. Cushing O. and Mary, Jan. 30, 1824.
Harrison Otis, ch. Cushing O. and Mercy L., bp. May 15, 1831. C.R.3.
Henery, s. Thomas B. and Lucy, Mar. 11, 1789.
Horace Cushing, s. Charles Jr. and Rhoda, Dec. 29, 1824.
Horace Cushing, s. Charles Jr. and Rhoda, July 23, 1830.
Huldah, d. Will[ia]m and Eliz[abeth], Sept. 3, 1780.
Ichabod, ch. Jo[h]n and Judith, bp. Sept. 30, 1753. C.R.1.
James, s. Cornelius and Mehitable, Mar. 2, 1683.
James, s. James and Hannah, Feb. 27, 1719.
James, s. Benja[min] and Leah, Nov. 16, 1735.
James, s. James Jr. [dup. omits Jr.] and Hannah, Mar. 14, 1753.
James, s. Bartlett and Deborah, Jan. 12, 1805.
James, s. Elisha and Abigail, May 23, 1810.
James Buffinton, s. Elijah and w., bp. Sept. 4, 1796. C.R.2.
James Edwin, s. Cushing O. and Mary, May 8, 1821.
James Edwin, ch. Cushing O. and Mercy L., bp. May 15, 1831. C.R.3.
James Prat, s. Benja[min] Jr. and Sarah, Aug. 23, 1799.
James Pratt, ch. Benjamin Jr., bp. Oct. 10, 1813. C.R.1.
James Sylvester, s. Joseph and Meriam, Apr. 14, 1800.
Jane, d. Cornelius Briggs "alias wade [" (a natural son of Sarah Wade) he removed to Maine," written later] and Jane, Sept. 14, 1739.
Jane, d. John Jr. and Judith, Jan. 18, 1783.
Jenne, [ch.] John 3d, bp. Oct. 8, 1786. C.R.1.
Jerusha, d. Corn[elius] and Jerusha, June 29, 1764.
Joa, [ch.] John 3d, bp. Oct. 8, 1786. C.R.1.
Job, s. James and Hannah, Oct. 28, 1722. [Brigs, C.R.2.]
Job, s. James and Hannah, bp. June 24, 1733. C.R.2.
Joe, d. [sic] John Jr. and Judith, Oct. 29, 1784.
John, s. Joseph Sr. and Deborah, Dec. 18, 1709.
John, ch. Joseph and Deborah, bp. Aug. 10, 1712. C.R.2.
John, s. John and Deborah, bp. Oct. 25, 1714 [sic, 1713]. C.R.2.
John, s. James [(Brigs) C.R.2.] and Hannah, Sept. 28, 1717.
John, s. James and Hannah, Jan. 1, 1718.
John, s. Cornelius Briggs "alias wade" [" (a natural son of Sarah Wade) he removed to Maine," written later] and Jane, Jan. 30, 1737.

BRIGGS, John Jr. [h. Judith], Nov. 17, 1744.
John, s. John and Abigail, June 11, 1751.
Jo[h]n, ch. Jo[h]n and Judith, bp. Sept. 30, 1753. C.R.1.
John, s. Will[ia]m and Eliza[beth], Feb. 24, 1770.
John, s. Elisha and Abigail, Nov. 4, 1803.
John, s. Henry and Betsey, Oct. 14, 1827.
John Doane, s. John and Jane, Apr. 3, 1827.
John R., ———, 1827. G.R.14.
Joseph, s. Cornelious and Mary, Apr. 29, 1679.
Joseph, s. Joseph Sr., bp. May 29, 1715. C.R.1.
Joseph, ch. Jo[h]n and Judith, bp. Sept. 30, 1753. C.R.1.
Joseph, s. John and Abigal, Jan. 29, 1756. [Brigs, C.R.2.]
Joseph, s. James Jr. and Rhoda, Feb. 1, 1777.
Joseph, s. Joseph and Meriam, Oct. 25, 1807.
Joseph Otis, s. Barnabas W. and Deborah, Nov. 9, 1836.
Joseph Worring, s. Elisha and Abigail, Jan. 27, 1808. [Joseph Warren Brigs, C.R.2.]
Josiah, s. Charles and w., bp. May 1, 1796. C.R.2.
Juda, d. John, bp. Oct. 30, 1763. C.R.1.
Judith, d. Joseph Jr. and Judeth, May 20, 1725.
Judith [———], w. John Jr., May 4, 1754.
Judith, d. Jo[h]n, bp. July 7, 1754. C.R.1.
Judith, d. John Jr. and Judith, July 16, 1788.
Juliette Frances, d. Barnabas W. and Deborah, Sept. 28, 1846.
Leah, d. Benja[min] and Leah, Sept. 22, 1720.
Lemuel, s. Will[ia]m and Eliza[beth], Mar. 25, 1765.
Lloyd, s. Cushing O. and Mary, Ap[r]. 8, 1830.
Lloyd, ch. Cushing O. and Mercy L., bp. May 15, 1831. C.R.3.
Lucy, d. James Jr. [dup. omits Jr.] and Hannah, Apr. 15, 1751.
Lucy, twin d. James and Hannah, July 7 [dup. July 6], 1755.
Lucy [———], w. John, ——— [1789]. G.R.2.
Lucy, d. John Jr. and Judith, June 4, 1799.
Lucy Ann, d. Charles Jr. and Rhoda, Aug. 7, 1827.
Lucy Turner, d. Henry and Betsey, Jan. 23, 1830. [w. Nathaniel Cushing Nash, G.R.14.]
Luther, s. James Jr. and Rhoda, Jan. 25, 1779.
Lydia, d. John and Abigail, Feb. 24, 1763.
Margret, d. John (Brigs) and Abigail, bp. Mar. 27, 1748. C.R.2.
Margret, d. John and Abigail, bp. May 14, 1749. C.R.2.
Mary, d. Joseph Sr. and Deborah, Aug. 26, 1707.
Mary, d. Joseph Jr. and Mary (d. ——— Garrett), Oct. 9, 1711.
Mary, ch. Joseph and Deborah, bp. Aug. 10, 1712. C.R.2.
Mary, d. Cornelius and Jerusha, Dec. 18, 1753.
Mary, d. Joseph and Meriam [Miriam, G.R.6.], Feb. 4, 1814.

BRIGGS, Mary, d. Henry and Betsey, Oct. 25, 1817.
Mary, ch. Henry and Betsey dec'd, bp. June 6, 1834. C.R.2.
Mary Foster, d. Elisha and Abigal, Mar. 5, 1797.
Mary Jane, d. Charles Jr. and Rhoda, July 11, 1821.
Mary Thomas, d. Cushing O. and Mary, Apr. 11, 1828.
Mary Thomas, ch. Cushing O. and Mercy L., bp. May 15, 1831. C.R.3.
Moses, s. Ezra and Lydia, bp. Oct. 4, 1767. C.R.1.
Nancy L. [———], w. George H. [Apr. —, 1820]. G.R.14.
Nathanael, s. Joseph Sr., bp. Sept. 24, 1727. C.R.1.
Nathaniel, s. Ezra, bp. Nov. 14, 1763. C.R.1.
Otis, s. Bartlett and Deborah, Feb. 2, 1809.
Paul, s. Benja[min] and Rebecca, Jan. 25, 1765.
Paul, s. Benja[min] Jr. and Sarah, Mar. 22, 1797.
Paul Dean, s. Paul and Siba, May 7, 1823.
Polly, d. James Jr. and Rhoda, Apr. 10, 1775. [w. Silas Litchfield, G.R.6.]
Polly, d. Benja[min] Jr. and Sarah, June 29, 1794.
Polly, d. John Jr. and Judith, Sept. 24, 1795.
Rachel, d. James and Hannah, Dec. 23, 1726.
Rachel, d. Benja[min] and Leah, Aug. 13, 1730.
Rachel, d. Will[ia]m and Eliza[beth], Aug. 19, 1755. [Brigs, C.R.2.]
Rachel, d. Ezra, bp. June 7, 1759. C.R.1.
Rebecca, d. John and Abigal, Aug. 24, 1759.
Rebecca, d. Benja[min] and Rebec[c]a, Oct. 3, 1769.
Rhoda, d. Bartlett and Deborah, Jan. 20, 1814. [w. Rufus Curtis, G.R.6.]
Ruben, s. Cornelius Briggs "Alias wade" ["(a natural son of Sarah Wade) he removed to Maine," written later] and Jane, Apr. 18, 1741.
Ruth, d. Will[ia]m and Eliza[beth], Aug. 13, 1757.
Sabera, d. John and Abigal, Sept. 10, 1757. [Ceberry Briggs, C.R.2.]
Samuel, s. Cornelus and Jerusha, Jan. 12, 1762.
Sarah, d. Cornelius Briggs "alias wade [waid, C.R.1]" ["(a natural son of Sarah Wade) he removed to Maine," written later] and Jane, May 9, 1742.
Sarah, d. James Jr. [dup. omits Jr.] and Hannah [dup. Hanah], Nov. 3, 1748.
Sarah, twin d. James and Hannah, July 7 [dup. July 6], 1755.
Sarah, twin d. John, bp. Apr. 25, 1758. C.R.1.
Sarah, d. Ezra, bp. June 12, 1768. C.R.1.
Sarah, d. Benja[min] Jr. and Sarah, Apr. 20, 1793.
Sarah, d. Henry and Betsey, Jan. 5, 1832.

BRIGGS, Sarah, ch. David and Charlotte, ——— [rec. after ch. b. Apr. 23, 1837].
Sarah Ann, d. John and Jane, Oct. 9, 1823.
Sarah Jacobs, d. Elisha and Abigail, Mar. 17, 1795. [Sarah J. Poole, G.R.14.]
Sarah Smith, d. Elisha and w., bp. Oct. 18, 1801. C.R.2.
Selina Curtis, d. James S. and Selina, Oct. 26, 1824.
Seth, s. James and Hannah, Aug. 28, 1721.
Shadrach, s. Joseph and Meriam, Feb. 4, 1799.
Shadrack, s. James Jr. and Rhodia, Aug. 16, 1769.
Soffa, d. Benja[min] Jr. and Sarah, Apr. 7, 1795.
Sophia, d. John, bp. May 26, 1793. C.R.1.
Sophia, w. Thomas Ellms, ———, 1796. G.R.2.
Sophy, d. John Jr. and Judith, Apr. 24, 1791.
Susanna, d. Cornelius, bp. Nov. 11, 1744. C.R.1.
Susanna, d. John Jr. and Judith, Feb. 20, 1781.
Thankfull, d. Joseph Sr., bp. June 30, 1717. C.R.1. [Thankful, ch. Joseph and Deborah, C.R.2.]
Thankfull, ch. Jo[h]n and Judith, bp. Sept. 30, 1753. C.R.1.
Thomas, s. Thomas Barker and Lucy, June 20, 1785.
Thomas Barker, s. James and Hannah, July 13, 1757. [Brigs, C.R.2.]
Thomas Wales, s. Henry and Betsey, Mar. 23, 1825.
Walter E., ch. James P. and Adeline, Mar. 3, 1840.
William, s. James and Hannah, July 23, 1731. [Brigs, C.R.1.]
Will[ia]m, s. Will[ia]m and Eliza[beth], Mar. 15, 1760.
William [Nov. —, 1816]. C.R.1.
William Thomas, s. Cushing O. and Mary, Dec. 1, 1815.
William Thomas, ch. Cushing O. and Mercy L., bp. May 15, 1831. C.R.3.
———— [————], w. ————, —— [1753]. C.R.1.
————, d. Barnabas W., shipwright, and Deborah O., Sept. 27, 1846.

BRIGS (see Bridges, Brige, Briges, Brigg, Briggs), James, s. James (Briges), Feb. 2, 1687.
John, s. Capt. John, Apr. 28, 1687. [Bridges, C.R.2.]
Ruth, d. Cornelius, bp. Sept. —, 1757. C.R.2.

BROCK (see Brocke, Broocke, Brook, Brooke, Brookes, Brooks), Grace, ch. Francis, bp. ————, 1704. C.R.2.

BROCKE (see Brock, Broocke, Brook, Brooke, Brookes, Brooks), Mary, d. Francise, Dec. 15, 1699. [Brock, d. Francis, C.R.2.]

BROOCKE (see Brock, Brocke, Brook, Brooke, Brookes, Brooks), Barsheba, d. Francise, May 21, 1703. [Barshua Brock, ch. Francis, C.R.2.]
Grace, d. Francise, July 27, 1701.

BROOK (see Brock, Brocke, Broocke, Brooke, Brookes, Brooks), Elizabeth, d. Gilbert, bp. June 21, 1646. C.R.2.
Hannah, d. W[i]ll, bp. Sept. 14, 1645. C.R.2.
Hannah, d. Gilbert, bp. Oct. 2, 1659. C.R.2.
Johanna, d. W[illl[ia]m, bp. Oct. 16, 1650. C.R.2.
Mary, d. William, bp. Nov. 28, 1647. C.R.2.
Mary, d. Gilbert, bp. July 15, 1649. C.R.2.
Nathaniel, s. Will[iam], bp. Mar. 29, 1646. C.R.2.
Rachel, d. Gilbert, bp. July 7, 1650. C.R.1.
Sarah, d. Gilbert, bp. June 21, 1646. C.R.2.
Sarah, d. W[i]ll[ia]m, bp. May 26, 1650. C.R.2.

BROOKE (see Brock, Brocke, Broocke, Brook, Brookes, Brooks), Bathshebah, d. Gilbert, bp. Apr. 8, 1655. C.R.1.
Deborah, d. William, bp. Mar. 18, 1654. C.R.2.
Phebe, d. Gilbert, bp. Sept. 5, 1652. C.R.2.
Rebecca, d. Gilbert, bp. Apr. 12, 1657. C.R.2.
Thomas, s. William, bp. June 28, 1657. C.R.2.

BROOKER, Alice [? m.], ———, 1774. G.R.14.

BROOKES (see Brock, Brocke, Broocke, Brook, Brooke, Brooks), William, s. Nathaniell, bp. July 5, 1685. C.R.2.

BROOKS (see Brock, Brocke, Broocke, Brook, Brooke, Brookes), Abigail, d. Gilbert and Abigail, bp. Apr. 20, 1729. C.R.2.
Adam, s. Nath[anie]l Jr. and Deborah, May 2, 1788.
Avis Keen, ch. Adam and Hepzibah, Nov. 2, 1838 [? in Scituate]. C.R.4.
Benjamin, s. Gilbert and Hannah, bp. July 31, 1720. C.R.2.
Betty, d. Will[ia]m (Brook) [dup. Jr.] and Betty, July 10, 1782.
Charles, ch. W[illia]m and Sally, bp. Apr. 7, 1833. C.R.3.
Charles Frederick, s. Nathaniel and Charlotte, Feb. 24, 1828.
Charles Stockbridge, s. Gilbert and Abigail, bp. Jan. 20, 1733. C.R.2.
Charlotte Elizabeth, d. Nath[anie]l and Charlotte, Oct. 10, 1830.
Charlotte Elizabeth, ch. Nath and Charlotte, bp. ———, 1833. C.R.2.
Cynthia, d. Nath[anie]l Jr. and Deborah, Aug. 1, 1798.
Deborah, d. Will[ia]m and Mary, May 26, 1761.

BROOKS, Deborah, ch. Adam and Hepzibah, Apr. 19, 1830.
Delia Maria, d. William Jr. and Sally, Sept. 18, 1828.
Ebenezer, s. Gilbert, bp. Mar. 23, 1722. C.R.2.
Edward Wanton, s. Nath[anie]l and Charlotte, Sept. 19, 1837.
Elijah, s. William Jr. and Betty, Feb. 25, 1793.
Elijah F., ch. Elijah and Marie, Apr. 2, 1834, in Marshfield.
Eliza, d. William Jr. and Sally, May 1, 1830.
Elizabeth, d. Nathanaell, Oct. —, 1687. [Elizybeth Brookes, d. Nathaniell, C.R.2.]
Elizabeth, d. Gilbert and Abigail, bp. Jan. 1, 1727–8. C.R.2.
Elizabeth, d. Nat[hanie]ll and Elizabeth, bp. Nov. 6, 1743. C.R.2.
Elizabeth, d. Nath[anie]ll Jr. and Eliza[beth], Nov. 1, 1744.
Eliza[beth], d. Will[ia]m and Mary, Aug. 27, 1757. [Aug. 22, P.R.4.]
Elizabeth B., ch. Adam and Hepzibah, Feb. 12, 1819.
Elvira, d. Nath[anie]l and Charlotte, ——— [rec. between ch. b. Oct. 10, 1830, and ch. b. Sept. 19, 1837].
Eunice, d. William Jr. and Sally, Aug. 27, 1818.
Eunice, ch. Cap[t]. W[illia]m, bp. Aug. 3, 1823. C.R.2.
Experience, d. Gilbert and Abigail, bp. May 16, 1731. C.R.2.
Gilbart, s. Will[ia]m and Mary, Jan. 24, 1755. [Gilbert, C.R.2. P.R.4.]
Gilbert, s. Nathanaell, Nov. 9, 1690.
Gilbert, s. Gilbert and Elizabeth, bp. July 13, 1718. C.R.2.
Gilbert, s. William Jr. and Betty, Feb. 18, 1785.
Gracey Jewett, d. W[illia]m and Sally, Oct. —, 1835.
Hannah, d. Nathanael, Nov. 4, 1679. [Hanna Brooke, d. Nathanell, C.R.2.]
Hannah, d. Will[ia]m and Mary, Sept. 16, 1740.
Harriet Elizabeth, d. Will[ia]m Jr. and Sally, Sept. 9, 1824.
Harriet Elizabeth, ch. William and Sally, bp. Sept. 2, 1827. C.R.3.
James, s. William Jr. and Sally, Feb. 13, 1827.
Joanna, d. Thomas, Sept. 5, 1695.
Joanna, d. Will[ia]m and Mary, Nov. 21, 1748.
John, s. Gilferd and Abigail, bp. May 9, 1736. C.R.2.
John, s. Gilbert Jr. and Deborah, bp. Aug. 17, 1740. C.R.2.
John Adams, ch. Adam and Hepzibah, Feb. 20, 1826.
John Thaxtor, s. William Jr. and Sally, Sept. 26, 1822. [John Thaxter, ch. Cap[t]. W[illia]m, C.R.2.]
Jonathan, s. Nath[anie]l Jr. and Deborah, May 14, 1793.
Lucy, d. Nath[anie]ll Jr. and Sarah, Dec. 18, 1756.
Lucy, d. William Jr. and Betty, May 16, 1787.
Lucy, d. Simeon and Hannah, Nov. 18, 1808.
Lydia, d. Nath[anie]l [Nathanael, C.R.2.] and Mary, Apr. 24, 1726.

BROOKS, Lydia, d. Nath Jr., bp. July 3, 1757. C.R.2.
Marie E., ch. Elijah and Marie, Sept. 24, 1830, in Marshfield.
Martha W., d. Nath[aniel] and Rebecca, July 25, 1842.
Mary, d. Nathanaell, "the middle of" Oct., 1681. [Brookes, d. Nathaniell, C.R.2.]
Mary, d. Nath[anie]l and Mary, Nov. 11, 1727.
Mary, d. Will[ia]m and Mary, Mar. 17, 1746. [w. Benj[amin] Delano, G.R.14.]
Mary Ann Wing, ch. Adam and Hepzibah, Sept. 27, 1834 [? in Scituate]. C.R.4.
Mehitabel, d. [Tailer] and Meriam, bp. Feb. 22, 1740-1. C.R.2.
Mercy, d. Nathanaell, Dec. 2, 1685. [Brookes, d. Nathaniell, C.R.2.]
Mercy, d. Gilbert (Broks) and Abigail, bp. Feb. 10 1722[-3]. C.R.2.
Mercy, d. Nath[anie]l and Mary, Oct. 17, 1731.
Michael, s. Nath[anie]l and Mary, Aug. 23, 1729. [Micael, s. Nathan[ie]ll (Brook) and Mary, C.R.2.]
Miriam, d. William, bp. June 6, 1652. C.R.2.
Miriam, d. Tailor and Miriam, bp. July 31, 1743. C.R.2.
Nathan, s. William Jr. and Betty, Jan. 8, 1798.
Nathanael, s. Nathan[ie]l and Mary, bp. Oct. 21, 1722. C.R.2.
Nathanaell, s. Nathanaell, Aug. —, 1693.
Nathaniel Milton, s. Nathaniel and Charlotte, Jan. 27, 1826.
Nath[anie]l Milton, ch. Nath and Charlotte, bp. ——, 1833. C.R.2.
Nath[anie]ll, s. Nath[anie]ll and Mary, Aug. 30, 1723.
Nath[anie]ll, s. Nath[anie]ll Jr. and Sarah, May 19, 1755. [Nath[anie]l Broks, s. Nath[aniel], C.R.2.]
Nath[anie]ll, s. Nath[anie]l Jr. and Deborah, Apr. 7, 1796.
Noah, s. Nath[anie]ll [Nath[a]n[ie]l, C.R.2.] and Mary, Sept. 30, 1720.
Noah, s. Tailor and Miriam, bp. Nov. 4, 1744. C.R.2.
Patience, d. Will[ia]m and Mary, Oct. 5, 1738. [Brook, C.R.2.] [Brooks, P.R.4.]
Philenda [dup. Philondia], d. Will[ia]m Jr. and Betty, Oct. 3, 1778.
Rachel, d. Gilbert, bp. July 20, 1740. C.R.2.
Rebecca C. [dup. omits C.], d. Nathaniel, farmer, and Rebecca, June 8, 1844.
Rufus, s. Simeon and Hannah, Feb. 21, 1813.
Ruth, d. Gilbert (Brook) and Abigail, bp. May 2, 1725. C.R.2.
Sally, d. Will[ia]m (Brook) Jr. and Betty, Nov. 12, 1776.
Sally, d. William [Cap[t]. William, C.R.2.] Jr. and Sally, Apr. 28, 1816.

BROOKS, Samuel, s. Gilbert and Deborah, bp, Mar. 6, 1742-3.
    C.R.2.
Sarah, d. Will[ia]m and Mary, Sept. 24, 1742.
Sarah, d. Simeon and Hannah, Mar. 9, 1806.
Sarah Swift, ch. Adam and Hepzibah, Apr. 8, 1824.
Sardis, s. Nathaniel Jr. and Deborah, Sept. 2, 1784.
Semion, s. Nath[anie]l Jr. and Sarah, Aug. 13, 1775.
Seth, s. Will[ia]m and Mary, Jan. 9, 1745.
Seth, s. William Jr. and Betty, Aug. 11, 1789.
Silas Swift, ch. Adam and Hepzibah, May 5, 1817. [May 20,
    C.R.4.]
Simeon, s. Nath[anie]l and Mary, Apr. 7, 1733.
Simeon (see Semion).
Stephen, s. Nath[anie]l [Nat[hanie]ll, C.R.2.] and Mary, Sept. 14,
    1737.
Stephen, s. Nath[anie]l Jr. and Deborah, Aug. 29, 1790.
Stephen, ch. Adam and Hepzibah, July 25, 1820.
Susanna, d. W[illia]m and w., bp. Jan. 22, 1748-9. C.R.2.
Taylor, s. Nath[anie]ll and Mary, Aug. 28, 1718. [Tailer, s.
    Nathanaell and Mary, C.R.2.]
Temprance [dup. Temprince Brook], d. Will[ia]m Jr. and Betty,
    Oct. 8, 1780.
Thomas, s. Thomas, June 26, 1688.
William, s. Nathanael, July —, 1683.
William, s. Gilbart (Brooke) [Gilbert (Brook), C.R.2.] and Eliza-
    beth, July 12, 1714. [[h. Mary (Braman)] G.R.14.]
William, s. Will[ia]m and Mary, Feb. 19, 1752.
William, s. Will[ia]m (Brook) Jr. and Betty, Mar. 12, 1775.
William Torrey, s. William Jr. and Sally, Sept. 22, 1813.
———, ch. Deborah, Mar. 20, 1673-4.
———, s. Nathaniel and Charlotte, Oct. 7, 1824.
———, d. Nath[aniel] and Rebecca P., Mar. 7, 1847.

BROUGHTON, Mary [———], w. Daniel, — [1842]. G.R.10.

BROWN (see Browne), Abednego Wade, s. Ebenezer and Mabel,
    Nov. 17, 1809.
Abednego Wade, s. Ebenezar, bp. June 2, 1811. C.R.1.
Abel, s. Jonathan and Sarah, Aug. 12, 1803.
Abijah, s. John and Nancy, Sept. 12, 1808.
Abner, s. Jonathan, bp. July 19, 1741. C.R.1.
Alfred, s. Andrew and Polly, June 4, 1814.
Amelia Whittam, ch. Benjamin Jr. and Margrett, Apr. 10, 1840.
Andrew, s. Andrew and Polly, Mar. 17, 1812.

BROWN, Andrew I. [? J.] [dup. Jackson], s. W[illia]m, shoemaker, and Sarah B. [dup. S.], Mar. 8, [18]46.
Anna, d. Benjamin and Anna, July 9, 1803.
Anna, ch. Benjamin and Anna, bp. Sept. 22, 1811. C.R.1.
Barnabas Franklin, s. John and Nancy, Mar. 28, 1814.
Bela, s. Jonathan and Sarah, Aug. 21, 1812.
Bela Francis, s. John 2d and Clarissa, Apr. 23, 1841.
Benjamin, s. Abijah and Eleanor, Nov. 24, 1774.
Benjamin, s. Benjamin and Anna, Mar. 21, 1802. [Capt. Benjamin [h. Margaret], G.R.9.]
Benjamin, ch. Benjamin and Anna, bp. Sept. 22, 1811. C.R.1.
Benjamin 3d, ch. Benjamin Jr. and Margrett, Aug. 10, 1828, in Boston. [[h. Catharine H.] G.R.7.]
Betsey, d. Jonathan and Sarah, Jan. 3, 1799.
Betsey, d. Ebenezer and Mabel, Sept. 6, 1814. [Betsy, d. Ebenezar, C.R.1.]
Betsey [twin d. ———], Aug. 22, 1836.
Betty, d. Abijah and Vashti, May 2, 1791.
Caroline Augusta, ch. Benjamin Jr. and Margrett, Dec. 18, 1830, in Boston.
Caroline Little, d. Benjamin and Anna, Aug. 16, 1818.
Caroline Little, ch. Benjamin, bp. Aug. 19, 1821. C.R.1.
Catherine H. [———], w. Benjamin Jr., ——— [1831]. C.R.3. [Catharine H., Mar. 3, 1831, G.R.7.]
Charles, s. Joseph and Mercy, Feb. 18, 1796. [[h. Lucy] G.R.8.]
Charles, s. Jonathan and Sally [dup. Sarah], Apr. 19, 1801.
Charles Edward, ch. Charles 2d and Martha J., June 30, 1828, at Cape Ann.
Charles F., s. Joseph Jr. and Emily, Aug. 13, 1848.
Clarissa [———], w. John [Oct. —, 1799]. G.R.2.
Ebenezer, s. Abijah and Eleanor, May 23, 1782.
Ebenezer, ——— [1810]. C.R.3.
Ebenezer, s. Ebenezer and Mabel, May 29, 1818.
Edward Everett, ch. Samuel and Harriet F. [dup. Hannah T.], Oct. 29, 1845.
Edwin, ch. Charles 2d and Martha J., Aug. 26, 1837.
Edwin, ch. Enos and Deborah, Oct. 3, 1838.
Edwin, s. Enos and Deborah [Oct. —, 1840]. G.R.2.
Edwin Young, ch. Charles 2d and Martha J., Dec. 3, 1840.
Elbridge Gerry, s. John and Nancy, July 28, 1817.
Elisha James, ch. Abel and Judith, June 7, 1839.
Eliza Ann, d. Charles and Lucy, Sept. 12, 1831.
Eliza Webb, d. John and Nancy, Oct. 22, 1821.
Ellen, d. Charles and Lucy, Aug. 1, 1835.

BROWN, Emeline Holbrook, ch. Benjamin Jr. and Margrett, Feb. 9, 1835, in Boston.
Emily A., d. Joseph Jr. and Emily, Apr. 26, 1840.
Emily S. [――――], w. Joseph, Jan. 31, 1819. G.R.2.
Enos, s. Jonathan and Sarah, July 22, 1810.
Enos Holbrook, ch. Benjamin Jr. and Margrett, Mar. 23, 1832, in Boston.
Fanny, d. Andrew and Polly, Aug. 11, 1808.
Frank, "22nd Reg. Mass. Vols.," s. John and Clarissa [Apr. ―, 1841]. G.R.2.
George Davis, s. John 2d and Clarissa, Nov. 28, 1838. ["29th Reg. Mass. Vols.," G.R.2.]
George W., s. Joseph Jr. and Emily, Aug. 30, 1838.
George Washington, s. Benjamin and Anna, June 10, 1815.
George Washington, ch. Benjamin, bp. Aug. 19, 1821. C.R.1.
Hannah Wetherell, ch. Benjamin and Anna, bp. Sept. 22, 1811. C.R.1.
Hannah Witherell, d. Benjamin and Anna, Oct. 22, 1805.
Harriet Louisa, d. Samuel and Harriet F., Aug. 22, 1837.
Henrietta Frances, ch. Benjamin Jr. [dup. corker, omits Jr.] and Margrett [dup. Margaret], Dec. 30, 1845.
Henry, ch. Samuel and Louisa, Mar. 5, 1834.
Henry Lewis, ch. Lewis and Lydia B., June 6, 1842.
James, s. Andrew and Polly, Jan. 1, 1805.
James, ―― [1830]. C.R.3.
James Lufkin, ch. Charles 2d and Martha J., Oct. 29, 1830, at Cape Ann.
Jane H. [――――], w. Peleg T. [Sept. ―, 1838]. G.R.2.
John, s. Abijah and Eleanor, Nov. 27, 1777.
John, s. John and Nancy, Sept. 5, 1804.
John, s. Jonathan and Sarah, July 14, 1808.
John, ch. John and w., bp. June 7, 1812. C.R.1.
John Edward, s. John 2d and Clarissa, Oct. 9, 1833.
Jonathan, s. Jonathan and w., bp. July 16, 1738. C.R.1.
Joseph, s. Jonathan and Mary, June 15, 1769. [father of Charles, C.R.3.]
Joseph, s. Joseph and Mercy, Oct. 26, 1814. [[h. Emily S.] G.R.2.
Joseph H., s. Joseph Jr. and Emily, June 28, 1842.
Joseph Northey, s. Abijah and Eleanor, Apr. 14, 1776.
Josiah, s. Jonathan and Sarah, July 19, 1805.
Julia F. [――――], w. William [Jan. ―, 1804]. G.R.8.
Julia Merritt, ch. Benjamin Jr. and Margrett, July 13, 1842.
Knight, s. Jonathan, bp. June 2, 1745. C.R.1.
Knite, s. Jonathan, bp. Nov. 4, 1750. C.R.1.

BROWN, Laura A., ch. William and Sarah S., Feb. 8, 1838.
Lewis, s. Jonathan and Sarah, Dec. 1, 1814. [[h. Lydia B.] G.R.2.]
Louiza Amanda, ch. Lewis and Lydia B., Oct. 25, 1839.
Lucindia G., ch. Charles 2d and Martha J., Jan. 18, 1835, at Cape Ann.
Lucy, d. Abijah and Eleanor, Aug. 29, 1771.
Lucy [———], w. Charles [Mar. —, 1793]. G.R.8.
Lucy [———], w. Charles, —— [1802]. C.R.3.
Lydia B. [———], w. Lewis, ——, 1819. G.R.2.
Lyman Eliot, ch. Benjamin Jr. and Margrett, Apr. 3, 1838. [Lyman Elliot, G.R.9.]
Mabel Wade, d. Ebenezer and Deborah, Jan. 28, 1822.
Mahala D., d. Abednego [dup. adds W.], yeoman, and Mahala [dup. Maha], Aug. 3, 1844.
Marcena Webb, s. John and Nancy, Oct. 5, 1823.
Margaret [———], w. Capt. Benjamin, Feb. 25, 1805. G.R.9.
Margarett Ann, ch. Benjamin Jr. and Margrett, June 27, 1826, in Boston.
Mary, d. Jonathan, bp. Aug. 30, 1747. C.R.1.
Mary, d. Andrew and Polly, May 14, 1801.
Mary Ann, grand d. John [Feb. —, 1834]. C.R.1.
Mary C., d. Charles A., sailor, and Polly, Jan. 28, 1845.
Mercey [———], w. Joseph, —— [1777]. G.R.8.
Mercy Pierce, d. Ebenezer and Mabel, Aug. 2, 1812.
Moses L., ch. Charles 2d and Martha J., Sept. 9, 1832, at Cape Ann. ["He was a Mason" [h. Sophia M. (Litchfield)] G.R.7.]
Nahum, s. Andrew and Polly, Dec. 11, 1802.
Nahum, s. Andrew and Polly, Apr. 7, 1810.
Nancy, d. John and Nancy, Nov. 30, 1806.
Nancy, ch. John and w., bp. June 7, 1812. C.R.1.
Nancy O. [———], w. Joseph H. [July —, 1849]. G.R.2.
Patience Vinal [———], w. Edward, —— [1841]. C.R.3.
Patty, d. Joseph and Mercy, June 18, 1805.
Peleg Thomas, s. John 2d and Clarissa, Sep[t]. 24, 1836.
Priscilla B., ch. William and Sarah S., Oct. 8, 1841.
Robert, s. J[o]nothan, bp. Mar. 23, 1760. C.R.1.
Ruth, d. Abijah and Eleanor, Dec. 15, 1779.
Sally, d. Mary, bp. Oct. 22, 1775. C.R.1.
Sally, d. Jonathan and Sarah, Aug. 11, 1797.
Samuel, s. Jonathan, bp. June 3, 1739. C.R.1.
Sam[ue]l, s. Jonath[a]n, bp. July 7, 1754. C.R.1.
Samuel, s. Joseph and Mercy, Oct. 28, 1808.
Samuell, s. Samuell, Jan. 8, 1704.
Sarah, d. Andrew and Polly, Dec. 11, 1806.

BROWN, Sarah [twin d. ———], Aug. 22, 1836.
Sarah Corene, ch. Samuel and Harriet F., Sept. 6, 1839.
Sarah F., ch. William and Sarah S., Dec. 7, 1839.
Susan Clapp, d. Mary, Sept. 28, 1821.
Susanna, d. Jona[than], bp. Oct. 9, 1757. C.R.1.
Thomas Webb, s. John and Nancy, June 23, 1810.
Thomas Webb, ch. John and w., bp. June 7, 1812. C.R.1.
Warren Lufkin, ch. Abel and Judith, Oct. 27, 1841.
Wilbur Parker [dup. Parke], s. Charles 2d, stone cutter, and Martha G. [dup. J., second dup. E.] (b. Gloucester), Jan. 8, 1848.
William, s. Joseph and Mercy, Jan. 21, 1802. [[h. Julia F.] G.R.8.]
William, s. Andrew and Polly, Aug. 7, 1817.
William F. [Nov. —, 1829]. G.R.8.
William Francis, ch. Abednego W. and Mahala, May 10, 1842.
William J., ch. William and Sarah S., Feb. 29, 1844.
——— [———], w. Geo[rge] W., — [1815]. C.R.1.
———, [twin] s. Enos and Deborah, Aug. 12, 1837.
———, [twin] d. Enos and Deborah, Aug. 12, 1837.
———, s. John 2d and Clarissa, Apr. 25, 1844.
———, s. Ebenezer, farmar, and Judith, Jan. 15, 1848.

BROWNE (see Brown), Ebenezer, ch. Samuel, bp. June 3, 1711. C.R.1.
Hannah, ch. Samuel, bp. June 3, 1711. C.R.1.
Jonathan, s. Murriah, wid., bp. Aug. 29, 1714. C.R.1.

BROWNELL, Clara E., ———, 1824. G.R.14.
Nathan P., M.D., ———, 1825. G.R.14.

BRUCE, ———, d. James and Susan, Apr. 5, 1845.

BRYAN (see Briant, Bryant), Judith, d. Joseph, bp. Nov. 5, 1704. C.R.2.
Martha, d. John, bp. ———, 1695. C.R.2.

BRYANT (see Briant, Bryan), Abigail, d. Samuel and Abigail, bp. July 21, 1723. C.R.2.
Abigail, inf. Benjmin and w., bp. June 7, 1748. C.R.2.
Abigal, d. Sam[ue]ll and Mary, Dec. 31, 1747. [Abigail, C.R.2.]
Agatha, d. John Sr., Mar. 12, 1677-8. [Briant, C.R.2.]
Albert, Rev. [Jan. —, 1838]. C.R.3. [[h. Mary Emmons (Torrey)] ———, 1838, G.R.7.]
Ann, ch. David, bp. Mar. 23, 1738-9. C.R.2.
Ann, [ch.] Peleg and Mary, bp. Apr. 3, 1748. C.R.2.
Benjamin, s. Thomas, Oct. 13, 1708.

BRYANT, Benjamin, s. Thomas and Mary, bp. Dec. 10, 1710. C.R.2.
Benja[min], s. Benja[min] and Abigail, Oct. 17, 1734.
Betty, d. Benja[min] and Abigail, Feb. 15, 1739.
Consider, s. Benja[min] and Abigal, June 9, 1742.
Daniel, s. John, bp. Feb. 5, 1659. C.R.2.
David, s. John Jr., Aug. 17, 1684. [Briant, C.R.2.]
David, s. David, Feb. 14, 1706–7.
David, ch. David and Hannah, bp. Oct. 1, 1710.
David, s. David Jr. and Hannah, bp. Sept. 6, 1730. C.R.2.
Deborah, d. John and Deborah, June 17, 1709.
Dorothy, d. Daniell, Mar. 5, 1692–3.
Edward, s. Capt. Peleg, bp. June 10, 1753. C.R.2.
Elijah, s. Sam[ue]ll and Mary, Nov. 8, 1751. [Briant, s. Sam[ue]ll, C.R.2.]
Elijah, s. Joshua Jr. and Abiel, Apr. 11, 1782.
Elisha, s. Daniell, June 30, 1701.
Eliza, d. Gridley and w. [Oct. —, 1826]. C.R.1.
Elizabeth, d. John (Briant), Aug. —, 1665.
Elizabeth, d. Daniell, Feb. 4, 1690–1.
Elizabeth, d. David, Feb. 6, 1708–9.
Elizabeth, ch. David and Hannah, bp. Oct. 1, 1710. C.R.2.
Foster, s. Zine and Unice, Mar. 17, 1799.
George, s. Benja[min] and Abigail, June 15, 1736.
Gridley, s. Zine and Unice, Aug. 26, 1789. [[h. Maria W.] G.R.2.]
Gridley James Fox [h. Louisa Bryant (Braid)], Aug. 29, 1816. G.R.2.
Hannah, d. John, Jan. 25, 1645.
Hannah, ch. John, bp. Mar. 23, 1650. C.R.2.
Hannah, d. Thomas and Mary, bp. Aug. 7, 1720. C.R.2.
Hannah, d. David and Hannah, bp. Nov. 4, 1733. C.R.2.
Hannah Barker, d. Nath[aniel], bp. June 25, 1769. C.R.1.
Henry E., s. Snow, painter, and Eliza A., July 22, 1849, in S. Scituate.
Hosea, s. Joshua Jr. and Abiel, Sept. 25, 1784.
Ira, s. Sam[ue]ll [Samuel Jr., C.R.2.] and Mary, Aug. 28, 1750.
Ira, s. Joshua Jr. and Abiel, Sept. 3, 1777.
John, s. John, Aug. 17, 1644.
John, ch. John, bp. Mar. 23, 1650. C.R.2.
John, s. John Jr., Mar. 29, 1677–8.
John, s. John and Deborah, Oct. 13, 1707.
John, s. Samuell and Abigail, bp. Dec. 21, 1718. C.R.2.
John, s. John, bp. Dec. 1, 1751. C.R.2.

BRYANT, John, s. Sam[ue]ll and Mary, Jan. 8, 1757.
John, s. Joshua Jr. and Abiel, Oct. 25, 1787.
Jonathan, s. David and Hannah, bp. June 6, 1731. C.R.2.
Joseph, s. John, bp. Apr. 16, 1671. C.R.2.
Joseph, s. Joseph, Jan. 3, 1695-6.
Joseph, s. Zine and Unice, Apr. 28, 1791.
Joshua, s. John Jr., Nov. 14, 1687. [Briant, C.R.2.]
Joshua, s. Samuel [Sam[ue]ll, C.R.2.] and Abigail, Jan. 6, 1712-13.
Judith, d. Joseph, Jan. 24, 1698.
Lemuel, s. Thomas and Mary, bp. Feb. 25, 1721-2. C.R.2.
Lillis, d. Benja[min] and Abigal [Abigail, C.R.2.], Apr. 22, 1738.
Lucy, d. Benja[min] and Abigail, Mar. 25, 1732. [Luce, C.R.2.]
Margaret, d. Jonathan and Elizabeth, Apr. 15, 1707.
Margaret, ch. Jonathan and Elizabeth, bp. May 27, 1711. C.R.2.
Maria W. [———], w. Gridley, Dec. 15, 1794. G.R.2.
Martha, d. John, Feb. 26, 1651.
Martha, d. John Jr., Aug. 22, 1691.
Martha, d. Peleg, bp. Oct. 2, 1757. C.R.2.
Mary, d. John, Feb. 24, 1649.
Mary, d. John, bp. Jan. 19, 1661. C.R.2.
Mary, d. John Jr., bp. Oct. 31, 1681. C.R.2.
Mary, d. John Jr., Sept. 3, 1682.
Mary, d. David [d. David and Hannah, C.R.2.], May 4, 1711.
Mary, d. Thomas [d. Thomas and Mary, C.R.2.], Nov. 16, 1711.
Mary, d. Benja[min] and Abigal [Abigail, C.R.2.], June 29, 1730.
Mary Ewell, d. Peleg and w., bp. July 15, 1744. C.R.2.
Mercy, d. Daniell, Nov. 21, 1688.
Moley, d. Sam[ue]ll and Mary, July 23, 1753. [Molley, d. Sam[ue]l, C.R.2.]
Nancy, d. Zine and Unice, Aug. 29, 1784.
Nathanael, s. Thomas and Mercy, bp. Nov. 29, 1724. C.R.2. [Nathaniel, G.R.14.]
Nathaniel, s. Nathaniel of Marshfield and w. (d. Capt. Barker), bp. July 7, 1765. C.R.1.
Noah, s. Joshua Jr. and Abiel, Dec. 30, 1793.
Noah, s. Joshua and w., bp. July 1, 1798. C.R.2.
Patience, d. Hannah, wid., bp. May 22, 1773. C.R.1.
Peleg, s. Thomas and Mary, bp. July 27, 1718. C.R.2.
Peleg, s. Peleg and w., bp. Oct. 19, 1746. C.R.2.
Prince, s. Benj[a]m[in] and Abigail, bp. July 27, 1746. C.R.2.
Rachell, d. Daniell, July 3, 1695.
Rachell, d. Daniell, Jan. 10, 1696-7.
Rhoda, d. Peleg and Mary, bp. Dec. 3, 1749. C.R.2.
Ruth, d. Joseph, Feb. 18, 1693-4.

BRYANT, Ruth, d. Jonathan and Elizabeth, Mar. 15, 1709.
Ruth, ch. Jonathan and Elizabeth, bp. May 27, 1711. C.R.2.
Ruth, d. Elizabeth, bp. Sept. 13, 1730. C.R.2.
Ruth, ch. David, bp. Mar. 25, 1735. C.R.2.
Ruth, d. Benj[a]m[in] and Abigail, bp. Aug. 5, 1744. C.R.2.
Sally, d. Joshua Jr. and Abiel, Mar. 5, 1776.
Sally, w. Charles Ellms, July 13, 1809. G.R.6.
Samuel, s. Sam[ue]ll and Abigail, bp. July 29, 1716. C.R.2.
Samuel, s. Sam[ue]ll and Mary, Dec. 26, 1748.
Samuell, s. John, Feb. 6, 1653. [Samuel, C.R.2.]
Samuell, s. John Jr., Jan. 15, 1689. [Briant, C.R.2.]
Sarah, d. John, Sept. 29 [dup. Oct. —], 1648. [Sept. 29, P.C.R.]
Sarah, [ch.] Thom[a]s and Sarah, bp. May [? 17], 1747. C.R.2.
Sarah Mary, ch. John, bp. Mar. 23, 1650. C.R.2.
Seth, s. Thomas [s. Thomas and Mary, C.R.2.], Feb. 12, 1713-14.
Snow, s. Sam[ue]ll and Mary, Oct. 6, 1758.
Snow, s. Joshua Jr. and Abiel, Dec. 9, 1779.
Snow, s. Snow and Deborah, Nov. 19, 1820.
Thirza, d. Joshua Jr. and Abiel, Jan. 7, 1791. [Thirzby, C.R.2.]
Thomas, s. Thomas and Mary, bp. Apr. 29, 1716. C.R.2.
Zebulon, s. Zine and Unice, Sept. 5, 1786.
Zina, s. Sam[ue]ll and Mary, Jan. 1, 1755. [Zine Briant, C.R.2.]

BUCK (see Bucke), Abigal, d. Thomas and Hannah, Oct. 20, 1723.
Anna, d. Thomas, bp. Sept. 18, 1709. C.R.1.
Benjamin, s. John, Mar. 15, 1665.
Benjamin, ch. John, ——, 1666.
Charles, s. Christana, bp. July 16, 1775. C.R.1.
Christiana, d. Joseph, bp. Nov. 12, 1752. C.R.1.
Debora, d. Isack, July 17, 1665.
Deborah, d. John, Nov. 15, 1670.
Deborah, d. Joseph, bp. Oct. 25, 1747. C.R.1.
Desire, d. Thomas, Oct. 10, 1717.
Elisabeth, d. Thomas, July 9, 1716. [Elizabeth, C.R.1.]
Elisabeth, d. Thomas and Hannah, Aug. 17, 1721. [Elizabeth, C.R.1.]
Elizabeth, d. John, July 16, 1653.
Elizabeth, ch. John, bp. Oct. 4, 1663. C.R.2.
Ephraim, bp. ——, 1701. C.R.2.
Hannah, d. John, Aug. 9, 1661.
Hannah, ch. John, bp. Oct. 4, 1663. C.R.1.
Isaac, s. Isaac [s. Isaac and Mary, C.R.2.], Feb. 13, 1717.
Isaack, s. Isaac and Mary, bp. Sept. 25, 1748. C.R.2.

BUCK, Isack, s. Isack Jr., Apr. 8, 1689. [Isaac, s. Isaac, C.R.2.]
James, s. Isaac [s. Isaac and Mary, C.R.2.], Oct. 13, 1719.
James, s. Isaac and Mary, bp. Nov. 3, 1723. C.R.2.
John, s. John, Sept. 6, 1659.
John, ch. John, bp. Oct. 4, 1663. C.R.2.
Jonathan, s. Thomas (Bucke) and Hannah, Sept. 1, 1714.
Jonathan, s. Jonathan and Rachel, bp. July 3, 1742. C.R.1.
Joseph, s. John, June 26, 1657.
Joseph, ch. John, bp. Oct. 4, 1663. C.R.2.
Joseph, twin s. Thomas, Sept. 7, 1719.
Joseph, s. Joseph, bp. Nov. 11, 1750. C.R.1.
Lemuel, s. Jonathan, bp. Oct. 4, 1747. C.R.1.
Lusanna, d. Joseph and Leah, bp. July 3, 1743. C.R.1.
Lusanna, d. Isaac Jr. and Mary, Sept. 18, 1746.
Margeret, d. Isaac, June 8, 1716. [Margaret, C.R.1.]
Margrett, d. Isack, Aug. 7, 1687. [Margeret Bucke, d. Isaace, C.R.2.]
Mary, d. John, June 26, 1655.
Mary, ch. John, bp. Oct. 4, 1663. C.R.2.
Mary, d. Thomas, bp. Sept. 18, 1709. C.R.1.
Mary, d. Isaac, bp. Oct. 26, 1714. C.R.1.
Mary, d. Isaac and Mary, bp. June 13, 1725. C.R.2.
Mary, d. Joseph, bp. July 22, 1744. C.R.1.
Mary, d. Isaac Jr. and Mary, Aug. 14, 1744.
Mary, d. Isaac, bp. June 7, 1752. C.R.2.
Rachel, d. Jonathan, bp. Aug. 5, 1744. C.R.1.
Rachel, July 31, 1746. P.R.2.
Rachell, d. John, Aug. 22, 1674. [Rachel Bucke, C.R.2.]
Reuben (see Ruben).
Robard [dup. Robert], s. John, June 16, 1672. [Robert, C.R.2.]
Ruben, s. Isaa[c] Jr. and Mary, May 16, 1742.
Sarah, d. Isaac Jr. and Mary, bp. Sept. 2, 1750. C.R.2.
Seth, s. Thomas and Hannah, May 21, 1727.
Susanah [dup. Susanna], d. John, July 19, 1664. [Susanna, C.R.2.]
Thomas, bp. ——, 1701. C.R.2.
Thomas, twin s. Thomas, Sept. 7, 1719.
Thomas, s. Isaac and Mary, bp. June 17, 1722. C.R.2.
Thomas, s. Isaac and Mary, bp. June 4, 1727. C.R.2.
Thomas, s. Jonathan, bp. Sept. 25, 1743. C.R.1.

BUCKE (see Buck), Abigail, d. Isaac Jr. and Eunice, Aug. 7, 1685.
Abigail, d. Isaace, bp. Apr. 22, 1688. C.R.2.

BUCKE, Abigail, d. Thomas, Sept. 29, 1691.
Abigail, d. Isaac and Mary, Oct. 22, 1714. [Buck, C.R.1.]
Deborah, d. Thomas, May 10, 1689.
Hannah, d. Thomas, Mar. 2, 1708–9.
Isaac, s. Isaac, bp. July 1, 1683. C.R.2.
John, s. Thomas, Apr. 27, 1695.
Mary, d. Thomas, June 12, 1684.
Mary, d. Thomas, Jan. 5, 1706–7.
Mary, d. Isaac and Mary, Sept. 1, 1713.
Sarah, d. Thomas, Jan. 26, 1711–12. [Buck, C.R.1.]
Thomas, s. Thomas, Sept. 15, 1682.

BUKER (see Bouker, Bowker), Jonathan, s. Lazarus, bp. June 7, 1752. C.R.2.

BUMPAS (see Bumpasse, Bumpus), Benjamin, s. Jacob, Nov. 13, 1677.
Benjamin, s. Sarah, bp. Apr. 7, 1678. C.R.2.
Jacob, s. Jacob, July 6, 1680. [Bumpus, C.R.2.]
James, s. John, bp. June 16, 1678. C.R.2.
Samuell, s. John, bp. Apr. 30, 1676. C.R.2.

BUMPASSE (see Bumpas, Bumpus), John, s. John, bp. Sept. 28, 1673. C.R.2.
Mary, d. John, bp. Aug. 20, 1671. C.R.2.

BUMPUS (see Bumpas, Bumpasse), Icabod, s. Jacob, bp. June 26, 1687. C.R.2.
Isaac, s. John, bp. Mar. 27, 1681. C.R.2.
Job, s. John, bp. Apr. 29, 1683. C.R.2.

BURDET (see Burdit, Burditt), Elizabeth, ch. Henry and Lydia, bp. Sept. 1, 1723. C.R.2.
Francis, s. Henry, bp. Aug. 18, 1728. C.R.2.
Joshua, s. Henry and Lydia, bp. June 26, 1726. C.R.2.
Ruth (Burded), d. Henry and Lydia, bp. Nov. 7, 1731. C.R.2.
Thankfull, ch. Henry and Lydia, bp. Sept. 1, 1723. C.R.2.
William, ch. Henry and Lydia, bp. Sept. 1, 1723. C.R.2.

BURDIT (see Burdet, Burditt), Elizabeth, d. Henery, Feb. 20, 1717.

BURDITT (see Burdet, Burdit), William, s. Henry and Lydia, Sept. 27, 1713.

BURGES, Silence, d. Cesar and Meriah, negros, May 13, 1712.
Silence, d. Cesar, negro, bp. May 15, 1720. C.R.1.

BURKE, Catharine [————], w. Martin, —— [1834]. G.R.10.

BURNETT, Betsey B., ch. Thomas and Mary Ann, May 24, 1835, in Novacotia E.
Lucy, [twin] d. Thomas, seaman (b. Cape Breton), and Mary A., Aug. 16, 1848.
Mahitable, ch. Thomas and Mary Ann, Dec. 22, 1833, in Novacotia E.
Thomas M., s. Thom[as] W., sailor, and Mary A., Apr. 1, 1845.
————, [twin] d. Thomas, seaman (b. Cape Breton), and Mary A., Aug. 16, 1848.

BURNS, James, s. James, bp. Apr. 11, 1745. C.R.1.

BURREL (see Burrell), Mary, d. ————, bp. June 21, 1752. C.R.2.

BURRELL (see Burrel), Adelaide I. [? J.], d. Isaac Jr., cordwainer, and Mabel, Jan. 21, [18]46.
Charles Jacob, ch. Isaac Jr. [and] Mabel, Feb. 7, 1842.
Edmond, s. Isaac Jr. and w., June 19, 1810.
Isaac, s. Isaac Jr. and w., July 13, 1806.
James S., s. Isaac Jr. and w., July 20, 1814.
John H., s. James [*sic*] Jr. and w., July 8, 1817.
Joseph, s. Isaac Jr. and w., Nov. 5, 1818.
Joseph H. [dup. Henry], twin ch. Isaac Jr. [and] Mabel, Dec. 2, 1843.
Julia Ann, d. Isaac Jr. and w., Aug. 11, 1812.
Julia Ann, d. Gracy [spinster, crossed out], Dec. 31, 1844.
Mabel C., ch. Isaac Jr. [and] Mabel, Feb. 16, 1839.
Olive, d. Isaac Jr. and w., Apr. 15, 1808.
William H. [dup. Hughes], twin ch. Isaac Jr. [and] Mabel, Dec. 2, 1843.

BURROUGHES (see Burroughs, Burrows), Mary, d. Jeremiah, bp. Apr. 5, 1657. C.R.2.

BURROUGHS (see Burroughes, Burrows), Elizabeth, d. Jeremy, bp. May 27, 1655. C.R.2.
Jeremiah, s. Jeremy, bp. May 23, 1652. C.R.2.
John, s. Jeremy, bp. Mar. 5, 1653. C.R.2.

BURROWS (see Burroughes, Burroughs), James Henry, ch. Thomas J. and Betsey W., June 16, 1843.
Lydia B. [dup. Beedle], d. Thom[as] [dup. adds J.], sailor, and Betsey [dup. adds W.], June 28 [dup. June 29], 1845.

BURROWS, Sarah Lincoln, ch. Thomas J. and Betsey W., July 9, 1839.
Thomas J., ch. Thomas J. and Betsey W., Aug. 22, 1837.
W[illia]m Thomas, ch. Thomas J. and Betsey W., Nov. 22 [? 21], 1841.

BUTLER, Bridget, ——, 1824. G.R.10.
Elizabeth, d. Israel and Elizabeth, bp. July 12, 1730. C.R.2.
Patrick, brother of Bridget, ——, 1843. G.R.10.
Sarah, d. Israel and Eliz[abe]th, bp. July 15, 1733. C.R.2.

BUTTARLY (see Butterly), Christopher, —— [1832], in Rush, Co. Dublin, Ire. G.R.10.

BUTTERLY (see Buttarly), Joseph, —— [1819], in Rush, Co. Dublin, Ire. G.R.10.

BYRAM (see Byrum), Nicholas, s. Seth, bp. Aug. 7, 1768. C.R.1.
Sarah, d. Seth, bp. Nov. 2, 1766. C.R.1.

BYRUM (see Byram), Seth, s. Seth and Sarah, May 1, 1763. [Byram, C.R.1.]
Stephen, s. Seth and Sarah, Aug. 9, 1764. [Byram, C.R.1.]

CAHILL, Ann, d. Martin, bp. Nov. 18, 1733. C.R.1.

CAIN, Ephraim, ch. Ephraim and Hannah of Middleborough, bp. Dec. 19, 1708. C.R.2.
Mary, ch. Ephraim and Hannah of Middleborough, bp. Dec. 19, 1708. C.R.2.

CALDWELL, Nellie, w. Capt. John L. Manson, —— [1835]. G.R.6.

CAMBEL, Sarah, d. James and Sarah, bp. Apr. 4, 1725. C.R.2.

CAME, Benjemen, s. Josiah, bp. May 6, 1683. C.R.2.

CARLILE, William, [ch.] Will[ia]m, bp. May 9, 1779. C.R.1.

CARR, Charlotte [——], w. Elias, Oct. 16, 1813. G.R.6.
Elias, h. Charlotte, Feb. 8, 1808. G.R.6.
Sarah H., ——, 1827. G.R.7.

CARROLL, Margaret, w. Martin Burke, —— [1839]. G.R.10.

CASH (see Cask), Jonathan, s. Abner and Irana, June 8, 1762. [Cask, C.R.1.]

CASK (see Cash), Sarah, d. Abner (Cash) and Irana, Aug. 29, 1759. [Cass, c.r.1.]

CASS (see Cash, Cask).

CASSEL, Ezekiel, s. Timothy and Deborah of Newport, R.I., bp. Oct. 17, 1725. c.r.2.

CASSWELL, John, s. Jo[h]n and Elizabeth, bp. Sept. 6, 1747. c.r.1.

CASTEL, Derius, twin s. Elizabeth, Oct. 16, 1757.
Meribah, twin d. Elizabeth, Oct. 16, 1757.
Susanna, d. Elizabeth, May 25, 1759.

CAZNEAUR (see Cosnow), John, s. Sevario, shoemaker, and Elizabeth, Nov. 13, 1844.

CHADWICK (see Chadwicke), John, s. John, Nov. 2, 1702.
Marcy, d. John, Dec. 2, 1704.

CHADWICKE (see Chadwick), Daniell, s. John, Sept. 15, 1711.
Richard, s. John, Nov. 28, 1708.
Thomas, s. John, Feb. 15, 1706-7.

CHAMBERLIN (see Chamberline), Joseph, s. Nathanaell, July 21, 1699.
William, Apr. 7, 1652. c.r.4.

CHAMBERLINE (see Chamberlin), Eunice, d. Nathanaell, July 20, 1698.
Freedom, s. Nathanaell, June 15, 1697.

CHANDELER (see Chandeller, Chandler, Chanler, Chanlor), Mary, d. Benjamin, bp. Mar. 16, 1678-9. c.r.2.

CHANDELLER (see Chandeler, Chandler, Chanler, Chanlor), Keturah, d. Benjaman, bp. May 20, 1683. c.r.2.

CHANDLER (see Chandeler, Chandeller, Chanler, Chanlor), Benjamin, s. Benjeamin, bp. Apr. 12, 1685. c.r.2.
Hannah Maria, d. Sceva and Hannah, Mar. 24, 1834.
John, s. Benjamin, bp. Oct. 3[worn], 1676. c.r.2.
Mary A. [? m.], —— [1803]. c.r.3.
Mary Baker, d. Sceva and Hannah, Sep[t]. 14, 1832.
Mercy Allen, d. Seva and Hannah, Sept. 18, 1838.
Sceva [h. Hannah] [Dec. —, 1804]. g.r.6.
Seth, s. Sceva and Hannah, Aug. 15, 1829.

CHANDLER, ———, s. Sceva and Hannah, Sep[t]. 4, 1836.
———, ch. Seva and Hannah, Aug. 9, 1843.

CHANLER (see Chandeler, Chandeller, Chandler, Chanlor), Sammuell, s. Benjamin, Nov. 30, 1674. [Samuell, s. Benjemin, c.r.2.]

CHANLOR (see Chandeler, Chandeller, Chandler, Chanler), Martha, d. Benjamen, Feb. 16, 1672. [Chandler, d. Benjamin, c.r.2.]

CHAPMAN, Hannah B. [———], w. Timothy B., ———, 1835. g.r.19.
John, s. Ralph, bp. Sept. 27, 1657. c.r.2.
Ralph, s. Ralph, bp. Sept. 27, 1657. c.r.2.
Sarah, d. Ralph, bp. Sept. 27, 1657. c.r.2.

CHASE, ———, ch. Charles H. and Lenthia, July 10, 1843.

CHETTENDEN (see Chitanden, Chitenden, Chittenden, Chittentun), Israell, s. Israell Jr., Aug. 14, 1715.

CHILD (see Childe, Childs), Jane, d. Richard of Marishfield, bp. May 16, 1669. c.r.2.

CHILDE (see Child, Childs), Joseph, s. Richard of Marishfield, bp. Oct. 27, 1667. c.r.2.

CHILDS (see Child, Childe), Sally [? m.] [Jan. —, 1783]. c.r.1.

CHIPMAN, Charles [h. Elizabeth C. (Tilden)], Sept. 20, 1809. g.r.7.
Charles Edward, ch. Charles and Elizabeth C., Apr. 14, 1832.
Daniel M., brother of Charles, Nov. 10, 1819. g.r.7.
Elizabeth C., d. Charles and Elizabeth C. T., Nov. 6, 1836. g.r.7.
Nancy Jenkins, d. Charles, bp. June 21, 1840. c.r.3.
William Wirt, ch. Charles and Elizabeth C., May 9, 1834.

CHITANDEN (see Chettenden, Chitenden, Chittenden, Chittentun), Israel, s. Gedion (Chitenden) and Mehetable, Aug. 14, 1781.

CHITENDEN (see Chettenden, Chitanden, Chittenden, Chittentun), Deborah, d. Gedion and Mehetable, Sept. 10, 1777.

CHITTENDEN (see Chettenden, Chitanden, Chitenden, Chittentun), Alatheah, d. Joseph, July —, 1697.
Anna, d. Iserell, Sept. 22, 1686.

CHITTENDEN, Anna, d. Israel and Mary, Feb. 22, 1726.
Anna, d. Israel, bp. Oct. 29, 1727. C.R.1.
Anne, d. Isaac and Peirces, Aug. 17, 1751.
Calvin, s. Isaac and Peirces, Sept. 24, 1746.
Charles Jenkins, s. Israel (Chittenen) and Sally, Sept. 4, 1808.
Deborah, d. Iserell, Mar. 13, 1683-4.
Desire, d. Nath[anie]l, bp. Dec. 11, 1757. C.R.1.
Elizabeth, d. Isack, Sept. 9, 1658.
Elizabeth, d. Henry, Oct. —, 1673.
Elizabeth, d. Iserell, Apr. 13, 1693.
Elizabeth, d. Thomas and Elizabeth, Mar. 12, 1708.
Elizabeth, d. Thom[a]s, bp. July 14, 1717. C.R.1.
Elizebeth, d. Isaace, bp. July 16, 1682. C.R.2.
Gidion, s. Israel Jr. and Deborah, Mar. 20, 1749. [Gideon, C.R.1.]
Hannah, d. Israel and Mary, Jan. 31, 1736.
Hannah, d. Israel, bp. May 8, 1737. C.R.1.
Harriet, d. Nath[anie]l and Ruth, Oct. 19, 1794.
Harriot, d. Nath[anie]ll and w., bp. Aug. 28, 1796. C.R.2.
Isaac, s. Israel Jr., Sept. 28, 1719.
Isaac, bp. Sept. 8, 1743, a. 79. C.R.1.
Isaac, s. Nath[anie]ll [Nath[anie]l, C.R.1.] and Desire, Oct. 3, 1753.
Isack, s. Iserell, Mar. 27, 1681.
Isacke, s. Isacke, Sept. 30, 1663.
Isaiah, s. Nath[anie]l dec'd and w., bp. Nov. 11, 1759. C.R.1.
Iserell, s. Iserell, July 16, 1690.
Israel, s. Israel, bp. Apr. 26, 1719. C.R.1.
Israel, s. Israel Jr. and Deborah, Sept. 6, 1742.
Israel, s. Israel Jr. and Deborah, bp. Oct. 23, 1743. C.R.1.
Israel, s. Israel and Sally, Sept. 9, 1805.
Israell, s. Isacke, Oct. 10, 1651.
Jael, d. Thom[a]s, bp. July 14, 1717. C.R.1.
Jaell, d. Stephen, Jan. 22, 1691.
Joseph, s. Henry, Mar. 8, 1656-7.
Lucy, d. Nath[anie]l and Ruth, Dec. 1, 1792.
Lucy, d. Nath[anie]ll and w., bp. Apr. 13, 1794. C.R.2.
Luther, s. Nath[anie]l, bp. June 20, 1756. C.R.1.
Luther, s. Nath[anie]ll and Ruth, Jan. 22, 1789.
Martha, d. Stephen, July 15, 1694.
Mary, d. Isacke, Aug. 17, 1648.
Mary, d. Joseph, Dec. —, 1684.
Mary, d. Israel and Mary, Mar. 31, 1722.
Mary, d. Nath[anie]ll and Ruth, Jan. 17, 1786.
Mehetabel, d. Thom[a]s, bp. July 14, 1717. C.R.1.
Mehetable, d. Stephen, June 8, 1686.

CHITTENDEN, Mehetable, d. Thomas and Elizabeth, Mar. 2, 1709-10.
Nathanael, s. Joseph, Dec. —, 1694.
Nathaniel, s. Israel, bp. June 20, 1725. C.R.1.
Nathaniel, s. Nath[anie]ll and Ruth, Jan. 16, 1778.
Nath[anie]ll, s. Israel and Mary, May 22, 1724.
Nath[anie]ll, s. Nath[anie]ll and Desire, Sept. 19, 1750.
Nath[anie]ll, s. Nath[anie]ll and Desire, Dec. 4, 1751. [Nath[a]niel, s. Nath[anie]l, C.R.1.]
Nicholas, s. Iserell, Feb. 4, 1678-9. [Nicolas Chittendun, s. Israell, C.R.2.]
Nicholas, s. Israel and Mary, May 2, 1731. [Nicolas, C.R.1.]
Nicolas, s. Israel Jr. and Deborah, June 22, 1746. [Nicholas, C.R.1.]
Rebecka, twin d. Isack, Feb. 25, 1646.
Rebekah, d. Stephen, Dec. 5, 1680.
Ruth, d. Henery, bp. July 16, 1682. C.R.2.
Ruth, d. Joseph, Jan. —, 1689.
Ruth, d. Nath[anie]ll and Ruth, Mar. 13, 1776.
Sally, d. Nath[anie]ll and Ruth, Apr. 18, 1783.
Samuel Turner, s. Israel and Sally, May 21, 1807.
Sarah, twin d. Isack, Feb. 25, 1646.
Sarah, d. Stephen, Mar. 12, 1688.
Sarah, d. Steph[en], bp. May 2, 1708. C.R.1.
Sarah, d. Tho[ma]s and Eliza[beth], Dec. 1, 1712.
Sarah, d. Thom[a]s, bp. July 14, 1717. C.R.1.
Stephen, s. Tho[mas] and Eliza[beth], Dec. 15, 1722.
Stephen, s. Tho[ma]s, bp. Sept. 18, 1726. C.R.1.
Steven, s. Isacke, Nov. 5, 1654.
Susanna, d. Henry, Jan. 12, 1663-4.
Susannah, d. Henery, bp. July 16, 1682. C.R.2.
Temperance, d. Nath[anie]l and Ruth, Aug. 1, 1780.
Thomas, s. Stephen, Nov. 14, 1683.
Tho[ma]s, s. Tho[mas] and Eliza[beth], Dec. 17, 1718.
Tho[ma]s, s. Tho[ma]s and Sarah, Mar. 30, 1748.

CHITTENTUN (see Chettenden, Chitanden, Chitenden, Chittenden), Deborah, d. Israell, bp. Sept. 5, 1686. C.R.2.
Hannah, d. Israel, bp. Aug. 14, 1687. C.R.2.
Isaac, s. Israell, bp. June 25, 1682. C.R.2.
Rebeckah, d. Steven and Mehitabel, bp. July 9, 1682. C.R.2.

CHOYCE, Petter, "A negro slave of John booth," Oct. 15, 1699.

CHUBBOCK (see Chubbuck, Chubuck), Anthony, s. Anthoney and Lucy, Jan. 8, 1808.

CHUBBUCK (see Chubbock, Chubuck), Abby Brooks, d. Anthony and Lucy, Aug. 26, 1824.
Almera, ch. Anthony and Cynthia, Jan. 2, 1844.
Anthony, s. David and Ruth, Nov. 15, 1784, in Hingham. [Chubuck [h. Cynthia] [h. Lucy], G.R.6.]
Anthony, ch. Anthony and w., bp. July 7, 1811. C.R.1.
Celia Little, ch. Anthony and Cynthia, Aug. 22, 1837.
Charles A., ch. Anthony Jr. and Mary L., Aug. 22, —— [rec. between ch. b. July 26, 1831, and ch. b. Jan. 7, 1833].
Charles A., ch. Anthony Jr. and Mary L., Jan. 7, 1833.
Charles Thomas, s. Francis G. and Lydia, Nov. 30, 1829.
Daniel L., s. Martin C., caulker, and Serana C., June 9, 1849.
David, s. David and Ruth, May 31, 1797.
Francis Gardiner, s. David and Ruth, Feb. 19, 1801.
Francis Gardner, s. Francis G. and Lydia, Dec. 24, 1827. [Chubuck, G.R.6.]
Henry Harrison, ch. Anthony and Cynthia, Oct. 1, 1840.
Henry Turner, s. Francis G. and Lydia, July 16, 1832. [Chubuck, G.R.6.]
Jane Turner, d. Anthony and Lucy, Oct. 26, 1812.
Julia Ann, d. Martin, caulker, and Serena C., Sept. 2, 1844.
Lucy Otis, d. Anthony and Lucy, July 25, 1810.
Lydia [————], w. ————, —— [1800]. C.R.1.
Marting, s. David and Ruth, Nov. 5, 1786, in Hingham.
Mary, d. David and Ruth, Nov. 14, 1807.
Mary L., ch. Anthony Jr. and Mary L., July 26, 1831.
Melzar, s. David and Ruth, Jan. 25, 1783, in Hingham.
Nancy, d. David and Ruth, Jan. 4, 1795.
Perez, s. David and Ruth, —— 24, 1803.
Ruth, d. David and Ruth, Nov. 10, 1790.
Ruth, d. David and Ruth, Apr. 29, 1799.
Temperance, d. David and Ruth, Oct. 5, 1792, in Abington.
Thomas, s. David and Ruth, Jan. 7, 1789, in Abington.
Will[ia]m Cushing, s. David (Chubbock) and Ruth, Mar. 23, 1805.
William Kingsbury, s. A[nthony] and Lucy, Nov. 16, 1831.
————, s. Martin T., corker, and Serena C., Mar. 19, 1845.

CHUBUCK (see Chubbock, Chubbuck), Abby Brooks, d. Anthony and Lucy, Dec. 26, 1819.
Cynthia [————], w. Anthony [Oct. —, 1798]. G.R.6.
Frances M. [Sept. —, 1831]. G.R.6.
Martin Thomas, s. Anthony and Lucy, May 16, 1816.
———— [————], w. ————, —— [1816]. C.R.1.

CHURCH, Abigail, d. Nathanaell, Dec. 16, 1666.
Abigail, d. Nathaniell, Mar. 22, 1700–1.
Abigal, d. Nath[anie]ll and Jerusha, Feb. 11, 1726. [Abigail, d. Nathan[ie]l, C.R.2.]
Alice, d. Nathanaell, Aug. 23, 1679.
Benjamin, s. Cornelius B. and Huldah, July 22, 1805.
Caleb, s. Nathaniell, Apr. 4, 1712.
Caleb, s. Nathanaell and Judith, bp. June 27, 1714. C.R.2.
Charles, s. Nathanaell, Mar. —, 1683–4.
Charles, s. Richard, July 26, 1723. [Charls, C.R.2.]
Charles, s. Nath[anie]ll and Jerusha, Dec. 9, 1735. [Charls, C.R.2.]
Constant, s. Nath[anie]ll and Jerusha, July 28, 1737.
Constant, ch. Nathanael and Jerusha, bp. May 8, 1743. C.R.2.
Cornelius, s. Cornelius B. and Huldah, Aug. 25, 1802.
Cornelius Briggs, s. Lemuel and Susanna, Oct. 28, 1778.
Deborah, d. Nathaniell, Oct. —, 1705.
Elizabeth, d. Joseph and Grace, bp. July 31, 1743. C.R.2.
Elizabeth, d. Nath[anie]ll and Mehitable, May 27, 1753 [*sic*, see Joseph].
Esther, d. Cornelius B. and Huldah, Oct. 9, 1813.
Hannah, d. Richard, Oct. 22, 1699.
Henaietta, d. Thomas and Hannah, Dec. 16, 1789.
Huldah, d. Cornelius B. and Huldah, June 7, 1811.
Jerusha, d. Nath[anie]ll [Nathan[ie]l Jr., C.R.2.] and Jerusha, Mar. 8, 1732.
Jerusha, d. Thomas and Hannah, Mar. 16, 1795.
John, s. Cornelius B. and Huldah, June 24, 1809.
Joseph, s. Nathanaell [Nathaniel, C.R.2.], Mar. —, 1681–2.
Joseph, s. Nathaniell [s. Nathanael and Judith, C.R.2.], May 22, 1709.
Joseph, s. Joseph and Grace, bp. July 22, 1744. C.R.2.
Joseph, s. Joseph and Grace, bp. Oct. 5, 1746. C.R.2.
Joseph, s. Nath[anie]ll Jr. and Mehitable, Nov. 3, 1752 [*sic*, see Elizabeth].
Judith, d. Nathaniell, Oct. —, 1703.
Lemuel, s. Nath[anie]ll [Nathan[ie]ll Jr., C.R.2.] and Jerusha, Jan. 28, 1738.
Lemuel, s. Nath[anie]ll [Nathanael C.R.2.] and Jerusha, Dec. 6, 1742.
Lemuel, s. Lemuel and Susanna, Sept. 19, 1772.
Lemuel, s. Cornelius B. and Huldah, Oct. 22, 1823.
Lusanna, d. Richard and Anna, Feb. 9, 1724.
Lydia, d. Nath[anie]ll and Jurusha [d. Nathanall and Jerusha, C.R.2.], Sept. 20, 1722.

CHURCH, Lydia, d. Lemuel and Susanna, Sept. 9, 1768.
Lydia, d. Cornelius B. and Huldah, Aug. 11, 1821.
Mary, d. Nathan[ie]ll and Judith, bp. Oct. 26, 1718. C.R.2.
Mary, d. Thomas and Mary, bp. Nov. 29, 1747. C.R.2.
Mary, d. Nath[anie]ll and Mary, Feb. 23, 1760.
Mary Perry, d. Thomas and Hannah, Apr. 25, 1782.
Nathanaell, s. Nathanaell, Feb. 10, 1670-1. [Nathaniel, Nathaniel, C.R.2.]
Nathanaell, s. Nathanaell, Mar. 7, 1698-9.
Nathaniel, s. Nath[anie]ll and Jerusha, Jan. 20, 1723. [Nathanael, s. Nathanael Jr., C.R.2.]
Nath[anie]ll, s. Nath[anie]ll and Mehitable, May 20, 1755.
Nath[anie]ll, s. Nath[anie]ll and Mary, Dec. 10, 1763.
Rebecca, d. Lemuel and Susanna, July 9, 1770.
Richard, s. Nathanaell [Nathaniel, C.R.2.], Mar. 24, 1668-9.
Richard, s. Richard, Nov. 5, 1697.
Richard, s. Richard and Anna, Sept. 1, 1721.
Ruth, d. Richard, Dec. 8, 1701.
Ruth, d. Richard dec'd, bp. Oct. 1, 1710. C.R.2.
Sarah, d. Nathanaell, Oct. 31, 1686.
Sarah, d. Nath[anie]ll [Nathan[ie]l Jr., C.R.2.] and Jerusha, Apr. 11, 1730.
Sarah, d. Nath, bp. ——, 1755. C.R.2.
Sarah Jones, d. Thomas and Hannah, Mar. 31, 1793.
Silva, d. Joseph and Grace, bp. May 6, 1750. C.R.2.
Susan, d. Cornelius B. and Huldah, Aug. 10, 1807.
Susanna, d. Lemuel and Susanna, Oct. 9, 1775.
Thomas, s. Nath[anie]ll [dup. Jr.] and Jerusha, Jan. 20 [dup. June 20], 1720.
William, s. Nath[anie]ll [Nathan[ie]l, C.R.2.] and Jerusha, Mar. 4, 1728.
William, s. Nath[anie]ll [Nathan[ie]l, C.R.2.] and Jerusha, Nov. 24, 1734.
William, s. Nath[anie]ll and Jerusha, Jan. 16, 1743.
William, s. Lemuel and Susanna, Aug. 8, 1789.
——, d. Nathan[ie]ll and Judith, bp. Apr. 25, 1708. C.R.2.

CLAP (see Clape, Clapp), Abigail, d. Joseph, May 16, 1699.
Abigail, ch. Joseph, bp. Feb. 27, 1744-5. C.R.2.
Abigail, d. Nathan[ie]ll Esq. and Desire, bp. Feb. 10, 1750-1. C.R.2.
Abigaill, d. Samuell, Oct. —, 1679. [Abigall, d. Samuel, C.R.2.]
Abigal, d. Thomas, Jan. 29, 1659. [Abigail Clappe, C.R.2.]
Abigal, d. Benja[min] and Grace, Aug. 21, 1736. [Abigail, C.R.1. C.R.2.]

CLAP, Abijah, s. David and Deborah, Sept. 25, 1727. [Habijah, C.R.1.]
Albert, s. Samuel, Feb. 16, 1791.
Allen, ch. Allen, bp. Sept. 10, 1825. C.R.2.
Anna, d. Joseph [d. Joseph and Abigail, C.R.2.], Mar. 1, 1705–6.
Annah, ch. Joseph, bp. Oct. 13, 1776. C.R.1.
Anne, d. Joshua and Lydia, Aug. 30, 1771.
Augustus, s. Tho[ma]s Esq. [Col. T., C.R.1.] and Ester, Mar. 28, 1752.
Barnard, s. Joseph, bp. Sept. 14, 1766. C.R.1.
Bela, s. Joshua and Lydia, July 2, 1760.
Benja[min], s. Benja[min] and Grace, Oct. 13, 1737.
Benjamine, s. Joseph, Apr. 26, 1710.
Betty, d. Joseph Jr. and Hannah, Oct. 13, 1740.
Caleb, s. Joshua and Lydia, May 9, 1764.
Calven, s. Tho[ma]s and Mary, Feb. 27, 1740. [Calvin, C.R.1.]
Calvin, s. Tho[ma]s Esq. and Esther, Oct. 28, 1749.
Chandler, s. Tho[ma]s Esq. [Col. Tho[ma]s, C.R.1.] and Ester, Dec. 8, 1754.
Charles, s. Joseph Jr., bp. Oct. 14, 1759. C.R.1.
Charles, s. Joseph, bp. July 31, 1763. C.R.1.
Charles, s. Galen and Patience, Mar. 16, 1774.
Cloea, d. John and Cloea, May 26, 1770.
Constant, s. John [Capt. John, C.R.2.] and Mercy, June 1, 1743.
David, s. Samuell, Nov. —, 1684.
David, s. David and Deborah, Mar. 20, 1720.
Deborah, d. Samuell, Feb. —, 1686–7.
Deborah, d. David and Deborah, Dec. 2, 1714.
Deborah, d. Increase and Delight, Jan. 19, 1761.
Deborah, d. James and Elizabeth, May 29, 1786.
Desire, d. Nathan[ie]ll and Desire, bp. May 24, 1741. C.R.2.
Dwelle, s. David Jr., bp. July 28, 1745. C.R.2.
Dwelly, s. David Jr. and Ruth, Aug. 12, 1741.
Elijah, s. Benja[min] and Grace, Oct. 6, 1746.
Elijah, s. Joseph [Joseph Sr. [?], C.R.2.] and Sarah, Feb. 16, 1757.
Elijah, s. John and Cloea, Apr. 25, 1766.
Elisha, s. Joseph, Mar. 9, 1713–14.
Enice, s. Galen and Patience, July 26, 1765.
Esther, d. John, bp. Sept. 25, 1764. C.R.1.
Eunice, d. Nath[anie]l Esq., bp. Apr. 15, 1753. C.R.2.
Galen, s. David and Deborah, Feb. 5, 1732.
Galen, s. David, bp. Aug. 5, 1733. C.R.1.
George, s. John Jr. and Mercy, Oct. 7, 1726.
Hannah, d. Joseph Jr. and Hannah, Nov. 8, 1733.

CLAP, Hannah, d. Nath[anie]ll and Desire, Nov. 11, 1739.
Hannah, d. Tho[ma]s Esq. and Esther, Oct. 24, 1746.
Hannah, d. Jo[seph] and Sarah, Sept. 19, 1748.
Hannah, d. Galen and Patience, Feb. 22, 1772.
Hannah, d. Galen and Patience, Aug. 7, 1776.
Harriot, d. Allen and w., bp. Mar. 5, 1809. C.R.2.
Henry, s. Leonard, bp. June 5, 1803. C.R.1.
Increase, s. David, bp. Sept. 21, 1735. C.R.1.
Incres, s. David and Deborah, Mar. 20, 1734.
Isaac, s. Jo[h]n and Mercy, Apr. 18, 1736.
James, s. David and Deborah, July 20, 1723.
James, s. David, bp. Aug. 22, 1725. C.R.1.
James, s. Increase and Delight, Apr. 10, 1759.
James, s. James and Elizabeth, May 19, 1789.
Jane, d. Samuell, Nov. —, 1689.
Job, s. Joseph, Nov. 6, 1712.
John, s. Thomas, Oct. 18, 1658. [Clappe, C.R.2.]
John, s. Samuell, Sept. "ye last," 1677.
John, s. Samuell, bp. Oct. 6, 1678. C.R.2.
John, s. Stephen, Oct. 14, 1697.
John, s. Stephen [and] Temperance, bp. ——, 1701. C.R.2.
John, s. John, Sept. 4, 1707.
John, s. John and Mercy, Oct. 8, 1728.
John, s. John and Mercy, bp. Jan. 14, 1732-3. C.R.2.
Jo[h]n, s. Jo[h]n and Mercy, July 5, 1734.
John, s. John and Cloea, Sept. 23, 1780.
Jonathan Blackman, s. Elisha and Leah, Sept. 25, 1737.
Joseph, s. Joseph, July 15, 1701.
Joseph, s. Joseph Jr. and Hannah, Feb. 21, 1734.
Joseph, s. Joseph and Hannah, bp. June 6, 1736. C.R.2.
Joseph, s. Joseph, bp. June 5, 1773. C.R.1.
Joseph Stowers, s. John and Cloea, Aug. 26, 1768.
Joshua, s. David and Deborah, Nov. 16, 1713.
Joshua, s. David and Deborah, Jan. 1, 1729.
Joshua, s. David, bp. Aug. 30, 1730. C.R.1.
Julia, ch. Allen, bp. Sept. 28, 1823. C.R.2.
Leonard, s. Leonard, bp. Nov. 1, 1801. C.R.1.
Lewis, s. Benja[min] and Deborah, Jan. 5, 1764.
Lewis, inf. Lewis and w., bp. May 8, 1788. C.R.1.
Lucy, d. Galen and Patience, Mar. 13, 1761.
Lucynde, d. Sam[ue]ll Jr. and Lucy, —— [rec. after ch. b. July 30, 1752]. [Lucinda, d. Samuel Jr., bp. June 2, 1754, C.R.2.]
Luther, s. Joseph, bp. May 6, 1764. C.R.1.
Lydia, d. Joshua and Lydia, Sept. 14, 1758.

CLAP, Lydia, d. Joshua and Lydia, July 3, 1762.
Lydia, d. John and Cloea, July 10, 1778.
Mabel, ch. Joseph, bp. Oct. 13, 1776. C.R.1.
Marthew Short, s. Joshua and Lydia, Oct. 4, 1766.
Mary, d. Joseph, Mar. 6, 1696–7.
Mary, d. David, Oct. 13, 1717.
Mary, d. Sam[ue]ll Jr. [Samuel, C.R.2.] and Sarah, Oct. 8, 1731.
Mary, d. Thomas, abt. ——, 1739.
Mary, d. Nat[hanie]ll and Desire, bp. Jan. 25, 1746–7. C.R.2.
Mary, d. John and Jerusha, bp. Sept. 15, 1754. C.R.1.
Mary Leonard, d. Leonard, bp. Nov. 10, 1799. C.R.1.
Mercy, d. John and Mercy, Sept. 25, 1740.
Mercy, ch. Joseph, bp. Oct. 13, 1776. C.R.1.
Michael, s. Sam[ue]ll Jr. and Sarah, Nov. 27, 1726. [Micael Clap, C.R.2.]
Michel, s. Michel and Sarah, Oct. 15, 1760.
Nabbe, d. Increas and Delight, Apr. 22, 1764. [Nabba, d. Increase, C.R.1.]
Nathaniel, s. Stephen, Sept. 11, 1709. [Nathanael, s. Stephen and Temperance, C.R.2.]
Nath[aniel], s. Nath, bp. June 20, 1756. C.R.2.
Noah, s. David and Deborah, Oct. 7, 1725.
Noah, s. David, bp. Aug. 25, 1728. C.R.1.
Noah, ch. Abijah and w., bp. Apr. 29, 1750. C.R.1.
Patience, d. Galen and Patience, Aug. 30, 1769.
Polly Bowker, ch. Allen, bp. Oct. 5, 1817. C.R.2.
President, ——, 1827.
Rachel, d. Jo[h]n and Mercy, Feb. 16, 1730.
Rachel, d. Nath[aniel] Esq., bp. Mar. 2, 1755. C.R.2.
Rachel, d. Col. John and Cloea, Aug. 30, 1763.
Rachell, d. Stephen, May 29, 1701. [Rachel, d. Stephen and Temperance, C.R.2.]
Rebeckah, d. Joseph, Oct. 2, 1703.
Rufus, s. Tho[ma]s Esq. [Col. T., C.R.1.] and Ester, Jan. 24, 1759.
Ruth, d. Jo[h]n and Mercy, Nov. 16, 1729.
Ruth, d. Joseph Jr. and Hannah, Apr. 14, 1738.
Ruth, d. Capt. Jo[h]n, bp. Sept. 18, 1757. C.R.1.
Samuel, s. Joseph, Nov. 18, 1695.
Samuel, s. John Jr. and Mercy, July 25, 1725.
Samuel, s. Sam[ue]ll and Sarah, Dec. 25, 1739. [Sam[ue]ll, C.R.2.]
Sarah, d. Joseph, May 15, 1708.
Sarah, d. Sam[ue]ll Jr. and Sarah [d. Samuel and Hannah, C.R.2.], Nov. 15, 1728.
Sarah, d. Job and Penelopie [Penelope, C.R.1.], June 4, 1759.

CLAP, Sarah, d. Galen and Patience, Apr. 30, 1763.
Seth Sutten, s. Lewis and Thankful, Mar. 22, 1805.
Silvanus, s. Nat[hanie]ll and Desire, bp. Jan. 23, 1742–3. C.R.2.
Solon, s. Lewis and Thankfull, July 17, 1807.
Stephen, s. Stephen [s. Stephen and Temperance, C.R.2.], Oct. 4, 1706.
Stephen, s. Sam[ue]ll Jr. [Sam[ue]l, C.R.2.] and Lucy, July 30, 1752.
Susanna, d. Elisha and Leah, Apr. 29, 1736.
Susanna, [ch.] Nath[anie]ll and Desire, bp. Oct. 30, 1748. C.R.2.
Temperance, d. Nat[hanie]ll and Desire, bp. Feb. 17, 1744–5. C.R.2.
Thomas, s. Stephen, June 20, 1703.
Thomas, s. Stephen, bp. Aug. 6, 1704. C.R.2.
Thomas, s. John [s. John and Hannah, C.R.2.], Nov. 11, 1705.
Thomas, s. Galen and Patience, Aug. 3, 1767.
William, s. Sam[ue]ll and Sarah, Dec. 3, 1733.

CLAPE (see Clap, Clapp), Hannah, d. Samuell, bp. June 11, 1682. C.R.2.
Thomas, s. Samuell, bp. June 11, 1682. C.R.2.

CLAPP (see Clap, Clape), Abigail Mott, d. Allen and Marcy G., Apr. 18, 1834.
Albart, [twin] s. Leonard and Betsey, Jan. 15, 1804.
Albert (see Alfred).
Albert, ch. Rufus and Nancy, Nov. 22, 1842.
Albert T., s. Albert and Priscilla, Sept. 4, 1824.
Alexander, s. Dwelle and Bettey, Oct. 10, 1767.
Alexander, s. Alexander and Bethiah, Feb. 1, 1807.
Alfred, [twin] s. Leonard and Betsey, Jan. 15, 1804.
Alfred, ch. Alfred and Catharine, July —, 1834. [July 2, P.R.9.] [Albert, July 2, P.R.13.]
Alfred, ch. Alfred dec'd and Catherine, bp. July 5, 1840. C.R.1.
Alfred, s. Rufus, farmer, and Nancy, July 11, 1847.
Alice Chase (see Allice Chase Clap).
Alice M. [———], w. George H., ———, 1830. G.R.14.
Allen, s. Alexander and Bethiah, Jan. 26, 1801. [[h. Mercy G.] G.R.8.]
Allice Chase, d. Albart and Prisilla, Sept. 29, 1814.
Andrew, ch. Elijah 3d and Temperance, June 22, 1837.
Ann [———], w. Geo[rge] P. [May —, 1819]. G.R.15.
Ann M., ch. George and Deborah, Nov. 2, 1840.
Ann Rozena, ch. Thomas 3d and Ann R., May 30, 1842.

CLAPP, Anna W. [———], w. Charles, ——— [1818]. c.r.3.
Annah, d. Allen and Charlottee, Jan. 2, 1815. [Annah Brooks Clap, c.r.2.]
Antonette, d. Natha[nie]ll and Anna, Feb. 27, 1822.
Arathusa, d. James and Elizabeth, Jan. 12, 1799.
Arathusa, d. Will[ia]m L. and Serena, Sept. 14, 1824, in Philadelphia.
Artemas, s. Roger and Peggey, Apr. 4, 1794.
Augustus, s. Leonard and Betsey, Sept. 15, 1807.
Bathsheba, d. Dwelly and Rachel, Oct. 17, 1791.
Bathsheba, d. Elijah Jr. and Martha, Nov. 16, 1811.
Benj[ami]n, s. Benj[ami]n and Judeth, Feb. 17, 1804.
Benjamin, ch. Judith, wid., bp. June 2, 1816. c.r.1.
Benj[a]min F., s. James, shoemaker, and Eliza, May 9, 1846.
Bethiah, d. Elijah and Martha, Aug. 3, 1783.
Bethiah, d. Joseph 2d and Lydia, Nov. 24, 1830.
Betsey, d. James (Clap) and Elizabeth, Mar. 4, 1785.
Betsy, d. Silvanus and Elisabeth, Feb. 5, 1771.
Betsy [———], w. ———, ——— [1773]. c.r.1. [Betsey, w. Leonard, g.r.11.]
Betty, d. Dwelle and Bettey, Oct. 28, 1769.
Caleb Nichols, s. Tilden and Penelope, Nov. 10, 1839.
Cassius, s. Roger and Peggy, July 16, 1796.
Catherine Mandana, ch. Alfred dec'd and Catherine, bp. July 5, 1840. c.r.1.
Catherine Maria, ch. John and Lucy, Sept. 5, 1834.
Cerene, d. Alexander and Bethiah, Dec. 29, 1802.
Chandler, s. Leonard and Betsey, Dec. 25, 1808. [Capt. Chandler [h. Hannah], g.r.6.]
Charles, s. David and Elizabeth, July 28, 1795.
Charles, s. Benjamin and Judeth, Oct. 15, 1813.
Charles, ——— [1814]. c.r.3.
Charles, ch. Judith, wid., bp. June 2, 1816. c.r.1.
Charles, ch. James S. and Elizabeth, Dec. 7, 1838.
Cha[rle]s H., s. Cha[rle]s, ——— [1845]. c.r.3.
Charles Whitcomb, ch. Hervey and Hannah, Nov. 2, 1835.
Charlottee, d. Allen and Charlottee, Apr. 9, 1809.
Christiana, d. Job and Lydia, Dec. 20, 1825.
Clara A., d. Gorham, painter, and Lydia, Sept. 7, 1847.
Couff, s. Couff and Floro, Feb. 5, 1744.
Daniel, s. James (Clap) and Elisabeth, Apr. 27, 1791.
David, s. David and Mary, July 24, 1752. [Clap, s. David dec'd and Mary, c.r.2.]
David Jr., s. David and Elizabeth, Jan. 22, 1783.

CLAPP, David, s. Joseph S., shipwright, and Sally, Sept. 16, 1844.
Davis, ch. James S. and Elizabeth, Dec. 2, 1833.
Deborah, d. Increase, bp. May 15, 1763. C.R.1.
[D]eborah, d. Lewis and Lydia, Mar. 2, 1796.
Deborah Ann, d. Nath[anie]ll and Anna, Aug. 13, 1819.
Desire, d. Silvanus and Elisabeth, Dec. 4, 1775.
Dwelle, s. Dwelle and Bettey, Feb. 12, 1763.
Edwin, ch. John and Lucy, May 15, 1831.
Edwin, ch. James S. and Elizabeth, Feb. 6, 1844.
Elijah (see Elisha).
Elijah, s. Thomas and Marcy, Sept. 26, 1801. [[h. Harriet] G.R.5.]
Elijah, s. Elijah Jr. and Martha, Mar. 9, 1807, in Boston.
Elijah Thomas, s. Elijah 3d and Harriet, Sept. 8, 1826.
Elisha, s. David and Elizabeth, July 9, 1790.
Elisha, s. David and w., bp. Feb. 3, 1794. C.R.2.
Elisha, s. David and Elizabeth, Mar. 9, 1794. [Elijah, C.R.2.]
Eliza, d. Dwelly and Rachel, June 27, 1802.
Elizabeth, d. David and Elizabeth, Mar. 6, 1784.
Elizabeth, d. Rachel, wid., bp. Oct. 2, 1793. C.R.1.
Elizabeth, ch. Franklin and Clara, Nov. 24, 1840.
Elizabeth Brooks, d. Stephen and Delight, Sept. 12, 1819.
Elizabeth Frances, d. Leonard and Betsey, Mar. 13, 1814.
Ellen Maria, ch. Joseph and Lucy, Mar. 6, 1832.
Emeline, d. James S., shoemaker (b. Hanover), and Elizabeth (b. Weymouth), Feb. 20, 1849, in S. Scituate.
Emely, d. Thomas and Marcy, Jan. 23, 1819.
Emilia, d. Thomas and Marcy, Sept. 14, 1799.
Emily Fisher [? m.], —— [1824]. G.R.2.
Emma W., d. Cha[rle]s, —— [1849]. C.R.3.
Erstine Follen, s. Allen D., tanner, and Deborah, June 3, 1846.
Eugene H., ch. William A. and w., Oct. 14, 1843.
Eunice, ch. James S. and Elizabeth, Apr. 27, 1836.
Fanny, d. David and w., bp. Nov. 2, 1794. C.R.2.
Frances Augusta, ch. John and Lucy, Feb. 11, 1824.
Frank Allen, s. Nathaniel B. and Anna B., Nov. 5, 1839.
Frank Otis, s. Rufus, yeoman, and Nancy (b. Marshfield), Apr. 24, 1849.
Franklin, s. Thomas and Marcy, July 21, 1812.
Galen, s. Capt. John and w., bp. June 5, 1791. C.R.2.
Galen, s. Roger and Peggey, Mar. 14, 1792.
Georganna M., ch. Charles and Anna W., Aug. 4, 1839.
George, s. Elijah Jr. and Martha, Jan. 5, 1814.
George, ch. Franklin and Clara, Feb. 10, 1844.

CLAPP, George A., s. George, blacksmith, and Deborah B., Nov. 9, 1845.
George B., ch. George and Deborah, Jan. 23, 1839.
George C., ch. Chandler [dup. sailor] and Hannah C. [dup. omits C.], Nov. 7, 1845.
George Henry, s. Tilden and Penelope, Sept. 29, 1828. [[h. Alice M.] G.R.14.]
George Henry, ch. George P. and Ann, July 18, 1841.
George Parker, s. Henry and Martha, Feb. 18, 1817. [[h. Ann] G.R.15.]
Hanah, d. Sam[uel], Jan. 15, 1673.
Hannah, d. Thomas and Marcy, Oct. 9, 1803.
Hannah C. [———], w. Chandler, —— [1818]. C.R.1. [w. Capt. Chandler, ——, 1817, G.R.6.]
Hannah M., ch. Seth and Nancy, May 23, 1839.
Hannah Stone, d. Stephen and Delight, Mar. 8, 1821.
Hannah Wilder, d. Michael T. and Hannah, Aug. 6, 1827.
Harriet [———], w. —— [Aug. —, 1801]. C.R.3.
Harriet Augusta, d. Elijah 3d and Harriet, June 23, 1832.
Harriet C. [———], w. Elijah, —— [1802]. C.R.3.
Harriet Ford, d. Thomas and Marcy, Nov. 22, 1821.
Harry, s. Alexander and Bethiah, Feb. 23, 1797.
Helena, ch. Allen, bp. July 1, 1821. C.R.2.
Helena, ch. James S. and Elizabeth, Nov. 25, 1828.
Henry, s. Leonard and Betsey, May 29, 1802. [[h. Frances (Perry)] G.R.2.]
Henry, ch. Franklin and Clara, Jan. 29, 1839.
Henry O., s. Henry, merchant, and Frances, Apr. 15, 1847.
Henry Thomas, ch. Thomas 3d and Ann R., Apr. 1, 1840.
Hervey, s. Thomas and Marcy, Feb. 26, 1814.
Hiram, s. Job and Lydia, July 28, 1822.
Howard, s. Thomas and Mary, Feb. 3, 1810.
Howard, s. Elijah 3d and Harriet, July 6, 1829.
Ida U., d. Thomas, shipwright, and Usulia C., May 14, 1847.
James Henry, ch. James S. and Elizabeth, Mar. 9, 1831.
Jane Franklin, ch. Hervey and Hannah, May 19, 1833.
Job, s. Alexander and Bethiah, Jan. 31, 1799.
Job, s. Benjamin and Judeth, Apr. 5, 1810.
Job, ch. Judith, wid., bp. June 2, 1816. C.R.1.
John, ch. John and Lucy, Dec. 31, 1828.
Joseph, s. Sam[uel], Dec. 14, 1668.
Joseph, s. Perkins and Rachel, Oct. 5, 1804. [[h. Lucy (Clapp)] G.R.14.]
Joseph, s. Alexander and Bethiah, June 1, 1809.

CLAPP, Joseph, s. Albert and Priscilla, Sept. 4, 1827.
Joseph Church, s. David and Elizabeth, July 22, 1780.
Joseph Henry, s. Joseph 2d and Lydia, Dec. 20, 1833.
Joseph Stowers, s. Elijah Jr. and Martha, Nov. 10, 1808.
Joseph T., s. Tilden, shoemaker, and Penelope, Mar. 29, 1844 [dup. 1845].
Joseph W., ch. Chandler and Hannah C., May 19, 1843.
Jotham, s. James and Elizabeth, Oct. 8, 1795.
Judeth, d. Benj[ami]n and Judeth, Mar. 24, 1806.
Judith Otis, ch. Judith, wid., bp. June 2, 1816. C.R.1.
Julia, d. Elijah 2d and Harriet, Aug. 17, 1843.
Lazarus B. Damon, s. Allen Jr. and Marcy G., Feb. 7, 1824.
Leonard [h. Betsey], —— [1766]. G.R.12.
Leonard, s. Leonard and Betsey, Mar. 18, 1800.
Levi, s. Dwelly and Rachel, Aug. 11, 1778.
[L]ewis, s. Lewis and Lydia, Jan. 6, 1794.
Louisa, ch. Franklin and Clara, Jan. 13, 1836.
Louiza, d. Thomas and Marcy, Mar. 24, 1815.
Lucenday, d. David and Elizabeth, July 31, 1785.
Lucinda, d. Dwelly and Rachel, Mar. 2, 1805.
Lucinda, d. Tilden and Penelope, July 28, 1834.
Lucretia, ch. Allen, bp. July 1, 1821. C.R.2.
Lucy, d. Dwelle and Bettey, Dec. 27, 1774.
Lucy, d. Thomas and Marcy, Dec. 23, 1805.
Lucy, d. Allen and Charlottee, Jan. 9, 1808. [w. Joseph Clapp, G.R.14.]
Lucy A., d. Tilden and Penelope, May 28, 1837.
Lucy Ann, ch. John and Lucy, Mar. 29, 1822.
Lucy Briggs, [twin] d. Leonard and Betsey, July 17, 1805 [*sic*, see Sally Briggs Clapp]. [w. Calvin Damon, G.R.14.]
Lucy Briggs, ch. Leonard, bp. Aug. 28, 1808. C.R.1.
Lucy Frances, ch. Joseph and Lucy, Mar. 30, 1829.
Lucy Frances, d. Hiram and Nancy, July 3, 1846.
Lucy V. [——], w. Ozias [July —, 1832]. G.R.6.
Luther Litchfield, s. Tilden and Penelope, Dec. 23, 1826.
Lydia [? m.], ——, 1799. G.R.8.
Lydia, d. Benj[ami]n and Judeth, Jan. 3, 1808.
Lydia, d. Alexander and Bethiah, Oct. 29, 1811.
Lydia, ch. Judith, wid., bp. June 2, 1816. C.R.1.
Lydia Ellms, d. Tilden and Penelope, May 14, 1841.
Lydia Holmes, d. Lewis and Lydia, July 13, 1789. [Clap, C.R.1.]
Lydia Otis, ch. John and Lucy, Feb. 21, 1826.
Mandana Catharine, ch. Alfred and Catharine, Oct. 12, 1830. [Mandana Catherine, P.R.13.]

CLAPP, Marcy, d. Thomas and Marcy, Jan. 22, 1808.
Maria, d. Franklin B., farmer, and Clara (b. Cohassett), Aug. 11, 1849.
Maria A., ch. James S. and Elizabeth, June 13, 1841.
Maria Foster, ch. Chandler and Hannah C., June 13, 1839.
Martha, d. Elijah Jr. and Martha, June 1, 1805, in Boston.
Martha Foster, d. Silas and Ruth C., Oct. 17, 1815.
Mary, d. Silvanus and Elisabeth, Sept. 5, 1781.
Mary, d. David and Elizabeth, Nov. 22, 1781.
Mary, d. Elijah Jr. and Martha, Aug. 13, 1803, in Boston.
Mary C. [? m.], ——, 1842. G.R.8.
Mary Elmes, d. Silas and Ruth C., Oct. 31, 1820.
Mary Ellms, d. Joseph 2d and Lydia, Sept. 16, 1838.
Mary F., d. Henry, merchant, and Frances, July 30 [1845].
Mary Gould, d. Allen Jr. and Marcy G., Jan. 11, 1826.
Mary Leonard, d. Leonard and Betsey, Sept. 26, 1798.
Melatiah, s. Silvanus and Elisabeth, Mar. 19, 1769.
Melatiah, s. Stephen and Delight, Feb. 13, 1815.
Mercy Ford, d. Elijah 2d and Harriet, June 12, 1837.
Mercy G. [——], w. Allen [Mar. —, 1800]. G.R.8.
Michael, s. Michael T. and Hannah, Nov. 12, 1825.
Molly, d. Galen and Patience, Dec. 20, 1758.
Nance, d. John, bp. June 5, 1763. C.R.1.
Nancy Anna, ch. Rufus [dup. farmer] and Nancy, Sept. 20, 1845.
Nathaniel, s. Silvanus and Elisabeth, Mar. 1, 1785.
Nathaniel, s. David and Elizabeth, Nov. 7, 1787.
Nathaniel Briggs, s. Nath[anie]ll and Anna, Aug. 28, 1815.
Nichols, s. Silas and Ruth C., June 20, 1823.
Oriana, ch. Chandler and Hannah C., Nov. 14, 1837. [Orianna, Nov. 13, G.R.12.]
Otis Parsons, s. Stephen and Delight, Mar. 12, 1818.
Owen, s. Paul and w., Mar. 22, 1833.
Paul, s. Alexander and Bethiah, Jan. 26, 1791.
Peleg Ford, s. Elijah 3d and Harriet, Jan. 27, 1835.
Penelope [——], w. Tilden L., —— [1805]. G.R.14.
Perez, [twin] s. Dwelly and Rachel, Aug. 24, 1793.
Perkins, s. Elijah and Martha, Oct. 3, 1779.
Perkins, s. Perkins and Rachel, Feb. 11, 1809.
Polly (C[l]app), d. Dwelly and Rachel, Aug. 18, 1781.
Polly, d. Allen and Charlottee, Jan. 15, 1817.
Rachel, d. Silvanus and Elisabeth, Apr. 9, 1778.
Rachel [——], w. Perkins, —— [1783]. G.R.14.
Rachel, d. Dwelly and Rachel, Sept. 2, 1798.
Rachel, d. Perkins and Rachel, Feb. 17, 1807.

CLAPP, Rachel, d. Perkins and w., bp. June 5, 1808. C.R.2.
Rachel Stowers, ch. John and Lucy, Feb. 7, 1820.
Rhoda, d. Tilden and Penelope, Oct. 1, 1832.
Rhoda Nicholls, d. Tilden and Penelope, Oct. 29, 1830.
Roger, s. Dwelle and Bettey, May 29, 1765.
Rogers, s. Dwelly and Rachel, Dec. 2, 1785.
Rufus, s. Leonard and Betsey, Apr. 10, 1817. [[h. Nancy (Hall)] G.R.6.]
Ruth, d. Dwelle and Bettey, Feb. 20, 1772.
Ruth, d. David and Elizabeth, June 5, 1792.
Ruth, d. Dwelly and Rachel, Oct. 15, 1796.
Ruth Litchfield, d. Joseph 2d and Lydia, Mar. 16, 1835.
[S]alley, d. Lewis and Lydia, May 14, 1799.
Sally, d. Elijah and Martha, May 18, 1781.
Sally, d. Dwelly and Rachel, Apr. 8, 1784.
Sally Briggs, [twin] d. Leonard and Betsey, July 15, 1805 [*sic*, see Lucy Briggs Clapp].
Sally Briggs, ch. Leonard, bp. Aug. 28, 1808. C.R.1.
Salome Litchfield, d. Allen and Marcy G., Mar. 3, 1829.
Sammuell, s. Sam[uel], May 14, 1667.
Sam[ue]ll, s. Perkins and w., bp. June 5, 1808. C.R.2.
Sarah J., d. Franklin, farmer, and Clara, Dec. 30, 1846.
Sarah Tilden, ch. John and Lucy, Feb. 10, 1818.
Serena, d. James and Elisebeth, Sept. 15, 1793.
Silas, s. Alexander and Bethiah, Dec. 10, 1793.
Silas Damon, s. Silas and Ruth C., Oct. 14, 1818.
Stephen, s. Silvanus and Elisabeth, July 20, 1787.
Stephen, s. Stephen and Delight, Oct. 5, 1824.
Stephen G., s. Stephen G., painter, and Lydia (b. Malden), Sept. 14, 1849, in S. Scituate.
Stephen Gorham, s. Stephen and Delight, Aug. 27, 1816.
Steven, s. Sam[uel], Mar. 4, 1670.
Susan F., d. Tilden and Penelope, Dec. 23, 1843.
Susanna, [twin] d. Dwelly and Rachel, Aug. 24, 1793.
Sylvanus, s. Nathaniel and Anna, Oct. 18, 1831.
Temperance, d. Stephen and Delight, Aug. 26, 1822.
Temperance, ch. Elijah 3d and Temperance, June 22, 1832.
Temprance, d. Silvanus and Elisabeth, June 9, 1773.
Thomas, s. Leonard and Betsey, Feb. 25, 1812.
Thomas, s. Perkins and Rachel, Apr. 22, 1812.
Thomas, s. Thomas and Marcy, Jan. 22, 1824.
Thomas Jenkins, s. Elijah and Martha, Jan. 19, 1791. [[h. Mary C.] G.R.14.]
Tilden, s. Dwelly and Rachel, Dec. 2, 1807.

CLAPP, William, ch. Allen, bp. Oct. 25, 1812. C.R.2.
William, s. Allen and Charlottee, Sept. 7, 1813.
William, s. Thomas [dup. 3d] and Annrosena [dup. Ann R.], Nov. 20, 1846. [———, 1847, G.R.7.]
William Otis, s. Joseph 2d and Lydia, June 10, 1840.
William Thomas, s. Harvey [second dup. Hervey], shoemaker, and Hannah, Aug. 6 [dup. Aug. 7], 1844.
Xoa, d. Alexander and Bethiah, Dec. 12, 1804.
Xoa Allen, d. Allen and Marcy G., Dec. 12, 1831.
———, ch. Hervey and Hannah, July 4, 1840.

CLARA (see Clary, Cleary), ———, s. Mary, Mar. 25, 1848.

CLARK (see Clarke, Clerk), Abigail, d. Thomas and Allice, bp. Nov. 24, 1723. C.R.2.
Alice, d. Thom[a]s (Clerk) and Allice, bp. Feb. 25, 1721–2. C.R.2.
Ann, d. Thomas, Dec. 23, 1682.
Ann, ch. Thomas and Martha, bp. Sept. 9, 1705. C.R.2.
Charity, d. Thomas (Clarke), May 20, 1692.
Charity, ch. Thomas and Martha, bp. Sept. 9, 1705. C.R.2.
Daved, s. Thomas, Mar. 24, 1694.
David, ch. Thomas and Martha, bp. Oct. 8, 1710. C.R.2.
Deborah, d. Thomas, July 28, 1690.
Deborah, ch. Thomas and Martha, bp. Sept. 9, 1705. C.R.2.
Ezekiel, s. Thomas and Allice, bp. July 24, 1726. C.R.2.
Ezra, s. Thomas (Clarke) and Allice, bp. Sept. 4, 1720. C.R.2.
Joseph, s. Thomas, Jan. 5, 1684.
Joseph W. [h. Beulah], ——— [1778]. G.R.15.
Mary, ch. Thomas and Martha, bp. Oct. 8, 1710. C.R.2.
Nathaniell, s. Thomas, Mar. 28, 1704.
Samuel, ch. Thomas and Martha, bp. Oct. 8, 1710. C.R.2.
Samuell, s. Thomas, Feb. 11, 1701–2.
Thomas, s. Thomas Jr., Oct. 2, 1703.

CLARKE (see Clark, Clerk), John, s. Thomas Jr., Oct. 22, 1707.
Joseph, s. Thomas Jr. and Alice, May 7, 1711.
Marcy [dup. Clark], d. Thomas, Nov. 5, 1677.
Martha, d. Tho[mas], bp. July 28, 1678. C.R.2.
Mary, d. Thomas, Mar. 18, 1696–7.
Mary, d. Thomas Jr. and Alice, Sept. 23, 1708.
Rachell [dup. Clark], d. Thomas, Mar. 24, 1678–9. [Rachel Clarke, C.R.2.]
Seth, s. Thomas Jr. and Alice, Nov. 4, 1712.
Thomas [dup. Clark], s. Thomas, Jan. 7, 1680.
Thomas, s. Thomas, bp. June 11, 1682. C.R.2.

CLARY (see Clara, Cleary), Catharine, d. James and Rosanna, Aug. 2, 1825.
Mary Ann, d. James and Rosanna, Mar. 25, 1823, in Cornwallis, Nova Scotia.

CLEARY (see Clara, Clary), Charles M., s. James and Roxanna, Mar. 3, 1842.
Emma Frances [dup. and second dup. Clary], d. James, yeoman, and Roxana [dup. and second dup. Roxanna], Oct. 2, 1844.
James, s. James and Rosanna, Nov. 16, 1836.
John, s. James and Rosanna, Sept. 12, 1827.
Margaret Oconer, d. James and Rosanna, Aug. 25, 1834.
Mercy Vinal, d. James and Rosanna, Mar. 2, 1832.
Rosanna, d. James and Rosanna, Nov. 2, 1829.
Thomas Edward, s. James and Rosanna, Mar. 21, 1839.

CLEMENT (see Clements), Hannah [———], w. Theodore, ——— [1807]. C.R.1.

CLEMENTS (see Clement), Mary A., w. Ephraim Young, July 22, 1828. G.R.6.

CLERK (see Clark, Clarke), Caleb, ch. Thomas and Allice, bp. May 3, 1719. C.R.2.
John, ch. Thomas and Allice, bp. May 3, 1719. C.R.2.
Joseph, ch. Thomas and Allice, bp. May 3, 1719. C.R.2.
Martha, ch. Thomas and Allice, bp. May 3, 1719. C.R.2.
Mary, ch. Thomas and Allice, bp. May 3, 1719. C.R.2.
Seth, ch. Thomas and Allice, bp. May 3, 1719. C.R.2.

CLIFFT (see Clift, Clifte, Clyft), Lydia, d. William, July 13, 1697.

CLIFT (see Clifft, Clifte, Clyft), Amos, ch. Sam[ue]ll and Lydia of Marshfield, bp. Aug. 12, 1739. C.R.2.
Lydia, ch. William and Lydia, bp. July 14, 1706. C.R.2.
Lydiah, d. W[illia]m of Marshfield, bp. Jan. 12, 1728–9. C.R.2.
Mary, d. William and Lydia, bp. Aug. 31, 1707. C.R.2.
Mary, ch. Sam[ue]ll and Lydia of Marshfield, bp. Aug. 12, 1739. C.R.2.
Samuel, s. Will[ia]m and Lydia of Marshfield, bp. Oct. 23, 1709. C.R.2.
Silva "alias Zilpha," d. W[illia]m of Marshfield, bp. Aug. 18, 1734. C.R.2.
William, ch. William and Lydia, bp. July 14, 1706. C.R.2.
Willes, s. W[illia]m and Judith of Marshfield, bp. June 6, 1731. C.R.2.
Zilpha (see Silva).

CLIFTE (see Clifft, Clift, Clyft), William, s. William, Apr. 30, 1700.

CLYFT (see Clifft, Clift, Clifte), Joseph, [ch.] William and Judith of Marshfield, bp. Aug. 8, 1736. c.r.2.
Mary, d. W[illia]m and Lydia of Marshfield, bp. Aug. 21, 1715. c.r.2.
Nathanael, s. William (Clift) of Marshfield, bp. Sept. 11, 1726. c.r.2.
William, s. William (Clift) Jr. and Judith of Marshfield, bp. July 30, 1721. c.r.2.
Wills, s. William and Judeth, bp. July 26, 1724. c.r.2.

COBB, Hannah, d. ———, bp. Oct. 5, 1639. c.r.1.
Mary, d. Henery, Mar. 24, 1637. p.c.r.

COBURN, Ama, d. Saul and Patience, Apr. 29, 1785.

COCKE (see Cocks, Cook), James, s. Robert, Dec. 1, 1693.
Jane, d. Robert, May 11, 1697.
Margarett, d. Robert, June 6, 1699.
Mary, d. William and Mary, w. T[homas] Curtis, July —, 1676.
William, s. Robert, Aug. 25, 1695.

COCKS (see Cocke, Cook), Mary, d. W[illia]m and Mary of Hanover, bp. Mar. 31, 1728. c.r.2.

COFFIN, Charles J., ch. Peter and Anne (Martin), ——— [1811]. g.r.14.

COLAMER (see Collamare, Collamer, Collamore, Collimor, Collmore, Collomare, Collomore, Colomer), Abigaill [dup. Abigail Collamore], d. Peter and Abigail, Aug. 4, 1695. [Abigail Collomar, c.r.2.]
Anthony, s. Peter, June 16, 1699. [Collomar, c.r.2.]
Elizabeth, d. Anthony, Dec. 11, 1679. [Elizebeth Collimer, c.r.2.]
Isaac, s. Peter, July 24, 1707. [Collomare, s. Peter (Colomare) and Abigail, c.r.2.]
Martha, d. Anthony, May 12, 1677. [Collimer, d. Anthonie, c.r.2.]
Samuell, s. Peter and Abigail, Aug. 21, 1712. [Samuel Collomar, c.r.2.]
Sarah, d. Peter and Abigail, May 22, 1697. [Collomar, c.r.2.]

COLBY, Elvira F., ———, 1846. g.r.6.

COLE, Abigal, d. David and Sarah, Mar. 9, 1743.
Ambrose, s. Ambrose, Feb. 1, 1695-6.

COLE, Ambrose, s. Will[ia]m and Rachel, June 27, 1779.
Amelia F. [? m.], ——, 1835. G.R.6.
Amos, ch. Ambrose, bp. Oct. 23, 1726. C.R.1.
Amose, s. Ambrose Jr. and Eliza[beth], Oct. 26, 1722.
Andrew, s. Braddock and Betsey, July 16, 1820.
Ann, d. Ambrose, Dec. 9, 1701.
Augustus, s. Charles and Esther, Nov. 24, 1789. [[h. Sally] C.R.3.]
Augustus, s. Augustus and Sally J., Jan. 1, 1828.
Augustus H., s. Ambrose, —— [1811]. C.R.1.
Benjamin, s. Ambros, bp. Jan. 28, 1750. C.R.1.
Bradock, s. Will[ia]m and Rachel, Dec. 9, 1788. [Braddock, C.R.1.] [Braddock [h. Betsey (Waterman)], Dec. 9, 1787, P.R.2.]
Charles, s. James and Sarah, Sept. 1, 1759.
Charles, s. Charles and Esther, Mar. 3, 1799.
Charles, [twin] s. Augustus and Sally J., Apr. 2, 1831.
Charlotte, d. Will[ia]m and Rachel, June 4, 1768.
David, s. Ambrose, Oct. 19, 1704.
David, s. David and Sarah, Oct. 16, 1737.
David, s. Will[ia]m and Rachel, May 11, 1776.
Desire, d. Ensign and Sarah, May 8, 1732.
Desire, d. Ensign, bp. Aug. 5, 1733. C.R.1.
Desire, d. James and Sarah, Apr. 14, 1756.
Easther, [twin] d. Augustus and Sally J., Apr. 2, 1831.
Eliza Waterman, d. Braddock and Betsey, May 11, 1823.
Elizabeth, d. Ambrose Jr. and Elizabeth, June 26, 1721.
Elizabeth, ch. Ambrose, bp. Oct. 23, 1726. C.R.1.
Eliza[beth], d. David and Sarah, Feb. 9, 1739.
Elizabeth, bp. July 22, 1739, a. 73. C.R.1.
Elizabeth, d. Will[ia]m and Rachel, June 26, 1774.
Enoch, s. James and Sarah, Apr. 5, 1766.
Enoch, twin s. Charles [James, C.R.2.] and Esther, June 1, 1801.
Enoch Edward, s. Enoch, yeoman, and Roxanna W., Apr. 2, 1849.
Ensign, s. Ensign and Sarah, Aug. 16, 1737.
Ensing, s. Ambrose, Nov. 2, 1698.
Esther, d. Charles and Esther, Dec. 3, 1793.
George Henry, s. Braddock and Betsey, Jan. 6, 1816.
George Henry, ch. Braddock, bp. Sept. 2, 1821. C.R.1.
Gridley, s. Will[ia]m and Rachel, Mar. 9, 1784.
Gridley, s. Gridley, bp. Nov. 3, 1808. C.R.1.
Gridley, s. Braddock and Betsey, Oct. 28, 1813.
Gridley, ch. Braddock, bp. Sept. 2, 1821. C.R.1.
Hannah Chandler, d. Charles [Cha[n]dler, C.R.2.] and Esther, May 3, 1797.

COLE, Henry Otis, ch. Joseph O. and Sarah W., Aug. 2, 1844.
James, s. Ambrose and Abigal, Sept. 2, 1716.
James, s. James and Sarah, Oct. 2, 1750.
Jonathan, s. Ambrose and Silence, Aug. 20, 1709.
Jonathan, s. Jona[than] and Sarah, July 22, 1739.
Joseph Otis, s. Braddock and Betsey, Apr. 11, 1818.
Joseph Otis, ch. Braddock, bp. Sept. 2, 1821. C.R.1.
Lucy, d. Ensign and Sarah, Nov. 10, 1742.
Lydia, d. David and Sarah, Sept. 20, 1733. [Lidia, C.R.1.]
Lydia Vinal, d. Braddock and Betsey, Nov. 5, 1825. [Nov. 4, P.R.2.]
Mahittable, d. Ja[me]s and Sarah, Nov. 6, 1753. [Mehitabel, C.R.2.]
Mary, d. Jona[than] and Sarah, Nov. 21, 1733.
Mary, d. Ja[me]s and Sarah, Sept. 1, 1746.
Mary [――――], w. Ambrose, ―― [1782]. C.R.1.
Mary Clapp, twin d. Charles [James, C.R.2.] and Esther, June 1, 1801.
Mehitable (see Mahittable).
Mercy James, d. Augustus and Sally J., Oct. 23, 1825.
Nabby, d. James and Sarah, Sept. 1, 1763.
Nancy, d. Charles and Esther, July 6, 1803.
Nancy, d. Charles and w., bp. Aug. 5, 1804. C.R.2.
Noah D., ――, 1836. G.R.14.
Oliver, s. William and Rachel, Oct. 16, 1771.
Polly, d. Gridley and Polly, Jan. 22, 1811.
Rachel, d. Will[ia]m and Rachel, Jan. 27, 1782.
Ruth, d. Ensign and Sarah, Oct. 1, 1734.
Salley, d. Charles and Esther, July 10, 1787. [Sally [w. Benjamin Merritt], G.R.14.]
Sally, d. David and Charlotte, July 12, 1779.
Sally [――――], w. Augustus, ―― [1791]. C.R.3.
Sarah, d. Jona[than] and Sarah, Aug. 26, 1736.
Sarah, d. James and Sarah, Aug. 22, 1748.
Sarah James, d. Augustus and Sally (James), May 28, 1820.
Sarah James, d. Capt. Augustus, bp. Sept. 7, 1823. C.R.1.
Thomas Otis, s. Braddock and Betsey, Nov. 3, 1830.
Thomas Otis, s. Braddock and Betsey, bp. Nov. 4, 1832. C.R.1.
William, s. Ambrose, Sept. 1, 1693.
William, s. David and Sarah, Nov. 28, 1735. [Apr. 28, P.R.2.]
William, s. Will[ia]m and Rachel, Apr. 7, 1766. [William Jr., P.R.2.]
William, ch. Gridley, bp. Mar. 24, 1814. C.R.1.
William Gridley, s. Gridly [Gridley, C.R.1.] and Polly, Dec. 4, 1808.

COLEMAN (see Colemen, Colman), Amiel, s. Joseph, bp. July 22, 1792. C.R.1.

Benjamin, [twin] s. Thomas, June [3], 1704. [Benjaman Colman, s. Thomas and Mary, June 3, C.R.4.

Comfurt, [twin] d. Thomas, June [3], 1704. [Comfort Colman, d. Thomas and Mary, June 3, C.R.4.]

David, s. Joseph, bp. June 4, 1769. C.R.1.

Deborah Foster, d. Amial and Betsey, Oct. 19, 182[worn] [1820].

Elisabeth, d. Joseph, bp. Oct. 8, 1786. C.R.1.

Elizabeth, d. Amial and Betsey, July 16, 1813.

Hannah Rich, d. Joseph Jr., bp. Apr. 3, 1803. C.R.1.

Hariot, d. Amial and Betsey, June 24, 1819.

James, s. Thomas, July 24, 1694. [Jeames, s. Thomas (Çolmam) and Margret, C.R.4.]

John, s. Thomas and Mary, Apr. 28, 1706. [Colman, C.R.4.]

John, s. Jo[h]n, bp. May 29, 1737. C.R.1.

John, s. Joseph, bp. Aug. 3, 1788. C.R.1.

Joseph, s. Thomas, Feb. 18, 1685. [Colman, s. Thomas and Margaite, Feb. 18, 1683, C.R.4.]

Joseph, s. Jo[h]n, bp. Oct. 19, 1740. C.R.1.

Lilias, d. Thomas, July 24, 1686. [Colman, d. Thomas (Coalman) and Margaite, C.R.4.]

Molly, ch. Joseph, bp. May 8, 1768. C.R.1.

Moses Rich, s. Joseph Jr. and Lydia, Dec. 22, 1806.

Nancy, d. Joseph, bp. Oct. 8, 1786. C.R.1.

Nathan Jenkins, s. Amial and Betsey, Jan. 10, 1817.

Rebekah, d. Thomas, Jan. 9, 1681. [Coalman, d. Thomas and Margarte, C.R.4.]

Sarah, d. Thomas, Apr. 10, 1682. [Coalman, d. Thomas and Margarte, C.R.4.]

Sarah Jenkins, d. Amial and Betsey, Apr. 26, 181[5].

Thankfull, d. Zackakiah, Feb. 20, 1701–2.

Thomas, s. Thomas, Mar. 15, 1688. [Colman, s. Thomas (Coalman) and Margrate, C.R.4.]

William, s. Thomas, Feb. 15, 1692. [Colman, s. Thonas and Margret, C.R.4.]

COLEMEN (see Coleman, Colman), Lydeah, d. Joseph, bp. Aug. 20, 1780. C.R.1.

COLLAMARE (see Colamer, Collamer, Collamore, Collimor, Collmore, Collomare, Collomore, Colomer), Samuel, s. Anthony, bp. Apr. 3, 1737. C.R.2.

COLLAMER (see Colamer, Collamare, Collamore, Collimor, Collmore, Collomare, Collomore, Colomer), Abigal, d. Anthony and Susanna, Jan. 23, 1732. [Abigail Collomare, c.r.2.]

Abigal, d. Antho[n]y and Susannah, Apr. 7, 1746. [Abigail Collamar, c.r.2.]

Anthony, s. Anthony and Susannah, July 4, 1735. [Collomare, c.r.2.]

Anthony, s. Anthoney and Marcy, Jan. 19, 1759.

Barker, s. Antho[ny] and Mercy, Aug. 15, 1767.

Betty, d. Jo[h]n and Margret, Apr. 14, 1740. [Collomare, c.r.2.]

Davis, s. Isaac and Thankfull, Oct. 23, 1743. [David Collomare, c.r.2.]

Enoch, s. Jo[h]n and Margaret, June 27, 1745. [Collamar, s. John and Margret, c.r.2.]

Ezekel, s. Peter and Eliza[beth], Jan. 3, 1756.

Hannah, d. Tho[ma]s and Hannah, Apr. 16, 1740. [Collomare, c.r.2.]

Hannah, d. Antho[ny] and Mercy, Feb. 23, 1763.

Isaac, s. Isaac and Thankfull, May 13, 1736. [Collomare, c.r.2.]

John, s. Peter, Dec. 2, 1704. [Collomar, c.r.2.]

John, s. John and Margaret, July 15, 1742. [Collomare, s. John and Margret, c.r.2.]

John, s. Antho[ny] and Mercy, Aug. 11, 1772.

Joseph, s. Isaac and Thankfull, Nov. 27, 1737. [Collomare, c.r.2.]

Joshua, s. Isaac and Thankfull, Nov. 16, 1740. [Collomar, s. Isaac (Collomare), c.r.2.]

Lusanna, d. Anthony and Susannah, May 21, 1742. [Collomare, d. Anthony and Susanna, c.r.2.]

Lydia, d. Tho[ma]s and Hannah, Jan. 30, 1747. [Collomar, c.r.2.]

Martha, d. Tho[ma]s and Hannah, Aug. 19, 1744. [Collamer, c.r.2.]

Mary, d. Peter, Feb. 14, 1702–3. [Collomar, c.r.2.]

Mary, d. Jo[h]n and Margret, Dec. 7, 1735. [Collomare, d. John and Margaret, c.r.2.]

Mary, d. Antho[ny] and Mercy, Aug. 18, 1770.

Mercy, d. Antho[ny] and Marcy, Mar. 16, 1761.

Peleg, s. Isaac and Thankfull, Sept. 1, 1745.

Peter, s. Peter, Jan. 20, 1700–1. [Collomar, c.r.2.]

Peter, s. Isaac and Thankfull, Oct. 8, 1734. [Collomare, c.r.2.]

Rebecca, d. Isaac and Thankfull, July 25, 1742. [Collomare, c.r.2.]

Samuel, s. Anthony and Susannah, Mar. 28, 1737.

COLLAMER, Samuel, s. Antho[ny] and Mercy, July 18, 1765.
Sarah, d. Jo[h]n and Margaret, Apr. 23, 1733. [Collomare, d. John and Margret, C.R.2.]
Submit, d. Tho[ma]s and Hannah, Sept. 18, 1753. [Collamore, C.R.2.]
Susana, d. Isaac and Thankfull, July 28, 1751.
Susannah, d. Anthony and Susannah, Jan. 17, 1739. [Susanna Collomare, C.R.2.]
Thankfull, d. Isaac and Thankfull, Jan. 8, 1738. [Collomare, C.R.2.]
Thomas, s. Peter and Abigail, Feb. 19, 1709–10. [Collomar, C.R.2.]
Thomas, s. Thomas and Hannah, June 10, 1738. [Collomare, C.R.2.]

COLLAMORE (see Colamer, Collamare, Collamer, Collimor, Collmore, Collomare, Collomore, Colomer), Almira Amanda, d. John and Polly, Feb. 6, 1827.
Andrew Fuller, s. John and Michal, Sept. 11, 1817.
Anthony, s. Enoch and Hannah, Jan. 15, 1787.
Betsey, d. John and Michal, Nov. 15, 1807.
Davis, s. John and Michal, Oct. 7, 1824.
Ebenezar, s. John and Michal, Sept. 5, 1809.
Enoch, s. Enoch and Hannah, May 17, 1782.
George Enoch, s. John and Polly, Aug. 16, 1828.
Gilman, s. Enoch and Hannah, June 22, 1789.
Gilman C., s. John and Polly, Mar. 29, 1834.
Hannah, d. Enoch and Hannah, June 22, 1777.
Horace, s. Enoch and Hannah, Nov. 4, 1791. [Collmomore, s. Capt. Enoch, C.R.2.]
John, s. Enoch and Hannah, July 9, 1775.
John, [twin] s. John and Michal, Aug. 13, 1802.
Lucinda, d. John and Michal, Mar. 28, 1813.
Lucinda, [twin] d. John and Michal, Aug. 30, 1815.
Lusanna, d. Enoch and Hannah, Nov. 27, 1794.
Mary, d. John and Michal, May 7, 1806.
Michal, [twin] d. John and Michal, Aug. 13, 1802.
Sarah, d. Enoch and Hannah, Sept. 27, 1779.
Sarah, d. John and Michal, July 26, 1804.
Sophia, d. Enoch and Hannah, Nov. 28, 1784.
William Ward, s. John and Polly, Feb. 20, 1830.
Williams, s. John and Michal, July 23, 1811.
Williams, [twin] s. John and Michal, Aug. 30, 1815.

COLLIER, Alben, s. Isaac, bp. Sept. 25, 1793. C.R.1.
Ann Jane, ch. Isaac Jr., bp. June 17, 1810. C.R.1.

COLLIER, Anna, d. Isaac [and] Tamsin, June 25, 1786. [Anne, G.R.2.]
Bridgit, d. Tho[ma]s and Bridgit, May 9, 1740. [Bridget, C.R.1.]
Charles W. [Mar. —, 1835]. G.R.2.
Cynthia, d. Isaac and Tamsin, June 3, 1794.
Elisabeth, d. Isaac and Tamsin, Oct. 30, 1779. [Elizabeth, C.R.1.]
Elisha, s. Isaac and Tamsin, July 8, 1788. [Elisha H., G.R.2.]
Elisha, s. Isaac, bp. Sept. 25, 1793. C.R.1.
Eliza, d. Isaac and Betsy, Apr. 29, 1801.
Eliza, ch. Isaach, bp. May 29, 1803. C.R.1.
Eliza A. [? m.], Dec. 8, 1816. G.R.2.
Elizabeth, d. W[illia]m, bp. Nov. 21, 1756. C.R.1.
Elizabeth (see Elisabeth).
Ephraim Bosworth, s. Tho[ma]s and Bridgit, June 13, 1748.
Garshum, s. Tho[ma]s and Bridgit, Apr. 31 [*sic*], 1738. [Gershom Colier, C.R.1.]
Isaac, s. William and Judeth, June 13, 1750.
Isaac, s. Isaac and Tamsin, May 29, 1773.
Isaac, s. Isaac, bp. Dec. 24, 1802. C.R.1.
Isaac Jr., s. Isaac and Betsy, Dec. 4, 1805.
James, s. Isaac and Tamsin, Aug. 29, 1775.
James S., twin s. Jonathan and Abigail, Oct. 21, 1793.
Jane, d. Tho[ma]s and Bridgit, Apr. 9, 1744.
Jenny, d. Isaac and Tamsin, Feb. 19, 1782.
John L., twin s. Jonathan and Abigail, Oct. 21, 1793.
Jonathan, s. William and Judith, Mar. 8, 1758.
Joseph H., s. Isaac and Betsy, Apr. 16, 1798.
Joseph Haydon, ch. Isaach, bp. May 29, 1803. C.R.1.
Judey, [twin] d. Isaac and Tamsin, Mar. 2, 1784.
Judith, d. W[illia]m, bp. Sept. 8, 1754. C.R.1.
Judith, d. Isaac, bp. Oct. 8, 1786. C.R.1.
Julia Ann [? m.], —— [1821]. G.R.2.
Lucy Vinal, d. Peleg and Lucy, July 25, 1808.
Marcy Vinal, d. Peleg and Lucy, Feb. 9, 1811.
Mary, d. Tho[mas] and Bridgit, Apr. 22, 1746.
Mary, d. Isaac and Tamsin, June 21, 1792.
Mary, d. Isaac, bp. Sept. 18, 1793. C.R.1.
Mary A., d. Rev. W[illia]m, —— [1810]. G.R.2.
Mary Lincoln, d. Peleg H., seaman, and Mary, June 13 [dup. Mar. 13], 1833.
Moses, s. Isaac and Tamsin, Aug. 29, 1777.
Moses, s. Moses and Rachel, Nov. 8, 1803.
Naby, d. Jonathan and Abigail, Sept. 22, 1800.
Nancy, d. Isaac and Betsy, Feb. 7, 1808.

COLLIER, Peleg, [twin] s. Isaac and Tamsin, Mar. 2, 1784.
Peleg, ch. Isaac, bp. Oct. 8, 1786. C.R.1.
Peleg, ch. Peleg H. and Mary, June 13, 1835.
Peleg Haydon, s. Peleg and Lucy, Sept. 9, 1809. [Peleg Hayden, h. Mary (Mann), G.R.6.]
Rachel Curtis, d. Moses and Rachel, Sept. 24, 1801.
Rachel Curtis, d. Moses, bp. Nov. 28, 1802. C.R.1.
Ruthe, d. Jonathan and Abigail, Sept. 21, 1789.
Saley, d. Jonathan and Abigail, Oct. 2, 1791.
Sarah, d. W[illia]m, bp. Oct. 29, 1752. C.R.1.
Tamson, d. Isaac and Betsy, June 16, 1803.
Tho[ma]s, s. Tho[ma]s and Bridgit, Apr. 17, 1736.
Will[ia]m, s. Tho[ma]s (Colleer) and Bridgit, May 11, 1742.
William, s. Isaac and Tamsen [Tamsan, C.R.1.], Oct. 11, 1771.
W[illia]m, Dec. 4, 1811. G.R.2.
William James, ch. Isaac Jr., bp. June 17, 1810. C.R.1.

COLLIMOR (see Colamer, Collamare, Collamer, Collamore, Collmore, Collomare, Collomore, Colomer), Mary, d. Antony, Nov. 10, 1667. [Collimer, d. Anthony, C.R.2.]
Peter, s. Antony, May 6, 1671. [Collymer, s. Anthony, C.R.2.]

COLLMORE (see Colamer, Collamare, Collamer, Collamore, Collimor, Collomare, Collomore, Colomer), Betty, d. Benja[min], bp. Nov. 20, 1757. C.R.2.
Ezekiel, s. Peter, bp. Apr. 24, 1757. C.R.2.

COLLOMARE (see Colamer, Collamare, Collamer, Collamore, Collimor, Collmore, Collomore, Colomer), Lydia, [ch.] Thomas and Hannah, bp. July 18, 174[sic, 1742]. C.R.2.

COLLOMORE (see Colamer, Collamare, Collamer, Collamore, Collimor, Collmore, Collomare, Colomer), Benja[min], s. Benja[min], bp. June 20, 1756. C.R.2.
Hannah, d. Benja[min], bp. June 20, 1756. C.R.2.
Mary, d. Benja[min], bp. June 20, 1756. C.R.2.
Sarah, d. Benja[min], bp. June 20, 1756. C.R.2.

COLMAN (see Coleman, Colemen), Abigal, d. James and Abigail, Dec. 16, 1740.
Alice Little, d. David and Alice, Jan. 8, 1801.
Almeda, d. David and Alice, Nov. 5, 1809.
Amelia Francis [dup. Frances], d. Moses R., mariner, and Polly, Dec. 19, 1835.
Ammiel, s. Joseph and Mercy, Oct. 23, 1789.
Ammiel, s. Ammiel and Betsey, Jan. 10, 1823.

COLMAN, Catharine Hall, d. Joseph Jr. and Deborah, Mar. 3, 1831. [Catherine H., w. Benj[amin] Brown, C.R.3.]
Catherine Hall, ch. Joseph Jr. and Deborah, bp. June 30, 1833. C.R.3.
David, s. Joseph and Mercy, Aug. 4, 1773.
David, s. David and Alice, May 7, 1814.
Deborah [―――], w. Joseph Jr. [Nov. ―, 1802]. C.R.3.
Deborah Tilden, d. Joseph Jr. and Deborah, Sept. 14, 1825.
Deborah Tilden, ch. Joseph Jr. and Deborah, bp. June 30, 1833. C.R.3.
Edward, s. Elisha and Polly, Feb. 20, 1813.
Elijah, s. Elisha and Polly, Sept. 2, 1823.
Elisha, s. Molly, Sept. 8, 1786.
Elisha, s. Elisha and Polly, Nov. 21, 1811.
Elisha F., ch. Elisha Jr. and Amanda F., May 28, 1843.
Elizabeth, d. Joseph and Mercy, May 5, 1784.
Elizabeth (see ――― Colman).
Frank Noyes, s. Moses R., mariner, and Polly, Apr. 30, 1846.
George Thompson, [twin] s. Joseph Jr. and Deborah, Mar. 20, 1840.
Hulda, d. Leah, bp. May 27, 1764. C.R.1.
Hulde, d. Leah, Nov. 22, 1762.
James, s. James and Abigal, Oct. 2, 1738.
James Gordon, s. Ammiel and Betsey, Aug. 20, 1827.
Jane Ann, d. Elisha and Polly, May 1, 1827.
John, s. John and Leah, Jan. 31, 1736.
John, s. Joseph and Mercy, Feb. 11, 1782.
John, bp. Aug. 25, 1797, in 94th y. C.R.1.
Joseph, s. John and Leah, Oct. 3, 1739.
Joseph, s. Joseph and Mercy, Aug. 1, 1767. [Coleman, C.R.1.]
Joseph, s. Joseph Jr. and Lydia, Mar. 12, 1798. [Coleman, C.R.3.]
Joseph Thomas, s. Joseph Jr. and Deborah, Oct. 17, 1822.
Joseph Thomas, ch. Joseph Jr. and Deborah, bp. June 30, 1833. C.R.3.
Leah, d. Jo[h]n and Leah, May 8, 1733.
Leah, d. Jo[h]n, bp. June 9, 1734. C.R.1.
Leah, d. Joseph and Mercy, Feb. 3, 1775. [Coleman, C.R.1.]
Lilles, d. Joseph and Mercy, Mar. 9, 1780.
Lillis, d. John and Leah, Nov. 28, 1741. [Lilis Coleman, C.R.1.]
Lydia, d. Joseph Jr. and Lydia, Aug. 14, 1794.
Margret, d. James and Abigail, Oct. 30, 1728.
Mary, d. John and Leah, Oct. 24, 1730.
Mary, d. Jo[h]n, bp. June 9, 1734. C.R.1.
Mary, d. David and Alice, Feb. 13, 1803. [w. Justin Litchfield, G.R.7.]

COLMAN, Mary Maria, ch. Moses R. and Polly, Sept. 24, 1830.
Mercy, d. Joseph and Mercy, Aug. 24, 1771. [Marcy Coleman, c.r.1.]
Mercy, d. Joseph Jr. and Lydia, July 22, 1800.
Mercy, d. Ammiel and Betsey, July 14, 1826.
Mercy Tilden, d. Joseph Jr. and Deborah, Apr. 30, 1837.
Molly, d. Joseph and Mercy, Sept. 2, 1765.
Moses Barrett, ch. Moses R. and Polly, Feb. 17, 1833.
Moses Barrett, ch. Moses R. and Polly, Jan. 31, 1839.
Moses Parker, s. Joseph Jr., bp. May 7, 1809. c.r.1.
Nancy, d. Joseph Jr. and Lydia, Jan. 23, 1792.
Nancy, d. Joseph Jr. and w., bp. Sept. 16, 1793. c.r.1.
Perry P., s. Joseph Jr. and Lydia, Apr. 23, 1808.
Polly [——], w. Elisha, —— [1783]. c.r.1.
Polly, d. Joseph Jr. and Lydia, June 13, 1796.
Polly, d. Elisha and Polly, Oct. 4, 1820.
Prudence, d. James and Abigal, Dec. 25, 1733.
Sarah, d. James and Abigal, Apr. 29, 1732.
Sarah, d. John Jr. and Sarah, June 16, 1766.
Sarah Elizabeth, ch. David and Eliza F., June 16, 1837.
Sarah Howland, d. James and Abigal, July 14, 1744.
Seth W., s. Elisha and Polly, Mar. 16, 1815.
Susan Maria, d. Joseph Jr. and Deborah, Apr. 6, 1828. [w. Dea. John H. Young, c.r.3.]
Susan Maria, ch. Joseph Jr. and Deborah, bp. June 30, 1833. c.r.3.
Thomas, s. James and Abigal, July 3, 1730.
Waterman, s. Ammiel and Betsey, May 27, 1824.
William, s. James and Abigal, May 15, 1736.
William, s. Elisha and Polly, July 7, 1818.
William E., s. W[illia]m, housewright, and Lucy W., Mar. 28, 1847.
William Gridley, ch. Moses R. and Polly, Mar. 10, 1843.
——, [twin] d. Joseph Jr. and Deborah, Mar. 20, 1840. [Elizabeth, c.r.3.]
——, s. Moses R., sailor, and Patty, Apr. 30, 1845.

COLOMER (see Colamer, Collamare, Collamer, Collamore, Collimor, Collmore, Collomare, Collomore), Sarah, d. Anthony, ——, 1673. [Collymer, c.r.2.]

COMSIT, Zilpha, "indian girl," bp. May 25, 1764. c.r.1.

CONANT, Anne [? m.], ——, 1790. g.r.7.
Thomas, Rev., ——, 1785. g.r.7.

CONOPHY, Annie [? m.], ——, 1849. G.R.10.

CONVERSE, Jane B., —— [1812]. G.R.14.

COOK (see Cocke, Cocks), Abby Ann Ruth, d. Russell [dup. Russel], tailor (b. Tiverton, R.I.), and Mary B. [dup. V.], Feb. 23, 1842, in Boston.
Abigail F., d. Ichabod and Mary, Dec. 24, 1813.
Albert F., s. Russell [dup. Russel], tailor (b. Tiverton, R.I.), and Mary B. [dup. V.], Nov. 26, 1849. [Albert Francis, ch. Russel and Mary, C.R.3.]
Alfred, s. Tobias and Lucy, Oct. 11, 1821.
Angeline Mills, ch. Richard and Mabel, Feb. 1, 1843.
[A]nna, d. Robart and Juda, Oct. 31, 1785.
[C]aroline, d. Robert and Juda, Oct. 8, 1801.
Catherine, d. Ichabod and Mary, Dec. 20, 1822.
Catherine Hall, d. Robert, master mariner, and Eliza, July 13, 1848.
[C]harles, s. Robert and Juda, Oct. 20, 1798.
Charles, s. Robert Jr. and Lucy, Mar. 2, 1822. [Charles [R.], P.R.19.]
Charles Freeman, ch. Josiah H. F. and Philenda, Apr. 10, 1833.
Charles Henry, s. Charles and Clarissa, Oct. 9, 1824.
Clarissa Cushing, d. Charles and Clarissa, Oct. 16, 1822.
Constant Little, ch. Josiah H. F. and Philenda, Mar. 4, 1835.
Cynthia B., d. Ichabod and Mary, July 13, 1816.
[D]eborah, d. Robert and Juda, Sept. 20, 1781.
Ebed S., s. Ichabod Jr., sailor, and Lucinda A., Nov. 21, 1846.
Edward Otis, s. Russell [dup. Russel], tailor (b. Tiverton, R.I.), and Mary B. [dup. V.], Sept. 5, 1839, in Boston.
Edwin Pason, ch. Ichabod Jr. and Lucinda A., May 21, 1843, in Cohasset.
Eliza [————], w. Robert, —— [1817]. G.R.6.
Eliza Ann, d. William and Eliza, Dec. 29, 1830.
Eliza Jane, d. Robert, gentleman [dup. mariner], and Eliza [second dup. crossed out, adds D.], May 9, 1844.
Emiley, d. Ichabod and Mary, Dec. 19, 1811.
[E]mily, d. Robert and Juda, Aug. 7, 1794.
Fanny, d. Henry and Fanny, Feb. 16, 1822.
Fanny, ch. Henry dec'd and Fanny, bp. May 6, 1827. C.R.3.
Francis Marion, ch. Josiah H. F. and Philenda, Sept. 11, 1838.
George Clarke, ch. Robert and Eliza, May 2, 1842.
George Henry, s. Russell [dup. Russel], tailor (b. Tiverton, R.I.), and Mary B. [dup. V.], Nov. 18, 1843, in Boston.
Harriet, d. Henry and Fanny, Dec. 24, 1823.

Cook, Harriet, ch. Henry dec'd and Fanny, bp. May 6, 1827. c.r.3.
Henry, s. Robert and Juda, Aug. 17, 1796.
Henry, s. Henry and Fanny, July 7, 1820.
Henry, ch. Henry dec'd and Fanny, bp. May 6, 1827. c.r.3.
[I]chabod, s. Robert and Juda, Dec. 11, 1779.
Ichabod, s. Ichabod and Mary, Apr. 6, 1821.
[I]srael, [twin] s. Robert and Juda, Nov. 31 [*sic*], 1789.
James Damon, s. Ichabod [dup. Jr.], mariner, and Lucinda, Mar. 15, 1844.
James J., s. Robert and Eliza, Sept. 29, 1846. g.r.6.
John Nowel, s. Ichabod and Mary, Sept. 10, 1809.
Josiah Hatsel Freeman, s. Tobias and Lucy, Aug. 9, 1811.
[J]uda, d. Robert and Juda, May 7, 1792.
Langdon W., "Co. D. 42 Mass Regt." [h. Lydia M. (Doane)], ——, 1847. g.r.2.
Lucenda [dup. Lucinda] A., d. Ichabod Jr., sailor, and Lucenda [dup. Lucinda] A., Mar. 6, 1848.
Lucy, d. Tobias and Lucy, Dec. 29, 1807.
Mary [————], w. Ichabod [Nov. —, 1779]. g.r.2.
Mary, d. Ichabod and Mary, Jan. 23, 1808.
Mary Ann, d. Tobias and Lucy, Aug. 9, 1813.
Mary Thomas, d. Russell [dup. Russel], tailor (b. Tiverton, R.I.), and Mary B. [dup. V.], Aug. 29, 1834.
Mary V. [————], w. Russel [dup. w. Dea. Russell] [Sept. —, 1807 [dup. 1806]]. c.r.3.
Mercy Lincoln, d. Charles and Clarissa, July 28, 1830.
Nana, d. Robert, bp. July 26, 1778. c.r.1.
Nancy Sutton, d. Ichabod and Mary, June 5, 1806.
Orlando Dill, ch. Robert and Eliza, Mar. 18, 1838.
Richard, s. Tobias and Lucy, Oct. 14, 1819.
[R]obert, [twin] s. Robert and Juda, Nov. 31 [*sic*], 1789.
Robert, s. Tobias and Lucy, Nov. 27, 1816.
Robert, ch. Robert and Eliza, June 10, 1840.
Russel [dup. Dea. Russell] [h. Mary V.], —— [1810]. c.r.3. [Cooke [h. Mary Vinal (Otis)], Apr. 21, 1810, g.r.7.]
[S]alley, d. Robert and Juda, Aug. 30, 1783.
Samuel W., s. Ichabod and Mary, Apr. 4, 1819. [[h. Sarah L.] "Company C. 38$^{\underline{th}}$ Regt. Mass. Vol.," g.r.2.]
Sarah Jane, d. Samuel W., shoemaker, and Sarah L., Sept. 25, 1848.
Sarah L. [————], w. Samuel W., —— [1823]. g.r.2.
[T]obias, s. Robert and Juda, Nov. 9, 1787.
Tobias White, s. Tobias and Lucy, Aug. 12, 1809.

Cook, [W]illiam, s. Robert and Juda, May 1, 1800. [[h. Eliza] G.R.2.]
William Ambrose, s. William and Eliza, Feb. 22, 1835.
William Russell, s. Russell [dup. Russel], tailor (b. Tiverton, R.I.), and Mary B. [dup. V.], Dec. 2, 1836, in Boston.
——, d. William and Eliza, Jan. 13, 1827.
——, ch. Richard [dup. mariner] and Mabel, Aug. 31, 1844.
——, s. Robert and Eliza, July 30, 1849.

COPELAND (see Copland), Elisabeth, d. Ebenezar and Sarah, Feb. 6, 1800.
Joseph, ch. Joseph and Elizabeth, bp. Aug. 6, 1737. C.R.2.
Sarah, d. Ebenezar [Eben[eze]r, C.R.2.] and Sarah, Oct. 6, 1797.

COPLAND (see Copeland), Ebenezer, s. Joseph and Eliza[beth], Oct. 20, 1753. [Copeland, s. Joseph and Elis[abeth], C.R.2.]
Elisha, s. Joseph and Eliza[beth], Dec. 20, 1759.
Elizabeth, d. Joseph and Eliza[beth], May 6, 1736. [Copeland, C.R.2.]
Hannah, d. Joseph and Eliza[beth], Feb. 24, 1742. [Copeland, C.R.2.]
Huldah, d. Ebenezer and w., bp. Sept. 30, 1804. C.R.2.
Joseph, s. Joseph and Eliza[beth], Aug. 22, 1749. [Copeland, C.R.2.]
Lidia, d. Joseph and Eliza[beth], July 20, 1747. [Lydia Copeland, d. Joseph and Elisabeth, C.R.2.]
Mary, d. Joseph and Eliza[beth], Nov. 3, 1740. [Copeland, C.R.2.]
Rebeca, d. Joseph and Eliza[beth], Aug. 30, 1755. [Rebeckah Copeland, C.R.2.]
Rhoda, d. Joseph and Eliza[beth], Apr. 22, 1745. [Rhode Copeland, C.R.2.]
Ruth, d. Joseph and Eliza[beth], Sept. 16, 1738. [Copeland, C.R.2.]
Sarah, d. Joseph and Eliza[beth], Jan. 2, 1758.
Will[ia]m, s. Joseph and Eliza[beth], Sept. 21, 1751. [Copeland, C.R.2.]

CORBETT, Francis A., ch. James and Hannah J., Jan. 18, 1845.
George, ch. Thomas L. and Relief, Mar. 10, 1834.
Hannah J., ch. James and Hannah J., June 23, 1839.
Mary A., ch. James and Hannah J., Nov. 24, 1842.
William M., ch. Thomas L. and Relief, Aug. 17, 1837.
——, d. James, shoemaker and Hannah, Jan. 18, 1844.

CORLEW (see Corloo, Corlow, Curloo), Betheah Woodard, d. Bill and Sarah, Oct. 6, 1797.

CORLEW, Jane, ——, 1786. G.R.14.
Jane, d. William, bp. Sept. 30, 1804. C.R.2.
Joseph E., M.D. [h. Susan W.], ——, 1818. G.R.14.
Marget, d. Bille and Sarah, Aug. 13, 1800.
Sally, d. Bille and Sarah, Sept. 6, 1795.
Susan W. [———], w. Joseph E., M.D., ——, 1823. G.R.14.

CORLOO (see Corlew, Corlow, Curloo), Polly, d. Will[ia]m and Margrett, Nov. 25, 1783.

CORLOW (see Corlew, Corloo, Curloo), Anne, d. Will[ia]m and Margrett, Mar. 25, 1779. [Corlew, G.R.14.]
Betsey, d. Thomas and Abigail, Feb. 14, 1796.
Bille, s. Will[ia]m and Margreat, Nov. 8, 1770.
Charles, s. Will[ia]m and Margret, Nov. 29, 1776.
Elijah, s. Will[ia]m and Margreat, Nov. 27, 1772.
Jenny, d. Will[ia]m and Margrett, June 16, 1786.
[J]oseph, s. Will[ia]m and Margrett, July 25, 1781. [Corlew, G.R.14.]
Noah, s. Thomas and Abigail, June 23, 1793.

CORNISH, Abigail, d. Joseph and Patience of Hanover, bp. May 26, 1728. C.R.2.
Josiah, s. Joseph and Patience of Hanover, bp. Aug. 6, 1727. C.R.2.

CORTHEL (see Corthell), Levi, s. Robert and Mary, bp. June 20, 1742. C.R.2.
Mary, d. Robert, bp. May 13, 1744. C.R.2.
Robert, s. Robert and Mary, bp. May 17, 1741. C.R.2.

CORTHELL (see Corthel), Deborah [———], w. Theophelis [Sept. —, 1781]. G.R.2.
Eliza H., d. John E., butcher, and Eliza W., Apr. 13, 1848.
Eliza W. [? m.], ——, 1816. G.R.14.
John, ch. John E. and Eliza W., Sept. 15, 1836.
John E., ——, 1812. G.R.14.
Joseph H., ch. John E. and Eliza W., Nov. 21, 1838.
Theopilus [h. Deborah], —— [1779]. G.R.2.

COSNOW (see Cazneaur), John F., ch. Sylvester and Elizabeth, Dec. 4, 1844.
Sylvester, ch. Sylvester and Elizabeth, Sept. 5, 1841.

COURTIS (see Courtisse, Curtice, Curtis, Curtise, Custis), Anna, d. Richard, bp. July 4, 1652. C.R.2.
Elizabeth, d. Thomas, bp. Aug. 19, 1649. C.R.2.

COURTIS, Elizabeth, d. Richard, bp. July 4, 1652. C.R.2.
Samuel, s. Thomas of York, bp. Sept. 4, 1670. C.R.2.

COURTISSE (see Courtis, Curtice, Curtis, Curtise, Custis), Deborah, d. William, bp. May 18, 1662. C.R.2.

COWEN (see Cowing), Balch, s. Israel, bp. July 28, 1728. C.R.1.
Caleb, s. John Jr., July 9, 1696.
Iserell, s. John, Dec. 10, 1664.
Iserell, s. Iserell, Jan. 21, 1693.
Israel, s. Israel and Lydia, Sept. 29, 1724.
Israell (Cowing), s. John Jr., Sept. 7, 1701.
John, s. John, July 10, 1662.
John, s. John Jr., Oct. 9, 1692.
Joseph, s. John, Dec. 3, 1657.
Joseph, s. John Jr., Apr. 18, 1690.
Joshua, s. John Jr., July 9, 1694.
Lydia, d. Israel and Lydia, Mar. 12, 1726.
Mary, d. John, May 14, 1659.
Rebekah, d. John, May 10, 1666.
Sarah, d. John Jr., July 9, 1688.

COWING (see Cowen), Betsey, d. Israel and Becka, July 29, 1796.
Charles, s. Israel and Desire, July 14, 1773.
David, s. Gethelus and Lucy, Aug. 16, 1768.
Deborah, d. Job and Deborah, Dec. 22, 1733.
Desier, d. Gethelus and Lucy, Mar. 11, 1771.
Elizabeth, d. Israell, Mar. 13, 1697.
Eliza[beth], d. Job and Deborah, Apr. 14, 1740.
Garthelus, ch. Hannah, wid., bp. July 19, 1719. C.R.1.
Gathelus, s. Israell and Hannah, Feb. 4, 1708-9.
Gethelious, s. Job and Deborah, Sept. 4, 1745. [Gathelus, C.R.1.]
Hannah, d. Israell, Aug. 21, 1694.
Hannah, d. Job and Deborah, Mar. 19, 1737.
Hannah, d. Job, bp. Apr. 23, 1738. C.R.1.
Hannah, d. Job and Deborah, July 12, 1752.
Israel, s. Israel, bp. May 5, 1728. C.R.1.
Israel, s. Job and Deborah, Sept. 10, 1750.
Israel, s. Israel and Desire, Oct. 27, 1770.
Israell, s. Israell, Oct. 23, 1699.
Job, s. Israell and Hannah, Mar. 8, 1713-14.
Job, ch. Hannah, wid., bp. July 19, 1719. C.R.1.
Job, s. Job and Deborah, Sept. 18, 1742.
Joseph, s. Israell, Mar. 1, 1715.
Joseph, ch. Hannah, wid., bp. July 19, 1719. C.R.1.

Cowing, Joseph, s. Joseph, bp. July 28, 1745. C.R.1.
Josiah, s. Israell, May 19, 1704.
Lydia, d. Israel, bp. May 5, 1728. C.R.1.
Mary, d. Israell, Dec. 28, 1691.
Mary, d. John, Apr. 1, 1705.
Mary, d. Job and Deborah, Feb. 19, 1735.
Mary, d. Job, bp. May 30, 1736. C.R.1.
Rachel, ch. Hannah, wid., bp. July 19, 1719. C.R.1.
Rachel, d. Job, bp. June 26, 1748. C.R.1.
Sarah, d. Israell, Dec. 21, 1717.

CRANE, Ed. W., —— [1844]. C.R.1.

CROCKER, John, s. ——, bp. "Jun." [June] 11, 1637. C.R.1.

CROOKER, Egatha, d. Elijah and Egatha, Oct. 23, 1765.
Elijah, s. Elijah and Egatha, Dec. 2, 1761.
Elisha, s. Elijah and Egatha, July 28, 1769.
Eliza J., d. Joseph, mariner, and Morgianna, Aug. 29, 1845, in Boston.
Gemaliel, s. Elijah and Egatha, Aug. 26, 1767.
Joseph, s. Elijah and Egatha, Oct. 15, 1763.
Phillips, s. Elijah and Egatha, Dec. 22, 1771.
Sally, d. Capt. Crooker of Boston, bp. Oct. 22, 1775. C.R.1.

CROUCH, Patience, ch. Mary, bp. Nov. 5, 1732. C.R.1.

CUDDWORTH (see Cudworth), James, s. ——, bp. May 3, 1635. C.R.1.

CUDWORTH (see Cuddworth), Abial, s. John and Elizabeth [dup. Elisabeth], Oct. 19, 1786 [dup. 1787]. [Abiel, G.R.2.]
Abiel, ch. John, bp. Aug. 14, 1796. C.R.1.
Abiel, s. Abiel and Joanna, Aug. 28, 18[worn] [rec. before ch. b. May 9, 1816].
Abigail, d. Jeames and Mary, Mar. 9, 1680 [? in Scituate]. C.R.4.
Abigail, d. James [James Jr., C.R.1.] and Abigail, Apr. 21, 1745.
Abigail, d. Joseph and Elisabeth, Aug. 12, 1779.
Abigall, d. John, Oct. 7, 1718.
Alexander, s. Joseph, bp. May 24, 1778. C.R.1.
Alexandria, ch. Joseph and Elisabeth, Nov. 12, 1777.
Almira [——], w. Samuel S., July 25, 1820. G.R.2.
Anna (Cudwerth), d. Zeph[ania]h and Elisabeth, Sept. 6, 1797.
Barnard, s. John and Elizabeth [dup. Elisabeth], Dec. 18, 1792 [dup. 1793].
Barnard, ch. John, bp. Aug. 14, 1796. C.R.1.

SCITUATE BIRTHS

CUDWORTH, Benjamin, s. Nathanil, bp. May 13, 1716. C.R.I.
Benja[min], s. Benja[min] and Mary, June 16, 1744.
Benja[min], s. Benjamin and Mary, Aug. 22, 1753.
Benjamin, s. Israel and Marcy, Sept. 18, 1785.
Benjamin, s. Isreal and Mercy, bp. July 21, 1788. C.R.I.
Benjamin, s. Israel [Dea. Israel, C.R.2.] and Mabel, Oct. 3, 1836.
Benjamin Holms, s. Melzer and Lydia, June 12, 1807.
Bethia, d. Jonathan, Nov. 25, 1671.
Betsey, d. Zeph[ania]h and Elisabeth, Mar. 18, 179[worn].
Betsey, d. Urbane and Deborah O., Dec. 17, 1820.
Betsy, d. Zephaniah, bp. Sept. 28, 1794. C.R.I.
Betty, d. James 3d and Rachel, Nov. 18, 1749.
Betty, ch. David and Abigail, bp. June 4, 1753. C.R.I.
Charles, s. John and Elizabeth [dup. Elisabeth], Mar. 17, 1780.
Cynthia, d. Zephaniah and Elisabeth, June 22, 1776.
Cynthia (see Zintha).
David, ch. David and Abigail, bp. June 4, 1753. C.R.I.
David, s. Joseph and Elisabeth, May 12, 1776.
Deborah, d. Israel Jr., bp. Feb. 24, 1739. C.R.I.
Deborah, d. Jonathan and Hannah, Oct. 6, 1747.
Desire, ch. David and Abigail, bp. June 4, 1753. C.R.I.
Elijah, s. Joseph and Elisabeth, July 29, 1788. [[h. Lucy] G.R.14.]
Elijah, s. Elijah and Lucy, Sept. 17, 1818.
Elisabeth, d. Joseph and Elisabeth, Apr. 7, 1783.
Eliza L. [———], w. Samuel C., ———, 1819. G.R.14.
Elizabeth, ch. Hannah dec'd, wid., bp. June 2, 1717. C.R.I.
Elizabeth, d. James and Elizabeth, Aug. 18, 1718.
Elizabeth, d. Jo[h]n Jr. and Mary, Dec. 12, 1738.
Elizabeth, ch. Israel and Mary, bp. Nov. 18, 1739. C.R.I.
Elizabeth, d. James Jr., bp. May 1, 1743. C.R.I.
Eliza[beth], d. Benja[min] and Mary, June 13, 1743.
Elizabeth (see Elisabeth).
Elizabeth [dup. [E]lisabeth], d. John and Elizabeth [dup. Elisabeth], May 16, 1788.
Elizabeth, ch. John, bp. Aug. 14, 1796. C.R.I.
Elizabeth, d. Elijah and Lucy, July 30, 1824.
Elizebeth, d. Jeames and Mary, Mar. 4, 1677 [? in Scituate]. C.R.4.
Esther, d. Elijah and Lucy, May 4, 1834.
Hanah, d. Jonathan, May 8, 1674.
Hannah, d. Nath[anie]l, bp. Aug. 10, 1718. C.R.I.
Hannah, d. Israel, bp. June 5, 1743. C.R.I.
Hannah, d. Jona[than], bp. Apr. 26, 1745. C.R.I.
Hannah, d. Israel, bp. Aug. 4, 1754. C.R.I.

CUDWORTH, Hannah, d. Joseph and Lydia, Nov. 18, 1773 [dup. 1774].
Hannah, ch. Joseph and w., bp. Apr. 6, 1777. C.R.1.
Harriet Tileston, d. Israel and Mabel, Oct. 28, 1830.
Henery, s. Jonathan, bp. Feb. 28, 1749. C.R.1.
Hulda, d. John Jr. and Mary, Apr. 18, 1735.
Israel, s. Jonathan, Oct. 18, 1683.
Israel, s. Nath[anie]l, bp. June 6, 1708. C.R.1.
Israel, ch. Hannah dec'd, wid., bp. June 2, 1717. C.R.1.
Israel, s. Martha, wid., bp. June 28, 1741. C.R.1.
Israel, d. Israel, bp. July 3, 1748. C.R.1.
Israel, s. James [James Jr., C.R.1.] and Abigale, Mar. 15, 1757.
Israel, s. Israel and Marcy, Jan. 13, 1788. [Isreal, s. Isreal and Mercy, C.R.1.] [Dea. Israel [h. Mabel], C.R.3.]
Israel, [twin] s. Israel and Mabel, Aug. 1, 1828.
Israell, s. Nathaniell and Sarah, Sept. 8, 1706.
James, s. Jonathan, Jan. —, 1682.
James, s. James and Elisabeth, Feb. 26, 1714.
James, s. John, Sept. 21, 1715.
James, s. James, bp. Aug. 10, 1718. C.R.1.
James, s. James 3d and Rachel, Mar. 28, 1748.
James, —— [1781]. C.R.1. [[h. Marcy] G.R.6.]
James, s. Zeph[ania]h [Zepheniah, C.R.1.] and Elisabeth, Feb. 7, 1782.
James Winchel, ch. Israel Jr. and Mabel, bp. June 1, 1828. C.R.3.
James Winchell, s. Israel Jr. and Mabel, Sept. 12, 1824.
Jane, d. Abiel and Joanna, Nov. 18, 1825.
Jeames, s. Jeames and Mary, June 3, 1665 [? in Scituate]. C.R.4.
Joanna, d. James Jr., Aug. 8, 1671. [Johanna, d. Jeames and Mary, C.R.4.]
Joanna [————], w. Abiel [Oct. —, 1784]. G.R.2.
Joanne, d. Abiel and Joanna, Nov. 20, 1821. [Joann, G.R.2.]
Job Clapp [dup. omits Clapp], s. John and Elizabeth [dup. Elisabeth], July 14, 1783.
Job Clapp, ch. John, bp. Aug. 14, 1796. C.R.1.
Johanna, d. Nath[anie]l, bp. Sept. 9, 1722. C.R.1.
John, s. Jeames and Mary, May 2, 1674 [? in Scituate]. C.R.4.
John, s. John, May 16, 1706.
John, s. John [dup. Jr.] and Elizabeth, Jan. 12, 1773.
John, ch. John and w., bp. May 19, 1776. C.R.1.
John, s. Elijah and Lucy, May 5, 1831.
Jonathan, s. James, bp. Sept. 16, 1638. C.R.1.
Jonathan, s. Jonathan, Apr. 15, 1679.
Jonathan, s. Nathaniell [Nathaniel, C.R.1.] and Sarah, Oct. 4, 1710.

CUDWORTH, Jonathan (Cudw[or]th), s. Jonathan, bp. Sept. 21, 1750. C.R.1.
Jonathan, s. Jonathan and Hannah, Nov. 5, 1752.
Joseph, s. Jo[h]n Jr. and Mary, Sept. 3, 1740.
Joseph, s. Joseph and Lydia, Oct. 17, 1772.
Joseph, ch. Joseph and w., bp. Apr. 6, 1777. C.R.1.
Joseph, s. Elijah and Lucy, Feb. 26, 1820.
Joseph, s. Elijah and Lucy, May 5, 1828.
Kezia, d. James and Abigail, Nov. 24, 1749. [Keziah, d. James Jr., C.R.1.]
Kezia, d. Zeph[ania]h and Elisabeth, Feb. 11, 1787. [Keziah, d. Zepheniah, C.R.1.]
Laban, s. Elijah and Lucy, Dec. 25, 1821.
Lucy, d. Benja[min], bp. Apr. 21, 1751. C.R.1.
Lucy, d. James 3d and Rachel, Sept. 30, 1756.
Lucy, d. Joseph and Elisabeth, Feb. 24, 1785.
Lucy, d. Zeph[ania]h, bp. Dec. 13, 1789. C.R.1.
Lucy, d. Zeph[ania]h and Elisabeth, Oct. 30, 1790.
Lucy [———], w. Elijah [May —, 1792]. G.R.14.
Lucy, d. Elijah and Lucy, Sept. 20, 1816.
Lydia, d. Joseph and Lydia, June 17, 1768.
Lydia, ch. Joseph and w., bp. Apr. 6, 1777. C.R.1.
Lydia Vinal, d. Israel Jr. [Dea. Israel, C.R.3.] and Mabel, July 19, 1826.
Lydia Vinal, ch. Israel Jr. and Mabel, bp. June 1, 1828. C.R.3.
Mabel, d. Benja[min], bp. Aug. 7, 1748. C.R.1.
Mabel [———], w. [dup. adds Dea.] Israel, ——— [1795]. C.R.3.
Mabel, [twin] d. Israel and Mabel, Aug. 1, 1828.
Mable, d. Benja[min] and Mary, Dec. 9, 1741. [Mabel, C.R.1.]
Marcy, d. Jonathan, bp. Apr. — [1746]. C.R.1.
Marcy, d. Benjamin and Mary, Jan. 7, 1761.
Marcy, d. John and Elizabeth [dup. Elisabeth], Apr. 14, 1782. [Mercy, C.R.1.]
Marcy Eliza[bet]h, d. Israel and Mabel, Jan. 2, 1834. [Mercy Elizabeth, C.R.3.]
Marcy Little, d. Israel and Marcy, July 17, 1795.
Margarett, d. John, Dec. 5, 1703.
Maria Sanford, d. Israel Jr. and Mabel, Dec. 13, 1822.
Maria Sanford, ch. Israel Jr. and Mabel, bp. June 1, 1828. C.R.3.
Mary, d. James, bp. July 23, 1637. C.R.1.
Mary, d. Jeames and Mary, Mar. 14, 1667 [? in Scituate]. C.R.4.
Mary, d. Israell, Oct. 17, 1678.
Mary, d. John, Feb. 19, 1709–10.
Mary, d. John Jr. and Mary, Aug. 15, 1736.

CUDWORTH, Mary, d. Benja[min] and Mary, Sept. 23, 1749.
Mary, d. John and Elizabeth [dup. Elisabeth], July 19, 1779.
Mary, d. Israel [Isreal, C.R.1.] and Marcy, Oct. 12, 1789.
Mary, ——, 1814. G.R.2.
Mary Ann, d. Elijah and Lucy, July 24, 1826. [w. Augustus Gardner, G.R.14.]
Mary B. [? m.], ——, 1819. G.R.2.
Melser, s. James Jr., bp. Sept. 15, 1754. C.R.1.
Melzar, s. Zeph[ania]h and Elisabeth, May 11, 1784.
Melzar, s. Zepheniah, bp. Apr. 9, 1786. C.R.1.
Mercy (see Marcy).
Nathanell, s. Jonathan, Sept. 7, 1667.
Nathaniel, s. Benja[min] and Mary, May 30, 1747. [Nathanael, C.R.1.]
Nathaniell, s. Nathaniell and Sarah, Oct. 18, 1712. [Nathaniel, s. Nathaniel, C.R.1.]
Noah, s. Zeph[ania]h and Elisebeth, Oct. 4, 1778.
Oliver, s. Benja[min], bp. Jan. 13, 1756. C.R.1.
Peter, s. Joseph and Elisabeth, Mar. 18, 1790.
Phebe, d. Joseph and Lydia, July 3, 1770.
Phebe, ch. Joseph and w., bp. Apr. 6, 1777. C.R.1.
Polly, [twin] d. Joseph and Elisabeth, Mar. 20, 1781.
Polly Briggs, d. Abial and Joanna, Aug. 8, 1819.
Priscilla, d. Joanna, bp. July 15, 1744. C.R.1.
Rachel, d. Nathan[ie]l, bp. Apr. 10, 1720. C.R.1.
Rachel, d. James and Rachel, Oct. 7, 1746.
Rachel, d. James [James Jr., C.R.1.] and Abigail, Apr. 8, 1747.
Rachel, d. James 3d and Rachel, Oct. 17, 1754.
Rachell, d. Jonathan, Oct. 11, 1689.
Rebecca, d. John and Eliza[beth], Aug. 30, 1775. [Rebeccah, C.R.1.]
Ruth, d. Israel, bp. June 3, 1739. C.R.1.
Sally, [twin] d. Joseph and Elisabeth, Mar. 20, 1781.
Samuel, s. James, bp. July 5, 1741. C.R.1.
Samuel, s. James 3d and Rachel, Sept. 14, 1751.
Samuel C. [h. Eliza L.], ——, 1821. G.R.14.
Samul Stilman, s. Abial and Joanna, May 9, 1816. [Samuel S. [h. Almira], G.R.2.]
Sarah, d. Jeames and Mary, Apr. 13, 1669 [? in Scituate]. C.R.4.
Sarah, d. Jonathan, ——, 1676.
Sarah, d. Nathaniell [Nathaniel, C.R.1.] and Sarah, Sept. 12, 1708.
Sarah, d. John, Dec. 3, 1713.
Sarah (Cudw[or]th), d. Israel, bp. June 23, 1751. C.R.1.
Sarah, d. Benja[min], bp. July 12, 1752. C.R.1.

CUDWORTH, Thirza, d. John and Elizabeth [dup. Elisabeth], July 23, 1795.
Thirza, ch. John, bp. Aug. 14, 1796. C.R.1.
Timothy, s. Mary, Nov. 10, 1738.
Urbane, s. John and Elisabeth, Sept. 2, 1800.
Urbane, s. Urbane and Deborah O., Aug. 19, 1823.
Xoe, d. John and Elizabeth [dup. Elisabeth], May 26, 1790.
Zephaniah, s. James and Abigail, Feb. 13, 1752. [Zepheniah, C.R.1.]
Zepheniah, s. James and Elizebeth, Dec. 17, 1719. [Zephaniah, C.R.1.]
Zintha, [ch.] Zephaniah and w., bp. May 31, 1778. C.R.1.
Zoa, ch. John, bp. Aug. 14, 1796. C.R.1.

CUMMINGS, ———, d. Jeremiah, farmer (b. Ireland), and Mary (b. Ireland), Aug. 6, 1848, in Boston.
———, s. Jeremiah, farmer (b. Ireland), and Mary (b. Ireland), Oct. 16, 1849, in Hopkinton.

CURLOO (see Corlew, Corloo, Corlow), Danil, s. Edward and Abigail, Oct. 26, 1746.
Edward, [twin] s. Edward and Abigail, Aug. 26, 1736.
John, s. Edward and Abigal, June 30, 1732.
Thomas, [twin] s. Edward and Abigal, Aug. 26, 1736.
Will[ia]m, s. Edward and Abigail, Nov. 18, 1744.

CURRAN, Barbara [———], w. John, ——— [1842], in Co. Galway, Ire. G.R.10.

CURRELL (see Currill), Henry, s. Gilbert, farmer, and Martha, Sept. 15, 1845.
Mary E., ch. Gilbert and Martha, June 31 [*sic*], 1843.

CURRILL (see Currell), George Gilbert [dup. Currell], s. Gilbert, shoemaker, and Martha [second dup. (b. Maine)], Nov. — [dup. Nov. 9, second dup. Sept. 9], 1849.

CURTICE (see Courtis, Courtisse, Curtis, Curtise, Custis), Anna d. Richard, May 12, 1649.
Benjamin, s. Benjamin Jr. and Hannah, bp. Apr. 27, 1718. C.R.2.
Bezaleel, ch. John and Experience, bp. Oct. 10, 1714. C.R.2.
Caleb, s. Benj[a]m[in] and Hannah, bp. May 8, 1726. C.R.2.
Deborah, d. Richard, Apr. 16, 1661.
Elijah, s. Sam[ue]ll and Rebecca, bp. July 20, 1735. C.R.2.
Elisha, s. Joseph and Rebecca, bp. July 14, 1706. C.R.2.
Elisha, s. Elisha and Martha, bp. Apr. 3, 1737. C.R.2.

CURTICE, Elizabeth, d. Richard, Jan. 12, 1651.
Elizabeth, d. John and Experience, bp. May 28, 1721. C.R.2.
Hanna, d. John, bp. July 9, 1682. C.R.2.
Hannah, d. Benj[a]m[in] and Hannah, bp. Mar. 1, 1724. C.R.2.
James, s. Benj[a]m[in] and Rebecca, bp. Sept. 8, 1734. C.R.2.
John, s. Richard, Dec. 9, 1653. [Courtis, C.R.2.]
Luke, s. Benjamin and Hannah, bp. Mar. 11, 1722. C.R.2.
Luther, s. Elisha and w., bp. Apr. 9, 1749. C.R.2.
Lydia, d. John, bp. May 29, 1757. C.R.2.
Margret, d. W[illia]m and Margret, bp. Feb. 26, 1726-7. C.R.2.
Martha, d. Richard, Mar. 15, 1657. [Courtisse, C.R.2.]
Martha, d. Elisha and Sarah, bp. June 2, 1745. C.R.2.
Mary, d. Richard, Jan. 9, 1655. [Courtis, C.R.1.]
Mehitabel, d. Elisha and Martha, bp. May 18, 1735. C.R.2.
Mehittabell, d. William, bp. Mar. 23, 1677. C.R.2.
Melzar, s. Simeon and w., bp. Apr. 28, 1745. C.R.2.
Nathanael, s. Benj[a]m[in] Jr. and Hannah of Hanover, bp. Mar. 31, 1728. C.R.2.
Peleg, s. Joseph and Rebeckah, bp. Oct. 12, 1712. C.R.2.
Samuell, s. William, bp. Nov. 29, 1685. C.R.2.
Sara, d. William, bp. Sept. 5, 1680. C.R.2.
Sarah, d. Richard, July 20, 1663. [Courtisse, C.R.2.]
Sarah, d. Elisha and Sarah, bp. Dec. 19, 1742. C.R.2.
Simeon, s. Simeon, bp. July 10, 1743. C.R.2.
Susannah, ch. John and Experience, bp. Oct. 10, 1714. C.R.2.
Thomas, s. Richard, Mar. 18, 1659. [Curtisse, C.R.2.]
Thomas, s. Benjamin (Curtise) Jr. and Hannah, bp. Sept. 4, 1720. C.R.2.
William, s. John, bp. May 17, 1685. C.R.2.
William, s. W[illia]m, bp. Nov. 29, 1724. C.R.2.
Zechariah, [ch.] Elisha and w., bp. Nov. 25, 1739. C.R.2.

CURTIS (see Courtis, Courtisse, Curtice, Curtise, Custis), Abba Sophia, ch. Seth and Ruth, Jan. 6, 1820, in Hanover.
Abby S., d. Peleg, carpenter, and Abby S., Sept. 25, 1849, in S. Scituate.
Abel, s. William and Margret, Nov. 24, 1719. [Curtice, C.R.2.]
Abigail, d. Samuel (s. Thomas of York) and Elizabeth, Jan. 17, 1703-4. [Curtise, C.R.2.]
Abigail [———], w. Charles, —— [1775]. C.R.3.
Abigail, d. Charles and Abigail, Jan. 9, 1818.
Abigail, ch. Charles, bp. Aug. 1, 1824. C.R.1.
Abigail L., d. Norton, shoemaker, and Mary [dup. adds P.], Aug. 29, 1844.
Abigail Soule, d. Elijah and Rachel, Oct. —, 17[torn].

Curtis, Abner, s. Tho[ma]s and Ruth, Sept. 11, 1742.
Abner, s. Eli and Desire, May 31, 1762.
Adeline, d. Job and Bethiah, Apr. 19, 1830.
Albert Cushing, ch. Frederick and Ann Maria, July 4, 1834, in Hingham.
Ammiel, s. Sam[ue]ll 3d and Ruth, Aug. 5, 1781. [Amiel, C.R.1.]
Amos, s. Sam[ue]ll Jr. and Anna, July 15, 1722. [Curtice, C.R.2.]
Amos, s. Amos and Mary, Feb. 4, 1747. [Curtice, C.R.2.]
Amos, s. Sam[ue]l Jr. and Hetee, Aug. 2, 1784.
Amos Turner, s. Eli Jr. and Deborah, Jan. 10, 1805.
Anna, d. Samuell Jr., Apr. 14, 1711. [Ann Curtice, d. Sam[ue]ll Jr. and Ann, C.R.2.]
Anna Maria, ch. Frederick and Ann Maria, June 20, 1836.
Arthur, s. Norton, shoemaker, and Mary P., June 16, 1849.
Asa, s. John, bp. Oct. 30, 1743. C.R.1.
Asa, s. Eli and Desier, Mar. 13, 1773.
Asa, s. Gamaliel and Patience, Mar. 16, 1789.
Asa Franklin, s. Asa and Jane, Jan. 22, 1812.
Bartlit, s. Elijah and Abigal, Dec. 1, 1758.
Benjamin, s. William, Jan. —, 1666–7. [Courtisse, C.R.2.]
Benjamin, s. Benjamin, Dec. 14, 1692.
Benjamin, s. Samuel (s. Thomas of York), May 2, 1699.
Benja[min], s. Benja[min] and Rebecca, May 12, 1728. [Curtice, s. Benj[a]m[in] and Rebeccae, C.R.2.]
Benjamin, s. Benja[min] Jr. and Mary, Sept. 15, 1762.
Benjamin F., s. Asa F., yeoman, and Catherine, Feb. 15, 1849.
Beriah, s. Tho[ma]s and Ruth, Mar. 9, 1745.
Bethiah, d. Job and Bethiah, Aug. 13, 1806.
Betsey, d. Charles and Abigail, Oct. 30, 1801.
Betsey Gannett, d. Charles Jr. and Cynthia, July 16, 1824.
Bezaleel, s. John (s. William Sr.) and Experience, Sept. 29, 1711.
Calvin, s. Elisha and Sarah, bp. Sept. 27, 1747. C.R.2.
Catherine Parker, ch. Asa F. and Catherine, Feb. 16, 1837.
Charles, s. Benja[min] and Rebecca, July 26, 1744. [Charls Curtice, C.R.2.]
Charles, s. Sam[ue]ll [Sam[ue]l, C.R.1.] (s. William) and Elenor, Aug. 14, 1757.
Charles, s. Thomas and Lusannah, July 17, 1767.
Charles, s. Sam[ue]ll 3d [Samuel Jr., C.R.1.] and Ruth, Nov. 5, 1778.
Cha[rle]s, Capt., —— [1790]. C.R.3.
Charles, s. Charles and Betsey, Nov. 27, 1793.
Charles, s. James Jr. and Desire, June 13, 1809. [Curtice, C.R.2.]
Charles Augustus, ch. Seth and Ruth, Aug. 21, 1817.

CURTIS, Charles E., s. Nehemiah R. and w., Dec. 17, 1814.
Charles Thomas, s. Charles Jr. and Cynthia, Dec. 31, 1815.
Charles Thomas, s. Charles Jr. and Cynthia, July 20, 1818.
Charles Wesley, s. Charles [dup. Jr., second dup. omits Jr., adds T.], bricklayer [dup. mason], and Martha, May 16, 1846. [s. Charles T. and Martha W., G.R.7.]
Charlotte [———], w. Chandler, —— [1795]. C.R.1.
Charlotte Ann, d. Shadrach B. and Charlotte, Feb. 24, 1829.
Christefer, s. Sam[ue]ll and Rachel, Sept. 27, 1754. [Christopher Curtice, C.R.2.]
Clara M. [———], w. Job E., June 5, 1849. G.R.2.
Clarissa Wade, d. Eli 3d and Clarissa, Nov. 2, 1821.
Cushing Otis, s. James Jr. and Desire, Dec. 3, —— [Dec. 3, written in pencil]. [s. Cap[t]. James, bp. Nov. 7, 1824, C.R.2.]
Cynthia (see Zintha).
Cynthia, d. Gamaliel and Patience, June 5, 1785.
Cynthia, d. Elijah and Phebe, Nov. —, 1805.
Cynthia, d. Charles Jr. and Cynthia, July 17, 1822.
David, s. Benjamin and Mary, June 26, 1708. [Curtice, C.R.2.]
Deborah, d. Thomas (s. Rich[ard]), Feb. 17, 1697.
Deborah, d. Benjamin and Mary, Aug. —, 1704.
Deborah, d. Sam[ue]l Jr. and Anna, Feb. 21, 1717. [Curtice, s. Sam[ue]ll and Anna, C.R.2.]
Deborah, d. Eli Jr. and Deborah, Oct. 2, 1799.
Deborah [———], w. George, —— [1814]. C.R.1.
Dennis Jr. [h. Thirza (Winslow)], Oct. 1, 1816, in Pembroke.
Desier, d. Eli and Desier, July 28, 1767.
Desire Otis, d. James Jr. and Desire, Mar. 27, 1813.
Diana [———], w. Rufus, —— [1779]. G.R.6.
Ebenezer, s. Benjamin, Aug. 1, 1694.
Edward Pason, s. Thomas and Druzilla, Aug. 6, 1837.
Edwin, s. Job and Bethiah, July 28, 1821.
Elener, d. Sam[ue]ll (s. William) and Elener, Sept. 14, 1751. [Elinore, d. Sam[ue]l, C.R.1.]
Elener, d. Sam[ue]ll (s. William) and Elenor, Nov. 21, 1761.
Elenur, d. Sam[ue]ll 3d and Ruth, Oct. 26, 1783.
Eli, s. Tho[ma]s Jr. and Ruth, Feb. 23, 1733.
Eli, s. Eli and Desire, Mar. 9, 1760.
Eli, s. Eli Jr. and Deborah, Sept. 29, 1787.
Eli, s. Eli Jr., bp. July 27, 1794. C.R.1.
Eli, s. Eli 3d and Clarissa, Oct. 28, 1815.
Elijah, s. Benja[min] and Rebecca, May 25, 1735.
Elijah, s. Elijah and Abigal, Jan. 16, 1761.
Elijah, s. Elijah and Rachel, Nov. —, 1787.

CURTIS, Elijah Stowers, s. Elijah and Rachel, Aug. —, 179[torn].
    [Curtice, s. Elijah Jr., bp. Sept. 16, 1792, C.R.2.]
Elisha, s. Joseph and Rebekah, Feb. 20, 1704–5.
Eliza Ann, d. Charles Jr. and Cynthia, Nov. 2, 1820.
Elizabeth, d. Samuel (s. Thomas of York), Oct. 10, 1694.
Elizabeth, d. William (s. John) and Rachel, Nov. 18, 1722.
Eliza[beth], d. Sam[ue]ll and Rachal, Nov. 14, 1746. [Elisabeth Curtice, C.R.2.]
Ellen L., d. Luther, tanner, and Sarah, July 30, 1844.
Ellen Maria, ch. Eli Jr. and Melvina, Mar. 6, 1843.
Ellony, d. Sam[ue]l Jr., bp. Jan. 31, 1784. C.R.1.
Emeline Frances, ch. Norton and Mary P., Mar. 1, 1837.
Emely, d. Gam[alie]l and Patience, Feb. 11, 1795.
Emma Souther, d. George, carpenter, and Deborah (b. Hingham), June 9, 1846, in Medford.
Enoch, s. Sam[ue]ll and Rachel, Sept. — [illegible]. [Curtice, s. Sam[ue]l, bp. Oct. 29, 1752, C.R.2.]
Frances Maria, ch. Seth and Ruth, May 29, 1823, in Hanover.
Francis J., ch. Frederick and Ann Maria, June 25, 1840.
Frederick H., "A naval veteran," ——, 1838. G.R.19.
Frederick Nichols, ch. Frederick and Ann Maria, Oct. 21, 1831, in Quincy.
Fredrick, s. James Jr. and Desire, Dec. 23, 1807. [Frederick Curtice, C.R.2.]
Gamaliel, s. John, bp. Sept. 11, 1763. C.R.1.
George, s. Sam[ue]ll [Samuel, C.R.1.] (s. William) and Rhoda, Aug. 24, 1776.
George, s. Charles Jr. and Cynthia, Mar. 12, 1827.
George Henry, s. George, carpenter, and Deborah (b. Hingham), Dec. 25, 1843, in Medford.
George Howard [oward, written in pencil], s. Thomas, drovier, and Drusilla, May 22 [184–].
George Little, s. Shadrach B. and Charlotte, Mar. 3, 1837.
George Washington, ch. Joseph and Deborah, Feb. 22, 1841.
Hannah, d. John (s. Richard) [and Miriam (Brooks)], May 28, 1681.
Hannah, d. Nehemiah and Joanna [Joannah, C.R.1.], Feb. 26, 1766.
Hannah Adams, ch. Norton and Mary P., Dec. 21, 1833.
Hannah Merritt, d. Ammil and Hannah, Apr. 12, 1811.
Harriet, ch. James Jr., bp. Nov. 2, 1820. C.R.2.
Harriet, ch. Asa F. and Catherine, Jan. 6, 1840.
Harriet Atwood Briggs, ch. Rufus and Rhoda, July 22, 1838.
Harriet Dunbar, ch. Amos T. and Polly, May 5, 1832.

CURTIS, Harriet M., d. Lewis N., shoemaker, and Harriet T., Oct. 29, 1847.
Harriet T. [――――], w. Lewis N., ―― [1822]. C.R.3.
Harriot, d. Job and Bethiah, Feb. 25, 1814.
Harriot Clark, d. James Jr. and Desire, Feb. 15, 1817.
Henrietta, d. Nehemiah R. and w., Apr. 1, 1809.
Henry, ch. Joseph and Deborah, Feb. 23, 1833.
Henry J., s. Stephen and Mary S., June 2, 1822.
Henry M., s. Fredrick, shipwright, and Ann M., Jan. 15, 1845.
Henry Norton, ch. Norton and Mary P., Apr. 23, 1838.
Henry W., ch. Frederick and Ann Maria, Jan. 11, 1846.
Hervey, s. Charles and Abigail, June 21, 1808.
Hetee, d. Sam[ue]l Jr. and Hetee, Sept. 3, 1786.
Hiram, s. Job and Bethiah, Nov. 25, 1809.
Ichabod, s. John, bp. Jan. 13, 1773. C.R.1.
Jael, d. Will[ia]m and Margret, Aug. 14, 1721. [Curtice, C.R.2.]
James, s. Benja[min] and Rebecca, Feb. 2, 1732.
James, s. Elijah and Ziporah, ――, 17[sic] [rec. before ch. b. Apr. 23, 1782].
James, ch. Asa F. and Catherine, Sept. 28, 1841.
James Henry, s. Asa and Jane, Mar. 7, 1814.
James Irving, s. T. Jefferson, inn keeper, and Jane, Jan. 28, 1849.
James Otis, s. James Jr. and Desire, Nov. 1, 1804.
James W., ch. James and Wealthy, Feb. 12, 1834, in Abington.
Jane, d. Asa and Jane, Jan. 31, 1821.
Jane T. [? m.], ――, 1814. G.R.6.
Jeal, d. Tho[ma]s Jr. and Ruth, June 29, 1732.
Jesse, s. Joseph and Rebekah, Oct. 17, 1709. [Curtice, s. Joseph and Rebeccah, C.R.2.]
Job, s. Benja[min] and Rebecca, Mar. 9, 1726. [Curtice, C.R.2.]
Job, s. Sam[ue]ll and Rachel, July 3, 1748. [Curtice, s. Samuel and Rachel, C.R.2.]
Job, s. Job and Bethiah, Dec. 10, 1807.
Job Edwin, ch. Norton and Mary P., Oct. 12, 1842. [[h. Mary C.] [h. Clara M.] G.R.2.]
John, s. William, Feb. ―, 1670–1.
John, s. William Jr. (s. John) and Rachell, Apr. 16, 1708. [s. W[illia]m and Elizabeth, C.R.1.]
John, s. John and Experience, May 14, 1709. [Curtice, C.R.2.]
Jo[h]n, s. Jo[h]n (grand s. W[illia]m Sr.) and Sarah, May 6, 1737.
John, s. John and Sarah, Aug. 4, 1767.
John, s. Asa and Jane, Oct. 1, 1816.
John, s. W[illia]m Sr., ――――. [This entry crossed out.]
John A., s. Luther and Sarah, Jan. 2, 1834.

CURTIS, John Merritt, s. Ammiel and Hannah, Apr. 30, 1809.
Jonathan, s. Benja[min] Jr. and Mary, Mar. 22, 1765.
Joseph, s. William, May —, 1664. [Courtis, C.R.2.]
Joseph, s. Joseph, Mar. 23, 1693-4.
Joseph, s. Eli 3d and Clarissa, Jan. 26, 1824.
Joseph, ch. Eli Jr. and Melvina, Mar. 7, 1840.
Joseph Bowker, ch. Joseph and Polly, July 21, 1814.
Joseph H., ch. Joseph and Deborah, Feb. 7, 1844.
Josiah, s. Joseph, Apr. 5, 1696-7. [Curtise, C.R.2.]
Julia, d. Elijah and Phebe, Mar. 16, 1809.
Julia Adeline, ch. Amos T. and Polly, ———, 1843.
Julia Ann, d. Job and Bethiah, Feb. 28, 1827.
Julia F., d. James, shoemaker, and Ruth, Feb. 26, 1844 [dup. 1845].
Julia T., d. Nehimeah R. and w., Oct. 19, 1820.
Julia T., ch. Thomas J. and Jane L., Aug. 11, 1843.
Julia T., ———, 1844. G.R.6.
Leaffy, ch. Joseph and Polly, Nov. 29, 1808.
Lefy, d. Peleg Jr. and Ruth, Mar. 31, 1783.
Lendal, s. Benja[min] Jr. and Mary, July 24, 1775.
Lewis Nichols, s. Charles and Abigail, Mar. 3, 1812. [[h. Harriet T. (Litchfield)] G.R.7.]
Lewis Nichols, ch. Charles, bp. Aug. 1, 1824. C.R.1.
Lorenzo, s. Thomas, drover, and Priscilla [Druscilla, written above in pencil], June 17, 1847.
Lot, s. Jo[h]n, bp. July 16, 1749. C.R.1.
Lucinda B., d. Stephen and Lucinda, Apr. 28, 181[worn] [1817].
Lucinda B., d. Stephen and Mary S., Oct. 4, 1819.
Lucy, d. Benja[min] Jr. and Mary, Aug. 25, 1766.
Lucy, d. Samuel [Sam[ue]ll, C.R.1.] (s. William) and Rhoda, June 23, 1783.
Lucy C. [? m.], ———, 1814. G.R.14.
Lucy Nichols, d. James Jr. and Desire, Mar. 24, 1815.
Lusannah, d. Tho[ma]s and Lusannah, Apr. 6, 1761.
Lusannah, ch. Thomas and Lusannah, bp. May 29, 1768. C.R.1.
Luther, s. Eli and Desire, Jan. 10, 1766.
[L]uther, s. Eli Jr. and Deborah, Nov. 28, 1789.
Luther, s. Eli Jr. and Deborah, July 6, 1797. [[h. Sarah] G.R.6.]
Luther Nichols, s. Eli 3d and Clarissa, June 28, 1819.
Lydia, d. Benjamin, Feb. 27, 1695-6. [Curtise, C.R.2.]
Lydia, d. Elijah and Rachel, May 16, 1796. [Curtice, C.R.2.]
Lydia, d. Job and Bethiah, Apr. 9, 1823.
Lydia Bowker, d. Job and Bethiah, May 6, 1825.
Lydia Cole, d. Charles and Abigail, Feb. 15, 1814.
Lydia Cole, ch. Charles, bp. Aug. 1, 1824. C.R.1.

CURTIS, Lydia Warner, d. Charles Jr. and Cynthia, Jan. 15, 1831.
Mabel, ch. Thomas and Lusannah, bp. May 29, 1768. C.R.1.
Mabel, d. Charles Jr. and Cynthia, Oct. 4, 1828.
Marcy, d. Tho[ma]s, bp. Aug. 6, 1738. C.R.1.
Marcy, d. Thomas, bp. Apr. 29, 1770. C.R.1.
Maria, d. Ruth, wid., bp. Jan. 27, 1806. C.R.1.
Martha, d. Joseph and Rebekah, Feb. 14, 1701. [Curtise, C.R.2.]
Martha, d. Samuell Jr. and Anna, Aug. 3, 1713. [Curtice, C.R.2.]
Martha Ann, d. Thomas and Druzilla, Oct. 11, 1831.
Martha Augusta, d. Ammiel and Hannah, July 30, 1814.
Martin, s. Charles and Abigail, Sept. 26, 1806.
Martin, ———, 1807. G.R.14.
Martin Shiverick, ch. Martin and Lucy C., Sept. 27, 1835.
Mary, d. Benjamin (s. William), Aug. 22, 1691.
Mary, d. Thomas (s. Rich[ard]) and Mary, Mar. 6, 1701–2.
Mary, d. Benja[min] and Rebecca, Aug. 15, 1737. [Curtice, C.R.2.]
Mary, d. Benja[min] Jr. and Mary, Sept. 7, 1771.
Mary, d. Sam[ue]l Jr. [Sam[ue]ll, C.R.2.] and Hetee, Nov. 26, 1791.
Mary, d. Eli Jr. and Deborah, Jan. 20, 1795.
Mary, d. Sam[ue]l 3d and Ruth, Oct. 9, 1796.
Mary, d. Elijah and Rachel, Sept. —, 1798.
Mary, [twin] d. Asa and Jane, July 5, 1825.
Mary, ch. Sam[uel] and Mehitabel (Young), ———.
Mary Bailey, d. Charles and Abigail, Jan. 30, 1816.
Mary Bailey, ch. Charles, bp. Aug. 1, 1824. C.R.1.
Mary C.[———], w. Job E., Nov. 23, 1845. G.R.2.
Mary Jane, d. Nehemiah and Mercy, Oct. 1, 1810. G.R.6.
Mary Norton, ch. Norton and Mary P., Oct. 2, 1835.
Mary P. [———], w. Norton [Sept. —, 1813]. C.R.3.
Mary Thaxter, ch. Frederick and Ann Maria, July 4, 1838.
Mary Turner, ch. Amos T. and Polly, July 30, 1828.
Mary Turner, d. Amos and Mary, bp. Oct. 7, 1832. C.R.1.
Mehetabel, ch. Sam[uel] and Mehitabel (Young), ———.
Mehetable, d. William, Dec. —, 1675.
Mehitable, d. Sam[ue]ll and Anna, Sept. 9, 1726. [Mehitabel Curtice, d. Samuel and Anna, C.R.2.]
Mercy, d. John (s. Richard) [and Miriam (Brooks)], Jan. 12, 1678–9. [Marey [or Marcy] Curtice, C.R.2.]
Meriam, d. Jo[h]n (grand s. W[illia]m Sr.) and Sarah, Oct. 20, 1734. [Miriam, C.R.1.]
Merria, d. Sam[ue]ll 3d and Ruth, Mar. 29, 1801.
Miriam, d. William, Apr. —, 1673.
Miriam, d. Sam[ue]ll Jr. and Anna, Jan. 1, 1715. [Curtice, C.R.2.]

CURTIS, Molly Vinal, d. Sam[ue]ll (s. William) and Rhoda, May 3, 1780.
Nahum, s. Job and Bethiah, June 11, 1816.
Nancy, d. John and Sarah, July 27, 1779.
Nathaniel Wade, s. Eli 3d and Clarissa, Aug. 7, 1817.
Nehemiah, s. John and Sarah, July 31, 1769.
Nehemiah, s. Shadrach B. and Anna, Mar. 7, 1826.
Nehemiah, s. Shadrach B. and Charlotte, June 8, 1833.
Nehemiah R., s. Nehemiah R. and w., July 26, 1817.
Nehemiah Randol, s. Elijah and Ziprah, Apr. 23, 1782.
Noah, s. Eli Jr. and Deborah, Sept. 30, 1801.
Norton, s. Charles and Abigail, Feb. 17, 1810.
Norton, ch. Charles, bp. Aug. 1, 1824. C.R.1.
Patience Wade, d. Gamaliel and Patience, Mar. 1, 1787.
Paul, s. Elijah and Rachel, Dec. 26, 1800. [Curtice, C.R.2.]
Peleg, s. Benjamin and Mary, Sept. —, 1710. [Curtice, C.R.2.]
Peleg, ch. Joseph and Polly, Oct. 18, 1818.
Phebe Cushing, d. James Jr. and Desire, Feb. 28, 1806. [Curtiss, C.R.2.]
Philip, s. Peleg Jr. and Ruth, June 5, 1786.
Phillip, s. Job and Bethiah, Jan. 11, 1812.
Polley, d. Eli Jr. and Deborah, July 24, 1792.
Polly, d. Sam[ue]l Jr. and Hetee, Dec. 31, 1789.
Rachel, d. William (s. John) and Rachel, June 6, 1717.
Rachel, d. Sam[ue]ll (s. William) and Rhoda, Jan. 28, 1774.
Rachel, d. Elijah and Rachel, May 2, 178[torn].
Rachell, d. William Jr. (s. John) and Rachell, July 24, 1710. [Rachel Curtois, C.R.1.]
Rebecca, d. Benja[min] and Rebecca, Aug. 17, 1730. [Curtice, C.R.2.]
Rebecca, d. Elisha and Sarah, bp. Apr. 28, 1754. C.R.2.
Rebecca, d. Benja[min] Jr. and Mary, Aug. 10, 1760.
Rebeckah, d. Joseph, May 9, 1699. [Rebecca Curtise, C.R.2.]
Reuben, s. Asa and Jane, Oct. 6, 1818.
Rhoda, d. Samuel and Rhoda, bp. Sept. 23, 1770. C.R.1.
Richard, s. Joseph and Rebekah, Nov. 8, 1702. [Curtise, C.R.2.]
Rufus [h. Rhoda (Briggs)], ——, 1805. G.R.6.
Ruth, d. Thomas (s. Rich[ard]), Apr. 19, 1699. [Curtise, C.R.2.]
Ruth, d. Benjamin, June 14, 1700.
Ruth, d. Thomas (s. Rich[ard]) and Mary, Feb. 24, 1711–12.
Ruth, d. Tho[ma]s Jr. and Ruth, Sept. 28, 1735.
Ruth, d. Thomas, bp. Jan. 19, 1772. C.R.1.
Ruth, d. Samuel [dup. Sam[ue]ll] 3d and Ruth, May 9 [dup. May 3], 1793.

CURTIS, Ruth, d. Charles and Abigail, Feb. 2, 1803.
Ruth Augusta, ch. Seth and Ruth, Mar. 9, 1827, in Hanover.
Ruth Ferguson, ch. Norton and Mary P., Feb. 12, 1840.
Ruth M., d. Luther and Sarah, Aug. 17, 1838.
Salley, d. Sam[ue]l 3d and Ruth, Dec. 16, 1798.
Sally, second w. Jonathan Stetson, ———, 1783. G.R.14.
Samuel, s. Samuel (s. Thomas of York), Sept. 26, 1695. [Curtise, ch. Sam[ue]ll Sr., C.R.2.]
Samuel, s. William Jr. (s. John) and Rachell, Mar. 10, 1711–12.
Samuel, s. William (s. John) and Rachel, Jan. 4, 1719.
Samuel, s. Sam[ue]ll [Sam[ue]l, C.R.1.] (s. William) and Elener, June 13, 1754.
Samuel, s. Sam[ue]l Jr. and Hetee, Nov. 1, 1781.
Samuel, s. Sam[ue]l 3d and Ruth, Aug. 24, 1786. [Sam[ue]ll, s. Sam[ue]ll Jr., C.R.1.]
Samuel, ch. Sam[uel] and Mehitabel (Young), ———.
Samuel Deane, s. James Jr. and Desire, Sep[t]. 3, ——— [Sep[t]. 3, written in pencil] [rec. after ch. b. Feb. 15, 1817]. [bp. Nov. 2, 1820, C.R.2.]
Samuell, s. William, June —, 1681.
Samuell, s. Samuell Jr., June 24, 1708. [Samuel Curtice, s. Samuel and Anna, C.R.2.]
Sam[ue]ll, s. Benja[min] and Rebecca, Apr. 2, 1724. [Samuel Curtice, C.R.2.]
Sam[ue]ll, s. Amos and Mary, Feb. 19, 1745. [Samuel Curtice, C.R.2.]
Sam[ue]ll, s. Sam[ue]ll· and Rachel, June 15, 1750. [Samuel Curtice, C.R.2.]
Sam[ue]ll, s. Sam[ue]ll 3d and Ruth, Nov. 13, 1788. [Samuel, s. Sam[ue]ll Jr., C.R.1.]
Sarah, d. William, Aug. —, 1679.
Sarah, d. Benjamin, Dec. 20, 1697.
Sarah, d. Jo[h]n (grand s. W[illia]m Sr.) and Sarah, Mar. 16, 1732.
Sarah, d. John and w., bp. Aug. 12, 1733. C.R.1.
Sarah, d. Benja[min] Jr. and Mary, Sept. 22, 1757.
Sarah, d. John and Sarah, Feb. 12, 1777.
Sarah [———], w. Luther, ———, 1806. G.R.6.
Sarah E., d. Luther and Sarah, Oct. 21, 1835.
Sarah Elizabeth, d. Luther and Sarah, Aug. 15, 1832.
Sarah Elizebeth [dup. Elizabeth], d. Norton, cordwainer, and Mary P., Oct. 7, 1846.
Sarah Otis, d. James Jr. and Desire, Apr. 10, 1811. [w. Capt. Turner Litchfield, G.R.2.]
Selina Briggs, ch. Asa F. and Catherine, ——— [rec. after ch. b. Sept. 28, 1841].

CURTIS, Seth, s. Eli and Desier, June 4, 1769.
Shadrach Briggs, s. Nehemiah and Polly, June 19, 1796.
Shadrach Briggs, s. Shadrach B. and Anna, Sept. 22, 1823.
Silina, d. Gamaliel and Patience, June 7, 1797.
Simeon, s. Sam[ue]ll Jr. and Anna, June 1, 1720. [Curtice, C.R.2.]
Simeon, s. Tho[mas] and Ruth, June 27, 1739.
Sophia, d. Sam[ue]l Jr. and Mehitabel [dup. Hetee], Dec. 21, 1778.
Stephen, s. William, Sept. —, 1677.
Stephen, s. William, bp. Dec. 1, 1678. C.R.2.
Stephen, s. Benja[min] Jr. and Mary, Oct. 21, 1768.
Stephen, s. Peleg Jr. and Ruth, Feb. 9, 1792.
Sussana, d. Benjamin and Mary, Mar. 23, 1702. [Susanna Curtise, C.R.2.]
Thankfull, d. Joseph and Rebekah, Jan. 17, 1707-8. [Curtise, d. Joseph and Rebecca, C.R.2.]
Thirza I. [? J.], d. James H., and Thirza C., Mar. 19, 1845.
Thomas, s. Thomas (s. Rich[ard]) and Mary, Mar. 5, 1703-4.
Thomas, s. Thomas Jr. and Ruth, Dec. 8, 1729.
Thomas, ch. Thomas and Lusannah, bp. May 29, 1768. C.R.1.
Thomas, s. Charles and Abigail, Nov. 10, 1804.
Thomas, s. Asa and Jane, Oct. 22, 1823.
Thomas, [twin] s. Asa and Jane, July 5, 1825.
Thomas, s. Asa and Jane, Oct. 8, 1826.
Thomas H., ———, 1845. G.R.6.
Thomas J., ———, 1808. G.R.6.
Thomas Whitney, s. Thomas and Druzilla, Oct. 9, 1829.
Warren Cooper, s. Thomas and Druzilla, ———, 1839.
Washington, ch. James and Ruth, Sept. 7, 1847.
William, s. William, Jan. —, 1668-9. [Courtis, C.R.2.]
William, s. John (s. Richard) [and Miriam (Brooks)], Sept. 15, 1683.
William, s. Benjamin and Mary, July —, 1706.
William, s. William Jr. (s. John) and Rachell, Sept. 28, 1714.
William, s. Jo[h]n, bp. Aug. 4, 1754. C.R.1.
William, s. Samuel [Sam[ue]ll, C.R.1.] (s. William) and Rhoda, Nov. 1, 1771.
William, s. Gamaliel and Patience, Oct. 21, 1790.
William H., ch. Dennis Jr. and Thirza, July 1, 1844.
Zebiah, d. Jo[h]n, bp. Dec. 28, 1746. C.R.1.
Zintha, d. Elijah and Abegal, May 21, 1757. [Cynthia Curtice, C.R.2.]
———, ch. Ammiel and Hannah, bp. Nov. 22, 1812. C.R.1.
——— [———], w. Nichols, ——— [1822]. C.R.3.
———, d. Henry, mariner, and Theresa C., Mar. 19, 1844.

CURTIS, ———, s. Thomas J., mariner, and Jane, Apr. 12, 1844.
———, s. Rufus, shoemaker, and Rhoda, Jan. 1, 1845.
———, d. Eli Jr., farmer, and Melvina, Jan. 10, 1848.

CURTISE (see Courtis, Courtisse, Curtice, Curtis, Custis), Benjamin, ch. Benjamin, bp. ———, 1696. C.R.2.
Benjamin, ch. Sam[ue]ll Sr., bp. ———, 1701. C.R.2.
Deborah, d. Benjamin, bp. July 16, 1704. C.R.2.
Ebenezer, ch. Benjamin, bp. ———, 1696. C.R.2.
Elizabeth, ch. Sam[ue]ll Sr., bp. ———, 1696. C.R.2.
Joseph, s. Joseph, bp. ———, 1697. C.R.2.
Mary, ch. Benjamin, bp. ———, 1696. C.R.2.
Sarah, ch. Benjamin, bp. ———, 1699. C.R.2.
William, s. Benjamin and Mary, bp. Aug. 12, 1705. C.R.2.

CUSHEIN (see Cushen, Cushin, Cushing), John, s. John, Apr. 28, 1662. [Cushion, C.R.2.]

CUSHEN (see Cushein, Cushin, Cushing), Benjamen, s. John, Feb. 4, 1678. [Benjamin Cushin, C.R.2.]
Caleb, s. John, Jan. 6, 1672. [Cusheen, C.R.2.]
Deborah, d. John, Sept. 7, 1674. [Debeorah Cushin, C.R.2.]
James, s. John, Jan. 27, 1668. [Cushion, C.R.2.]
Jerimiah, s. John, July 13, 1666. [Jeremiah Cushin, C.R.2.]
John, s. John, Sept. 14, 1674. P.C.R.
Joseph (Cusen), s. John, Sept. 23, 1677.
Joshua, s. John, Aug. 27, 1670. [Cushion, C.R.2.]
Mathew, s. John, Feb. 16, 1664. [Cushion, C.R.1.]
Sarah, d. John, Aug. 26, 1671. [Cusheen, C.R.2.]
Thomas, s. John (Cushin), Dec. 26, 1663. [Cushion, C.R.2.]

CUSHIN (see Cushein, Cushen, Cushing), Joseph, s. John, bp. May 12, 1678. C.R.2.
Mary, d. John, bp. Oct. 3 [worn], 1676. C.R.2.

CUSHING (see Cushein, Cushen, Cushin), Abigail, d. James Jr. and Sarah, Nov. 8, 1766.
Abigail, d. "Nath^n" Esq. and Abigail, June 4, 1775.
Abigail, ch. Charles W. and Deborah (Jacob), Nov. 24, 1808 [? in Hingham]. P.R.14.
Abigal, d. Jo[h]n and Mary, June 8, 1748. [Abigail, d. Hon. John Jr. and Mary, C.R.2.]
Albert, s. Pickels [Pickles, C.R.2.] Jr. and Rachel, Sept. 3, 1810.
Alice, d. Joseph and Lydia, ———, 1756.
Allice, d. Dea. Cushing Jr., bp. June 19, 1757. C.R.2.
Allyne, s. Joseph and Desire, Dec. 9, 1811.

CUSHING, Almira, d. George and Nancy, Feb. 13, 1812, in Boston.
Andrew, s. George and Nancy, Sept. 24, 1814.
Ann Jane, d. Elnathan and Mary, May 7, 1809.
Ann Jane, ch. Elnathan, bp. Sept. 2, 1810. C.R.2.
Anna, d. Joseph and Desire, Jan. 20, 1809.
Barker, s. Jo[h]n Jr. and Deborah, Oct. 5, 1750.
Barker, s. John Jr. and Deborah, Mar. 23, 1757.
Bela, s. Pickels and Abigail, Dec. 20, 1773.
Benjamin, s. John Jr. [s. John and Deborah, C.R.2.], Apr. 17, 1706.
Benjamin, s. James Jr. and Mary, Dec. 15, 1741.
Benjamin, ch. James Jr., bp. Nov. 6, 1743. C.R.2.
Bethiah, d. Jo[h]n and Mary, Mar. 29, 1740.
Bethyah, d. James Jr. and Sarah, Dec. 1, 1764.
Betsey, d. Nath[anie]l and Ellis, July 24, 1791.
Betsey, d. Nath[anie]ll and w.; bp. Oct. 13, 1793. C R.2.
Betsey [――――], w. Zeba [Mar. ―, 1802]. G.R.9.
Caleb, s. Joseph Jr. and Lydia, July 1, 1750.
Caleb, s. Joseph [Dea. Joseph Jr., C.R.2.] and Lydia, Oct. 7, 1754.
Caroline, d. Thomas and Ruth, Jan. 27, 1800.
Charles, s. Jo[h]n Jr. and Mary, Aug. 13, 1734. [Charls, C.R.2.]
Charles, s. Pickles and Abigail, Feb. 21, 1781.
Charles, s. Francis and Lucy, Dec. 14, 1789.
Charles W. [h. Deborah (Jacob) (d. James)], Nov. 7, 1766 [? in Hingham]. P.R.14.
Charles W., ch. Charles W. and Deborah (Jacob), Oct. 26, 1811 [? in Hingham]. P.R.14.
Charles W., s. Elnathan and Louisa M., Aug. 23, 1840.
Charlotte, d. Hawkes and Ruth, July 12, 1786.
Charlotte Elizabeth, d. Elnathan, carpenter, and Louisa, Sept. 26, 1848.
Charlotte Vose, d. Georog and Nancy, Feb. 12, 1809, in Boston.
Chauncy, s. Nath[anie]l and Ellis, Aug. 27, 1794.
Christiana, d. Elnathan and Mary, Mar. 15, 1815.
Christina, d. Elnathan and Mary, June 25, 1817.
Christopher, s. Hon. "Nath{n}" Esq. and Abigail, May 20, 1773.
Christopher, s. George and Nancy, May 3, 1820.
Clarissa, d. Thomas [Dea. Tho[ma]s, C.R.2.] and Ruth, Feb. 16, 1814.
Clearissa, d. Hawkes and Ruth, May 21, 1784.
Content, d. James and Mary, July 19, 1722.
Content, d. Ja[me]s Jr. and Mary, Mar. 22, 1761.
Daniel, s. James Jr. and Sarah, Aug. 17, 1769.

CUSHING, David, ch. Charles W. and Deborah (Jacob), Sept. 5, 1801 [? in Hingham]. P.R.14.
David Jacob, s. Nath[anie]l [Nath[anie]ll, C.R.2.] and Hannah, Feb. 13, 1805.
David Lincoln, s. Elnathan and Mary, Mar. 25, 1819.
Debby, d. Nath[anie]l and Ellis, Dec. 31, 1774.
Deborah, d. Jo[h]n Jr. [d. John and Elizabeth, C.R.2.], Nov. 16, 1718.
Deborah, d. John Jr. and Deborah, Jan. 20, 1748.
Deborah, d. Joseph [Dea. Joseph, C.R.2.] Jr. and Lydia, July 3, 1752.
Deborah, d. Fra[nc]is and Temperance, Dec. 9, 1774.
Deborah Richmond [d. Charles W. and Deborah (Jacob)], w. Rufus Farrow, Jan. 18, 1796, in Hingham. P.R.14.
Debreh, d. John Jr., Apr. 2, 1693.
Edward, s. Jo[h]n Jr. and Mary, Sept. 6, 1736.
Edward, s. Jo[h]n Jr. and Deborah, Oct. 18, 1752.
Edward, s. John Jr. and Deborah, June 21, 1762.
Edward, s. Nath[anie]l Jr. and Hannah, May 2, 1794. [Eldward, s. Nath[anie]ll Jr. and w., C.R.2.]
Elijah, s. John Jr., Mar. 7, 1697–8.
Elijah, s. Elijah and Elizabeth, bp. Feb. 6, 1725. C.R.2.
Eliza, d. Pickels [Pickles, C.R.2.] Jr. and Rachel, May 1, 1813.
Eliza[beth], d. Jo[h]n Jr. and Deborah, Apr. 9, 1744. [Elisabeth, C.R.2.]
Elizabeth [w. Noah Jenkins], Aug. —, 1784. P.R.17.
Ella F., d. Fredrick, ship carpenter (b. Boston), and Cynthia, May 18, 1847.
Ellen Augusta, d. Elnathan and Louisa M., Dec. 16, 1838.
Elnathan, s. Elnathan and Mary, Aug. 27, 1807.
Elnathan, ch. Elnathan, bp. Sept. 2, 1810. C.R.2.
Elnathan Hobart, s. Elnathan and Louisa M., Sept. 24, 1835.
Elvira, d. Pickels Jr. and Rachel, Sept. 15, 1818.
Elvira, d. Pickels Jr. and Rachel, July 5, 1821.
Emely Seagrave, d. Zeba and Betsey, May 2, 1833.
Emily, d. Thomas [Dea. Thomas, C.R.2.] and Ruth, May 20, 1811.
Emma S. T., d. Elnathan, shipwright, and Louisa [dup. adds M.], Dec. 18, 1845.
Eunice, ch. Charles W. and Deborah (Jacob), Sept. 29, 1806 [? in Hingham]. P.R.14.
Eunice Susan Thurston, d. Elnathan, carpenter, and Louisa, Dec. 18, 1845.
Everett, ch. John and Harriet, Oct. 11, 1828, in Lowell.
Everett [ch. John and Harriet], ———, 1830. G.R.2.

CUSHING, Ezekiell, s. Jeremiah, Apr. 27, 1698.
Fanny, d. "Nath^n" Esq. and Abigail, June 26, 1780.
Fatima, ch. Charles W. and Deborah (Jacob), Nov. 19, 1797 [? in Hingham]. P.R.14.
Fatima, ch. Charles W. and Deborah (Jacob), Oct. 2, 1799 [? in Hingham]. P.R.14.
Frances, d. Elnathan and Mary, Mar. 22, 1811.
Francis, s. Jo[h]n Jr. and Deborah, Oct. 21, 1745.
Francis, s. Francis and Temperance, Aug. 24, 1773.
Frederick, s. Zeba and Emely, July 22, 1820, in Boston.
George, s. Joseph Jr. and Lydia, July 5, 1736.
George, d. George and Lydia, Sept. 8, 1776.
George Frederick [George Frederick, crossed out], d. Fredrick, shipwright, and Cintha, May 18, 1847.
George Frederick, s. Fredrick, carpenter (b. Boston), and Cynthia, Sept. 21, 1849.
George King, s. Thomas and Ruth, Jan. 25, 1805.
George King, s. George and Nancy, Nov. 29, 1806, in Boston. [sister [*sic*] of Nancy, C.R.3.] [[h. Lucretia] G.R.14.]
Hannah, d. Jeremiah, Mar. 26, 1687. [Cushin, d. Jeremyah, C.R.2.]
Hannah, d. Jo[h]n [Jo[h]n Esq., C.R.1.] and Mary, Sept. 2, 1738.
Hannah [———], w. Capt. Nathaniel, ——— [1769]. G.R.2.
Hannah, d. George and Lydia, July 16, 1774.
Hannah, d. Nathaniel and Hannah, June 29, 1809.
Hannah Augusta, d. Nathaniel 3d and Olive, Aug. 23, 1826.
Hannah Briggs, d. Zeba and Betsey, Jan. 18, 1827.
Harriet, d. Pickels Jr. and Rachel, Aug. 10, 1805. [Harriot, d. Pickles and w., C.R.2.]
Harriet, ch. John and Harriet, Sept. 15, 1831, in Lowell.
Harrison, s. Thomas [Dea. Thomas, C.R.2.] and Ruth, Sept. 20, 1808.
Hawke, s. Joseph Jr. and Lydia, Feb. 13, 1744. [Hawkes, C.R.2.]
Hayward Peirce, s. Nath[anie]ll Jr. and Jane, May 3, 1812. [Hayward Pierce, ch. Nath[anie]l 2d, C.R.2.] [Hayward Peirce, G.R.14.]
Henry A., ch. Zatu and Betsey P., Sept. 26, 1839.
Ignatius, s. Jeremiah, Sept. 22, 1689.
Isaac, s. Hawkes and Ruth, Dec. 28, 1775.
Isaac, s. George and Nancy, Aug. 15, 1817.
Isabella Jane, d. Elnathan and Louisa M., Aug. 17, 1831.
Isabella Jane, d. Elnathan and Louisa, ——— [1834]. G.R.14.
James, s. James and Mary, Sept. 16, 1716.
James, s. James Jr. and Mary, Jan. 9, 1739.

CUSHING, James, ch. James Jr., bp. Nov. 6, 1743. C.R.2.
James, ch. Charles W. and Deborah (Jacob), Apr. 10, 1820 [? in Hingham]. P.R.14.
James, ch. Joshua and Sally, Aug. 4, 1830.
Jane, d. Nath[anie]ll Jr. and Jane, Sept. 26, 1808.
Jeremiah, s. Jeremiah, Sept. 4, 1695.
Jerusha Gay, d. Elnathan and Lillis, Mar. 25 [dup. Mar. 26], 1805.
John, s. John Jr., July 17, 1695.
John, s. Jo[h]n Jr. and Elizabeth, Aug. 16, 1722.
John, s. John Jr. and Deborah, Jan. 23, 174[worn] [? 1743].
John, s. Nath[anie]l [Nath[anie]ll, C.R.2.] and Hannah, June 14, 1800.
John, s. Joseph and Desire, Dec. 31, 1804.
John [h. Harriet (Morrill)], ——, 1805. G.R.2.
John, ch. Joshua and Sally, May 10, 1832.
John, ch. Joshua and Sally, Sept. 15, 1834.
John Peak, s. Nathaniel 3d and Olive, Mar. 19, 1836.
Joseph, s. Joseph and Mercy, Nov. 25, 1711.
Joseph, s. Joseph Jr. and Lydia, Nov. 18, 1733.
Joseph, s. Pickels and Abigail, Mar. 12, 1768.
Joseph, s. Joseph and Desire, Dec. 19, 1794.
Joseph Bowers, ch. Charles W. and Deborah (Jacob), Oct. 25, 1817 [? in Hingham]. P.R.14.
Joshua Warren, ch. Joshua and Sally, May 31, 1829.
Josiah, s. John and Sarah, Jan. 29, 1714.
Josiah, s. Thomas and Ruth, Sept. 9, 1806.
Josiah Thomas, s. Elnathan and Mary, Jan. 1, 1821.
Julia, d. Pickels Jr. [Pickles, C.R.2.] and Rachel, July 19, 1807.
Lamuel, s. Hawkes and Ruth, Apr. 4, 1780.
Leafy, d. Joseph and Desire, Nov. 16, 1791. [Leafe, C.R.2.]
Leafy M., ch. Martin and Laura A. (Holt), ——, 1848. G.R.14.
Lemuel, s. Joseph Jr. and Lydia, Nov. 16, 1746.
Lemuel (see Lamuel).
Lidia, d. James and Mary, Dec. 15, 1714. [Lydia, C.R.1.]
Louiza Maria, d. Elnathan Jr. and Louiza M., Dec. 2, 1827.
Luce, d. Hon. John Esq. and Mary, bp. June 28, 1747. C.R.2.
Lucretia [———], w. George K. [Sept. —, 1776]. G.R.14.
Lucy, d. Jo[h]n and Mary, Dec. 30, 1745.
Lucy, d. Ja[me]s Jr. and Mary, Dec. 30, 1747. [Luce, C.R.2.]
Lucy, d. Ja[me]s Jr. and Mary, May 11, 1755.
Lucy, d. Pickels and Abigail, July 6, 1771.
Lucy, d. Francis and Temporince, July 28, 1779.
Lucy, d. Joseph and Desire, Aug. 12, 1793.
Lydia (see Lidia).

CUSHING, Lydia, d. Ja[me]s Jr. and Mary, Dec. 3, 1743.
Lydia (Cush), d. Dea. Cush[ing], bp. Feb. 29, 1756. C.R.2.
Lydia, d. George and Lydia, Jan. 29, 1786.
Lydia H., d. Pickels Jr. and Rachel, Apr. 22, 1816. [Lydia King, d. Pickles Jr., C.R.2.]
Mabel, ch. Charles W. and Deborah (Jacob), Sept. 25, 1803 [? in Hingham]. P.R.14.
Margaret Wade, [twin] d. Nathaniel 3d and Olive, Oct. 22, 1829.
Maria L., d. Geo[rge], —— [1814]. C.R.3.
Maria Louisa, ch. George and Nancy, bp. Oct. 19, 1828. C.R.3.
Maria Louiza, d. George and Nancy, May 5, 1824.
Marten, s. Pickles and Abigail, Feb. 13, 1783.
Martha Ann [————], w. John P., —— [1848]. G.R.2.
Martin, s. Joseph and Desire, July 9, 1810. [[h. Laura A. (Holt)] G.R.14.]
Martin Leonard, s. Leonard and Mary C., June 15, 1823.
Mary, d. John Jr., Nov. 24, 1700.
Mary, d. Jo[h]n Jr. and Mery, Sept. 6, 1730.
Mary, d. Ja[me]s Jr. and Mary, June 6, 1752.
Mary, d. John Jr. and Deborah, July 21, 1759.
Mary, d. George and Lydia, Aug. 10, 1778.
Mary, d. Francis and Lucy, July 14, 1788.
Mary, d. Pickles Jr. and w., bp. Dec. —, 1800. C.R.2.
Mary, d. Pickels Jr. and Rachel, Apr. 19, 1803.
Mary Davis, d. Leonard and Mary C., Nov. 16, 1821.
Mary Jacob, d. Nathaniel 3d and Olive, Dec. 11, 1824.
Mary Stockbridge, d. Elnathan and Lillis, Jan. 26, 1803.
Mary Stockbridge, d. Elnanathan [sic] and w., bp. May 20, 1804. C.R.2.
Mary Thomas, d. Elnathan and Louisa M., Sept. 23, 1833. [w. Jesse D. Webb, G.R.14.]
Matilda, d. Joseph and Desire, Nov. 29, 1801.
Matilda, d. Joseph and w., bp. Oct. 9, 1803. C.R.2.
Mercy, d. Jo[h]n [John Jr., C.R.2.] and Sarah, Oct. 24, 1716.
Mercy, d. Joseph Jr. and Lydia, Apr. 30, 1739.
Nabbe, d. Pickels and Abigail, Apr. 3, 1776.
Nabbe, d. Pickels and Abigail, June 10, 1778.
Nancy, d. Hawkes and Ruth, June 6, 1782.
Nancy [————], w. Geo[rge], —— [1782]. C.R.3. [[June —, 1782] G.R.14.]
Nancy, d. George and Nancy, Nov. 23, 1803, in Boston.
Nathan, s. Joseph Jr. and Lydia, Sept. 24, 1741 [dup. 1742].
Nathan, s. Nath[anie]ll Jr. [Nath[anie]l 2d, C.R.2.] and Jane, May 29, 1814.

CUSHING, Nathaniel, s. Joseph Jr. and Lydia, June 9, 1751.
Nath[anie]l, s. Nath[anie]l and Ellis, Oct. 25, 1779. [[h. Jane (Peirce)] G.R.14.]
Nathaniel, s. Nath[anie]l Jr. and Hannah, Feb. 11, 1796.
Nathaniel Grafton, s. Nathaniel 3d and Olive, Apr. 2, 1828.
Nathaniel Grafton, s. Nathaniel 3d and Olive, June 8, 1831.
Nathaniell, s. John and Deborah, July 9, 1709. [Nathanael, s. John (Chushing) and Deborah, C.R.2.]
Nath[anie]ll, s. Jo[h]n Jr. and Elizebeth, Aug. 12, 1724. [Nathanael, s. John and Elizabeth, C.R.2.]
Nath[anie]ll, s. John Jr. and Mary, May 16, 1768.
Nath[anie]ll, s. Nath[anie]ll Jr. and Jane, Dec. 6, 1809. [Nathaniel, ch. Nath[anie]l 2d, C.R.2.] [Nathaniel, G.R.14.]
Nazerath, d. John Jr., Sept. 11, 1703.
Olive Wade, d. Nathaniel 3d and Olive, Feb. 23, 1833.
Parker Warren, ch. Warren B. and Eveline, May 14, 1840.
Perez, s. Nath[anie]l and Ellis, Nov. 1, 1781.
Pickels, s. Pickels and Abigail, May 20, 1769.
Pickles s. Joseph Jr. [Dea. Joseph, C.R.2.] and Lydia, Feb. 18, 1743.
Polley, d Nath[anie]l and Ellis, Nov. 28, 1777.
Rachel, d. Ja[me]s Jr. and Mary, June 15, 1757.
Rachel, d. George and Lydia, Mar. 21, 1781.
Rebecca, d. Joseph and Desire, Jan. 31, 1799.
Robart, s. Jo[h]n Jr. and Deborah, June 4, 1747. [Robert, C.R.2.]
Robart, s. John Jr. and Deborah, Feb. 4, 1755. [Robert, C.R.2.]
Robert, s. George and Lydia, May 26, 1783.
Roland, s. John [Hon. John, C.R.2.] and Mary, Jan. 9, 1743.
Roland, s. John and Mary, Feb. 26, 1749.
Roland, s. Pickles and Abigail, May 7, 1785.
Roland, s. Pickels Jr. and Ruth, Dec. 3, 1794.
Ruth, d. Hawkes and Ruth, Nov. 10, 1772.
Ruth, ch. Tho[ma]s and Ruth, ——, 1797. G.R.14.
Ruth, w. Thomas Totman, —— [1799]. G.R.14.
Ruth T., d. Pickels Jr. and Ruth, June 21, 1797. [Ruth Thomas, d. Picles and w., C.R.2.]
Ruth Turner, d. Thomas and Ruth, Feb. 6, 1797.
Sally Wade, [twin] d. Nathaniel 3d and Olive, Oct. 22, 1829.
Samuel, s. Benja[min] and Jean, Nov. 15, 1769.
Samuel, s. Nath[anie]l and Ellis, July 29, 1787.
Samuel F. M., s. Elnathan and Louisa M., Apr. 14, 1843.
Samuel West, s. Nath[anie]l and Hannah, Jan. 4, 1798. [Sam[ue]ll West, s. Nath[anie]ll and w., C.R.2.]
Sam[ue]ll, s. Ja[me]s Jr. and Mary, Sept. 3, 1745. [Samuel, C.R.2.]

CUSHING, Sarah, d. John Jr., Jan. 8, 1689–90.
Sarah, d. James and Mary, Nov. 30, 1718.
Sarah, d. Jo[h]n Jr. and Elizabeth, Mar. 26, 1720.
Sarah, d. John Jr. and Elizabeth, bp. May 1, 1720. C.R.2.
Sarah, d. James and Mary, bp. June 12, 1726. C.R.2.
Sarah, d. Ja[me]s Jr. and Mary, Apr. 14, 1750.
Sarah, d. Hawkes and Ruth, Feb. 5, 1778.
Sarah, d. Pickles and Abigail, Sept. 9, 1787.
Sarah Hatch, ch. Joshua and Sally, Oct. 13, 1833.
Sophia Bradford, ch. Charles W. and Deborah (Jacob), June 28, 1814 [? in Hingham]. P.R.14.
Stephen, s. Joseph and Desire, Jan. 17, 1797.
Susan E., ch. Martin and Laura A. (Holt), ———, 1845. G.R.14.
Susanna, w. W. J. Newcomb, ——— [1828]. G.R.2.
Temperance, d. Francis and Temperance, Apr. 11, 1777.
Thomas, s. Joseph Jr. and Lydia, June 22, 1748.
Thomas, s. Joseph [Dea. Joseph, C.R.2.] Jr. and Lydia, May 29, 1749.
Thomas, s. Hawke and Ruth, Oct. 25, 1770.
Warren, s. Nath[anie]l and Ellis, Dec. 14, 1785.
William, s. John Jr. and Elizabeth, Sept. 23, 1725.
William, s. Jo[h]n Jr. and Mary, Mar. 1, 1732.
Will[ia]m, s. Pickels Jr. and Ruth, Nov. 21, 1792.
Williams, s. Elnathan and Mary, Jan. 22, 1813.
Zeba [h. Betsey], ——— [1790]. G.R.8.
———, s. John Jr. and Debarh, Feb. 29, 1692.
———, d. John and Mary, June 20, 1742.
———, s. Pickles Jr. and w., bp. June 7, 1795. C.R.2.

CUSTIS (see Courtis, Courtisse, Curtice, Curtis, Curtise), Nabby, d. Benja[min] Jr. and Mary, May 30, 1778.

DAGGETT (see Dogget, Doggett).

DAGON (see Degon), Elizabeth, d. Richard (Degon), May 16, 1693.

DALBY (see Dolby), Caroline J., d. John [dup. adds S.], housewright, and Cynthia [dup. adds B.], Aug. 11, 1846.
Cynthia B. [———], w. John [June —, 1816]. G.R.2.
James Thomas, ch. John S. and Cynthia B., Nov. 27, 1839, in Philadelphia.
John [h. Cynthia B.], June 6, 1810. G.R.2.
Samuel Price, ch. John S. and Cynthia B., Oct. 22, 1842, in Roxbury.
Sarah A. B., ch. John S. and Cynthia B., Feb. 18, 1844.

DAMAN (see Damen, Damin, Damman, Dammon, Damon),
Alven, s. Melzer and Bathshaba, Feb. 21, 1810. [Alvan
Damon, ch. Melzar, C.R.2.]
Anna, d. Simeon and Lucy, Aug. 12, 1796.
Anna Lenthel Eells, d. Calvin and Desire, Mar. 16, 1788.
Anna Lenthel Ells, d. Galen and Jenne, Apr. 1, 1790.
Arvilla, [twin] d. John and Elizabeth, Mar. 24, 1791. [Dammon, C.R.1.]
Baker, s. Silvanus and Lydia, Aug. 1, 1790.
Caleb, s. Reuben and Lydia, May 6, 1782. [Damon, G.R.2.]
Calvin, s. Calvin and Mercy, Apr. 4, 1792.
Calvin, s. Galen and w., bp. July 15, 1804. C.R.2.
Daniel, s. Simeon and Lucy, Nov. 25, 1788. [Damon [h. Mahala (Damon)], G.R.18.]
David, twin s. Jacob and Abigail, Sept. 18, 1815.
Delight Bowker, d. Simeon and Lucy, Oct. 25, 1786.
Desire Ells, d. Calvin and Mercy, Oct. 7, 1790.
Dimmic Bowker, s. Galen and Jenne, Sept. 1, 1795. [Demick Bowker, C.R.2.]
Ebenezer, s. Experience, Nov. 6, 1698.
Edward Ells, s. Edward and Celia, Mar. 1, 1781.
Elijah, s. Simeon and Lucy, Jan. 1, 1783. [Damon [h. Sally], G.R.14.]
Eliza Ellms, d. Henry and Elizabeth, Aug. 7, 1831.
Elizabeth, d. John and Elizabeth, Aug. 24, 1780.
Experience, s. Experience, Apr. 7, 1693.
Galen, s. Galen and Jenne, Aug. 5, 1793. [Damon, G.R.14.]
George, s. Zadock and Thankful, Mar. 11, 1788.
George Henry, s. Henry and Elizabeth, Nov. 6, 1833.
Hannah, d. Josiah and Lucy, Dec. 21, 1799.
Harris, s. Edward and Celia, Feb. 21, 1786.
Henry, s. Reuben and Lydia, Jan. 12, 1797.
Henry, s. Henry and Anna, Apr. 20, 1812. [Damon, G.R.6.]
Ichabod, s. Experience, June 26, 1690.
Isaac, s. Stephen and Hannah, Sept. 20, 1777.
Jacob, twin s. Jacob and Abigail, Sept. 18, 1815.
James, s. Josiah and Lucy, Dec. 13, 1801.
Jane, d. Josiah and Lucy, Aug. 24, 1790.
Jane, d. Josiah and Lucy, Sept. 9, 1793.
Joanna, ch. Melzar, bp. June 4, 1813. C.R.2.
Job, s. Eells and Huldah, Nov. 9, 1785.
John, s. Experience (Damen), May 7, 1687.
John, s. Josiah and Lucy, Nov. 7, 1796. [Damon, G.R.2.]
John Wade, s. Zadock and Thankful, Nov. 12, 1792.

DAMAN, Joseph, s. Reuben and Lydia, Oct. 8, 1787.
Jude Litchfield, d. Simeon and Lucy, Aug. 19, 1792.
Judith, d. John and Eliza[be]th, Dec. 13, 1784.
Levi, s. Edward and Celia, Aug. 25, 1782.
Lucinda, d. Silvanus and Mary, Oct. 14, 1777.
Lucretia, [twin] d. John and Elizabeth, Mar. 24, 1791. [Dammon, C.R.1.] [Damon, C.R.3.]
Lucy, d. Josiah and Lucy, Oct. 30, 1783.
Lucy, d. Edward and Celia, Aug. 21, 1784.
Lucy, d. Simeon and Lucy, Nov. 19, 1784.
Lucy, d. Reuben and Lydia, June 3, 1802.
Lydia, d. Silvanus and Lydia, Dec. 20, 1785.
Lydia, d. Simeon and w., bp. May 22, 1791. C.R.2.
Lydia, d. Reuben and Lydia, July 13, 1799.
Lydia, ch. Melzar, bp. July 7, 1816. C.R.2.
Martha A., d. William and Charlottee, Aug. 20, 1828.
Martin, s. Zadock and Thankful, Mar. 10, 1798. [Damon [h. Sylvia], G.R.2.]
Mary, d. Silvanus and Lydia, May 10, 1784.
Mary Collier, d. Galen and Jenne, Dec. 1, 1791.
Nancy, d. Zadock and Thankful, May 4, 1781.
Nancy, d. Josiah and Lucy, Feb. 26, 1785.
Patience, d. Experience, Apr. 6, 1696.
Polley, d. Reuben and Lydia, Oct. 10, 1784.
Rebecca, d. Silvanus and Lydia, Apr. 4, 1793.
Reuben, s. Reuben and Lydia, July 4, 1792.
Rhoda, d. Reuben and Lydia, June 12, 1780.
Rodha, d. Ichabod, bp. May 21, 1769. C.R.1.
Ruth, d. Simeon and Lucy, Oct. 4, 1790.
Ruth, d. Silvanus and Lydia, June 26, 1797.
Ruth Tilden, d. Calvin and Mercy, Dec. 3, 1795.
Ruth Tillden, d. Calvin and w., bp. May 10, 1795. C.R.2.
Sally, d. John and Elizabeth, Sept. 14, 1789.
Samuel Litchfield, s. Simeon and Lucy, Aug. 9, 1794. [Samuell Litchfield, s. Simion, C.R.2.]
Sarah, d. Silvanus and Lydia, May 12, 1795.
Sarah, d. Elijah (Damon) and Sally, Oct. 15, 1814.
Silas, s. Reuben and Lydia, July 20, 1789.
Silvanus, s. Israel and Sarah, June 12, 1756. [Dammon, C.R.1.]
Simeon, s. Simeon and Lucy, Aug. 25, 1781.
Snell, s. Zadock and Thankful, Sept. 5, 1796.
Susannah, d. Galen and w., bp. July 15, 1804. C.R.2.
Temperance, d. Silvanus and Lydia, May 24, 1788.
Thaatssy, d. Henry and Anna, May 26, 1808.

SCITUATE BIRTHS 125

DAMAN, Thankful, d. Zadock and Thankful, Oct. 20, 1783.
William, s. Silvanus and Lydia, Mar. 14, 1782.
William, s. Zadock and Thankful, Apr. 8, 1790. [Damon, G.R.2.]
Zadock, s. Zadock and Thankful, Oct. 1, 1785.
——, s. William and Charlotte, Aug. 20, 1831.

DAMEN (see Daman, Damin, Damman, Dammon, Damon),
Abigail, d. Zechariah, Oct. —, 1692.
Daniel, s. Zechariah, Mar. —, 1688.
Daniell, s. Jo[h]n, Feb. —, 1652.
Deborah, d. Jo[h]n, Apr. 25, 1645.
Ebineizer, s. John, Jan. 11, 1665.
Experance, s. John, Apr. 17, 1662.
Hannah, d. John, Dec. 2, 1672.
Hannah, d. Zechariah, Nov. —, 1694.
Hannah, d. Experience and Patience, Nov. 5, 1700.
Hannah, d. Daniell and Bathsheba, Apr. 24, 1713. [Dammon, d. Daniel and Barsheba, C.R.2.]
Icabud, s. John, Apr. 8, 1668.
John, s. Jo[h]n, Nov. 3, 1647.
John, s. Zechariah, June —, 1684.
John, s. Ichabod and Sarah, Jan. 26, 1709–10.
Margrett, d. John, July 20, 1670.
Martha, d. Zechariah, July —, 1682.
Martha, d. Zechariah (Damon) and Mehetable, Sept. 5, 1714.
Mary, d. John, July —, 1651.
Mary, d. Zechariah, Mar. —, 1690.
Mary, d. Experience and Ruth, Nov. 29, 1713.
Mehetable, d. Zechariah, Feb. —, 1696.
Ruth, d. Experience and Ruth, Aug. 4, 1712.
Sarah, d. Ichabod and Sarah, Mar. 19, 1711–12.
Silence, d. Experience and Patience, Oct. 29, 1702.
Sillance, d. John, Jan. 2, 1663.
Zachary, s. John, Feb. —, 1649.
Zechariah, s. Zechariah, June —, 1686.

DAMIN (see Daman, Damen, Damman, Dammon, Damon),
Martha, d. Zechariah, bp. June 25, 1682. C.R.2.

DAMMAN (see Daman, Damen, Damin, Dammon, Damon),
Reubin, s. Caleb (Daman) and Hannah, Feb. 13, 1759.

DAMMON (see Daman, Damen, Damin, Damman, Damon),
Abiel, s. Dan[ie]l and Jemima, bp. June 9, 1734. C.R.2.
Abigail, d. Zechariah (Damon) and Mehitabel, bp. Aug. 30, 1724. C.R.2.

DAMMON, Amos, s. Amos, bp. May 19, 1754. C.R.2.
Bathsheba, d. Danniel and Judith, bp. May 1, 1748. C.R.2.
Benjamin, s. Ebenezar (Damon) of Marshfield, bp. Mar. 26, 1738. C.R.2.
Daniel, s. Daniel and Judith, bp. Aug. 22, 1742. C.R.2.
Elijah, s. Ichabod, bp. Aug. 5, 1733. C.R.1.
Elizebeth, [ch.] John and w., bp. Sept. 21, 1788. C.R.1.
Ezekiel, ch. John and Eliz[abeth] of Marshfield, bp. Mar. 28, 1731. C.R.2.
Isaac, s. Dan[ie]ll (Damon) [s. Dan[ie]ll and Barshebah, C.R.2.], Sept. 17, 1718.
Israel, ch. Israel and Sarah, bp. Sept. 17, 1749. C.R.1.
Jael, d. Zecheriah and Mehitabel, bp. May 4, 1718. C.R.2.
Joan, d. Melzar and Bathshaba, Feb. 15, 1813.
Joanna, d. Joseph and Joanna, bp. Nov. 4, 1750. C.R.2.
John, s. John, Jan. 30, 1716.
John, ch. Jo[h]n, bp. Oct. 23, 1720. C.R.1.
John, s. Josiah, b. Dec. 24, 1752. C.R.1.
Joseph, s. Joseph, bp. Nov. 6, 1743. C.R.2.
Joseph, s. Joseph and Joanna, bp. May 18, 1746. C.R.2.
Josiah, s. Josiah, bp. June 20, 1756. C.R.1.
Judith, [ch.] John and w., bp. Sept. 21, 1788. C.R.1.
Leafa, d. Joseph and Joanna, bp. Nov. 4, 1750. C.R.2.
Leah, d. Josiah, bp. June 16, 1754. C.R.1.
Lusanna, ch. John and Eliz[abeth] of Marshfield, bp. Mar. 28, 1731. C.R.2.
Luther, s. David and Mary, bp. Sept. 21, 1755. C.R.1.
Mary, d. Zech[ariah] and Mehitabel, bp. Jan. 1, 1720–21. C.R.2.
Mercy, d. John, bp. July 22, 1722. C.R.1.
Mercy, d. John (Damon) and Elizabeth of Marshfield, bp. Apr. 28, 1723. C.R.2.
Molly, d. David, bp. July 2, 1758. C.R.1.
Rebecca, d. Zechariah and Mehitabel, bp. May 3, 1730. C.R.2.
Relief, ch. John and Eliz[abeth] of Marshfield, bp. Oct. 1, 1721. C.R.2.
Rubin, s. Ichabod, bp. Oct. 15, 1738. C.R.1.
Ruth, d. Joseph and Joanna, bp. Nov. 4, 1750. C.R.2.
Ruth, d. David, bp. May 18, 1760. C.R.1.
Sally, d. John, bp. Oct. 17, 1790. C.R.1.
Samuel, [ch.] Daniel and Sarah, bp. Apr. 15, 1750. C.R.2.
Sarah, d. Zecheriah and Mehittable, bp. May 14, 1727. C.R.2.
Sarah, ch. Israel and Sarah, bp. Sept. 17, 1749. C.R.1.
Sarah, d. Josiah, bp. Aug. 24, 1760. C.R.1.
Seth, s. Israel, bp. July 7, 1751. C.R.1.

SCITUATE BIRTHS 127

DAMMON, Temperance, ch. Jo[h]n, bp. Oct. 23, 1720. C.R.1.
Temporance, d. Jo[h]n, Mar. 19, 1718.
Thankfull, d. Experience Jr., bp. Sept. 9, 1722. C.R.1.
Zadock, s. Caleb, bp. Jan. 13, 1754. C.R.1.
Zechariah, s. John, bp. Feb. 17, 1720. C.R.1.
Zechariah, s. Zechariah and Mehitabel, bp. Aug. 25, 1723. C.R.2.
Zecheriah, s. Daniel and Jemima, bp. Dec. 6, 1731. C.R.2.

DAMON (see Daman, Damen, Damin, Damman, Dammon),
    Abbie W. [———], w. James, ———, 1818. G.R.2.
Abiel, s. Daniel and Jemima, Apr. 11, 1732.
Abigail, d. Joshua and Wealthy, Apr. 1, 1794.
Abigail, d. John Jr. and w., Feb. 2, 1818.
Abigail, d. Jacob and Abigail, Dec. 15, 1819.
Abigail Frances, ch. Galen and Serena, Dec. 26, 1840.
Abner, s. Ichabad Jr. and Ruth, June 30, 1766.
Adeline, d. John Jr. and w., Feb. 20, 181[blotted] [1810].
Albion, ch. Daniel and Lydia, Oct. 3, 1836.
Alexander, s. Doane and Sally, Oct. 5, 1816.
Alexander Doane, ch. Alexander and Mary B., Sept. 8, 1840.
Alfred, s. Isaac B. and Mary Ann, Mar. 6, 1836.
Alice [? m.] [Mar. —, 1767]. G.R.14.
Almira, d. William Jr. and Charlotte, Oct. 7, 1822.
Almira, d. Galen and Serena, July 4, 1833.
Alonzo W., s. Davis, housewright, and Lucy, Feb. 11, 1847.
Alpheus, ch. Daniel and Lydia, Sept. 11, 1839.
Amos, s. Daniel and Jemima, Aug. 1, 1729. [Dammon, s.
    Daniel and Jemimah, C.R.2.]
Andrew Jackson, ch. John C. and Polly, June 14, 1843. [" 39th
    Regt. Mass. Vol's.," G.R.2.]
Anna A., d. Joshua S., farmer (b. Hanover), and Elizabeth W.
    (b. Braintree), Mar. 13, 1849, in S. Scituate.
Anna Cook, d. Henry and Anna, Nov. 10, 1813.
Arabella A., ch. Austin and Lydia A. [Feb. —, 1845]. G.R.15.
Aseneth, d. Ichabaud Jr. and Ruth, Sept. 3, 1751. [Asenath
    Dammon, d. Ichabod 3d, C.R.1.]
Austin, s. Josiah Jr. and Mary, May 26, 1818. [[h. Lydia A.]
    G.R.15.]
Bailey Daniels, s. Isaac B. and Mary Ann, Nov. 20, 1834.
Barshua, d. Daniel and Jemima, Apr. 30, 1722. [Barsheba
    Dammon, C.R.2.]
Bathsheba, d. Joshua and Wealthy, Dec. 4, 1791.
Betsey, d. Luther and Alice, Aug. 9, 1806.
Caleb, s. Ichabod and Judah, Apr. 1, 1722.
Caleb, ch. Ichabod Jr., bp. July 12, 1730. C.R.1.

DAMON, Caleb, s. Caleb and Hannah, Aug. 11, 1749.
Caleb, s. Amos, bp. Apr. 5, 1752. C.R.2.
Caleb Lincoln, s. Caleb and Sally, Mar. 24, 1826.
Calven, s. Zach[a]r[iah] Jr. and Anna (Lenthal), Mar. 2, 1760.
Calvin, s. Galen and Jenne, Feb. 3, 1802. [[h. Lucy B. (Clapp)] G.R.14.]
Calvin, s. Calvin and Jane, July 24, 1818.
Calvin A., ch. Calvin and Lucy, May 8, 1834.
Caroline (Dam[o]n), d. Galen and Serena, May 5, 1831.
Caroline A., d. William and Charlotte, July 29, 1835.
Celia, d. Harris and Ruth T., Oct. 17, 1819.
Celia Sylvester, d. Harris and Ruth T., Oct. 17, 1819.
Charles, s. William and Agatha, Mar. 18, 1812. [[h. Polly] G.R.14.]
Charles, ch. James and Sally, May 1, 1841.
Charles Henry, s. Isaac N. and Judith L., Aug. 19, 1818.
Charles Henry, s. Galen Jr. and Serena, Mar. 22, 1821.
Charles Henry, s. John 2d and Almira, Apr. 12, 1839.
Charles Henry, ch. Charles and Polly, Nov. 16, 1840.
Charlotte, d. William and Charlotte, Jan. 29, 1825.
Clarrissa, twin d. Sam[ue]ll and w., bp. May 15, 1791. C.R.2.
Daniel, s. Joshua and Wealthy, June 2, 1808.
Daniel Edwin, ch. Daniel and Lydia, Aug. 2, 1829.
Daniell, s. Daniell, Apr. 23, 1716. [Daniel Dammon, s. Daniel and Barshebah, C.R.2.]
David, s. Experience and Ruth, Apr. 29, 1717.
David, ch. Ruth, wid., bp. Oct. 1, 1732. C.R.1.
David, s. Robert and Mary, bp. Sept. 30, 1753. C.R.2.
David, s. Luther and Alice, Nov. 28, 1799.
Davis, s. Elijah and Sally, July 5, 1812. [[h. Lucy (Damon)] [h. Ruth (Damon)] G.R.14.]
Deborah, d. John and Temperance, Jan. 25, 1728.
Deborah, d. Jo[h]n, bp. Oct. 10, 1731. C.R.1.
Deborah, d. Jo[h]n and Temperance, May 14, 1734.
Doane [dup. Daman], s. Josiah and Lucy, Feb. 14, 1792.
Doane, s. Henry and Anna, Sep[t]. 15, 1826.
Edward, s. Zacher[iah] Jr. [Zech[ariah], C.R.2.] and Anna (Lenthall), Apr. 19, 1755.
Edwin White, s. John 2d and Almira, Apr. 8, 1837. ["A member of Co. C. U.S. Engineers," G.R.2.]
Eells, s. Zach[a]r[iah] Jr. and Anna (Lenthall), Feb. 12, 1758.
Eleanor Curtis, d. Hanary and Elanor, Dec. 15, 1803. [Elenor Curtis, ch. Henry, C.R.1.]
Elisabeth, d. Amos, bp. June 1, 1755. C.R.2.
Eliza Ann, d. Galen and Serena, June 6, 1827.

DAMON, Elizabeth Calief, ch. James S. and Elizabeth, Apr. 5, 1828.
Elizabeth Cudworth, d. Henry (Daman) and Anna, Oct. 4, 1809.
Elizabeth J[osephine], d. Abigail, Nov. 24, 1846.
Elva Josephine, d. Sylvanus and Caroline, Mar. 18, 1849.
Emeline, d. John 2d and Rebecca, Mar. 5, 1828.
Ensign Barnes, s. Joshua Jr. and Matilda, Dec. 2, 1829.
Eunice (see Unice).
Eunice Bowker, d. J[acob] and Abigail, Nov. 18, 1825.
Eveline Jane, ch. Calvin and Lucy, Apr. 11, 1830.
Experience (see Sparance).
Franklin, s. Henry and Anna, May 1, 1821. [[h. Jerusha] G.R.6.]
Franklin Jacobs, s. Isaac N. and Judith L., Apr. 10, 1826.
Freeman, s. John Jr. and w., Apr. 18, 1801.
Freeman, s. Jacob and Abigail, Aug. 9, 1822.
Galen, s. Zach[a]r[iah] and Anna (Lenthal), Sept. 25, 1766.
Galen, s. Galen Jr. and Serena, Apr. 20, 1819.
Galen Francis, d. Galen and Serena, July 18, 1836.
George, s. Galen Jr. and Serena, Mar. 22, 1823.
George Bates, s. Nathaniel and Lucy, June 9, 1828.
George F., ch. George and Sarah, Aug. 6, 1841, in Hanover.
George W., s. William and Charlotte, Mar. 27, 1833.
Georgianna, d. Franklin, sail maker, and Jerusha, Sept. 13, 1845.
Hannah, d. Caleb and Hannah, Dec. 28, 1747. [Dammon, C.R.1.]
Hannah, d. Israel, bp. Apr. 15, 1753. C.R.1.
Hannah, d. W[illia]m, bp. June 1, 1755. C.R.2.
Hannah Hayden, d. Isaac B. and Mary Ann E., Dec. 1, 1816.
Hannah Loring, d. Isaac N. and Judith L., Dec. 19, 1815.
Hannah S. [———], w. John, —— [1816]. G.R.2.
Heman S., s. Isaac B. and Mary Ann E., Sept. 7, 1826.
Henry [dup. Daman], s. Josiah and Lucy, Apr. 14, 1780. [Capt. Henry Damon [h. Eleanor], G.R.6.]
Henry Wade, s. Joshua Jr. and Matilda, Apr. 27, 1827.
Hiram, s. Doane and Sally, Jan. 26, 1818.
Horace James, s. Isaac N. and Judith L., Dec. 17, 1832.
Hosea, s. Elijah and Sally, Apr. 29, 1819. [[h. Martha J.] G.R.14.]
Howard, s. Galen and Jenne, Feb. 11, 1799. [Daman, C.R.2.]
Howard, ch. James S. and Elizabeth, Jan. 20, 1840.
Howard F., ch. Calvin and Lucy, Apr. 6, 1832.
[I]chabad, s. Ichabad Jr. and Ruth, Jan. 14, 1764. [Echabod, s. Echabod, C.R.1.]
Ichabod, s. Ichabod and Judah, Nov. —, 1724.
Ichabod, ch. Ichabod Jr., bp. July 12, 1730. C.R.1.
Isaac, s. Isaac and Lydia, June 13, 1748. [Dammon, s. Isaack and Lydya, C.R.2.]

DAMON, Isaac Baker, s. Isaac B. and Mary Ann E., June 20, 1821.
Isaac Newton, s. Isaac N. and Judith L., Apr. 25, 1813.
Israel, s. Ichabod and Judah, Nov. 17, 1719.
Israel, ch. Ichabod Jr., bp. July 12, 1730. C.R.1.
Israel [dup. Daman], ch. Will[ia]m and Agatha, June 17, 1807.
Israel Davis, ch. Israel [dup. yeoman, second dup. farmer] and Susan W. [second dup. omits W.] (Farrington), May 9, 1844.
Jacob, s. John and Unice, Aug. 19, 1783.
Jael, d. Zachary (Dammon) and Mehetable, Mar. 19, 1717.
James, s. John 2d and Rebecca, Aug. 10, 1819. [[h. Abbie W.] G.R.2.]
James Doane, s. James and Sally, May 8, 1827.
James Sullivan, s. Galen and Jenne, Feb. 19, 1806.
Jane, d. Galen and Jenne, Apr. 2, 1812.
Jane, d. Calvin and Jane, Aug. 8, 1816, in Charleston.
Jane Tilden, d. Harris and Ruth T., Oct. 18, 1827.
Jefferson, s. Joshua and Wealthy, Oct. 19, 1802.
Jefferson, s. Jacob and Abigail, Aug. 16, 1817.
Jemima, d. Daniel and Jemima, Mar. 9, 1723. [Dammon, d. Dan[ie]l and Jemimah, C.R.2.]
Jemimah, d. Amos, bp. June 20, 1756. C.R.2.
Jerusha [———], w. Franklin, ———, 1820. G.R.6.
Jesse, s. James and Sally, Oct. 25, 1834.
Jesse, s. James and Sally, June 29, 1836.
Joanna, d. Experience and Ruth, May 4, 1722.
John, s. Daniel and Judiah, Mar. 26, 1744 "N. S." [Dammon, s. Daniel and Judith, C.R.2.]
John, s. John and Unice, July 26, 1774.
John, s. Josiah and Lucy, Dec. 7, 1795.
John Bryant, s. John 2d and Almira, July 11, 1835.
John Cudworth, s. Josiah Jr. and Elizabeth, July 8, 1814.
John J., s. John Jr. and w., Dec. 8, 1799.
John Martin, ch. Martin and Sylvia, Apr. 2, 1839.
Jonathan, s. Experience and Ruth, Jan. 9, 1725.
Jonathan, ch. Ruth, wid., bp. Oct. 1, 1732. C.R.1.
[Jo]nathan, s. Ichabad Jr. and Ruth, Dec. 6, 1761.
Jonathan, s. Echabod, bp. July 31, 1763. C.R.1.
Joseph, s. Daniel and Barshua, Dec. 16, 1720. [Dammon, s. Daniel and Barshebah, C.R.2.]
Joseph, s. William and Agatha, Oct. 28, 1809.
Joseph, s. James and Sally, Feb. 23, 1838.
Joshua, s. Joshua and Wealthy, Apr. 14, 1797.
Joshua F., s. Israel, farmer, and Susan W., Oct. 13, 1846.
Joshua Flagg, s. Joshua Jr. and Matilda, Sept. 9, 1824.

DAMON, Josiah, s. Ichabod and Sarah, Dec. 20, 1714.
Josiah [dup. Daman], s. Josiah and Lucy, July 7, 1788
Josiah, ch. John C. and Polly, July 13, 1839.
Judith, ch. Ichabod Jr., bp. July 12, 1730. C.R.1.
Judith, d. Joshua and Wealthy, Nov. 26, 1786.
Judith Sparance, d. Daniel and Mahala, Sept. 19, 1823.
Julia, d. Galen and Serena, Mar. 11, 1830.
Julia Ann, d. Harris and Ruth T., Dec. 4, 1828.
Julia Ann, ch. James S. and Elizabeth, Oct. 10, 1836.
Keziah, d. Ichabad Jr. and Ruth, Apr. 9, 1754. [Dammon, d. Ichabod 3d, C.R.1.]
Lazrus Bowker, s. Galen and Jenne, Feb. 13, 1797. [Lazerus Bowker Daman, C.R.2.]
Levi, s. Harris and Ruth T., Jan. 17, 1821.
Levi Harris, s. Harris and Ruth T., Nov. 9, 1823.
Lincoln D., s. Sylvanus, sailor, and Caroline, Nov. 23 [1845].
Lucinda, twin d. Sam[ue]ll and w., bp. May 15, 1791. C.R.2.
Lucinda F., d. Luther, shoemaker, and Lucy, Aug. 15, 1849, in S. Scituate.
Lucius, s. James, mariner, and Sarah [dup. Sally], Jan. 20 [dup. Jan. 19], 1844.
Lucretia, d. John Jr. and Lucretia, Dec. 11, 1822.
Lucy, d. Isaac, bp. May 15, 1757. C.R.2.
Lucy, twin ch. William and Agatha, Feb. 8, 1805.
Lucy [———], w. Luther [July —, 1809]. G.R.14.
Lucy, d. Luther and Alice, June 9, 1816. [w. Davis Damon, G.R.14.]
Lucy, d. Elijah and Sally, Feb. 23, 1817.
Lucy A. [dup. Augusta], d. Charles, farmer, and Patty [dup. Polly], June 24, [18]25.
Lucy A., d. Davis, housewright, and Lucy, July 22, 1845.
Lucy Doane, d. Henry and Anna, Oct. 20, 1815.
Lucy Judson, d. Nathaniel and Lucy, July 19, 1826.
Lucy S., d. John Jr. and w., Oct. 24, 1798.
Luther, s. Luther and Alice, Sept. 10, 1801. [[h. Lucy] G.R.14.]
Lydia, d. Isaac and Lydia, Apr. 18, 1751.
Lydia, twin ch. William and Agatha, Feb. 8, 1805.
Lydia A. [———], w. Austin [Mar. —, 1825]. G.R.15.
Lydia A., ch. George and Sarah, Feb. 15, 1844.
Lydia James, ch. Daniel and Lydia, Jan. 21, 1834.
Lydia Rogers, d. Caleb and Sally, May 11, 1827.
Lydia Thomas Jones, d. Melzar and Bathsheba, June 4, 1816.
Mahala, d. Joshua and Wealthy, Apr. 23, 1789. [w. Daniel Damon, G.R.18.]

DAMON, Mahala, d. Daniel and Mahala, Sept. 6, 1818.
Mahittable, d. Zackariah Jr., June 18, 1716. [Mehetabel Dammon, d. Zechariah, C.R.2.]
Malina Cook Farrow, d. Allen Jr., farmer, and Rachel (Binney), July 27, 1846.
Malzar, s. John and Unice, Apr. 4, 1776.
Marcus Morton, s. James and Sally, July 16, 1830.
Maria L., ch. Austin and Lydia A., —— [1847]. G.R.15.
Marsena Webb, s. Josiah Jr. and Mary, Jan. 9, 1820.
Martha, d. Experience and Ruth, Dec. 17, 1715.
Martha [————], w. G. H., —— [1827]. C.R.1.
Martha J. [————], w. Hosea, ——, 1823. G.R.14.
Mary, d. John and Temperence, Jan. 5, 1721.
Mary, d. Robert, bp. May 10, 1752. C.R.2.
Mary Ann Elizabeth, d. I[saac] B. and Mary Ann E., Apr. 7, 1824.
Mary Bryant, d. Luther and Alice, June 21, 1804.
Mary Collier, ch. James S. and Elizabeth, Aug. 12, 1831.
Mary Eells, d. Harris and Ruth T., Aug. 1, 1822.
Mary Eells, d. Harris and Ruth T., Dec. 19, 1825.
Mary Eliza, ch. Alexander and Mary B., —— [rec. after ch. b. Sept. 8, 1840].
Mary Jane, d. William Jr. and Charlotte, Oct. 18, 1820.
Mary L., d. Harris and Ruth T., Mar. 11, 1831.
Mary Sophia, d. Nathaniel and Lucy, Oct. 19, 1830.
Mehetable, d. Calvin and Jane, Sept. 9, 1820.
Mehitable (see Mahittable).
Merril, d. John Jr. and w., Apr. 20, 1808.
Naby, d. John and Unice, Apr. 22, 1778.
Nancy, d. Luther and Alice, Apr. 29, 1810.
Nancy, d. John Jr. and w., Feb. 10, 1815.
Nancy Watson, d. William and Charlotte, Nov. 1, 1841.
Nathan, s. Jo[h]n and Temperance, July 17, 1724.
Nathaniel James, s. Nathaniel and Lucy, Sept. 28, 1823.
Nath[anie]ll, s. Zacher[iah] Jr. and Anna (Lenthal), Feb. 14, 1750. [Nathaniel Dammon, s. Zachariah Jr. and Anna (Lenthal), C.R.2.]
Obidiah, s. John Jr. and w., Nov. 6, 1813.
Pheba, d. Henry and Anna, July 20, 1819.
Philenda Litchfield, d. Leah Jr., May 9, 1781.
Polly, d. John and Unice, Aug. 20, 1780.
Polly, d. John Jr. and w., Jan. 22, 1806.
Priscilla, ch. James S. and Elizabeth, Sept. 27, 1842.
Quincy Adams, s. Isaac N. and Judith L., Dec. 17, 1828.
Rachel, d. Experience and Ruth, July 17, 1718.

DAMON, Rachel, ch. Ruth, wid., bp. Oct. 1, 1732. C.R.1.
Rachel Binney, d. Henry and Anna, July 5, 1823.
Rebekah, d. John 2d and Rebecca, Nov. 14, 1824.
Reuben (see Ruben).
Robert, s. Daniel and Jemima, Mar. 3, 1726. [Dammon, s. Daniel and Jemimah, C.R.1.]
Robert Ensign, s. James and Sally, Nov. 4, 1828.
Ruben, s. Ichabod and Judah, Aug. 30, 1736.
Ruth, d. Ichabad Jr. and Ruth, June 10, 1749.
Ruth, d. Ichabad 3d and Ruth, bp. July 1, 1750. C.R.1.
Ruth, d. Luther and Alice, Jan. 13, 1798. [w. Davis Damon, G.R.14].
Ruth T. [———], w. Harris [Dec. —, 1794]. G.R.14.
Sally [———], w. Elijah, ———, 1784. G.R.14.
Sally, d. Doane and Sally, July 5, 1819.
Samuel, s. Calvin and Jane, Dec. 6, 1822.
Sarah, d. Henry and Anna, July 5, 1817.
Sarah, d. Doane and Sally, Aug. 7, 1821.
Sarah Allen, d. James and Sally, Oct. 2, 1832.
Sarah L., d. Nathaniel and Lucy, May 31, 1833.
Sarah L., d. Nathaniel and Lucy, June 5, 1835, in Marshfield.
Sarah M., ch. George and Sarah, Sept. 29, 1839, in Hanover.
Serena, d. Galen Jr. and Serena, June 16, 1825.
Seth, s. Experience Jr. and Thankfull, Mar. 1, 1725.
Seth, s. Experience, bp. Sept. 28, 1726. C.R.1.
Silvanus, s. Isaac B. and Mary Ann E., Nov. 28, 1814.
Simeon, s. Dan[ie]l, bp. Aug. 30, 1752. C.R.2.
Simeon, ch. Daniel and Lydia, July 9, 1831.
Solomon Loring, s. Isaac N. and Judith L., Sept. 30, 1811.
Sophia J. [———], w. William, May 5, 1821. G.R.2.
Sparance, d. Joshua and Wealthy, July 3, 1799.
Stephen, s. Isaac and Lydia, Sept. 3, 1744. [Dammon, C.R.2.]
Stephen, s. Zacher[iah] Jr. and Anna (Lenthall), Jan. 24, 1753.
Susan, d. Galen and Jenne, Mar. 2, 1804.
Susan, ch. James S. and Elizabeth, July 17, 1834.
[Su]sanna, d. Ichabad Jr. and Ruth, Feb. 17, 1759. [Susanna Dammon, d. Ichabod 3d, C.R.1.]
Susannah Collamore, d. Elijah and Sally, May 30, 1824.
Sylvia, ch. Martin and Sylvia, Dec. 21, 1842.
Tamsin Dunbar, d. Isaac N. and Judith L., Oct. 23, 1823.
Thankful W., d. William and Charlotte, Oct. 29, 1838.
Thankfull, d. Experience Jr. and Thankfull, May —, 1721.
Thirza, d. John 2d and Rebecca, July 21, 1818.
Thirza C. [C., written in pencil], d. Josiah Jr. and Mary, July 3, 1822.

DAMON, Truman, s. John Jr. and w., Feb. 13, 1804.
Unice, d. John and Unice, Feb. 23, 1772.
Virgil, s. Josiah Jr. and Mary, Sept. 27, 1823.
Walter Lincoln, s. Caleb L., shoemaker, and Abigail, Dec. 13, 1846.
Wealthy, d. Joshua and Wealthy, Aug. 19, 1783.
William, s. Ichabad Jr. and Ruth, Oct. 18, 1756. [Dammon, s. Ichabod 3d, C.R.1.]
William [dup. Daman], s. Will[ia]m and Agatha, June 12, 1803. [[h. Sophia J.] G.R.2.]
William, s. Israel, —— [1841]. C.R.1.
William Rogers, s. Isaac B. and Mary Ann, Apr. 20, 1829, in Marshfield, ["in Civil war," G.R.6].
Xoe, d. John 2d and Rebecca, Sept. 5, 1822.
Zacharyer, s. Zacher[iah] Jr. and Anna (Lenthall), Sept. 27, 1749. [Zechariah Dammon, s. Zechariah and Anna (Lenthall), C.R.2.]
[torn]ln, s. Lucy, Oct. 30, 1795.
—— [worn], ch. Ruth, wid., bp. Oct. 1, 1732. C.R.1.
——, ch. Israel and Susan W. (Farrington), Feb. 20, 1842.
——, d. William, sailor, and Mary, Apr. 8, 1844.
——, s. Caleb, shoemaker, and Abigail, Sept. 6, 1849.

DANA, Charles, ch. Henry B. and Harriett C., Nov. 17, 1834.
Emily, ch. Henry B. and Harriett C., Nov. 6, 1838.
Francis, ch. Henry B. and Harriett C., Sept. 17, 1831.
Harriet S., ch. Henry B. and Harriett C., Mar. 14, 1822.
Henry, ch. Henry B. and Harriett C., Mar. 27, 1816.
Henry, ch. Henry B. and Harriett C., Aug. 14, 1825.
Lucy, ch. Henry B. and Harriett C., Aug. 2, 1829.
William B., ch. Henry B. and Harriett C., Jan. 27, 1817.

DARBY (see Dorby).

DAVIS (see Daviss), Elizabeth, d. Trustrum, Mar. 20, 1695–6.

DAVISS (see Davis), Nicolas, s. Nicholas (Davis) and Grace of Kingston, bp. Aug. 3, 1729. C.R.2.

DAWES (see Daws), Ebenezer [s. Rev. Ebenezer and Betty], "born after his father's decease," ——, 1792.
William [dup. Daws], s. Rev. Ebenezer and Betty, Apr. 9, 1790.

DAWS (see Dawes), Ebenezer, s. Rev. Ebenezer and Betsey, Mar. 1, 1791.

SCITUATE BIRTHS 135

DEANE (see Deans), Charles Frederick, s. Rev. Samuel and Stella, Mar. 21, 1813.
Helen Maria, d. Rev. Samuel and Stella, Apr. 9, 1819.
Helen Maria, d. Rev. Samuel and Stella, Apr. 21, 1821. [w. Dennis Rockwell, G.R.14.]
Helen Maria, ch. Rev. Sam[ue]l, bp. Sept. 1, 1822. C.R.2.
John Milton, s. Rev. Samuel and Stella, June 13, 1816.
John Milton, ch. Rev. Samuel, bp. Nov. 9, 1817. C.R.2.
Martha Phillips, d. Rev. Samuel and Stella, June 22, 1811.
Martha Phillips [?], ch. Rev. Sam[ue]l, bp. Aug. 2, 1812. C.R.2.
Samuel, Rev. [h. Stella], Mar. 31, 1784, in Mansfield. G.R.14.
Stella [———], w. Rev. Samuel, ——— [1787]. G.R.14.

DEANS (see Deane), Ephraim, s. Jonas, May 22, 1694.
Thomas, s. Jonas, Oct. 29, 1691.

DEGON (see Dagon), Thomas, s. Richard, June 14, 1694.

DELANO, Alfred Otis, ch. Benjamin F. and Jane, ———. [———, 1839, G.R.14.]
Benjamin [h. Mary (Brooks)], June 24, 1746, in Pembroke. G.R.14.
Benj[ami]n Franklin, s. William and Sarah, Sept. 17, 1809. [[h. Jane Foster] G.R.14.]
Benja[min] Franklin, ch. W[illia]m dec'd and Sarah, bp. Oct. 6, 1822. C.R.2.
Charlotte, ch. Benj[amin] F. and Jane, ———, 1845, in Portsmouth, N.H. G.R.14.
Edward Hart, s. William and Sarah, Aug. 12, 1811. ["Naval Constructor at Pensacola, Norfolk & Charlestown Navy Yards" [h. Mary Randall (James)], G.R.14.]
Edw[ar]d Hart, ch. W[illia]m dec'd and Sarah, bp. Oct. 6, 1822. C.R.2.
Hannah Maria, ch. William H. and Sarah, June 22, 1835. [Hannah Mary, G.R.14.]
Lucy Snow, d. William and Sarah, Sept. 14, 1815. [d. William and Sarah (Hart), ———, 1814, G.R.14.]
Lucy Snow, ch. W[illia]m dec'd and Sarah, bp. Oct. 6, 1822. C.R.2.
Mary, d. Benja[min] and Mary, Dec. 15, 1776.
Mary, d. William and Sarah, Nov. 7, 1803.
Mary Elisabeth, d. Will[i]am and w., bp. May 20, 1804. C.R.2. [Mary Elizabeth, d. William and Sarah (Hart), ———, 1803, G.R.14.]
Mary Frances, ch. William H. and Sarah, Jan. 6, 1832.
Prudence Clark, d. William and Sarah, May 25, 1807. [d. William and Sarah (Hart), ———, 1806, G.R.14.]

DELANO, Sarah, d. Benja[min] and Mary, Mar. 30, 1782. [[w. Samuel Foster] Mar. 30, 1783, P.R.5.]
Sarah, d. William and Sarah [Sarah (Hart), G.R.14.], Jan. 18, 1813.
Sarah, ch. W[illia]m dec'd and Sarah, bp. Oct. 6, 1822. C.R.2.
Sarah Ann, ch. William H. and Sarah, July 6, 1829.
Sarah Ann, ch. W[illia]m H., bp. July 1, 1832. C.R.2.
William, s. Benja[min] and Mary, Oct. 4, 1770. [[h. Sarah (Hart)] G.R.14.]
William, s. William and Sarah, Nov. 3, 1804.
William Hart, s. William and w., bp. Oct. —, 1804. C.R.2.
———, d. Benjamin F., shipwright, and Jane, Apr. 22, 1844.

DEXTER, Abigail H., d. Thomas and Abigail, June 29, 1818.

DILL, William A. [Dec. —, 1848]. G.R.6.

DILLINGHAM, Mariah, d. Tho[ma]s and Remembranc, July 17, 1764.
Thomas, s. Tho[ma]s and Remembranc, Oct. 18, 1769.

DOANE (see Done), Henry, s. Joshua and Lydia, May 12, 1820.
Horace William, s. Joshua and Lydia, May 23, 1816.
John, s. John and Lucy, Nov. 6, 1765. [Done, C.R.1.]
John, s. Joshua and Lydia, Dec. 1, 1829.
John, ——— [1831]. G.R.2.
Joshua, s. John and Lucy, July 20, 1793.
Lucy A., d. Luther and Lucy, Sept. 2, 1847.
Lydia, d. Joshua and Lydia, Mar. 19, 1824.
Maria, d. John and Lucy, Aug. 22, 1800.
Nancy, d. John and Lucy, May 27, 1787.
Thomas Stoddard, s. Joshua and Lydia, Apr. 1, 1831.
———, d. Horace, marriner, and Susan, Apr. 3 [184–].
———, d. Horace, sailor, and Susan, Apr. 1, 1848.

DODSON, Anthony, s. Jonathan, Sept. 27, 1696.
Deborah, d. Jonathan, Mar. 12, 1698.
Gershom, s. Anthony, Feb. 14, 1653.
Gershom, s. Jonathan, Dec. 8, 1704.
Hannah, d. Jonathan, Mar. 21, 1703.
Jonathan, s. Anthony, Dec. 20, 1659.
Jonathan, s. Jonathan, Mar. 14, 1695.
Margarite, d. Antony, bp. Nov. 23, 1656. C.R.2.
Mary, d. Jonathan, May 12, 1699.
Sarah, d. Anthony, Aug. 26, 1652.
Sarah, d. Jonathan, July 15, 1701.

DOGGET (see Doggett), Experience, d. Jo[h]n, bp. Sept. 11, 1738. C.R.1.
Echabod, s. John, bp. Dec. 16, 1770. C.R.1.
Jemima, d. Jo[h]n, bp. May 31, 1730. C.R.1.
John, s. Jo[h]n, bp. May 14, 1731. C.R.1.
Thomas, s. Jo[h]n, bp. Sept. 10, 1745. C.R.1.

DOGGETT (see Dogget), Abigail, d. Capt. Jo[h]n, bp. Aug. 7, 1757. C.R.1.
[A]bner, s. John and Abigal, Aug. 16, 1749. [Dogget, s. John and Abigail, C.R.1.]
David, s. John, bp. July 23, 1732. C.R.1.
David, s. Jo[h]n, bp. July 14, 1734. C.R.1.
[E]benezer, s. John and Abigal, July 9, 1752. [Dogget, C.R.1.]
Jemima, d. Capt. Jo[h]n, bp. Oct. 3, 1736. C.R.1.
John, s. Jo[h]n, bp. Sept. 22, 1754. C.R.1.

DOHERTY (see Dorothy, Doughtie, Doughty, Dougty, Douty), Cornelius, Dec. 20, 1815, in Co. Donegal, Ire. G.R.10.
Mary [———], w. Daniel [Nov. —, 1846]. G.R.10.

DOLBY (see Dalby), Savillion Fuller [dup. Dalby], s. John [dup. adds S.], carpenter (b. England), and Cynthia [dup. adds B.], May 22, 1849.

DONE (see Doane), Ginny, ch. John, bp. Sept. 1, 1776. C.R.1.
James, ch. John, bp. Sept. 25, 1775. C.R.1.
Joshua, ch. John, bp. Sept. 25, 1775. C.R.1.
Lucy, ch. John, bp. Oct. 6, 1765. C.R.1.
Nancy, ch. John, bp. Sept. 1, 1776. C.R.1.

DORBY, Eleazer, s. Eleazer [(Dorbey) C.R.1.] Jr. and Mary, Mar. 31, 1722.
Jonathan, Rev., Sept. 14, ———.

DOROTHY (see Doherty, Doughtie, Doughty, Dougty, Douty), Charles, s. John and Molley, Dec. 7, 1777.
Eunice, d. John and Molley, Dec. 7, 1775.
John, s. John and Molley, June 10, 1770.
Joseph, s. John and Molley, Feb. 3, 1772.
Molley, d. John and Molley, Jan. 13, 1767.
Prudence, d. John and Molley, Apr. 15, 1773.

DORR, Lucy E. [———], w. William [May —, 1848]. G.R.14.

DOTEN, Lydia Robbins, d. James and Harriet, Mar. 21, 1833.

DOUGHTIE (see Doherty, Dorothy, Doughty, Dougty, Douty), Mary, d. James, June 23, 1650.

DOUGHTY (see Doherty, Dorothy, Doughtie, Dougty, Douty), Elizabeth, d. James, Nov. 5, 1654.
James, s. James, Feb. 21, 1651.
Lidia, d. James, Feb. 14, 1658. [Lydia, c.r.2.]
Martha, d. James, bp. Apr. 12, 1657. C.R.2.
Robard, s. James, Feb. 14, 1667.
Sammuell, s. James, Sept. 29, 1664.
Sarah, d. James, Apr. 2, 1662.
Susana, d. James, Feb. 15, 1670.
Susanna, d. Thom[as], negro, bp. July 15, 1722. C.R.1.

DOUGLAS (see Douglass), [B]etsey, d. John and Lydia, June 17, 1772.
[E]lijah, s. John and Lydia, Sept. 29, 1770.
Lendall, s. John and Lydia, Feb. 28, 1768.
[torn]ry [Mary], d. John and Lydia, Sept. 31 [*sic*], 1773.

DOUGLASS (see Douglas), [L]ydia, d. John (Douglas) and Lydia, Sept. 13, 1766.

DOUGTY (see Doherty, Dorothy, Doughtie, Doughty, Douty), Thomas, s. Susanna, negro, bp. Aug. 22, 1725. C.R.1.

DOUTY (see Doherty, Dorothy, Doughtie, Doughty, Dougty), Judith, ch. [Thom[as] and] Susanna, negro, bp. Dec. 4, 1720. C.R.1.
Margaret, ch. [Thom[as] and] Susanna, negro, bp. Dec. 4, 1720. C.R.1.
Priscilla, ch. [Thom[as] and] Susanna, negro, bp. Dec. 4, 1720. C.R.1.
Sarah, d. Susanna, bp. June 9, 1727. C.R.1.
Susanna, ch. [Thom[as] and] Susanna, negro, bp. Dec. 4, 1720. C.R.1.

DRAKE, Beza W., s. Beza, laborer, and Elizabeth, Nov. 3, 1844.

DREW, Joseph S., —— [1815]. C.R.1.
Theodore Clement, s. Joseph, ship carpenter (b. Duxbury), and Lucy, May 14, 1844, in Medford.
——, s. Joseph S., ship joiner, and Lucy, Apr. 26, 1845.

DUMBER (see Dunbar, Dunber), ——, s. James H., cooper, and Mabel T., Apr. 25 [184–], in Boston.

DUNBAR (see Dumber, Dunber), Atwood Litchfield, s. Cyrus and Sally, Apr. 9, 1805. [[h. Mercy] G.R.6.]
Betsey, d. Cyrus and Sally, Mar. 13, 1810. [Betsy, C.R.1.]
Cyrus, s. Cyrus and Sally, July 3, 1808 [*sic*, see Polly]. [bp. July 10, 1807, C.R.1.]
Cyrus Hood, s. Cyrus and Sally, Feb. 29, 1812.

DUNBAR, David [h. Margaret (Bennet)], ——, 1731. G.R.6.
Elisha, s. Elisha and Fanny, Oct. 29, 1784.
Eliza, w. Seth Webb, —— [1795]. G.R.6.
Eliza, d. [Capt. Jesse, C.R.1.] Jesse and Sally, Mar. 28, 1797. [w. Capt. Seth Webb, G.R.6.]
Frederic, [ch.] Ezekiel and w., bp. Jan. 18, 1778. C.R.1.
Hosea, s. Cyrus and Sally, Dec. 4, 1817.
James Hervey, s. Cyrus and Sally, May 10, 1814.
James Hervey, s. Cyrus and Sally, Apr. 7, 1815. [James Harvey, C.R.1.] [James H. [h. Mabel T.], G.R.7.]
Jesse Jr., ——, 1791. G.R.6.
Jesse, s. Jesse and Sally, Sept. 9, 1792.
John Wetherell, s. Jesse and Sally, Jan. 8, 1799. [John Witherell, s. Capt. Jesse, C.R.1.]
Josephine, d. Cyrus H., seaman, and Lucy [dup. adds A.], Oct. 13, 1848.
Lucy Atwood, ch. Cyrus H. and Lucy A., July 27, 1840.
Mabel Thomas, ch. James H. and Mabel T., Dec. 6, 1837. [Dec. 9, G.R.7.]
Mabel Thomas, ch. James H. and Mabel T., Nov. 29, 1839.
Mabel Thomas, ch. Cyrus H. and Lucy A., Oct. 3, 1842.
Olivia (see —— Dunbar).
Orianna, ch. Cyrus H. [dup. Jr., omits H., sailor] and Lucy A., July 13, 1845.
Polly, d. Cyrus and Sally, May 20, 1808 [*sic*, see Cyrus]. [bp. July 1, 1808, C.R.1.]
Sally, d. Jesse and Sally, Aug. 7, 1789. [Sarah, G.R.5.]
Sally, d. Cyrus and Sally, Apr. 11, 1803.
Sally Dilino, d. Jesse and Sally, Jan. 24, 1801. [Sally Delano, d. Capt. Jesse, C.R.1.]
Sarah, d. [Capt. J., C.R.1.] Jesse and Sally, Feb. 13, 1802.
Sarah Ann, d. Bethana, Dec. 20, 1827.
William Jr., "Co. A. 35 Mass. Vols," —— [1828]. G.R.2.
——, ch. James H., cooper, and Mabel T., May 5, 1844. [Olivia, G.R.7.]

DUNBER (see Dumber, Dunbar), Amos, s. Benja[min] and Rebecca, Mar. 4, 1751.
Annear, d. Benja[min] and Rebecca, Sept. 10, 1747.
Bennit, s. David and Margreat, Sept. 15, 1766.
David, s. David and Margreat, Nov. 20, 1756.
Elisha, s. Benja[min] and Rebecca, June 13, 1743.
Elisha, s. David and Margreat, July 31, 1762.
Ezekel, s. Benja[min] and Rebecca, Apr. 9, 1749.

DUNBER, Jesse, s. David and Margreat, Aug. 28, 1760.
Lucy, twin d. David and Margreat, Oct. 4, 1769.
Lusanna, d. Ezekiel, bp. Aug. 20, 1780. C.R.1.
Mary, d. Benja[min] and Rebecca, Dec. 17, 1738.
Melzer, s. Benja[min] and Rebacca, Dec. 16, 1753.
Obed, s. Benja[min] and Rebecca, Nov. 8, 1740.
Obed, s. Benja[min] and Rebecca, Sept. 5, 1745.
Peleg, s. Benja[min] and Rebecca, Feb. 2, 1755.
Ruben, twin s. David and Margreat, Oct. 4, 1769.
Seth, s. Benja[min] and Rebecca, Sept. 4, 1737.

DUNHAM, Eliazer, s. Eliazar, bp. May 20, 1683. C.R.2.
Elizabeth, d. Joseph and Jane, Feb. 21, 1732. [Dunnam, C.R.2.]

DUNN, Ann [? m.], —— [1810]. G.R.10.
Patrick [h. Mary (Welsh)] [Feb. —, 1831]. G.R.10.

DWELLE (see Dwelly), Elizabeth, ch. Jedediah and Elizabeth, bp. Nov. 30, 1729. C.R.2.
Luce, d. Jedidiah and Elizabeth, bp. Apr. 4, 1731. C.R.2.
Lucy, d. Abner, bp. June 1, 1777. C.R.1.
Lusanna, d. Joseph (Dwelly) and Mary, bp. Nov. 8, 1730. C.R.2.
Richard, s. Richard and Margaret, bp. Mar. 7, 1725–6. C.R.2.
Ruth, d. John and Judeth, bp. July 10, 1726. C.R.2.
Sarah, d. Abner and Sarah, bp. Dec. 1, 1726. C.R.2.
Sarah, d. Joseph, bp. Oct. 5, 1746. C.R.2.

DWELLY (see Dwelle), Abnah, ch. John, bp. ——, 1701. C.R.2.
Abner, s. John, Mar. 7, 1699–[1]700.
Abner, s. Jedediah [Jedidiah, C.R.2.] and Eliza[beth], Mar. 6, 1733.
Abner, s. Abner and Eliza[beth], Jan. 10, 1758.
Abner, ch. Abner and w., bp. Aug. 27, 1775. C.R.1.
Benjamin, s. John and Rachell [Rachel, C.R.2.], May 22, 1708 [*sic*, see Mary].
Benjamin, s. John (Dwelley) and Judith, bp. Nov. 2, 1729. C.R.2.
Bradbury, d. Abner and Sarah, July 17, 1722. [Bradberry, C.R.2.]
Bradbury, s. Joseph and Mary, Nov. 26, 1735. [Dwelle, C.R.2.]
Charles House, s. Abner, bp. Oct. 8, 1786. C.R.1.
Deborah, d. John and Rachell, July 25, 1703.
Deborah, d. Jedediah and Eliza[beth], Sept. 22, 1728. [Dwelle, C.R.2.]
Deborah, d. Abner and Eliza[beth], Nov. 13, 1768.
Deborah, ch. Abner and w., bp. Aug. 27, 1775. C.R.1.
Drusilla, d. Joseph and Mary, Dec. 11, 1733. [Drusella, C.R.2.]
Elizabeth, d. Richard [Richard Jr., C.R.2.], Aug. 25, 1687.
Elizabeth, d. Jeddediah and Eliza[beth], Apr. 27, 1726.

DWELLY, Elizabeth, d. Abner and Eliza[beth], Sept. 18, 1762.
Elizabeth, ch. Abner and w., bp. Aug. 27, 1775. C.R.1.
Grace, d. Richard [d. Richard and Grace, C.R.2.], Feb. 16, 1715.
Ichabod, s. John, Dec. 30, 1696 [*sic*, see Obadiah]. [Icabod, C.R.2.]
Jedediah, s. Jedediah and Eliza[beth], Mar. 15, 1737. [Jedidiah Dwelle, s. Jedidiah and Elizabeth, C.R.2.]
Jedediah, s. Abner and Eliza[beth], Oct. 5, 1760.
Jedidiah, s. John, Sept. 5, 1698.
John, s. John, Jan. 15, 1693-4.
John, ch. John, bp. ——, 1697. C.R.2.
John, s. Jo[h]n and Judeth, Nov. 17, 1722. [Dwelle, s. John and Judith, C.R.2.]
John, s. Joseph dec'd and Mary, bp. Apr. 9, 1749. C.R.2.
Joseph, s. John, Feb. 18, 1705.
Joseph, s. Joseph and Mary, Oct. 14, 1737.
Joshua, s. Richard, June 2, 1689.
Joshua, s. Jedediah and Eliza[beth], July 20, 1736. [Dwelle, s. Jedidiah and Eliz[abeth], C.R.2.]
Lemuel, s. John and Rachel, June 25, 1717.
Lemuel, s. Joseph and Mary, Aug. 10, 1741.
Lott, s. Eliza[beth], wid., Apr. 6, 1740. [Lot Dwelle, C.R.2.]
Lucy, d. Abner and Eliza[beth], Sept. 19, 1766.
Lusanah, d. Jedediah and Eliza[beth], Mar. 20, 1730.
Lusanna, d. John and Rachell, Dec. 19, 1711. [Dwelle, d. John and Rachel, C.R.2.]
Lydia, d. Richard, Apr. 16, 1695.
Margaret, d. Richard, June 10, 1696.
Margrett, ch. Richard dec'd and Aimy, bp. June 4, 1710. C.R.2.
Mary, d. Richard, Mar. 29, 1684. [Dwelley, d. Richard Jr., C.R.2.]
Mary (Delly), d. John and Rachell, May 18, 1708 [*sic*, see Benjamin]. [Dwelly, d. John and Rachel, C.R.2.]
Mary, d. Joseph and Mary, Jan. 15, 1731. [Dwelle, C.R.2.]
Mercy, d. John and Rachell [Rachel, C.R.2.], Sept. 24, 1714.
Nabby, d. Abner, bp. Aug. 18, 1782. C.R.1.
Obadiah, s. John, Feb. 21, 1696-7 [*sic*, see Ichabod].
Obadiah, ch. John, bp. ——, 1699. C.R.2.
Rachel, ch. John, bp. ——, 1697. C.R.2.
Rachell, d. John, Sept. 27, 1695.
Richard, s. Richard, Nov. 23, 1685. [Dwelley, s. Richard Jr., C.R.2.]
Richard, s. Richard and Grace, Feb. 9, 1713-14.
Ruth, d. Richard, July 27, 1691.

DWELLY, Ruth, ch. Richard dec'd and Aimy, bp. June 4, 1710.
C.R.2.
Ruth, d. Joseph and Mary, Jan. 8, 1743. [Dwelle, C.R.2.]
Samuel, s. Richard, July 25, 1693.
Samuel, ch. Richard dec'd and Aimy, bp. June 4, 1710. C.R.2.
Samuell, s. Richard, bp. Dec. 2, 1683. C.R.2.
Simeon, s. John and Rachell, Dec. 22, 1701.
Simeon, s. John and Judith, bp. May 2, 1725. C.R.2.
Thankfull, d. John and Rachel, Dec. 12, 1706.
William, s. Abner and Sarah, Apr. 13, 1724.
William, s. Abner, bp. May 18, 1783. C.R.1.

DYER, Sarah R. [? m.], ——— [1828]. G.R.14.

EAMES, Mercy, d. Antony, bp. Nov. 6, 1757. C.R.2.

EDWARDS, ———, ch. Robert W. and Emeline, May 13 [1844].
———, ch. Robert W. and w., ——— [rec. before ch. b. May 13, 1844].

EELLS, Abigail, d. John and Abiah, bp. Nov. 4, 1750. C.R.2.
Anna Lenthall, d. Nath[anie]ll and Hannah, Oct. 16, 1721. [Anna Lenthal, d. Nathanael and Hannah, C.R.2.]
Benja[min] Hatch Tower, [ch.] Sam[ue]ll and w., bp. July 2, 1809. C.R.2.
Benjamin, ch. Nathaniel, bp. Aug. 16, 1818. C.R.2.
Desire, d. North and Ruth, June 8, 174[torn] [1743].
Desire, d. North and Ruth, Oct. 12, 1744.
Edward, s. Nathanaell and Hannah, Jan. 3, 1712–13.
Elizabeth J., ——— [1818]. G.R.15.
Hannah, d. Nathanaell [Nathanael, C.R.2.] and Hannah, Jan. 24, 1714–15.
Hannah, [ch.] John and Abiah, bp. May 5, 1734. C.R.2.
Hannah North, d. Sam[ue]l and Hannah of Hanover, bp. Jan. 18, 1736–7. C.R.2.
Hannah North, d. Samuel and Hannah of Hanover, bp. Feb. 5, 1737–8. C.R.2.
Hannah Shiverick, d. Nathaniel and Nabby, Feb. 4, 1802. [Hannah Schiverick Eelles, d. Nath[anie]ll Jr. and w., C.R.2.]
John, s. Nathaniell [Nathanael, C.R.2.] and Hannah, Feb. 15, 1708–9.
John, s. John and Abiah, bp. Mar. 5, 1737–8. C.R.2.
Joseph, s. John and Abiah, bp. June 21, 1747. C.R.2.
Lenthall, d. John and Abiah, bp. May 19, 1745. C.R.2.
Lusanna, d. John and Abiah, bp. Dec. 19, 1742. C.R.2.
Martha Turner, d. Nathaniel and Nabby, June 16, 1811.

EELLS, Mary, d. Nath[anie]ll and Hannah, May 8, 1716.
Mary, d. Nathaniel and Nabby, May 1, 1815.
Nathaniel, s. Nathaniel and Nabby, Feb. 4, 1809. [Nath[anie]ll, s. Nathaneel and w., C.R.2.]
Nathaniell, s. Nathaniel and Hannah, Jan. 31, 1710–11. [Nathanael, s. Nathanael and Hannah, C.R.2.]
Nath[anie]ll, s. North and Ruth, Jan. 1, 1746. [Nathanael, C.R.2.]
North, s. Nath[anie]ll [Nathanaell, C.R.2.] and Hannah, Sept. 22, 1718.
North, s. North and Ruth, June 1, 1752.
Robert Lenthall, s. Sam[ue]l and Hannah, bp. Feb. 13, 1731–2. C.R.2.
Rolen Turner, s. Nathaniel and Nabby, Jan. 19, 1804.
Rusha, —— [1786]. G.R.15.
Ruth, d. North, bp. Apr. 24, 1755. C.R.2.
Samuel, s. Samuel and Hannah of Hanover, bp. June 15, 1735. C.R.2.
Samuel, s. North and Ruth, Sept. 14, 1748.
Samuel, s. Nath[anie]ll and Sarah, Aug. 9, 1783.
Samuell, s. Nathanaell and Hannah, Feb. 19, 1706–7. [Samuel, s. Nathanael and Hannah, C.R.2.]
Sarah, d. Nathaniell [Nathanael, C.R.2.] and Hannah, Aug. 1, 1705.
Sarah, d. Sam[ue]ll and Hannah of Hanover, bp. June 24, 1733. C.R.2.
Sarah, d. John and Abiah, bp. May 8, 1743. C.R.2.
Sarah, d. Waterman, bp. ——, 1755. C.R.2.
Sarah, d. Nathaniel and Nabby, June 3, 1813.
Sarah, ch. Nath[anie]l, bp. June 19, 1814. C.R.2.
Thankfull, d. North and Ruth, Sept. 25, 1749.
Thankfull, d. North and Ruth, Nov. 22, 1750. [Thankful, C.R.2.]
Waterman, s. John and Abiah, bp. Aug. 13, 1732. C.R.2.
William Witherel, s. Sam[ue]ll [Sam[ue]l, C.R.2.] and Hannah, Dec. 14, 1730.
Zilpah Turner, d. Nathaniel [Nath[anie]ll, C.R.2.] and Nabby, Mar. 20, 1807.

ELEMS (see Ellmes, Ellms, Elmes, Elms, Emms), ——, inf. Jonathan and Elisabeth, bp. June 4, 1748. C.R.2.

ELLIOT, Abigail [——], w. William [June —, 1783]. G.R.2.

ELLIS, David, s. Mordeca, bp. Sept. 2, 1744. C.R.1.
Rebecca, d. Mordecai and Sarah, bp. July 19, 1741. C.R.1.
Sarah, d. Mordecai, bp. Nov. 7, 1742. C.R.1.

SCITUATE BIRTHS

ELLMES (see Elems, Ellms, Elmes, Elms, Emms), Ann, d. Robert and Ann, Oct. 12, 1733. [Elms, C.R.1.]
Anson, s. Ebenezer and Judith, Nov. 17, 1809.
Archabel, s. Ebenezer and Judith, Jan. 9, 1806.
Cushing (Cvesing) Otis, s. Ebenezer and Judith, Feb. 14, 1801.
Ebenezer, s. Cushing O., yeoman, and Mary, July 19, 1844.
Eliza[beth], d. Joseph and Eliza[beth], July 24, 1743. [Elms, C.R.1.]
Joanna, d. Jo[h]n and Mary, Sept. 1, 1734. [Elms, C.R.1.]
John, s. John and Mary, Nov. 24, 1728. [Elmes, C.R.1.]
Jonathan, s. Jo[h]n and Mary, Jan. 4, 1726.
Joseph, s. Joseph and Elizabeth, Mar. 15, 1732. [Ellms [h. Mary (Lincoln)], G.R.8.]
Marget, d. Ebenezer and Judith, Dec. 15, 1799.
Mary, d. Jo[h]n and Mary, Jan. 3, 1724.
Mercy Ellen, d. Joshua O., farmer, and Sarah J., June 20, 1848.
Nancy, d. Ebenezer and Judith, May 23, 1798.
Nath[anie]ll, s. Joseph and Elizabeth, June 11, 1738.
Nicholas, s. John and Mary, Apr. 22, 1732. [Nicolas Elms, C.R.1.]
William, s. Benjamin and Elizabeth, Oct. 5, 17[worn, 1795, written in pencil].
Zibiah, d. Robert and Ann, June 17, 1735. [Zebiah Elms, C.R.1.]

ELLMS (see Elems, Ellmes, Elmes, Elms, Emms), Allony, d. Robert Jr., bp. Mar. 25, 1781. C.R.1.
Ann Stephen, d. Charles and Polly, Jan. 20, 1811.
Anna, d. Jonath[an], bp. May 23, 1708. C.R.1.
Benjamin T., s. Thomas and Sophia, Oct. 24, 1830.
Caroline, d. William and Caroline, Sept. 27, 1820.
Caroline Baker [? m.], ——, 1826. G.R.6.
Charles, s. Charles and Polly, June 21, 1805. [[h. Sally (Bryant)] G.R.6.]
Charles, s. Joseph N. and Elizabeth, Aug. 7, 1813. [Ellmes, s. Joseph Jr., C.R.1.] [Ellms, G.R.8.]
Charles Cook, s. William and Caroline, June 13, 1835.
Cynthia [———], w. Capt. Daniel, —— [1776]. G.R.6.
Eliza Allen, d. William and Caroline, Aug. 9, 1839.
Elizabeth, d. Joseph N. and Elizabeth, Mar. 28, 1807.
Elizabeth, d. Nath[anie]l and Nancy, Apr. 22, 1824.
Elizabeth, d. Cushing O. and Susan, Sept. 1, 1827.
Harriet Atwood, ch. Joseph and Harriet, Dec. 4, 1831.
Harriet Rebecca, d. Thomas and Sophia, Oct. 15, 1840.
Harriet T., d. Daniel, farmer, and Lusanna H., Sept. 5, 1846.
Henry Lincoln, s. William and Caroline, Apr. 10, 1837.

ELLMS, Isaac, s. Cushing O. and Susan, Apr. 16, 1830.
James Horace, s. William and Caroline, Apr. 14, 1841.
John Briggs, s. Ebenezer W. and Judith, May 22, 1796. [Elms, s. Ebenezar Woodworth, c.r.1.]
Jonathan, s. Jo[h]n and Mary, bp. Aug. 20, 1727. C.R.1.
Joseph [h. Elizabeth (Sutton)], ——, 1700. G.R.8.
Joseph, s. Joseph N. and Elizabeth, Oct. 7, 1805.
Joseph Hatch, s. Nathaniel and Nancy, Apr. 19, 1826.
Joshua Otis, s. Charles and Polly, Nov. 4, 1808.
Katharine, d. Robert, bp. Jan. 21, 1738. C.R.1.
Lincoln, s. Lewis and Xoa, Oct. 31, 1828.
Lincoln Barnes, s. William and Caroline, Apr. 1, 1827.
Lincoln Barnes, s. William and Caroline, Apr. 1, 1830.
Lizzie Cynthia, d. Daniel, farmer, and w., July 21, 1849.
Lois L. [——], w. Samuel, —— [1775]. G.R.8.
Louisa B., ch. Nathaniel and Nancy, July 6, 1838. G.R.14.
Lucy Ann, ch. Noah C. and Lucy, May 8 [?], 1836.
Lucy Ann, ch. Noah and Lucy N., bp. Sept. 24, 1837. C.R.3.
Lucy Jackson, d. Nathaniel and Nancy, Dec. 28, 1835.
Maria [? m.], ——, 1809. G.R.6.
Mary, d. Charles and Polly, July 17, 1802.
Mary, d. William and Caroline, Sept. 10, 1826.
Mary Briggs, d. Thomas and Sophia, Apr. 17, 1836.
Nancy [——], w. Nathaniel, Sept. 18, 1800. G.R.14.
Nancy, d. Cushing O. and Susan, Aug. 1, 1824.
Nath[anie]l, s. Joseph, bp. Oct. 28, 1739. C.R.1.
Nathaniel [h. Elizabeth (Wade)], ——, 1766. G.R.8.
Nathaniel, s. Nathaniel and Nancy, May 27, 1829.
Noah Franklin, ch. Noah C. and Lucy, Apr. 27, 1833.
Noah Franklin, ch. Noah and Lucy N., bp. Nov. 23, 1834. C.R.3
Olive Sophia, d. Thomas and Sophia, Dec. 21, 1832.
Polly, d. Samuel (Eellms) and Louis, July 14, 1814.
Robert, s. Jonathan (Eellms), bp. Aug. 14, 1709. C.R.1.
Robert, s. Joseph N. and Elizabeth, Oct. 22, 1808. [Elmes, s. Joseph Jr., C.R.1.] [Ellms, G.R.6.]
Rodolphus, s. Lewis and Xoa, Feb. 1, 1833.
Samuel, s. John and Betsey, Sept. 2, 1772.
Sarah A., d. Joshua O. and Sarah I. [? J.], Dec. 31 [184–].
Sarah Pratt, d. Thomas and Sophia, Oct. 13, 1831.
Thomas Tilden, s. William and Caroline, Oct. 6, 1824.
Timothy, s. Joseph N. and Elizabeth, Mar. 4, 1811. [Elmes, s. Joseph Jr., C.R.1.]
William, s. William and Caroline, Nov. 25, 1822.
William, s. William and Caroline, Mar. 13, 1833.

ELLMS, ——— [———], w. Otis, ——— [1798]. c.r.1.
———, d. Cushing, shoemaker, and Mary, Apr. 8, 1845.

ELMES (see Elems, Ellmes, Ellms, Elms, Emms), Anna, d. Jonathan and Patience, Oct. 17, 1704.
Betsey, d. Samuel and Louis, Sept. 19, 1808.
Charles, s. Robert Jr. and Sarah, Aug. 15, 1772. [Elms, c.r.1.]
Daniel, s. Robert Jr. and Sarah, June 2, 1774. [Elms, c.r.1.]
Daniel, s. Daniel and Cynthia, May 30, 1817.
Desire, d. Jonathan and w., bp. Oct. 31, 1748. c.r.2.
Ebenezar W., s. Ebenezer W. and Judith, Sept. 4, 1793. [Ebenezer Woodworth Elms, ch. Ebenezer Woodworth, c.r.1.]
Ebenezer Woodworth, ch. Robert Jr. and Sarah, Mar. 7, 1770.
Eleanor, d. Robert Jr. and Sarah, Feb. 14, 1781.
Elizabeth, d. Nathaniel and Elizabeth, Oct. 23, 1800.
Hannah, d. Rodulphus (Elms), Dec. 25, 1653.
Hannah, d. Eben[eze]r W. and Judith, Nov. 27, 1794.
Hannah, d. Samuel and Louis, Sept. 11, 1797.
Hariot, d. Daniel and Cynthia, Dec. 2, 1807.
Hipsabah, d. Samuel and Louis, Jan. 4, 1802.
Howard, s. Nathaniel Jr. and Nancy, Dec. 6, 1821. [Ellms, g.r.14.]
Joanna, d. Rodulphus, Mar. 28, 1651.
John, s. Rodulphus, July 6, 1655.
John, s. Jonathan, Apr. 3, 1698.
John, s. Jonathan and Eliza[beth], May 17, 1750. [Elms, c.r.1.]
John, s. Samuel and Luis, Feb. 4, 1796.
John Stephens Spurr, s. Robert Jr. and Sarah, Mar. 1, 1776. [John Stevens Spur Elms, c.r.1.]
Jonathan, s. Rodulphus, Sept. 27, 1663.
Jonathan, s. Jonathan, Mar. 16, 1695-6.
Joseph, s. Rodulphus, Mar. 26, 1658. [Mar. 16, p.c.r.]
Joseph, s. Jonathan, Dec. 2, 1701.
Joseph Northey, s. Robert Jr. and Sarah, May 16, 1778. [Joseph Northy Elms, c.r.1.]
Judeth, d. Ebenezar and Judith, Nov. 11, 1789.
Katharine, d. Rodalphus, Mar. [22], 1698.
Lewis, s. Samuel and Louis, Feb. 5, 1804. [Ellms, g.r.14.]
Lincoln, s. Samuel and Louis, Aug. 15, 1793.
[L]ucy, d. Nath[anie]l and Elizabeth, Sept. 21, 1791.
Lucy, d. Daniel and Cynthia, Apr. 25, 1809.
Lydia, d. Dr. James, wid. William Vinal, ——— [1810]. c.r.1.
Lydia, d. Daniel and Cynthia, Oct. 20, 1811.
Martha, d. Samuel and Louis, Mar. 15, 1806.

ELMES, Mary, d. Rodulphus, June 9, 1648.
Mary, d. Rodolphus Jr., Nov. [8], 1696.
Mary, d. Nathaniel and Elizabeth, July 17, 1799.
Melzar James, s. Daniel and Cynthia, July 11, 1814. [Ellms, G.R.6.]
Nathaniel, s. Nath[anie]l and Elizabeth, Dec. 4, 1794. [Ellms [h. Nancy], G.R.14.]
Noah Cudworth, s. Daniel and Cynthia, Sept. 15, 1803.
Patience, d. Jonathan, Jan. 29, 1699–[1]700.
Robert, s. Jonathan and Patience, Sept. 26, 1707.
Robert, s. Robert Jr. and Sarah, Apr. 24, 1765.
Rodolphus, s. Rodolphus, July [6], 1700.
Rodulphus, s. Rodulphus, May 27, 1668.
Salley, d. Ebenezar W. and Judith, July 17, 1791.
Sarah, d. Rodulphus, Sept. 29, 1645.
Sarah, d. Robert Jr. and Sarah, May 30, 1768.
Sarah, d. Samuel and Louis, Nov. 25, 1811.
Sibbiah, d. Jonathan, Aug. 19, 1694.
[T]homas, s. Nathaniel and Elizabeth, Feb. 6, 1789. [Ellms [h. Sophia (Briggs)], G.R.2.]
Waitestill, d. Rodulphus, Feb. 9, 1660.
Winnefree, d. Samuel and Louis, Dec. 11, 1800.

ELMS (see Elems, Ellmes, Ellms, Elmes, Emms), Consider, s. Jona[than], bp. Feb. 25, 1752. C.R.2.
Cynthia [? m.], ―― [1786]. C.R.1.
John Spur, s. Robert, bp. May 13, 1744. C.R.1.
Joseph, s. Joseph and Eliz[abeth], bp. Nov. 3, 1734. C.R.1.
Joseph, s. Joseph, bp. ―― 25, 1806. C.R.1.
Judith, ch. Ebenezar Woodworth, bp. July 6, 1794. C.R.1.
Mary, d. Jo[h]n and Mary, bp. Aug. 20, 1727. C.R.1.
Patience, d. Robert, bp. Mar. 27, 1737. C.R.1.
Rhoda, d. Jo[h]n, bp. July 30, 1738. C.R.1.
Robert, s. Robert, bp. Aug. 23, 1741. C.R.1.
Robert, ch. Robert Jr. and w., bp. Dec. 24, 1769. C.R.1.
Sally, ch. Ebenezar Woodworth, bp. July 6, 1794. C.R.1.
Sarah, ch. Robert Jr. and w., bp. Dec. 24, 1769. C.R.1.

EMERSON, Jeremiah L. [h. Mary], Aug. 27, 1806. G.R.2.
Mary [――――], w. Jeremiah L., Jan. 23, 1808. G.R.2.

EMMS (see Elems, Ellmes, Ellms, Elmes, Elms), Samuel, s. Samuel and Abig[ai]l, bp. Dec. 11, 1743. C.R.1.

ENSIGNE, Hannah, d. John, bp. May 29, 1670. C.R.2.

EUEL (see Ewel, Ewell, Ewill), Ann, d. Rebeca, bp. Oct. 5, 1729. c.r.1.
Elizabeth, d. Jo[h]n, bp. Oct. 5, 1729. c.r.1.
John, s. Jo[h]n, bp. Sept. 14, 1735. c.r.1.
Malachi, s. Jo[h]n, bp. May 8, 1743. c.r.1.
Rachel, d. Jo[h]n, bp. July 1, 1733. c.r.1.
Sarah, d. Jo[h]n, bp. Nov. 10, 1728. c.r.1.

EWEL (see Euel, Ewell, Ewill), Deborah, d. John, bp. Oct. 10, 1773. c.r.1.
Gershom, ch. Gershom (Ewell), bp. Apr. 28, 1723. c.r.1.
Henry, s. Jo[h]n, bp. Aug. 14, 1737. c.r.1.
James, s. John Jr. and w., bp. July 16, 1758. c.r.1.
Job, ch. Gershom (Ewell), bp. Apr. 28, 1723. c.r.1.
Malachi, s. John, bp. July 26, 1772. c.r.1.
Melzar, s. John, bp. May 27, 1764. c.r.1.
Melzar, s. John, bp. Sept. 7, 1766. c.r.1.
Peleg, s. Jo[h]n, bp. June 7, 1741. c.r.1.
Peleg, s. Peleg, bp. Jan. 13, 1772. c.r.1.
Perez, s. Peleg and w., bp. Nov. 26, 1769. c.r.1.
Rachel, d. Jo[h]n, bp. July 6, 1760. c.r.1.
Releif, ch. Gershom (Ewell), bp. Apr. 28, 1723. c.r.1.
Sarah, d. John, bp. Aug. 20, 1769. c.r.1.
Seth, ch. Gershom (Ewell), bp. Apr. 28, 1723. c.r.1.

EWELL (see Euel, Ewel, Ewill), Amelia, ch. Luther and Sarah T., Apr. 26, 1843.
Ann A., ch. D. R. and w., Oct. 27, 1843.
Bethia, d. Henry, Sept. 27, 1653.
Bethiah, d. Gershom and Mary, Mar. 3, 1682-3.
Betsey, d. Gershom and Hannah, June 25, 1794. [Betsy, c.r.2.]
Charles, s. John and Releaf, Nov. 1, 1803.
Charles, s. John and Releaf, July 16, 1805.
Charles F., s. Walter F., housewright, and Emeline B., Nov. 26, 1847.
Charllotte, d. Elijah S. and Ruth, Feb. 13, 1818.
Daniel R., ch. Luther and Sarah T., Sept. 13, 1840, in Pembroke.
Deborah, d. Henry, June 4, 1663.
Elijah Souther, s. Gershom and Hannah, Sept. 30, 1787.
Elijah Souther, s. Elijah S. and Ruth, July 27, 1816.
Eliza, d. John and Releaf, Jan. 6, 1800.
Francis, s. John and Releaf, Dec. 3, 1808.
George, s. John and Releaf, Aug. 10, 1812.
Gershom, s. Gershom and Mary, Jan. 24, 1691-2.
Gershom, s. Gershom and Relief, Jan. 16, 171[6].

EWELL, Gershom, s. Jo[h]n, bp. Oct. 26, 1746. C.R.1.
Gershon, s. Henry, Nov. 14, 1650.
Hannah, d. Henry, June 21, 1649. [June 22, P.C.R.]
Hannah, d. Gershom and Mary, Feb. 1, 1694-5.
Hannah, d. Jo[h]n, bp. Oct. 18, 1747. C.R.1.
Hannah, d. Gershom and Hannah, Apr. 4, 1783.
Hellen, d. Elijah S. and Ruth, July 20, 1822.
Henry Thomas, s. John and Releaf, Mar. 9, 1807.
Huldah L., d. Elijah S. and Ruth, June 13, 1820.
Ichabod, s. Henry, June —, 1659.
Job, s. Gershom and Relief, Jan. 19, 1720.
John, s. Gershom and Mary, June 27, 1699.
John, s. John, bp. Aug. 15, 1762. C.R.1.
John, s. Gershom and Hannah, Nov. 17, 1777.
John, s. John and Releaf, Apr. 20, 1801.
Louisa I. [? J.], ch. Luther and Sarah T., Oct. 3, 1838, in Pembroke.
Lucy A. [dup. Ann], d. Luther, farmer, and Sarah T., Aug. 15, 1846.
Lucy Sylvester, d. John and Releaf, July 28, 1798.
Luther I. [? J.], ch. Luther and Sarah T., Oct. 12, 1837, in Pembroke.
Lydia, d. Gershom and Hannah, July 11, 1789.
Lydia, d. Gershom and Hannah, Nov. 9, 1792. [[w. Josiah Stoddard] Nov. 15, G.R.14.]
Mary, d. Gershom and Mary, Aug. 14, 1685.
Mary A., ch. Luther and Sarah T., July 1, 1834, in Pembroke.
Mercy S., ch. Luther and Sarah T., Oct. 5, 1831, in Marshfield.
Nabby, d. Gershom and Hannah, Jan. 13, 1775.
Nabby, d. Gershom and Hannah, Feb. 22, 1781.
Penelope, d. Gershom and Mary, Apr. 18, 1697.
Perez, s. Gershom and Hannah, Jan. 3, 1779.
Rebekah, d. Gershom and Mary, Apr. 2, 1690.
Sally, d. Gershom and Hannah, July 16, 1785.
Sarah, d. Gershom and Mary, Feb. 2, 1687-8.
Sarah T., ch. Luther and Sarah T., July 26, 1830, in Marshfield.
Seth, s. Gershom and Relief, Sept. 16, 1719.
Susan T. [dup. F.], d. Luther, farmer, and Sarah [dup. adds T.], Dec. 19, 1844.
Susanna, d. John and Releaf, Oct. 2, 1814.
Vesta P., d. Luther, farmer, and Sarah T., Mar. 21, 1848.
Walter H., s. Walter F., housewright, and Emeline, Feb. 24, 1846.
——, d. Luther, shoemaker (b. Marshfield), and Sarah T. (b. Pembroke), Dec. 18, 1849, in S. Scituate.
——, d. Walter F., carpenter (b. Marshfield), and Emeline, Dec. 25, 1849, in S. Scituate.

EWILL (see Euel, Ewel, Ewell), Abia, d. Henery, Sept. 27, 1653. P.C.R.

FARINGTON, ———, ch. Harvey and Sarah, Nov. 20, 1843.

FARRAR (see Farrow), Abial, s. Charles H., farmer, and Mary G., June 18, 1847. [Abiel, "A private of Co. M. 1st. Mass. Ha Art'y," G.R.14.]
Albert F., s. James J., farmer, and Lucy, Aug. 16, 1844.
Charles A., s. Charles H., yeoman, and Mary G., Apr. 21, 1849, in S. Scituate.
Johanna, d. Thom[a]s, bp. June 20, 1756. C.R.2.
Lucy [? m.], ——— [1791]. G.R.14.
Thomas, s. Tho[ma]s, bp. Apr. 5, 1752. C.R.2.
———, s. James I. [? J.], farmer, and Lucy, Feb. 28, [18]46.

FARROW (see Farrar), Abby Fatima, d. Rufus and Deborah R., Dec. 16, 1835. [Abba Fatima, P.R.14.]
Abial, h. Bethia Cushing, Nov. 29, 1763. P.R.15.
Abial, s. Abial and Bethiah, Apr. 12, 1790.
Abigail, d. Benj[a]m[in] and Leah, bp. Apr. 23, 1732. C.R.2.
Abigail, d. Abial and Bethiah, Mar. 18, 1798.
Albert N., s. Isaac S. (Farrar), mason, and Mary B. (b. Lynn), Mar. 13, 1849, in S. Scituate.
Allen, ——— [1788]. C.R.3.
Allen, s. Allen and Rebekah, Nov. 3, 1816, in Roxbury.
Benjamin Franklin, s. A[bial] Jr. and Lucy, Apr. 1, 1829.
Bethiah, d. Abial and Bethiah, Nov. 7, 1786.
Charles Henry, s. Abiel Jr. and Lucy, June 16, 1822.
Christian, ch. Benj[a]m[in], bp. Aug. 20, 1738. C.R.2.
Deborah Jacob, d. Rufus and Deborah R., Sept. 24, 1832.
Deering, s. Tho[ma]s Jr. and Rebecca, July 18, 1784.
Elizabeth Phillips, d. Allen and Rebekah, July 9, 1823.
Gustavus Henry, ch. James J. and Lucy, Dec. 14, 1831.
Hannah, d. Allen and Rebekah, June 24, 1827.
Henry Richmond, ch. Richmond and Abigail G., June 25, 1837.
Isaac, s. Abial Jr. and Lucy, Apr. 27, 1814.
James, s. Allen and Rebekah, Mar. 1, 1820.
James Jacob, s. Abiel and Nabby [ch. Abial and Abby, P.R.15.], Feb. 24, 1807.
Jemima, d. Thomas and Jemimah, bp. May 4, 1746. C.R.2.
Leah, d. Benja[min] [d. Benj[a]m[in] and Leah, C.R.2.], Dec. 9, 1722.
Louisa, d. Rufus and Deborah R., Sept. 12, 1840.
Lucy James, ch. James J. and Lucy, July 7, 1833.

FARROW, Lucy M., ch. William and Sally, Dec. 11, 1842.
Mandana, d. Rufus and Deborah R., Sept. 29, 1830.
Martha, d. Thomas and Jemimah, bp. Feb. 14, 1747–8. C.R.2.
Martha, d. Thomas, bp. May 19, 1754. C.R.2.
Mary L., ch. James J. and Lucy, Dec. 28, 1840.
Nabby, d. Tho[ma]s Jr. and Rebecca, May 27, 1786.
Nathan, s. Tho[ma]s Jr. and Rebecca, Feb. 20, 1783.
Nathaniel, s. Abial and Bethiah, Nov. 4, 1788.
Rachel, d. Benj[a]m[in], bp. July 18, 1731. C.R.2.
Rachel B., d. Allen Jr., mariner, and Rachel B., Mar. 13, 1844.
Rebecca, d. Tho[ma]s Jr. and Rebecca, Nov. 16, 1777.
Rebekah, d. Allen and Rebekah, Feb. 28, 1813, in Roxbury.
Richmond, s. Abial and Nabby, ———, 1813. [ch. Abial and Abby, May 21 or 22, P.R.15.]
Rufus, s. Abial and Bethiah, Oct. 31, 1794. [h. Deborah R. Cushing, Oct. 30, P.R.14.] [Oct. 30, P.R.15.]
Rufus Brooks, ch. James J. and Lucy, Aug. 14, 1829.
Samuel, s. Tho[ma]s Jr. and Rebecca, Feb. 5, 1789.
Sarah, d. Benjmin and Leah, bp. June 19, 1726. C.R.2.
Sarah, d. Tho[ma]s Jr. and Rebecca, Mar. 4, 1780.
Sarah Ellen, ch. James J. and Lucy, Feb. 2, 1837.
Sophia Bradford, d. Rufus and Deborah R., May 17, 1825. [May 17, 1826, P.R.14.]
Tamar, d. Benj[a]m[in], bp. Aug. 11, 1734. C.R.2.
Thomas, s. Benjamin, Apr. 10, 1721.
Thomas, s. Thomas Jr. [and] Rebecca, Sept. 6, 1775.
Thomas, s. Abial and Bethiah, July —, 1796. [July 18, P.R.15.]
William, s. Abial and Bethiah, Jan. 25, 1793. [Jan. 29, P.R.15.]
William Cushing, s. Abial Jr. and Lucy, Aug. 12, 1816.
William H., ch. James J. and Lucy, May 12, 1839.
———, s. Benj[amin] F. (Farrar), yeoman, and Eliza E., Nov. 8, 1849, in S. Scituate.

FAUNCE, Bathsheba, [ch.] Thomas and Hannah of Plymouth, bp. May 5, 1734. C.R.2.
Daniel, s. Thomas and Hannah of Plymouth, bp. July 1, 1739. C.R.2.
Hannah, ch. Thomas and Hanah of Plymouth, bp. Oct. 16, 1737. C.R.2.

FAXON, Ethan Allen, ch. Asaph A. and Mercy L., Sept. 29 [29, written in pencil over 30], 1841.
Eunice Adelaid [dup. Allen], d. William T., butcher, and Harriet, Dec. 12, 1847.
Frank Allen, s. Asaph A., butcher, and Mercy L., May 29, 1848.

FAXON, James D., ch. Asaph A. and Mercy L., Apr. 29, 1843.
Susan E., ch. Asaph A. [dup. butcher] and Mercy L., Dec. 3, 1845.
William H., s. William T., butcher (b. Braintree), and Harriet, Apr. 10, 1849. [W[illia]m Henry, s. W[illia]m F. and Harriet, G.R.2.]

FERGUSON (see Furguson), Charles Martin, ch. William and Lydia, Aug. 16, 1843.
Emeline [dup. Furguson], ch. William [dup. stage driver] and Lydia, Mar. 10, 1847.
Harvey, ch. William and Lydia, Nov. 24, 1841.
Mary Eliza, d. William, stage driver (b. Manchester), and Lydia C. [dup. omits C.], Jan. 1, 1849.
William Clarence, ch. William and Lydia, May 20, 1840.

FIELD, John, s. Jo[h]n, bp. Aug. 19, 1739. C.R.1.

FIESH (see Fish), Jonathan, s. Jonathan and Marey, Dec. 18, 1744.
Mary, d. Jonathan and Mary, Dec. 25, 1747. [Fish, C.R.1.]
Nathaniel, s. Jonathan and Mary, Sept. 13, 1749.

FISH (see Fiesh), Anne E. [———], w. Rev. W. H., ———, 1815. G.R.14.
Charlottee, d. Charles and Zibiah, June 3, 1791.
Jonathan, s. Jonathan, bp. Sept. 3, 1749. C.R.1.
Mary, d. Ebenezar [and] Deborah of Duxbury, bp. July 9, 1738. C.R.2.
Mary, ch. Jonathan, bp. Oct. 15, 1752. C.R.1.
Nathaniel, ch. Jonathan, bp. Oct. 15, 1752. C.R.1.
Stephen, s. Jonathan, bp. May 3, 1754. C.R.1.
William H., Rev., ———, 1812. G.R.14.
———, s. Thom[a]s of Duxboro, bp. Jan. 25, 1711. C.R.1.

FITTS, Isaac N., ch. Luke G. and Lydia, June 29, 1829.
John A., ch. Luke G. and Lydia, June 14, 1836.
Luke G., ch. Luke G. and Lydia, Feb. 14, 1831.
Lyman A., ch. Luke G. and Lydia, Dec. 31, 1837.
Matilda, ch. Luke G. and Lydia, Apr. 30, 1828.
Seth O., ch. Luke G. and Lydia, Sept. 6, 1840.
Welcome W. D., ch. Luke G. and Lydia, Mar. 10, 1833.

FLYNN, Mary [———], w. Thomas, ——— [1817]. G.R.10.
Thomas [h. Mary], ——— [1814], in Rush, Co. Dublin, Ireland. G.R.10.

FOGG, Betsey [———], w. Ebenezer T., ———, 1791. G.R.14.
Charles Edward, s. Ebenezer T. and Betsey, Feb. 18, 1825.
Cha[rle]s Edward, ch. Eben[eze]r T. Esq., bp. Aug. 5, 1827. C.R.2.
Ebenezer T. [h. Betsey], ———, 1795. G.R.14.
Ebenezer Thayer, s. Ebenezer T. [Ebenezer T. Esq., C.R.2.] and Betsey, Oct. 31, 1826.
Elizabeth Ann, d. Ebenezer T. and Betsey, May 8, 1829
George Parsons, s. Eben[eze]r T. [Thayer, C.R.2.] and Betsey, June 27, 1821. [[h. Lucy S.] G.R.14.]
Horace Tower, s. Ebenezer T. and Betsey, Sept. 7, 1823.
Horace Tower, ch. Eben[eze]r T. Esq., bp. Aug. 5, 1827. C.R.2.
Isabella Thayer, d. Ebenezer T. and Betsey, Sept. 15, 1831. [w. Ebenezer Nye [of] Cincinnati, O., G.R.14.]
Lucy S. [———], w. George P., ———, 1828. G.R.14.

FOLKE, Sarah, d. John, bp. Oct. 13, 1661. C.R.2.

FOORD (see Ford), Daniel, ch. Dr. Peleg, bp. Oct. 27, 1805. C.R.1.
Harriet, ch. Dr. Peleg, bp. Oct. 27, 1805. C.R.1.
Margaret, d. John and Martha, Apr. 3, 1714.

FORD (see Foord), Abba, d. Charles and Lydia, Sept. 14, 1821.
Abigail Turner, d. Dr. Peleg and Marcy, Sept. 31, 1811. [Foord, C.R.1.]
Charles, ch. Charles and Lydia, Dec. 22, 1803, in Marshfield.
Colman, ch. Charles and Lydia, Oct. 3, 1811, in Marshfield [*sic*, see Gera Jenkins Ford].
Daniel, s. Dr. Peleg and Marcy, June 14, 1804.
David Barnes, s. Michael and Sarah, Nov. 10, 1820.
Frances [dup. Francis] Maria, d. Cha[rle]s and Lydia, Dec. 9, 1828.
Gera, ch. Charles and Lydia, May 13, 1805, in Marshfield.
Gera Jenkins, ch. Charles and Lydia, Apr. 4, 1812, in Marshfield [*sic*, see Colman]. [[h. Philenda D.] [Apr. —, 1813] G.R.14.]
Gideon, ——— [1808]. G.R.14.
Hannah, d. Peleg, Dec. 23, 1717.
Hannah, d. Peleg, bp. Aug. 31, 1719. C.R.1.
Harriat, d. Dr. Peleg and Marcy, Nov. 24, 1801. [Harriet, w. Elijah Clapp, G.R.5.]
Isabella G., ch. Gideon and Mary, Mar. 1, 1838.
James, s. Micah [Michael] and Rhoda, May 3, 1780.
John James, s. Peleg, shipcarpenter, and Mary Ann, Aug. 16, 1849.

FORD, Joseph F., ch. Gideon and Mary, June 4, 1845.
Lillis, ch. Charles and Lydia, Apr. 30, 1815, in Marshfield.
Lucy, d. Micah [Michael] and Rhoda, Oct. 26, 1782.
Lydia, d. Michael and Rhoda, Apr. 14, 1786.
Maria, ch. Charles and Lydia, Mar. 7, 1807, in Marshfield.
Mary A. [———], w. Peleg [Jan. —, 1809]. G.R.5.
Mary Ann, ch. Peleg and Mary Ann, Oct. 11, 1838.
Mary E., ch. Gideon and Mary, Nov. 3, 1832, in Marshfield.
Mary L. [? m.], ——— [1811]. G.R.14.
Michael, s. Michael and Rhoda, Jan. 22, 1784.
Michael, s. Michael and Sarah, Oct. 23, 1814.
Nancy, d. Dr. Peleg and Marcy, May 31, 1806. [Foord, C.R.1.]
Nathan, ch. Charles and Lydia, Dec. 16, 1813, in Marshfield.
Peleg, s. Dr. Peleg and Marcy, July 25, 1809. [Foord, C.R.1.] [Ford [h. Mary A.], G.R.5.]
Peleg, ch. Peleg and Mary Ann, Jan. 31, 1840.
Peleg [h. Annie Maria (Turner)], ———, 1843. G.R.14.
Philenda D. [———], w. Gera J. [May —, 1819]. G.R.14.
Rhoda, d. Micah [Michael] and Rhoda, Feb. 7, 1776.
Sanders, ch. Charles and Lydia, Nov., 9, 1817, in Marshfield.
Sarah, d. Micah [Michael] and Rhoda, Nov. 16, 1777.
Sophia, ch. Charles and Lydia, Feb. 16, 1809, in Marshfield. [Sophronia, G.R.2.]
Sophronia, d. Charles and Lydia, Oct. 7, 1819.
William Cowper, s. Michael and Sarah, Aug. 7, 1817.
———, s. Charles and Lydia, Aug. 20, 1823.
———, s. Charles and Lydia, Aug. 9, 1825.

FORESTER, ———, ch. ———, Dec. 1 [1844].

FOSTER (see Fostor), Abigail, d. John and Sarah, Mar. 6, 1766.
Abigal, d. Joseph and Abigal, Feb. 2, 1738. [Abigail, d. Joseph and Abigail, C.R.2.]
Alfred B., s. Seth and Abigail, July 23, 1803. [Alfred Brunson, s. Capt. Seth and w., C.R.2.] [Alfred B., ch. Seth and Nabby (Otis), P.R.5.]
Amy, d. Samuel and Polly, Mar. 29, 1802 [*sic*, see Henry].
Augusta C. [———], w. Philip [Oct.—, 1830]. G.R.14.
Bathshua, d. Elisha and Temperance, Jan. 13, 1742. [Barsheba, d. Elisha and Temperance, C.R.2.]
Benj[ami]n Palmer, s. Dr. Freeman and Esther, Feb. 12, 1802.
Benjamin Palmer, s. Daniel and Leafy, Dec. 17, 1831.
Betsey [———], w. Walter [Dec. —, 1795]. G.R.14.
Betty, d. Joseph and Abigal [Abigail, C.R.2.], May 19, 1741.
Caroline, d. Seth and Abigail [Nabby (Otis), P.R.5.], Sept. 18, 1801.

FOSTER, Caroline, d. Daniel and Leafy, July 9, 1835.
Charles, s. Elisha and Grace, Feb. 21, 1781.
Charles, s. Timothy and Hannah, July 15, 1809.
Charles Thomas, s. Charles and Eunice, Feb. 22, 1813.
Ch[arle]s Thomas, ch. Charles, bp. Sept. 5, 1824. C.R.2.
Charlotte O., d. Seth and Abigail [Nabby (Otis), P.R.5.], Apr. 4, 1806.
Daniel, s. Elisha and Grace, May 25, 1787.
Deborah [? m.], May 12, 1790. G.R.13.
Elisabeth, d. Hatherly and Ba[th]shua, Feb. 14, 1721. [Elizabeth, d. Hatherly and Barshua, C.R.2.]
Elisha, s. Hatherly and Bathsheba [Barshubah, C.R.2.], May 28, 1708.
Elisha, s. Elisha and Temperance [Temperance, C.R.2.], Apr. 28, 1745.
Elisha, s. Elisha and Grace, July 17, 1775. [Elisha Jr., P.R.5.]
Elisha, s. Elisha Jr. and Sally, Sept. 27, 1805.
Elizabeth (see Elisabeth).
Ellen, d. Timothy and Deborah, Aug. 31, 1833.
Esther S., d. Dr. Freeman and Esther, Jan. 22, 1813. [Esther Stephens, P.R.5.]
Eunice, ch. Charles and Eunice (Ruggles), Feb. 9, 1817. P.R.5.
Francis, s. Timot[hy] and w., bp. Aug. 13, 1809. C.R.2.
Freeman, s. Elisha and Grace, July 17, 1777. [Dr. Freeman [h. Esther], G.R.15.] [June 8, P.R.5.]
Freeman, s. Dr. Freeman and Esther, July 14, 1800. [Freeman Jr., P.R.5.]
George, s. Elisha Jr. [Capt. Elisha, C.R.2.] and Sally, May 9, 1812.
Gracey Berstow, d. Elisha Jr. and Sally, Jan. 7, 1808. [Grace Turner ["Barstow," written above "Turner"], d. Elish and w., C.R.2.] [Grace B., ch. Elisha and Sally, P.R.5.]
Hannah, d. Timothy and Hannah, Oct. 16, 1817. [Hannah Clap, C.R.2.]
Harriet, d. Seth and Abigail, Jan. 17, 1808. [Harriette, C.R.2.] [Harriet, ch. Seth and Nabby (Otis), P.R.5.]
Harris, s. Samuel and Polly, Dec. 24, 1799.
Hatherly, s. Joseph and Abigal, Apr. 21, 1737.
Henry, s. Samuel and Polly, Feb. 3, 1802 [sic, see Amy].
Henry, s. Elisha Jr. and Sally, May 4, 1823. [May 3, P.R.5.]
Henry, ch. Cap[t]. Elisha, bp. June 6, 1824. C.R.2.
Jacob, s. John and Sarah, May 16, 1770.
James, s. John Jr. and Abigail, June 18, 1799.
James O., s. Seth and Abigail, May 17, 1813. [s. Capt. Seth, C.R.2.] [James Otis, ch. Seth and Nabby (Otis), P.R.5.]
Jane, d. Seth and Abigail, Oct. 1, 1810. [w. Benj[amin] F. Delano, G.R.14.] [ch. Seth and Nabby (Otis), P.R.5.]

FOSTER, John, s. Hatherly and Bathsheba [Barsheba, C.R.2.], Jan. 12, 1711–12.
John, s. Elisha and Temporance [Temperance, C.R.2.], Mar. 25, 1740.
John, s. John and Sarah, Apr. 14, 1768. [[h. Abigail (Southworth)] G.R.13.]
John, s. John Jr. and Abigail, July 12, 1795.
Joseph, s. Hatherly, Aug. 8, 1702.
Joseph, s. Joseph and Abigal [Abigail, C.R.2.], Feb. 27, 1742.
Joseph, s. Timothy and Hannah, Aug. 18, 1814.
Joseph Thomp[so]n, s. Dr. Freeman and Esther, Apr. 10, 1804. [Apr. 17, P.R.5.]
Joshua Turner, s. Elisha Jr. and Sally, Jan. 30, 1810. [s. Capt. Elisha, C.R.2.] [Jan. 31, P.R.5.]
Josiah, s. John and Sarah, Apr. 1, 1782.
Lucinda, d. Jacob and Joanna, Mar. 11, 1796.
Margaret, d. Joseph and Abigal, May 20, 1734. [Margret, d. Joseph and Abigail, C.R.2.]
Margarett, d. Hatherly, Aug. 20, 1699. [Margaret, C.R.2.]
Mary, d. Elisha and Temperance, Dec. 2, 1750.
Mary, d. Elisha, bp. Dec. 8, 1751. C.R.2.
Mary, d. Elisha Jr. and Sally, May 3, 1821. [May 4, P.R.5.]
Mary, ch. Cap[t]. Elisha, bp. June 6, 1824. C.R.2.
Mary Jacobs, d. Timothy and Hannah, Oct. 6, 1811.
Mary Louiza, d. Samuel and Sarah, May 23, 1823. [Mary Loisa, C.R.2.] [Mary Louisa, P.R.5.]
Mary M., d. Thomas A., caulker (b. Boston), and Judith R. (b. Boston), June 17, 1848.
Mary Otis, d. Samuel and Polly, Aug. 19, 1797.
Molly, d. Ebenezer and Mary, bp. Oct. 14, 1770. C.R.1.
Pegge, d. Elisha and Grace, Aug. 5, 1772. [Peggy, P.R.5.]
Philip, s. Elisha Jr. and Sally, Oct. 17, 1818. [[h. Augusta C.] G.R.14.] [Oct. 28, P.R.5.]
Philip, ch. Cap[t]. Elisha, bp. Nov. 7, 1819. C.R.2.
Ruth, d. Hatherly, May 14, 1704.
Ruth, d. Hatherly and Barshua, bp. Aug. 4, 1717. C.R.2.
Ruth, d. Elisha and Temperance, Jan. 12, 1754.
Sally, d. Elisha Jr. [Cap[t]. Elisha, C.R.2.] and Sally, Mar. 17, 1816.
Samuel, s. Elisha and Grace, Jan. 27, 1779.
Sarah, d. Elisha and Temperance, Mar. 31, 1749.
Sarah, d. John and Sarah, May 23, 1778.
Sarah [? m.], ———, 1782. G.R.14.
Sarah A., d. Thomas A., caulker (b. Boston), and Judith R. (b. Boston), May 30, 1846.

FOSTER, Sarah Delano, d. Samuel and Sarah, May 22, 1810.
Sarah Southworth, d. John [John Jr., C.R.2.] and Abigail, Jan. 16, 1804.
Seth, s. Elisha and Grace, June 21, 1770.
Seth, s. Daniel and Leafy, Feb. 14, 1830.
Steel, s. Joseph and Abigal [s. Capt. Joseph and Abigail, C.R.2.], Dec. 17, 1750.
Temperance, d. Elisha and Grace, Dec. 22, 1782.
Temperance, ch. Elisha and Grace, May 25, 1787. P.R.5.
Temperance, d. Elisha and Grace [Dec. —, 1796]. G.R.14.
Temperance F., d. Dr. Freeman and Esther, July 10, 1806.
Temporance, d. Elisha and Temperance, Mar. 25, 1747. [Temperance, d. Elishah and Temperance, C.R.2.]
Temporence Freeman, d. Timothy and Hannah, Oct. 5, 1804. [Temperance Freeman, C.R.2.] [Temperance, w. Francis Turner, G.R.14.]
Timothy, s. Edward, bp. Mar. 7, 1635. C.R.1.
Timothy, s. Edward, bp. Apr. 22, 1638. C.R.1.
Timothy, s. Hatherly and Bathsheba [Barshua, C.R.2.], Mar. 4, 1706.
Timothy, s. Joseph and Abigal [Abigail, C.R.2.], Mar. 23, 1744.
Timothy, s. John and Sarah, Dec. 3, 1775.
Walter, s. Elisha and Grace, Jan. 22, 1789. [[h. Betsey] G.R.14.]
Walter, s. Charles and Eunice, July 31, 1823.
Walter, ch. Charles, bp. Sept. 5, 1824. C.R.2.
William, s. Timothy and Hannah, Mar. 30, 1807.

FOSTOR (see Foster), Joseph, s. John (Foster) and Sarah, July 5, 1772.

FOX, Annie M. [? m.], Mar. 13, 1847. G.R.19.

FOXWELL, Martha, d. ———, bp. Apr. 22, 1638. C.R.1.
Mary, d. ———, bp. Aug. 30, 1635. C.R.1.

FRANK (see Franke), Hervey, colored, s. Joseph, laborer, colored (b. Portugal), and Clarissa (b. Hingham), Sept. 4, 1849, in S. Scituate.

FRANKE (see Frank), Margaret, d. Franke, negro, and Margaret, Apr. 19, 1705.

FREEMAN, Alfred, s. Joshua and Alice, Mar. 6, 1814.
Alfred, ———, 1822. G.R.14.
Alice, d. John and Harriet, Nov. 9 [184–].
Asher, s. Asher and Dinah, Feb. 20, 1790.

FREEMAN, Charles Henry, s. Lemuel and Betsey, Mar. 20, 1818.
Diana C. [―――], colored, w. Parmenus Pierce, July 11, 1827.
  G.R.14.
Elizabeth Gundeway, d. L[emuel] and Betsey, Nov. 25, 1824.
Hariat, d. Prince and Abigail, Jan. 28, 1794. [Harriot, C.R.2.]
James, s. Asher and Dinah, Feb. 11, 1786.
James Robert, ch. Richard and Celia, Sept. 23, 1843.
John, s. Joshua and Alice, Nov. 1, 1810.
Joseph, s. Joshua and Alice, Nov. 22, 1806.
Joshua, s. Asher and Dinah, Oct. 8, 1784.
Joshua, s. Joshua and Alice, Dec. 23, 1808.
Joshua F., colored, s. John, laborer, colored, and Harriet, Mar. 10, 1849, in S. Scituate.
Lecta, d. Prince and Abigail, Aug. 28, 1795.
Lemuel, s. Asher and Dinah, May 5, 1777.
Lemuel, s. Thirza, Jan. 28, 1830. ["45 Reg't. M.V.M. (Colored),"
  G.R.14.]
Mary, d. Thirza, Dec. 18, 1844.
Mary E. [―――], w. Edw[ard] F., ―――, 1841. G.R.14.
Nancy, d. Asher and Dinah, Apr. 20, 1788.
Olive, d. Betsey, Dec. 29, 1830.
Prince (F[r]eeman), s. Prince and Abigail, Mar. 30, 1808.
Richard, s. Lemuel and Betsey, Feb. 29, 1812.
Samuel, s. Lemuel and Betsey, Nov. 4, 1821.
Sarah, d. Asher and Dinah, Jan. 26, 1781.
Stanley, s. Prince and Abigail, "Black people," bp. Jan. 24, 1790.
  C.R.1.
William Henry, ch. Richard and Celia, Dec. 10, 1841, in Hanover.
Zilpha Gundeway, d. Lem[ue]l and Betsey, Jan. 1, 1815.
[torn]nna, d, Thirza, May 20, 1837.
―――, ch. John and Harriet, Feb. 18, 1844.
―――, s. Richard, shoemaker, and Celia, Apr. 26, 1844.
―――, s. Richard and Celia, Apr. 21, 1848.

FRENCH, George, s. Melvin and Theatsey, Oct. 1, 1833.
Henry F., ch. Freeman and Joanna, Sept. 6, 1825, in Hingham.
Joanna W., ch. Freeman and Joanna, Sept. 8, 1827, in Hingham.
Lydia H., ch. Freeman and Joanna, July 13, 1841.
Mary J., ch. Freeman and Joanna, Aug. 13, 1838, in Abington.
Melvin, s. Melvin and Theatsey, Mar. 12, 1829.
Phineas, s. Melvin and Theatsey, Mar. 22, 1831.
Sarah E., ch. Freeman and Joanna, Apr. 8, 1832, in Abington.

FROST, Martha S. [w. George O[tis] Torrey], Nov. 10, 1821, in
  Saco [Me]. P.R.24.

FULLER, Mary Elizabeth, d. Milton and Rachel, July 26, 1826, in Boston.
Mary Elizabeth, ch. Dr. Milton and Rachel, bp. Nov. 4, 1832. C.R.1.
Rachel Aphia, d. Milton and Rachel, July 28, 1824, in Westminster.
Rachel Aphia, ch. Dr. Milton and Rachel, bp. Nov. 4, 1832. C.R.1.
Samuel, s. Samuel, bp. Feb. 11, 1637. C.R.1.

FURGUSON (see Ferguson), Esther C. [dup. Ferguson], d. W[illia]m, stage driver, and Lydia, May 1, 1845.

GAD, Lucretia Leonard, d. Polly, June 5, 1818.

GALLOW, Bethyah Woodard, d. Will[ia]m Jr. and w., bp. Oct. 29, 1797. C.R.2.
Margaret, d. Will[ia]m and w., bp. Sept. 21, 1800. C.R.2.

GAMMON, Edward "a native of Waterford, Ireland," Jan. 12, 1826. G.R.10.
Patrick, ―― [1822]. G.R.10.

GANITT (see Gannet, Gannett, Gannit, Gannitt), Samuell, s. Mathew (Gannett) Jr., Feb. 13, 1714.

GANNET (see Ganitt, Gannett, Gannit, Gannitt), Benjamin, s. Sam[ue]l, bp. June 6, 1777. C.R.1.
Hanah, d. Joseph, Aug. 4, 1684.
Hannah, d. Sam[ue]l, bp. Nov. 4, 1759. C.R.1.
Hannah, d. Samuel, bp. Oct. 9, 1763. C.R.1.
Isaac, s. Elkaney (Gannett) and Marcy, Sept. 27, 1796.
Joseph, s. Joseph, bp. July 31, 1719. C.R.1.
Joseph, s. Joseph of Bridgwater, bp. Oct. 7, 1722. C.R.1.
Lucy, d. Sam[ue]ll, bp. Sept. 26, 1773. C.R.1.
Mary, d. Matthew Jr., bp. Apr. 15, 1722. C.R.1.
Mary, ch. Matthew Sr., bp. July 15, 1722. C.R.1.
Matthew, ch. Matthew Sr., bp. July 15, 1722. C.R.1.
Matthew, s. Elkaney (Gannett) and Marcy, Apr. 5, 1787.
Samuel, ch. Matthew Sr., bp. July 15, 1722. C.R.1.
Sarah, d. Samuel, bp. Sept. 28, 1766. C.R.1.
Susanna, d. Matthew, bp. Apr. 25, 1759. C.R.1.
Thomas, s. Samuel and Mercy, July 5, 1793.

GANNETT (see Ganitt, Gannet, Gannit, Gannitt), Abby J., d. Seth, blacksmith, and Martha, Dec. 7, 1846.
Abigail, d. Matthew, bp. Oct. 22, 1749. C.R.1.
Beckey, d. Joseph and Ruth, Mar. 18, 1796.

GANNETT, Benjamin, s. Sam[ue]l and Sarah, bp. July 14, 1754. C.R.1.
Catharine, d. Elkanah and Marcy, Sept. 12, 1805.
Charlotte, d. Elkanah and Marcy, June 20, 1801.
Clarissa, d. Elkanah and Marcy, Nov. 12, 1791.
Cole, s. Joseph and Ruth, Apr. 6, 1794.
Deborah, d. Joseph, Feb. —, 1690–1.
Deborah, d. Matthew Jr., Dec. 13, 1712. [Gannet, C.R.1.]
Deborah T. [———], w. Thomas, —— [1796]. G.R.6.
Edward, s. Matthew and Sybil, June 1, 1810.
Elisabeth [dup. crossed out, Ganitt], d. Mathew (Ganitt) Jr. [dup. crossed out, (Ganett) Jr.], Feb. 1, 1718. [Elizabeth Gannet, d. Matthew Jr., C.R.1.]
Elizabeth, d. Elkanah and Marcy, Oct. 19, 1793.
Elizabeth, d. Matthew and Sybil, Oct. 6, 1808.
Elkanah, s. Matthew and Submit, May 20, 1761.
Ellen, ch. Freeman and Elvira, —— [rec. after ch. b. Nov. 13, 1844].
Elvira, d. Freeman, shoemaker, and Elvira, Nov. 13, 1844.
Freeman Howard, ch. Freeman and Elvira, ——, 1842.
Freman, s. Joseph and Ruth, Oct. 6, 1803. [Freeman, G.R.2.]
George King, s. Joy and Mary, Dec. 27, 1828, in Cohasset.
Hannah, d. Mathew, Mar. 29, 1702.
Howard, s. Joseph and Ruth, May 23, 1808.
Isabelle, d. Elkanah and Marcy, Dec. 5, 1798.
Jared, s. Elizabeth, Dec. 13, 1827.
Joseph, s. Joseph, Apr. —, 1686.
Joseph, s. Joseph, Sept. 3, 1693.
Joseph, s. Matthew, bp. July 14, 1754. C.R.1.
Joseph, s. Sam[ue]l, bp. Dec. 4, 1757. C.R.1.
Joseph, s. Samuel and Sarah, July 1, 1768. [[h. Ruth] G.R.2.]
Joseph, s. Joseph and Ruth, Sept. 21, 1810.
Joy, s. Joseph and Ruth, June 10, 1798.
Judith [? m.], —— [1788]. G.R.2.
Lewis, s. Elkanah and Marcy, Sept. 20, 1799.
Louiza Joy, d. Joy and Mary, Nov. 3, 1827, in Cohasset.
Lucy Thomas, ch. Joseph Jr. and Mercy J., ——.
Marcy [? m.], —— [1769].
Marcy Jones, d. Thomas and Lucy, Jan. 23, 1814. [Mercy J., w. Joseph Jr., G.R.2.]
Mary [———], w. Samuel, —— [1770]. G.R.2.
Mary Rogers, d. Joy and Mary, Dec. 29, 1832.
Matthew, s. Joseph, Oct. 12, 1688.
Mercy (see Marcy).
Mercy, d. Elkanah and Marcy, June 21, 1789.

GANNETT, Nabby, d. Joseph and Ruth, June 25, 1800.
Prince, s. Matthew, bp. Oct. 30, 1756. C.R.1.
Ruth, d. Mathew and Submit, Mar. 20, 1771.
Seth, s. Matthew and Submit, bp. Nov. 1, 1747. C.R.1.
Seth, s. Joseph and Ruth, Mar. 1, 1806.

GANNIT (see Ganitt, Gannet, Gannett, Gannitt), Caleb, s. Joseph and Hannah, Dec. 17, 1720. [Gannet, C.R.1.]
Samuel, s. Matthew and Mary, Apr. 26, 1721.

GANNITT (see Ganitt, Gannet, Gannett, Gannit), Mary, d. Mathew, Oct. 31, 1716.
Mathew, s. Mathew, Apr. —, 1685.
Mathew, s. Mathew, Dec. 17, 1718.
Seth, s. Mathew Jr., Sept. 18, 1716. [Gannet, s. Matthew Jr., C.R.1.]

GARDNER, Abby S., d. Thomas H., shoemaker (b. Hingham), and Deborah, Mar. 13, 1849, in S. Scituate.
Abigail L., ch. John and Ruth, Sept. 18, 1829, in Hanson.
Angus, ch. John and Ruth, July 19, 1827, in Hanson.
Augustus [h. Mary A. (Cudworth)], ——, 1833. G.R.14.
Benjamin T., ch. John and Ruth, Dec. 2, 1834.
Caroline, ch. John and Ruth, Jan. 14, 1825, in Hanson.
Eliza A. [ch. Reuben and Polly], ——, 1824.
Eliza H., ch. Horatio N. and Martha, Nov. 17, 1840.
Elizabeth [———], w. John Jr. [Aug. —, 1824]. G.R.15.
Emma Augusta, ch. Stephen and Maria, Aug. 13, 1836.
Estella, d. Horatio N., blacksmith (b. Hingham), and Martha (b. Newburyport), July 6, 1849, in S. Scituate.
Helen, ch. Stephen and Maria, Nov. 12, 1837.
Henrietta, d. Horatio N., blacksmith, and Martha, Apr. 25, 1847.
Henry, ch. John and Ruth, Oct. 7, 1841.
Henry C., ch. Thomas H. and Sally, Mar. 13, 1841, in Hanover.
Henry H., ch. Samuel and Elizabeth, July 10, 1840.
Henry H., " Co. G. 18th. Regt M. V. M.," Aug. 15, 1841. G.R.15.
Jared P., ch. John and Ruth, Sept. 1, 1832, in Hanson. [Gardener, G.R.15.]
John [h. Ruth], Feb. 27, 1799. G.R.15.
John, ch. John and Ruth, Aug. 7, 1822, in Hanson. [John Jr., G.R.15.]
John D., ch. Thomas H. and Sally, Mar. 24, 1843.
Lucy A., d. Reuben, stagedriver, and Lucy, Mar. 3, 1848.
Martha Ann, ch. Horatio N. and Martha, Dec. 22, 1838.
Mary A., ch Thomas H. and Sally, June 20, 1837, in Ab ngton.

GARDNER, Mary Ann, d. Thomas H. and Deborah, July 23, 1846.
Mary E., d. John Jr., factory clerk (b. Hanover), and Elizabeth, Apr. 3, 1849, in S. Scituate.
Mary Nothey, d. Reubin and Polly, Oct. 31, 1811.
Reuben, s. Reuben and Polly, Nov. 8, 1809.
Robert C., ch. Thomas H. and Sally, June 23, 1839, in Abington.
Ruth [———], w. John, Dec. 7, 1801. G.R.15.
Ruth C., ch. John and Ruth, Aug. 12, 1838.
Sarah Maria, ch. Stephen and Maria, Feb. 25, 1835.
Sophia, ch. Stephen and Maria, Dec. 31, 1833.
Sydnia, ch. Horatio N. and Martha, Apr. 8, 1843.
Wilber F., s. John Jr., tack maker, and Elizabeth, Jan. 3, 1848.
———, twin ch. John and Ruth, Oct. 1, 1839.
———, twin ch. John and Ruth, Oct. 1, 1839.
———, s. H., blacksmith, and Marthy, Mar. 29, 1844.
———, s. Harrison, shoemaker, and Sally, Apr. 4, 1844.

GARRET (see Garrett), Jo[h]n, s. John, Jan. 17, 1741.
Lidiah, d. John, bp. Sept. 30, 1688. C.R.2.
Ruth, d. Joseph, bp. July 9, 1682. C.R.2.

GARRETT (see Garret), Anne, d. Richard, Oct. 8, 1696.
Deborah, d. Richard, Feb. 22, 1697-8.
Elizabeth, d. Joseph, Aug. 14, 1686.
Jael, d. Joseph, Apr. 2, 1692.
John, s. Richard, Nov. 25, 1651.
John, s. Richard, Dec. 23, 1706.
Joseph, s. Richard, Mar. 10, 1648-9. [Garret, C.R.2.]
Joseph, s. Joseph, Apr. 10, 1690.
Lydia, d. John, June 27, 1687.
Mary, d. Richard, Nov. 5, 1655.
Mary, d. Joseph, Apr. 18, 1683.
Nathaniell, s. Richard, bp. May 14, 1654. C.R.2.
Richard, s. John, Jan. 4, 1689.
Ruth, d. Joseph, Dec. 24, 1680.

GEORGE, Frank, ——— [1835], in Fayall. G.R.10.
Phebe, d. Emme, bp. June 17, 1744. C.R.1.

GIBBONS, Helen, w. Seth Webb Jr., ———, 1826. G.R.6.

GIBBS, Ann, d. John, Dec. 11, 1719.
Anne, d. John, bp. Oct. 8, 1721. C.R.1.
John, s. John and Rachel, Aug. 22, 1760.

GILBERT, A. B., Oct. 8, 1826. G.R.11.
Abby W., d. Edwin, merchant, and Abigail, Nov. 8, 1846.

GILBERT, Alanson A. C. [h. Mary (Studley)] [h. Mary Frances] [Mar. —, 1827]. G.R.2.
E. W., May 7, 1848. G.R.11.
F. B., Apr. 4, 1810. G.R.11.
Frederick A., s. Edwin B., merchant [dup. trader], and Abigail, Jan. 7, 1844 [dup. 1845].
Mary Frances [———], w. A[lanson] A. C. [May —, 1841]. G.R.2.
Mary S. [———], w. A. A. C. [Oct. —, 1828]. C.R.1.
———, s. Edwin B., merchant (b. Sharon), and Abigail E., Nov. 12, 1849, in S. Scituate.

GILFORD, Agatha, d. W[illia]m and Elizabeth, bp. Nov. 2, 1718. C.R.2.
Elizabeth, d. W[illia]m and Eliz[abeth], bp. May 16, 1725. C.R.2.
John, s. William and Elizabeth, bp. Apr. 12, 1725. C.R.2.
Susannah, d. Will[ia]m and Eliz[abeth], bp. June 2, 1717. C.R.2.
William, s. Will[ia]m and Elizabeth, bp. June 2, 1717. C.R.2.

GILKEY (see Gilkie), Jacob, s. James, bp. June 21, 1752. C.R.2.
James, s. James and Grace, bp. July 24, 1743. C.R.2.
James, s. James and Grace, bp. Sept. 9, 1750. C.R.2.
Rachel, d. James and Grace, bp. May 24, 1741. C.R.2.

GILKIE (see Gilkey), John, s. James and Grace, bp. June 16, 1745. C.R.2.
Lucresia, d. James and Grace, bp. Jan. 24, 1747–8. C.R.2.

GINKINGS (see Jenken, Jenkens, Jenkiens, Jenkings, Jenkins), Edward, s. Thomas, Aug. 3, 1683. [Jenken, C.R.2.]
Hanah, d. Thomas, July 21, 1679.
Thomas, s. Thomas, Jan. 15, 1681. [Ginkins, C.R.2.]

GLASS, Consider [h. Sarah], ——, 1793. G.R.3.
Consider, Capt., —— [1813]. C.R.1.
Sarah [———], w. Consider, ——, 1795. G.R.6.

GLEASON, Elizabeth C. R. [? m.] [Feb. —, 1824]. G.R.15.

GLINES, Andrew Perry, Jan. 31, 1820, in Wentworth, N.H. P.R.16.
Isaac [Sept. —, 1765]. P.R.16.
Isaac, h. Hannah (Kimball), Apr. 2, 1792, in Northfeild, N.H. P.R.16.
Mary Arianna, Oct. 31, 1823, in Wentworth, N.H. P.R.16. [Mary Ariannah, P.R.22.]

GLOVER, Catherine Jacobs, d. Martin C. and Sophronia, July 29, 1839.
Ellen Jane, d. Martin C. and Sophronia, Mar. 30, 1841.

GLOVER, Henry, s. Martin C. and Sophronia, July 29, 1833.
Martin Colburn, s. Martin C. and Sophronia, Aug. 28, 1824.
Sophronia, d. Martin C. and Sophronia, July 29, 1826.
———, ch. Martin C. and Sophronia, Apr. 12, 1843.

GOLD, William, s. Rachel, bp. Aug. 5, 1744. C.R.1.

GOODRIDGE, Martha, ——— [1792]. G.R.6.

GOODSPEED, Nathanael, ch. Nathan[ie]ll and Sarah of Rochester, bp. Aug. 29, 1708. C.R.2.
Stephen, ch. Nathan[ie]ll and Sarah of Rochester, bp. Aug. 29, 1708. C.R.2.
Thankfull, d. Nath[anie]l, bp. Apr. 18, 1737. C.R.1.

GORDAK, Henrietta A., d. Dr. W[illia]m and Martha H., w. Geo[rge] H. French [May —, 1828]. G.R.11.
Martha H. [———], w. Dr. W[illia]m [Aug. —, 1805]. G.R.11.

GORDON, James (see James Blankinship).

GOTHAM, Elnathan Cushing, ch. Henry and Ann Jane, Mar. 20, 1839.
Henrietta, ch. Henry and Ann Jane, Apr. 5, 1835.
Maria M., ch. Henry and An Jane, Nov. 16, 1843.
———, s. Henry, millwright, and Ann J., Apr. 10, 1844.

GRANDERSON (see Grandison), Charles, ———, 1805. G.R.14.
Harriet [? m.], ———, 1793. G.R.14.
Reuben, negro, s. Coff, Feb. 20, 1781.

GRANDISON (see Granderson), Abigail, ch. Charles and Harriet, June 26, 1839.
George, ch. Charles and Harriet, Jan. 28, 1831.
Harriet, ch. Charles and Harriet, Jan. 1, 1834.
Harriet, ch. Charles and Harriet, May 26, 1835.
Mary, ch. Charles and Harriet, May 7, 1832.

GRASSIE, Frances [? m.], ——— [1834]. G.R.10.

GRAY, Ann L. [? m.], ———, 1820. G.R.7.
Anthony, ———, 1816. G.R.7.
Elizabeth, d. Tho[ma]s of Ireland, bp. Oct. 18, 1741. C.R.2.
George, s. Thomas and Sarah of Ireland, bp. Nov. 23, 1735. C.R.2.
Lydia, d. Sarah, bp. Apr. 26, 1767. C.R.1.
Mary, d. James and w., bp. Nov. 24, 1745. C.R.2.
Sarah, d. Thomas and Sarah, bp. Aug. 13, 1738. C.R.2.
Thomas Baldwin, s. Anthoney, cordwainer, and Ann, June 29 [1844].

GREEN (see Greene), Abigail M., d. Andrew, sailor, and Louis, Aug. 10, 1844.
Albert S., s. Thomas B., farmer, and Amelia B., Aug. 29, 1847.

GREENE (see Green), Lydia Frances [———], w. Albert S., Mar. 8, 1841. G.R.15.
Tho[ma]s B., Capt., Apr. 25, 1810. G.R.15.

GRIFFIN, Bristah, s. Antho[n]y and Meriah, Nov. 28, 1752.
David, s. Polly, Apr. 21, 1817.
Jemima, d. Antho[n]y and Meriah, Aug. 23, 1750.

GRIGGS, Elizabeth W. [———], w. Reuben, Mar. 22, 1819. G.R.14.

GROSE (see Gross), Deborah, d. Edmond and Olive, Dec. 31, 1756.
Elijah, s. Edmond and Olive, Aug. 16, 1760.
Joshua, s. Edmond and Olive, Apr. 8, 1758.

GROSS (see Grose), Charles, ch. Ansel G. and Rebecca, June 15, 1828, in Hanover.
Deborah Sylvester, d. Lewis and Deborah F., Feb. 10, 1826.
Dexter, ch. Ansel G. and Rebecca, — 9, 1830, in Hanover.
Edmond, s. Edmond and Olive, Dec. 3, 1739.
Edmund, s. Edmund and Oliffe, bp. Sept. 6, 1741. C.R.2.
Elisha, s. Edmond and Olive, Mar. 16, 1749.
George H., s. Henry A., shoemaker (b. Hanover), and Julia A., Nov. 22, 1849, in S. Scituate.
George W., ch. H. and w., Jan. 4, 1844.
George Webster, ch. Ansel G. and Rebekah, Jan. 14, 1844.
Helen M., ch. Ansel G. and Rebekah, Feb. 1, 1838.
Henry A., ch. Ansel G. and Rebecca, Mar. 12, 1826, in Hanover.
Jacob, s. Elisha and Deborah, Jan. 20, 1793.
James Lewis, s. Lewis and Deborah F., Apr. 18, 1828.
John, s. Edmond [Edmund, C.R.2.] and Olive, Nov. 13, 1738.
John, s. E[l]isha and Deborah, Jan. 26, 1790.
John D., ch. Ansel G. and Rebekah, Dec. 1, 1840.
John Edward, s. John and Roxana, May 12, 1819.
Lewis, s. Elisha and Deborah, July 16, 1795.
Lucinda Wilder, d. John and Roxanna, Sep[t]. 2, 1829.
Lucy, d. Edmond and Olive, Nov. 22, 1751.
Martha, d. Edmond and Olive, Jan. 13, 1743.
Mary, d. Edmond and Olive, June 6, 1748.
Mary E., ch. Ansel G. and Rebekah, Sept. 20, 1836.
Nelson, ch. Ansel G. and Rebecca, Aug. 12, 1832, in Hanover.
Olive, d. Edmon and Olive, Oct. 23, 1740.

GROSS, Olive, d. Edmund and Olive, bp. Mar. 6, 1742–3. C.R.2.
Rebekah Jane, ch. Ansel G. and Rebekah, Sept. 20, 1834.
Roxana Wilder, d. John and Roxana, Dec. 1, 1822.
Thomas, s. Edmond and Olive, Jan. 3, 1745.

GROSVENER (see Grosvenor), Deborah, d. Rev. Ebenezer [Rev. Eben, C.R.1.] and Elizabeth, Jan. 10, 1765.
Ebenezer, s. Rev. Eben[eze]r and Elizabeth, Mar. 11, 1768. [Grosvenor, C.R.1.]
Eliza[beth], d. Rev. Ebenezer and Eliza[beth], Dec. 3, 1769. [Grosvenor, C.R.1.]
Lucy, d. Rev. Ebenezer and Eliza[beth], June 4, 1766. [Grosvenor, d. Rev. Eben, C.R.1.]
Nancy, d. Ebenez[e]r and Eliza[beth], Feb. 17, 1773. [Grosvenor, d. Rev. Eben[ezer], C.R.1.]
Peter Clark, s. Rev. Ebenezer and Eliza[beth], Aug. 9, 1771. [Grosvenor, s. Rev. Eben, C.R.1.]

GROSVENOR (see Grosvener), Elizabeth, d. Rev. Eben, bp. June 18, 1775. C.R.1. [Elesebeth, P.R.26.]
Mary, d. Rev. Eben, Apr. 3, 1777. C.R.1.
Sally, d. Rev. E., July 29, 1779. C.R.1.

GUILD, Luthera, d. Josiah, bootmaker (b. Bellow Falls, Vt.), and Mary (b. Marshfield), July 27, 1849, in S. Scituate.

GUNDERWAY, Almira, ch. Jeremiah and Celia, Dec. 30, 1801.
Celia, ch. Jeremiah and Celia, Sept. 17, 1815.
Ezekiel, ch. Jeremiah and Celia, Oct. 17, 1804.
Ezekiel E., ch. Jeremiah Jr. and Lydia, Aug. 22, 1841.
Ferdinand, ch. Jeremiah and Celia, Jan. 19, 1810.
Jeremiah, ch. Jeremiah and Celia, May 26, 1807.
Samuel, ch. Jeremiah and Celia, Oct. 19, 1812.
Samuel, ch. Jeremiah Jr. and Lydia, Nov. 26, 1837.
Thomas H., ch. Jeremiah Jr. and Lydia, Dec. 21, 1838.

GURNEY, Anna, ch. Benoi and Mary S., Dec. 27, 1831.
Benoi, ch. Benoi and Mary S., Apr. 26, 1811.
Benoi, ch. Benoi and Mary S., Sept. 18, 1822.
Catharine M., ch. Benoi and Mary S., Aug. 18, 1825.
Eliza A. W., ch. Benoi and Mary S., Dec. 14, 1837.
Mary S., ch. Benoi and Mary S., Oct. 23, 1815.
Rebecca A., ch. Benoi and Mary S., Feb. 25, 1827.
Reuben S., ch. Benoi and Mary S., Apr. 28, 1824.
Silas, ch. Benoi and Betsey, Jan. 3, 1842.

GURNEY, Tryphosa H., ch. Benoi and Mary S., Oct. 14, 1829.
Winfield S., s. Benoi, pedler, and Betsey, May 16, 1846.

HALL, Abigail, d. John, Sept. 5, 1708.
Abigail, d. John, bp. Oct. 29, 1710. C.R.1.
Almira, d. Mathew and w., bp. Mar. 14, 1827. C.R.1.
Asa, ch. Robert and Catharine J., Oct. 16, 1833.
Bridget, d. Mathew, fisherman (b. Ireland), and Mary (b. Ireland), Sept. 20, 1837, in Ireland.
Catharine, ch. Mercy, wid., bp. Nov. 5, 1820. C.R.1.
Catherine, d. John of Marshfild, bp. June 6, 1725. C.R.1.
Catherine [———], w. Robert, Oct. 3, 1810. G.R.6.
Catherine, d. Mathew, fisherman (b. Ireland), and Mary (b. Ireland), Oct. 16, 1835, in Ireland.
[Catherine] ch. Robert and Catharine J., May 30, 1842.
Cattern, d. John, Oct. 27, 1723.
Charlotte [———], w. Harvey, ——— [1805]. C.R.1.
Elizabeth, d. John, June 24, 1710.
Jane, d. Mathew, fisherman (b. Ireland), and Mary (b. Ireland), Sept. 17, 1843, in Ireland.
John, s. John, Jan. 4, 1712–13.
Joseph Ewell, ch. Robert and Catharine J., Nov. 29, 1837.
Mary, d. John, Aug. 28, 1706.
Mary, d. John, bp. Oct. 29, 1710. C.R.1.
Nancy, w. Rufus Clapp, ———, 1826. G.R.6.
Rachel, d. Jo[h]n, Dec. 26, 1721.
Rachel, d. John, bp. Apr. 14, 1723. C.R.1.
Richard, s. Mathew, fisherman (b. Ireland), and Mary (b. Ireland), Aug. 16, 1839, in Ireland.
Robert [h. Catherine], Apr. 13, 1806. G.R.6.
Robert, ch. Mercy, wid., bp. Nov. 5, 1820. C.R.1.
Robert Henry, ch. Robert and Catharine J., Sept. 30, 1831.
Sally, d. Sally, wid., bp. Sept. 7, 1817. C.R.1.
Sarah, d. John, May 14, 1719.
Susan Hopkins, d. Sally, wid., bp. Sept. 7, 1817. C.R.1.
Susanna, d. John, May 1, 1717.
Timothy, s. John, Dec. 5, 1714.

HAMATT (see Hammatt), Thompson Philips, ch. Maj. W[illia]m, bp. June 8, 1822. C.R.2.

HAMILTON, Alexander, s. Leonard and Ruth, Jan. 6, 1824.
Almira, d. Sally B., Nov. 27, 1833.
Angeline Frances, d. Silas and Deborah, June 29, 1833.
Asa George, s. Silas and Sarah, Oct. 27, 1788.

HAMILTON, Barnabas Morro, s. Leonard and Ruth, Nov. 27, 1808.
Cordelia, d. Silas and Deborah, Aug. 7, 1836.
Emely, d. Leonard and Ruth, Sept. 17, 1820.
George Washington H., s. Leonard and Ruth, July 27, 1822.
Leonard, s. Silas and Sarah, Feb. 23, 1786.
Leonard, s. Leonard and Ruth, Nov. 10, 1813.
Rebekah Colburn, d. Leonard and Ruth, Sept. 19, 1815.
Rebekah Frances, d. Silas and Deborah, Dec. 31, 1830.
Ruth Morrice, d. Leonard and Ruth, Sept. 30, 1817.
Sally Bailey, d. Leonard and Ruth, Nov. 10, 1811.
Silas, s. Silas and Sarah, Aug. 20, 1791.
Silas, s. Leonard and Ruth, July 27, 1807.
William, s. Leonard and Ruth, Aug. 2, 1826.

HAMMATT (see Hamatt), John Howland, ch. W[illia]m Esq., bp. Aug. 15, 1825. C.R.2.

HAMMON (see Hammond, Hamon), Agatha, ch. Jedidiah, bp. May 17, 1724. C.R.2.
Benjamin, s. Jedediah, July 28, 1718.
Benj[a]m[in], ch. Jedidiah, bp. May 17, 1724. C.R.2.
Frederick, ch. Experience, bp. Nov. 4, 1810. C.R.1.
Joseph, ch. Jedidiah, bp. May 17, 1724. C.R.2.
Joseph, s. Joseph, bp. Mar. 14, 1741. C.R.1.
Joseph, ch. Experience, bp. Nov. 4, 1810. C.R.1.
Olive, d. Experience, bp. Aug. 5, 1810. C.R.1.
Sally, ch. Experience, bp. Nov. 4, 1810. C.R.1.
Sarah, [ch.] Benj[a]m[in] and Sarah, bp. Feb. 26, 1737-8. C.R.2.
Seth, s. Joseph, bp. Apr. 22, 1744. C.R.1.
Thankful, d. Joseph and Thankful, Aug. 13, 1738. [Thankfull, d. Joseph and Thankfull, C.R.1.]

HAMMOND (see Hammon, Hamon), Agatha (see Eagatha).
Benjamin, s. Benja[min], bp. Oct. 19, 1740. C.R.1.
Eagatha, d. Jos[eph] and Thank[fu]l, Aug. 15, 1764. [Agatha Hamon, bp. July 15 [*sic*], C.R.1.]
Egatha, d. Jedediah and Elizabeth, Sept. 13, 1713.
Experance, s. Joseph and Thankfull, Dec. 17, 1757. [Experience, C.R.1.]
Experience, s. Exper[ien]ce and Lettice, Aug. 11, 1789.
Frederick, s. Experience and Lettice, July 28, 1795.
Fredrick, s. Jos[eph] and Thankfull, Nov. 10, 1761. [Frederick Hamon, C.R.1.]
Joanna, d. Jedediah (Hamon) and Elizabeth, Mar. 9, 1721.
John, s. Experience and Lettice, Aug. 11, 1789.

HAMMOND, Joseph, s. Jedediah and Elizabeth, Dec. 1, 1714.
Joseph, s. Experence and Lettice, Dec. 10, 1801.
Ollive, d. Experence and Lettice, July 22, 1798.
Polly, d. Experience and Lettice, Feb. 26, 1781.
Sarah, d. Exper[ien]ce and Lettice, Jan. 25, 1793.
Thomas, s. Exper[ien]ce and Lettice, Jan. 15, 1785.
Will[ia]m, s. Jos[eph] and Thankfull, Aug. 26, 1760.
William, s. Experience and Lettice, Feb. 18, 1783.

HAMON (see Hammon, Hammond), Belea, s. Joseph and Thankfull, Jan. 29, 1756.
David, s. Joseph and Thankfull, Sept. 4, 1753. [Hammond, C.R.1.]
Joanna, d. Joseph (Haymon) and Thankful, Apr. 11, 1746. [Hammon, C.R.1.]
Joseph, s. Joseph and Thankful, Nov. 24, 1748. [Hammon, C.R.1.]
Lettes, d. Joseph and Thankful, Apr. 14, 1740. [Lettice Hammond, C.R.2.]
Lucy, d. Joseph and Thankful, Apr. 17, 1751. [Hammond, C.R.1.]
Seth, s. Joseph and Thankful, Mar. 1, 1743.
William, s. Joseph, b. Aug. 15, 1762. C.R.1.

HANKS, Elizabeth, d. Benjamin and Abigail, bp. ——, 1711. C.R.2.

HANMER, Abigail, d. Benjamin, Apr. 28, 1719.
Abigail, ch. Benj[a]m[in] and Abigail, bp. Oct. 21, 1722. C.R.2.
Hannah, d. John, bp. July 24, 1659. C.R.2.
Joseph, s. Benjamin and Abigal, Nov. 11, 1716.
Joseph, ch. Benj[a]m[in] and Abigail, bp. Oct. 21, 1722. C.R.2.
Rebecah, d. Joseph, May 27, 1685.

HARKEN, Unice, —— [1801]. G.R.10.

HARLOW, Charles E., ch. James M. and Elizabeth J., Oct. 29, 1843.
Ella J., d. James M. and Betsey J., Jan. 6, 1847.
George E., s. James M., shoemaker (b. Boston), and Betsey (b. Ft. Independence), Dec. 2, 1849, in S. Scituate.
Henry W., ch. James M. and Elizabeth J., Nov. 12, 1840, in Randolph.
James F. Bradlee, ch. James M. and Elizabeth J., Apr. 25, 1837, in Randolph.
Mary, d. Sam[ue]ll and Mary, June 22, 1717.
William B., ch. James M. and Elizabeth J., Sept. 24, 1839, in Randolph.

HARRIS, Abraham [h. Mary],———, 1778, in N. Carolina. G.R.14.
Desire, d. Abraham and Polly, Nov. 14, 1818.
Edwin, ch. Samuel and Sarah, Jan. 18, 1839.
Enoch, s. Abraham and Polly, June 1, 1812.
Enoch, ch. Abr[aha]m, bp. Sept. 27, 1814. C.R.2.
James, s. Abraham and Polly, Dec. 19, 1825.
Laura, d. Abraham and Polly, May 6, 1833.
Lucy, d. Abraham and Polly, Oct. 8, 1820.
Mary [———], w. Abraham, —— [1788]. G.R.14.
Mary Frances, ch. Samuel and Sarah, May 14, 1841.
Samuel, s. Abraham and Polly, Jan. 16, 1814.
Samuel, ch. Abrah[a]m, bp. Nov. 12, 1815. C.R.2.
Sarah Eastman, ch. Samuel and Sarah, Jan. 16, 1840.
Stephen, s. Abraham and Polly, Apr. 3, 1810.
Stephen, ch. Abrah[a]m, bp. Nov. 12, 1815. C.R.2.
William F., s. William and Clarissa, May 7, 1846.

HARRUB (see Hurrub), Charles, s. Isaac M. and Mercy, Mar. 25, 1835.
Darias, Apr. 18, 1812. G.R.6.
Ellen, d. Darius and M. F., bp. Dec. 5, 1847. C.R.3.
George, s. Isaac M. and Mercy, Feb. 12, 1830.
Isaac Thomas, s. Isaac M. and Mercy, July 5, 1827.
Maria Louisa, d. Isaac M. and Mercy, Dec. 5, 1836.
Mary T. Thomas Manson, ch. Darius and Matilda T. [Matilda F., C.R.3.], Mar. 17, 1844.
Matilda F. [———], w. Darius [Feb. —, 1815]. C.R.3.
Matilda Fidirike, ch. Darius and Matilda F., bp. Jan. 7, 1844. C.R.3.
Matilda Frederica, d. Isaac M. and Matilda, Aug. 7, 1839.
Mercy Bailey, d. Isaac M. and Mercy, Mar. 20, 1832.
Wilhelmina Concordia, d. Isaac M. and Matilda, May 6, 1842.
Wilhelmine Concordea, ch. Darius and Matilda, bp. Jan. 7, 1844. C.R.3.

HART, Peter [May —, 1809]. G.R.15.
Sarah, d. Edmund and Elizabeth (Clark), w. W[illia]m Delano, Aug. 18, 1778, in Boston. G.R.14.

HARVEY, Sarah M. [———], w. Joseph H., Jan. 24, 1833. G.R.2.

HASKINGS (see Haskins, Hoskins), Edward, s. Isaac, calker, and Sally, Aug. 3, 1846.

HASKINS (see Haskings, Hoskins), Betsey Arnold, d. Lemuel and Betsey R., Mar. 14, 1810.
Esther F., d. Isaac, caulker, and Sally, Nov. 20, 1844.

HASKINS, Isaac Hall, s. Lemuel and Sally, May 16, 1803. [[h. Sally F.] [h. Esther Stevens] G.R.15.]
Lemuel, s. Lemuel and Salley, July 20, 1799.
Lemuel F., ch. Isaac H. and Esther S., Mar. 19, 1840.
Ruth Delano, d. Lemuel and Betsey R., Aug. 26, 1813.
Sally Chase, d. Lemuel and Sally, June 3, 1801.
Sally F. [———], w. Isaac H. [Mar. —, 1816]. G.R.15.
William, s. Lemuel and Sally, Mar. 18, 1805.
William Cushing, ch. William and Hannah, Feb. 18, 1838.
Zilpah Bryant, d. Lemuel and Sally, Dec. 29, 1806.

HATCH, Abbie Caroline, d. Israel and Abigail [Dec.—, 1842]. G.R.15.
Abiall, s. James, May 19, 1704.
Abigail, d. Thomas, Nov. 10, 1678.
Abigail Phillips, d. Luther and Abigail P., Jan. 14, 1824.
Abigal, twin ch. Thomas and Hannah, Aug. 8, 1709.
Abigall, ch. Thomas, bp. June 25, 1682. C.R.2.
Abigil, d. Hezekiah and Patience, Nov. 12, 1741. [Abigail, C.R.2.]
Adeline, d. Marshal and Debby, Dec. 16, 1814. [Adeline H., w. ——— Litchfield, G.R.11.]
Adeline, d. Samuel and Marcy, July 20, 1821.
Aderline, ch. William and Mary Ann, Mar. 31, 1840. [Adeline, G.R.14.]
Agatha, d. Benja[min] and Mercy, June 14, 1762.
Anna, d. Jeremiah, Oct. 6, 1677.
Anna, d. Israel and Bethiah, Nov. 27, 1734.
Anna, d. Nehemiah and Mary, bp. July 19, 1747. C.R.2.
Annah, d. Nehemiah and Mary, July 16, 1748.
Anson, s. Jonathan Jr. and Mercy, July —, 1796.
Anthony Emes, s. Benja[min] Jr. and Mercy, Apr. 18, 1753.
Antipas, s. Walter, Oct. 26, 1658.
Artimissa, d. Jonathan Jr. and Mercy, May 19, 1791.
Arvilla, d. Jona[tha]n and Lucy, Nov. 10, 1783.
Asa Lawrence, s. Anson and Deborah, Jan. 3, 1825.
Augustus, s. Samuel, farmer, and Corselia [C[orelia], G.R.4.] M., Feb. 24, 1848.
Benja[min], s. Jo[h]n Jr. and Grace, June 28, 1721.
Benjamin, s. Joseph and Mary, Apr. 23, 1722.
Benja[min], s. Benja[min] Jr. and Mercy, Mar. 1, 1750.
Benjamin Jacob, s. Sam[ue]l [Sam[ue]ll, C.R.1.] and Marcy, Sept. 14, 1826.
Bethia, d. Walter, Mar. 31, [16]61. [Bethaia, C.R.2.]
Bethiah, d. Israel Jr. and Bethiah, Nov. 22, 1727 [*sic*, see Elizabeth].

HATCH, Betsy Turner, d. Jonathan Jr. and Marcy, May 19, 1802.
Charles, s. Benja[min] Jr. and Mer[c]y, Jan. 18, 1755.
Charles, s. Turner, farmer, and Elizabeth, Nov. 26 [dup. Nov. 25], 1844.
Chattureh, d. Thomas, Apr. 8, 1672.
Cushing, ch. Turner and Elizabeth F., Dec. 7, 1840.
Daniel, s. Hezekiah [Bezaliel, C.R.2.] and Patience, Feb. 19, 1735.
Daniel, s. Jona[tha]n and Lucy, Mar. 30, 1769.
Daniel, s. Jonathan Jr. and Lucy, Aug. 21, 1774. [[h. Nancy] G.R.2.]
Daniel [June —, 1800]. G.R.2.
Daniel, s. Daniel and Nancy, July 20, 1809.
David, s. Israell, Apr. 9, 1707.
David, [twin] s. Thomas and Hannah, Aug. 8, 1709.
David, ch. Israel and Elizabeth, bp. June 8, 1712. C.R.2.
David, s. David and Mary of Bridgwater, bp. June 14, 1730. C.R.2.
David, s. David and Eliza[beth], May 2, 1735.
David, s. David, bp. Aug. 19, 1739. C.R.1.
Debby, d. Daniel and Nancy, Apr. 23, 1805.
Deborah, d. Jeremiah, Mar. 24, 1678.
Deborah, d. Jeremiah Jr. and Deborah, bp. Nov. 4, 1722. C.R.2.
Deborah, d. Hezekiah and Deborah, Mar. 18, 1746.
Deborah, d. Benja[min] and Mercy, May 10, 1765.
Deborah, d. John and Deborah, Apr. 1, 1781.
Deborah, d. Marshal and Debby, Mar. 27, 1817.
Deborah Lincoln, d. Jonathan Jr. and Marcy, Apr. 3, 1798.
Deborah Litchfield, d. Anson and Merriel, Apr. 3, 1828.
Deborah Nash, ch. Thomas M. and Eunice, Jan. 20, 1840.
Desire, d. Samuell, Sept. 25, 1698.
Desire, d. Michael and Pricilla, Sept. 8, 1736.
Desire, d. David and Eliza[beth], Jan. 24, 1740.
Drusilla, d. Hezekiah and Deborah, Feb. 11, 1748.
Drusilla, d. Jonathan and Lucy, June [5], 177[2].
Ebenezer, s. Samuell, Apr. 6, 1684.
Eleazer [h. Hannah B.], —— [1800]. G.R.14.
Eleazer, ——, 1835. G.R.14.
Elijah, s. John and Deborah, Dec. 4, 1791.
Elisha, s. Sammuell, Nov. 7, 1692.
Elizabeth, d. Jerimiah, Mar. 10, 1668.
Elizabeth, d. Samuell, June 16, 1690.
Elizabeth, d. Israell, Jan. 22, 1703-4.
Elizabeth, ch. Israel and Elizabeth, bp. June 8, 1712. C.R.2.
Elizabeth, d. Israel Jr. and Bethiah, May 12, 1728 [*sic*, see Bethiah].

HATCH, Elizabeth, d. David and Eliza[beth], May 18, 1738.
Elizabeth, d. David, bp. Aug. 19, 1739. C.R.I.
Elizabeth F., ch. Turner and Elizabeth F., Dec. 25, 1836.
Elizebeth, d. Jerimya, bp. Sept. 9, 1683. C.R.2.
Eunice (see Unice).
Eunice Jacob, d. Samuel and Marcy, Aug. 24, 1813.
Eunice Jacob, ch. Sam[ue]ll, bp. Oct. 2, 1814. C.R.I.
Eunice Jacobs, ch. Thomas M. and Eunice, Jan. 10, 1842.
Ezekell, s. Samuel, May 14, 1695.
Febe, d. Jerimyah, Apr. 8, 1671.
George, s. John and Deborah, Aug. 11, 1783.
George, s. Warren and Sarah, May 1, 1818.
George Anson, ch. Turner and Elizabeth F., Feb. 28, 1839.
Grace, d. Jo[h]n Jr. and Grace, May 4, 1726.
Grace, d. Benja[min] Jr. and Mercy, Feb. 26, 1747.
Hanah, d. Thomas, July 26, 1673.
Hanah, d. Samuell, Feb. 15, 1681–2. [Hannah, C.R.2.]
Hanna, d. Wid. Hatch, bp. June 14, 1646. C.R.2.
Hannah, d. Walter, Mar. 3, 1651.
Hannah, d. Thomas, bp. June 24, 1683. C.R.2.
Hannah, d. Thomas, Apr. 12, 1703.
Hannah, d. Nehemiah, bp. Aug. 15, 1736. C.R.I.
Hannah B. [———], w. Eleazer, —— [1794]. G.R.14.
Hannah C., d. Turner, farmer, and Elizabeth S., Feb. 18, 1849, in S. Scituate.
Harriet C., ch. William and Mary Ann, July 10, 1841. [w. Amos T. Litchfield, G.R.14.]
Harriot, d. Daniel and Nancy, Nov. 7, 1811.
Henry Turner, ch. Turner and Elizabeth F., May 5, 1833.
Hesaciah, s. Thomas, Jan. 1, 1701–2.
Ichabod, s. Benja[min] Jr. and Mercy, May 8, 1767.
Isaac, s. Jeremiah Jr., Apr. 23, 1697.
Isaac, ch. Isaac and Lydia, bp. Sept. 30, 1722. C.R.2.
Isaace, s. Samuel, bp. May 1, 1687. C.R.2.
Isack, s. Samuell, Dec. 20, 1687.
Israel, ch. Israel and Elizabeth, bp. June 8, 1712. C.R.2.
Israel, s. Israel Jr. and Bethiah, Aug. 8, 1730.
Israel [h. Abigail F.] [Sept. —, 1818]. G.R.15.
Israell, s. Israell, May 5, 1701.
Isriell, s. Walter, Mar. 25, 1667.
James, s. Jerimiah, May 4, 1674.
James, s. James, Nov. 19, 1698.
Jane, d. Walter, Mar. 7, 1655.
Jane, d. Israel Jr., bp. July 11, 1732. C.R.2.

HATCH, Jane, d. Benja[min] and Jerusha, Dec. 29, 1746.
Jedediah, s. Jeremiah Jr., May 15, 1700.
Jeremiah, s. Thomas, Mar. 2, 1684–5.
Jeremiah, s. Jeremiah and Deborah, bp. June 27, 1725. C.R.2.
Jeremy, s. Jeremy, bp. Apr. 20, 1662. C.R.2.
Jerimiah, s. Jerimiah, Aug. 31, 1660.
Jerimiah, s. Jerimiah Jr., Aug. 10, 1694.
Joannah, d. Jerimiah, bp. June 10, 1679. C.R.2.
Johanah, d. Jerimiah, Mar. 21, 1662.
John, s. Walter, July 8, 1664.
John, s. Jerimiah, Jan. 4, 1666.
John, s. Jerimiah Jr., Apr. 10, 1690.
John, s. John, Oct. 20, 1697.
John, s. Roduphas, Mar. 16, 1702–3.
John, inf. s. John Jr. and Grace, bp. Feb. 20, 1719–20. C.R.2.
John, s. Israel Jr. and Bethiah, May 27, 1739.
John, s. Michael [Micael, C.R.2.] and Priscilla, Apr. 12, 1741.
John, s. Benja[min] Jr. and Mercy, Dec. 9, 1745.
John, s. Micheal and Pricilla, May 8, 1751.
John, s. Michael, bp. May 30, 1756. C.R.2.
John, s. John and Deborah, Mar. 6, 1772.
John, s. Jonath[an] and w., bp. Dec. 8, 1805. C.R.2.
John Willian, ch. William and Mary Ann, Aug. 1, 1838.
Jonathan, s. Israell, Oct. 28, 1709.
Jonathan, ch. Israel and Elizabeth, bp. June 8, 1712. C.R.2.
Jonathan, s. Hezekiah and Patience [Hannah, C.R.2.], May 26, 1739.
Jona[tha]n, s. Jona[tha]n and Lucy, July 27, 1764.
Joseph, s. Walter, Dec. 9, 1669.
Joseph, s. Thomas, May 6, 1682.
Joseph, s. Rodulphas, May 14, 1705.
Joseph, s. Benja[min] and Jerusha, May 28, 1754.
Joseph, s. Daniel and Nancy, Mar. 11, 1803.
Joseph H., ch. William and Mary Ann, Nov. 24, 1842.
Joshua, s. Micheal and Pricilla [s. Micael and Priscilla, C.R.2.], July 13, 1746.
Josiah, s. Samuell, May 30, 1680. [Josia, s. Samuel, C.R.2.]
Josiah, ch. Isaac and Lydia, bp. Sept. 30, 1722. C.R.2.
Judith, w. Col. Samuel Tolman, —— [1798]. G.R.15.
Julia, d. Marshal and Debbey, June 1, 1820.
Julia, d. Marshal and Deborah, Dec. 29, 1823.
Keturah (see Chattureh).
Keturah, d. Thomas, bp. June 24, 1683. C.R.2.
Leonard Clapp, ch. Turner and Elizabeth F., Apr. 18, 1835.

HATCH, Lidia, d. Thomas, bp. May 20, 1683. C.R.2.
Lidia, d. Jerimia, bp. Aug. 22, 1686. C.R.2.
Lidya, ch. Israel and Elizabeth, bp. June 8, 1712. C.R.2.
Lucretia Thomas, ch. Thomas M. and Eunice, Feb. 28, 1838.
Lucy, d. David and Eliza[beth], Mar. 29, 1746.
Lucy, d. Jona[tha]n and Lucy, Jan. 27, 1767. [[w. Simeon Litchfield] G.R.2.]
Lucy, d. Daniel and Nancy, July 31, 1807.
Lusannah Ruggles, d. George and w., bp. July 2, 1809. C.R.2.
Luther J., ch. Turner and Elizabeth F., Oct. 19, 1842.
Lyda, d. Jerimiah, Dec. 5, 1669.
Lydia, d. William, Apr. 28, 1653.
Lydia, d. William Sr. (s. Tho[ma]s), Jan. 7, 1654.
Lydia, d. William, bp. July 6, 1656. C.R.2.
Lydia, d. Thomas, Dec. 9, 1666.
Lydia, d. Israell, Oct. 16, 1699.
Lydia, d. Sam[ue]ll Jr. and Elizabeth, May 24, 1706.
Lydia, d. Samuel and Elizabeth, bp. Aug. 29, 1708. C.R.2.
Lydiah, d. Isaac and Penelipa, bp. Jan. 4, 1729–30. C.R.2.
Marcy, d. Jerimiah, Apr. 15, 1665.
Marcy Turner, d. Jonathan Jr. and Marcy, July 18, 1805.
Marcy Turner, d. Samuel and Marcy, Apr. 20, 1816. [Mercy Turner, C.R.1.]
Margarett, d. Thomas, Aug. 26, 1677.
Margeret, d. Thomas, bp. June 24, 1683. C.R.2.
Marshal, s. Jona[than] and Lucy, June 18, 1781. [Marshall, C.R.1.]
Marshall, s. Turner, farmer, and Elizabeth F., Dec. 4, 1846.
Martha, d. Nehemiah and Martha, July 13, 1738.
Mary, d. W[i]ll, bp. Oct. 3, 1652. C.R.2.
Mary, d. Jerimiah [Jeremy, C.R.2.], Feb. 14, 1658.
Mary, d. Thomas, Jan. 19, 1668.
Mary, ch. Thomas, bp. June 25, 1682. C.R.2.
Mary, d. John Jr. and Grace, Nov. 1, 1723.
Mary, d. Nehemiah and Martha, Apr. 21, 1734.
Mary, d. Benja[min] Jr. and Mercy, Jan. 27, 1741.
Mary Ann, d. Samuel and Eunice, Jan. 24, 1809.
Mary Ann, ch. Sam[ue]ll, bp. Oct. 2, 1814. C.R.1.
Mary Ann [———], w. William [May —, 1817]. G.R.14.
Mary Ann, ch. William and Mary Ann, Oct. 26, 1836. [w. David W. Turner, G.R.14.]
Mary Jane, d. Anson and Merriel, May 25, 1832.
Mathea, d. Thomas, Aug. 12, 1696.
Mehetable, d. John and Hannah, Feb. 11, 1712–13. [Mehetabal, d. John Jr. and Hannah, C.R.2.]

HATCH, Melzer, s. John and Deborah, Oct. 22, 1773.
Mercie [————], w. Samuel [Mar. —, 1786]. G.R.4.
Mercy, d. Jerimia, bp. May 4, 1679. C.R.2.
Mercy, d. Hezekiah and Patience, May 30, 1734.
Mercy, d. Benja[min] Jr. and Mercy, Mar. 7, 1743.
Mercy, d. John and Deborah, Nov. 11, 1777.
Mercy, d. John and Deborah, July 2, 1785.
Mercy Thomas, ch. Thomas M. and Eunice, Sept. 14, 1843.
Mercy Turner (see Marcy Turner Hatch).
Michael, s. Michael and Pricilla, Aug. 2, 1735.
Michael, s. Michael and Pricilla, Nov. 28, 1737. [Micael, s. Micael and Priscilla, C.R.2.]
Michaell, s. Thomas and Hannah, July 30, 1712.
Micheal, s. Micheal and Pricilla, July 21, 1748. [Macael, s. Michael and w., C.R.2.]
Molle Northey, d. Nehemiah and Mary, Feb. 27, 1749. [Molly Northy, C.R.2.]
Nancy [————], w. Daniel, —— [1777]. G.R.2.
Nancy, d. Daniel and Nancy, —— [rec. before ch. b. Mar. 11, 1803].
Naomy, d. Benja[min] and Jerusha, May 5, 1748.
Nathan, s. Jeremiah and Frances, bp. June 30, 1728. C.R.2.
Nehemiah (Hath), s. Thomas and Hannah, June 11, 1707.
Orra, d. Daniel and Nancy, Nov. 6, 1816.
Patience, d. Hezekiah and Patience, Feb. 19, 1736.
Penellope, d. Isaac and Penelope, bp. Feb. 20, 1725. C.R.2.
Persis, d. John and Deborah, Nov. 2, 1789.
Phebe (see Febe).
Phebe, d. James, June 17, 1701.
Phoebe, d. William, bp. Mar. 19, 1653. C.R.2.
Pricilla, d. Michael and Pricilla, Oct. 26, 1738. [Priscilla, d. Micael and Priscilla, C.R.2.]
Rachel, d. David and Eliza[beth], Oct. 12, 1748.
Rebecca, d. Benja[min] and Jerusha, Sept. 24, 1742.
Rebekah [? m.], —— [1798]. C.R.1.
Rhoda, d. Micheal and Pricilla, June 30, 1756.
Rhoda, d. Michael, bp. July 10, 1757. C.R.2.
Rodea, d. Micheal and Pricilla, June 8, 1753.
Rodulphus, s. Thomas, Dec. 26, 1674.
Rodulpus, ch. Thomas, bp. June 25, 1682. C.R.2.
Ruben, s. Nehemiah and Martha, Aug. 14, 1732.
Ruben, s. Nehemiah and Mary, Jan. 9, 1746.
Ruth, d. Sam[ue]ll Jr. and Elizabeth, Oct. 21, 1709.
Ruth, d. Hezekiah and Patience, Mar. 3, 1743.

HATCH, Ruth, d. Hezekiah and Deborah, July 20, 1752.
Samuel, s. Walter, Dec. 22, 1653.
Samuel, s. Samuel [Sam[ue]ll, C.R.2.] Jr. and Elizabeth, May 24, 1723.
Samuel, s. Isaac and Penelopy, bp. Aug. 1, 1736. C.R.2.
Samuel, s. Samuel and Marcy, May 10, 1824.
Samuel, s. Samuel, bp. Sept. 11, 1825. C.R.1.
Samuel Oakman, s. John and Deborah, Jan. 25, 1779.
Samuell, s. Samuell, Nov. 10, 1678. [Samuel, s. Samuel, C.R.2.]
Sarah, d. Thomas, May 23, 1664.
Sarah, d. Thomas, bp. May 20, 1683. C.R.2.
Sarah, d. Isaac of Hanover, bp. May 26, 1728. C.R.2.
Sarah, d. Isaac and Penelopa, bp. Sept. 15, 1734. C.R.2.
Sarah, d. Michael and Pricilla [d. Mical and Priscilla, C.R.2.], Apr. 14, 1742.
Sarah, d. Michael and Pricilla, Apr. 17, 1743.
Sarah, d. Jona[than] and Lucy, Nov. 8, 1761.
Sarah, d. Warren and Sarah, May 25, 1813.
Sarah Jacobs (Hacth), d. Samuel [Sam[ue]ll, C.R.1.] and Marcy, Dec. 20, 1818.
Sela, d. Benja[min] and Mercy, Apr. 16, 1758.
Seth, s. Isaac and Penelipah, bp. Dec. 24, 1727. C.R.2.
Shadruch, s. James, May 26, 1706.
Stephen, s. Isaac and Sarah, bp. May 20, 1722. C.R.2.
Stephens, s. Jeremiah Jr., Aug. 11, 1708.
Submit, d. Benja[min] and Jerusha, July 9, 1744.
Surviah, d. Thomas, Apr. 16, 1705.
Susanna, d. Michael and Pricilla, Aug. 24, 1733.
Thankfill, d. Micheal and Pricilla, May 14, 1745. [Thankfull, ch. Micael and Priscilla, C.R.2.]
Thankfull, d. Micael, bp. May 27, 1744. C.R.2.
Thomas, s. Thomas, Dec. 4, 1670.
Thomas, s. Jerimiah, Dec. 15, 1672.
Thomas, ch. Thomas, bp. June 25, 1682. C.R.2.
Thomas, s. Jerimiah Jr., Oct. 20, 1692.
Thomas, s. Thomas, Mar. 30, 1698.
Thomas, s. Hezekiah and Patience, May 10, 1732.
Thomas, s. Michael and Pricilla, July 8, 1734.
Thomas, s. David and Eliza[beth], May 20, 1743.
Thomas Marshal, s. Marshal and Debbey, July 16, 1812.
Turner, s. Jonathan Jr. and Mercy, Aug. 4, 1794.
Turner, s. Jonathan and Polly, July 13, 1813.
Unice, d. Hezekiah (Hattch) and Deborah, Apr. 27, 1745.
Warren, s. John and Deborah, Aug. 20, 1775.

HATCH, Warren, s. John and Deborah, July 2, 1787.
Warren, s. Warren and Sarah, July 13, 1816.
Willard Rogers, s. Samuel, farmer, and Corelia M. (b. Boston), Aug. 15, 1849, in Marshfield.
William, s. William, bp. Apr. 29, 1660. c.r.2.
William, s. Jabez "late" of Marshf[ie]ld, bp. Apr. 10, 1757. c.r.1.
William, s. Jonathan and Polly, Nov. 6, 1815. [[h. Mary Ann] g.r.14.]
William Smith, s. Anson and Merriel, Jan. 12, 1827.
Zephaniah, s. Thomas and Hannah, June 19, 1711.
Zephaniah, s. David and Eliza[be]th, Mar. 18, 1732.
—— Turner, d. Jonathan Jr. and w., bp. Oct. 30, 1803. c.r.2.
——, ch. David, bp. June 18, 1736. c.r.2.

HATHAWAY, H. W., —— [1849]. g.r.15.
Joseph T. [Oct. —, 1813]. g.r.15.
Marcy T. [? m.] [July —, 1819]. g.r.15.

HATHORNE (see Hawthorn, Hawthorne), Helen Thomas, ch. Thomas and Rachel, Apr. 11, 1827.
Jane Anderson, ch. Thomas and Rachel, July 1, 1834.
Mary Elizabeth, ch. Thomas and Rachel, Sept. 23, 1831.
Rebecca Bates, ch. Thomas and Rachel, Nov. 1, 1836.
Susan Rebecca, ch. Thomas and Rachel, Nov. 10, 1838.
William Porter, ch. Thomas and Rachel, July 8, 1829.

HAWTHORN (see Hathorne, Hawthorne), Sarah Ann, ch. Robert and Grace, July 15, 1838.
Thomas, ch. Robert and Grace, Apr. 28, 1840.

HAWTHORNE (see Hathorne, Hawthorn), Eliza, ch. Robert (Hawthorn) and Grace, July 29, 1825.
Grace, ch. Robert (Hawthorn) and Grace, June 18, 1827.
James, ch. Robert (Hawthorn) and Grace, Sept. 19, 1832.
Jane Mattesan, ch. Robert (Hawthorn) and Grace, Jan. 27, 1830.
John, ch. Robert (Hawthorn) and Grace, Dec. 6, 1823.
John Elijah, ch. Samuel (Hathorne) and Jane D., Sept. 23, 1832.
Mary, ch. Robert (Hawthorn) and Grace, Feb. 28, 1833.
Mary, ch. Robert (Hawthorn) and Grace, Oct. 1, 1836.
Robert, ch. Robert (Hawthorn) and Grace, Oct. 18, 1828.
William, ch. Robert (Hawthorn) and Grace, Mar. 4, 1835.

HAYDEN (see Heyden, Heydon, Hughden), Anna, d. Will[ia]m and Anna, Sept. 2, 1746.
Benjamin, s. Ezekel and Betty, Aug. 7, 1765.
Benjamin F., s. Peleg and Rhoda, May 8, 1802.
Benjamin Franklin, ch. Benjamin F. and Almira, Nov. 15, 1838.

HAYDEN, Charles Walter, s. Elisha and Martha, Mar. 10, 1822.
Cha[rle]s Walter, ch. Elisha, bp. Oct. 5, 1823. C.R.2.
Daniel, s. Ezekel and Betty, Nov. 9, 1763.
Deborah, d. Elisha and Martha, Sept. 11, 1807. [Heyden, C.R.2.]
Desire, twin d. William and Anna, Apr. 20, 1749.
Elisha, s. Elisha and Martha, Oct. 31, 1805. [Heyden, C.R.2.]
Emma, ch. Benjamin F. and Almira, July 26, 1841.
Ezra, s. Will[ia]m and Anna, May 17, 1754.
Fanna, d. Joseph, bp. Aug. 5, 1764. C.R.1.
Fanny, d. Benjamin and Ruth, ———— [rec. before ch. b. Dec. 4, 1795].
George B. [h. Louisa J.], ————, 1826. G.R.14.
Henry, s. Peleg and Rhoda, Sept. 19, 1786.
James, s. Benjamin and Ruth, Dec. 4, 1795.
Joshua, s. Ezekel and Betty, July 12, 1767.
Joshua s. Daniel and Nancy, July —, 1790.
Louisa J. [————], w. George B., ————, 1835. G.R.14.
Lucy, ch. Benjamin F. and Almira, Nov. 24, 1842.
Luther, s. Will[ia]m Jr. and Sarah, Apr. 19, 1767. [Heyden, C.R.1.]
Mabel, d. Will[ia]m Jr. and Sarah, Oct. 12, 1768.
Martha, d. Elisha and Martha, Sept. 23, 1814.
Martha, ch. Elisha, bp. June 9, 1816. C.R.2.
Mary, d. ———— and w., bp. Dec. 9, 1737. C.R.2.
Mary Ann, d. Elisha and Martha, June 29, 1811. [Heyden, C.R.2.]
Mary E. [————], w. Bartlett, ———— [1833]. G.R.14.
Nancy [————], w. Thomas O., July 30, 1845. G.R.7.
Peleg, s. Peleg and Rhoda, Dec. 15, 1792.
Prudance, twin d. William and Anna, Apr. 20, 1749.
Rhoda, d. Peleg and Rhoda, Oct. 13, 1789.
Rhoda Ann, ch. Benjamin F. and Almira, Jan. 2, 1835.
Roland Litchfield, ch. Benjamin F. and Almira, Dec. 27, 1835.
Serene, d. Peleg and Rhoda, Nov. 26, 1795.
Tameson, d. Will[ia]m and Anna, Sept. 12, 1751.
Thomas O. [h. Nancy], Aug. 1, 1840. G.R.7.
William, s. Will[ia]m and Anna, Nov. 9, 1744.
William, s. Elisha and Martha, Sept. 3, 1809.
William, s. Elisha and Martha, July 25, 1817.
William, ch. Elisha, bp. July 4, 1819. C.R.2.
William Wert, ch. Benjamin F. and Almira, Nov. 24, 1837.

HAYES, Mary T. [————], w. Oliver P., May 23, 1825. G.R.2.
Oliver P. [h. Mary T.], Jan. 30, 1818. G.R.2.
Priscilla [————], w. ————, ———— [1793]. C.R.1. [Pricilla, w. Jonathan, G.R.2.]

HAYWARD, Laura, —— [1844]. C.R.3.
Maria F. [——], w. Ward L., ——, 1839. G.R.7.
Ward L. [h. Maria F.], ——, 1839. G.R.7.

HEALY, Lydia, d. Benj[a]m[in], bp. May 31, 1766. C.R.1.
Timothy, s. Benj[a]m[in], bp. July 20, 1766. C.R.1.

HEARSEY (see Hearsy, Hersey, Hersy), Abigail, ch. William and Abigail of Abington, bp. July 18, 1725. C.R.2.
Isaac, ch. William and Abigail of Abington, bp. July 18, 1725. C.R.2.
Sarah, Aug. 26, 1768 [in Hingham or Scituate]. P.R.7.
William, ch. William and Abigail of Abington, bp. July 18, 1725. C.R.2.

HEARSY (see Hearsey, Hersey, Hersy), Mary, d. William (Hearsie) of Abington, bp. Mar. 9, 1728–9, in Hanover. C.R.2.

HENCHMAN (see Hinchsman, Hinksman), Deborah, ch. Joseph, bp. Dec. 3, 1704. C.R.2.
Edmond, ch. Joseph, bp. Dec. 3, 1704. C.R.2.
Hannah, d. Joseph and Mary, bp. July 29, 1705. C.R.2.
Mary, ch. Joseph, bp. Dec. 3, 1704. C.R.2.
Sarah, ch. Joseph, bp. Dec. 3, 1704. C.R.2.
Thomas, ch. Joseph, bp. Dec. 3, 1704. C.R.2.

HERRENDEEN, Hezekiah, s. Hezekiah and w. of Marshfield, bp. June 23, 1717. C.R.2.

HERSEY (see Hearsey, Hearsy, Hersy), Otis [h. Nancy A. (Merritt)], ——, 1816. G.R.14.

HERSY (see Hearsey, Hearsy, Hersey), Molly, d. Hannah, bp. May 12, 1751. C.R.1.

HEYDEN (see Hayden, Heydon, Hughden), Benjamin, ch. Ezekiel and w., bp. Feb. 26, 1775. C.R.1.
Betsy, d. Joseph, bp. May 8, 1774. C.R.1.
Daniel, ch. Ezekiel and w., bp. Feb. 26, 1775. C.R.1.
Elkanah, d. [sic] Will[ia]m Jr., bp. Sept. 1, 1776. C.R.1.
Esther, d. Joseph, bp. May 12, 1771. C.R.1.
James, ch. Ezek[iel], bp. Sept. 15, 1776. C.R.1.
Joshua, ch. Ezekiel and w., bp. Feb. 23, 1775. C.R.1.
Lucy, d. Joseph Jr., bp. June 7, 1767. C.R.1.
Nabbee, d. Ezra, bp. Sept. 15, 1776. C.R.1.
Nancy, ch. Ezek[iel], bp. Sept. 15, 1776. C.R.1.

HEYDEN, Ruth, d. W[illia]m Jr., bp. Nov. 4, 1770. C.R.1.
Temperance, d. Joseph, bp. May 12, 1771. C.R.1.
William, s. Ezra, bp. May 9, 1779. C.R.1.

HEYDON (see Hayden, Heyden, Hughden), Anna, d. Ezra, bp. Aug. 11, 1782. C.R.1.

HICK (see Hicke), Ephraim, s. Daniel, bp. Apr. 30, 1665. C.R.2.

HICKE (see Hick), Daniell, s. Daniell, bp. May 19, 1661. C.R.2.

HIGHLAND (see Hiland, Hilland, Hyland), Elizabeth, d. Thomas, bp. Sept. 24, 1665. C.R.2.
Mary, d. Tho[mas] Jr., bp. June 21, 1668. C.R.2.

HILAND (see Highland, Hilland, Hyland), Benjamin, s. John (Hyland) and Elizabeth, Sept. 30, 1711. [Hyland, C.R.1.]
Edmond, s. Samuel Jr. and Mehetable, Aug. 29, 1811.
Elizabeth, d. John, Feb. 2, 1697-8.
Henrey, s. Samuel Jr. and Mehetable, July 14, 1809.
James, s. John, Mar. 10, 1701-2.
John, s. John, July 4, 1704.
Lydia Bates, d. Samuel Jr. and Mahetable, Oct. 15, 1819.
Peleg, s. Samuel Jr. and Mahetable, Feb. 11, 1817. [Hyland [h. Mary J.], G.R.8.]
Ruth, d. John, Sept. 19, 1695.
Samuel Bennett, s. Samuel Jr. and Mahetable, June 18, 1814.
Sarah, d. John and Elizabeth, Jan. 9, 1706-7.
Thomas, s. John (Hyland) and Elizabeth, Jan. 23, 1708-9.

HILL, Abigail, ch. Daniel and Elizabeth, Jan. 19, 1826, in Boston.
Charles, ch. Daniel and Elizabeth, July 29, 1828, in Boston.
Daniel, ch. Daniel and Elizabeth, Jan. 31, 1821, in Boston.
Daniel E., s. Daniel Jr., carpenter, and Lydia S., Sept. 16, 1844.
Elizabeth, ch. Daniel and Elizabeth, May 13, 1824, in Boston.
George, ch. Daniel and Elizabeth, Nov. 17, 1835.
Joseph [h. Lois], —— [1776]. G.R.15.
Joseph, ch. Daniel and Elizabeth, June 27, 1837.
Lydia [? m.], ——, 1821. G.R.8.
Lydia M., d. Daniel Jr., housewright, and Lydia, Nov. 6, 1846.
Martha C., ch. Daniel and Elizabeth, Mar. 18, 1822, in Boston.
Olive, ch. Daniel and Elizabeth, Apr. 13, 1830, in Boston.
Sarah M., ch. Daniel and Elizabeth, Jan. 1, 1833, in Boston.
Susanna S., ch. Daniel and Elizabeth, May 27, 1823, in Boston.

HILLAND (see Highland, Hiland, Hyland), Elizabeth, d. Thomas, Aug. 15, 1665.

HILLAND, John, s. Thomas, Mar. 17, 1670-1. [Highland, C.R.2.]
Mary, d. Thomas, May 15, 1667.
Ruth, d. Thomas, June 15, 1673. [Highland, C.R.2.]
Thomas, s. Thomas, Jan. 25, 1662-3. [Highland, C.R.2.]

HINCHSMAN (see Henchman, Hinksman), Hannah, d. Joseph, Aug. 10, 1698.
William (Hincksman), s. Joseph, Apr. 2, 1696.

HINCKLEY (see Hinkley), Elizabeth, d. ———, bp. Sept. 6, 1635. C.R.1.
Samuell, s. Samuel, bp. Feb. 10, 1638. C.R.1.

HINKLEY (see Hinckley), Samuel, s. Samuell, bp. Feb. 4, 1637. C.R.1.

HINKSMAN (see Henchman, Hinchsman), Deborah, d. Joseph, Jan. 31, 1692.
Edmond, s. Joseph, Nov. 9, 1700.
Elizabeth, d. Joseph, July 17, 1685.
Joseph, s. Joseph, Sept. 22, 1694.
Mary, d. Joseph, June 22, 1689.
Sarah, d. Joseph, Sept. 1, 1702.
Thomas, s. Joseph, May 9, 1691.

HOBARD (see Hobart, Hubard), Abigall, [twin] ch. Iserell, May 20, 1678.
Nathanell, [twin] ch. Iserell, May 20, 1678. [Nathaniell Hubard, s. Israell, C.R.2.]

HOBART (see Hobard, Hubard), Abigall, d. Israell, Jan. 14, 1683-4. [Abigail Hobird, C.R.2.]
Iserell, s. Iserell, May 16, 1682. [Israell Hoburd, s. Israell, C.R.2.]
Israell, s. Israell, Feb. 5, 1686-7. [Hubird, s. Israel, C.R.2.]
Jaell, d. Israel, June 26, 1680. [Jael Huburd, d. Israell, C.R.2.]
Louisa P. [———], w. ———, ——— [1822]. C.R.3.

HOBSON, Andrew [dup. adds Jackson], s. Aaron, shoemaker (b. Raleigh, N.C.), and Sarah (b. Raleigh), Nov. 24, 1833.
Eliza A., d. Aaron, shoemaker (b. Raleigh, N.C.), and Sarah (b. Raleigh), June 13, 1826.
John B., s. Aaron, shoemaker (b. Raleigh, N.C.), and Sarah (b. Raleigh), Apr. 14, 1829.
Sarah M., d. Aaron, shoemaker (b. Raleigh, N.C.), and Sarah (b. Raleigh), Nov. 2, 1836. [Sarah N., w. Geo[rge] H. Sylvester, C.R.3.]

HOLBROKE (see Holbrook, Holəbroke, Holebrook, Holebrooke, Hollbrook, Hoolbrok), Samuel, s. Sam[ue]l Jr., bp. Jan. 13, 1754. C.R.1.

HOLBROOK (see Holbroke, Holebroke, Holebrook, Holebrooke, Hollbrook, Hoolbrok), Abiezer, s. John Jr. and Sarah, Sept. 16, 1719.
Abigail, d. John Jr. and Sarah, Apr. 7, 1724.
Desire, d. Sam[ue]ll (Holbrok) and Janes [*sic*, Jane], Dec. 28, 1726.
Elijah, ch. Sam[uel], bp. Jan. 26, 1777. C.R.1.
Elisha, s. Jo[h]n Jr. and Sarah, May 25, 1716.
Elisha, s. Samuel, bp. Mar. 20, 1765. C.R.1.
Ezekiel, s. Jo[h]n Jr. and Sarah, May 29, 1727.
Jane, ch. Sam[uel], bp. Jan. 26, 1777. C.R.1.
Josiah, s. Sam[ue]l Jr., bp. Nov. 7, 1756. C.R.1.
Luce, d. Jo[h]n Jr. and Sarah, Jan. 15, 1729.
Lydia, d. Sam[ue]ll and Jane, June 13, 1722.
Lydia, d. Sam[ue]l, bp. July 14, 1723. C.R.1.
Mabel, d. William, bp. Aug. 30, 1778. C.R.1.
Martha, d. John Jr. and Sarah, Nov. 11, 1721.
Mary, d. Sam[ue]l Jr., bp. Mar. 29, 1755. C.R.1.
Prisila, d. Sam[ue]ll and Jane, Apr. 18, 1724.
Samuel, s. Sam[ue]ll and Jane, Feb. 1, 1729.
Samuel, s. Samuel, bp. June 28, 1730. C.R.1.
Samuel [Aug. —, 1779]. C.R.1.
Sarah, d. Sam[ue]l Jr., bp. May 6, 1759. C.R.1.
William, s. Sam[ue]ll [Samuel, C.R.1.] and Jane, Dec. 21, 1733.
William, s. Samuel Jr. and Sarah, bp. Nov. 5, 1752. C.R.1.
William, s. William, bp. May 13, 1781. C.R.1.
——— [———], w. Samuel, —— [1783]. C.R.1.

HOLDUM, Mary (see Mary Oldam).

HOLEBROKE (see Holbroke, Holbrook, Holebrook, Holebrooke, Hollbrook, Hoolbrok), Mary, d. Samuel (Holebrooke) and Jane, Jan. 22, 1712. [Holbrook, C.R.1.]
Thomas, s. John (Holebrook) Jr. and Sarah, Apr. 7, 1712.

HOLEBROOK (see Holbroke, Holbrook, Holebroke, Holebrooke, Hollbrook, Hoolbrok), John, s. John (Holebrooke) Jr. and Sarah, June 13, 1710.

HOLEBROOKE (see Holbroke, Holbrook, Holebroke, Holebrook, Hollbrook, Hoolbrok), Hannah, d. Samuel (Holbrook) Jr. and Jane, Oct. 23, 1710. [Holbrook, C.R.1.]

HOLLBROOK (see Holbroke, Holbrook, Holebroke, Holebrook, Holebrooke, Hoolbrok), Abigall, d. John, May 11, 1675.

HOLLBROOK, Bethiah, d. Samm[uel], Apr. 2, 1681. [Holbrooke, d. Samuel, C.R.2.]
Bethiah, d. Samuell Jr., Apr. 28, 1716. [Holbrook, d. Sam[ue]l Jr., C.R.1.]
Deborah, d. John, Aug. 22, 1683.
Elizabeth, d. John, Feb. 2, 1672.
Elizabeth, d. Samm[uel], Dec. 14, 1678.
Experience, d. John, Jan. 22, 1677.
Hannah, d. John, Jan. 11, 1679.
John, s. John, Nov. 19, 1686.
Mary, d. Samm[uel], Nov. 2, 1686. [Holbrooke, d. Samuell, C.R.2.]
Sammuell, s. Samm[uel], Feb. 9, 1683.
Sarah, d. John, July 11, 1680.
Thomas, s. John, June 27, 1713.

HOLMES (see Holms, Homes), Abigal, d. Jo[h]n and Susannah, Feb. 21, 1720.
Deborah, twin d. Jo[h]n and Susannah, June 22, 1719.
Hannah, d. Josiah (Holms) of Marshfield, bp. Mar. 26, 1738. C.R.2.
Hannah, d. John and Hannah, Aug. 3, 1754.
Mary [———], w. Heman, —— [1777]. C.R.3.
Ruth, twin d. Jo[h]n and Susannah, June 22, 1719.
Sally Bailey, d. Bailey and Fanny, Sept. 28, 1832.
Sally Bailey, ch. Bailey dec'd and Fanny, bp. Sept. 6, 1835. C.R.3.
Sarah, d. John and Hannah, Nov. 10, 1756. [Homes, C.R.2.]

HOLMS (see Holmes, Homes), Nathanaell, s. John of Pembrooke, "adopted" s. Sam[ue]ll Lappam, bp. July 20, 1735. C.R.2.

HOLT, Laura A., w. Martin Cushing, ——, 1817. G.R.14.

HOMES (see Holmes, Holms), Abraham, ch. W[i]ll[ia]m, bp. Apr. 14, 1661. C.R.2.
Isaack, ch. W[i]ll[ia]m, bp. Apr. 14, 1661. C.R.2.
Israel, ch. W[i]ll[ia]m, bp. Apr. 14, 1661. C.R.1.
Josiah, ch. William, bp. Apr. 27, 1661. C.R.2.
Mary, ch. William, bp. Apr. 27, 1661. C.R.2.
Rebecca, ch. W[i]ll[ia]m, bp. Apr. 14, 1661. C.R.2.
Sarah, ch. W[i]ll[ia]m, bp. Apr. 14, 1661. C.R.2.

HOOLBROK (see Holbroke, Holbrook, Holebroke, Holebrook, Holebrooke, Hollbrook), Jane, d. Sam[ue]ll and Jane, Jan. 8, 1719. [Holbrook, d. Samuel, C.R.1.]

HORTON, Edwin B., s. Simmons, shoemaker, and Mary A. B., Apr. 24, 1848.

HORTON, George S. [dup. Simmons], s. Simmons, shoemaker, and Mary A., Aug. 28, 1844.
Henry F., s. Simmons, shoemaker, and Mary A., July 19, 1846.

HOSKINS (see Haskings, Haskins), Martha, d. John, Apr. 8, 1708.
Samuell, s. John, June 7, 1699.

HOUSE, Abigail, d. Benja[min], bp. Aug. 3, 1729. C.R.1.
Abigal, d. Benja[min] and Abigal, Feb. 21, 1728.
Abigal, d. Benja[min] and Rachel, Apr. 30, 1765. [Abigail, d. Benja[min] Jr., C.R.1.]
Abner, s. Benja[min] and Abigal, Sept. 22, 1739.
Abner, s. Benja[min] Jr. and Rachel, Aug. 19, 1758.
Abner, s. Abner and Rebecca, Dec. 8, 1783.
Ann S., ch. Freeman and Marie, Aug. 14, 1841.
Benjamin, s. Joseph, July 1, 1704.
Benja[min], s. Benja[min] and Abigall, Nov. 2, 1725.
Benjamin, s. Benjamin Jr. and Rachel, Aug. 21, 1761.
Charles, s. Benj[amin] Jr., bp. Aug. 30, 1767. C.R.1.
David, s. Samuel, Mar. 7, 1697-8.
David, s. Joseph, Apr. 4, 1709.
David, ch. Samuell and Sarah, bp. Apr. 22, 1711. C.R.2.
Deborah, d. Joseph and Lydia, bp. Dec. 16, 1722. C.R.2.
Deborah, d. Benja[min] and Abigall, Mar. 24, 1732.
Deborah, d. Benja[min], bp. June 24, 1733. C.R.1.
Deborah, d. Benjamin Jr. and Rachel, Sept. 23, 1751.
Delight, d. Benj[ami]n [Benjamin Jr., C.R.1.] and Rachel, May 1, 1770.
Elisabath, [triplet] d. John, Apr. 16, 1706. [Elizabeth, C.R.1.]
Elizabeth, d. Samuell, bp. Oct. 23, 1636. C.R.1.
Elizabeth, d. Samuel and Sarah, Dec. 19, 1704.
Elizabeth, ch. Samuell and Sarah, bp. Apr. 22, 1711. C.R.2.
Elizabeth, d. Joseph and Lydia, bp. June 12, 1726. C.R.2.
George F., ch. Freeman and Marie, Oct. 26, 1828.
George F., ch. Freeman and Marie, Aug. 12, 1831, in Abinton.
Hannah, d. Benja[min] and Abigal, June 10, 1736.
Hannah, d. Benja[min] Jr. and Rachel, May 23, 1756.
Henry W., ch. Freeman and Marie, Aug. 6, 1839, in Hanover.
James, s. Samuel and Sarah, Mar. 15, 1702.
James, ch. Samuell and Sarah, bp. Apr. 22, 1711. C.R.2.
James F., ch. Freeman and Marie, Apr. 5, 1826, in Hingham.
James L., s. James, carriage builder, and Hannah N. [dup. omits N.], Oct. 2, [18]45.
John, s. Sammuell, Sept. 22, 1672.
John, [triplet] s. John, Apr. 16, 1706.
John, s. Samuel and Sarah, Dec. 27, 1709.

House, John, ch. Samuell and Sarah, bp. Apr. 22, 1711. c.r.2.
Joseph, s. Sammuell, Apr. 10, 1667.
Joseph, s. Samuel, Apr. 17, 1696.
Joseph, [triplet] s. John, Apr. 16, 1706.
Joseph, ch. Samuell and Sarah, bp. Apr. 22, 1711. c.r.2.
Joseph, s. Benja[min] [Benj[ami]n Jr., c.r.1.] and Rachel, Oct. 16, 1762.
Joshua, s. Joseph and Lydia, bp. Aug. 2, 1724. c.r.2.
Lucy, d. Coombs and Deborah, Nov. 9, 1798.
Lydia, d. Joseph and Lydiah, bp. Feb. 6, 1720–21. c.r.2.
Marie E., ch. Freeman and Marie, Sept. 1, 1834, in Braintree.
Mary, d. Samuel [Sam[ue]ll, c.r.2.] and Sarah, Oct. 27, 1711.
Pamelia M. [dup. W.], d. Freeman, shoemaker, and Maria [dup. Marie], Apr. 16, 1845 [dup. 1846].
Peleg, s. Benja[min] and Abigall, Mar. 6, 1730.
Peleg, s. Benja[min], bp. June 13, 1731. c.r.1.
Peleg, s. Benja[min] Jr. and Rachel, Feb. 17, 1754.
Rachel, d. Benja[min] Jr. and Rachel, Sept. 16, 1750.
Rachel, d. Benja[min] Jr. and Rachel, June 17, 1760.
Rebackah, d. Sammuell, Apr. 12, 1670.
Rebecca, ch. Samuell and Sarah, bp. Apr. 22, 1711. c.r.2.
Rebekah, d. Samuel and Sarah, Apr. 2, 1700.
Sammuell, s. Sammuell, Mar. 28, 1665.
Samuel, s. Samuel, Nov. 10, 1693.
Samuel, s. Samuel and Sarah, Dec. 20, 1706.
Samuel, ch. Samuell and Sarah, bp. Apr. 22, 1711. c.r.2.
Sarah, d. Samuel [Sam[ue]ll, c.r.2.] and Sarah, Mar. —, 1713–14.
Susan, ch. James and Hannah, Apr. 22, 1836.

HOWARD, Charles, s. Perez and Hannah, Oct. 4, 1798.
Mary A., d. Franklin, tailor, and Mary C., Feb. 3, 1847. [Mary Adeline, c.r.3.]
Perez, s. Perez and Hannah, Dec. 14, 1796.
Stillman, s. Perez and Hannah, Sept. 22, 1799.
———, d. Franklin, tailor (b. Bridgewater), and Helen A., Nov. 30, 1849.

HOWLAND, Fidelia, ch. Luther and Fidelia, Apr. 12, 1843.
Jacob, s. Jacob and Sally, July 3, 1823, in Plymouth.
Luther, s. Consider and Ruth, Oct. 28, 1796.
Mary P., ch. Luther and Fidelia, Nov. 18, 1844.
Ruth, d. Luther, farmer, and Fidelia, Aug. 28, 1846.
Sally, d. Charles and Deborah, w. Ira Litchfield of Boston, Feb. 23, 1808. g.r.2.
Sally Ann, d. Jacob and Sally, Aug. 1, 1829.
Samuel Stephenson, s. Jacob and Sally, May 22, 1826.

HUBARD (see Hobard, Hobart), Rebekah, d. Israell, bp. May 26, 1678. C.R.2.

HUGHDEN (see Hayden, Heyden, Heydon), Abigail [Hayden ?], ch. Joseph, bp. Sept. 4, 1763. C.R.1.
Lettice [Hayden ?], ch. Joseph, bp. Sept. 4, 1763. C.R.1.
Pamelia [Hayden ?], ch. Joseph, bp. Sept. 4, 1763. C.R.1.

HUMPHREY (see Humphries, Humphris), Clarissa, w. Harvey Winslow, Aug. 14, 1799, in Hingham [Hingham, written in pencil].
John [? of Fredericksburg, Va.], ——— [1838]. C.R.1.

HUMPHRIES (see Humphrey, Humphris), Noah, s. John and Mary, Nov. 7, 1777.

HUMPHRIS (see Humphrey, Humphries), Cynthia, d. John and Mary, May 21, 1784.
Edward, s. Edward and Ann, Mar. 23, 1742.
Edward, s. John and Mary, Sept. 29, 1775.
[E]leanor, d. John and Mary, Jan. 24, 1787.
Francis, s. John and Mary, Feb. 9, 1782.
Hannah, d. Richard and Lydia, May 13, 1780.
Jenney, d. John and Mary, Mar. 10, 1780.
John, s. Edward and Ann, June 10, 1749.
Lois, d. John and Mary, Sept. 13, 1773.
Margaret, d. Edward and Ann, Nov. 15, 1741.
Mary, d. Edward and Ann, Aug. 19, 1748.
Nancy, d. John and Mary, Mar. 16, 1789.
Peleg, s. Richard and Lydia, Jan. 6, 1778.
Richard, s. Edward and Ann, Mar. 19, 1744.
Richard, s. Richard and Lydia, Mar. 20, 1776.

HUNT, Adeline E., ch. William and w., Jan. 21, 1844.
Catharine [———], w. William E., ———, 1831. G.R.8.
George H., s. Henry H., shoemaker, and Adaline, Mar. 1, 1848.
  [George H. W., s. Henry L. and Adeline, G.R.14.]
Henry L. [h. Adeline], May 19, 1817. G.R.14.
Howland Litchfield, s. Samuel and Hannah L., Sept. 21, 1821.
John, s. John and w., bp. Nov. 2, 1740. C.R.2.
Lucinda [———], w. Daniel T., ——— [1823]. G.R.15.
Lucy F., d. William E. and Mary N., Nov. 5, 1849.
Mary M. [———], w. W[illia]m E., ——— [1819]. G.R.11.
Samuel Judson, s. Samuel and Hannah L., Aug. 11, 1826.
William Eustis, s. Samuel and Hannah L., Feb. 23, 1824. [[h. Catharine] G.R.8.]

HURRUB (see Harrub), Ellen [dup. Harrub], d. Darius, farmer, and Matilda [dup. adds T.], July 21, 1846.

HUTCHINSON, Albert, ch. Jesse D. and Patience, Apr. 10, 1840, in Dorchest[er].
Harriet Louisa, ch. Jesse D. and Sarah L., May 10, 1843.
Jesse D. [h. Patience V.] [h. Sarah L.], ——, 1807. G.R.7.
Julia A., d. Jesse D., stone cutter, and Sarah L., Apr. 12, 1847.
Mary F., ch. Jesse D. and Patience, Mar. 17, 1837, in Dorchest[er].
Nelson Vinal, ch. Jesse D. and Sarah L., Apr. 24, 1845.
Patience V. [———], w. Jesse D., ——, 1812. G.R.7.
Sarah L. [———], w. Jesse D., —— [1822]. C.R.3. [——, 1823, G.R.7.]
——, s. Jesse D., yeoman, and Sarah L., Apr. 24, 1844.

HYDE, Ada M., d. James, carver, and Adeline, May 5, 1845.
Ann Eliza, ch. James and Adeline, ——, 1843.
George Edward, s. James, carver (b. Charlestown), and Adeline, June 29, 1849.

HYLAND (see Highland, Hiland, Hilland), Abby Carrol, ch. Henry and Olive H., May —, 1837.
Abigail, d. Amasa and Polly, Jan. 19, 1828.
Abigail C. V., ch. Henry and Olive H., June 21, 1840.
Abner, s. Will[ia]m and Mary, Aug. 29, 1761.
Amasa, s. Will[ia]m and Mary, May 23, 1760.
Amasa, s. Samuel and Hannah, Feb. 7, 1795.
Amasa, s. Amasa and Polly, Dec. 28, 1825.
Andrew Murray, ch. Peleg and Mary J., Apr. 6, 1841.
Anne, d. John and Elizabeth, June 4, 1710.
Anne, ch. John, bp. Aug. 31, 1712. C.R.1.
Barden, s. Samuel and Hannah, June 18, 1784.
Bardin, s. Bardin and Rebecca, Oct. 8, 1815.
Bathsheba, ch. Benja[min] and w., bp. May 10, 1752. C.R.1.
Benjamin, ch. Benja[min] and w., bp. May 10, 1752. C.R.1.
Benjamin, s. Benja[min], bp. Feb. 21, 1755. C.R.1.
Celenda, d. Samuel and Hannah, Feb. 14, 1799.
Clarissa, d. Amasa and Polly, Dec. 12, 1816.
Deborah, d. James, bp. June 24, 1754. C.R.1.
Deborah [———], w. Isaiah, ——, 1810. G.R.6.
Ebenezer, s. Samuel Jr. and Mahetable, June 13, 1823.
Edmond, ch. Edmund and Hannah A., Dec. 16, 1843.
Edmund, s. Samuel and Hannah, Dec. 2, 1789.
Eliza E., d. Samuel Jr. and Mahitabel, Mar. 9, 1828. [d. Samuel and Mehitable, w. Benj[amin] F. Farrar, G.R.8.]

HYLAND, Elizabeth, ch. John, bp. Aug. 31, 1712. C.R.I.
Elizabeth, ch. James and Mary, bp. July 24, 1737. C.R.I.
Elizabeth [———], w. Samuel, —— [1807]. G.R.8.
Elizabeth, d. Amasa and Polly, Nov. 10, 1830.
Ellen M., d. Edmund and Hannah, June 20, 1848.
Georgiana Amanda, ch. Henry and Olive H., Aug. 23, 1832.
Henry Puffer, ch. Henry and Olive H., —— [rec. after ch. b. June 21, 1840].
Irene A., d. Edmand, housewright, and Hannah A., Feb. 14, 1846.
Isaiah, s. Samuel and Hannah, Feb. 5, 1782.
Isaiah, s. Bardain and Rebacca, Nov. 10, 1807.
Isaiah, h. Deborah, ——, 1807. G.R.6.
James, ch. John, bp. Aug. 31, 1712. C.R.I.
James Gregory, s. Bardin and Rebekah, Dec. 15, 1810.
Joanne, d. Samuel Jr. and Mahetable, July 16, 1825.
John, ch. John, bp. Aug. 31, 1712. C.R.I.
John, s. Will[ia]m and Mary, May 19, 1756.
John Bardine, s. Isaiah and Deborah, Dec. 5, 1830.
John Ellms, s. Bardin and Rebekah, Feb. 24, 1813.
Laban Rose, s. Isaiah and Deborah, Dec. 26, 1832.
Lorenzo F., s. Peleg and Mary J., Oct. 4, 1845.
Lucy, d. Will[ia]m and Mary, Feb. 26, 1755.
Lucy, d. Samuel and Hannah, Apr. 4, 1792.
Mary, ch. James and Mary, bp. July 24, 1737. C.R.I.
Mary Ann, d. Amasa and Polly, Apr. 6, 1821.
Mary E., d. Peleg and Mary J., Mar. 15, 1843.
Mary J. [———], w. Peleg, ——, 1820. G.R.8.
Mehetable, ch. James and Mary, bp. July 24, 1737. C.R.I.
Mehetebel, ch. John, bp. Aug. 31, 1712. C.R.I.
Mehitable [———], w. Samuel, —— [1788]. G.R.8.
Olive H. [? m.], —— [1811]. G.R.7.
Olive Hammond, ch. Henry and Olive H., Sept. 25, 1830.
Oliver, s. Amasa and Polly, Sept. 1, 1823.
Rebecca E., d. Isaiah and Deborah, —— [1835]. C.R.3.
Rhoda, d. James, bp. May 11, 1756. C.R.I.
Saberry, ch. Benja[min] and w., bp. May 10, 1752. C.R.I.
Samuel, s. Will[ia]m and Mary, Mar. 22, 1758.
Samuel, s. Samuel and Hannah, Sept. 26, 1786. [[h. Mehitable] [h. Elizabeth] G.R.8.]
Samuel, s. Samuel Jr. and Mahetabel, Nov. 22, 1832.
Sarah, ch. John, bp. Aug. 31, 1712. C.R.I.
Sarah, ch. James and Mary, bp. July 24, 1737. C.R.I.
Sarah, d. Samuel and Hannah, Mar. 23, 1797.
Serena B., ch. Peleg and Serena, Aug. 19, 1837.

HYLAND, Thomas, ch. John, bp. Aug. 31, 1712. C.R.I.
William, s. John, bp. Sept. 18, 1715. C.R.I.
Will[ia]m, s. Will[ia]m and Mary, Apr. 24, 1753.
William, s. Amasa and Polly, Jan. 1, 1819.

INGHAM, John, s. Thomas, bp. Oct. 4, 1663. C.R.2.
Sarah, d. Thomas, Jan. 21, 1647.
Sarah, d. Thomas, bp. Mar. 22, 1656. C.R.2.
Thomas, s. Thomas, Mar. 1, 1678.

JACKESON (see Jackson), Hannah, d. Jonathan, Jan. 30, 1692.
Jonathan, s. Jonathan (Jackson), June 3, 1685.
Sarah, d. Jonathan, Feb. 14, 1688.

JACKSON (see Jackeson), Anna "who was borne tow or three years before," d. Samuell, bp. Mar. 25, 1638. C.R.I.
Betsey G. [———], w. Henry, —— [1824]. C.R.3.
Charles Henry, ch. Henry T. and Betsey G., Dec. 11, 1841.
Deborah, d. Jonathan and Mahitable, Dec. 23, 1765.
Ebenezer Ellms, s. Rowland and Elenor, Nov. 22, 1815.
Elenor, d. Rowland and Elenor, Jan. 4, 1803.
Elizabeth Otis, d. Rowland and Elenor, Sept. 5, 1821. [w. James L. Merritt, G.R.2.]
Helen Eliza, d. Henry, shipcarpenter [dup. shipwright], and Betsey G. [dup. omits G.], Aug. 11, 1846.
Henry, s. Rowland and Elenor, June 11, 1817.
Jonathan, s. Sam[uel], May 7, 1647.
Jonathan, s. Jonathan and Deborah, Feb. 14, 1733.
Jonathan, s. Jona[than], bp. Mar. 31, 1734. C.R.I.
Jonathan, s. Rowland and Elenor, Jan. 2, 1812.
Jonathan, ch. Roland, bp. Oct. 10, 1813. C.R.I.
Lydia, d. Jona[than] and Mahitable, May 3, 1761.
Mehetable, d. Rowland and Elenor, Oct. 1, 1808. [Mehitabel, G.R.6.]
Mehitable, d. Roland, bp. Oct. 6, 1812. C.R.I.
Melzar Cudworth, s. Rowland and Elenor [Eleanor, C.R.3.], Mar. 4, 1819.
Nancy, d. Rowland and Elenor, Oct. 28, 1823.
Polly, d. Rowland and Elenor, Jan. 26, 1806.
Polly, ch. Roland, bp. Oct. 10, 1813. C.R.I.
Robert Ellms, s. Rowland [Roland, C.R.I.] and Elenor, June 6, 1813.
Roland, s. Jona[than] and Mahitable, Dec. 8, 1778.
Roland, ch. Roland, bp. Oct. 10, 1813. C.R.I.
Rowland, s. Rowland and Elenor, Aug. 26, 1804.

JACKSON, Samuel, s. Jona[tha]n and Mahitable [s. Jonathan Jr. and Mehetable, C.R.1.], June 26, 1758.
Sarah, d. Jona[than] and Sarah, Apr. 15, 1730.
Sarah Northey, d. Rowland and Elenor, Mar. 1, 1810.
Sarah Nothey, ch. Roland, bp. Oct. 10, 1813. C.R.1.
Ward, s. Jonathan and Mahitable, Nov. 16, 1768.
William Thomas, ch. Henry T. and Betsey G., June 11, 1843.

JACOB (see Jacobs), Abby (see Nabe).
Abigil, d. Joseph and Mary, Dec. 1, 1753. [Abigail, d. Dea. Joseph, C.R.2.]
Andrew, s. Loring and Merial, July 29, 1813.
Anne, d. Benja[min] and Mary, July 6, 1738. [Ann, C.R.1.]
Anne, d. Benja[min] and Mary, May 30, 1743. [Ann, C.R.1.]
Anne, d. Benja[min] and Mary, Nov. 25, 1753.
Belea, s. Elisha and Lusanna, May 1, 1770.
Benjamin, s. David [Dea. Jacob, C.R.1.], Apr. 10, 1709.
Benja[min], s. Elisha and Lusanna, Sept. 29, 1766.
Betsey Turner, d. Walter and Betsey, June 27, 1802. [Betsy Turner, C.R.2.] [Betsey T. Jacobs, G.R.14.]
Braddock, s. Elisha and Lusanna, May 6, 1764. [Jacobs, May 4, P.R.7.]
Celinda, d. James H. and Lusannah, Nov. 3, 1813.
Charles, s. John and Hannah, May 26, 1770.
Charles, s. Walter and Betsey, Jan. 27, 1817.
Clarissa Richmond, d. Ichabod R. and Clarissa, Mar. 19, 1818.
David, s. David, Oct. 28, 1690.
David, s. Joshua and Mary, Jan. 16, 1729.
Deborah, d. David, Apr. 22, 1698.
Deborah, d. Joseph [Dea. Joseph, C.R.2.] and Mary, May 12, 1747.
Deborah, d. James and Deborah, June 22, 1776.
Dexter, ch. Huldah, bp. June 6, 1824. C.R.2.
Edward Foster, s. Elisha and Lusanna, Oct. 23, 1774.
Elisha, s. David, Oct. 30, 1696.
Elisha, s. [Dea., C.R.1.] David and Sarah, Oct. 7, 1711.
Elisha, s. Joseph and Mary, Aug. 29, 1735.
Elisha, s. Elisha and Lusanna, Aug. 12, 1760.
Elisha, s. Joseph and Hannah, Oct. 11, 1790.
Elizabeth, d. Mary of Hingham, bp. July 8, 1666. C.R.2.
Elizabeth, d. Joshua Jr. and Eliza[beth], Oct. 24, 1767.
Eunice (see Unice).
Eunice, d. James and Deborah, Feb. 3, 1785.
Fanney, d. John and Hannah, Nov. 18, 1776. [Fanny, sister Hannah J. Turner dec'd, C.R.3.]

JACOB, Frances Maria, d. Walter and Betsey, Apr. 26, 1811.
Francis, s. John and Hannah, Oct. 2, 1766.
Freeman, ch. Huldah, bp. June 6, 1824. C.R.2.
Geo[rge] Ward, ch. Cap[t]. Josh[u]a Jr., bp. Nov. 3, 1816. C.R.2.
Hannah, d. David, Apr. 27, 1704.
Hannah, d. Joseph and Mary, May 9 [?], 1739.
Hannah, d. John and Hannah, Apr. 4, 1763.
Hannah, d. Joseph and Hannah, Mar. 11, 1783.
Ichabod Ritchmond, s. Ja[me]s and Deborah, June 27, 1774.
James, s. Joshua and Mary, Mar. 6, 1742.
James, s. James and Deborah, Jan. 3, 1773.
James Harvy, s. Joseph and Hannah, Apr. 2, 1787.
John, s. Joshua and Mary, May 23, 1735. [Col. John [h. Hannah], G.R.14.]
John, s. John and Hannah, Sept. 22, 1759.
Joseph, s. David [s. David and Sarah, C.R.2.], Aug. 16, 1707.
Joseph, s. Joseph [Dea. Joseph, C.R.2.] and Mary, May 5, 1745.
Joseph, s. Joseph and Mary, July 12, 1755.
Joseph, s. Joseph [Dea. Joseph, C.R.2.] and Mary, May 5, 1757.
Joseph, s. Joseph and Hannah, Nov. 6, 1781.
Joshua, s. David, Mar. 31, 1702.
Joshua, s. Joshua and Mary, June 23, 1737.
Joshua, s. Joshua Jr. and Eliza[beth], Sept. 22, 1765.
Lamuel, s. John and Hannah, June 10, 1761.
Lamuel, s. Elisha and Lusanna, Mar. 4, 1762.
Loring, s. Joshua Jr. and Eliza[beth], May 5, 1771.
Loring, s. Loring and Merial, June 16, 1812.
Lucy, d. Joshua and Mary, Nov. 3, 1748. [Luce, C.R.2.]
Lucy, d. Joshua Jr. and Eliza[beth], Apr. 16, 1773.
Lusanna, d. Elisha and Lusanna, Nov. 20, 1777.
Lydia, d. David, Aug. 1, 1700.
Lydia, d. Joseph [Dea. Joseph, C.R.2.] and Mary, May 30, 1743.
Lydia, d. Elisha and Lusanna, Aug. 25, 1768.
Mary, d. David, July 15, 1692.
Mary, d. Joshua and Mary, July 17, 1732.
Mary, d. Benja[min] and Mary, Sept. 8, 1739.
Mary, d. Joseph [Dea. Joseph, C.R.2.] and Mary, Jan. 27, 1751.
Mary, d. John and Hannah, July 20, 1768.
Mary Ann, d. Walter and Betsey, June 4, 1800.
Mary Ann, d. Loring and Merial, Nov. 15, 1815.
Mary Sheffield, d. Ichabod Richmond and Clarisa, Sept. 24, 1806.
Micah, s. James and Deborah, July 17, 1782.
Nabe, d. James and Deborah, June 19, 1780. [Abby, second w. Abial Farrow, P.R.15.]

JACOB, Nathaniel, s. Joseph and Mary, Oct. 7, 1748. [Nathanael, s. Dea. Joseph and w., C.R.2.]
Nathaniel, s. Joseph and Mary, Apr. 6, 1750. [Nathanael, s. Dea. Joseph and Mary, C.R.2.]
Polly Corpes, d. Elisha and Lusanna, May 29, 1772.
Pricilla, d. Benja[min] and Mary, Feb. 8, 1746-7. [Priscilla, C.R.1.]
Pricilla, d. Benja[min] and Mary, Mar. 21, 1749.
Releaff, d. Joseph and Mary, Jan. 16, 1737. [Relief, C.R.2.]
Rhoda, d. Joshua Jr. and Elisabeth, Aug. 7, 17778 [*sic*, 1778].
Richmond, s. Ichabod R. and Clarissa, Oct. 4, 1808.
Roland, s. John and Hannah, Mar. 17, 1772.
Rowland Turner, s. Walter and Betsey, Nov. 6, 1808.
Ruth, d. Joseph and Hannah, Dec. 13, 1784.
Sarah, d. David, Sept. 12, 1694.
Sarah, d. Joshua and Mary, Nov. 2, 1727.
Sarah, d. Joseph [Dea. Joseph, C.R.2.] and Mary, May 14, 1741.
Sarah, d. Benja[min] and Mary, Jan. 10, 1756.
Sarah, d. John and Hannah, Dec. 15, 1764.
Sarah, d. Ichabod R. and Claressa, Feb. 18, 1810.
Silvester, s. Joshua Jr. and Elisabeth, Sept. 1, 1782.
Thomas, s. Ichabod Richmond and Claressa, July 8, 1812.
Thomas Marshal, s. James and Deborah, Sept. 22, 1777.
Unice, d. Joshua and Mary, July 23, 1740. [Eunice, C.R.2.]
Walter, s. John and Hannah, Dec. 27, 1774.
Walter, s. Walter and Betsey, Sept. 17, 1804.
Warren, s. John and Hannah, Mar. 29, 1778.

JACOBS (see Jacob), Adeline Ford, d. Benj[ami]n R. and Tryphosa, Oct. 18, 1827.
Adeline Ford, d. Benj[ami]n R. and Tryphosa, Apr. 3, 1829.
Ame Cushing, d. Capt. Joshua Jr. and w., bp. June 29, 1806. C.R.2.
Andrew, ch. Warren and Tamson, Feb. 8, 1843.
Ansel, Dec. 20, 1789. P.R.7.
Augustus, ch. Benjamin 2d and Lydia M. P., July 24, 1843.
Aurelia Felton, d. Thomas M. and Hannah, June 22, 1823.
Barton Richmond, s. Ichabod R. and Clarissa, June 23, 1823.
Bela Tower, s. Joshua [Joshua Jr., C.R.2.] and Hannah, Mar. 18, 1808.
Benjamin [dup. Jacob], s. Ichabod R. and Clarissa, Sept. 17, 1814 [dup. 1815].
Benja[min] Hearssy, s. Braddock and w., bp. Feb. 24, 1793. C.R.2. [b. Dec. 9, 1792, P.R.7.]
Benjamin Randall, s. Lemuel and Sarah, Apr. 24, 1790. [[h. Tryphosa] G.R.14.]

JACOBS, Benjamin Warren, s. Benj[ami]n R. and Tryphosa, Mar. 8, 1825.
Betsey [———], w. Walter [Feb. —, 1778]. G.R.14.
Charles Sumner, Apr. 27, 1810 [in Littleton]. P.R.7.
Clarissa, d. David and Olive, Aug. 15, 1825.
Clarrissa, d. Joseph and w., bp. Aug. 18, 1793. C.R.2.
David, s. David and Olive, Jan. 7, 1827.
David How, s. Thomas M. and Hannah, Apr. 5, 1820.
David R., s. Joshua and Hannah, July 24, 1817. [David Richmond, C.R.2.]
Deborah Richmond, d. Perez and w., bp. July 1, 1798. C.R.2.
Edward, s. Edward F. and Priscilla, Jan. 11, 1803.
Edward, s. Foster and w., bp. Nov. 3, 1805. C.R.2.
Edwin, s. Michael and Huldah, Mar. 6, 1826.
Elisha, s. Edward F. and Priscilla [s. Foster and w., C.R.2.], Mar. 12, 1808.
Eunice C., d. Joshua and Hannah, Feb. 23, 1806.
Franklin, s. Loring and Mary, Mar. 21, 1803.
Frederick, s. Edward F. and Priscilla, Oct. 29, 1817.
George Edward, s. Edward and Adeline, Nov. 29, 1827.
George Hiram, Oct. 5, 1805 [in Littleton]. P.R.7.
George Ward, s. Joshua and Hannah, Aug. 7, 1815.
Hannah [———], w. Col. John, Dec. 18, 1788. G.R.14.
Hannah, d. Braddock and w., bp. Sept. 1, 1799. C.R.2. [b. June 26, P.R.7.]
Hannah Deane, d. Benj[ami]n R. and Tryphosa, Apr. 5, 1823.
Hannah W., d. Joshua Jr. and Hannah, Feb. 4, 1798. [Hannah Waterman, C.R.2.]
Henry, s. Edward F. and Priscilla, Aug. 24, 1813.
Howard Bowker, s. Edward and Adeline, June 14, 1833.
Joanna, May 28, 1797. P.R.7.
Joanna, d. Braddock and w., bp. Sept. 1, 1799. C.R.2.
John Q., ch. Warren and Tamson, Jan. 23, 1840.
Joshua, s. Joshua [Capt. Joshua Jr., C.R.2.] and Hannah, Nov. 19, 1801.
Julia Ann, d. Michael and Huldah, Sept. 13, 1823.
Lemuel, s. Lemuel and Sarah, Apr. 1, 1788.
Lucy Clapp, d. Edward F. and Priscilla [d. Foster and w., C.R.2.], May 14, 1805.
Lucy E., d. Andrew, farmer, and Sophronia, Apr. 30, 1849, in S. Scituate.
Lusanna, Aug. 7, 1801. P.R.7.
Lydea, d. Braddock and w., bp. Oct. 4, 1795. C.R.2. [Lydia, b. Feb. 22, P.R.7.]

JACOBS, Lydia Smith, d. Edward F. and Priscilla, June 29, 1811.
Martha, d. Loring and Merial, Sept. 28, 1817.
Mary, d. Joshua Jr. and w., bp. July 13, 1800. C.R.2.
Mary C., ch. Warren and Tamson, Oct. 29, 1837.
Mary James, d. Joshua and Hannah, Jan. 3, 1800.
Mary Priscilla, d. Edward F. and Priscilla, Oct. 26, 1820.
Mary Wilder, May 30, 1803 [in Littleton]. P.R.7.
Merial, d. Loring and Merial, Oct. 18, 1822.
Nabby Sophia, d. Ichabod R. and Clarissa, Apr. 10, 1821.
Nancy, d. Lemuel and Sarah, Sept. 1, 1793.
Polly, d. Joshua (Jacob) and Elisabeth, Aug. 26, 1780.
Pyam, s. Joshua and Hannah, Jan. 5, 1813. [Piam, ch. Cap[t].
    Josh[u]a, C.R.2.]
Sarah, d. Lemuel and Sarah, Feb. 1, 1786.
Sarah, June 9, 1788. P.R.7.
Sarah R., d. Benj[ami]n R. and Tryphosa, Dec. 11, 1820.
Sophia, Oct. 9, 1807 [in Littleton]. P.R.7.
Temperance T., d. Benj[amin] R. and Tryphosa, Aug. 2, 1832.
Theophilus, s. Joshua and Hannah, Dec. 15, 1803. [Thophilus,
    s. Capt. Joshua Jr. and w., C.R.2.]
Thomas Richmond, s. Thomas M. and Hannah, Nov. 24, 1825.
Tryphosa [———], w. Benj[amin] R., —— [1792]. G.R.14.
Warren H., ch. Warren and Tamson, Jan. 10, 1835.
Washington, s. Loring and Merial, Nov. 19, 1825.
William C., s. Joshua and Hannah, Nov. 15, 1810. [W[illia]m
    Cushing, ch. Cap[t]. Josh[u]a, C.R.2.]
William Fly, s. David and Olive, Feb. 12, 1828.
———, ch. Benj[amin] R. and Tryphosa, Oct. 15, 1835.
———, s. Andrew, farmer, and Sophronia, Apr. 2, 1844.
———, s. George, mariner, and Matilda, Jan. 13, 1844 [dup. 1845].

JAMES, Abigail DeWolfe, d. Arnold and Sally, Dec. 5, 1822.
Albert, s. William Jr. and Welthea, Feb. 7, 1827.
Alfred, s. Joshua and Sarah, Feb. 25, 1827. [[h. Caroline Rich]
    G.R.14.]
Almira, d. John [Maj. John, C.R.2.] and Paitence, Mar. 11, 1805.
Anna Appleton, [twin] d. Will[ia]m Jr. and Welthea, Jan. 2, 1822.
Anne Appleton, ch. W[illia]m Jr., bp. Oct. 2, 1825. C.R.2.
Benjamin, s. John [s. John and Eunice, C.R.2.], May 12, 1711.
Benjamin, s. Benja[min] and Mercy, Feb. 23, 1744.
Benjamin, s. Benja[min] and Sarah, May 10, 1774.
Benjamin, s. Elisha Jr. and Lydia Young [(Little)], Aug. 22, 1814.
Betsey, d. William and Molly, July 17, 1784.
Betsy, d. William and w., bp. Sept. 16, 1792. C.R.2.
Charles, s. John and Hannah, June 30, 1775.

JAMES, Charles, s. John and Patience, Aug. 18, 1800.
Charles, s. Maj. John and w., bp. Sept. 30, 1804. C.R.2.
Charles Prouty, s. Elisha Jr. and Lydia, Jan. 18, 1827.
Charlotte Otis, d. John 3d and Sally C., Sept. 27, 1815.
Edward, s. Elisha Jr. and Lydia Young [(Little)], May 1, 1817.
    ["Member of Co K. 7 Reg. Mass. Vols.," G.R.5.]
Elisha, s. John [s. James and Eunice, C.R.2.], Apr. 5, 1715.
Elisha, s. John Jr. and Prudence, Aug. 13, 1744.
Elisha, s. Elisha and Sarah, July 3, 1780.
Elisha, s. Benja[min] and Sarah, Apr. 29, 1785. [Dr. Elisha, C.R.3.] [Dr. Elisha [h. Lydia Young (Little)], G.R.5.]
Eliza, d. John [Maj. John, C.R.2.] and Paitence, Aug. 14, 1807.
Elizabeth, d. Arnold and Sally, Mar. 4, 1815, in Bristol, R.I.
Emely, d. Joshua and Sarah, Feb. 6, 1819. [Emily, G.R.14.]
Emily, ch. Joshua, bp. Sept. 3, 1820. C.R.2.
Eunice (see Unes).
Eunice, d. John Jr. and Prudence, Mar. 9, 1747.
Eunice, d. John and Prudence, bp. Apr. 3, 1748. C.R.2.
Francis, s. Elisha Jr. and Lydia Young [(Little)], July 16, 1819.
Frederick Augustus, s. W[illia]m and Welthea, Nov. 27, 1832.
Galen, s. John and Patience, Sept. 29, 1790.
George, s. John and Hannah, Feb. 15, 1771.
Hannah, d. John and Hannah, Sept. 5, 1768.
Hannah, d. William and Molly, Nov. 7, 1786.
Hannah, d. John [Capt. John, C.R.2.] and Patience, Mar. 30, 1792.
Hannah, d. William and w., bp. Sept. 16, 1792. C.R.2.
Hannah Packard, d. W[illia]m and Welthea, Sept. 5, 1835.
Harriet, d. John and Patience, Jan. 1, 1796.
Harriet A. Newel, d. Arnold and Sally, Apr. 1, 1818.
Harriot Mareah, d. John 3d and Sally C., July 25, 1817.
Helen, d. Joshua and Sarah, Dec. 23, 1823.
Henry Hayden, s. Arnold and Sally, Mar. 2, 1812, in Nantucket.
Henry Packard, s. Will[ia]m Jr. and Welthea, Aug. 4, 1823.
Hervey, s. Thomas and Sarah, Dec. 31, 1796.
Horace, s. John and Patience, Jan. 3, 1794. [Horrace, C.R.2.]
John, s. John and Rhoda, bp. July 18, 1731. C.R.2.
John, s. John, Jan. 10, 1676–7.
John, s. John, bp. Apr. 7, 1678. C.R.2.
John, s. John [s. John and Eunice, C.R.2.], June 5, 1709.
John, s. Jo[h]n Jr. and Rhoda, July 12, 1731.
John, s. John 3d and Sarah, Jan. 15, 1759.
John, s. John and Hannah, July 27, 1766.
John, s. Benja[min] and Sarah, Sept. 12, 1776. [[h. Abigail (Turner)] G.R.5.]

JAMES, John, s. Thomas and Sarah, Apr. 18, 1784.
John, s. John and Patience, Jan. 19, 1789.
John, s. Elisha Jr. and Lydia Young [(Litttle)], Aug. 22, 1824.
Joseph, s. John and Hannah, July 11, 1773.
Joseph, s. John and Patience, Nov. 27, 1802.
Joseph, s. Maj. John and w., bp. Sept. 30, 1804. C.R.2.
Joshua, s. Elisha and Sarah, June 20, 1787. [Dea. Joshua [h. Sally], G.R.14.]
Josiah Leavitt, s. William and Molly, Oct. 9, 1791. [Josiah Levitt, C.R.2.]
Lucy, d. John Jr. and Prudence, Oct. 8, 1751.
Lucy, d. Elisha and Sarah, Jan. 14, 1782.
Lucy, d. John and Paticence, Dec. 30, 1797.
Lydia, d. John and Eunice, May 13, 1713.
Lydia, d. John Jr. and Prudence, Nov. 27, 1749.
Lydia, d. William and Molly, June 27, 1780.
Lydia, d. William and w., bp. Sept. 16, 1792. C.R.2.
Lydia J., d. Dr. James, w. James Vinal, —— [1810]. C.R.3.
Lydia Little, d. Elisha Jr. and Lydia Young [(Little)], Feb. 11, 1810. [d. Elisha 3d, C.R.1.] [d. Elisha and Lydia, wid. James M. Vinal, G.R.5.]
Lydia Y. [——], w. Dr. Elisha, —— [1790]. C.R.3.
Marcy, d. Benja[min] and Sarah, July 27, 1778.
Martha Ann Taylor, d. Arnold and Sally, July 31, 1808, in Nantucket.
Mary, d. John, Oct. 5, 1704.
Mary, d. Thomas and Sarah, Feb. 2, 1795.
Mary, d. John [Maj. Jo[h]n, C.R.2.] and Paitence, Mar. 9, 1810.
Mary, d. Elisha Jr. and Lydia Young [(Little)], Nov. 26, 1821.
Mary Dana, d. Elisha Jr. and Lydia, May 18, 1829.
Mary Randal, d. William Jr. and Welthea, Jan. 12, 1820. [Mary Randall, d. William and Wealthy (Alden), w. Edward H[art] Delano, in Quincy, G.R.14.]
Mary Randall, ch. W[illia]m Jr., bp. Oct. 2, 1825. C.R.2.
Mercy, d. Benja[min] and Mercy, Sept. 11, 1737.
Milton, s. Thomas and Sarah, May 23, 1804, in Londonderry, N.H.
Molly, d. William and Molly, May 27, 1782.
Molly, d. William and Molly, Oct. 12, 1796.
Polly, d. Benja[min] and Sarah, Apr. 25, 1781.
Polly, d. William and w., bp. Sept. 16, 1792. C.R.2.
Prudence, d. Jo[h]n Jr. and Prudence, Dec. 23, 1740.
Rhoda, d. Jo[h]n Jr. and Prudence, Sept. 29, 1742. [Rhode, C.R.2.]
Sally, d. Benjamin and Sarah, Feb. 1, 1772.

JAMES, Sally [———], w. ———, —— [1786]. G.R.6. [w. Dea. Joshua, G.R.14.]
Samuel, s. Samuel, Aug. 4, 1712.
Samuel P. Jones, s. Arnold and Sally, Feb. 9, 1820.
Sarah, d. John and Hannah, Mar. 22, 1764.
Sarah, d. Capt. Elisha and Sarah, May 4, 1777.
Sarah, d. Thomas and Sarah, Dec. 25, 1785.
Sarah Wales, d. Elisha Jr. and Lydia Young [(Little)], Feb. 8, 1812.
Stanton, s. Capt. Elisha and Sarah, Dec. 11, 1774.
Staunton, s. Jo[h]n Jr. and Prudence, Oct. 13, 1738. [Stanton, C.R.2.]
Temperance, d. Elisha and Sarah, Dec. 30, 1785.
Thomas, s. John [Capt. John, C.R.2.] Jr. and Prudence, June 9, 1753.
Thomas, s. Thomas and Sarah, Feb. 24, 1782.
Thomas, s. John and Paitence, June 30, 1812.
Thomas Scott, s. Dr. Elisha [dup. Jr. omits Dr.] and Lydia Y. [dup. omits Y.], May 8, 1832.
Unes, d. John, Mar. 25, 1703.
Unes, d. John, Feb. 5, 1706-7. [Eunice, d. John and Eunice, C.R.2.]
Welthea [———], w. William [Aug. —, 1792]. G.R.14.
Welthea Alden, d. Will[ia]m Jr. and Welthea, July 6, 1830.
Will[ia]m, s. John Jr. and Prudence, June 1, 1746.
William, s. William and Molly, Mar. 1, 1789. [[h. Welthea] G.R.14.]
William, ch. William and w., bp. Sept. 16, 1792. C.R.2.
William Alden, s. William Jr. and Welthea, Mar. 7, 1818.
William Henry, s. Will[ia]m Jr. and Welthea, Apr. 19, 1825.
Zipporah, d. John, Aug. 22, 1717. [Ziphorah, d. John and Eunice, C.R.2.]
———, [twin] d. Will[ia]m Jr. and Welthea, Jan. 2, 1822.

JENKEN (see Ginkings, Jenkens, Jenkiens, Jenkings, Jenkins), Hannah, d. Tho[mas], bp. May 16, 1680. C.R.2.

JENKENS (see Ginkings, Jenken, Jenkiens, Jenkings, Jenkins), Elijah, ch. Elijah and w., bp. Nov. 8, 1801. C.R.1.
Eliza, ch. Elijah and w., bp. Nov. 8, 1801. C.R.1.
George, ch. Capt. Coleman, bp. Sept. 13, 1823. C.R.1.
Hannah Robins, d. Samuel Jr., bp. Oct. 5, 1800. C.R.1.
John, s. Capt. Oliver, bp. June 4, 1799. C.R.1.
Joshua, ch. Capt. Coleman, bp. Sept. 13, 1823. C.R.1.
Lydia, d. Luther and Leah, Sept. 29, 1814.
Martha, d. Sam[ue]ll (Jenkins) and Rebecca, Mar. 16, 1750. [Jenkins, d. Sam[ue]l, C.R.1.]
Sarah, d. Sam[ue]ll and Rebecca, July 16, 1761.

JENKIENS (see Ginkings, Jenken, Jenkens, Jenkings, Jenkins), Joshua, s. Joshua, bp. July 8, 1770. C.R.1.

JENKINGS (see Ginkings, Jenken, Jenkens, Jenkiens, Jenkins), Abigail, ch. Sam[ue]l Jr. and w., bp. May 31, 1778. C.R.1.
David, s. Edward, Mar. 15, 1715.
Echabod, s. Daniel, bp. July 12, 1770. C.R.1.
Mary, d. Edward, Sept. 18, 1717.
Nethaneel, ch. Sam[ue]l Jr. and w., bp. May 31, 1778. C.R.1.
Samuel, ch. Sam[ue]l Jr. and w., bp. May 31, 1778. C.R.1.

JENKINS (see Ginkings, Jenken, Jenkens, Jenkiens, Jenkings), Abagil, d. Sam[ue]ll Jr. and Abagil, Nov. 15, 1773.
Abigal, d. Sam[ue]ll and Rebecca, Feb. 24, 1759 [*sic*, see Calab].
Abigail, d. Tho[ma]s, bp. May 9, 1756. C.R.1.
Abigail, d. Sam[ue]l, bp. May 25, 1760. C.R.1.
Abigail Young, d. Peleg and Mary (Thomas), July 17, 1815.
Alice Baker, d. Colman and Betsy, July 22, 1803.
Alice Baker, ch. Colman and w., bp. Nov. 8, 1812. C.R.1.
Alpheus Briggs, s. Cha[rle]s and Jane, July 21, 1806.
Andrew Jackson, s. Perez T. and Nancy, Feb. 23, 1815.
Anna, d. Edward, Sept. 13, 1708.
Anna, ch. Thomas Jr. and Sarah, bp. May 6, 1739. C.R.1.
Anna, d. Tho[ma]s, bp. Oct. 16, 1748. C.R.1.
Annie E., d. Joshua P. and Eliza W., Nov. 4, 1847.
Asa, s. Edward, bp. June 8, 1777. C.R.1.
Aurelia, d. Peleg and Mary (Thomas), May 21, 1809.
Aurelia, d. Peleg and Mary (Thomas), Apr. 25, 1813.
Baley, s. Tho[ma]s Jr. and Hannah, Feb. 3, 1779. [Bailey [h. Rachel], G.R.14.]
Barthshaba, d. Daniel and Eliza[beth], July 14, 1766. [Bashaba Jenkings, C.R.1.]
Barthshaba, d. Daniel and Eliz[abe]th, Jan. 21, 1772. [Bathshaba Jenkings, C.R.1.]
Benjamin, ch. Edward and w., bp. Aug. 25, 1776. C.R.1.
Bethiah, d. Samuel Jr. and Hannah, Dec. 24, 1803. [Jenkens, d. Sam[ue]ll, C.R.1.]
Betsey [? m.], ———, 1780. G.R.6.
Betsey (see Elisabeth).
Betsey, ch. Colman and w., bp. Nov. 8, 1812. C.R.1.
Betsy, d. Colman and Betsy, Aug. 1, 1809.
Calab, s. Sam[ue]ll and Rebecca, Oct. 9, 1758 [*sic*, see Abigail]. [Caleb, s. Sam[ue]l, C.R.1.]
Caleb, s. Sam[ue]ll [Sam[ue]l, C.R.1.] and Rebecca, Apr. 24, 1754.

JENKINS, Caleb Morton, s. Caleb and Elizabeth, Nov. 1, 1802.
Caleb Turner, s. Caleb M., ship joiner, and Jane P., Feb. 21, 1849.
Calven, s. Calven, bp. May 26, 1793. C.R.1.
Calvin, s. James and Mary, June 22, 1758.
Calvin, s. Calvin and Elisabeth, July 1, 1789.
Calvin, s. Calvin Jr. and Mary, Sept. 6, 1824. [Calvin 3d, s. Calvin 2d and Lucy [dup. s. Calvin and Mary (Cudworth)], C.R.3.]
Calvin, ch. Calvin Jr. and Mary, bp. May 6, 1827. C.R.3.
Charles, s. Edward and Martha, Sept. 13, 1764.
Charles, ch. Edward and w., bp. Aug. 25, 1776. C.R.1.
Charles, s. Charles and Jane, Dec. 11, 1788.
Charles E., s. Colman and Betsey, July 2, 1817.
Chloe, d. Gideon and Mary, Mar. 6, 1802.
Clarissa, d. Gidion and Mary, Oct. 29, 1799.
Colman, s. Gera and Lilles, Nov. 22, 1774. [Coleman, C.R.1.]
Colman Sr. [dup. Capt. Coleman], —— [1775]. C.R.1.
Colman, ——, 1779. G.R.6.
Colman, s. Colman and Betsy, May 27, 1805.
Colman, ch. Colman and w., bp. Nov. 8, 1812. C.R.1.
Colman Jr., ——, 1838. G.R.6.
Commings, s. Sam[ue]ll Jr. and Abigel, —— [rec. between ch. b. Sept. 22, 1779, and ch. b. Feb. 4, 1782].
Content, d. Edw[ar]d and Martha, Sept. 10, 1726.
Content, d. Edward, bp. Dec. 19, 1750. C.R.1.
Cummings, s. James Jr. and Ruth, May 19, 1782. [Commings, C.R.1.]
Daniel, s. Edw[ar]d and Abigal, June 9, 1728.
Daniel, s. Edward, bp. July 26, 1730. C.R.1.
Daniel, s. Daniel and Eliza[beth], Apr. 25, 1760.
Daniel, s. Eli and Rebekah, June 2, 1808.
David Sanford, s. Calvin and Elisabeth, Mar. 10, 1800. [Jenkens, s. Calven, C.R.1.] [Jenkins, s. Calvin and Elizabeth, C.R.3.] [Jenkins, h. Eliza Cushing (Jenkins), P.R.17.]
David Sanford, ch. David S. and Eliza C., bp. Oct. 5, 1834. C.R.3. [[h. Mercy A.] b. Apr. 17, G.R.7.] [David Sanford Jr., b. Apr. 17, P.R.17.]
Davis, s. Joshua and Ruth, Jan. 23, 1781.
Davis, s. Ruth, wid., bp. Oct. 8, 1786. C.R.1.
Davis (Jinkings), s. Davis and Nancy, Apr. 10, 1806.
Deborah, twin ch. Dan[ie]l, bp. Nov. 6, 1774. C.R.1.
Desire, d. David, bp. Sept. 22, 1745. C.R.1.
Diana Elizabeth, ch. Colman Jr. and Diana, Aug. 22, 1835.

JENKINS, Ebenezer, s. Sam[ue]ll and Rebecca, Mar. 8, 1745.
Ebenezer, s. Samuel, bp. Apr. 6, 1746. C.R.1.
Ebenezer, s. Joshua, bp. May 19, 1776. C.R.1.
Edmond Raymond, s. Eli and Rebekah, Nov. 4, 1798.
Edward, s. Edward and Marthas, Nov. 25, 1713.
Edward, s. Sam[ue]ll [Sam[ue]l, C.R.1.] and Rebecca, Dec. 4, 1741.
Edward, ch. Edward and w., bp. Aug. 25, 1776. C.R.1.
Edward, s. Charles and Jane, Oct. 10, 1796.
Edward Henry, s. Edward H. and Nancy, Mar. 16, 1825.
Edward Little, ch. Reuben Y. and Sarah, July 24, 1842.
Eli, s. Daniel and Eliza[beth], Aug. 5, 1768. [Jenkings, C.R.1.]
Elijah, s. Gera and Lilles [Lillis, C.R 1.], Oct. 5, 1766.
Elijah, s. Charles and Jane, Nov. 3, 1793.
Elijah, s. Elijah and Marcy, June 20, 1800.
Elijah, s. Noble E. and Mercy, Jan. 30, 1824.
Elisabeth, d. Calvin and Elisabeth, June 28, 1782. [Betsey, d. Dea. Calvin, C.R.3.]
Elisabeth Davis, d. Caleb and Elizabeth, Apr. 1, 1794.
Elisha James, s. Peleg and Polly, Oct. 26, 1825.
Eliza, d. Elijah and Marcy, Jan. 20, 1798.
Eliza, d. Noah and Betsey, Oct. 1, 1804.
Eliza Ann, ch. David S. and Eliza C., bp. Aug. 12, 1832. C.R.3. [b. Nov. 21, 1831, P.R.17.]
Eliza C. [———], w. David S., ——— [1804]. C.R.3. [Eliza Cushing, w. David Sanford, Oct. 1, P.R.17.]
Eliza W. [? m.], ———, 1823. G.R.6.
Elizabeth, d. David and Elizabeth, bp. Nov. 13, 1743. C.R.1.
Elizabeth, d. Daniel and Eliza[beth], Aug. 17, 1761.
Elizabeth [———], w. Caleb, ——— [1763]. G.R.6.
Elizabeth (see Elisabeth).
Elizabeth Tilson, d. Perez T. and Nancy, May 28, 1825.
Ellice, ch. Edward and w., bp. Aug. 25, 1776. C.R.1.
Emily, d. Calvin and Elisabeth, Nov. 16, 1793. [Emila, d. Calven, C.R.1.] [Emily, d. Calvin and Elizabeth, C.R.3.]
Everett, s. Noble E. and Mercy, Jan. 10, 1820.
Everline, d. Eli and Rebekah, June 8, 1805.
Frances Maria, d. Elijah and Marcy, Sept. 27, 1805. [Jenkens, d. Capt. Elijah, C.R.1.] [Jenkins, G.R.6.]
Francis C., Aug. 1, 1831. G.R.11.
Gedion, s. James and Mary, Sept. 21, 1753. [Gideon, C.R.1.]
George, s. Samuel Jr. and Abagil, Sept. 22, 1779.
George Colman, ch. Colman Jr. and Diana, Mar. 19, 1833.
Gera, s. Thomas, bp. May 16, 1742. C.R.1.
Gera, s. Gera and Lilles, Nov. 2, 1770.

JENKINS, Gera, s. Gera, bp. Nov. 24, 1771. C.R.1.
Gideon (see Gedion).
Gideon, s. Gideon and Mercy, July 28, 1785.
Hannah, d. T., bp. July 12, 1752. C.R.1.
Hannah C., ——, 1797. G.R.14.
Hannah Cynthia Briggs, d. Charles and Jane, [Dec.] 5, 180[7].
Hannah Rich, d. Perez T. and Nancy, Apr. 23, 1823.
Hannah Robbins, d. Samuel Jr. and Hannah, July 31, 1799.
Harvey Hatch, s. Bailey (Jinkins) and Rachel, Oct. 24, 1814.
Hervey Hatch, ch. Bailey, bp. Oct. 7, 1821. C.R.2.
Henriatte, twin d. Davis and Nancy, Mar. 8, 1811.
Henry, s. Eli and Rebekah, Jan. 28, 1801.
Henry, twin s. Davis and Nancy, Mar. 10, 1811.
Henry T., "Co F. 43 Reg't.," ——, 1836. G.R.14.
Henry T., s. Noah, yeoman, and Rachel T., Sept. 5, 1844.
Horace, s. Luther and Leah, Feb. 6, 1817.
Horatio, s. Charles and Jane, July 25, 1804.
Horatio N., —— [1833]. C.R.1.
Isaac, s. James [James Jr., C.R.1.] and Ruth, Oct. 19, 1784.
Isaac Nuton, s. Davis and Nancy, Aug. 4, 1816.
Israel, s. Gera and Lilles, Oct. 3, 1777.
James, s. Edw[ar]d and Martha, Feb. 15, 1718.
James, s. James and Mary, July 3, 1749.
James, s. James Jr. and Ruth, Sept. 16, 1779.
James, s. Calvin [Calven, C.R.1.] and Elisabeth, Apr. 10, 1797.
James, s. Luther and Lear, Oct. 10, 1808.
James, s. Cummings and Rachel, Sept. 15, 1811.
Jane Collier, d. Charles and Jane, Mar. 10, 1803.
Jane Collier, d. Edward H. and Nancy, Feb. 1, 1820.
Jeanny Morton, d. Caleb and Elizebeth, Sept. 28, 1801.
Joaana Morton, d. Caleb and Eliz[abe]th, Sept. 20, 1807.
John, s. Tho[ma]s, bp. Aug. 24, 1746. C.R.1.
John, s. Gera and Lilles, Aug. 21, 1773.
John, twin s. James and Ruth, Mar. 8, 1792.
John, s. Elijah and Marcy, Sept. 18, 1802. [Jenkens, C.R.1.] [Jenkins, G.R.6.]
John, s. Luther and Lear, Oct. 29, 1806.
Joseph, s. Sam[ue]ll [Sam[ue]l, C.R.1.] and Rebecca, Oct. 5, 1757.
Joseph, s. Joseph and Abigail, July 28, 1791.
Joseph, s. Colman and Betsy, May 6, 1813.
Joseph Francis, ch. Colman Jr. and Diana, Aug. 1, 1831.
Joseph Stetson, s. Elijah and Marcy, Nov. 11, 1803. [Jenkens, C.R.1.]
Joshua, s. Sam[ue]ll [Samuel, C.R.1.] and Rebecca, July 25, 1744.

JENKINS, Joshua, s. Davis and Nancy, Sept. 17, 1813.
Joshua, s. Colman and Betsey, Nov. 20, 1821.
Josiah, s. Gideon and Mercy, Dec. 1, 1791.
Leah, d. Luther and Leah, Aug. 2, 1810.
Lemuel, ch. Edward and w., bp. Aug. 25, 1776. C.R.1.
Lilles, d. Gera and Lilles, July 6, 1776. [Lillis, d. Jera, C.R.1.]
Lilles, d. Gera and Lilles, May 3, 1781.
Lizzie, d. Peleg T., merchant, and Elizabeth [beth, written in pencil] M., Apr. 6, 1845.
Louise Litchfield, d. Howard, carpenter, and Rachel C., May 24, 1844.
Lucy, ch. Edward and w., bp. Aug. 25, 1776. C.R.1.
Lucy, d. Charles and Jane, Mar. 6, 1787.
Lucy, twin d. James and Ruth, Mar. 8, 1792.
Lucy, d. James and Ruth, June 11, 1794.
Luther, s. Gideon and Mercy, Dec. 3, 1780.
Luther, s. Luther and Lear, Sept. 10, 1804.
Lydia, ch. Thomas Jr. and Sarah, bp. May 6, 1739. C.R.1.
Lydia, d. Gera and Lilles, June 1, 1784.
Mable, d. Calvin and Elisabeth, July 28, 1795. [Mabil, d. Calven, C.R.1.]
Margarette P. [――――], second w. Capt. Perez, Apr. 20, 1824. G.R.6.
Maria, d. Elijah and Marcy, Apr. 27, 1796.
Maria, d. Capt. Elijah, bp. Mar. ―, 1800. C.R.1.
Maria, twin d. Colman and Betsy, May 4, 1811. [Jenkens, C.R.1.]
Martha, d. Edw[ar]d and Martha, Feb. 15, 1724.
Martha, d. Samuel, bp. Oct. 17, 1756. C.R.1.
Mary, d. Edward, Jan. 31, 1706.
Mary, d. Tho[ma]s, bp. Apr. 1, 1744. C.R.1.
Mary, d. James and Mary, Feb. 9, 1747.
Mary, d. James and Mary, bp. Apr. 10, 1748. C.R.1.
Mary, d. Joshua, bp. Apr. 19, 1772. C.R.1.
Mary [――――], w. Calvin Jr., ―― [1790]. C.R.3.
Mary, d. Cummings and Rachel, June 3, 1809.
Mary, twin d. Colman and Betsy, May 4, 1811. [Jenkens, twin ch. Coleman, C.R.1.] [Jenkins, w. Joel L. Manson, G.R.6.]
Mary Joanna, w. Capt. Joshua L. Jordan, ―― [1831]. G.R.6.
Mercy, d. Gideon and Mercy, Mar. 19, 1789.
Mercy A. [――――], w. David S. [May ―, 1838]. G.R.6.
Mercy Hall, d. Noble E. and Mercy, Dec. 27, 1821.
Nancy, d. Gideon and Mercy, Mar. 3, 1783.
Nancy, d. Samuel Jr. and Abagil, Sept. 11, 1783.
Nancy (Jenkings), d. Davis and Nancy, Oct. 25, 1807.

JENKINS, Nancy Brown, d. Edward H. and Nancy, June 12, 1823.
Nancy Colman, d. Perez T. and Nancy, Mar. 9, 1817.
Nathan Delano, s. Perez T. and Nancy, July 3, 1819.
Nathan Dileno, s. Caleb and Elizabeth, June 16, 1796.
Nathaniel, s. Sam[ue]ll [Sam[ue]l, C.R.1.] and Rebecca, Mar. 11, 1748.
Nathaniel, s. Sam[ue]ll and Rebecca, Oct. 28, 1752. [Nathanael, s. Samuel, C.R.1.]
Nath[anie]ll, s. Samuel Jr. and Abagil, Feb. 3, 1776.
Noah, s. Danil and Eliz[abe]th, Aug. 20, 1776. [Jenkings, s. Daniel, C.R.1.] [h. Elizabeth Cushing, P.R.17.]
Noah, s. Noah and Betsey, May 15, 1810. [May —, 1811, P.R.17.]
Noble Everett, s. Charles and Jane, Jan. 26, 1791.
Oliver, s. Gera and Lilles, Dec. 28, 1767. [Jenkings, C.R.1.]
Paul, s. Daniel and Eliza[beth], Nov. 24, 1762. [Jenkings, C.R.1.]
Peleg, s. James and Mary, Feb. 11, 1751.
Peleg, s. Gideon and Mercy, Jan. 10, 1779.
Peleg Andrew, s. Peleg T., carpenter, and Elizebeth M., Sept. 10, 1848.
Peleg Foard, s. Caleb and Eliz[a]b[e]th, Apr. 27, 1805. [Peleg Ford, C.R.1.]
Peleg Thomas, s. Peleg and Mary (Thomas), Oct. 20, 1817.
Perez, s. Perez T. and Nancy, Mar. 23, 1813. [Capt. Perez [h. Margarette P. (second w.)], G.R.6.]
Perez Tilson, s. Caleb and Elizabeth, Dec. 22, 1791.
Polle, d. James Jr. and Ruth, Nov. 5, 1775. [Polly, C.R.1.]
Rachel [———], w. Bailey, ———, 1787. G.R.14.
Rachel Woodward, d. Bailey and Rachel, Apr. 1, 1812.
Rebecca, d. Sam[ue]ll [Sam[ue]l, C.R.1.] and Rebecca, Sept. 17, 1747.
Reuben Young, s. Peleg and Mary (Thomas), July 7, 1810.
Rhoda, d. Tho[ma]s, bp. Nov. 19, 1758. C.R.1.
Ruth, d. James Jr. and Ruth, June 15, 1777.
Ruth, d. Joshua and Ruth, Dec. 24, 1778.
Ruth, d. James and Ruth, Feb. 14, 1788.
Ruth, d. Davis and Nancy, Dec. 5, 1809.
Sally, d. Calvin and Elisabeth, Aug. 31, 1787.
Sally, d. Calven, bp. May 26, 1793. C.R.1.
Sally B., d. Colman and Betsey, Aug. 5, 1814.
Sally Bosman, d. Colman, bp. Oct. 1, 1815. C.R.1.
Samuel, s. Edward and Martha, Aug. 13, 1710.
Samuel, s. Sam[ue]ll and Rebecca, Mar. 8, 1742.
Samuel, s. Sam[ue]l, bp. Apr. 17, 1743. C.R.1.
Samuel, s. Samuel Jr. and Abagil, July 10, 1772.

JENKINS, Samuel, s. Samuel Jr. and Hannah, June 5, 1801. [Sam[ue]ll, s. Sam[ue]ll Jr., C.R.1.]
Samuel B., ch. Samuel L. and Ruth, Aug. 21, 1838, in Cohassett.
Samuel Lincoln, s. Luther and Leah, Aug. 22, 1812.
Sarah, d. Thomas, bp. Dec. 30, 1739. C.R.1.
Sarah, d. Sam[ue]ll Jr. and Abagil, Feb. 4, 1782.
Sarah, d. Charles and Jane, Oct. 14, 1785.
Sarah Bailey, d. Joseph and Abigail, Apr. 2, 1794.
Sarah L., d. Noah, farmer, and Rachel T., Jan. 6, 1845.
Sarah Welch Litchfield, d. Howard, carpenter, and Rachel C., Aug. 16, 1846.
Sarah White, d. Caleb and Elizabeth, Jan. 11, 1799.
Shadrach, s. Gideon and Mary, Jan. 14, 1796.
Silas, s. Daniel and Eliza[beth], Dec. 11, 1764. [Jenkings, C.R.1.]
Silas, twin ch. Dan[ie]l, bp. Nov. 6, 1774. C.R.1.
Solon, s. Gideon and Mary, Dec. 1, 1793.
Sopha, d. Samuel Jr. and Abigal, Apr. 15, 1786.
Sophia, d. Commings and Rachel, Feb. 12, 1814.
Sophronia, d. Colman and Betsy, Oct. 1, 1801.
Sophronia, ch. Colman and w., bp. Nov. 8, 1812. C.R.1.
Thankfull, d. Edward and Martha, May 17, 1712.
Thomas, s. Edward, Mar. 5, 1707.
Thomas, ch. Thomas Jr. and Sarah, bp. May 6, 1739. C.R.1.
Thomas, s. Tho[ma]s Jr. and Hannah, Apr. 20, 1767.
Thomas Bailey, [twin] s. Bailey and Rachel, Aug. 7, 1807. [Jenkens, C.R.2.]
Turner Hatch, s. Bailey and Rachel, Jan. 19, 1810.
William, ch. Edward and w., bp. Aug. 25, 1776. C.R.1.
William [of] N. York, —— [1816]. C.R.1.
William Cole, s. Cummings and Rachel, July 4, 1816.
William Collier, s. Cha[rle]s and Jane, June 29, 1799.
William H., s. Colman and Betsey, July 6, 1819. [[h. Lucy G. (Porter)] G.R.6.]
William Woodward, [twin] s. Bailey and Rachel, Aug. 7, 1807. [Jenkens, C.R.2.]
—— [——], wid. ——, —— [1761]. C.R.1.

JENNINGS, Elizabeth C., w. Geo[rge] M. Young, Sept. 17, 1828. G.R.6.

JEWETT, Edwin Cooper, ch. Rev. Paul, bp. Aug. 14, 1836. C.R.3.
Eleanor Punchard, d. Rev. Paul and Gracey, June 30, 1829.
Henry Paul Blatchford, s. Rev. Paul and Gracey, Jan. 29, 1828.
William James, ch. Rev. Paul and Gracey, bp. June 23, 1833. C.R.3.

JOAN (see Jones), Mary, d. William and Dorothy, June —, 1668.

JOHNSON, Benjamin, s. Humphry [Humfrey, C.R.2.], Aug. 27, 1657.
John, s. Humphrey, Mar. —, 1653.
Josepth, s. Humphrey, June 24, 1655. P.C.R. [Joseph, s. Humfrey, C.R.2.]
Margret, d. Humphrey, Dec. 22 [1659]. [Margaret, d. Humfrey, C.R.2.]
Mary, d. Humfrey, bp. Apr. 19, 1662. C.R.2.

JONES (see Joan), Abby Frances, ch. John H. and Almira C., Feb. 12, 1840.
Abigail, d. Eben[eze]r and Jane of Marshfield, bp. Dec. 20, 1730. C.R.2.
Adeline, d. John Jr. and Sarah (Tower), Oct. 6, 1823.
Alonso, s. Samuel P. and Pemela, June 16, 1790.
Alonzo, s. Samuel Paine and Pemelia, Nov. 9, 1791.
Alonzo, s. Samuel Paine and Pemelia, June 18, 1793.
Alonzo, s. Alonzo and Fanney, July 5, 1814.
Amos, s. John and Ruth, Nov. 27, 1742.
Aurelia Jenkins, d. Thomas F. and Mabel, Sept. 25, 1820.
Benjamin Parker, s. Parker and Judith O., Dec. 12, 1829.
Betsey, d. Alonzo and Fanny, May 5, 1826.
Betty, [ch.] Elisha and Sarah of Marshfield, bp. July 22, 1739. C.R.2.
Betty, d. John, bp. Sept. 19, 1756. C.R.2.
Charles, s. Charles and Esther, May 10, 1810.
Christopher B., s. Christopher B. and Lucy, Feb. 2, 1813.
Consider, twin ch. Ebenezar and Jane of Marshfield, bp. June 24, 1739. C.R.2.
Content, ch. Elisha and Sarah of Marshfield, bp. Mar. 23, 1734-5. C.R.2.
Cushing, s. Charles and Elizabeth, Aug. 26, 1822.
Cushing, s. Charles and Elizabeth, Dec. 5, 1824.
Deborah, d. Elisha, bp. Oct. 23, 1726. C.R.1.
Diana, d. Alonzo and Fanny, Nov. 25, 1824.
Ebenezar, s. Eben[eze]r and Jane of Marshfield, bp. Sept. 7, 1735. C.R.2.
Elezebeth Rachel, d. Samuel Paine and Pemelia, May 18, 1789.
Elisha, s. Elisha and Sarah of Marshfield, bp. May 4, 1735. C.R.2.
Eliza Vinal, d. Alonzo and Fanny, Dec. 9, 1820.
Eliza Vinal, d. Alonzo, "adopted" ch. Rev. P. Jewett, bp. June 1, 1828. C.R.3.
Elizabeth (see Elezebeth Rachel).

JONES, Ellen F., ch. Ezekiel Jr. and Betsey, Aug. —, 1843.
Ellen R. [? m.] [Jan. —, 1828]. G.R.14.
Emme Thomas, d. Ezekiel and Lucy W., Jan. 7, 1827. [Emma T., G.R.6.]
Esther Hayden, d. Alonzo and Fanny, July 18, 1816.
Ezekiel, s. Samuel Paine and Pemelia, Feb. 28, 1795. [Capt. Ezekiel, "The last Scituate Veteran of the Navy of 1812. Raised from the ranks in the Navy to a Captaincy in the U.S. Rev. Marine," G.R.6.]
Ezekiel, s. Ezekiel and Lucy W., Apr. 31 [sic], 1814.
Fanny Woodbury, d. Alonzo and Fanny, Sept. 25, 1818.
Francis E., s. Charles, trunk maker, and Charlotte A., Sept. 12, 1846.
George Henry, s. Thomas F. and Mabel, Aug. 2, 1828.
George W., s. John and Sally, bp. Nov. 8, 1836. C.R.1.
George Washington, s. Samuel Paine and Pemelia, Aug. 4, 1804.
Gustavus, s. John Jr. and Sarah (Tower), Mar. 25, 1820.
Hannah, d. Isaac and Hannah, Nov. 11, 1720.
Hannah, ch. Isaac and Hannah, bp. May 26, 1723. C.R.2.
Hannah, d. Ebenezar and Jane of Marshfield, bp. Dec. 29, 1728. C.R.2.
Hannah J., d. Christopher B. and Lucy, July 26, 1817.
Hannah Thomas, ch. John C. and Sally, June 28, 1833.
Harriet Dunbar, d. Ezekiel Jr. and Betsey, bp. May 31, 1841. C.R.1.
Helen T. [? m.], July 18, 1818. G.R.6.
Isaac, s. Isaac and Hannah, bp. July 7, 1717. C.R.2.
Isaac, s. Isaac and Hannah, bp. Oct. 11, 1724. C.R.2.
Isaac, s. John and Lucy, Dec. 26, 1796.
John Cogresell, s. Samuel Paine and Pemelia, Aug. 21, 1805.
John Henry, s. John Jr. and Sarah (Tower), Sept. 25, 1815.
John Lincoln, s. Christopher B. and Lucy, Dec. 11, 1814.
John Quincy, ch. John [Capt. John, G.R.6.] C. and Sally, Oct. 23, 1828.
John Quincy, ch. John C. and Sally, bp. Nov. 4, 1832. C.R.1.
Joseph, s. Elisha, bp. Oct. 29, 1727. C.R.1.
Joseph Hayden, s. Samuel Paine and Pemelia, Apr. 6, 1799.
Lucy, d. John and Lucy, Dec. 13, 1800.
Lucy W. [————], w. Capt. Ezekiel, —— [1789]. G.R.6.
Lucy White, d. Ezekiel and Lucy W., July 4, 1816.
Marcellus, ch. Thomas and Abigail C., Sept. 9, 1836.
Mary, d. Isaac and Hannah, Oct. 11, 1718.
Mary, d. Charles and Esther, May 6, 1808.
Mary Ann, d. Alonzo and Fanny, Mar. 13, 1823.

JONES, Mary Lincoln, d. Christopher B. and Lucy, Nov. 19, 1809.
Mary Thomas, d. Thomas F. and Mabel, May 23, 1822.
Mary Vining, ch. Charles and Mary J., Nov. 8, 1840.
Melvina, ch. John C. and Sally, bp. Nov. 4, 1832. C.R.1.
Melvinia, ch. John C. and Sally, Jan. 27, 1831.
Mercy Baker, ch. John C. and Sally, July 26, 1837.
Mercy Baker, d. John C. and Sally, bp. Aug. 12, 1838. C.R.1.
Noah Nichols, s. Charles and Elizabeth, Dec. 2, 1814.
Noah Nichols, ch. Charles, bp. June 12, 1825. C.R.2.
Pemelia, d. Samuel Paine and Pemelia, Mar. 20, 1783.
Pemelia Hayden, d. Ezekiel and Lucy W., June 28, 1818.
Pemelia Virginia, d. Ezekiel and Lucy W., Mar. 6, 1832, in Martha's Co., Va.
Sally, d. Samuel Paine and Pemelia, Aug. 22, 1785.
Sally [———], w. Capt. John C. [Oct. —, 1802]. G.R.6.
Sally Arnol, d. Alonzo and Fanney [Fanny, C.R.1.], June 15, 1812.
Samuel, s. John and Ruth, Jan. 14, 1739.
Samuel, s. Christopher B. and Lucy, July 4, 1807.
Samuel Paine, s. Samuel Paine and Pemelia, May 12, 1787.
Sarah, d. Isaac and Hannah, Jan. 18, 1722.
Sarah, d. Isaac and Hannah, bp. Sept. 11, 1726. C.R.2.
Sarah, d. Elisha, bp. Dec. 23, 1729. C.R.1.
Sarah Cushing, d. John Jr. and Sarah (Tower), Mar. 15, 1817.
Sarah Dunbar, ch. John C. and Sally, June 29, 1826.
Sarah Dunbar, ch. John C. and Sally, bp. Nov. 4, 1832. C.R.1.
Seth, twin ch. Ebenezar and Jane of Marshfield, bp. June 24, 1739. C.R.2.
Simeon, s. Eben[eze]r and Jane of Marshfield, bp. Dec. 31, 1732. C.R.2.
Sophia L. Brown, d. Alonzo [July —, 1840]. C.R.1.
Thomas, s. John and Lucy, Oct. 9, 1803.
Thomas Frances [sic], s. Samuel Paine and Pemelia, Apr. 28, 1797.
Thomas Francis, s. Thomas F. and Mabel, Mar. 6, 1826.
Waldo, s. John Jr. and Sarah (Tower), Aug. 23, 1831.
Walter C., s. Charles, trunk maker, and Charlotte A. (b. Boston), Sept. 7, 1849, in S. Scituate.
William, s. W[illia]m of Marshfield, bp. Feb. 24, 1754. C.R.2.
William, s. Charles and Elizabeth, July 18, 1819.
William, ch. Charles, bp. June 12, 1825. C.R.2.
William Stowell, ch. John C. and Sally, Sept. 24, 1841.
———, d. John H., trunkmaker, and Almira, Jan. 25, 1844.
———, s. Ezekiel Jr., mariner, and Betsey, Feb. 8, 1849.

JORDAN (see Jorden), Abia, d. Nath[anie]l and Abigail, Mar. 14, 1795.
Charles Lincoln, s. Charles N., shoemaker, and Catharine B., Aug. 7, 1844.
George, s. Nathaniel and Abigail, Sept. 20, 1785.
Hannah, d. Peleg and Rispah, Aug. 24, 1780.
Patience, ch. John and Patience, bp. July 15, 1722. C.R.2.
Peleg, s. Peleg and Rispah, June 4, 1784.
Polly, d. Nath[anie]l and Abigail, July 15, 1792.
Rebecca, d. Nath[anie]l and Abigail, Jan. 14, 1790.
Ruth, d. Nath[anie]l and Abigail, May 6, 1787.
Samuel, s. Peleg and Rispah, May 6, 1787.
——— [———], w. ———, ——— [1804]. C.R.1.

JORDEN (see Jordan), David, s. David and Lydia, Mar. 2, 1773.
Lydia, d. David and Lydia, Jan. 3, 1771.

JOSEPH, Antone, ——— [1816]. G.R.16.

JOSLIN (see Josline, Josling, Josselin, Joycelin), Abigail, d. Henery, bp. June 10, 1679. C.R.2.
Lydia, d. Henery Jr. and Hannah, Aug. 25, 1722.
Mary, d. Nathanaell and Frances, Mar. 13, 1712–13.
Mary, d. Nath[anie]ll, July 29, 1719.
Nath[anie]ll, s. Nath[anie]ll and Francis [*sic*], July 6, 1722.

JOSLINE (see Joslin, Josling, Josselin, Joycelin), Abigail, d. Henry, Apr. 12, 1677.
Abraham, s. Henry, Jan. 14, 1678–9. [Joslin, s. Henery, C.R.2.]
Anne, d. Henry, Feb. 22, 1680–1.
Charles, s. Henry, Mar. 15, 1682–3.
Henry, s. Henry, Mar. 24, 1696–7.
Jabez, s. Henry, Feb. 5, 1690–1.
Jemima, twin d. Henry, Dec. 17, 1695.
Joseph, s. Henry, Dec. 16, 1699.
Kezia, twin d. Henry, Dec. 17, 1695.
Mary, d. Henry, Jan. 22, 1684–5.
Nathanael, s. Henry, Feb. 10, 1686–7.
Rebekah, d. Henry, Mar. 25, 1689.
Rebekah, d. Henry, May 14, 1693.

JOSLING (see Joslin, Josline, Josselin, Joycelin), Thomas, s. Henry, Sept. —, 1702.

JOSSELIN (see Joslin, Josline, Josling, Joycelin), Harriet, d. Waterman and Melinda (Stetson), ———, 1835. G.R.14.
Waterman [h. Melinda (Stetson)], ———, 1792. G.R.14.

JOYCE (see Choyce).

JOYCELIN (see Joslin, Josline, Josling, Josselin), Anne, d. Henery, bp. June 25, 1682. C.R.2.

KEEN, Joseph, s. Joseph, Mar. 15, 1718.

KELLOGG, Mary H. [———], w. Milo, —— [1800]. G.R.14.

KELLY, Ann, d. James, bp. June 21, 1752. C.R.1.
David, ch. James and Eliz[abeth], Irish, bp. June 22, 1737. C.R.1.
Elizabeth, ch. James and Eliz[abeth], Irish, bp. June 22, 1737. C.R.1.
Elizabeth, d. James, bp. July 16, 1738. C.R.1.
James, ch. James and Eliz[abeth], Irish, bp. June 22, 1737. C.R.1.
James, s. James, bp. Mar. 16, 1744. C.R.1.
John, ch. James and Eliz[abeth], Irish, bp. June 22, 1737. C.R.1.
John, s. James, bp. Nov. 7, 1742. C.R.1.

KELTON, Mary K. [? m.], Apr. 16, 1803. G.R.2.
William H., Rev., "Pastor First Baptist Church" [h. Amelia (Simonds)], Sept. 26, 1835. G.R.2.

KEMPTON (see Kemton), Ephraim, s. Ephraim, bp. Apr. 8, 1649. C.R.2.
Ephraim, s. Ephraim, Oct. 1, 1649.
Joanna, d. Ephraim, bp. Nov. 9, 1645. C.R.2.
Manasseh, s. Ephraim, bp. Feb 9, 1650. C.R.2.
Mannasseh, s. Ephraim, Jan. 1, 1651.
Patience, d. Ephraim, bp. Nov. 21, 1647. C.R.2.
Patience, d. Ephraim, Oct. 2, 1648.
Ruth, d. Ephr[aim], bp. Sept. 24, 1654. C.R.2.

KEMTON (see Kempton), Joanna, d. Ephraim, Sept. 29, 1646. [Sept. 29, 1647, P.C.R.]

KENDER, Amanda Fitz Allen, d. W[illia]m and Hannah, Feb. 24, 1816, in Pembroke.
Bethiah Foster, d. William and Hannah, Aug. 27, 1810, in Pembroke.
Betsey Waterman, d. William and Hannah, June 23, 1827.
Hannah McFarland, d. W[illia]m and Hannah, June 27, 1824.
Mary Foster, d. William and Hannah, Jan. 22, 1813, in Pembroke.
Warren W., s. William J., furnace man, and Lucy J. (b. Chelsea, Vt.), Sept. 19, 1849, in S. Scituate.
William James, s. William and Hannah, Sept. 21, 1820.

KENT, Abigail, d. Ebenezer [Ebenezar, C.R.2.], Oct. 12, 1706.
Benjamin, s. John [s. John and Sarah, P.R.3.], Jan. 8, 1700.
Charlot Appelton, d. Samuel and Hannah, Jan. 12, 1800. [Charlotte Appleton, d. Sam[ue]ll and w., C.R.2.]
Ebenezer, s. John, May 28, 1699. [Ebnezer, s. John and Sarah, P.R.3.]
Ebenezer, [ch. Ebenezer] ——, 1717. [bp. Sept. 22, C.R.1.]
Elisabeth, d. John and Sarah, Jan. 8, 1697–8. P.R.3.
Elizabeth, d. Ebenezer, Sept. 6, 1710.
Ezekell, s. John, Oct. 8, 1705. [Ezekiel, s. John and Sarah, C.R.2.]
Hannah, d. John and Sarah, Mar. 5, 1696. P.R.3.
Hannah Willims, d. Sam[ue]ll and Hannah, Oct. 14, 1801. [Hannah Williams, C.R.2.]
Isaac, s. Ebenezer, Sept. 27, 1712.
John, s. John and Sarah, Sept. 29, 1694. P.R.3.
Mary, [ch. Ebenezer] ——, 1715. [bp. June 5, C.R.1.]
Mercy, d. Ebenezer, July 31, 1708.
Nathaniel, s. John and Sarah, Feb. 18, 1708.
Rachel, d. Sam[ue]ll, and Hannah, Oct. 21, 1805.
Samewell, s. John, Dec. 18, 1703. [Samuel, s. John and Sarah, P.R.3.]
Samuel King, s. Sam[ue]ll and Hannah, Sept. 12, 1803.
Sarah, d. John and Sarah, Oct. 11, [16]93. P.R.3.
Sarah, d. John [d. John and Sarah, P.R.3.], Sept. 10, 1702.
Seth, s. Ebenezer, bp. June 4, 1721. C.R.1.

KIMBALL, Deborah, —— [1796]. G.R.15.
Hannah K., d. Joseph and Mary of Canterbury, N.H., w. Isaac Glines, —— [1796]. G.R.2. [Jan. 18, in Canterbery, N.H., P.R.16.]

KINERICK, Deborah, d. George, bp. Nov. 25, 1638. C.R.1.

KING (see Kinge), Anna, d. Thomas, May ——, 1684.
Anna, d. John and Rebeckah, bp. Sept. 4, 1715. C.R.2.
Benjamin, s. John and Rebekkah, bp. Apr. 16, 1710. C.R.2.
Daniell, s. Thomas [Thomas Jr., C.R.2.], July ——, 1675.
Daniell, s. Daniell, May 15, 1704. [Daniel, C.R.2.]
Deborah, d. George [d. George and Deborah, C.R.2.], Apr. 7, 1711.
Ebenezer, s. Thomas Jr., Feb. 22, 1685. C.R.2.
Elisabath, d. Daniell, Apr. 30, 1702. [Elizabeth, d. Daniel, C.R.2.]
Elisha, s. John and Rebecca of Marshfield, bp. Oct. 6, 1717. C.R.2.
Elizabeth (see Elisabath).
Elizabeth, d. John and Rebeccah of Marshfield, bp. May 29, 1720. C.R.2.

KING, Georg, s. Thomas, Aug. —, 1682. [George, s. Thomas Jr., C.R.2.]
Hannah, d. Ecebod, May 17, 1702.
Hannah, d. Joseph of Marshfield, bp. Jan. 21, 1738-9. C.R.2.
Ichabod, s. Thomas [Thomas, Jr., C.R.2.], Oct. —, 1680.
Jane, d. Ichabod [d. Icabod and Hannah, C.R.2.], Feb. 17, 1705-6.
Jeane, d. Thomas, Nov. 14, 1673. [Jane, C.R.2.]
Jemima, d. Edward of Marshfield, bp. Sept. 18, 1670. C.R.2.
Jerusha, d. John and Rebecca, bp. Aug. 12, 1711. C.R.2.
John, s. Thomas [Thomas, Jr., C.R.2.], Apr. —, 1677.
John, s. John of Marshfield, bp. Apr. 1 [or 3], 1705. C.R.2.
John, s. John and Mary of Marshfield, bp. Aug. 13, 1732. C.R.2.
Joseph, s. John and Rebecca, bp. Apr. 11, 1708. C.R.2.
Lydia, d. George [d. George and Deborah, C.R.2.], Dec. 26, 1716.
Lydiah, [ch.] John and Mary of Marshfield, bp. July 2, 1738. C.R.2.
Mary, d. Daniel and Elizabeth, bp. July 28, 1706. C.R.2.
Mehetable, d. Daniell, Mar. 4, 1709-10. [Mehetabel, d. Dan[ie]ll and Elizabeth, C.R.2.]
Mercy, d. Thomas [Thomas Jr., C.R.2.], Nov. —, 1678.
Rebecca, [ch.] Joseph and Thankfull, bp. Aug. 8, 1736. C.R.2.
Rebekah, d. John and Rebèkah, bp. Aug. 25, 1706. C.R.2.
Rhoda, d. George and w. [Deborah, C.R.2.], July 27, 1713.
Robert, s. Daniell [s. Daniel and Elizabeth, C.R.2.], Dec. 14, 1707.
Sarah, d. Thomas [Thomas Jr., C.R.2.], Jan. 3, 1669.
Sarah, d. George [d. George and Deborah, C.R.2.], June 6, 1719.
Thomas, s. Thomas [Thomas Jr., C.R.2.], Aug. 30, 1671.
Thomas, s. Echabod, Dec. 17, 1703.
Thomas, s. John and Rebeckkah of Marshfield, bp. Aug. 23, 1713. C.R.2.
Thomas, ch. John of Marshfield, bp. Feb. 22, 1736-7. C.R.2.

KINGE (see King), Daniell, s. Thomas, Feb. 4, 1647. [Daniel King, C.R.2.]
George, s. Thomas, Dec. 24, 1642.
John, s. Thomas, May 30, 1652. [King, C.R.2.]
Rhode, d. Thomas, Oct. 11, 1639.
Sarah, d. Thomas, May 24, 1650. [King, C.R.2.]
Thomas, s. Thomas, June 21, 1645. [King, C.R.2.]

KIRK, James W., —— [1834]. G.R.14.

KNAPP, Charles A., ch. Otis and Mary, Feb. 28, 1828.
George O., ch. Otis and Mary, Oct. 15, 18[ ]. [[h. Abby L. (Stetson)] ——, 1802, G.R.15.]
James B., ch. Otis and Mary, Dec. 13, 1832 [*sic*, see Mary B.]. [Dec. 13, 1828, G.R.15.]

KNAPP, John H., ch. Otis and Mary, Aug. 20, 1836 [*sic*, see Robert C.].
Joseph F., ch. Otis and Mary, Feb. 8, 1840.
Lucy B., ch. Otis and Mary, June 5, 1823, in Abington.
Mary B., ch. Otis and Mary, Feb. 25, 1833 [*sic*, see James B.].
Robert C., ch. Otis and Mary, Feb. 20, 1837 [*sic*, see John H.].
Susan C., ch. Otis and Mary, Sept. 20, 1821.

LAMB, Ezekiel, Ind[ia]n, ch. James and Patience "(a Melatto)," bp. June 18, 1727. C.R.2.
James, Ind[ia]n, ch. James and Patience "(a Melatto)," bp. June 18, 1727. C.R.2.
Sarah, d. James, bp. July 15, 1722. C.R.1.

LAMBERT) (see Lumbert), Caleb, s. John and Ruth, bp. May 17, 1724. C.R.2.
Hannah, d. John, Apr. 10, 1697.
Huldah, [ch.] John and w., bp. Nov. 27, 1748. C.R.2.
James, s. James and Sarah, June 5, 1726.
John, s. John, Dec. 5, 1693.
John, s. John Jr. and Ruth, bp. Oct. 21, 1722. C.R.2.
Joseph, ch. John, bp. Aug. 26, 1737. C.R.2.
Joseph, s. James, bp. Aug. 6, 1738. C.R.2.
Joseph, s. Joseph and w., bp. Aug. 5, 1744. C.R.2.
Luce, [ch.] James and Sarah, bp. May 30, 1742. C.R.2.
Luke, s. James and Sarah, Mar. 21, 1730.
Lurana, d. John and w., bp. June 1, 1746. C.R.2.
Lydiah, d. James and Sarah, bp. Aug. 17, 1735. C.R.2.
Mary, d. John, Apr. 20, 1695.
Mary, d. James and Sarah, bp. June 3, 1733. C.R.2.
Samuel, s. Zaccheus Jr. and Zipporah, Sept. 4, 1794.
Sarah, d. James [(Lumbert) C.R.2.] and Sarah, Dec. 2, 1728.
Susanna, d. John, June 1, 1699.
Thomas, s. Thomas, bp. July 1, 1660. C.R.2.

LANE, Benjamin Turner, s. Benjamin Turner and Lucy, Sept. 25, 1791.
Fanny, d. Benja[min] T. and Lucy, Apr. 8, 1795.
George, s. Benja[min] and w., bp. July 1, 1804. C.R.2.
Joanna Turner, d. Capt. Benja[min] and w., bp. Sept. 29, 1799. C.R.2.
Lucy, d. Benjamin T., June 25, 1793.
Maria, d. Capt. Benja[min] and w., bp. Aug. 1, 1802. C.R.2.
Sarah Turner, d. Benja[min] T. [Benja[min] Turner, C.R.2.] and **Lucy,** Feb. 2, 1797.

LANGDON, John H., s. Daniel, ship carpenter (b. England), and Charlotte (b. Boston), Nov. 28, 1848.

LAPHAM (see Laphum, Lappam, Lappham, Lappum), Abiah F., d. Thomas Jr. and Abigal, Mar. 16, 1793.
Abiah Joice, d. Tho[ma]s Jr. and w., bp. Aug. 28, 1796. C.R.2.
Abigail, d. Stephen, bp. May 29, 1757. C.R.2.
Abigail, d. Thomas Jr., bp. June 30, 1802. C.R.2.
Abigal F., d. Thomas Jr. and Abigal, June 15, 1795.
Amos, s. Sam[ue]ll and Hannah, Dec. 1, 1717. [Lappam, s. Samuel and Hannah, C.R.2.]
Amos, s. Amos and Abagal, Mar. 13, 1761.
Batte, d. Jesse and Mercy, July 18, 1775.
Benjamin, s. Thomas Jr. and Sally, July 14, 1803.
Benjamin, ch. Thom[a]s, bp. Oct. 1, 1815. C.R.2.
Charles, s. Elisha and Sabre, bp. Aug. 30, 1767. C.R.1.
Charles H., ch. Charles H. and Bathsheba G., Mar. 28, 1832.
Cha[rle]s Henry, s. Charles and Temperance, Feb. 5, 1803.
Charles Henry, s. Charles and w., bp. June 24, 1804. C.R.2.
Charlotte, d. Charles and Temperance, Oct. 9, 1798.
Cynthia (see Zyntha).
Daniel Cushing, s. Michael and Sarah, Dec. 16, 1794.
David, s. Samuell, Apr. 3, 1706. [Lappam, s. Sam[ue]ll Lappan [*sic*], C.R.2.]
Elisha, s. Elisha, bp. May 6, 1764. C.R.1.
Elizabeth, d. Samuel and Hannah, Apr. 13, 1708. [Lappam, C.R.2.]
Fanna, ch. Elisha, bp. June 25, 1775. C.R.1.
George, s. Thomas Jr. and Abigal, Sept. 20, 1785.
George, s. Tho[ma]s Jr. and w., bp. July 3, 1791. C.R.2.
George, ch. Charles H. and Bathsheba G., Mar. 7, 1830.
Hannah, d. Samuell, Apr. 1, 1703.
Harriot, d. Thomas Jr. and Sally, Jan. 31, 1819.
Ichabod, s. Joseph and Patien, Oct. 22, 1711.
Israel, s. Thomas Jr. and Sally, June 30, 1808.
Israel, ch. Thom[a]s, bp. Oct. 1, 1815. C.R.2.
James Randal, s. Jesse and Mercy, June 8, 1772.
Joseph, s. Thomas, Sept. —, 1670.
Joseph, s. Joseph, Apr. 26, 1709.
Joshua, s. Samuel and Hannah, Dec. 22, 1710. [Lappam, s. Samuell and Hannah, C.R.2.]
Lidea Lincoln, d. Jessa and Mercy, Dec. 1, 1777.
Loring Cushing, s. Micah and w., bp. July 26, 1795. C.R.2.
Lucenda, d. Charles and Temperance, Sept. 5, 1809.
Lucy, d. Amos and Abagal, Apr. 6, 1756. [d. Amos and Abigail, C.R.1.]

LAPHAM, Lydia, d. Thomas, June 6, 1677.
Lydia, d. Sam[ue]ll and Hannah, Nov. 17, 1724. [Lappam, d. Samuel and Hannah, C.R.2.]
Lydia, d. Michael [Micah, C.R.2.] and Sarah, Dec. 13, 1799.
Lydia, d. Thomas Jr. and Sally, Mar. 31, 1816.
Mary, d. Samuell, Sept. 13, 1704. [Lappam, ch. Samuel, C.R.2.]
Mary, d. Thomas Jr. and Abigal, July 14, 1791.
Mary Souther, d. Michael and Sarah, Nov. 8, 1804.
Mercy, d. Samuell and Hannah, May 10, 1713. [Lappam, C.R.2.]
Molly, d. Amos and Abagal, Apr. 20, 1758.
Polly, d. Tho[ma]s Jr. and w., bp. Oct. 7, 1792. C.R.2.
Rachel, d. Thomas Jr. and Sally, Oct. 20, 1811. [Rachel C., G.R.14.]
Rachel Clap, ch. Thom[a]s, bp. Oct. 1, 1815. C.R.2.
Rebakah, d. Thomas Jr. and Abigail, Apr. 16, 1789.
Rebeckah, d. Tho[ma]s Jr. and w., bp. June 5, 1791. C.R.2.
Ruth, d. Thomas Jr. and Abigail, May 10, 1787.
Ruth, d. Tho[ma]s Jr. and w., bp. July 3, 1791. C.R.2.
Sally, d. Thomas Jr. and Sally, Oct. 9, 1806.
Sally, ch. Thom[a]s, bp. Oct. 1, 1815. C.R.2.
Samuel, s. Thomas, Apr. 12, 1676.
Sam[ue]ll, s. Sam[ue]ll and w., bp. Nov. 26, 1769. C.R.1.
Sarah, ch. Elisha, bp. June 25, 1775. C.R.1.
Sarah Tower, d. Michael and Sarah, July 11, 1797.
Temperance, d. Charles and Temperance, Sept. 25, 1806.
Temperance, d. Micah and w., bp. Nov. 1, 1807. C.R.2.
Thankfull, d. Sam[ue]ll and Hannah, May —, 1715.
William, s. Charles and Temperance, Dec. 31, 1795.
William, s. Charles and w., bp. Nov. 12, 1797. C.R.2.
William Turner, s. Will[ia]m and Avis W., Oct. 22, 1825.
Zyntha, ch. Elisha, bp. June 25, 1775. C.R.1.

LAPHUM (see Lapham, Lappam, Lappham, Lappum), Abigail, d. Tho[ma]s and Abiah, Mar. 28, 1757.
Charles, s. Tho[ma]s and Abiah, Mar. 14, 1765.
Charles, s. Jesse and Mercy, Dec. 25, 1769.
Israel, s. Thomas and Abiah, Oct. 18, 1752.
Jesse, s. Jesse and Mercy, July 19, 1767.
Michel, s. Tho[ma]s and Abiah, June 28, 1767.
Ruth, d. Tho[ma]s and Abiah, Apr. 30, 1754. [Lappum, C.R.2.]
Thomas, s. Tho[ma]s and Abiah, Feb. 15, 1759.

LAPPAM (see Lapham, Laphum, Lappham, Lappum), Amos, s. David and Rebecca, bp. July 11, 1731. C.R.2.
David, s. David and Rebecca, bp. July 5, 1730. C.R.2.

LAPPAM, Elisha, s. David and Rebecca of Marshfield, bp. July 7, 1734. C.R.2.
Elizabeth, [ch.] David and Rebecca of Marshfield, bp. May 23, 1736. C.R.2.
Hannah, ch. Samuel, bp. Oct. 22, 1704. C.R.2.
Rebecca, d. David and Rebecca of Marshfield, bp. May 6, 1733. C.R.2.
Samuel, s. Joshuah and Mary, bp. Oct. 22, 1738. C.R.2.
Thomas, s. David and Rebecca, bp. June 15, 1729. C.R.2.

LAPPHAM (see Lapham, Laphum, Lappam, Lappum), Elizabeth, d. Thomas, bp. May 6, 1638. C.R.1.
Joseph, s. Thomas, bp. Sept. 24, 1648. C.R.2.
Rebecca, d. Tho[mas], bp. Mar. 15, 1645. C.R.2.

LAPPUM (see Lapham, Laphum, Lappam, Lappham), Israel, ch. Thomas, bp. June 2, 1754. C.R.2.

LATHLY, Abigail, d. Philip dec'd, bp. Aug. 17, 1718. C.R.2.
William, "An apprentice Child to John Magoon," bp. Oct. 5, 1718. C.R.2.

LAWRENCE, John, —— [1845]. C.R.1.
Mary B. [? m.], ——, 1830. G.R.14.

LAWSON, Deborah, d. Deodate, July 27, 1694.
John, s. John, June 4, 1722.
Mordecai Hewet, s. Deodate, Apr. 22, 1700.
Richard, s. Deodate, June 23, 1696.

LEAVITT (see Levitt), Aaron, s. Aaron and Eunice, Oct. 29, 1819.
Charles, s. Aaron and Eunice, May 18, 1826.
Charles M., s. Charles M., shoemaker, and Matilda A., Nov. 27, 1846.
Cushman, s. Gad and Huldah, Aug. 11, 1795.
Ebenezer, s. Aaron and Eunice, Apr. 24, 1837.
Edwin Thomas, s. Charles M., shoemaker, and Matilda A. (b. Pembroke), Mar. 28, 1849.
Elizabeth, d. Aaron and Eunice, Apr. 25, 1835.
Emma J., ch. Jairus [dup. Jarius] and Lucy [dup. adds D.], July 13, 1845.
Eunice, d. Aaron and Eunice, Sept. 25, 1821. [w. Benjamin Leavitt, G.R.14.]
Frances J., d. George, shoemaker, and Eveline, Nov. 27, 1844.
Gad, s. Gad and Huldah, Sept. 2, 1793.
George, s. Moses and Olive, Sept. 27, 1818.

LEAVITT, George W., ch. Jairus and Lucy, July 11, 1842.
George W., s. George W., shoemaker, and Eveerline, Sept. 30, 1846.
Gilbert Warren, s. George W., shoemaker, and Eveline (b. Hanover), May 29, 1849, in S. Scituate.
Harrison Raymond, s. Isaac and Sarah, July 20, 1827.
Henry W., s. George W., shoemaker, and w., Dec. 24, 1847.
Hervey [h. Lydia H.], —— [1799]. G.R.15.
Huldah [———], w. Gad, —— [1767]. G.R.15.
Huldah G., d. Moses and Olive, Sept. 19, 1808.
Isaac, s. Isaac and Sarah, Aug. 24, 1822.
Jairus, ch. Jairus and Lucy, Sept. 22, 1833.
Jairus Warren, ch. Jairus and Lucy, Dec. 16, 1835.
John, s. Gad and Huldah, Sept. 9, 1791.
Kinsman, s. Aaron and Eunice, May 6, 1832.
Lucinda, d. Moses and Olive, Apr. 24, 1826.
Lucy D., ch. Jairus and Lucy, May 4, 1838.
Marcus Morton, s. Aaron and Eunice, Nov. 11, 1839.
Mary, d. Moses and Olive, Sept. 28, 1813.
Mary Ann, d. Aaron and Eunice, Sept. 17, 1829.
Nathan, s. Moses and Olive, Oct. 25, 1811.
Olive, d. Moses and Olive, June 15, 1822.
Sarah, d. Isaac and Sarah, Feb. 7, 1824.
Sarah A. [———], w. George W. [Jan. —, 1828]. G.R.14.
Soloman D., ch. Jairus and Lucy, June 17, 1840.
Stephen Gardner, s. Aaron and Eunice, July 8, 1824.

LECHFEILD (see Lechfeld, Lechfield, Leechfield, Lichfeild, Lichfield, Litchfeald, Litchfeeld, Litchfeild, Litchfelde, Litchfield, Litchfild), Exparance, s. Josiah, May 25, 1683.
Josiah, s. Josiah, Jan. 10, 1677.
Judith, d. Josiah, Apr. 25, 1687.
Nicholas, s. Josiah, Feb. 7, 1680. [Nicolas Leichfield, s. Josia, C.R.2.]
Sammuell, s. Josiah, Feb. 4, 1690.

LECHFELD (see Lechfeild, Lechfield, Leechfield, Lichfeild, Lichfield, Litchfeald, Litchfeeld, Litchfeild, Litchfelde, Litchfield, Litchfild), Dependance, d. Larance, Feb. 15, 1646.
Hanah, d. Josiah, Dec. 24, 1672.
Sarah, d. Josiah, Sept. 25, 1674.

LECHFIELD (see Lechfeild, Lechfeld, Leechfield, Lichfeild, Lichfield, Litchfeald, Litchfeeld, Litchfeild, Litchfelde, Litchfield, Litchfild), Thomas, s. Nicholas, bp. July 14, 1723. C.R.1.

LEE, Benjamin [dup. Benjmin F.], s. George, shoemaker, and Almira [dup. Myra], Nov. 23, 1844.
Emily S., d. George C., housewright, and Olive H. [dup. F.], Mar. 6, 1847. [Emily Susan, G.R.2.]
Francis Bates, ch. George C. and Olive F., Nov. 3, 1843.
George, s. Alice, June 22, 1804.
George H., ch. George and Myra, Sept. 17, 1841.
George W., "Co. G. 38 Mass. Vols.," ⸺ [1839]. G.R.2.
Hittee S., ch. George and Myra, June 2, 1838.
Isaac Cary, s. Stephen D., shoemaker, and Catharine E., Jan. 25, 1844.
James T., ch. George and Myra, Sept. 17, 1843.
Prudence C., ch. George and Myra, July 7, 1839.
Samuel J. Wyman, s. Stephen D., trader (b. Boston), and Catherine E. (b. Roxbury), Aug. 22, 1849.
Sarah H. [⸺], w. Washington [Oct. ⸺, 1782]. G.R.2.
Stephen D., s. Washington and Sarah H. [June ⸺, 1816]. G.R.2.
Washington [h. Sarah H.] [Apr. ⸺, 1777]. G.R.2.

LEECHFIELD (see Lechfeild, Lechfeld, Lechfield, Lichfield, Lichfield, Litchfeald, Litchfeeld, Litchfeild, Litchfelde, Litchfield, Litchfild), Bathsheba, d. Nicholas and Bathsheba, May 8, 1709.
James, s. Nicholas and Bathsheba, June 12, 1711.
Josiah, s. Nicholas and Bathsheba, Dec. 20, 1706.
Nicholas, s. Nicholas and Bathsheba, Mar. 10, 1707–8.

LEONARD, Charlotte E. [⸺], wid. Geo[rge] O., ⸺ [1806]. C.R.1.

LEVITT (see Leavitt), Betsey Pratt, d. Isaac and Sarah, Nov. 4, 1820.

LEWIS, Celinda [⸺], w. John, ⸺ [1812]. G.R.14.
George Otis, ch. Asa R. and Patience, Apr. 7, 1830.
James, ch. Asa R. and Patience, July 7, 1839.
John, s. Gorge Sr., Mar. 2, 1637. P.C.R. [Lewice, s. George, C.R.1.]
John [h. Celinda] [Oct. ⸺, 1815]. G.R.14.
Mary, ch. Asa R. and Patience, Dec. 22, 1833.
⸺, ch. Asa R. and Patience, July 18, 1832.

LICHFEILD (see Lechfeild, Lechfeld, Lechfield, Leechfield, Lichfield, Litchfeald, Litchfeeld, Litchfield, Litchfelde, Litchfield, Litchfild), Josiah, s. Josiah, Feb. 23, 1716.
Mary, d. Josiah, Oct. 10, 1715.

LICHFIELD (see Lechfeild, Lechfeld, Lechfield, Leechfield, Lichfeild, Litchfeald, Litchfeeld, Litchfeild, Litchfelde, Litchfield, Litchfild), Elisha, s. James and Ruth, bp. June 3, 1733. C.R.1.
Experience, s. Nicholas (Leechfield) and Bathsheba, Nov. 20, 1705.
John, s. Nicholas, bp. Sept. 24, 1721. C.R.1.
Josiah, s. Josiah, bp. Aug. [worn], 1679. C.R.2.
Josiah, ch. Mary, wid., bp. Sept. 28, 1718. C.R.1.
Lott, s. Josiah, bp. May 5, 1734. C.R.1.
Nicolas, s. Josiah, bp. May 6, 1739. C.R.1.
Ruth, d. Ruth, wid., bp. Mar. 23, 1734. C.R.1.
Ruth, d. Sam[ue]l, bp. July 18, 1736. C.R.1.

LINCLON (see Lincoln, Lincolne), Abigal, d. Isaac and Mary, Apr. 1, 1759.
Abraham, s. Jacob and Mary, Dec. 1, 1740. [Lyncoln, C.R.1.]
Caleb, s. Jacob and Mary, Jan. 8, 1737.
Caleb, s. Jacob and Mary, Sept. 6, 1743. [Lincoln, C.R.1.]
Eliza[beth], d. Jacob and Mary, Oct. 11, 1747. [Lincoln, C.R.1.]
Eliza[beth], d. Obediah and Jael, July 5, 1758.
Galen, s. Jacob and Mary, Jan. 17, 1735.
Galen, s. Obediah and Jael, Feb. 5, 175[6].
George, s. Isaac and Mary, Feb. 1, 1757.
George, s. Isaac and Mary, Oct. 22, 1764.
Hannah, d. Isaac and Mary, Dec. 8, 1762.
Isaac, s. Isaac and Abigal, Mar. 5, 1742. [Lincoln, C.R.2.]
Jacob, s. Jacob and Mary, Feb. 17, 1733.
Jacob, s. Isaac and Abigal, Feb. 15, 1747. [Lincoln, s. Isaac and Abigail, C.R.2.]
James, s. Isaac and Mary, June 20, 1752.
John, s. Isaac and Mary, Dec. 18, 1749.
Lydia, d. Jacob and Mary, Nov. 13, 1749. [Lincoln, C.R.1.]
Mary, d. Jacob and Mary, June 1, 1738. [Lincoln, C.R.1.] [Lincoln, w. Joseph Ellms, G.R.8.]
Mary, d. Isaac and Mary, June 9, 1754.
Obadiah, s. Jacob and Mary, July 30, 1731.
Sarah, d. Isaac and Abigal, June 15, 1744. [Lincoln, d. Isaac and Abigail, C.R.2.]
Solomon, s. Isaac and Abigal, Oct. 5, 1739. [Lincoln, s. Isaac and Abigail, C.R.2.]
Thomus, s. Jacob and Mary, Oct. 9, 1745. [Thomas Lincoln, C.R.1.]
Will[ia]m, s. Isaac and Abigal, Oct. 5, 1746. [Lincoln, s. Isaack and Abigail, C.R.2.]

LINCOLN (see Linclon, Lincolne), Abigail, d. Isaac and Abigail, bp. Mar. 8, 1740-1. C.R.2.
Bartlet, s. James and Hannah, Aug. 2, 1783.
Benjamin, s. Josh, bp. Aug. 3, 1755. C.R.2.
Caleb, s. Luke and Elizabeth, Aug. 1, 1730. [Lyncoln, C.R.1.]
Deborah, d. Joshua and Mercy, Apr. 12, 1740.
Deborah, d. George and Fanny, Apr. 9, 1822.
Dorothy, d. Luke and Elizabeth, June 4, 1722.
Elizabeth, d. Luke and Elizabeth, Sept. 19, 1728. [Lyncoln, C.R.1.]
Ephraim, s. Ephraim of Hingham, bp. May 19, 1717. C.R.1.
Hannah, d. Solomon [d. Solomon and Hannah, C.R.2.], July 25, 1707.
Hannah, d. Joshua and Mercy, Dec. 2, 1734.
Harriet E., d. Washington, yeoman, and Priscilla G. (b. Cohasset), Sept. 2, 1849, in S. Scituate.
Huldah, d. Joshua, bp. Mar. 22, 1753. C.R.2.
Isaac, s. Solomon and Hannah, Feb. 28, 1713-14.
James, s. James and Hannah, Aug. 7, 1776.
John, s. James and Hannah, Dec. 13, 1774.
John, s. John and Ruth, Jan. 2, 1780.
Joshua, s. Solomon [Soloman, C.R.2.] and Hannah, Feb. 8, 1711-12.
Joshua, s. Joshua and Mercy, Jan. 14, 1742.
Lucy, d. James and Hannah, May 14, 1778.
Luke, s. Luke and Elizabeth, Aug. 14, 1726. [Lyncoln, C.R.1.]
Lydia, d. James and Hannah, May 2, 1791. [Lydia E., G.R.14.]
Mark, s. Luke, bp. Aug. 20, 1732. C.R.1.
Martha Maria, d. George and Fanny, Sept. 24, 1827.
Mary, d. Joshua and Mercy, Apr. 11, 1744.
Mary, d. James and Hannah, Mar. 25, 1789.
Mary, w. Peleg F. Clapp, May 30, 1842. G.R.6.
Mercy, d. Joshua and Mercy, Mar. 1[blotted] [? 10], 1737.
Oliver [dup. Olover], s. James and Hannah, May 16, 1781 [dup. 1780].
Rachel, d. Luke and Elizabeth, Mar. 12, 1723.
Rachel (Loncoln), d. Joshua and Mercy, Sept. 2, 1736.
Seth, s. James and Hannah, Oct. 1, 1786.
Soloman F., ch. George and Fanny, Oct. 12, 1836.
Washington, s. George and Fanny, Aug. 3, 1825. [——, 1824, G.R.14.]
William, s. Luke, bp. June 4, 1738. C.R.1.

LINCOLNE (see Linclon, Lincoln), Deborah, d. Solomon, Feb. 29, 1716. [Lincoln, d. Soloman and Hannah, C.R.2.]
Jacob, s. Mordecai, bp. May 23, 1708. C.R.1.

LITCHFEALD (see Lechfeild, Lechfeld, Lechfield, Leechfield, Lichfeild, Lichfield, Litchfeeld, Litchfeild, Litchfelde, Litchfield, Litchfild), Meshek, twin ch. Lathrop, bp. July 5, 1778. C.R.1.
Shadreck, twin ch. Lathrop, bp. July 5, 1778. C.R.1.
LITCHFEELD (see Lechfeild, Lechfeld, Lechfield, Leechfield, Lichfeild, Lichfield, Litchfeald, Litchfeild, Litchfelde, Litchfield, Litchfild), Betty, d. Ephraim, bp. Aug. 2, 1778. C.R.1.
Percis, d. Barnabas, bp. Sept. 13, 1778. C.R.1.
LITCHFEILD (see Lechfeild, Lechfeld, Lechfield, Leechfield, Lichfeild, Lichfield, Litchfeald, Litchfeeld, Litchfelde, Litchfield, Litchfild), Abigail, d. Samuel Jr., bp. Apr. 26, 1747. C.R.1.
Rhoda, d. Experience, bp. May 15, 1757. C.R.1.
LITCHFELDE (see Lechfeild, Lechfeld, Lechfield, Leechfield, Lichfeild, Lichfield, Litchfeald, Litchfeeld, Litchfeild, Litchfield, Litchfild), Nicolas, s. Nicolas Jr., bp. May 18, 1745. C.R.1.
LITCHFIELD (see Lechfeild, Lechfeld, Lechfield, Leechfield, Lichfeild, Lichfield, Litchfeald, Litchfeeld, Litchfeild, Litchfelde, Litchfild), Abbie C. [? m.], Oct. 4, 1840. G.R.2.
Abial, s. Stephen and Rebecca, Dec. 20, 1806.
Abiel G., ch. Abiel and Lucy, Apr. 12, 1833.
Abigail, d. Sam[ue]ll, Feb. 23, 1716.
Abigail, d. Sam[ue]l Jr., bp. May 1, 1743. C.R.1.
Abigail, w. Charles Curtis [Oct. —, 1775]. G.R.7.
Abigail, ch. James, bp. Oct. 4, 1778. C.R.1.
Abigail, ch. James S. and Martha, Nov. 18, 1843.
Abigail Joy, d. Jairus and Martha, Apr. 26, 1830.
Abner (Litcfield), ch. Raina, wid., bp. Aug. 4, 1776. C.R.1.
Abner, s. Abner H. and Polly, Sept. 24, 1793.
Abner, s. Perez and Polly, Mar. 25, 1835.
Abner Hersy (Litchf[ie]ld), s. Isaac, bp. Apr. 22, 1759. C.R.1.
Adeline, d. Cushing, farmer, and Mary, Mar. 11, 1848.
Alfred, s. Israel and Fanny, Nov. 18, 1804.
Alfred B., ch. Billings and Thankful, Dec. 14, 1836.
Alice Colman, d. Davis and Alice L., Dec. 16, 1824, in Boston.
Alice L. [? m.], —— [1799]. C.R.1.
Alice L., Jan. 8, 1801. G.R.6.
Allen, s. Ward and Betsey, Aug. 30, 1788.
Allen, ch. Ward, bp. June 15, 1794. C.R.1.

LITCHFIELD, Almira, d. Nathan and Polly, July 21, 1803.
Almira, d. Roland and Lusanna, Dec. 6, 1803.
Amos, s. Nicolas, bp. July 22, 1753. C.R.1.
Amos Merritt, s. Orange and Elizabeth C., Feb. 6, 1831.
Amos T., ch. Joseph T. and Merrill, Jan. 13, 1839. [[h. Henrietta E.] G.R.14.]
Andrew, ch. Ephraim and w., bp. Sept. 15, 1776. C.R.1.
Andrew J., s. Alfred, farmer, and Mary, Aug. 15, 1845.
Angeline, d. Perez and Polly, Aug. 8, 1832.
Ann, d. Francis and Lucy, Dec. 23, 1808.
Ann Catherine, d. Rowland Jr. and Ann, Oct. 11, 1809.
Ann Elizabeth, d. Marshal [Marshall, C.R.3.] and Sophia, Aug. 21, 1838.
Ann Maria, d. Paul and Maria, Aug. 19, 1829. [w. —— Bailey, C.R.3.]
Anna, ch. James, bp. Nov. 24, 1771. C.R.1.
Anna, d. Joseph and Hannah, bp. Apr. 9, 1775. C.R.1.
Anna, d. Shadrach and Mary, Aug. 29, 1804.
Annie E. [————], w. Franklin, ——, 1842. G.R.8.
Anson B., ch. Joshua and Mary C., Sept. 17, 1837.
Artemas, s. Shadrach and Mary, Aug. 4, 1809.
Artium, s. Azotus and Marcy, Oct. 16, 1811.
Arville Hatch, d. Simeon and Lucy, Jan. 8, 1800.
Asa, s. Lawrence and Rachel, Mar. 20, 1787. [[h. Lucy (Litchfield)] G.R.11.]
Atwood, s. Nath[anie]l Jr. and Sarah, Feb. 14, 1781. [s. Nath[anie]ll, C.R.1.] [h. Olive (Vinal), P.R.6.]
Atwood, s. Atwood and Olive, Apr. 3, 1812. [Atwood Jr., P.R.6.]
Augusta Cook, d. Perez and Polly, Oct. 4, 1830.
Azotus, s. Daniel and Sarah, Nov. 12, 1774.
Barnabas, ch. Barnabas and w., bp. Nov. 5, 1775. C.R.1.
Barsheba (Litchf[iel]d), d. Josiah, bp. Sept. 9, 1750. C.R.1.
Basheba, d. Rufus and Rebekah, Sept. 9, 1818.
Bathsheba, ch. Nicholas, bp. Sept. 4, 1720. C.R.1.
Benjamin, ch. Lothrop, bp. Nov. 17, 1776. C.R.1.
Benjamin, s. Elijah and Elizabeth, May 8, 1802.
Benjamin, s. Meshech and Temperance, July 7, 1823.
Benjamin, s. Abram and Rachel, Jan. 9, 1829.
Benjamin B., s. Will, shoemaker, and Dianna, Dec. 21, 1849.
Benjamin B. Wisner, s. Marshal [Marshall, G.R.7.] and Sophia, Feb. 29, 1824.
Benjamin B. Wisner, s. Marshal and Sophia, June 26, 1829. [Benj[ami]n Blendensburgh Wisner, ch. Marshall and Sophia, C.R.3.]

SCITUATE BIRTHS 223

LITCHFIELD, Benjamin Blendenburgh Wisner, ch. Marshall and
Sophia, bp. Aug. 6, 1826. C.R.3.
Bernard, s. Elijah and Elizabeth, Mar. 2, 1795. [Bernerd [h.
Eliza], G.R.14.]
Bethiah (see Bithiah).
Bethsheba, d. Josiah and Susanna, Apr. 9, 1749.
Betsey C. [———], w. Harvey [Apr. —, 1817]. G.R.9.
Betsey Merritt, d. Thomas and Mabel, Oct. 24, 1826.
Betsy, d. Francis and Lucy, May 17, 1805.
Betsy Cushing, d. Barnard and Eliza, Nov. 22, 1825.
Billings (Litchfiel[d]), s. Francies and Lucy, Sept. 27, 1798.
Bithiah [dup. crossed out, Bethyah], d. Daniel and Sarah, Feb.
14 [dup. crossed out, Feb. 25], 1769. [Bethiah, C.R.1.]
C. L. [h. Mary S.] [Oct. —, 1818]. G.R.6.
Caleb, s. Isaac, bp. July 6, 1760. C.R.1.
Caleb D., s. Freeman, shoemaker, and Lydia, Dec. 1, 1849, in
S. Scituate.
Caleb Lincoln, s. Samuel and Roxana, Oct. 7, 1818, in Cohassett.
Canterbury, s. Isaac, bp. July 2, 1769.
Canterbury, s. Stmeon [*sic*, Simeon] and Lucy, Aug. 14, 1797.
Caroline, d. Hubbard and Eliza, June 14, 1836.
Caroline J. [———], w. George W., Aug. 11, 1845. G.R.8.
Caroline W., d. Turner, farmer, and Sarah O., Jan. 29, 1848.
Catharine, d. Daniel Jr. and Hannah, Jan. 1, 1811. [Catherine,
w. Alfred Clapp, G.R.8.]
Catherine, Jan. 1, 1811. P.R.13.
Catherine Ann, d. Sarah A., Aug. 15, 1846.
Ceile, d. Abner H. and Polly, June 19, 1783.
Charles (Litchf[ie]ld), s. Eleazar, bp. June 23, 1751. C.R.1.
Charles, s. Perez and Polly L., May 14, 1821.
Charles Alfred, ch. Alfred and Mary, June 16, 1833.
Charles Ammiel, [twin] s. Samuel and Roxana, Nov. 23, 1826.
Charles Francis, s. Rufus 2d and Lucy C., Mar. 31, 1828.
Charles Henry, s. Barnard and Eliza, June 7, 1828.
Charles Thomas, s. Melzar and Hannah, Aug. 4, 1831.
Charles Wells, s. Davis and Alice, July 14, 1830. ["Private in
Co. A. 28th. Regt. Conn. Vols., afterwards private in Co. B.
61st. Regt. Mass. Vols.," G.R.6.]
Charlotte, d. Nathan and Polly, June 28, 1797.
Charlotte, d. Elijah and Charlotte, Nov. 21, 1846.
Claricy, d. Nathan and Polly, Apr. 21, 1806. [Clarissa [w.
Francis Merritt], P.R.2.]
Cordelia B., ch. Joseph T. and Merrill, Dec. 31, 1837.
Cummings (Litch[fiel]d), s. Barnard and Eliza, Nov. 1, 1815.

LITCHFIELD, Cummins, ch. James, bp. Oct. 4, 1778. C.R.I.
Cushing, ―― [1812]. G.R.8.
Cushing Otis, ch. Turner and Sarah O., Dec. 19, 1834.
Cynthia (see Zinthe).
C[torn]ne, d. Abner and Lydia, Jan. 8, 1816.
D. Webster, s. Jairus and Martha, Apr. 3, 1833. [Daniel Webster, G.R.2.]
Daniel, s. Josiah and Susanna, Mar. 21, 1742.
Daniel, s. Josiah, bp. Oct. 9, 1743. C.R.I.
Daniel, ―― [1786]. C.R.I.
Daniel, s. Daniel and Sarah, July 10, 1788.
Daniel, s. Capt. Daniel, bp. Oct. 25, 1789. C.R.I.
Daniel, s. Daniel Jr. and Hannah, Aug. 28, 1823.
Daniel Clapp, s. Nath[anie]l and Deborah, June 14, 1815.
Daniel Clapp, [twin] s. Nath[anie]l and Deborah, July 5, 1822.
David, s. Tho[ma]s and Lydia, Sept. 21, 1768.
David Brigham, s. Marshal [Marshall, C.R.3.] and Sophia, Oct. 2, 1834.
Davis, s. Ward and Betsey, May 30, 1797.
Davis, s. Lawrence Jr. and Rebeccah, Sept. 17, 1809.
Davis Colman, s. Davis and Alice L., Mar. 26, 1821.
Debbe, d. Lawrence, bp. Oct. 5, 1800. C.R.I.
Debby, d. Lawrence and Rachel, Oct. 3, 1799. [Deby, P.R.19.]
Deborah, d. Sam[ue]ll Jr., bp. June 5, 1763. C.R.I.
Deborah [――――], w. Nymphas, ―― [1805]. G.R.2.
Deborah, d. Asa and Lucy, Aug. 14, 1829.
Deborah C. [――――], w. Nath[anie]l, ――, 1786. G.R.6.
Deborah Hatch, d. Nymphas and Deborah, Oct. 26, 1827.
Deby Clapp, d. Nath[anie]ll and Deborah, Jan. 24, 1809.
Desire, d. Eleazer, bp. Nov. 24, 1746. C.R.I.
Desire, ch. Ephraim and w., bp. Sept. 15, 1776. C.R.I.
Earnest [dup. Ernest] Howard, s. Joseph, shoemaker, and Jane, Mar. 19, 1848. [Ernest H., G.R.2.]
Edmand Quincy Sewall, ch. Turner and Sarah O., Apr. 10, 1839.
Edmund Quincy Sewall, s. Turner and Sarah, bp. July 5, 1840. C.R.I.
Edmund Quincy Sewall, ch. Turner [dup. farmer] and Sarah O., May 7, 1846.
Edmund Turner, s. Turner and Sarah, bp. July 7, 1844. C.R.I.
Edwin D., ch. Liba and Elizabeth, ――, 1846. G.R.14.
Edwin Richard, ch. Richard and Xoa, July 19, 1836.
Eleanor, d. John and Sarah, ――, 1792. G.R.8.
Eleazar, s. Eleazar, bp. June 7, 1759. C.R.I.
Eleazar, s. Eleazar and Deborah, June 8, 1793.
Eleazer, ch. Nicholas, bp. Sept. 4, 1720. C.R.I.

LITCHFIELD, Eleazer, s. Eleazer and Desire, Sept. 16, 1742. [Eleazar, s. Eleazar and Desire, C.R.1.]
Electa W. [————], second w. Howard [Mar. —, 1817]. G.R.6.
Elen G., ch. Joshua and Mary C., Nov. 13, 1838.
Eli, ch. Ephraim and w., bp. Sept. 15, 1776. C.R.1.
Elijah, s. Daniel and Sarah, June 3, 1767.
Elijah, s. Meshech and Temperance, Sept. 9, 1820.
Elijah, ch. Benjmin and Elizabeth, Dec. 5, 1825.
Elijah, ———, 1828. G.R.14.
Elisha, s. Nathan and Polly, July 2, 1810.
Eliza [————], w. Bernard, ——— [1799]. G.R.14.
Eliza [————], w. Enoch, Apr. 29, 1801. G.R.8.
Eliza, d. Stephen and Rebecca, Mar. 10, 1803.
Eliza, d. Stephen and Rebecca, Oct. 10, 1815.
Eliza Ann, d. Enoch Jr. and Eliza, Sept. 15, 1828.
Eliza Jane, d. Enoch Jr. and Eliza, Mar. 22, 1840.
Eliza Loring, ch. Martin and Eliza, Oct. 4, 1836.
Eliza Vinal, d. Atwood and Olive, July 19, 1821. [July 20, P.R.6.]
Elizabeth, d. Sam[ue]l Jr., bp. Nov. 4, 1744. C.R.1.
Elizabeth, d. Nicho[las][Nicolas, C.R.1.] Jr. and Sarah, Apr. 28, 1746.
Elizabeth, d. Tho[ma]s and Lydia, June 13, 1755.
Eliza[beth], d. Josiah Jr. and Tamesin, June 14, 1756. [Litchfeild, C.R.1.]
Elizabeth, d. Nicolas, bp. July 10, 1757. C.R.1.
Elizabeth [————], mother of Mrs. Henry Damon, ——— [1773]. C.R.3.
Elizabeth, d. James, bp. Nov. 6, 1774. C.R.1.
Elizabeth, d. Elijah and Elizabeth, Apr. 6, 1813.
Elizabeth [————], w. Liba, ———, 1824. G.R.14.
Elizabeth, d. Elizabeth, May 28, 1832.
Elizabeth L., ch. Joshua and Mary C., Nov. 2, 1840.
Ellen A., d. Isaac, blacksmith, and Priscilla, July 13, 1849.
Ellen Maria, d. Marshal H. and Frances M., Aug. 29, 1831.
Ellwood [dup. and second dup. Elwood] Mozart, ch. Sumner [second dup. Sunner, farmer] and Lillis, May 8, 1847.
Elmira Jane, d. Barnard and Eliza, Sep[t]. 11, 1836.
Elvira, d. Melzar and Hannah, Mar. 23, 1818.
Elvira, d. Abram and Rachel, June 2, 1834.
Elwyn E., ch. Howard, yeoman, and Rachael W., Dec. 30, 1848.
Emely, d. Silas and Polley, Mar. 31, 1795.
Emma B. [dup. Boardman], d. Henry [dup. Harvey], shipwright, and Betsey, July 6, 1846. [Emmie B., d. Harvey and Betsey C., G.R.9.]
Enoch (Litchfied), s. Isaac and Sarah, Sept. 22, 1802. [[h. Eliza] G.R.8.]

LITCHFIELD, Enos, s. Israel and Sarah, Dec. 17, 1785.
Enos, s. Israel and Sarah, Aug. 25, 1788.
Ephraim, s. Eleazer [Eleazar, C.R.1.] and Desire, Sept. 26, 1743.
Ephraim, s. Melzar and Hannah, Jan. 2, 1830.
Ernest (see Earnest Howard Litchfield).
Esther Cole, ch. Alfred and Mary, Jan. 14, 1830.
Esther Cole, ch. Alfred, bp. Sep[t]. 2, 1832. C.R.2.
Eunice, d. Eleazar and Deborah, Apr. 21, 1789.
Eunice, d. Silas and Polley, June 13, 1804.
Eunice [? m.], ———, 1819. G.R.6.
Evelina, d. Lawrence Jr. and Rebekah, May 22, 1814.
Evelina Francis, d. Rufus 2d and Lucy C., June 18, 1825.
Eveline, d. James S., caulker, and Martha L. [dup. omits L.], Oct. 5, 1848.
Fanny, d. Eleazar and Deborah, July 6, 1795.
Fanny Kilby, d. Luther and Anna, Aug. 13, 1815.
Festus, s. Israel and Sarah, Oct. 18, 1783.
Florence, d. John H., seaman, and Eliza D., Aug. 16, 1847.
Foster, s. Lawrence Jr. and Ruth, Nov. 30, 1791.
Foster, s. Leonard Jr. and Sarah C., Sept. 11, 1822.
Frances M. [———], w. M. H., ——— [1811]. C.R.1. G.R.2.
Frances Maria, d. Barnard and Eliza, Sep[t]. 12, 1831.
Francis, s. Nymphas and Deborah, Oct. 2, 1829.
Francis Doane, s. Melzar and Hannah, May 17, 1828.
Francis Henry, ch. Joseph and Jane, Mar. 6, 1844.
Francis Mason, s. Harvey, shipwright [dup. ship corpenter], and Betsey, June 27, 1844.
Franklin, s. Meshech and Temperence, Jan. 12, 1838. [[h. Annie E.] G.R.8.]
Freelove, d. Barnabas, bp. Aug. 12, 1781. C.R.1.
Freeman, s. Silas and Polley, Mar. 7, 1799.
Freeman [h. Lucy] [Mar. —, 1801]. G.R.8.
Freeman, s. Freeman and Lucy, Sept. 15, 1824.
Galen Lincoln, s. Leonard and Polly, Dec. 8, 1811.
Galen Watson, ch. Joseph and Jane, Jan. 17, 1842.
George, s. Francis and Lucy, July 10, 1780.
George, s. George and Polly, Aug. 12, 1808.
George Allen, ch. Richard and Xoa, Aug. 20, 1838.
George Briggs, s. Freeman and Lucy, Nov. 29, 1834.
George Emery, s. Justin and Mary, Oct. 10, 1828.
George Marshal, s. Marshal H. and Frances M., Oct. 15, 1837.
George Washington, ch. Samuel and Roxana, Feb. 22, 1837.
George William, s. Enoch Jr. and Eliza, Aug. 6, 1838. [[h. Caroline J.] G.R.8.]

LITCHFIELD, Grace, d. Rufus and Rebekah, Sept. 17, 1810. [Gracy, C.R.2.]
Hanna, d. Josia, bp. Sept. 5, 1680. C.R.2.
Hannah, d. Sam[ue]l Jr., bp. May 10, 1752. C.R.1.
Hannah, d. Nath[anie]ll and Priscilla, June 10, 1761. [mother of Abram, C.R.3.]
Hannah, ch. Nath[ani]el, bp. Oct. 6, 1765. C.R.1.
Hannah, d. Isaac and Hannah, Sept. 18, 1775.
Hannah, [ch.] Hannah, wid., bp. Nov. 1, 1778. C.R.1.
Hannah [―――], w. Daniel [Feb. ―, 1785]. G.R.8.
Hannah, d. James, bp. June 5, 1786. C.R.1.
Hannah, d. Melzar and Hannah, Oct. 21, 1821.
Harriet, d. Francis and Lucy, Dec. 5, 1800.
Harriet, d. Nymphas and Deborah, Dec. 2, 1824.
Harriet Augusta, d. Melzar and Hannah, July 25, 1826.
Harriet Cushing, d. Marshal and Sophia, Feb. 23, 1832. [d. Dea. Marshall [dup. and Sophia], w. James Brown, C.R.3.]
Harriet Thomas, d. Paul and Harriet, Sept. 30, 1822. [w. Lewis Nichols Curtis, G.R.7.]
Hartwell, s. Samuel and Roxana, Nov. 3, 1823.
Harvey, s. Israel and Sarah, Aug. 6, 1793.
Harvey Cushing, ch. Harvey and Betsey, July 28, 1838.
Harvy Whitcomb, ch. Joseph and Jane, Oct. 13, 1834.
Hayward [Howard], s. Semeon and Lucy, Jan. 13, 1804.
Hearsey, s. Abner H. and Polly, Oct. 6, 1788. [Hersey, G.R.6.]
Helen Amanda, d. Justin and Mary, Apr. 2, 1826.
Helen Augusta, d. Warren, farmer, and Helen M. [dup. omits M.], Nov. 3, 1849.
Helen Maria, d. Abram and Rachel, Mar. 25, 1825.
Henrietta E. [―――], w. Amos [Aug. ―, 1846]. G.R.14.
Henry D., ch. Benjmin and Elizabeth, Nov. 2, 1832, in Bath, Me.
Henry D., ch. Billings and Thankful, Apr. 13, 1842.
Henry Lincoln, s. Enoch Jr. and Eliza, Nov. 12, 1830.
Hersey (see Hearsey).
Hervey Thomas, s. Samuel and Roxana, Oct. 29, 1830.
Horrace, s. Marshall H. and Frances M., Sept. 30 [184–].
Hosea, s. Hersey and Eunice, July 25, 1813.
Howard (see Hayward).
Howard [h. Electa W.] [May ―, 1807]. G.R.6.
Howard, ch. Howard and Sophia, July 18, 1833.
Howar[d] E., ch. Liba and Elizabeth, Nov. 18, 1841.
Howland, s. Lawrence [Lawrance, C.R.1.] and Rachel, May 2, 1792.
Howland, s. Luther and Anna, Jan. 5, 1814.

LITCHFIELD, Hubbard, [triplet] s. Abner Hearsey and Polly, Aug. 11, 1796. [[h. Eliza] G.R.11.]
Ira, s. Stephen and Rebecca, Apr. 4, 1809.
Ira, s. Orange and Elizabeth C., Jan. 20, 1834.
Ira, ch. Orange and Elizabeth, bp. June 7, 1844. C.R.3.
Isaac, ch. Nicholas, bp. Sept. 4, 1720. C.R.1.
Isaac, s. Isaac and Hannah, Nov. 9, 1777.
Isaac, —— [1809]. G.R.6.
Isaac, s. Stephen and Keziah, Jan. 13, 1822.
Isabella, d. Simeon and Lucy, Sept. 17, 1801. [Isabel, w. Henry Merritt, G.R.14.]
Israel, s. Nicolas, bp. June 2, 1728. C.R.1.
Israel (Litchf[ie]ld), s. Josiah, bp. Sept. 22, 1754. C.R.1.
Israel, s. David and Sarah, May 30, 1810.
Israel, s. David, bp. Nov. 24, 1811. C.R.1.
Israel, s. Abram and Rachel, Nov. 26, 1827.
Isreal, s. Josiah (Lichchfield) and Susnna, July 1, 1753.
Jacob, s. Josiah and Susanna, Mar. 12, 1750.
Jacob, s. Josiah, bp. Sept. 29, 1751. C.R.1.
Jacob, s. Abner Hearsey and Polly, Dec. 21, 1780.
Jairus, s. Lawrence and Rachel, Sept. 7, 1784. [[h. Martha A. (Vinal)] Sept. 7, 1785, G.R.2.] [Sept. 7, 1784, P.R.19.]
Jairus, s. Leonard and Polly, Dec. 25, 1807.
Jairus Lincoln, ch. Lincoln and Isabelle, Jan. 17, 1841.
James, ch. Nicholas, bp. Sept. 4, 1720. C.R.1.
James, s. Josiah and Susannah, Nov. 12, 1734. [Lichfield, C.R.1.]
James, s. Nicho[las] [Nicolas, C.R.1.] Jr. and Sarah, Feb. 10, 1738.
James, s. James, bp. May 8, 1774. C.R.1.
James, ch. Elisha and w., bp. Sept. 10, 1775. C.R.1.
James [Apr. —, 1793]. G.R.8.
James, s. Josiah and Abigail, July 15, 1795.
James, s. Nathan and Polly, Feb. 13, 1799.
James, s. James and Lydia S., Dec. 3, 1823.
James Clapp, s. Nath[anie]ll and Deborah, Feb. 23, 1812.
James Franklin, s. Thomas and Mabel, Apr. 24, 1829.
James J., s. David and Sarah, July 8, 1814.
James Jenkins, s. David, bp. Oct. 10, 1813. C.R.1.
James Lawrence, ch. Joseph and Jane, Aug. 18, 1836.
James Studley, s. Lawrence Jr. and Rebecah, Oct. 24, 1811. [[h. Martha L. (Mott)] G.R.2.]
Jane, d. Hersey and Eunice [Jan. —, 1825]. G.R.6.
Jane Watson, d. Hubbard and Eliza, Aug. 8, 1828.
Joab Bester [Bestus], s. Enoch and Rebecca, Nov. 24, 1818.
Job (Litchf[ie]ld), s. Eleazar, bp. Sept. 2, 1753. C.R.1.

LITCHFIELD, John (Litchf[iel]d), s. Nicholas, bp. Nov. 3, 1751.
    C.R.1.
John, s. Eleazar, bp. May 23, 1756. C.R.1.
John, s. Eleazar and Deborah, Nov. 1, 1782.
John H., ch. Abner and Sarah, May 9, 1817, in New Bedford.
John Leonard, s. Leonard Jr. and Sarah C., Aug. 25, 1820. [[h.
    Julia F.] G.R.8.]
John Leonard, s. John L. and Julia H., Aug. 17, 1848.
John Quincy Adams, s. Allen and Marcy, Oct. 11, 1816.
John Ripley, s. Enoch Jr. and Eliza, Aug. 4, 1832.
Jonathan, s. Experience, bp. Nov. 24 [1760]. C.R.1.
Joseph, s. Josiah Jr. and Tamesin, Jan. 14, 1750.
Joseph (Litchf[ie]ld), s. Josiah Jr., bp. Feb. 4, 1753. C.R.1.
Joseph, s. Nathan and Polly, Mar. 9, 1813.
Joseph Addison, s. Leonard Jr. and Sarah C., Oct. 1, 1818.
Joseph Hatch, s. Nymphas and Deborah, Oct. 26, 1833.
Joseph Henry, s. Lincoln and Isabella [dup. Isabelle], June 26,
    1831.
Joseph L., ch. Joseph and Jane, June 23, 1838.
Joseph S., s. Freeman and Lydia, Sept. 7, 1846.
Joseph Stockbridge, s. Rufus 2d and Lucy, Feb. 14, 1832 [*sic*, see
    Lucy Stockbridge Litchfield].
Joseph Stockbridge, s. Rufus 2d and Lucy, Feb. 16, 1833.
Joseph Stockbridge, s. Rufus 2d and Lucy, Dec. 15, 1836.
Joseph Tilden, s. Rufus and Rebekah, June 19, 1804. [[h.
    Merrial (Litchfield)] G.R.14.]
Joseph Vinal, s. Atwood and Olive, July 20, 1818.
Josephine Romalina, d. Justin and Mary, June 18, 1834.
Josephine Romalina, ch. Justin and Mary, bp. Nov. 6, 1842. C.R.3.
Joshua, ch. Lothrop, bp. Nov. 17, 1776. C.R.1.
Joshua, s. Shadrach and Mary, Jan. 13, 1814.
Josiah, ch. Nicholas, bp. Sept. 4, 1720. C.R.1.
Josiah, s. Josiah and Susannar, Aug. 30, 1736. [Lichfield, C.R.1.]
Josiah, s. Josiah Jr. [and] Tamesin, Aug. 4, 1749.
Josiah, s. Josiah Jr., bp. Nov. 15, 1752. C.R.1.
Josiah, s. Josiah Jr. and Tamesin, Dec. 22, 1753.
Josiah, s. Daniel and Sarah, Mar. 6, 1777. [Joseah, C.R.1.]
Josiah, s. Daniel Jr. and Hannah, Sept. 5, 1816.
Juda, d. Joshua and w., bp. Oct. 7, 1792. C.R.2.
Julia, d. Rufus and Rebekah, May 9, 1812.
Julia Ann, d. Nath[anie]ll and Deborah, Sept. 2, 1810.
Julia Ann [———], w. George B., ——— [1842]. G.R.2.
Julia Franklin, d. Enoch Jr. and Eliza, Jan. 2, 1827. [w. John L.
    Litchfield, ———, 1826, G.R.8.]

LITCHFIELD, Julia W., ——— [1832]. C.R.3.
Julia Warren, ch. Warren and Julia, Dec. 7, 1841.
Justin, ——— [1790]. C.R.3.
Justin, s. Ward and Betsey, Apr. 30, 1799. [[h. Mary (Colman)] G.R.7.]
Justin, s. Justin and Mary, Aug. 3, 1839.
Justin Decatur, s. Justin and Mary, Mar. 31, 1822.
Justin Decatur, ch. Justin and Mary, bp. Nov. 6, 1842. C.R.3.
Larthroup, s. Nicho[las] Jr. and Sarah, July 31, 1741.
Laura, d. Thomas and Mabel, Nov. 7, 1812.
Laurance, s. Sam[ue]l Jr., bp. May 14, 1749. C.R.1.
Lawrance, ch. James, bp. Nov. 24, 1771. C.R.1.
Lawrence, ch. Lawrence, Feb. 24 [?], 1749. P.R.19.
Lawrence, ——— [1770]. C.R.1. [[h. Rebecca] G.R.8.]
Leavitt, s. James and Lydia S., Jan. 1, 1817.
Lenthell, d. Eleazar and Deborah, Apr. 10, 1785.
Leonard, s. Rowland and Lusanna, Dec. 20, 1782.
Leonard, s. Elijah and Elizabeth, Oct. 17, 1792.
Leonard F., s. John L., shoemaker, and Julia F., Apr. 8, 1844.
Leonard F., ch. John L. and Julia F., ———, 1846. G.R.8.
Lewis, s. Francis and Lucy, Aug. 16, 1782.
Lewis, s. Lawrence and Rachel, Nov. 11, 1794.
Lewis, s. Laurance, bp. July 3, 1796.
Lewis, s. James and Lydia S., Sept. 23, 1826.
Liba, s. Lawrence [Lawrance, C.R.1.] and Rachel, Sept. 30, 1779.
Liba, s. Daniel Jr. and Hannah, Feb. 21, 1815. [[h. Elizabeth] G.R.14.]
Liba, s. Thomas and Mabel, Feb. 17, 1822.
Liba, ch. Thomas and Mabel, bp. May 6, 1827. C.R.3.
Liba W., ch. Liba and Elizabeth, July 15, 1843.
Lillis, d. Daniel Jr. and Hannah, Nov. 7, 1818.
Lincoln, [triplet] s. Abner Hearsey and Polly, Aug. 11, 1796.
Loiza [dup. crossed out, Luiza], d. Barnard and Eliza [dup. crossed out, d. Elijah and Elizabeth], Mar. 18, 1821.
Lot, s. Josiah, bp. Aug. 29, 1756. C.R.1.
Lot, s. Amos and Bathsheba, June 10, 1781. [[h. Dolly] G.R.14.]
Lot, s. Rufus and Rebekah, Sept. 15, 1820.
Lothrop, s. Nicolas Jr., bp. Apr. 3, 1743. C.R.1.
Lothrop, ch. Lothrop, bp. Nov. 17, 1776. C.R.1.
Lott, s. Josiah and Susanna, Apr. 23, 1733.
Lott, s. Josiah and Susanna, Nov. 16, 1755.
Louis, d. Abner and Lydia, July 6, 1798.
Lucy, d. Josiah Jr. [dup. omits Jr.] and Tamesin [dup. Tamsin], Apr. 20, 1760 [dup. 1761].

LITCHFIELD, Lucy, d. Josiah, bp. July 10, 1763. C.R.1.
[L]ucy, d. Nath[anie]ll and Priscilla, Aug. 29, 1772.
Lucy, ch. Nathaneel, bp. July 9, 1775. C.R.1.
Lucy, ch. Lothrop, bp. Nov. 17, 1776. C.R.1.
Lucy, d. Barnabas, bp. June 5, 1786. C.R.1.
Lucy, d. Rowland and Lusanna, June 19, 1790.
Lucy, d. Simeon and Lucy, Apr. 1, 1794. [w. Asa Litchfield, G.R.11.]
Lucy, d. Simeon, bp. Aug. 23, 1795. C.R.1.
Lucy [―――], w. Freeman, ―― [1805]. C.R.3. [―― [1803], G.R.8.]
Lucy [? m.], ――, 1808. G.R.2.
Lucy, d. Shadrach and Mary, July 9, 1820.
Lucy Ann, d. Thomas and Mabel, Aug. 24, 1815.
Lucy Ann, ch. Thomas and Mabel, bp. May 6, 1827. C.R.3.
Lucy F., d. Freeman and Lucy, Feb. 9, 1823.
Lucy Lincoln, d. Francis and Lucy, ――, 1793.
Lucy Stockbridge, d. Rufus 2d and Lucy, June 15, 1831 [*sic*, see Joseph Stockbridge Litchfield].
Luther, s. Nath[anie]l, bp. Dec. 7, 1769. C.R.1.
[Lu]ther, s. Nath[anie]ll and Priscilla, Sept. 7, 1770.
Luther, ch. Nathaneel, bp. July 9, 1775. C.R.1.
Luther, s. Lot [and] Rachel, Feb. 8, 1778.
Luther, s. Lawrence and Rachel, Sept. 23, 1789.
Luther, s. Abram and Rachel, May 10, 1823.
Lydia, d. Tho[ma]s and Lydia, Apr. 5, 1761.
Lydia [―――], w. Abner, ―― [1773]. G.R.8.
Lydia, ch. Barnabas and w., bp. Nov. 5, 1775. C.R.1.
Lydia, d. Rowland and Lusanna, July 4, 1796.
Lydia, d. Hersey and Eunice, Jan. 29, 1817.
Lydia K. [? m.] [Apr. ―, 1816]. G.R.14.
Lydia Maria, ch. Billings and Thankful, Feb. 7, 1838.
Lydia Snow, d. James and Lydia S., Oct. 7, 1821.
Mabel, d. Thomas, bp. Nov. 18, 1753. C.R.1.
Mabel Thomas, d. Thomas and Mabel, Nov. 13, 1817.
Mabel Thomas, ch. Thomas and Mabel, bp. May 6, 1827. C.R.3.
Mable, d. Tho[ma]s and Lydia, Aug. 5, 1763. [Mabel, C.R.1.]
Mable, d. Rowland and Lusanna, Oct. 11, 1784.
Malezer, s. Melazer and Lucandia, July 11, 1798, in Littleton.
Marcy Allen, d. Allen and Marcy, Nov. 2, 1820.
Marcy Gould, ch. James S. and Martha, Aug. 8, 1839.
Margaret M., d. Melzar and Hannah, Sept. 20, 1819.
Maria, d. Meshech and Temperance, Apr. 3, 1819.
Maria Louiza, d. Rowland Jr. and Ann, Oct. 22, 181[worn] [rec. after ch. b. Oct. 11, 1809].

LITCHFIELD, Marietta J., d. Foster and Rebecca N., Nov. 14, 1846.
Marshal, s. Ward and Betsey, Jan. 9, 1795. [Marshall [dup. Dea. Marshall], C.R.3.] [Dea. Marshall [h. Sophia (Merritt)], G.R.7.]
Marshal, s. Marshal and Sophia, Aug. 20, 1822. [Marshall, ch. Dea. Marshall and Sophia (Merritt), G.R.7.]
Marshal, s. Marshal and Sophia, Dec. 5, 1827. [Marshall, ch. Marshall and Sophia, C.R.3.]
Marshall, ch. Marshall and Sophia, bp. Aug. 6, 1826. C.R.3.
Marshall Hatch, s. Simeon and Lucy, Sept. 19, 1807.
Martha [———], w. ———, —— [1804]. C.R.1. [w. William, G.R.2.]
Martha, d. Shadrach and Mary, Oct. 10, 1826.
Martha Jane, ch. Joseph T. and Merrill, Oct. 12, 1835.
Martha Reed, ch. Martin and Eliza, Feb. 3, 1841.
Martha Stockbridge, d. M[eshech] and Temperance, July 26, 1831.
Martha William, d. Will[ia]m and Patty, Oct. 24, 1833.
Martin, s. Simeon and Lucy, Apr. 19, 1796.
Mary, ch. Mary, wid., bp. Sept. 28, 1718. C.R.1.
Mary, d. Francis and Lucy, Oct. 27, 1795.
Mary, d. Rufus and Rebekah, Jan. 19, 1806.
Mary, d. Shadrach and Mary, May 31, 1817.
Mary (Litch[fiel]d), d. Nathaniel and Deborah, Feb. 26, 1818.
Mary Almira, d. Freeman and Lucy, Aug. 23, 1827.
Mary Ann, ch. Billings and Thankful, Mar. 20, 1835.
Mary Antoinette, ch. Alfred and Mary, Dec. 20, 1836.
Mary Brooks, ch. Lincoln and Isabelle [dup. Isabella], Nov. 19, 1833.
Mary Colman, d. Justin and Mary, July 23, 1824.
Mary Elizabeth, d. Orange and Elizabeth C., Jan. 29, 1827.
Mary Elizabeth, ch. Joseph T. and Merrill, Feb. 5, 1833.
Mary G. [? m.], —— [1805]. G.R.2.
Mary Jane, d. Simeon and Sophronia, July 4, 1839.
Mary L. [———], w. Perez [Aug. —, 1796]. G.R.6.
Mary Lincoln, d. Perez and Polly, Dec. 27, 1826.
Mary S. [———], w. C. L., ———, 1818. G.R.6.
Mary Smith, ch. Martin and Eliza, Mar. 15, 1832, in Roxbury.
Mary W. [———], w. Stephen [July —, 1800]. G.R.2.
Ma[torn] Franklin, d. Abner and Lydia, Apr. 16, 1818.
Melora Ann, d. Melzar and Hannah, Jan. 29, 1825.
Melvin Shaw, s. Enoch Jr. and Eliza, Sept. 28, 1822.
Melzar James, s. Melzar and Hannah, July 6, 1823.
Melzor, ch. Ephraim and w., bp. Sept. 15, 1776. C.R.1.
Mercy, d. Rowland and Lusanna, Mar. 9, 1793.
Mercy A., ———, 1825. G.R.6.

LITCHFIELD, Mercy Allen (see Marcy Allen Litchfield).
Meriel, w. Anson Hatch, Mar. 31, 1797. G.R.11.
Merriel, d. Lawrence and Rachel, Mar. 31, 1797.
Merrill (Litch[fiel]d), d. Barnard and Eliza, Jan. 7, 1814. [w. Joseph T. Litchfield, G.R.14.]
Milton, s. Israel and Sarah, Jan. 20, 1791. [[h. Abigail (Otis)] G.R.2.]
Milton Gray, ch. Sumner and Lillis, Mar. — [dup. Mar. 18], 1841.
Milton Gray, ch. Sumner and Lillis, Mar. 10, 1844.
Molly, d. Barnabas, bp. Dec. 8, 1776. C.R.1.
Myra Lincoln, d. Thomas and Mabel, Oct. 23, 1831. [Mira Lincoln [dup. Myra Lincoln, w. John Wade], C.R.3.]
Nathaniel (Litchf[ie]ld), s. Nath[anie]l, bp. Oct. 1, 1758. C.R.1.
Nathaniel, s. Nath[anie]l Jr. and Sarah, Mar. 25, 1783. [Nath[anie]ll, s. Nath[anie]ll Jr., C.R.1.]
Nath[anie]ll, s. Sam[ue]ll, Dec. 5, 1727.
Nath[anie]ll, s. Nath[anie]ll and Priscilla, Jan. 8, 1747.
Nath[anie]ll, s. Nath[anie]ll and Priscila, Dec. 20, 1754.
Nicholas, s. Josiah and Susanna, Jan. 8, 1738.
Nicholas, s. Nicho[las] Jr. and Sarah, Mar. 7, 1743.
Nichols, s. Lawrence Jr. and Rebecah, July 18, 1805.
Nicolas, ch. Nicholas, bp. Sept. 4, 1720. C.R.1.
Nimfus, s. Simeon and Lucy, Sept. 17, 1798. [Nymphas [h. Deborah], G.R.2.]
[No]ah, s. Nath[anie]ll [Nathaniel, C.R.1.] and Priscilla, Jan. 24, 1753.
Nymphas (see Nimfus).
Olive, d. Sam[ue]l Jr., bp. June 4, 1758. C.R.1.
Olive, w. Atwood, bp. June 3, 1810. C.R.1.
Olive, d. Daniel Jr. and Hannah, Dec. 31, 1820.
Ophelia, ch. Richard and Xoa, Aug. 8, 1834.
Oringe, s. Stephen and Rebecca, Dec. 12, 1800. [Orange, C.R.3.]
Otis, s. Daniel Jr. and Hannah, Mar. 15, 1826.
Otis, s. Daniel Jr. and Hannah, Apr. 2, 1828.
Otis Vinal, s. Atwood and Olive, Jan. 18, 1834. [Jan. 18, 1835, P.R.6.]
Parker Rich, s. Atwood and Olive, May 1, 1826.
Patience, d. Simeon and Lucy, Aug. 15, 1802.
Patty, ch. Elisha and w., bp. Sept. 10, 1775. C.R.1.
Patty, d. Nathan and Polly, Mar. 22, 1801.
Paul, s. Tho[ma]s and Lydia, Mar. 12, 1752.
Paul, s. Paul Litchfield, M.A., bp. Dec. 5, 1779. C.R.1.
Paul, s. Rowland and Lusanna, Jan. 20, 1799.
Paul, s. Paul and Harriet, Jan. 4, 1825.
Paul Briggs (Litch[fiel]d), s. Barnard and Eliza, Apr. 1, 1818.

LITCHFIELD, Penelope, d. Josiah (Lichfield) and Susanna, Feb. 17, 1746.
Penelopey, d. Josiah, bp. Oct. 25, 1747. C.R.1.
Perez, s. Eleazar and Deborah, May 30, 1791. [[h. Mary L.] G.R.6.]
Perez Lincoln, s. Perez and Polly L., Sept. 11, 1823.
Perez Lincoln, s. Perez and Polly, Sept. 19, 1837.
Perry Colman, s. Atwood and Olive, Sept. 20, 1828. [Litchfeld, Sept. 21, P.R.6.]
Peter, s. John and Sarah, Apr. 3, 1797.
Phebee (Litcfield), ch. Raina, wid., bp. Aug. 4, 1776. C.R.1.
Polley, d. Lawrence and Rachel, Jan. 26, 1782. [Polly, C.R.1.] [Polley, P.R.19.]
Polley, d. Ward and Betsey, Oct. 5, 1790.
Polley, ch. Ward, bp. June 15, 1794. C.R.1.
Polly, [triplet] d. Abner Hearsey and Polly, Aug. 11, 1796.
Polly, d. Atwood and Olive, Aug. 17, 1809.
Polly, d. George and Polly, June 1, 1811.
Polly Barnes, d. Leonard and Sarah C., Nov. 26, 1830.
Polly Otis, d. Atwood, bp. June 3, 1810. C.R.1. [ch. Atwood and Olive (Vinal), b. Aug. 17, 1809, P.R.6.]
Priscilla, d. Nath[anie]ll [Nath[anie]l, C.R.1.] and Priscilla, Oct. 12, 1749 [*sic*, see Priscilla].
Priscilla, d. Nath[anie]ll and Priscilla, June 24, 1750 [*sic*, see Priscilla]. [Litchf[ie]ld, d. Nath[anie]l, C.R.1.]
Priscilla (Litchf[ie]ld), d. Sam[ue]l Jr., bp. July 7, 1754. C.R.1.
Priscilla, d. Nath[aniel] and Priscilla, May 25, 1759.
Priscilla, ch. Nath[ani]el, bp. Oct. 6, 1765. C.R.1.
Priscilla, d. Daniel Jr. and Hannah, Dec. 24, 1812.
Priscilla H., d. Francis and Clarrissa, Dec. 2, 1845.
Prissilla Vinal, d. Daniel Jr. and Hannah, Oct. 30, 1807.
Rachel [———], w. Lawrence, Sept. 5, 1758. P.R.19.
Rachel, d. Abner H. and Polly, Dec. 6, 1785.
Rachel N., ch. Warren [dup. farmer] and Helen [dup. Hellen], Apr. 11, 1845.
Raina (Litcfield), ch. Raina, wid., bp. Aug. 4, 1776. C.R.1.
Rawson, s. Azotus and Marcy, Feb. 2, 1814.
Rebecca [———], w. Laurence [Lawrence, G.R.8.], ——— [1775]. C.R.1.
Rebecca [———], w. Rufus, ——— [1779]. C.R.3.
Rebecca, d. Stephen and Rebecca, Apr. 25, 1798.
Rebecca, d. Rufus and Rebekah, May 12, 1816.
Rebecca Cudworth (Litchf[iel]d), d. Orange and Elizabeth C., Feb. 19, 1840.

LITCHFIELD, Rebecca Cudworth, ch. Orange and Elizabeth, bp. June 7, 1844. C.R.3.
Rebecca L., ch. Simeon and Sophronia, Apr. 3, 1841.
Rebeckah Hiland L., d. Shadrach and Mary, July 6, 1823.
Remember, d. Sam[ue]l, bp. Aug. 14, 1737. C.R.1.
Reuben D., s. Freeman and Lucy, Nov. 10, 1837.
Richard, s. Shadrach and Mary, Aug. 29, 1807.
Richard, s. Shadrach and Mary, July 6, 1812.
Richmond, s. Orange and Elizabeth C., July 28, 1824
Roland, s. Tho[ma]s and Lydia, Mar. 19, 1759.
Roland, s. Paul, bp. June 14, 1778. C.R.1.
Rowland, s. Rowland and Lusanna, Aug. 6, 1786 [Roland, C.R.3.]
Roxana, [twin] d. Sam[ue]l and Roxana, Nov. 23, 1826.
Rufus, s. Amos and Bathsheba, June 21, 1779.
Rufus, s. Eleazar and Deborah, Apr. 30, 1797.
Rufus, s. Rufus and Rebekah, Feb. 17, 1814.
Ruth, d. Tho[ma]s and Lydia, Oct. 2, 1772.
Ruth, d. David and Sarah, Apr. 21, 1803.
Ruth, ch. David and Sarah, bp. Oct. 4, 1811. C.R.1.
Ruth Clapp, d. Lawrence Jr. and Ruth, Aug. 25, 1795.
R[torn]h, d. Abner and Lydia, July 29, 1800.
Sabre, d. James, bp. June 5, 1786. C.R.1.
Sal, d. Daniel and Sarah, Apr. 2, 1779.
Sally, d. Nathaniel Jr. and Sarah, Nov. 7, 1778.
Sally, d. Hersey and Eunice, May 9, 1815.
Salome, d. Elijah and Elizabeth, Oct. 20, 1796.
Salome, d. Leonard Jr. and Sarah C., July 4, 1824.
Salome, d. John H. and Eliza, Nov. 13, 1848.
Salome Angeline, d. Barnard and Eliza, Dec. 3, 1833.
Salome Roberts, ch. John H. and Eliza, May 11, 1841.
Samuel, s. Sam[ue]ll, Oct. 11, 1715.
[Sa]muel, s. Nath[anie]ll and Priscilla, Apr. 5, 1757.
Samuel (Litchf[ie]ld), s. Nath[anie]l, bp. Oct. 1, 1758. C.R.1.
Samuel, s. Abner H. and Polly, May 29, 1791.
Samuel, s. Lawrence Jr. and Rebeccah, Apr. 15, 1807. [[h.. Cordelia (Studley)] G.R.2.]
Samuel Hubbard, s. Sam[ue]l and Roxana, Oct. 11, 1820, in Springfield, Vt.
Sarah, d. Josia, bp. Sept. 5, 1680. C.R.2.
Sarah, d. Sam[ue]ll, June 5, 1718.
Sarah, d. Josiah and Susanna, Feb. 14, 1744.
Sarah, d. Josiah, bp. Oct. 13, 1745. C.R.1.
Sarah, d. Nicho[las] Jr. and Sarah, Oct. 14, 1748.

LITCHFIELD, Sarah, d. Nicholas Jr., bp. Nov. 5, 1749. C.R.1.
Sarah, d. Tho[ma]s and Lydia, Aug. 3, 1767.
Sarah, d. Daniel and Sarah, bp. May 29, 1768. C.R.1.
Sarah, d. Foster and Lucy P., Aug. 29, 1820.
Sarah Abigail, d. Leon[ar]d Jr. and Sarah C., Oct. 25, 1825.
Sarah Adeline, d. Justin and Mary, Oct. 29, 1836.
Sarah Ann, d. James and Lydia S., Oct. 20, 1819.
Sarah Caroline, ch. Harvey and Betsey, Aug. 22, 1834.
Sarah E. [———], w. William H., May 31, 1828. G.R.8.
Sarah Foster (Litch[fiel]d), d. Foster and Lucy (Peakes), July 20, 1821.
Sarah Merritt, d. Marshal [Marshall, C.R.2.] and Sophia, June 15, 1826.
Sarah Tilden, d. Atwood and Olive, Nov. 16, 1823.
Sarah Turner, ch. Turner and Sarah O., Dec. 22, 1840.
Sarah Turner, ch. Turner and Sarah O., Feb. 15, 1842. [Sara T., G.R.2.]
Sarah W., d. Howard, farmer, and Rachel, Aug. 16, 1846.
Sarah Whitcomb, d. Barnard and Eliza, July 20, 1823.
Sela, d. Isaac, bp. June 16, 1765. C.R.1.
Serena Clapp, [twin] d. Nath[anie]l and Deborah, July 5, 1822.
Serissa, d. Israel and Fanny, Apr. 14, 1803.
Seth, s. Daniel Jr. and Hannah, Dec. 25, 1808.
Siba, d. Lawrence and Rachel, Nov. 14, 1802.
Siba, ch. Lawrence, bp. Jan. —, 1814. C.R.1.
Sibae, d. Israel and Sarah, Apr. 6, 1780.
Silas, s. Daniel and Sarah, July 12, 1772.
Silas D., s. Freeman and Lucy, Oct. 29, 1830.
Simeon, s. Isaac, bp. Nov. 9, 1766. C.R.1. [[h. Lucy (Hatch)] b. Aug. 30, G.R.2.]
Simeon, s. Simeon and Lucy, Apr. 10, 1795.
Solon, s. Perez and Polly L., Sept. 6, 1825.
Sophia [———], w. Tho[ma]s, —— [1787]. C.R.3.
Sophia, d. Israel and Sarah, Aug. —, 1797. [w. Thomas Litchfield, G.R.7.]
Sophia [———], w. [dup. adds Dea.] Marshall, —— [1798]. C.R.3.
Sophia, d. Simeon and Lucy, Sept. 1, 1809.
Sophia L. [———], w. Howard L., —— [1810]. C.R.1.
Sophia Marshal, d. Marshal and Sophia, Aug. 5, 1833. [Sophia Marshall, ch. Marshall and Sophia, C.R.3.] [Sophia M., w. Moses L. Brown, G.R.7.]
Sophia Otis [? m.], ——, 1794. G.R.2.
Sophronia, d. James and Lydia S., May 17, 1818.

LITCHFIELD, Stephen, s. Isaac and Hannah, July 8, 1771.
Stephen, s. Stephen and Rebecca, Aug. 24, 1795.
Stephen, ch. Warren and Helen, Oct. 7 [dup. Oct. 27], 1847.
Stilman, s. Hersey and Eunice, Oct. 27, 1819.
Sumner, s. Milton and Abigail, Jan. 15, 1821.
Sumner Otis, ch. Sumner and Lillis, Aug. 12, 1842.
Susan E., ch. Billings and Thankful, Feb. 24, 1841.
Susan Huntington, d. Justin and Mary, Aug. 24, 1831.
Susan Huntington, ch. Justin and Mary, bp. Nov. 6, 1842. C.R.3.
Susanna, ch. Nicholas, bp. Sept. 4, 1720. C.R.1.
Susanna, d. Josiah, bp. Sept. 27, 1741. C.R.1.
Susannah (Littchfield), d. Josiah and Susanna, Mar. 4, 1740.
Susannah, d. James and w., bp. Dec. 14, 1766. C.R.1.
Sylvia N., d. Abram and Rachel, Dec. 29, 1830.
Temprance [———], w. Meshach, —— [1794]. G.R.16.
Thaddeus Lawrence, s. Leonard and Sarah C., Nov. 6, 1827.
Thankful Vinal, d. Atwood and Olive, May 20, 1831.
Thankful (Litch[fie]ll), d. Daniel (Litchf[i]e[l]d) [dup. crossed out, adds and Sarah], Oct. 23, 1770. [Thankful Litchfield, d. Dan, C.R.1.]
Thankfull, d. Daniel and Sarah, July 18, 1785.
Theophilus, s. Eleazar and Deborah, Apr. 7, 1787.
Thomas, s. Ward and Bestey, Dec. 4, 1785. [[h. Mabel (Vinal)] [h. Sarah (Litchfield)] G.R.7.]
Thomas, —— [1787]. C.R.3.
Thomas, ch. Ward, bp. June 15, 1794. C.R.1.
Thomas, s. Thomas and Mabel, Sept. 23, 1824. [[h. Sarah (Merritt)] G.R.7.]
Thomas, ch. Thomas and Mabel, bp. May 6, 1827. C.R.3.
Thomas Curtis, s. Leonard and Polly, Mar. 14, 1810.
Thomas Emery, s. Davis and Alice L., Sept. 17, 1823, in Boston.
Thomas Jefferson, s. David and Sarah, Sept. 20, 1807.
Thomas Jefferson, ch. David and Sarah, bp. Oct. 4, 1811. C.R.1.
Thomas Porter, s. Hubbard and Eliza, Jan. 20, 1831.
Thomas Tilden, s. Allen and Marcy, Sept. 20, 1818.
Turner, s. Stephen and Rebecca, May 1, 1811. [Capt. Turner [h. Sarah O. (Curtis)], G.R.2.]
Turner, ch. Turner and Sarah O. [Sarah Otis, C.R.1.], Mar. 23, 1837.
Walter, s. Marshal H. and Frances M., Oct. 20, 1840.
Ward, s. Tho[ma]s and Lydia, May 9, 1757. [Dea. Ward [h. Betsey (Merritt)], G.R.7.]
Ward, s. Ward and Betsey, Sept. 11, 1783.
Ward, ch. Ward, bp. June 15, 1794. C.R.1.

LITCHFIELD, Ward, s. Thomas and Mabel, Sept. 11, 1819.
Ward, ch. Thomas and Mabel, bp. May 6, 1827. C.R.3.
Warren, s. Bar[n]abas and w., bp. May 1, 1769. C.R.1.
Warren, s. Stephen and Rebecca, June 4, 1813.
Warren, s. Warren, yeoman, and Helen, Feb. 27, 1844. [Warren Jr., "A member of Co. C. 43, Mass. Vols.," s. Warren and Helen M., G.R.2.]
Warren Studley, s. Samuel 2d, yeoman, and Cordelia, Oct. 26, 1844. [s. Samuel and Cordelia S., "A member of Co. G. 38 Mass. Vol's.," G.R.2.]
Wealthy (Litchf[ie]ld), d. Experience, bp. Oct. 1, 1758. C.R.1.
Webster, s. Orange and Elizabeth C., Feb. 23, 1837.
Webster, ch. Orange and Elizabeth, bp. June 7, 1844. C.R.3.
[W]illiam, s. Nath[anie]ll and Priscilla, Mar. 9, 1766. [Litchfeeld, s. Nath[anie]l, C.R.1.]
William, s. Joseph Litchfield, A.M., bp. Aug. 12, 1781. C.R.1.
W[torn]n [dup. crossed out, William], s. Abner and Lydia, Dec. 15, 1801.
William, s. David and Sarah, Sept. 1, 1805.
William, ch. David and Sarah, bp. Oct. 4, 1811. C.R.1.
William, s. Meshech and Temperance, Feb. 25, 1826.
William, s. Samuel and Roxana, Nov. 12, 1833.
William C., ch. Cummings and Lydia, Mar. 31, 1840.
William Gertrude [*sic*], ch. Joseph and Jane, Mar. 12, 1840.
William Gridley, s. Atwood and Olive, Apr. 11, 1815.
William Hubbard, s. Hubbard and Eliza, Sept. 15, 1825. [[h. Sarah E.] G.R.8.]
William Price, ch. James S. and Martha, Nov. 12, 1841.
Winnett Atkins, d. Milton and Abigail, Sept. 1, 1823.
Xoa, d. Israel and Sarah, Feb. 19, 1782.
Xoa Jane, d. Thomas and Sophia, Nov. 20, 1839. [Zoa Jane, G.R.7.]
Xoa Jane, ch. Thomas and Sophia, bp. Nov. 6, 1842. C.R.3.
[Z]acheus, s. Nath[anie]ll and Priscilla, Dec. 21, 1763.
Zacheus, ch. Nath[ani]el, bp. Oct. 6, 1765. C.R.1.
Zenas Holbrook, s. Enoch Jr. and Eliza, Apr. 3, 1824.
Zinthe, d. Daniel and Sarah, Aug. 16, 1782. [Zintha, C.R.1.]
Zoa Jane (see Xoa Jane).
[torn]g, s. Abner and Lydia, May 12, 1812.
———, ch. Josiah Jr. and prob. Abigail (Studley) (second w.), —— [rec. after ch. b. Apr. 20, 1760.] [This entry written in pencil.]
——— [———], w. Joab, —— [1761]. C.R.1.
——— [———], w. Harvey, —— [1795]. C.R.3.

LITCHFIELD, ———, ch. Israel and Sarah, Feb. 10, 1796.
——— [———], w. Lincoln [Apr. —, 1803]. C.R.1.
——— [torn], d. Abner and Lydia, July 5, 1803.
——— [torn], d. Abner and Lydia, July 25, 1804.
——— [torn], d. Abner and Lydia, Jan. 21, 1806.
——— [torn], s. Abner and Lydia, May 12, 1807.
——— [torn], s. Abner and Lydia, Sept. 29, 1809.
———, brother of Mrs. Roland Turner, ——— [1824.] C.R.1.
———, s. Paul and Maria, Feb. 5, 1832.
———, ch. Freeman and Lucy, ———, 1839.
———, s. Samuel and Roxana, Feb. 12, 1842.
———, ch. Josiah and Harriet, Sept. —, 1842.
———, ch. Richard and Xoa, Feb. 28, 1843.
———, ch. Harvey and Betsey, May —, 1843.
———, d. Billings, house wright, and Thankful, Jan. 12, 1844.
———, ch. Turner and Sarah O., Apr. 23, 1844.
———, s. Howard, mariner, and Sophia, Dec. 19, 1844.
———, ch. Josiah Jr. and prob. Abigail (Studley) (second w.), ———. [This entry written in pencil.]

LITCHFILD (see Lechfeild, Lechfeld, Lechfield, Leechfield, Lichfeild, Lichfield, Litchfeald, Litchfeeld, Litchfeild, Litchfelde, Litchfield), Horvey, s. Silas (Litchfield) and Polly, Aug. 12, 1807. [Harvey [h. Betsey C.], G.R.9.]

LITTLE, Annah [ch. Ephraim], Aug. 23, 1673. P.R.1.
Barnabas [ch. Ephraim], Feb. 8, 1691–2. P.R.1.
Barnabas, s. David, bp. July 7, 1717. C.R.1. [[ch. David and Elizabeth] b. May 20, P.R.1.]
Barnabas, s. David, bp. June 5, 1726. C.R.1. [[ch. David and Elizabeth] b. Feb. 18, 1725, P.R.1.]
David [ch. Ephraim], Mar. 17, 1681. P.R.1.
David, s. David and Elizabeth, Sept. 2, 1712. [Sept. 4, P.R.1.]
Elizabeth [———], w. David, Sept. 29, 1686. P.R.1.
Elizabeth, d. David and Elizabeth, Jan. 17, 1719.
Ephraim, May 10, 1650. P.R.1.
Ephraim [ch. Ephraim], Sept. 27, 1676. P.R.1.
Ephraim, s. David and Elizabeth, Apr. 9, 1708.
Ephraim, s. David, bp. Oct. 5, 1712. C.R.1.
James [h. Lydia], ———, 1758. G.R.6.
James [ch. James and Lydia], ———, 1787. G.R.6.
John [ch. Ephraim], Mar. 17, 1683. P.R.1.
Lydia [———], w. James, ———, 1756. G.R.6.
Lydia Young, w. Elisha James, Oct. 10, 1790. G.R.5.
Mary [ch. Ephraim], July 7, 1685. P.R.1.

LITTLE, Mary, d. David and Elisabeth, Feb. 12, 1721.
Mercy [ch. Ephraim], Feb. 26, 1678. P.R.1.
Nathaniell, s. David, Feb. 2, 1714. [Nathaniel, C.R.1.] [Nathaniel [ch. David and Elizabeth], Feb. 3, P.R.1.]
Ruth [ch. Ephraim], Nov. 23, 1686. P.R.1.
—— [ch. Ephraim], June 19, 1675. P.R.1.

LOMBORD (see Lumbard), Samuel, s. Zackeus, bp. May 7, 1769. C.R.1.
Zacheus, s. Zacheus, bp. Dec. 31, 1769. C.R.1.

LORING, Eunice A. [——], w. Samuel, Aug. 8, 1841. G.R.19.
Samuel [h. Eunice A.], Nov. 12, 1835. G.R.19.

LOTHROP (see Lothropp), ——, s. —— and w., Aug. 1, 1775. P.R.26.

LOTHROPP (see Lothrop), Bernabas, s. John, bp. June 6, 1636. C.R.1.

LOW, Elizabeth S., w. Capt. Hiram Newcomb, Jan. 22, 1826. G.R.2.

LOWEL (see Lowell), Elizabeth, d. John of Boston, bp. Aug. 21, 1664. C.R.1.
Joseph, s. John of Boston, bp. May 25, 1662. C.R.2.
Patience, d. John of Boston, bp. June 7, 1662. C.R.2.
Phebe, d. John of Rehoboth, bp. Aug. 11, 1667. C.R.2.

LOWELL (see Lowel), John, s. John of Boston, bp. June 17, 1660. C.R.2.
Zacheus, s. John of Rehoboth, bp. May 16, 1669. C.R.2.

LOYS [?], Bethaia, d. John of Marblehead, bp. Sept. 18, 1670. C.R.2.

LUCAS, Mary, d. Jane of Marshfield, bp. Oct. 23, 1726. C.R.2.

LUMBARD (see Lombord), Mary, d. Bernard, bp. Oct. 8, 1637. C.R.1.

LUMBERT (see Lambert), James, ch. James and Sarah, bp. Aug. 24, 1729. C.R.2.

MacCLOUD (see Macloud, McCloud, McLoud), ——, s. Roderick and Mehittable, Jan. 12, 1847.

MACK, Esther [——] [w. Capt. John], ——, 1769. G.R.6.
John, s. John and Esther, Feb. 8, 1806.
John, ch. Esther, wid., bp. Sept. 30, 1810. C.R.1.
Joseph Haydon, s. John and Esther, Aug. 15, 1809.

MACK, Joseph Haydon, ch. Esther, wid., bp. Sept. 30, 1810.
C.R.1.
Maria Mallaville, ch. Joseph H. and Rosanna, June 4, 1837.

MACKFARLAND, Hannah, d. John and Martha of Duxborough,
bp. Aug. 7, 1709. C.R.2.
John, s. John and Martha of Duxboroug, bp. June 8, 1707. C.R.2.

MACLOUD (see MacCloud, McCloud, McLoud), Simeon I., s.,
John, seaman (b. Pictou, N.S.), and Susan, July 19, 1848.

MAGGOONE (see Magone, Magoon, Magoone, Magoun), Eliab,
s. John, bp. July 4, 1675. C.R.2.

MAGONE (see Maggoone, Magoon, Magoone, Magoun), Elias, s.
John, Aug. 17, 1673.
John, s. John, July 14, 1668.

MAGOON (see Maggoone, Magone, Magoone, Magoun), Abigal,
d. Jo[h]n Jr. and Abigal, Feb. 28, 17[*sic*] [rec. between ch. b.
Jan. 16, 1732, and ch. b. Aug. 6, 1735]. [Abigail Magoone, d.
John Jr. and Abigail, bp. May 20, 1733, C.R.2.]
Hannah, d. John, bp. July 23, 1671. C.R.2.
Hannah, d. John Jr. and Abigal [Abigail, C.R.2.], May 17, 1737.
Isaac, s. John (Magoone), Aug. —, 1675.
John, s. John, bp. July 18, 1669. C.R.2.
Jo[h]n, s. Jo[h]n Jr. and Abigall, Aug. 6, 1735. [Magoone, s. John
and Abigail, C.R.2.]
Lusanna, d. John Jr. and Abigall, Jan. 16, 1732.

MAGOONE (see Maggoone, Magone, Magoon, Magoun), David,
ch. Elias and Hannah, bp. July 22, 1705. C.R.2.
Elias, s. Elias of Duxborough, bp. June 20, 1708. C.R.2.
James, ch. James dec'd and Sarah, bp. Sept. 18, 1709. C.R.2.
John, s. John [s. John and Hannah, C.R.2.], July 10, 1705.
Lusanna, d. John and Abigail, bp. May 24, 1730. C.R.2.
Mary, ch. Elias and Hannah, bp. July 22, 1705. C.R.2.
Sarah, ch. James dec'd and Sarah, bp. Sept. 18, 1709. C.R.2.
Thomas, ch. James dec'd and Sarah, bp. Sept. 18, 1709. C.R.2.

MAGOUN (see Maggoone, Magone, Magoon, Magoone), Hulda,
w. Jonathan Stetson, ——, 1771. G.R.14.

MAINE, Henry W., s. W[illia]m, shoemaker, and Lydia, Aug. 2,
1846.

MAJER (see Myer), Otto J., s. John, weaver, and Ann, Aug. 20,
1846.

MALLUS (see Mellus), John, s. Will[ia]m and Sarah, May 3, 1721. [Mellues, C.R.1.]
Sarah Hart, d. William and Mary, bp. Nov. 15, 1741. C.R.2.
William, s. Will[ia]m, Dec. 3, 1718. [Mellus, C.R.1.]

MAN (see Mann), Abigail, d. Richard, Feb. 23, 1698-9.
Barnabus, s. Nath[anie]ll (Mann) and Abigail, Feb. 14, 1793. [Barnabas, C.R.1.]
Benjamin, s. Thomas, Feb. 19, 1697.
Benjamin, ch. Thomas, bp. Aug. 22, 1708. C.R.1.
Charles, s. Nathaniel and Abigail, Nov. 16, 1790. [Mann, C.R.1.]
Charlotte, d. Josiah and Sagey, Jan. 22, 1779. [Charlottee Mann, C.R.1.]
David, s. Thomas, bp. July 26, 1719. C.R.1.
David, s. Tho[ma]s Jr. and Deborah, Nov. 9, 1719.
Deborah, ch. Thomas, ———, 1719.
Deborah, twin d. Thomas Jr. and Deborah, Feb. 20, 1721.
Deborah, inf. Josiah and Mary, bp. May 13, 1748. C.R.2.
Deborah, d. Tho[ma]s [Thomas Jr., C.R.1.] and Deborah, Oct. 6, 1749.
Deborah, ch. Josiah, bp. Feb. 28, 1759. C.R.1.
Deborah, d. Tho[ma]s and Deborah, June 29, 1766. [Mann, C.R.1.]
Delight [ch. Joseph], ———, 1732. [bp. Sept. 24, C.R.1.]
Ebenezar, s. Thom[a]s, bp. June 9, 1727. C.R.1.
Ebenezer, s. Tho[ma]s Jr. and Deborah, Dec. 28, 1725.
Elizabeth, d. Thomas, Mar. 10, 1692.
Elizabeth, d. Richard, Aug. 27, 1696.
Elizabeth, ch. Thomas, bp. Aug. 22, 1708. C.R.1.
Ensigne, ch. Thomas, bp. Aug. 22, 1708. C.R.1.
Ephraim, s. Joseph, ———, 1728. [bp. Aug. 4, C.R.1.]
George, s. David, bp. May 15, 1754. C.R.1.
Hanah, d. Richard, Apr. 13, 1689.
Isaah, s. Tho[ma]s and Deborah, Feb. 7, 1756. [Isaiah, s. Thomas Jr., C.R.1.]
Isaiah, s. Thomas Jr., bp. Jan. 20, 1750. C.R.1.
John, s. Richard, Apr. 7, 1684.
John, s. Tho[ma]s and Deborah, May 10, 1761.
Joseph, s. Thomas, Dec. 27, 1694.
Joseph, ch. Thomas, bp. Aug. 22, 1708. C.R.1.
Joseph, s. Joseph and Mary, Oct. 10, 1722.
Josiah, s. Richard, Dec. 10, 1654.
Josiah, s. Thomas, Mar. 11, 1679. [Josia, C.R.2.]
Josiah, s. Tho[ma]s Jr. and Deborah, Dec. 9, 1715.

SCITUATE BIRTHS 243

MAN, Josiah, s. Thomas Jr. and Deborah (Joy), ———, 1716.
Josiah, s. Josiah (May) and Sagey, June 19, 1783.
Luce, d. Tho[ma]s and Deborah, Dec. 23, 1752. [Lucy, d. Tho[ma]s Jr., C.R.1.]
Lucy, d. Josiah and Sagey, July 19, 1786.
Lucy, d. Josiah and Zilpha, July 16, 1821.
Margaret, ch. Josiah, bp. Feb. 28, 1759. C.R.1.
Margaret, d. Josiah and Sagey, June 19, 1771.
Martha, d. Benjamin and Martha, bp. Apr. 24, 1726. C.R.2.
Mary, d. Thomas, Mar. 15, 1688.
Mary [ch. Joseph], ———, 1730. [bp. Sept. 13, C.R.1.]
Nathanell, s. Richard, Sept. 23, 1646.
Nathanell, s. Richard, Oct. 27, 1693 [*sic*, see Richard].
Rebachat, d. Richard, Mar. 22, 1686.
Richard, s. Richard, Feb. 5, 1652.
Richard, s. Richard, Mar. 10, 1693-4 [*sic*, see Nathanell].
Sarah, d. Thomas, Nov. 15, 1684.
Sarah, twin d. Thomas Jr. [dup. omits Jr.] and Deborah, Feb. 20, 1721.
Sarah, d. Tho[ma]s [Tho[ma]s Jr., C.R.1.] and Deborah, May 14, 1758.
Sarah, d. Josiah and Sagey, Sept. 5, 1776. [Mann, C.R.1.]
Seth, s. Joseph and Mary, ———, 1724.
Seth, s. Joseph and Mary, bp. May 30, 1725. C.R.1. C.R.2.
Susanna, d. Josiah and w., bp. July 8, 1750. C.R.2.
Thomas, s. Richard, Aug. 15, 1650.
Thomas, s. Thomas, Apr. 5, 1681.
Thomas, s. Tho[ma]s Jr. and Deborah, Nov. 26, 1717. [Capt. Thomas Mann [h. Deborah], G.R.6.]
Thomas, s. Tho[ma]s Jr., ———, 1718.

MANLEY, Harriet E. [? m.], ———, 1824. G.R.7.

MANN (see Man), Abigail, d. Nathaniel (Man) and Abigail, May 30, 1802.
Abigail, d. Nathaniel, bp. May 13, 1804. C.R.1.
Abigail Billings, d. Charles and Mary D., Oct. 11, 1825.
Almeda Cushman, d. Charles and Mary D., Aug. 15, 1836.
Barne, ch. Jonathan and w., bp. Oct. 13, 1776. C.R.1.
Benjamin, s. Josiah and Zilpha, May 17, 1836.
Betsey, d. Jona[than] and Mary, Nov. 25, 1777.
Briggs, s. John and Rebekah, Jan. 7, 1807.
Charles, s. Josiah and Zilpha, July 17, 1833.
Charles Dexter, s. Charles and Mary D., Nov. 17, 1838.
Deborah [dup. Man], d. Josiah and Mary, Oct. 2, 1754.

MANN, Desire, d. Jona[than] and Mary, July 18, 1781.
Edmon Billings, s. Nathaniel and Abigail, May 12, 1786.
Edmund Cooper, s. Josiah and Zilpha, July 13, 1828.
Edward Billings, s. Nathanel and w., bp. July 31, 1791. C.R.1.
Elizabeth, d. Jonathan, bp. May 11, 1777. C.R.1.
Emily A., ch. Thomas D. and Lucy, Sept. 5, 1838.
George, s. Jonathan and Mary, Dec. 23, 1766.
George, ch. Jonathan and w., bp. Oct. 13, 1776. C.R.1.
George, ——, 1819. G.R.6.
Isaiah, s. John and Patience, Dec. 23, 1789.
John, s. Thomas, bp. May 15, 1763. C.R.1.
John, s. John and Patience, Nov. 1, 1785.
Jonathan [dup. Man], s. Josiah and Mary, Mar. 28, 1744 [dup. 1745]. [Man, bp. July 15, 1744, C.R.1.]
Jonathan, s. Jona[than] and Mary, Apr. 15, 1783.
Josiah [dup. Man], s. Josiah and Mary, May 12, 1745 [dup. 1746]. [Man, bp. July 28, 1745, C.R.1.]
Josiah, s. Josiah Jr., bp. June 5, 1771. C.R.1.
Josiah, s. Josiah and Zilpha, Feb. 11, 1831.
Leah, d. Jona[than] and Mary, June 15, 1779.
Leoisa, d. John and Rebeckah, Oct. 1, 1804.
Louiza Adams, d. Charles and Mary D., Mar. 26, 1833. [Louisa Adams, G.R.14.]
Lydia Curtis, d. John and Rebekah, Dec. 24, 1808.
Margaret, ch. Josiah and w., bp. Oct. 20, 1776. C.R.1.
Mary [dup. Man], d. Josiah and Mary, Dec. 28, 1748. [Man, C.R.2.]
Mary, ch. Jonathan and w., bp. Oct. 13, 1776. C.R.1.
Mary, d. Nath[anie]ll and Abigail, Nov. 21, 1804.
Mary, w. Peleg Hayden Collier, w. Bela Brown, ——, 1810. G.R.6.
Mary Ann Howard, d. Charles and Mary D., June 2, 1829.
Melinda, d. Nath[anie]ll (Man) and Abigail, Apr. 18, 1807.
Nancy, d. John and Patience, Nov. 21, 1797.
Nath[anie]l [dup. Nathanil Man], s. Josiah and Mary, Oct. 9, 1759. [Nath[anie]l Man, C.R.1.]
Nathaniel, s. Nath[anie]ll and Abigail, Mar. 30, 1798.
Noah, s. Jona[than] and Mary, Feb. 22, 1787.
Patience, d. John and Patience, Apr. 5, 1782.
Peleg, s. John and Patience, Feb. 3, 1784.
Polley, d. Jona[than] and Mary, Dec. 30, 1775.
Polly, d. John and Patience, Aug. 12, 1792.
Rebeca, d. Nath[anie]ll and Abigail, Mar. 28, 1800.
Rebecca [———], w. John [Oct. —, 1769]. G.R.6.

MANN, Rebecca H., d. Josiah and Zilpha, Dec. 7, 1822.
Rebekah Davis, d. Charles and Mary D., Feb. 5, 1821.
Reubin, s. John and Rebekah, Nov. 21, 1811.
Sally, d. John and Patience, Dec. 16, 1787.
Samuel A., ch. Thomas D. and Lucy, May 3, 1842.
Sarah Franklin, d. Nath[anie]ll and Abigail, Nov. 16, 1809.
Sarah French, d. Nath[anie]ll, bp. June 27, 1813. C.R.1.
Sarah Wales, d. Charles and Mary D., Mar. 2, 1841.
Susannah [dup. Susanna Man], d. Josiah and Mary, Dec. 16, 1752. [Susannah Man, C.R.1.]
Theodore Billings, s. Nath[anie]ll and Abigail, Aug. 12, 1795.
Thomas, s. John and Patience, June 17, 1795.
Thomas, ——, 1796. G.R.6.
Thomas Eliot, "Member of Co. F. 47th. Regt. Mass. Vol.," ——, 1820. G.R.6.
—— [——], w. ——, —— [1770]. C.R.1.
——, ch. Josiah and Zilpha, June 11, 1840.

MANNING, Venus, colored, —— [1777]. G.R.14.

MANSAL (see Mansel, Mansell), John, s. John (Mansail) Jr. and Sarah, Feb. 1, 1768.

MANSEL (see Mansal, Mansell), Abigal, d. John and Leah, June 1, 1752.
Ann, d. John and Leah, June 29, 1749.
Jean, d. John and Leah, Sept. 25, 1759. [Jane, C.R.1.]
John, s. John and Leah, Aug. 9, 1745.
Joseph, s. John and Leah, Dec. 9, 1750.
Leah, d. John and Leah, Sept. 8, 1755.
Lillis, d. John and Leah, Oct. 22, 1763. [Lylis, C.R.1.]
Lucy, d. John and Leah, June 11, 1766.
Mary, d. John and Leah, Dec. 27, 1761.
Peleg, s. John and Leah, Sept. 23, 1757.
Ruth, d. John and Leah, Oct. 22, 1768.
Will[ia]m, s. John and Leah, Jan. 23, 1754.
William, s. Jo[h]n, bp. July 10, 1755. C.R.1.

MANSELL (see Mansal, Mansel), Abigail, ch. John and Leah, bp. Sept. 30, 1753. C.R.1.
Ann, ch. John and Leah, bp. Sept. 30, 1753. C.R.1.
John, ch. John and Leah, bp. Sept. 30, 1753. C.R.1.
Joseph, ch. John and Leah, bp. Sept. 30, 1753. C.R.1.

MANSON, Ann Ellms, d. John and Abigail T., Oct. 13, 1834.
Anne Ellms, ch. John and Abigail, bp. June 5, 1841. C.R.1.

Manson, Benjamin Turner, s. Thomas L. and Mary, Jan. 22, 1829.
Charles, ch. Joel L. and Mary, July 22, 1845.
Charles [h. Emma B. (Pentz)], ――――, 1846. G.R.6.
Davis Jenkins, s. Nehemiah and Mercy, Sept. 12, 1820.
Edmund S., s. John and Abigail, Aug. 2, 1843.
Edmund Sewall, s. John and Abigail, bp. June 1, 1845. C.R.1.
Edward Everett, s. Thomas L. and Mary, July 7, 1835.
Edward Everett, s. Thomas L. and Mary, bp. May 2, 1841. C.R.1.
Edwin Chamberlin, s. William C., seaman, and Frances M. (b. Boston), July 10, 1849.
George, s. Nehemiah and Hannah, Sept. 28, 1810.
George, s. Thomas L. and Mary, bp. May 2, 1841. C.R.1.
George Horace, s. Thomas L. and Mary, May 6, 1832.
George Wales, s. John and Abigail T., Feb. 5, 1839.
George Wales, s. John and Abigail, June 21, 1840.
George Wales, ch. John and Abigail, bp. June 5, 1842. C.R.1.
Georgianna [――――], w. Benj[amin], ―――― [1832]. C.R.1. [Georgia W., w. B. T., G.R.6.]
Hannah Lincoln, d. Nehemiah and Mercy, Mar. 1, 1830.
Helen, d. John and Abigail T., Oct. 25, 1849.
Horace, ch. Joel L. and Mary, Oct. 25, 1849.
James, s. Nehemiah and Mercy, Oct. 16, 1824.
Joel Lincoln, s. Nehemiah and Hannah, Apr. 18, 181[3]. [[h. Mary (Jenkins)] G.R.6.]
John, s. Nehemiah and Hannah, July 9, 1794.
John, s. Capt. Nehemiah, bp. Feb. 1, 1802. C.R.1.
John, s. Nehemiah and Hannah, July 9, 1805.
John L., s. John and Abigail T., Feb. 25, 1837.
John Lincoln, s. John and Ann S., Nov. 29, 1832.
John Lincoln, ch. John and Abigail, bp. June 5, 1842. C.R.1.
Mary Lincoln, ch. Joel L. and Mary, May 30, 1842.
Mercy Lincoln, d. Nehemiah and Mercy, Sept. 9, 1818.
Nehemiah, s. Nehemiah and Hannah, Mar. 30, 1808.
Ruth, d. Nehemiah and Hannah, Feb. 7, 1799.
Ruth, d. Capt. Nehemiah, bp. June 9, 1801. C.R.1.
Ruth, d. Nehemiah and Hannah, Jan. 30, 1803.
Samuel Turner, s. Thomas L. and Mary, Jan. 13, 1826.
Sarah B. [? m.], ――――, 1814. G.R.6.
Thomas Lincoln, s. Nehemiah and Hannah, Nov. 19, 1796. [Capt. Thomas L. [h. Mary (Turner)], Nov. 19, 1797, G.R.6.]
Thomas Lincoln, s. Thomas L. and Mary, May 29, 1822.
William Cushing, s. Nehemiah and Mercy, Aug. 24, 1822.
William W., s. William C., sailor, and Frances M., May 20, 1847.

MARBELL (see Marble), David, s. Gershom and Waitstill, Jan. 31, 1704.
Ephraim, s. Gershom and Waitstill, May 2, 1702.
Nathaniell, s. Gershom and Waitstill, Mar. 1, 1706.

MARBLE (see Marbell), Abigail, ch. David and Abigail, bp. Nov. 23, 1735. C.R.2.
Charles Henry, s. Elijah, shoemaker, and Lydia, Sept. 14, 1844.
David, ch. David and Abigail, bp. Nov. 23, 1735. C.R.2.
Ephraim, s. David and Abigail, bp. Aug. 20, 1738. C.R.2.
John, s. Gershom, Apr. 25, 1700.
Luther, s. David and Abigail, bp. Aug. 15, 1736. C.R.2.

MARRITT (see Meret, Merit, Meritt, Merrett, Merrit, Merritt), Polley, d. Consider (Merritt) and Sarah, May 23, 1781.
William, s. Will[ia]m and Rhoda, Oct. 7, 1791. [This entry crossed out].

MARSH, Faustina [dup. Faustena Dora], d. John, shoemaker, and Lucy D., Nov. 12, 1848.
Horace Peirce, ch. Horace and Julia Ann, Nov. 10, 1837.
John [Dec. —, 1817]. G.R.2.
Joseph O. [dup. Owen], s. John, shoemaker, and Lucy D., Oct. 22, 1843.
Julia Ann, ch. John and Lucy D., June 2, 1841.
Polly E., w. Capt. Elijah Pratt, ——, 1819. G.R.2.
Sydney R. [dup. Russell], s. John, shoemaker, and Lucy D., Dec. 8, 1845.

MARTIN, Charles S., s. Antone, seaman (b. Island of Pico), and Matilda W., Apr. 30, 1849.
Dolly, —— [1779]. G.R.15.
Francis, s. Antony, sailor, and Matilda, Jan. 19, 1848.

MARVEL, Gershom, s. David, bp. Oct. 16, 1757. C.R.1.
Mary, d. David, bp. Apr. 7, 1754. C.R.1.
Mehitabel, d. David, bp. May 18, 1740. C.R.2.
Nathanael, s. David, bp. Oct. 16, 1748. C.R.1.
Rhode, d. David and w., bp. June 13, 1742. C.R.2.
Susanna, d. David, bp. Sept. 8, 1754. C.R.1.

MAYHEW (see Mayo), Jenny, d. Nath, bp. Dec. 4, 1757. C.R.2.

MAYO (see Mayhew), Abigail M., ch. Nathaniel and Sophia, July 25, 1828, at the Cape.
Abraham, ch. Nathaniel and Sophia, June 10, 1823, at the Cape.
Adeline, ch. Nathaniel and Sophia, Mar. 9, 1832, at the Cape.

MAYO, Anna Vinal, d. Lemuel and Anna, bp. June 6, 1773. C.R.I.
Emily, ch. Nathaniel and Sophia, Sept. 20, 1835.
Jane, d. Nath[anie]ll and Mary, Dec. 20, 1757.
John, s. Nath[anie]ll and Mary, Dec. 12, 1752.
Julia, ch. Nathaniel and Sophia, June 22, 1819, at the Cape.
Lemuel, s. Lemuel, bp. Oct. 1, 1786. C.R.I.
Lidia, d. Nath[anie]l and Mary, bp. Jan. 20, 1754. C.R.2.
Lucy, d. Lemuel, bp. May 26, 1776. C.R.I.
Lydia, d. Nath[anie]ll and Mary, Dec. 23, 1751.
Molly, d. Nath[anie]l and Mary, bp. Jan. 10, 1754. C.R.2.
Polly R., ch. Nathaniel and Sophia, Nov. 23, 1817, at the Cape.
Samuel R., ch. Nathaniel and Sophia, May 10, 1826, at the Cape.
Sarah B. [———], w. William, —— [1816]. G.R.8.
Sophia [———], w. Nathaniel, —— [1795]. G.R.2.
William, s. Nath[anie]ll and Mary, Dec. 4, 1759.
William [June —, 1809]. G.R.8.

McCARTHY, Dennis [h. Fanny], ——, 1826. G.R.10.
Fanny [———], w. Dennis, ——, 1832. G.R.10.

McCLOUD (see MacCloud, Macloud, McLoud), Alexander, s. John, mariner (b. Pictou, N.S.), and Susan, Oct. 3, 1849.

McKEE, Eliza J. [———], w. John, —— [1827]. G.R.15.
John [h. Eliza J.], —— [1830]. G.R.15.

McLOUD (see MacCloud, Macloud, McCloud), Alexander, s. John, sailor, and Susan, Dec. 3 [184–].
Eliza, ch. John and Susan C., Feb. —, 1842. [Eliza D., Feb. 21, G.R.6.]
Jesse D., ch. John and Susan C., Oct. 31, 1843.

MELLUS (see Mallus), Abigail, d. William (Mellues), bp. Apr. 11, 1725. C.R.I.

MERCER, Charles, s. Joel L. [L., written in pencil] and Mary, July 22, 1845.

MERCHANT, William, s. Will[ia]m of Boston, bp. [Apr.] 12, 1752. C.R.2.

MERET (see Marritt, Merit, Meritt, Merrett, Merrit, Merritt), Aimy, ch. Thomas (Merit) and Abigail, bp. Sept. 11, 1720. C.R.2.

MERIT (see Marritt, Meret, Meritt, Merrett, Merrit, Merritt), Abigail, ch. Thomas and Abigail, bp. Sept. 11, 1720. C.R.2.
Agatha, ch. Thomas and Abigail, bp. Sept. 11, 1720. C.R.2.

MERIT, Barnabas, s. Seth, bp. July 22, 1764. C.R.I.
Benjamin, s. Icabod and Mary, bp. Apr. 2, 1732. C.R.2.
Elisha, s. James, bp. Sept. 3, 1721. C.R.I.
Hannah, [ch.] Ichabod and Mary, bp. Aug. 4, 1734. C.R.2.
Henry, ch. Isaac and Jerusha, bp. June 22, 1729. C.R.I.
Isaac, s. Isaac, bp. Sept. 24, 1732. C.R.I.
James, s. James, bp. July 13, 1718. C.R.I.
Jerusha, ch. Isaac and Jerusha, bp. June 22, 1729. C.R.I.
Lusanna, d. Henry and Margret, bp. Oct. 8, 1729. C.R.2.
Martha, d. Henry Jr., bp. Oct. 1, 1727. C.R.I.
Mary, ch. Thomas and Abigail, bp. Sept. 11, 1720. C.R.2.
Mary, d. Icabod and Mary, bp. Oct. 11, 1730. C.R.2.
Nathan, s. Thomas, bp. Oct. 25, 1772. C.R.I.
Ruth, d. Jonathan Jr., bp. Feb. 16, 1752. C.R.I.
Sarah, d. Henry Jr., bp. July 21, 1725. C.R.I.
Seth, s. James, bp. Oct. 23, 1726. C.R.I.
Simeon, s. Jonathan and Mehitabel, bp. Nov. 9, 1735. C.R.2.
Thankfull, d. Jo[h]n Jr., bp. Aug. 2, 1730. C.R.I.

MERITT (see Marritt, Meret, Merit, Merrett, Merrit, Merritt), Charles, s. Tho[ma]s, bp. June 5, 1763. C.R.I.
Cynthia (see Zintha).
Deborah, d. Jonathan (Merritt) Jr. and Elizabeth, Apr. 14, 1711.
Elisha, ch. Elisha and w., bp. May 15, 1743. C.R.I.
Elizabeth, d. James Jr., bp. Dec. 26, 1742. C.R.I.
Elizabeth, d. Jonathan 3d and w., bp. May 15, 1743. C.R.I.
Elizabeth, d. Jonathan Jr., bp. May 29, 1763. C.R.I.
Gamaliel, s. Obediah, bp. June 5, 1763. C.R.I.
Hannah, d. Obadiah, bp. Jan. 30, 1753. C.R.I.
Isaac, s. Henry (brother of John) and Deborah, Sept. 29, 1702.
Joana, d. Consider (Merritt) and Sarah, June 2, 1783.
Lucy, d. Obadiah and Deborah, bp. May 27, 1753. C.R.I.
Mabel, twin d. Thomas, bp. July 3, 1768. C.R.I.
Molly, d. Tho[ma]s, bp. June 5, 1763. C.R.I.
Noah, s. Obediah, bp. June 5, 1763. C.R.I.
Sarah, d. Jonathan 3d, bp. Nov. 17, 1744. C.R.I.
Zintha, twin d. Thomas, bp. July 3, 1768. C.R.I.

MERRETT (see Marritt, Meret, Merit, Meritt, Merrit, Merritt), Laura, d. Malachi and Mercy, June 20, 1801.
Mercy, d. Malachi and Mercy, Jan. 22, 1791. [Merritt, C.R.I.]

MERRIT (see Marritt, Meret, Merit, Meritt, Merrett, Merritt), Asa, s. James, bp. Oct. 12, 1766. C.R.I.
Benjamin, s. Thomas, bp. Apr. 1, 1770. C.R.I.

MERRIT, [C]harles, s. Obediah and Deborah, June 21, 1756. [Merritt, C.R.I.]
Daniel, s. Jonathan Jr., bp. Sept. 28, 1755. C.R.I.
David, s. David and Hannah, Feb. 17, 1740. [Meritt, C.R.I.]
Deborah, twin d. Henery Jr. and Hannah, May 3, 1721. [Merit, twin d. Henry Jr., C.R.I.]
Deborah, d. Obediah [Obadiah C.R.I.] and Deb[ora]h, Aug. 30, 1763.
Delight, d. Isaac and Jerusha, May 8, 1734. [Merritt, C.R.I.]
Elisabeth, d. Jonatha[n] Jr. and Elisabeth, Apr. 2, 1719. [Elizabeth, C.R.I.]
Ensign, ch. Obediah, bp. July 2, 1775. C.R.I.
Gamaliel, s. Obediah and Deborah, Sept. 20, 1761.
Hannah, d. Obediah (Merritt) and Deborah, Aug. 20, 1747.
Hannah, d. David and Hannah, Feb. 25, 1748. [Merritt, C.R.I.]
Henery, s. Henery and Hannah, Nov. 13, 1715. [Henry Meritt, s. Henry (Merit) Jr., C.R.I.]
Henery, s. Isaac and Jerusha, Feb. 6, 1725.
Henery, s. Henery and Hannah, Aug. 19, 1728. [Henry Merit, s. Henry Jr., C.R.I.]
Isaac, s. Isaac and Jerusha, Mar. 19, 1731.
Israel, ch. Obediah, bp. July 2, 1775. C.R.I.
Jerusha, d. Isaac and Jerusha, July 8, 1727.
John, s. David and Hannah, Sept. 18, 1743.
[J]onathan, s. Obediah and Deborah, Aug. 20, 1754.
Joseph, s. Ichabod and Mary, Mar. 29, 1729.
Joshua, s. Jonathan Jr., bp. July 30, 1758. C.R.I.
Lucy, d. Obediah and Deborah, May 11, 1750.
Luke, s. Obediah and Deborah, Oct. 18, 1760.
Lydia, d. David and Hannah, Dec. 14, 1737. [Merritt, C.R.I.]
Malachi, s. Obediah and Deborah, July 21, 1757.
Malachi, ch. Obediah, bp. July 2, 1775. C.R.I.
[M]alechi, s. Obediah and Deborah, Aug. 15, 1765.
Martha, d. Hen[er]y Jr. and Hannah, Mar. 18, 1726.
Mary, d. Henery (Merritt) Jr. and Hannah, Oct. 18, 1717. [Merit, d. Henry Jr., C.R.I.]
Micah, s. Amos and w., bp. July 20, 1788. C.R.I.
Noah, s. Obediah and Deborah, Feb. 26, 1759.
Obediah, s. Jona[than] and Elizabeth, Mar. 9, 1723.
Paul, s. Seth, bp. May 28, 1758. C.R.I.
Penelopie, d. Henery Jr. and Hannah, Mar. 1, 1719. [Penelope Merit, d. Henry Jr., C.R.I.]
Priscilla, d. Elisha (Merritt) and Priscilla, June 7, 1744. [Meritt, C.R.I.]

MERRIT, Rachel, d. Isaac and Jerusha, May 5, 1729. [Merit, C.R.1.]
Ruth, d. Henery and Hannah, Mar. 18, 1730. [Merit, d. Henry Jr., C.R.1.]
Sarah, twin d. Henery Jr. and Hannah, May 3, 1721. [Merit, twin d. Henry Jr., C.R.1.]
Sarah, d. Henery Jr. and Hannah, Feb. 21, 1724.
Seth, s. James and Ruth, Aug. 14, 1724.
Simeon, s. Jonathan and Mehitable, Sept. 4, 1728.
Thankfull, d. Jo[h]n Jr. and Thankfull, July 18, 1729.

MERRITT (see Marritt, Meret, Merit, Meritt, Merrett, Merrit),
Aaron, s. Daniel and Mary, Mar. —, 1791.
Abigail, d. John (s. Henry Jr.) and Elizabeth, Nov. —, 1700.
Abigail, d. Thomas and Abigail, Sept. 21, 1714.
Abigail Billings, d. Billings and Abigail B., Sept. 2, 1820.
Abigail Billings, d. Billings and Abigail B., Aug. 21, 182[worn] [1824].
Abigail Brooks, d. Martin D. and Debby, Aug. 26, 1835. [Abbie B., Aug. 26, 1834, P.R.9.]
Abigail Hencock, d. Malichai and Marcy, Feb. 20, 1809.
Adna, s. Seth [Seth Jr., C.R.1.] and Susanna, Sept. 16, 1788.
Agatha (see Egatha).
Allen, s. Amos and Lydia, Apr. 7, 1796.
Allen, s. Melzar and Deborah, Oct. 25, 1821. [[h. Lydia (Alden)] G.R.2.]
Allen, s. Shadrach B. and Arvilla H., July 9, 1824.
Almena L., d. Israel and Celia, Mar. 4, 1818.
Ambros, [ch.] Amos and w., bp. Sept. 7, 1788. C.R.1.
Ambrose, s. Amos and Lydia, Apr. 17, 1781.
Ambrose, s. Ambrose and Kezia, Apr. 22, 1812.
Ambrose, s. Melzar and Deborah, Nov. 15, 1826.
Amos, s. James Jr. and Eliza[beth], May 1, 1755.
Amos, s. James Jr., bp. Oct. 30, 1756. C.R.1.
Amos, s. Amos and Lydia, Mar. 6, 1783.
Amos, [ch.] Amos and w., bp. Sept. 7, 1788. C.R.1.
Amos, s. Jonathan and Caroline W., June 19, 1835.
Amos Washington, s. James L. and Emely [Emily, C.R.1.], May 5, 1833.
Amy, d. Thomas and Abigal, Dec. 21, 1716.
Anna Brown, d. Nehemiah and Anna, Jan. 15, 1822.
Anne Brown, ch. Neh[emiah] and Anne, bp. Nov. 19, 1826. C.R.3.
Arvilla H. [———], w. Shadrach B., ——— [1800]. G.R.2.
Asa, s. James Jr. and Eliza[bet]h, July 4, 1761.

MERRITT, Asa, s. Asa and Betty, Oct. 31, 1792. [Merrit, C.R.1.]
Asa, s. Asa and Betsey, Oct. 7, 1820.
Asa James, s. Asa and Betsey, Nov. 22, 1828.
Bailey, s. Amos and Lydia, Sept. 18, 1804.
Barna, s. Seth and Susanna, Dec. 25, 1784.
Barna, ch. Seth Jr., and Susanna, bp. Sept. 13, 1789. C.R.1.
Beckey, d. James and Mary, Sep[t]. 9, 1785.
Belinda Torrey, d. Melzar and Deborah, Dec. 28, 1819.
B[e]nja[min], s. Consider and Sarah, Nov. 2, 1785. [[h. Sally (Cole)] G.R.14.]
Benjamin, s. Consider and w., bp. Sept. 6, 1796. C.R.2.
Benjamin, s. Benjamin and Sally, Aug. 28, 1823.
Benjamin F., s. Ensign and Sally, Oct. 24, 1821.
Betsey, w. Dea. Ward Litchfield, ———, 1760. G.R.7.
Betsey, d. Noah and Bettey, Nov. 18, 1789.
Betsey Briggs, d. Shadrach B. and Arvilla H., Apr. 3, 1829.
Betsy, d. Asa and Betty, Dec. 31, 1788. [Betsey, C.R.1.]
Betsy, d. Noah, bp. July 22, 1792. C.R.1.
Billings, s. Paul and Deborah, Dec. 5, 1787.
Billings, s. Martin D. and Debby, Sept. 24, 1830.
Billins, ch. Paul, bp. Oct. 25, 1789. C.R.1.
Caleb, s. Seth and Mercy, Mar. 11, 1770. [Merit, C.R.1.
Caroline, d. Jonathan and Caroline W., May 29, 1829.
Caroline [———], w. Amos W., ——— [1836]. G.R.2.
Celia, d. Israel and Celia, Sept. 10, 1804.
Charles, s. Tho[ma]s and Jean, Nov. 26, 1761.
Charles, s. Seth [Seth Jr., C.R.1.] and Susanna, Oct. 6, 1790.
Charles, s. Noah and Bettey, Oct. 2, 1791. [Meritt, C.R.2.]
Charles, s. Bailey and Lucy, Oct. 30, 1838.
Charles, ch. Bailey dec'd and Lucy, bp. Oct. 5, 1845. C.R.1.
Charles Henry, s. Francis and Clarissa, Aug. 21, 1827.
Charles Henry, s. Freeman and Hannah, Oct. 26, 1838.
Charles Torrey, s. Nehemiah and Anna [Anne, C.R.3.], Oct. 23, 1827.
Charlotte, d. Maj. Paul, bp. ——— [rec. between ch. bp. Nov. 24, 1799, and ch. bp. Aug. 31, 1800]. C.R.1.
Clarissa, d. Paul and Deborah, Feb. 15, 1800.
Clarissa [———], w. Francis, ———, 1806. G.R.14.
Clarissa, d. Francis and Clarissa, Mar. 26, 1831. [Clara, P.R.2.]
Consider, s. Elisha and Priscilla, Sept. 17, 1751. [Merit, C.R.1.]
Consider, s. Consider and Sarah, Jan. 3, 1791.
Consider, s. Consider and w., bp. Sept. 6, 1796. C.R.2.
Cynthia, d. Daniel and Mary, ——— [rec. before ch. b. Mar. 19, 1787]. [[Jan. —, 1785] G.R.14.]

MERRITT, Cynthia, d. Israel and Celia, Sept. 16, 1798.
Daniel, s. Daniel and Mary, Mar. 19, 1787.
Daniel H., s. William H., blacksmith, and Elizabeth R., Aug. 11, 1847.
David, s. John (s. Henry Jr.) and Elizabeth, Oct. —, 1703.
[David] Marble, s. George and Nabby, May 30, 1789, in Cohassett.
Debbey, d. Paul and Deborah, June 29, 1797. [Debbe, d. Capt. Paul, C.R.1.] [Deborah, P.R.21.]
Debby, d. Malichi, bp. Nov. 12, 1797. C.R.1.
Debby [―――], w. Martin, ―― [1797]. C.R.1. [w. Martin D., G.R.11.]
Debby, d. Malachi and Mercy, July 23, 1798.
Deborah, d. John (s. Henry Jr.), Dec. —, 1689.
Deborah, d. Henry (brother of John), Mar. 2, 1694.
Deborah, d. Melzar and Deborah, Mar. 23, 1816.
Deborah [―――], w. Kilburn B., ――, 1829. G.R.11. [Deborah L., P.R.23.]
Deborah Cushing, d. Martin D. and Debby, Oct. 26, 1822.
Deborah N., d. Joseph E., mason, and Hannah H., July 20, 1847.
Deborah Nowel, d. Ensign and Sally, June 7, 1808.
Dexter, s. Paul and Deborah, July 28, 1794. [[h. Abigail B. (Otis)] G.R.11.]
Diana [? m.], Aug. 24, 1803. G.R.11.
Ebenezer, s. John (s. Henry Jr.) and Elizabeth, Dec. 25, 1705.
Ebenezer, s. James and Mary, May 24, 1780.
Eben[eze]r, s. Gamaliel and Hannah, Jan. 10, 1793.
Ebenezer, ch. Hannah, wid., bp. May 30, 1802. C.R.1.
Edmund F., d. [*sic*] Munroe and Harriet, Oct. 17, 1846.
Edwin, s. Benjamin and Sally, Oct. 8, 1829.
Egatha, d. Thomas and Abigail, Feb. 11, 1711–12.
Elery L., ch. Francis and Clarissa, July 8, 1848. P.R.2.
Elijah, s. James and Mary, June 11, 1769.
Elisha, s. James (Merrit) and Ruth, July 14, 1720.
Elisha, s. Elisha and Priscilla, June 2, 1746. [Meritt, C.R.1.]
Elisha, s. Consider and Sarah, Apr. 22, 1779.
Elisha Foster, s. Elisha and Sebre, Sept. 2, 1821.
Elisha Litchfield, s. Francis and Clarissa, Aug. 20, 1829.
Eliza, d. Israel and Celia, June 26, 1800.
Eliza, d. Ambrose and Kezia, Sept. 24, 1806.
Eliza (see ―――― Merritt).
Eliza Ann, d. Caleb and Huldah, Sept. 13, 1803.
Eliza Ann, d. Caleb, bp. Sept. 15, 1805. C.R.1.
Eliza Washington, d. Consider Jr. and Betsey, Jan. 22, 1816.
Elizabeth, d. John (s. Henry Jr.), Feb. —, 1690–1.

MERRITT, Eliz[abeth], bp. Mar. 13, 1733, a. 63, "on her Death bed." C.R.1.
Elizabeth, d. Tho[ma]s and Jean [Jane, C.R.1.], Oct. 15, 1750.
Elizabeth, d. James Jr. and Eliza[beth], Apr. 11, 1757. [Merrit, C.R.1.]
Elizabeth, d. Tho[ma]s and Jean, July 20, 1758.
Elizabeth, d. Amos and Lydia, Feb. 18, 1801.
Elizabeth Litchfield, d. Elisha and Sebre, June 19, 1801.
Elizabeth Litchfield, d. Elisha and Sebre, Feb. 23, 1812.
Elizabeth R. [―――], w. William H., ――, 1822. G.R.14.
Ellen Augusta, d. Munroe and Harriet, Sept. 14, 1849.
Ellen M. [―――], w. John A. [Sept. ―, 1831]. G.R.11.
Ellen Mariah, d. Freeman and Hannah, June 8, 1837. [Ellen Maria, C.R.1.]
Emeline, d. Bailey and Lucy, Sept. 24, 1834.
Emeline Isabelle, d. H[enry] and Isabelle, June 8, 1831. [w. George R. Turner, G.R.14.]
Emely, d. Seth and Susanna, Feb. 14, 1800. [Emila, d. Dea. Seth, C.R.1.]
Emely Clapp, d. James L. and Emely, Aug. 24, 1823.
Emely Clapp, ch. James Lincoln, bp. Aug. 4, 1827. C.R.1.
Emerline, d. Israel and Celia, Apr. 13, 1813.
Emily [―――], w. Dea. James L. [Apr. ―, 1795.] G.R.2.
Emmeline, ch. Bailey dec'd and Lucy, bp. Oct. 5, 1845. C.R.1.
Ensign, s. Obediah and Deborah, Mar. 2, 1768.
Ezekiell, s. John (s. Henry Jr.) and Elizabeth, Mar. 22, 1709-10.
Fanny E. [―――], w. James, ――, 1828. G.R.14.
Foster, s. Shadrach B. and Aurilla [sic, Arvilla] H., June 2, 1835.
Francis, s. Consider and Sarah, Oct. 30, 1800. [[h. Clarissa] ――, 1801, G.R.14.] [[h. Clarissa (Litchfield)] Oct. 30, 1801, P.R.2.]
Francis, s. Francis and Clarissa, Jan. 18, 1823.
Freeman, s. Seth and Susanna, July 16, 1802.
Freeman Thomas, s. Freeman and Hannah, Jan. 26, 1832.
Freeman Thomas, ch. Freeman and Hannah, bp. Oct. 1, 1837. C.R.1.
Gamaliel, s. Gamaliel and Hannah, Jan. 10, 1783.
George, s. Shadrach B. and Arvilla H., Feb. 4, 1834.
George A., s. Allen, shoemaker, and Emeline (b. Abington), Nov. 7, 1849, in Abington.
George Billings, s. Dexter and Abigail B., June 12, 1827.
George Howard, s. H[enry] and Isabella, Sept. 11, 1842.
George M., s. Robert C., mason, and Martha, Aug. 25, 1846.
George Thomas, s. Jonathan and Caroline W., Mar. 16, 1827.

MERRITT, George W. Brown, s. Nehemiah and Anna, Feb. 27, 1833.
  [George Washington Brown, ch. Neh[emiah] and Anne, C.R.3.]
George Whitney, s. Dexter and Abigail B., Oct. 6, 1831.
Hannah, d. John (s. Henry Jr.), Feb. —, 1696–7.
Hannah, d. Henry Jr. and Hannah, Oct. 21, 1713. [Merit, C.R.1.]
Hannah, d. Gamaliel and Hannah, Apr. 16, 1784.
Hannah [? m.] [Oct. —, 1803]. G.R.11.
Hannah Chandler, d. Benjamin and Sally, Sept. 30, 1818.
Hannah Howard, d. Freeman and Hannah, Nov. 9, 1828.
Hannah Howard, ch. Freeman and Hannah, bp. Oct. 1, 1837.
  C.R.1.
Harriet [———], w. Monro, —— [1824]. C.R.3.
Harriett, d. Gam[a]l[ie]l, bp. Feb. 1, 1802. C.R.1.
Harvey, s. James L. and Emely, July 16, 1826.
Harvey, ch. James Lincoln, bp. Aug. 4, 1827. C.R.1.
Hatherly, s. James L. and Emely [Emily, C.R.1.], Apr. 15, 1837.
Hayward, s. Caleb, bp. Aug. 19, 1805. C.R.1.
Henery, s. Elisha and Priscilla, Jan. 21, 1748. [Merit, C.R.1.]
Henery, s. Consider and Sarah, May 9, 1798. [Henry [h. Isabel
  Litchfield], G.R.14.]
Henry, s. Henry (brother of John), Jan. 1, 1689.
Henry, s. John (s. Henry Jr.), May —, 1699.
Henry, s. Israel and Celia, Nov. 4, 1802.
Henry, s. Asa and Betsey, Sept. 4, 1825.
Henry, s. Ensign and Sally, Sept. 29, 1826.
Henry, s. Henry and Isabelle, July 26, 1829.
Howard, s. Shadrach B. and Arvilla H., Oct. 26, 1822.
Ichabod, s. John (s. Henry Jr.), Oct. —, 1695.
Ira, s. Amos and Lydia, Nov. 27, 1798.
Ira, s. Ambrose and Kezia, Dec. 7, 1804.
Ira, s. James L. and Emely, June 13, 1818.
Ira, ch. James Lincoln, bp. Aug. 4, 1827. C.R.1.
Isabelle, d. Paul and Deborah, Apr. 19, 1805. [Isabella, d.
  Maj. Paul, C.R.1.]
[I]srael, s. Obediah and Deborah, June 3, 1770.
Israel, s. Gamaliel and Hannah, Oct. 31, 1790.
Israel, ch. Hannah, wid., bp. May 30, 1802. C.R.1.
Israel, s. Israel and Celia, Sept. 31, 1809.
Jairus, s. Paul and Deborah, Nov. 30, 1785.
Jairus, ch. Paul, bp. Oct. 25, 1789. C.R.1.
James, s. Henry (brother of John), Nov. 14, 1691.
James, s. James, May 1, 1717.
James, s. James Jr. and Eliza[beth], Feb. 8, 1745.
James, s. James and Mary, Jan. 6, 1784.

MERRITT, James, s. Ensign and Sally, May 10, 1813.
James, s. Francis and Clarissa, Sept. 20, 1826. [[h. Fanny E.] ——, 1825, G.R.14.] [Sept. 20, 1825, P.R.2.]
James Cummings, s. Elisha and Sebre, Sept. 8, 1823.
James Edward, ch. Robert C. and Martha, Feb. 26, 1838.
James Hervey, s. Paul and Deborah, Mar. 14, 1790. [James Harvy Merrit, C.R.1.] [James H. Merritt, Mar. 19, G.R.11.]
James L. Sr., Dea., —— [1793]. C.R.1. [[h. Emily] G.R.2.]
James Lincoln, s. Amos and Lydia, Mar. 9, 1794.
James Lincoln, s. James L. and Emely, July 10, 1816.
James Lincoln, ch. James Lincoln, bp. Aug. 4, 1827. C.R.1. [[h. Elizabeth O. (Jackson)] G.R.2.]
Jean, d. Tho[ma]s and Jean, Aug. 28, 1752. [Jane, C.R.1.]
Jean, d. Tho[ma]s and Jean, Aug. 31, 1764. [Jane Meritt, C.R.1.]
Joanne, d. Consider Jr. and Betsey, Mar. 28, 1824.
Joce [?], d. Consider and w., bp. Sept. 6, 1796. C.R.2.
Joel, s. Dr. Seth, bp. Sept. 23, 1792. C.R.1.
Joel, s. Seth and Susanna, Sept. 28, 1792.
John, s. John (s. Henry Jr.), Aug. —, 1687.
John Adams, s. Paul [Maj. Paul, C.R.1.] and Deborah, Oct. 25, 1802.
John Adams, s. Martin D. and Debby, Nov. 19, 1826.
John Ensign, ch. Robert C. and Martha, Jan. 11, 1842.
John Quincy, s. Bailey and Lucy, Dec. 26, 1839.
John Wesley, s. Noah and Bettey, Jan. 6, 1805.
John Westly, s. Noah, bp. Mar. 20, 1808. C.R.1.
Jonathan, s. Henry (brother of John), Feb. 7, 1687.
Jonathan, s. John (s. Henry Jr.) and Elizabeth, May —, 1702.
Jonathan, s. Jonathan, Sept. 16, 1715. [Meritt, s. Jonathan (Merit) Jr., C.R.1.]
Jonathan, s. Obadiah, bp. Aug. 29, 1756. C.R.1.
Jonathan, s. Daniel and Mary, Nov. 14, 1794.
Jonathan, s. Jonathan and Caroline W., Aug. 12, 1830.
Joseph, s. Tho[ma]s and Jean, Mar. 17, 1756.
Joseph, s. Consider and Sarah, June 15, 1794.
Joseph, s. Consider and w., bp. Sept. 6, 1796. C.R.2.
Joseph, s. Daniel and Mary, Oct. 20, 1797.
Joseph, s. Noah and Bettey, Dec. 20, 1802.
Joseph, s. Ensign and Sally, Feb. 21, 1817.
Joseph, s. Consider Jr. and Betsey, Dec. 6, 1819.
Joseph Bailey, s. Bailey and Lucy, Nov. 27, 1830.
Joseph H., ——, 1825. G.R.8.
Joseph Howard, s. Elisha and Sebra, —— [rec. after ch. b. Sept. 8, 1823].

MERRITT, Joshua, s. Daniel and Mary, Aug. 30, 1789.
Joshua Young, s. Israel and Celia, Sept. 30, 1808.
Judith A. [―――], w. Hatherly, ―― [? 1837]. C.R.3.
Julia A., d. Israel and Celia, Sept. 12, 1816.
Julia Franklin, d. Elisha and Sebre, Jan. 5, 1804.
Kilburn Bailey, s. Martin D. and Debby, Nov. 25, 1824. [[h. Deborah] G.R.11.] [Kilborn B., P.R.23.]
Laura, d. Malachi, bp. Oct. 31, 1803. C.R.1.
Lavina, d. Gamaliel and Hannah, Aug. 13, 1786.
Lavina, ch. Hannah, wid., bp. May 30, 1802. C.R.1.
Leah, d. Henry (brother of John), Feb. 21, 1697.
Loring, s. Francis and Clarissa, Oct. 9, 1838.
Lucy, d. Priscilla, wid., bp. July 16, 1758. C.R.1.
Lucy, d. James and Mary, Jan. 10, 1778. [Merrit, d. James Jr., C.R.1.]
Lucy, d. Malachi, bp. Apr. 19, 1795. C.R.1.
Lucy, d. Malachi and Mercy, Jan. 13, 1796.
Lucy [―――], w. Bailey [Feb. ―, 1807]. G.R.2.
Lucy [―――], w. ―――, ―― [1808]. C.R.1.
Lucy, d. Ensign and Sally, June 28, 1819.
Lucy, w. Richard Nutter, ―― [1820]. G.R.6.
Lucy, d. Shadrach B. and Arvilla H., Nov. 5, 1821.
Lucy, d. Martin D. and Debby, Sept. 8, 1828.
Lucy [―――], w. Allen [Sept. ―, 1828]. C.R.1.
Lucy Bailey, d. Freeman and Hannah, Aug. 15, 1830.
Lucy Bailey, ch. Freeman and Hannah, bp. Oct. 1, 1837. C.R.1.
Luther, s. James and Mary, Mar. 19, 1775. [Merrit, C.R.1.]
Lydia [―――], w. Amos [Aug. ―, 1762]. C.R.1.
Lydia [―――], w. Dea. Amos, ―― [1767]. G.R.2.
Lydia, d. Amos and Lydia, May 15, 1787.
Lydia, [ch.] Amos and w., bp. Sept. 7, 1788. C.R.1.
Lydia Bailey, d. James L. [Simeon [?], C.R.1.] and Emely, July 8, 1829.
Mabel, d. James and Mary, July 26, 1787. [Merrit, d. James Jr., C.R.1.] [Merritt, w. Shadrach Wade, P.R.28.]
Madeline, d. Francis and Clarissa, Apr. 15, 1833. [Madeline I., P.R.2.]
Malachi, s. Malachi and Mercy, Nov. 6, 1793. [Merrit, C.R.1.]
Marcy, ch. Paul, bp. Oct. 25, 1789. C.R.1.
Maria, d. Amos and Lydia, June 1, 1803. [w. Paul Litchfield, C.R.3.]
Maria, d. Shadrach B. and Arvilla H., Mar. 15, 1831.
Martha [―――], w. ―――, ―― [1807]. C.R.1.
Martha, d. Consider Jr. and Betsey, Oct. 6, 1826.

MERRITT, Martha, d. Francis and Clarissa, July 17, 1835. [Martha R., July 15, P.R.2.]
Martha Hutson [Hudson], d. Elisha and Sebre, Aug. 3, 1805.
Martha Tilden, ch. Robert C. and Martha, Oct. 18, 1836.
Martin Bailey, s. Martin D. and Debby, Oct. 31, 1820.
Martin Daws, s. Paul and Deborah, June 26, 1792. [Martin Dawes, C.R.1.] [Martin D. [h. Debby], G.R.11.]
Mary, d. John (s. Henry Jr.), Nov. —, 1692.
Mary, d. Thomas and Abigail, Feb. 11, 1718.
Mary, d. James Jr. and Eliza[beth], July 24, 1749.
Mary, d. Noah, bp. Nov. 9, 1798. C.R.1.
Mary, w. Henry Bowker, ——, 1817. G.R.14.
Mary, d. Jonathan and Caroline W., Apr. 13, 1828.
Mary [———], w. O., July 30, 1828. G.R.6.
Mary Briggs, d. Caleb, bp. Apr. 24, 1810. C.R.1.
Mary Cole, d. Benjamin and Sally, July 26, 1816.
Mary E., d. Allen, shoemaker, and Emeline (b. Abington), Nov. 23, 1840, in Abington.
Mary E., d. Francis and Clarissa, July 2, 1841.
Mary Stodder, d. Caleb and Huldah, Aug. 17, 1806.
Mary Tilden, ch. Robert C. and Martha, May 8, 1840.
Melzar, s. Amos and Lydia, Sept. 24, 1791.
Melzar, s. Melzar and Deborah, Mar. 12, 1818.
Melzer, s. James Jr. and Eliza[beth], May 2, 1759. [Melzar Marit, C.R.1.]
Mercy, d. Paul and Deborah, Jan. 24, 1784.
Mercy (see Marcy).
Mercy C., d. Robert, mason, and Martha, May 30, 1848.
Micah, s. Amos and Lydia, Mar. 1, 1785.
Micah, s. Amos and Lydia, July 28, 1789. [Merrit, C.R.1.]
Molle, d. Tho[ma]s and Jean, June 5, 1760.
Monroe, s. James L. and Emely, Aug. 27, 1820. [Munroe, "Co. C. 4 Mass H. A.," "Member of Post 31 G.A.R.," G.R.2.]
Monroe, ch. James Lincoln, bp. Aug. 4, 1827. C.R.1.
Nabba, d. Tho[ma]s and Jean, Oct. 7, 1766. [Merrit, C.R.1.]
Nabbe, d. Seth and Susanna, Dec. 4, 1786.
Nabbe, ch. Seth Jr. and Susanna, bp. Sept. 13, 1789. C.R.1.
Nabby, d. James and Mary, Oct. 14, 1773. [Nabbee Merrit, d. James Jr., C.R.1.]
Nancy Ann, d. Benjamin and Sally, Feb. 6, 1821. [[w. Otis Hersey] G.R.14.]
Nehemiah, s. Jonathan Jr. and Elizabeth, Oct. 17, 1712. [Meritt, C.R.1.]
Nehemiah, s. Jonathan Jr., bp. Nov. 3, 1751. C.R.1.

MERRITT, Nehemiah, s. Nehemiah and Sarah, Apr. 26, 1796.
Nehemiah Thomas, s. Nehemiah and Anna, June 18, 1824.
Nehemiah Thomas, ch. Neh[emiah] and Anne, bp. Nov. 19, 1826. c.r.3.
Noah, s. Noah and Bettey, Mar. 15, 1788.
Noah, s. Noah and Bettey, Mar. 13, 1793.
Noah, s. Noah, bp. Aug. 2, 1795. c.r.1.
Obadiah, s. Noah and Bettey, Oct. 20, 1794.
Obadiah, s. Ensign and Sally, Apr. 9, 1824.
Orra, d. Bailey and Lucy, Dec. 11, 1840.
Orra Hatch, ch. Bailey dec'd and Lucy, bp. Oct. 5, 1845. c.r.1.
Otis, s. Malachi and Mercy, Mar. 31, 1804.
Paul, s. Seth and Mercy, Feb. 4, 1761. [Maj. Paul, c.r.1.]
Paul Brooks, s. Paul and Xoa, Oct. 7, 1824.
Perez, s. Seth [Dea. Seth, c.r.1.] and Susanna, Oct. 28, 1794.
Peter, s. Dea. Seth, bp. Sept. 17, 1797. c.r.1.
Peter, s. Seth and Susanna, Jan. 19, 1798.
Philipe, d. Amos and Lydia, Nov. 6, 1779.
Phillipe, [ch.] Amos and w., bp. Sept. 7, 1788. c.r.1.
Polly, d. Consider and w., bp. Sept. 6, 1796. c.r.2.
Polly, d. Noah and Bettey, Sept. —, 1797.
Polly, d. Noah and Bettey, Feb. 25, 1800.
Priscilla H., ch. Francis and Clarissa, Dec. 2, 1845. p.r.2.
Prissalla, d. Consider and Sarah, June 2, 1796. [Prissa, c.r.2.]
Prissilla, d. Benjamin and Sally, Sept. 26, 1814. [Priscilla, g.r.14.]
Rachell, d. Henry (brother of John), Apr. 29, 1699.
Rhoda, d. James and Mary, Nov. —, 1781.
Robert Cook, s. Ensign and Sally, Dec. 16, 1810.
Robert Thomas, ch. Robert C. and Martha, Mar. 8, 1834.
Roxa[?], d. Consider and w., bp. Sept. 6, 1796. c.r.2.
Roxana, d. Consider and Sarah, Mar. 19, 1788.
Ruth, d. John (s. Henry Jr.), May —, 1694.
Ruth, ch. James, bp. Mar. 23, 1739. c.r.1.
Ruth, d. James Jr. and Eliza[beth], Feb. 25, 1740.
Ruth, d. James and Mary, Nov. 28, 1770. [Merrit, d. James Jr., c.r.1.]
Ruth, d. Gamaliel and Hannah, Sept. 15, 1788.
Ruth, d. Ambrose and Kezia, Aug. 21, 1809.
Rutha, ch. Hannah, wid., bp. May 30, 1802. c.r.1.
Sally, d. Consider and Sarah, June 15, 1775.
Sally [———], w. Ensign, —— [1783]. g.r.6.
Sally, d. Ensign and Sally, Aug. 22, 1805.
Samuel, s. Gamaliel and Hannah, June 30, 1795.
Samuel, ch. Hannah, wid., bp. May 30, 1802. c.r.1.

MERRITT, Samuel Stetson, s. Caleb, bp. Aug. 8, 1814. C.R.1.
Sarah, d. Consider Jr. and Betsey, Mar. 28, 1818.
Sarah, w. Thomas Litchfield, June 15, 1826. G.R.7.
Sarah A., d. Francis, blacksmith, and Lydia V., July 7, 1846.
Sarah E., d. William H., blacksmith, and Elizabeth R., May 14, 1849, in S. Scituate.
Sarah T., d. Freeman and Hannah, Dec. 2, 1846.
Sebre [———], w. Elisha, ——— [1782]. C.R.1.
Seth, s. Seth, bp. Mar. 13, 1753. C.R.1.
Seth, s. Seth and Mercy, May 1, 1757. [Meritt, C.R.1.]
Seth, s. Caleb and Huldah, June 27, 1810.
Shadrach Briggs, s. Asa and Betty, May 4, 1797. [h. Arvilla H., G.R.2.]
Sophia, d. Nehemiah and Sarah, Aug. 6, 1798. [w. Dea. Marshall Litchfield, G.R.7.]
Susanna, d. Dea. Seth, bp. Feb. 18, 1799. C.R.1.
[Susy] Merritt, d. George and Nabby, Feb. 14, 1793, in Cohassett.
Thomas, s. John (s. Henry Jr.), Sept. —, 1688.
Thomas, s. Tho[ma]s and Jean, Apr. 2, 1754.
Thomas, s. Bailey and Lucy, Oct. 1, 1832. ["Veteran of Fire department," G.R.2.]
Whitman Bailey, s. Melzar and Deborah, Mar. 27, 1824.
William H., s. Consider Jr. and Betsey, Jan. 10, 1822. [[h. Elizabeth R.] ———, 1823, G.R.14.]
William Henry, s. Jonathan and Caroline W., Feb. 13, 1832.
William O., s. William O., yeoman, and Joanna, Sept. 1, 1844.
William Otis, s. Billings and Abigail B., Nov. 29, 1822.
William Pitt, s. Billings and A[b]igail B., Dec. 24, 1817.
William Pitt, ch. Billings, bp. Aug. 9, 1819. C.R.1.
Ziba, s. Seth and Susanna, Apr. 6, 1783.
Ziba, ch. Seth Jr. and Susanna, bp. Sept. 13, 1789. C.R.1.
[torn]ge, s. George and Naby, Dec. 9, 1797, in Cohassett.
———, s. Asa and Betsey, Feb. 16, 1817.
———, d. Martin D. and Debby, Nov. 7, 1819.
———, d. Francis and Clarissa, July 11, 1824.
———, ch. Robert C. and Martha, Jan. —, 1843.
———, ch. Jonathan and Caroline W., Jan. 1, 1844.
———, d. James H., carpenter, and Diana, Mar. 1, 1844. [Eliza, G.R.11.]

———, s. Jonathan and Caroline W. [dup. omits W.], Sept. 16, 1845.

MIGHELL (see Mighill), Grace, d. Tho[mas], bp. Feb. 10, 1688. C.R.2.
Samuell, s. Thomas, Dec. —, 1685. C.R.2.

MIGHILL (see Mighell), Mary, d. Thomas, May 27, 1683. C.R.2.

MILLER, Eunice K. [? m.], ———, 1837. G.R.6.
Olive P. [? m.], ———, 1843. G.R.6.

MINOT (see Minott), Sarah B. [————], w. Philip D., ——— [1812]. G.R.2.

MINOTT (see Minot), Angeline Frances, ch. Philip D. and Sarah, June 29, 1834.
Mary Jane, ch. Philip D. and Sarah, July 26, 1837.

MITCHEL (see Mitchell), Archibald, s. Archibald and Rhoda, Feb. 8, 1814. [Archibald Jr., G.R.2.]
Jane Tailor, d. Archibald and Rhoda, May 1, 1812.
Job, s. John and Lydia, July 19, 1743.
John, s. John and Lydia, Mar. 24, 1739.
Nancy, d. Archibald and Rhoda, Feb. 14, 1820.
Peter, s. Archibald and Rhoda, Oct. 20, 1826.
William, s. John and Lydia, Aug. 3, 1741.

MITCHELL (see Mitchel), Charles Henry, ch. Archabald and Mary, June 1, 1841.
Rhoda [————], w. Archibald, ——— [1775]. G.R.2.

MONAHAN, Patrick, "Co. C. 28 Mass Vols," ——— [1837]. G.R.10.

MONRO (see Monroe, Munroe), Benj[amin] Jr., s. Benj[amin] M., ——— [1833]. C.R.3.

MONROE (see Monro, Munroe), James Henry, ch. Lines T. and Almira, Oct. 20, 1838.
———, ch. Lines T. and Almira, Apr. 24, 1841.

MOOR (see Moore), John, s. John (More) and w. "from Ireland," bp. July 1, 1733. C.R.2.
Mary, d. John of Ireland, bp. July 18, 1731. C.R.2.

MOORE (see Moor), Thomas, s. W[illia]m (More) "a Stranger from Ireland," bp. Nov. 29, 1724. C.R.2.

MOREY, Penelope, d. Edmund, bp. Oct. 28, 1722. C.R.1.
Sarah, d. Edmund, bp. Oct. 28, 1722. C.R.1.
Susanna, d. Edmund, bp. Oct. 28, 1722. C.R.1.

MORIS (see Morris), William, s. Dennis and Ruth, bp. May 27, 1759. C.R.1.

MORRILL, Harriet, w. John Cushing, ———, 1808. G.R.2.

MORRIS (see Moris), Barnabas, s. William and Rhoda, Dec. 21, 1787.
Henry, s. William and Rebekah, Feb. 15, 1821, in Cohasset.
James H., s. William and Rebekah, Aug. 28, 1824.
John Gay, s. William and Rebekah, July 31, 1826.
Joseph Warren, s. William and Rebekah, Oct. 5, 1828.
Lemuel C., s. William and Rebekah, Aug. 22, 1819, in Cohasset.
Lemuel C., s. William and Rebekah, June 4, 1823.
Mary Adams, d. William and Rebekah, Mar. 25, 1833.
Nancy Rebekah, d. William and Rebekah, Aug. 1, 1830.
Ruth, d. William and Rhoda, July 26, 1789.
Sarah, d. William and Rhoda, Dec. 12, 1785.
William, s. William and Rhoda, Oct. 7, 1791.
William, s. William and Rebekah, Mar. 14, 1818, in Cohasset.

MORRISON, Sarah, d. Wid. Morrison, bp. May, 15, 1763. C.R.1.

MORSE, Mary, d. Marcus M., shoemaker (b. Hanover), and Mary A., Dec. 21, 1849, in S. Scituate.

MORTEN (see Morton), George, s. Gorge and Sarah, Nov. 6, 1747. [Morton, s. George, C.R.1.]
Rebecca, d. Gerorge and Sarah, Jan. 26, 1761.

MORTON (see Morten), Benjamin B., ch. John and Harriet A., Jan. 5, 1842.
Eli, s. George and Sarah, Apr. 13, 1758.
John, s. Gorge and Sarah, May 15, 1756.
Mary Ann, d. Silas and Elizabeth, Dec. 10, 1803.
Rebeccah, d. George, bp. June 5, 1763. C.R.1.
Sarah, d. Gorge and Sarah, Nov. 7, 1753.
Sarah E., ch. John and Harriet A., Aug. 17, 1843.

MOTT, Abigail, d. Stephen Jr. and Marcy, July 27, 1810, in Hull.
Alonzo, s. Joseph and Lydia, June 27, 1836.
Anna, d. Nath[anie]ll and Anna, Nov. 28, 1745. [Ann, d. Nath[anie]l, C.R.1.]
Anna, d. Nath[anie]ll and Anna, July 14, 1753. [Ann, d. Nath[anie]l, C.R.1.]
Areanna E., d. H. B. and M. N. [Jan. —, 1849]. G.R.2.
Atwood, s. Ebenezar [Ebenezer, C.R.1.] and Deborah, Sept. 18, 1736.
Betsey, d. Stephen and Nabby, Nov. 12, 1777. [Betsy, C.R.1.]
Deborah, d. Eben[eze]r and Deborah, Sept. 6, 1741.
Desire, d. John and Lydia, Dec. 15, 1744.

MOTT, Ebenezar, s. Eben[ezer] Jr., bp. Nov. 17, 1734. C.R.1.
Ebenezer, s. Ebenezer (Moott), Sept. 26, 1700.
Eliza, d. Stephen Jr., and Marcy, Apr. 20, 1802, in Hull.
Elizabeth, d. Ebenezer and Grace, July 17, 1716.
Elizabeth, d. John and Lydia, Oct. 11, 1747.
Fredrick, s. Joseph and Lydia, June 15, 1831, in Cohassett.
Grace, d. Ebenezer, Aug. 17, 1702.
Grace, d. Eben[eze]r and Deborah, Mar. 30, 1739.
Hannah, d. Atwood and Hannah, Feb. 8, 1763.
Hannah, [ch.] Atwood and Hannah, bp. Feb. 4, 1770. C.R.1.
Helen Mar, ch. Paul and Lydia, Jan. 16, 1843.
Henry, s. Joseph and Lydia, Jan. 25, 1825, in Cohassett.
Hosea B., ch. Joseph and Lydia, June 24, 1822, in Cohassett.
James Monroe, s. Stephen Jr. and Marcy, Oct. 15, 1822.
Jane, d. Stephen and Nabby, June 17, 1796.
John, s. Ebenezer and Grace, June 11, 1707.
John, s. John and Lydia [Lidia, C.R.1.], Dec. 15, 1732.
John, s. Stephen and Nabby, June 4, 1780.
Joseph, s. Stephen and Nabby, June 20, 1788.
Joseph Jr., s. Joseph and Lydia, Dec. 10, 1811, in Hingham.
Joseph Monrow, ch. Joseph Jr. and Judith, Feb. 12, 1840.
Joshua, s. Stephen and Nabby, Aug. 29, 1790.
Judith Annis, ch. Joseph Jr. and Judith, Mar. 29, 1843.
Leroy V., s. Paul, calker, and Lydia, July 7, 1847.
Lucy B., d. Paul, caulker (b. Hingham), and Lydia, Sept. 27, 1849.
Lucy Vinal, ch. Paul and Lydia, Sept. 27, 1849.
Lydia, d. John and Lydia, Aug. 18, 1734.
Lydia, d. Joseph and Lydia, Jan. 28, 1816, in Hingham.
Lydia Snow, d. Stephen and Nabby, Jan. 27, 1793.
Mabel N., d. Hosea, painter, and Mabel, Dec. 28, 1846.
Marcy Gould, d. Stephen Jr. and Marcy, Mar. 14, 1800, in Hull.
Martha Ann, d. Joseph and Lydia, Nov. 24, 1828, in Cohassett.
Martha Loring, d. Stephen Jr. and Marcy, Aug. 27, 1817. [w. James S. Litchfield, G.R.2.]
Mary, d. Ebenezer and Grace, Mar. 24, 1712–13.
Mary, d. Eben[ezer], bp. Nov. 17, 1734. C.R.1.
Mary, d. Stephen Jr. and Marcy, Oct. 14, 1804, in Hull.
Mary [———], w. Henry, ——— [1837]. G.R.2.
Mary L., ch. Paul and Lydia, Nov. 19, 1840.
Mercy [———], w. Stephen [Sept. —, 1779]. G.R.11.
Mercy Gould (see Marcy Gould Mott).
Micah, s. Ebenezer, bp. July 15, 1744. C.R.1.
Nabby, d. Stephen and Nabby, Jan. 6, 1774.
Nabby, ch. Stephen and w., bp. Apr. 14, 1776. C.R.1.

Mott, Nathanael, s. Ebenezer and Grace, June 23, 1720.
Nath[anie]ll, s. Nath[anie]ll and Anna, Sept. 21, 1749. [Nathaniel, s. Nath[anie]l, c.r.1.]
Otis, s. Joseph and Lydia, Aug. 11, 1819, in Cohassett.
Otis F., s. Otis, shoemaker, and Harriett N., Mar. 4, 1848.
Paul, s. Stephen and Nabby, Oct. 22, 1782.
Paul, s. Joseph and Lydia, Sept. 17, 1813, in Hingham.
Polly, d. Stephen and Nabby, Aug. 7, 1797.
Priscilla, [ch.] Atwood and Hannah, bp. Feb. 4, 1770. c.r.1.
Prissilla, d. Atwood and Hannah, July 22, 1760.
Rhoda, d. John and Lydia, Aug. 12, 1736.
Rhoda, d. Stephen and Nabby, May 6, 1785.
Ruth, d. John and Lydia, May 23, 1739.
Sarah, d. Atwood and Hannah, Nov. 16, 1758.
Sarah, [ch.] Atwood and Hannah, bp. Feb. 4, 1770. c.r.1.
Stephen, s. John and Lydia, May 29, 1741.
Stephen, s. John and Lydia, July 10, 1752.
Stephen, s. Stephen and Nabby, Sept. 15, 1775. [[h. Mercy] g.r.11.]
Stephen, s. Stephen Jr. and Marcy, Dec. 16, 1807, in Hull.
Thankfull, d. Ebenezer, bp. July 6, 1746. c.r.1.
Will[ia]m, s. Nath[anie]ll [Nathaniel, c.r.1.] and Anna, June 19, 1747.
William Wallace, ch. Joseph Jr. and Judith, Apr. 30, 1841.

MULLAN, James, s. Arthur and Mary, bp. Oct. 6, 1735. c.r.2.

MUNGO, E. R. [h. Mary T.] [Dec. —, 1790]. g.r.2.
Mary T. [————], w. E. R. [May —, 1798]. g.r.2.

MUNNIS, Addie Frances, ——— [1842]. g.r.2.

MUNROE (see Monro, Monroe), Ella I. [? J.], d. Lines T., farmer, and Almira, Sept. 24 [184–].
James Albert, s. James, shoemaker, and Mary, Aug. 30, 1844.
Joshua Litchfield, s. James (Monroe), shoemaker, and Mary, Jan. 29, 1848.
Mary A., d. James, cordwainer, and Nancy, May 21, 1846.
———, ch. James and Mary, ———, 1843.

MURPHY, Bridget Devlin [? m.], May 16, 1833. g.r.10.
Edward, Sept. 8, 1821. g.r.10.
John "Member of 28th. Mass. Vols.," ———, 1812, in Waterford, Ire. g.r.10.
Mary Kane [? m.], ———, 1825, in Galway, Ire. g.r.10.
Patrick, ———, 1819, in Waterford, Ire. g.r.10.
Peter, June 25, 1824. g.r.10.

MYER (see Majer), Rosabella, d. John, weaver (b. Germany), and Ann M. (b. England), June 8, 1849.

NAOMA, Thomas M., s. Thomas, sailor, and w., Feb. 12, 1848.

NASH, Abel, s. Simeon, bp. July 23, 1757. C.R.2.
Abigail, d. Elisha, bp. Sept. 19, 1756. C.R.1.
Bashaba, d. Noah, bp. Nov. 2, 1766. C.R.1. [Bathsheba, ch. Noah and Elizabeth (Cadworth), b. ——, 1765, G.R.2.]
Benjamin, s. Joseph Jr. and Lucy, May 25, 1803.
Betty, d. Noah and Eliza[beth], July 12, 1757. [Betsey, G.R.2.]
Charlotte A., ch. Lemuel M. and Mary, Aug. 6, 1831.
Church, ch. Simeon and Lydiah, bp. Aug. 10, 1746. C.R.2.
Clementine C. [? m.], ——, 1816. G.R.14.
David, s. Joseph and Hannah, May 11, 1712.
David, ch. Joseph and Hannah, bp. July 28, 1717. C.R.2.
David, s. David, bp. Feb. 11, 1753. C.R.1.
David, s. James and Ruth, June 14, 1794.
David, ch. James, bp. Mar. 25, 1796. C.R.1.
Debbe, d. Joseph, bp. May 13, 1781. C.R.1.
Debby Cushing, d. John and Debby, Oct. 17, 1797.
Deborah, d. Joseph and Deborah, Jan. 1, 1733.
Deborah, d. Joseph and Deborah, Dec. 28, 1736.
Deborah, d. Simeon, bp. Nov. 6, 1743. C.R.2.
Deborah, d. Joseph, bp. Oct. 13, 1765. C.R.1.
Deborah, d. James and Ruth, Feb. 29 [*sic*], 1791.
Deborah, ch. James, bp. Mar. 25, 1796. C.R.1.
Delight, d. Joseph and Deborah, Jan. 14, 1734.
Desire, d. Joseph and Thankful, bp. Mar. 5, 1758. C.R.1.
Ebenezer H., ch. Lemuel M. and Mary, May 28, 1829.
Elisha, s. Joseph and Hannah, July 4, 1722.
Eliza, d. John and Debby, Sept. 2, 1808.
Elizabeth, d. Joseph, Feb. 2, 1709–10.
Elizabeth, ch. Joseph and Hannah, bp. July 28, 1717. C.R.2.
Elizabeth, d. James and Sarah, Nov. 1, 1751.
Epherem, s. Joseph and Hannah, Jan. 19, 1715–16.
Eunice (see Unice).
Frederic Thayer, ——, 1849. G.R.14.
Hannah, d. Joseph, Mar. 7, 1704–5.
Hannah, ch. Joseph and Hannah, bp. July 28, 1717. C.R.2.
Hannah, ch. Hannah, wid., bp. June 30, 1745. C.R.1.
Hannah, d. Elisha, bp. Sept. 12, 1756. C.R.1.
Helen Louisa, Sept. 9, 1844. G.R.14.
Henry, s. John and Debby, Aug. 17, 1806.

NASH, Israel, s. Noah and Eliza[beth], Apr. 27, 1759. [bp. Apr. 22 [*sic*], C.R.1.] [Apr. 27, G.R.2.]
Israel, s. John and Debby, Mar. 8, 1811. [[h. Deborah Clapp Briggs] G.R.14.]
James, s. Joseph, Apr. 2, 1708.
James, ch. Joseph and Hannah, bp. July 28, 1717. C.R.2.
James, s. James and Sarah, Oct. 28, 1748.
James, s. James and Ruth, Nov. 1, 1779.
John, s. Joseph, Aug. 8, 1703.
John, ch. Joseph and Hannah, bp. July 28, 1717. C.R.2.
John, s. John and Hannah, Mar. 15, 1731.
John, ch. John and Hannah, bp. Dec. 2, 1733. C.R.1.
John, s. James and Sarah, Aug. 13, 1755.
John [May —, 1767]. G.R.2. [[h. Debby (Cushing)] May 29, G.R.14.]
John, s. John and Debby, July 29, 1799.
John Cushing, s. John K. and Sarah D., Feb. 26, 1839.
John King, s. John and Debby, Nov. 26, 1801.
Joseph, s. Joseph of Boston, June —, 1678.
Joseph, s. Joseph, Jan. 28, 1701–2.
Joseph, ch. Joseph and Hannah, bp. July 28, 1717. C.R.2.
Joseph, s. John and Hannah, Feb. 11, 1732.
Joseph, ch. John and Hannah, bp. Dec. 2, 1733. C.R.1.
Joseph, s. Joseph and Deborah, Feb. 4, 1739.
Joseph, s. Joseph, bp. Feb. 28, 1768. C.R.1.
Joseph, s. Solon and Sally, Apr. 9, 1795.
Joseph Parker, s. Joseph Jr. and Lucy, Dec. 18, 1800.
Joshua, s. James and Ruth, July 14, 1784.
Joshua, s. James, bp. Oct. 8, 1786. C.R.1.
Lemuel, s. Joseph Jr. and Lucy, July 1, 1806.
Lucy, d. Joseph and Deborah, Apr. 18, 1746.
Lucy, d. Joseph, bp. May 31, 1747. C.R.1.
Lucy, d. Noah and Eliza[beth], Feb. 27, 1761.
Lucy, d. Noah, bp. Oct. 23, 1763. C.R.1.
Lucy, d. Joseph [Joseph 2d, C.R.1.] and Lucy, Feb. 12, 1770.
Lucy, d. Solon and Sally, Sept. 21, 1797.
Lucy Ann, d. Joseph Jr. and Lucy, Feb. 5, 1811.
Lydia, d. Simeon, bp. July 23, 1757. C.R.2.
Mabel, d. Joseph Jr., bp. July 6, 1760. C.R.1.
Mary, d. Joseph and Hannah, Feb. 11, 1713–14.
Mary, d. Joseph and Hannah, Apr. 21, 1724.
Mary, d. James and Sarah, May 28, 1746.
Mercy, d. Joseph and Hannah, Feb. 25, 1718.
Mercy, d. Joseph and Deborah, Sept. 26, 1740. [Marcy, C.R.1.]

NASH, Miriam, d. David, bp. Sept. 7, 1746. C.R.1.
Nancy, d. Joseph, bp. Mar. 23, 1777. C.R.1.
Nancy, d. Joseph and Lucy, May 13, 1777.
Nathaniel Cushing, s. John and Debby, Apr. 6, 1804. [Nath[anie]ll Cushing, C.R.2.] [Nathaniel Cushing [h. Lucy T. (Briggs)], G.R.14.]
Noah, s. Jo[h]n and Hannah, Jan. 23, 1734. [h. Elizabeth (Cadworth), G.R.2.]
Noah, d. John, bp. July 20, 1735. C.R.1.
Noah, s. Noah, bp. Oct. 23, 1763. C.R.1. [Noah Jr., ch. Noah and Elizabeth (Cadworth), G.R.2.]
Oliver, ch. Simeon and Lydiah, bp. Aug. 10, 1746. C.R.2.
Penelope, d. David and Penelope, bp. Sept. 22, 1745. C.R.1.
Pricilla, d. John and Hannah, June 11, 1729.
Priscilla, ch. John and Hannah, bp. Dec. 2, 1733. C.R.1.
Rhoda, d. Joseph and Deborah, Feb. 14, 1742.
Ruth, d. James and Sarah, Dec. 13, 1758.
Ruth, d. James and Ruth, Aug. 28, 1777.
Sam[ue]ll, s. Simeon, bp. July 23, 1757. C.R.2.
Sarah, d. James and Sarah, Mar. 19, 1743.
Sarah, d. James, bp. June 3, 1744. C.R.1.
Sarah, d. James and Ruth, Jan. 8, 1788.
Sarah D. [? m.], ——, 1810. G.R.14.
Sarah M., ch. Lemuel M. and Mary, Oct. 30, 1839.
Seth, s. Jo[h]n, bp. May 31, 1738. C.R.1.
Simeon, s. Joseph and Hannah, May 8, 1717.
Simeon, s. Symion and Lydiah, bp. July 4, 1742. C.R.2.
Solon, s. Joseph [Joseph Jr., C.R.1.] and Lucy, Apr. 22, 1772.
Solon, s. Solon and Sally, May 1, 1800.
Thankful, d. Joseph 2d, bp. May 22, 1763. C.R.1.
Thomas, ch. Hannah, wid., bp. June 30, 1745. C.R.1.
Thomas, s. Simeon, bp. July 23, 1757. C.R.2.
Thomas, s. Joseph Jr. and Lucy, Sept. 13, 1808.
Thomas T., ch. Lemuel M. and Mary, July 6, 1838.
Tilon, s. Joseph [Joseph Jr., C.R.1.] and Lucy, Oct. 1, 1774.
Unice, d. Thomas and w., bp. July 26, 1767. C.R.1.
William, ch. Hannah, wid., bp. June 30, 1745. C.R.1.
William, s. Joseph Jr. and Lucy, Oct. 30, 1799.
William Agry, s. James and Ruth, Oct. 28, 1781.
William Henry, ——, 1847. G.R.14.
Zacheus, s. Jo[h]n and Hannah, July 12, 1736.
Zacheus, s. Jo[h]n, bp. May 31, 1738. C.R.1.
—— [——], w. ——, ——, 1797. G.R.6.
—— [h. ——], ——, 1807. G.R.6.

NASH, ——, s. ——, ——, 1828. G.R.6.
—— [——], w. ——, ——, 1832. G.R.6.
——, s. ——, ——, 1842. G.R.6.

NEAL (see Neale, Neel, Neele, Neil), Abagil, d. Job and Sarah, June 22, 1759.
Abigal, d. Joseph and Abigel, Feb. 6, 1721. [Abigail, d. Joseph and Abigail, C.R.2.]
Alice, d. Joseph Jr. and Alice, Sept. 2, 1741. [Allice "or Else," d. Joseph and Allice, C.R.2.]
Ann, d. Joseph Jr. and Alice, Feb. 3, 1738.
Anna, d. Job, bp. Oct. 26, 1755. C.R.2.
George, s. John "Late" of Ireland, bp. June 4, 1738. C.R.2.
Ichabod, s. John and Mary, bp. May 10, 1734. C.R.2.
Jane, d. John "Late" of Ireland, bp. Sept. 10, 1732. C.R.2.
Job, s. Joseph [s. Joseph and Abigail, C.R.2.], June 13, 1718.
Job, s. Job and Sarah, Sept. 22, 1746.
Job, s. Job and Sarah, Oct. 2, 1753.
John, s. John and Mary, bp. May 20, 1731. C.R.2.
John, s. John and Mary, bp. Apr. 29, 1732. C.R.2.
John, s. Job and Sarah, Dec. 12, 1744.
John, s. Joseph and Sarah, Mar. 9, 1795.
Joseph, s. Job and Sarah, Sept. 3, 1748.
Lucy, d. Job and Sarah, Sept. 28, 1761.
Lydia, d. Job and Sarah, Sept. 18, 1755.
Martha, d. John of Ireland, bp. Nov. 17, 1734. C.R.2.
Rebecca, d. Joseph and Alice, July 7, 1744.
Rebecca, d. Joseph and Allice, bp. May 11, 1746. C.R.2.
Sarah, d. Job and Sarah, Nov. 15, 1751.
Sarah, d. Joseph and Sarah, May 30, 1797.

NEALE (see Neal, Neel, Neele, Neil), Anne, d. Joseph, July 19, 1709.
Anne, ch. Joseph, bp. July 6, 1712. C.R.1.
John, s. Joseph, Nov. 7, 1705.
John, ch. Joseph, bp. July 6, 1712. C.R.1.
Joseph, s. Joseph, Sept. 29, 1707.
Joseph, ch. Joseph, bp. July 6, 1712. C.R.1.
Thomas, s. Joseph (Neal) and Abigail, Dec. 28, 1711.

NEEL (see Neal, Neale, Neele, Neil), Lydia, d. Joseph, Feb. 24, 1715–16. [Neale, C.R.1.]

NEELE (see Neal, Neale, Neel, Neil), Seth, s. Joseph and Abigall, Feb. 27, 1713. [Neale, C.R.1.]

SCITUATE BIRTHS 269

NEIL (see Neal, Neale, Neel, Neele), John, s. John and w. "(an Jreland man & woman)," bp. July 19, 1730. C.R.2.

NEW, Catherine M., ch. William E. and Eliza Ann, Apr. 15, 1835.

NEWALL (see Newel, Newell), Asenath, ch. Daniel and w., June 22, 1804.
Elizabeth, ch. Daniel and w., Feb. 9, 1798.
Fanny, ch. Daniel and w., Sept. 8, 1792.
Lucy, ch. Daniel and w., Nov. 12, 1808.
Mabel, ch. Daniel and w., Nov. 20, 1799.
Rebecca, ch. Daniel and w., July 16, 1794. [Rebeckah Newell [ch. Daniel and Susannah], G.R.8.]
Ruth, ch. Daniel and w., Apr. 18, 1796. [Newell [ch. Daniel and Susannah], G.R.8.]
Susan, ch. Daniel and w., Aug. 29, 1810.

NEWCOMB (see Newcombe, Newconb), Charles Henry, ch. Jacob C. and Roxana, Sept. 15, 1837.
David C. M., s. Enoch C., shoemaker (b. Hingham), and Sarah C. (b. Hingham), Dec. 23, 1849, in S. Scituate.
Eugene Clarance, d. Jacob C., shoemaker, and Roxana, Feb. 18, 1844.
Fred [ch. Capt. Hiram and Elizabeth S.], —— [1849]. G.R.2.
George Lewis, s. Levi and Joanne, Mar. 19, 1832. [s. Levi and Joann, C.R.1.] [Dr. George L., G.R.2.]
Henry Cook, s. Levi and Joanne [Joann, C.R.1.], Oct. 6, 1837.
Hiram, Capt. [h. Elizabeth S. (Low)], Sept. 24, 1822. G.R.2.
Joan [——], w. Levi [Mar. —, 1802]. G.R.2.
Joann Frances, d. Levi and Joanne, Jan. 8, 1829. [Joan Francis [*sic*], C.R.1.] [Joan F., d. Levi and Joan, G.R.2.]
John Briggs, s. Levi and Joanna, Nov. 27, 1840. [s. Levi and Joann, C.R.1.] ["7th Mass. Volunteers," G.R.2.]
Joshua, ch. Andrew and Mercy of Truerow, bp. Sept. 28, 1712. C.R.2.
Levi, h. Joan [Jan. —, 1791]. G.R.2.
Levi, s. Levi and Joanne, Feb. 8, 1822.
Levi, ch. Levi, bp. Aug. 4, 1827. C.R.1.
Martha Clara, d. Jacob, shoemaker (b. Hingham), and Roxanna, Oct. 30, 1848.
Mercy, ch. Andrew and Mercy of Truerow, bp. Sept. 28, 1712. C.R.2.
Sarah A., d. Levi and Joanna, Sept. 29, 1843. [Sarah Ann, d. Levi and Joann, C.R.1.]

NEWCOMB, Silas, s. Levi and Joanna [Joann, c.r.1.], Feb. 19, 1835.
Thomas Jefferson, ch. Jacob C. and Roxana, Aug. 18, 1840, in Hingham.
William James, s. Levi and Joanne, Mar. 28, 1824.
William James, ch. Levi, bp. Aug. 4, 1827. c.r.1.
Willy Augustus, s. William, shoemaker, and Ruth B. (b. Boston), June 14, 1849.
———, d. Levi and Joanne, July 5, 1827.
———, ch. Jacob C. and Roxana, June —, 1843.
———, ch. Jacob C., cordwainer, and Roxanna [dup. Roxana], Jan. —, 1845.

NEWCOMBE (see Newcomb, Newconb), Abigail, d. Andrew and Mercy of Truro, bp. Aug. 7, 1720. c.r.2.

NEWCONB (see Newcomb, Newcombe), Albert E., s. Jacob E., sailor, and Roxanna, Aug. 13, 1846.

NEWEL (see Newall, Newell), Barsheba, d. James, bp. Aug. 7, 1748. c.r.1.
Bashaba, [ch.] James Jr. dec'd and Jane, bp. Apr. 22, 1770. c.r.1.
Caleb, [ch.] James Jr. dec'd and Jane, bp. Apr. 22, 1770. c.r.1.
Daniel, s. James and Abigil, Dec. 6, 1752.
Daniel, s. Levi and Ruth, Apr. 21, 1772.
Jacob, [ch.] James Jr. dec'd and Jane, bp. Apr. 22, 1770. c.r.1.
James, s. James and Abigil, Dec. 23, 1740.
James, ch. James and Abigail, bp. Oct. 25, 1747. c.r.1.
James, [ch.] James Jr. dec'd and Jane, bp. Apr. 22, 1770. c.r.1.
Jenny, d. Wid. Newel, bp. Apr. 28, 1771. c.r.1.
Joshua, s. James and Abigil, Apr. 3, 1750.
Joshua, s. Mary, wid., bp. Dec. 6, 1772. c.r.1.
Levi, s. James and Abigil, July 19, 1746.
Levi, ch. James and Abigail, bp. Oct. 25, 1747. c.r.1.

NEWELL (see Newall, Newel), Anna, d. James and Mary, Jan. 26, 1703–4.
Basheba, d. Caleb, bp. Dec. 29, 1793. c.r.1.
Bathsheba, d. James and Mary, Mar. 2, 1706–7.
Hezekiah, s. James and Mary, May 8, 1702.
James, s. James and Mary, Jan. 6, 1699.
Jerusha, d. James and Mary, Sept. 29, 1691.
Joshua, s. James and Mary, Feb. 27, 1693.
Mary, d. James and Mary, Mar. 25, 1694.
Ruth, d. James and Mary, Nov. 7, 1695.
Ruth, d. Caleb and w., bp. Aug. 11, 1793. c.r.1.

NEWLAND, Lemuel, s. Marcy, bp. June 19, 1768. C.R.1.
Marcy, d. Priscilla, bp. July 29, 1739. C.R.1.

NEWMAN, Abigail, d. Thomas [of] Dorchester, bp. July 22, 1666. C.R.2.

NICHOLES (see Nicholles, Nicholls, Nichols, Nickalls, Nickolls, Nickols, Nicols), Sarah, d. Thomas, Mar. 25, 1668.

NICHOLLES (see Nicholes, Nicholls, Nichols, Nickalls, Nickolls, Nickols, Nicols), Joseph, s. Thomas, May 29, 1673.

NICHOLLS (see Nicholes, Nicholles, Nichols, Nickalls, Nickolls, Nickols, Nicols), Amos, s. Joseph and Bathsheba, Apr. 2, 1708. [Nickols, C.R.1.]
Caleb, s. Joseph and Bathsheba, Sept. 14, 1710. [Nicols, C.R.1.]
Noah, s. Joseph and Bathsheba, Feb. 6, 1712-13. [Nicols, C.R.1.]
Rachell, d. Joseph, Feb. 22, 1696-7.
Rebackah, d. Thomas, Mar. 17, 1670. [Rebecca Nicols, C.R.2.]
Susana, d. Thomas, Mar. 4, 1676.

NICHOLS (see Nicholes, Nicholles, Nicholls, Nickalls, Nickolls, Nickols, Nicols), Aderson F., ch. Benjamin and Sophronia, Oct. 24, 1843.
Andrew Jackson, ch. Benjamin and Sophronia, Oct. 13, 1840.
Bathsheba, d. Thomas, Mar. 24, 1681-2.
Benjamin, s. Noah Jr. and Bethiah, Dec. 31, 1807. [——, 1808, G.R.14.]
Benj[amin] Parker, ch. Benjamin and Sophronia, Jan. 1, 1837. [[h. Hannah C.] Dec. 31, G.R.19.]
Caleb, s. Caleb and Meriam [Mirriam, wid., C.R.1.], Mar. 4, 1776.
Caleb, s. Caleb and Rhoda, May 20, 1804.
Elias Oliver, ch. Benjamin and Sophronia, Apr. 1, 1839.
Elizabeth, d. Thomas, Sept. 12, 1690.
Hannah C. [——], w. Benjamin P., Nov. 4, 1844. G.R.19.
Henry, s. Caleb and Rhoda, Aug. 14, 1811.
Israel, s. Thomas, Sept. 12, 1683.
Israel, s. Noah Jr. and Bethiah, Jan. 26, 1805.
Israel, s. Israel and Ruth, Aug. 14, 1832.
Israell, s. Joseph, Jan. 14, 1705-6.
Jane W., ——, 1830. G.R.6.
Job, s. Joseph, May 2, 1716. [Nicols, C.R.1.]
Joseph, s. Joseph, July 6, 1699.
Leah, d. Joseph, May 21, 1703.
Mary, d. Thomas, Dec. 31, 1679.
Noah, s. Caleb and Meriam, July 29, 1773.

NICHOLS, Noah, ch. Mirriam, wid., bp. Nov. 10, 1776. C.R.1.
Noah Brooks, s. Noah Jr. and Bethiah, Jan. 25, 1801.
Noah Brooks, s. Israel and Ruth, Sept. 26, 1837.
Patience, d. Thomas, Feb. 25, 1685-6. [Nickolls, C.R.2.]
Penelope, ch. Mirriam, wid., bp. Nov. 10, 1776. C.R.1.
Penelope, d. Caleb and Rhoda, Feb. 21, 1806.
Polly, d. Caleb and Rhoda, May 4, 1809.
Rachel, ch. Mirriam, wid., bp. Nov. 10, 1776. C.R.1.
Rachel, d. Noah Jr. and Bethiah, June 20, 1802. [Nickols, C.R.1.]
Reuben, s. Caleb and Rhoda, Dec. 13, 1814.
Ruth [———], w. Israel, June —, 1809. G.R.6.
Ruth Merritt, d. Israel and Ruth, Dec. 4, 1830.
Sally, d. Noah Jr. and Bethiah, Apr. 30, 1810.
Sarah Elizabeth, d. Israel and Ruth, Sept. 29, 1834.
Sophronia [? m.], ———, 1815. G.R.14.
Sylva, d. Noah Jr. and Bethiah, Mar. 11, 1812.
Thomas, s. Joseph, June 10, 1701.
——— [———], mother of Israel, ——— [1775]. C.R.3.

NICKALLS (see Nicholes, Nicholles, Nicholls, Nichols, Nickolls, Nickols, Nicols), Bathsheba, d. Thomas, bp. June 19, 1681. C.R.2.
Susanna, d. Thomas, bp. June 19, 1681. C.R.2.

NICKOLLS (see Nicholes, Nicholles, Nicholls, Nichols, Nickalls, Nickols, Nicols), Israell, s. Thomas, bp. May 17, 1685. C.R.2.

NICKOLS (see Nicholes, Nicholles, Nicholls, Nichols, Nickalls, Nickolls, Nicols), Israel, s. Joseph, bp. Mar. 16, 1708. C.R.1.
Noah Brooks, s. Noah, bp. Nov. 28, 1802. C.R.1.

NICOLS (see Nicholes, Nicholles, Nicholls, Nichols, Nickalls, Nickolls, Nickols), Abigail, d. Noah and Zinthia. May 16, 1780. [Nichols, C.R.3. G.R.14.]
Anna, d. Rebecca, bp. Sept. 3, 1710. C.R.1.
Barsheba, d. Thomas, bp. Oct. 31, 1736. C.R.1.
Caleb, s. Israel and Eliza[beth], Mar. 17, 1741.
Cynthia (see Zinthea).
Elizabeth, ch. Thomas and w., bp. Oct. 8, 1732. C.R.1.
Elizabeth, d. Noah and Zinthia, Oct. 18, 1783.
Hannah, d. Israel and Eliza[beth], July 4, 1744. [Nichols, C.R.2.]
Israel, s. Israel and Eliza[beth], Oct. 2, 1748.
Jane, ch. Thomas and w., bp. Oct. 8, 1732. C.R.1.
Jane, ch. Israel of Hingham E. [East Church] and Desire, bp. May 25, 1746. C.R.1.

NICOLS, Joseph, ch. Thomas and w., bp. Oct. 8, 1732. C.R.1.
Lear, d. Israel and Eliza[beth], June 10, 1739.
Lucy, d. Noah and Zinthia, Oct. 5, 1787.
Mary, d. Tho[ma]s, bp. Oct. 30, 1743. C.R.1.
Noah, s. Israel and Eliza[beth], Sept. 1, 1746.
Rachel, d. Israel and Eliza[beth], Mar. 27, 1737.
Samuel, s. Israel and Eliza[beth], Oct. 13, 1752.
Thomas, s. Tho[ma]s, bp. July 6, 1745. C.R.1.
Thomus, s. Israel and Eliza[beth], Apr. 11, 1755. [Thomas, s. J[oh]n, C.R.2.]
Zinthea, d. Noah and Zinthie, Apr. 30, 1785.

NICOLSON, Hannah, d. Jom [? John or James], bp. May 16, 1756. C.R.2.
John, s. John and Lydia, Mar. 2, 1756.
Lydia, d. John and Lydia, July 9, 1752.
Lydia, d. John and Lydia, bp. Nov. 10, 1754. C.R.1.

NOONAN, Daniel, —— [1795], in Killeen, Co. Galway, Ire. G.R.10.
Mary [———], w. Daniel, —— [1796], in Killeen, Co. Galway, Ire. G.R.10.

NORRIS, Alfred H., —— [1815]. C.R.1.
Elizabeth Jenkins, d. W[illia]m L. and Serena, May 17, 1827.
Serena, d. William L. and Serena, Apr. 29, 1818, in Boston.
Serena, d. William L. and Serena, May 14, 1822, in Philadelphia.
William Mansfield, s. W[illia]m L. and Serena, Mar. 22, 1820, in Philadelphia.

NORTHEY (see Northy), Abraham, s. Elip[hale]t and Mary, Feb. 7, 1767.
Andrew, ch. Samuel and Eleanor, May 19, 1831.
Anna, d. James and Mary, Sept. 15, 1728.
Anna, d. Elip[hale]t and Mary, Jan. 4, 1770.
Betsey [dup. Betcy], d. Joseph and Betty, Feb. 17, 1787.
David, s. Elip[hale]t and Mary, Feb. 4, 1759.
Deborah, d. James and Mary, Apr. 20, 1732.
Ebenezer, s. James and Mary, Nov. 23, 1725.
Ebenezer, s. Capt. Joseph and Elezebeth, Jan. 30, 1786.
Edwin, ch. Samuel and Eleanor, Sept. 4, 1828.
Eleanor, d. Robert and Else, Apr. 12, 1791.
Elenor, d. Joseph and Elenor, June 13, 1739.
Eliphelet, s. Elip[hale]t and Mary, Aug. 10, 1757. [Eliphalet Northe, C.R.2.]

NORTHEY, Eliphelett, s. James and Mary, Jan. 24, 1723.
Eliza[beth], d. Joseph and Eliener, Mar. 12, 1747.
George, s. Joseph and Mercy P., Oct. 4, 1833.
Harriet Newell, ch. Samuel and Eleanor, Mar. 1, 1822.
Harvey, s. Joseph and Hannah, Dec. 16, 1826.
Harvey (see Hervey).
Henry Howard, s. Joseph and Hannah, Oct. 28, 1829.
Henry Howard, ch. Joseph, bp. July 15, 1832. C.R.1.
Hervey, ch. Joseph, bp. July 15, 1832. C.R.1.
James, s. James and Mary, Jan. 28, 1719.
Jane Parsons, ch. Samuel and Eleanor, Jan. 3, 1827.
Jesse, s. James and Mary, May 23, 1734.
John, s. Joseph and Eliner, July 26, 1759.
Joseph, s. Joseph and Elenor, June 24, 1733.
Joseph, s. Joseph and Eliener, Dec. 18, 1741.
Joseph, s. Robert and Else, Apr. 10, 1790.
Joseph, s. Joseph and Betty, May 6, 1794. ["foster bro. of poet Woodworth," C.R.1.]
Joseph, s. Joseph and Hannah, Oct. 10, 1824.
Joseph, s. Joseph, bp. July 15, 1832. C.R.1.
Lucy, ch. Samuel and Sally, Jan. 2, 1819.
Mary, d. Joseph and Elenor, Apr. 29, 1735.
Mary, d. Joseph and Eliener, Sept. 7, 1744.
Mary, d. Elip[hale]t and Mary, Sept. 3, 1761.
Mary Ann, ch. Samuel and Eleanor, Oct. 15, 1825.
Mehitable, d. James and Mary, Oct. 15, 1722.
Polly, d. Joseph and Betty, Sept. 9, 1792.
Ruth, d. Joseph and Eliener, Aug. 12, 1754.
Sally, d. Joseph and Betty, Dec. 20, 1789.
Sally, d. Robert and Else, May 8, 1793.
Sally, d. Robert and Else, June 10, 1798.
Sally, ch. Samuel and Sally, Feb. 20, 1821.
Samuel, s. Robert and Else, Apr. 11, 1786.
Samuel, s. Robert and Else, Apr. 25, 1795.
Samuel, ch. Samuel and Eleanor, Aug. 15, 1824.
Sarah, d. Joseph and Elenor, Mar. 7, 1736.
Thaddeus, ch. Samuel and Eleanor, Feb. 15, 1830.
William Hussey, ch. Samuel and Eleanor, Mar. 2, 1823.

NORTHY (see Northey), Anna, ch. James and Mary, bp. Oct. 18, 1741. C.R.2.
Bithiah, d. John, Dec. 18, 1682. [Bethiah, d. John and Sarah, Dec. 16, C.R.4.]
David, s. John [s. John and Sarah, C.R.4.], Apr. 6, 1678.

NORTHY, Deborah, ch. James and Mary, bp. Oct. 18, 1741. C.R.2.
Ebenezar, ch. James and Mary, bp. Oct. 18, 1741. C.R.2.
Eleanor, d. Robert and w., bp. Oct. 14, 1792. C.R.2.
Eliphalet, s. James and Mary, bp. Dec. 21, 1729. C.R.2.
James, s. John [s. John and Sarah, C.R.4.], Oct. 2, 1687.
James, s. Robert and w., bp. Oct. 14, 1792. C.R.2.
Jesse, ch. James and Mary, bp. Oct. 18, 1741. C.R.2.
John, s. John, Mar. 6, 1675. [s. John and Sarah, Mar. 6, 1674, C.R.4.]
Marcy (Nothe), d. Eliph[alet], bp. May 30, 1756. C.R.2.
Mary, d. James and Mary, Oct. 10, 1718.
Mary, ch. Joseph, bp. Nov. 14, 1737. C.R.1.
Mercy (see Marcy).
Robart, s. Elip[hale]t (Northey) and Mary, Sept. 12, 1764.
Sally, d. Robert and w., bp. Oct. 20, 1799. C.R.2.
Samuel, s. John, July 19, 1680 [Samuell, s. John and Sarah, C.R.4.]
Sarah, d. John, July 16, 1685. [d. John and Sarah, Aug. 16, C.R.4.]
Sarah, d. James and Mary, ——— [rec. between ch. b. Sept. 15, 1728, and ch. b. Apr. 20, 1732].
Sarah, ch. Joseph, bp. Nov. 14, 1737. C.R.1.
Sarah, ch. James and Mary, bp. Oct. 18, 1741. C.R.2.

NOTT, Azail Foster, s. Azail and Delilah, May 22, 1830. [Asahel F., h. Catharine M. ———, 1831, G.R.2.]
Catharine M. [———], w. Asahel F., ———, 1833. G.R.2.
Dawes Studley, s. Azael and Delilah, Sept. 26, 1834.
Francis, s. Azael and Delilah, Nov. 15, 1831.
John F., s. Ashael, farmer, and Delia, Sept. 29 [184–].

NUMUCH, Dinah, Indian, bp. Apr. 21, 1751. C.R.1.
Ezekiel, s. Dinah, bp. Apr. 21, 1751. C.R.1.

NUTTER, Lucy [———] of Boston, w. ———, ——— [1820]. C.R.1.

NYE, Ebenezer [h. Isabella Thayer (Fogg)], Mar. 20, 1819, in Falmouth. G.R.14.

OAKMAN, Elizabeth, [ch.] Sam[ue]l and Elizabeth of Marshfield, bp. Aug. 4, 1734. C.R.2.
Hiram, father of Col. O., ——— [1801]. C.R.1.
Israel, s. Sam[ue]l of Marshfield, bp. June 24, 1732. C.R.2.
Samuel, s. Sam[ue]l and Elizabeth of Marshfield, bp. Nov. 26 1727. C.R.2.

OAKMAN, Samyel Esq., Aug. 4, 1728. G.R.13.
Tobias, s. Samuel of Marshfield, bp. July 1, 1729. C.R.2.

OATICE (see Otis), Hanah, d. Steven, May 16, 1686.

OLDAM (see Oldham, Oldum, Ouldum), Abigaill, d. Thomas, Nov. 24, 1693.
Anna, d. Thomas, Mar. 19, 1695-6.
Desire, d. Thomas, Feb. 28, 1697-8.
Elizabeth, d. Thomas, May 5, 1677.
Elizabeth, d. Thomas, Oct. 4, 1691.
Grace, d. Thomas, Feb. 13, 1666-7. [Oldham, C.R.2.]
Hannah, d. Thomas, Mar. 7, 1664-5. [Oldhame, C.R.2.]
Isaac, s. Thomas, Apr. 9, 1669. [Isaack Oldham, C.R.2.]
Joshua, s. Thomas, June 20, 1684.
Lydia, d. Thomas, Aug. 11, 1679. [Oldham, C.R.2.]
Mary, d. Thomas, Aug. 20, 1658. [Oldham, C.R.2.]
Mary, d. Thomas, Apr. 1, 1686. [Holdum, d. Thomas Jr., C.R.2.]
Mercy, d. Thomas, July 28, 1689.
Ruth, d. Thomas, Dec. 5, 1674.
Sarah, d. Thomas, Mar. 13, 1670-1. [Oldham, C.R.2.]
Thomas, s. Thomas, Oct. 30, 1660. [Oldham, C.R.2.]
Thomas, s. Thomas, Jan. 30, 1698-9.

OLDHAM (see Oldam, Oldum, Ouldum), Elizabeth, d. Tho[mas], bp. Aug. 18, 1678. C.R.2.
Joseph, s. Jonathan and Patience, Sept. 1, 1780.
Joseph, s. Joseph and Gracey, Jan. 26, 1820.
Joshuah (Holdum), s. Thomas Jr., bp. Aug. 8, 1686. C.R.2.
Mehitabel, d. Joshua and Mehitabel, bp. Dec. 1, 1717. C.R.2.
Ruth, d. Tho[mas], bp. Aug. 18, 1678. C.R.2.
Ruth Bailey, d. Joseph and Ruth, Jan. 24, 1817.
Sarah, d. Thomas, bp. Apr. 5, 1662. C.R.2.
———, s. Joseph and Gracey, Jan. 21, 1822.

OLDUM (see Oldam, Oldham, Ouldum), Grace, d. Thomas, Feb. 27, 1703-4.

OLIVER, David, s. Thomas, Jan. 6, 1698-9.

ORCOT (see Orcott, Orcut, Orcutt), Martha, d. William, bp. Apr. 23, 1671. C.R.2.

ORCOTT (see Orcot, Orcut, Orcutt), Andrew, s. William of Marshfield, bp. Mar. 24, 1667. C.R.2.
John, s. William, bp. Apr. 18, 1669. C.R.2.
Joseph, s. William, bp. Dec. 9, 1672. C.R.2.

ORCUT (see Orcot, Orcott, Orcutt), Benjemen, s. William, bp. Mar. 9, 1680. C.R.2.
Deborah, d. William, bp. Oct. 7, 1683. C.R.2.
Elizabeth, d. William, bp. July 16, 1682. C.R.2.
Hanah, d. William, bp. Apr. 11, 1675. C.R.2.
Mary, d. William, bp. Apr. 11, 1675. C.R.2.
Thomas, s. William, bp. Oct. 2[worn], 1677. C.R.2.

ORCUTT (see Orcot, Orcott, Orcut), Deborah [———], w. Hosea V., ———, 1817. G.R.2.
Elijah, s. Emerson and Mary, June 5, 1737.
Elisha, s. Rhoda, Jan. 27, 1790.
Emerson, s. Emerson and Mary, July 24, 1745. [Orcut, C.R.1.]
Hannah, d. Emerson and Mary, Feb. 28, 1740.
Hannah, d. Seth and Rhoda, Apr. 6, 1785. [w. Josiah Stoddard, Apr. 5, G.R.14.]
William, s. Seth and Rhoda, Dec. 5, 1781.

O'REILLY, ———, ——— [1846]. C.R.1.

OSBORN (see Osborne, Ozburn), Celia E., ch. Henry A. and Clarissa, Oct. 14, 1841.
Clarissa, ch. Henry A. and Clarissa, Sept. 19, 1839.
Ebenezer, s. Ebenezer and w., bp. Aug. 1, 1802. C.R.2.
Ebenezer, s. Ebenezer Jr. and Mary, Oct. 13, 1825.
Edwin Francis, s. Caleb, shoemaker, and Mary A., May 23, 1844.
Edwin H., s. Joseph and Sophrona, Feb. 16, 1837.
Elizabeth, d. Ebenezer Jr. and Mary, Nov. 6, 1827.
Elizabeth W. [———], w. ———, ——— [1782]. C.R.1.
Esther W., ch. Henry A. and Clarissa, Dec. 9, 1843.
George, s. Ebenezer Jr. and Mary, Feb. 19, 1830.
Mabel, d. Eben[eze]r and Elizabeth, May 11, 1825.
Mary, d. Ebenezer Jr. and Mary, Sept. 13, 1823.
Olive F. Hudson, d. Eben[eze]r Jr. and Mary, Apr. 20, 1833.
Sarah Maria, d. Joseph and Sophrona, Jan. 10, 1834, in Hingham.
Sophrona E. L., d. Joseph and Sophrona, Jan. 10, 1829, in Hingham.
William Hyland, ch. Caleb and Mary A., Dec. 22, 1840.

OSBORNE (see Osborn, Ozburn), Caleb Leach, s. Eben[eze]r and Elizabeth, July 4, 1816.
Celia Elizabeth, d. Henry and Mary E., Oct. 16, 1833.
Edward F. [June —, 1844]. G.R.2.
Edwin H. [Feb. —, 1835]. G.R.2.
Elizabeth [———], w. Ebenezer, ——— [1781]. G.R.2.

OSBORNE, Henry Arnold, s. Eben[eze]r and Elizabeth, Apr. 20, 1814.
Laban Rose, s. Eben[eze]r and Elizabeth, June 4, 1819.
Mary A. [———], w. Caleb, —— [1821]. C.R.3.
William Hyland, ch. Caleb and Mary A., bp. July 10, 1842. C.R.3.

OSGOOD, David, s. Robert, Dec. 2, 1700.

OTIS (see Oatice), Abigail (see Nabby).
Abigail [———], w. Hon. Cushing, M.D., —— [1775]. G.R.14.
Abigail, [twin] d. Ensign and Lucy, Nov. 16, 1794.
Abigail Brooks, d. Ensign Jr. and Lucy, Jan. 2, 1816.
Abigail Ruth, d. David Jr. and Ruth, Apr. 16, 1820.
Abigail Thaxter, d. Joshua Jr. and Mary, Feb. 23, 1792. [w. Milton Litchfield, G.R.2.]
Abigail Tilden, d. Cushing [Dr. Cushing, C.R.2.] and Abigail, Jan. 25, 1811.
Abigall, d. Job, Aug. 28, 1703.
Abijah, ——, 1754. G.R.6.
Abijah, s. Abijah and Mary, Feb. 24, 1797.
Abijah, s. Abijah Jr. and Mary, July 13, 1828.
Adam, s. David and Mary, Oct. 2, 1798.
Almeda Little, d. James L. and Almeda, Jan. 27, 1829.
Almeda Little, d. Almeda, wid., bp. Nov. 4, 1832. C.R.1.
Alvin Hatch, s. Howland Jr., lumber dealer, and w., Sept. 27, 1848.
Amelia Mackey, d. Howland and Susan C., Aug. 25, 1833.
Amey, d. Ephraim and Sarah, Apr. 29, 1777. [Amy, C.R.4.]
Amos, s. Ensign, bp. June 12, 1737. C.R.1.
Amos, s. Ignatius and Thankful, bp. May 21, 1758. C.R.1.
Amos, s. Ignatious, bp. July 21, 1765. C.R.1.
Amos, ——, 1804. G.R.6.
Amos Shav, s. Abijah and Mary, Sept. 13, 1804.
Ann Smith, d. David Jr. and Ruth, July 4, 1816.
Anne, d. Joseph, Sept. 21, 1702.
Anne Vinal, d. David and Mary, May 2, 1794.
Barnabas, s. Joseph, bp. May 9, 1756. C.R.1.
Benjamin, s. Prince and Ruthy, Aug. 21, 1786.
[B]enjamin, s. Paul and Lucy, July 11, 1799.
Benjamin, s. David Jr. and Ruth, May 24, 1811.
Benjamin Howland, s. Prince H. and Hannah, May 6, 1817, in Canton.
Bethiah, d. Joseph, Nov. 20, 1703.
Betsey, d. John and Winnit, Sept. 26, 1791.

OTIS, Betty, d. David and Mary, July 31, 1785.
Celia Little, ch. David Jr. and Lucy, Apr. 20, 1841.
Celia Little, d. David Jr., master mariner, and Lucy, June 12, 1848.
Celia Little, ch. David Jr. and Lucy, ——— [rec. after ch. b. May 24, 1843].
Charles, s. Joseph, bp. Feb. 5, 1743. C.R.1.
Charles, s. Joseph, bp. Oct. 25, 1747. C.R.1.
Charles, s. Stephen, bp. Nov. 26, 1759. C.R.1.
Charles, s. Joseph Jr., bp. Apr. 18, 1779. C.R.1.
Cushing, s. Dr. James and Lucy, Mar. 7, 176[torn] [1769].
Cushing, ch. John C. and Philenia, Oct. 7, 1828.
Daniel, s. Eph[rai]m and Sarah, Nov. 6, 1788.
Daniel [h. Mary], ——— [1790]. G.R.21.
Daniel G., s. Daniel and Mary, Sept. 8, 1826.
David, s. Job, Aug. 5, 1716.
David, s. David and Mary, Mar. 3, 1774.
David, s. David Jr. and Ruth, Aug. 14, 1804.
David Harris, s. Ephraim and Sarah, Apr. 4, 1775.
Deborah, d. Joseph, Apr. 24, 1694.
Deborah, d. Isaac and Deborah, Oct. 16, 1723.
Deborah, d. Ignatius, bp. July 1, 1770. C.R.1.
Deborah, d. David and Mary, Oct. 20, 1777.
Deborah, d. Abijah and Mary, Sept. 12, 1806.
Delight, d. Joseph, Dec. 19, 1706.
Desire, d. Insine, Dec. 8, 1714.
Desire, d. Ensine, bp. June 9, 1717. C.R.1.
Desire, twin d. Ensigne [Ensign, C.R.1.] and Mary, Apr. 17, 1729.
Desire, d. Joshua and Hannah, Aug. 23, 1741.
Desire, d. Noah [Capt. Noah, C.R.1.] and Phebe, July 30, 1779.
Dorothy, d. Joseph, Apr. 24, 1698.
Edwin, s. Howland and Polly, June 9, 1819.
Elce, d. David and Mary, Jan. 4, 1788.
Elisabath, d. Joseph, Sept. 2, 1700.
Elisha, s. David and Mary, Nov. 15, 1778 [*sic*, see Mary].
Elisha, s. David Jr. and Ruth, Jan. 8, 1809.
Eliza Adam, d. Howland and Susan C., Dec. 25, 1831.
Elizabeth (see Elisabath).
Elizebeth, d. James and Lucy, Apr. 25, 1771.
Ellen M. [———], w. John F., ———, 1832. G.R.14.
Elsie (see Elce).
Ensign (see Insigne).
Ensign, s. Ensign and Mary, Apr. 25, 1723. [Ensine, s. Ensine, C.R.1.]

OTIS, Ensign, s. John and Jene, Jan. 9, 1747.
Ensign, ch. John and Jane, bp. Sept. 15, 1751. C.R.1.
Ensign Jr., s. Ensign and Lucy, Aug. 13, 1777. [[h. Lucy] G.R.6.]
Ephraim, s. Job, July 28, 1708.
Ephraim, s. Ephraim and Rachel, bp. June 9, 1734. C.R.2.
Ephraim, s. Ephr[ai]m and Sarah, Dec. 23, 1772, in Providence, R.I.
Ephraim, s. Daniel and Mary, June 18, 1819. [Ephriam, C.R.4.]
Eunice, d. David and Mary, May 27, 1796.
Ezekiel, s. Joshua Jr. and Mary, Feb. 8, 1783.
Fanna, d. Ignatius, bp. Dec. 4, 1763. C.R.1.
Franklin, s. John Jr. and Hannah, Feb. 16, 1806.
Genne, [twin] d. Ensign and Lucy, Nov. 16, 1794.
George, s. Joshua and Hannah, Sept. 20, 1744.
George, s. Joshua Jr. and Mary, Nov. 20, 1770.
George, ch. Joshua Jr. and w., bp. Mar. 5, 1775. C.R.1.
George, s. John T. and Sarah W., Dec. 23, 1830.
George A., s. Ephraim and Sarah, Aug. 29, 1781.
George Woshenton, s. Joshua Jr. and Mary, July 26, 1775.
Hannah, d. Joseph [Joseph Esq., C.R.1.], Dec. 10, 1709.
Hannah, d. Nathan[ie]ll and Hannah of New-London, bp. Sept. 7, 1718. C.R.2.
Hannah, d. Ensine, bp. Apr. 16, 1722. C.R.1.
Hannah, d. Isaac and Deborah, Mar. 9, 1730.
Hannah, d. Joshua and Hannah, May 3, 1739.
Hannah, d. Joshua and Hannah, July 28, 1751.
Hannah, d. Dr. James and Lucy, Feb. 24, 1767.
Hannah, d. John and Hannah, July 13, 1803.
Hannah Ensign, d. Ensign Jr. and Lucy, Mar. 7, 1807.
Harrison, s. John Jr. and Hannah, Apr. 5, 1811.
Harrison, s. John Jr., bp. Sept. 12, 1822. C.R.1.
Henry, s. Paul and Lucy, July 18, 1796.
Henry T. [ch. Ensign Jr. and Lucy], ——, 1814. G.R.6.
Henry T., s. Benj[amin] and Betsey A., May 9, 1845.
Henry Thomas, s. Ensign Jr. and Lucy, Dec. 7, 1813.
[H]ervy, s. Paul and Lucy, Sept. 19, 1802.
Howland, s. David and Mary, Feb. 7, 1790. [Capt. Howland [h. Polly], G.R.6.]
Howland, s. Howland and Polly, Mar. 8, 1817.
Ignatius, s. Ensign and Mary, Feb. 2, 1731.
Ignatius, s. Ensign, bp. July 30, 1732. C.R.1.
Insigne, s. Steven, Jan. 29, 1691.
[I]saac, s. Isaac and Deborah, Sept. 1, 1719.
Isaac, ch. Isaac and Deborah, bp. May 17, 1724. C.R.2.

OTIS, Isaac, twin ch. Ensign, bp. Oct. 4, 1727. C.R.1.
Isaac, s. Stephen, ———.
James, s. Joseph, Jan. 21, 1692–3.
James, s. Isaac and Deborah, Apr. 22, 1733. [bp. Apr. 19 [*sic*], C.R.2.]
James, s. Isaac and Deborah, Sept. 3, 1734.
James, s. Dr. James and Lucy, Apr. 21, 1765.
James, s. Abijah Jr. and Mary, Mar. 16, 1825, in Leeds, Eng.
James Edwin, s. Edwin, ship carpenter, and Margaret A. (b. Boston), Apr. 11, 1848.
James Little, s. Ensign Jr. and Lucy, Mar. 11, 1803.
Jane A., ch. Elisha and Mary B., Oct. 3, 1843.
Jane Turner, d. Ensign Jr. and Lucy, Nov. 8, 1818.
Jane Turner, d. Ensign Jr., bp. June 3, 1821. C.R.1.
Jane Willis, ch. John C. and Philenia, Mar. 31, 1831.
Jenny (see Genne).
Job, s. John, Mar. 20, 1677.
Job, s. Job, Mar. 28, 1702.
Job, s. Ignatius, bp. Mar. 14, 1779. C.R.1.
Job, s. Ephraim and Sarah, June 25, 1783.
Job, s. David and Mary, Jan. 21, 1792.
Job [h. Lydia], ———, 1802. G.R.6.
Job P., May 30, 1831. G.R.6.
Job Prince, s. Abijah and Mary, Mar. 11, 1802.
Job Prince, ch. Job P. and Lydia, May —, 1833.
John, s. Steven, Apr. 7, 1694.
John, s. Ensign and Mary, Apr. 11, 1725.
John, s. Ensign, bp. July 17, 1726. C.R.1.
John, s. John and Jane, Apr. 16, 1750.
John, ch. John and Jane, bp. Sept. 15, 1751. C.R.1.
John, s. Joseph and Mercy, July 9, 1754.
John, s. Noah and Febe, Feb. 17, 1769.
John, ch. Capt. Noah and w., bp. June 2, 1776. C.R.1.
John, s. John and Winnet, Jan. 9, 1788.
John, s. Joseph and Sarah N., May 2, 1834.
John Cushing, s. John Jr. and Hannah, Nov. 11, 1796.
John Cushing, ch. John Jr., bp. June 7, 1801. C.R.1.
John Ensign, s. Ensign Jr. and Lucy, Mar. 26, 1811. [———, 1812, G.R.6.]
John Forthergill, s. Daniel and Mary, Sept. 15, 1824. [[h. Ellen M.] G.R.14.] [John Fothergill, C.R.4.]
John Turner, s. Abijah and Mary, Apr. 30, 1799.
John Turner, s. John T. and Sarah W., July 3, 1822.
Johua, s. Stephen, ———.

OTIS, Joseph, s. Capt. Stephen, bp. June 20, 1708. C.R.1.
Joseph, s. [Capt. Stephen, C.R.1.] Stephen and Hannah, Mar. 16, 1709–10.
Joseph, s. Joseph, Oct. 1, 1712.
Joseph, ch. Joseph, bp. June 13, 1714. C.R.1.
Joseph, s. Joseph and w., bp. May 15, 1743. C.R.1.
Joseph, s. John and Winnet, Jan. 28, 1799.
Joshua, s. Capt. Stephen, bp. June 28, 1713. C.R.1.
Joshua, s. Joshua and Hannah, Apr. 11, 1737.
Joshua, s. Joshua and Hannah, Apr. 20, 1748.
Joshua, s. Josepha [*sic*, Joshua] Jr. and Mary, Mar. 27, 1778.
[J]osiah, s. Isaac and Deborah, Oct. 8, 1721.
Josiah, s. Isaac and Deborah, May 4, 1725.
Josiah Lyman, s. Prince H. and Hannah, June 25, 1821, in Augusta, Ga.
Judith, d. David and Mary, Mar. 15, 1782.
Lamuel, s. Joshua Jr., bp. Oct. 8, 1786. C.R.1.
Laura Cooper, d. Abijah Jr. and Mary, Aug. 20, 1836.
Lemuel, s. Prince and Ruthy, Sept. 6, 1783.
Lemuel Thomas, ch. David Jr. and Lucy, May 24, 1843.
Lidiah, d. Nathaniell, Jan. 24, 1716. [Lydiah, d. Nathan[ie]ll and Hannah, C.R.2.]
Lucy, d. Joshua, bp. Aug. 30, 1741. C.R.1.
Lucy, d. James and Lucy, June 15, 1763.
Lucy, d. Ensign, bp. Feb. 6, 1776. C.R.1.
Lucy [———], w. Ensign Jr., ———, 1782. G.R.6.
Lucy, d. Ensign and Lucy, Aug. 25, 1789.
Lucy Ann, ch. David Jr. and Lucy, June 4, 1837.
Lucy Bailey, d. Paul and Mable, May 22, 1809.
Lucy Little, d. Ensign Jr. and Lucy, Feb. 2, 1805.
Lydia (see Lidiah).
Lydia, d. Ignatius, bp. July 19, 1772. C.R.1.
Lydia [———], w. Job, ———, 1808. G.R.6.
Lydia Clapp, ch. Job P. and Lydia, Oct. —, 1834.
Lydia Dug[la]s, d. Abijah Jr. and Mary, Sept. 21, 1838.
Lydia James, d. Ensign Jr. and Lucy, Feb. 5, 1809.
Marcy, d. Job, Dec. 12, 1700.
Marcy, d. John and Winnet, Feb. 20, 1782.
Maria Thomas, d. James L. and Almeda, Aug. 29, 1830.
Margaret A., d. Edwin and Margaret Ann [written in pencil], **Jan.** 12, 1845.
Martha Watson, d. Abijah Jr., and Mary, July 31, 1832.
Mary, d. Steven, July 7, 1689.
Mary, d. Joseph, Mar. 20, 1696.

OTIS, Mary, d. Job, Nov. 26, 1705.
Mary, twin ch. Ensign, bp. Oct. 4, 1727. C.R.1.
Mary, twin d. Ensigne [Ensign, C.R.1.] and Mary, Apr. 17, 1729.
Mary, d. Jane, wid., bp. Dec. 30, 1752. C.R.1.
Mary, d. Ignatius, bp. Apr. 19, 1767. C.R.1. [d. Ignatius and Thankful [Mar. —], G.R.14.]
Mary, ———, 1771. G.R.6.
Mary, d. Joshua Jr. and Mary, June 28, 1773.
Mary, ch. Joshua Jr. and w., bp. Mar. 5, 1775. C.R.1.
Mary, d. David and Mary, Jan. 9, 1779 [*sic*, see Elisha].
Mary [————], w. Daniel, Feb. —, 1787, in New Bedford. C.R.4.
Mary, ———, 1795. G.R.6.
Mary Franklin, d. Paul and Mable, Oct. 25, 1811.
Mary Little, d. Joseph and Sarah N., Apr. 14, 1840.
Mary Turner, d. Abijah and Mary, Nov. 20, 1795.
Mary Vinal, d. David Jr. and Ruth, Sept. 11, 1806. [w. Russel Cooke, G.R.7.]
Mary Watson, d. Abijah Jr. and Mary, July 30, 1830.
Matilda Wade, d. David Jr. and Ruth, Aug. 30, 1813.
Mercy, ———, 1678. G.R.6.
Mercy (see Marcy).
Mercy, d. Joseph, bp. June 9, 1745. C.R.1.
Molly, d. Joseph, bp. Mar. 16, 1760. C.R.1.
Nabbe, d. Isaac and Deborah, Aug. 12, 1739. [Nabby, d. Dr. Isaac and Deborah, C.R.2.]
Nabbe, ch. Joseph Jr., bp. June 9, 1776. C.R.1.
Nabby, d. Dr. James and Lucy, Oct. 11, 177[3]. [Abigail [w. Seth Foster], P.R.5.]
Nabby, d. John and Winnet, Mar. 11, 1793.
Nathanaell, s. Joseph, Jan. 30, 1689-90.
Noah, s. Ensign, bp. June 30, 1734. C.R.1.
Noah, s. Noah and Febe, Nov. 27, 1766.
Noah, s. John Jr. and Hannah, Mar. 6, 1801.
Noah F., ch. John C. and Philenia, Mar. 4, 1835.
Oliver, s. Ignatius, bp. June 1, 1760. C.R.1.
Oliver, s. Ignatius, bp. Dec. 18, 1768. C.R.1.
Phebe, d. Noah and Phebe, Dec. 15, 1770.
Phebe, ch. Capt. Noah and w., bp. June 2, 1776. C.R.1.
Polle, d. Joshua and Mary, June 28, 1773.
Polley, d. Ephraim and Sarah, Aug. 5, 1770, in Providence, R.I.
Polley, d. Howland and Polly, Oct. 20, 1814.
Polly, d. David and Mary, Feb. 16, 1776.
Polly, d. John and Winnet, Feb. 10, 1784.
Prince Howland, s. Prince and Ruthy, Feb. 24, 1781.

OTIS, Priscila, d. Job and Mercy, Nov. 18, 1721. [Priscilla, c.r.1. g.r.6.]
Rachel Turner, d. Abijah and Mary, Oct. 27, 1800.
Rachell, d. Joseph, Dec. 1, 1713. [Rachel, c.r.1.]
Ruth, d. Job, Mar. 13, 1712. [w. Dr. Benjamin Stockbridge, g.r.6.]
Ruthy, d. Prince and Ruthy, Oct. 29, 1779.
Salle Barker, d. Joshua Jr., bp. Aug. 27, 1780. c.r.1.
Salley, d. John Jr. and Hannah, Jan. 31, 1809.
Sally, d. John and Winnet, Dec. 15, 1786.
Sally Barker, d. Joshua Jr. and Mary, Dec. 3, 1789.
Samuel, s. Joshua Jr. and Mary, May 18, 1785.
Samuel (see Lamuel).
Samuel Jenkins, s. John T. and Sarah W., Sept. 9, 1827.
Sarah, d. Job, Feb. 27, 1714.
Sarah, d. Job, Apr. 16, 1719.
Sarah, d. Noah and Phebe, Sept. 8, 1774.
Sarah, ch. Capt. Noah and w., bp. June 2, 1776. c.r.1.
Sarah, d. John Jr., bp. Sept. 12, 1822. c.r.1.
Sarah Ellms, d. Joseph and Sarah N., Apr. 18, 1831.
Sarah Foster, d. Joseph and Sarah N., Apr. 21, 1828.
Sarah H., d. Daniel and Mary, July 23, 1830.
Sarah Jenkins, d. John T. and Sarah W., July 9, 1824.
Sarah W. [———], w. Capt. John [Dec. —, 1799]. g.r.6.
Sarah White, d. John T. and Sarah W., Jan. 9, 1830.
Silas, s. John and Winnet, Apr. 12, 1795.
Sophia, d. John and Winnet, Apr. 5, 1794.
Stephen, s. Stephen, Nov. 3, 1697.
Stephen, s. Isaac and Deborah, Nov. 4, 1728.
Stephen, s. Eph[rai]m and Sarah, July 26, 1785.
Susan Maria, d. Howland and Susan C., Oct. 10, 1828, [in] Boston.
Thomas, s. Dr. James and Lucy, July 15, 1776.
Thomas, s. Daniel and Mary, July 12, 1822.
Thomas, s. David Jr. and Ruth, Mar. 23, 1823.
Thomas, s. Joseph and Sarah N., Jan. 24, 1842.
Thomus, s. Isaac and Deborah, May 29, 1736. [Thomas, ch. Dr. Isaac, c.r.2.]
Thomus, s. Isaac and Deborah, June 20, 1738. [Thomas, c.r.2.]
Washington, s. Joshua Jr., bp. Aug. 6, 1775. c.r.1.
William, s. Isaac and Deborah, May 23, 1726.
[W]illiam, s. Paul and Mable, Apr. 16, 1807.
William Watson, s. Abijah Jr. and Mary, Aug. 29, 1834.
Winnet, d. John and Winnet, June 12, 1780.
———, ch. Abijah Jr. and Mary, Jan. 20, 1841.

OULDUM (see Oldam, Oldham, Oldum), Calib, s. Thomas (Oldum), Jan. 27, 1701–2.

OZBURN (see Osborn, Osborne), Abigail Leach, d. Eben[eze]r and Elizabeth, Jan. 19, 1806.
Deborah, d. Eben[eze]r and Elizabeth, Aug. 19, 1811.
Ebenezer, s. Eben[eze]r and Elizabeth, May 28, 1801.
Eliza, d. Eben[eze]r and Elizabeth, Sept. 19, 1803. [Osborn, C.R.2.]
Joseph, s. Eben[eze]r and Elizabeth, Feb. 19, 1808.

PACKARD, Isaac B. [Mar. —, 1808]. G.R.14.

PAINE, Alfred Davis, ch. Alfred and Sophia, Mar. 1, 1839.
Lydia Holbrook, ch. Alfred and Sophia, Dec. 30, 1834.
Reuben H., ch. Alfred and Sophia, Dec. 10, 1843.

PALMER, Alice, d. John Jr. and Mary, Aug. 10, 1712.
Alice, d. John and w., bp. Aug. 21, 1715. C.R.2.
Amasa [h. Mary] [Feb. —, 1793]. G.R.15.
Anna, ch. John and Mary, bp. Oct. 8, 1710. C.R.2.
Anna, d. Sam[ue]l and Ann, bp. May 24, 1730. C.R.2.
Anna, d. Bezeliel [Bezaliel, C.R.2.] and Anna, Dec. 5, 1735.
Benja[min], s. Bezeliel [Bezalial, C.R.2.] and Anna, Jan. 18, 1737.
Benja[min], s. Bezeliel and Anna, Mar. 20, 1739.
Benjamin, [ch.] Bezalael and Anna, bp. May 30, 1742. C.R.2.
Bezaleel, s. John, June 10, 1675.
Bezaleel, s. Bezaleel and Elizabeth, July 14, 1706.
Bezaliel, ch. Bezaliel and Anna, bp. July 25, 1731. C.R.2.
Bezeliel, s. Bezeliel and Anna, Oct. 10, 1728.
Deborah, d. Elnathan and Mercy, Aug. —, 1710.
Deborah, ch. Elnathan and Mercy, bp. Sept. 4, 1715. C.R.2.
Elisha, s. Samuell and Anna, bp. May 8, 1720. C.R.2.
Elizabeth, d. John, Aug. 8, 1673.
Elnathan, s. John, Mar. 10, 1665–6.
Ephraim, s. Sam[ue]l and Anne, bp. Jan. 8, 1722–3. C.R.2.
Ephraim, s. Joseph and Jane, bp. Apr. 22, 1744. C.R.2.
Esther, w. Freeman Foster, Jan. 10, 1778. P.R.5.
Experience, d. John, Mar. 31, 1679.
Experience, ch. Joseph and Mary, bp. July 1, 1739. C.R.2.
Ezekiel, ch. Elnathan and Mercy, bp. Sept. 4, 1715. C.R.2.
Ezekiell, s. Elnathan and Mercy, Oct. 15, 1701.
Hannah, d. John, Mar. 25, 1671.
Hannah, d. John Jr., Aug. 8, 1695.
Huldah, d. Bezeliel [Bezaliel, C.R.2.] and Anna, Apr. 3, 1732.

PALMER, Huldah, d. Bezelael, bp. Oct. 5, 1755. C.R.2.
Isaac, ch. Joseph and Mary, bp. July 1, 1739. C.R.2.
Jane, d. Joseph and Jane, bp. June 2, 1751. C.R.2.
John, s. John, Mar. 17, 1668–9.
John, s. John Jr. and Mary, May —, 1706.
John, ch. John and Mary, bp. Sept. 23, 1711. C.R.2.
Joseph, s. Samuel and Anne [s. Sam[ue]ll and Ann, C.R.2.], May 7, 1711.
Joseph, s. Joseph and Jane, bp. Jan. 5, 1734–5. C.R.2.
Joshua, s. Josiah, Nov. 25, 1687.
Joshua, s. Sam[ue]ll and Anne, bp. July 22, 1716. C.R.2.
Joshua, s. Josiah Jr. and Sarah, Apr. 21, 1723.
Josiah, s. Josiah, Nov. 29, 1685.
Josiah, s. Josiah Jr. and Sarah, Mar. 1, 1724.
Luke, ch. Joseph and Jane, bp. June 30, 1747. C.R.2.
Lydya, ch. Joshua and Lydia, bp. July 7, 1747. C.R.2.
Martha, d. Jos[eph] and Jane, bp. Nov. 18, 1753. C.R.2.
Mary, d. John Jr. and Mary, Apr. —, 1704.
Mary, ch. John and Mary, bp. Sept. 23, 1711. C.R.2.
Mary, [ch.] Joseph and Jane, bp. May 16, 1742. C.R.2.
Mary, [ch.] Josehp [sic] and Jane, bp. May 15, 1748. C.R.2.
Mary [h. Amasa], —— [1804]. G.R.15.
Nathanael, ch. Bezaliel and Anna, bp. July 25, 1731. C.R.2.
Nath[anie]ll, s. Bezeliel and Anna, July 5, 1730.
Patience, d. John Jr. and Mary, Jan. 28, 1709–10.
Pricilla, d. Bezeliel and Anna, Feb. 22, 1742.
Prince, s. Sam[ue]ll and Ann, bp. May 22, 1726. C.R.2.
Prudence [? m.] [Feb. —, 1782]. G.R.15.
Ruth, d. John Jr., Jan. 26, 1699–1700.
Ruth, ch. John and Mary, bp. Sept. 23, 1711. C.R.2.
Samuel, s. John, Nov. —, 1683.
Samuel, s. Samuell and Anna, bp. Aug. 7, 1715. C.R.2.
Samuel, ch. Elnathan and Mercy, bp. Sept. 4, 1715. C.R.2.
Sarah, d. Elnathan, Dec. 26, 1698.
Sarah, ch. Elnathan and Mercy, bp. Sept. 4, 1715. C.R.2.
Sarah, d. Josiah and Sarah, May 13, 1726.
Sarah, d. Bazaleel, bp. July 15, 1753. C.R.2.
Sarah, d. Wid. Palmer, bp. Apr. 17, 1757. C.R.2.
Th[omas], s. Elnathan, Nov. 21, 1696.
Thomas, s. John and Mary, bp. July 8, 1716. C.R.2.
——, ch. Joshua and Lydia, bp. July 7, 1747. C.R.2.

PAMALICH (see Pammatuck), Bennony, s. Patience "an Indian woman," bp. Sept. 2, 1739. C.R.2.

PAMMATTUCK (see Pamalich), Benoni, s. Patience, ind[ia]n, Oct. 22, 1737.

PARKER, Alexander, s. William, Mar. 28, 1709.
Alexander, ch. W[illia]m and Rachel, bp. July 12, 1713. C.R.2.
Alice, d. Joseph, Aug. 31, 1684.
Catharine S. R., d. Perry L. and Polly, Dec. 30, 1823. [Catharine Scarboro Rich, ch. Perry Leatherbury, C.R.1.]
Elisha, s. W[illia]m and Rachel of Rochester, bp. July 28, 1717. C.R.2.
Elizabeth, d. Joseph, July 7, 1693.
George Washington, [twin] s. Perry L. and Polly, Dec. 10, 1826.
Joseph, s. Joseph, Mar. 31, 1690.
Josepth, s. Will[i]am, Oct. 4, 1658. P.C.R.
Joshua, ch. W[illia]m and Rachel, bp. July 12, 1713. C.R.2.
Josiah, s. William, Oct. 4, 1658.
Judith, d. Joseph, June 11, 1699.
Lillis Colman, d. Perry [Perrey, C.R.1.] L. and Polly, Feb. 22, 1822.
Lydia, d. William, May 9, 1653.
Lydia, d. William, bp. Apr. 13, 1656. C.R.2.
Martha, d. William, bp. June 13, 1647. C.R.1.
Martha, twin d. William, Apr. 30, 1702.
Mary, d. Will, Jan. 1, 1639.
Mary, ch. W[i]ll[ia]m, bp. May 16, 1647. C.R.2.
Mary, d. Joseph, Nov. 17, 1687.
Mary, twin d. William, Apr. 30, 1702.
Mary, twin d. William, Mar. 30, 1704.
Miles, s. William, June 25, 1655.
Miles, s. Joseph, June 21, 1702.
Miles, s. William [s. William and Rachel, C.R.2.], Sept. 13, 1706.
Miriam " alias Mary," ch. William and Rachel, bp. Sept. 16, 1705. C.R.2.
Nathanael, s. William, Apr. 1, 1698.
Nathanael, ch. William and Rachel, bp. Sept. 16, 1705. C.R.2.
Nathaniel, s. William, Mar. 8, 1662. [Mar. 8, 1661, P.C.R.]
Patience, d. Will[iam], Feb. —, 1648.
Patience, d. William, bp. May 6, 1649. C.R.2.
Perrey, ch. Perrey L. and w., bp. Oct. 27, 1822. C.R.1.
Perry L., s. Perry L. and Polly, July 5, 1820.
Polly [————], wid. ————, —— [1790]. C.R.1.
Rachel, ch. William and Rachel, bp. Sept. 16, 1705. C.R.2.
Rachell, d. William, July 2, 1700.
Ruth, d. Joseph Jr. and Charity, Jan. 29, 1711–12.
Ruth, d. Charity, bp. Oct. 25, 1714 [*sic*, 1713]. C.R.2.
Selina C. [————], w. Perry L. [Nov. —, 1824]. G.R.9.

PARKER, William, s. Will[iam], Dec. —, 1643.
William, ch. W[i]ll[ia]m, bp. May 16, 1647. C.R.2.
William, s. William, May 15, 1675.
William, twin s. William [ch. William and Rachel, C.R.2.], Mar. 30, 1704.
William Riley, [twin] s. Perry L. and Polly, Dec. 10, 1826.

PARRIS, Thomas, s. Thomas Jr. and Hannah, Nov. 30, 1725.

PARSONS, Jane, d. Moses and Rachel, July 19, 1813.
Joseph Palmer, s. Moses and Rachel, Oct. 15, 1809.
Mary, d. Moses and Rachel, June 24, 1819.
William, s. Moses and Rachel, Nov. 15, 1816.

PEAKES (see Peaks, Peek), Celia [———], w. Eleazar [dup. Eleazer], —— [1771]. C.R.3.
Diantha, d. William and Desire, June 21, 1807.
Eleazar, s. W[illia]m, bp. Oct. 7, 1750. C.R.1.
Eliazar, s. William, May 3, 1657.
Hannah, d. Eleazer and Hannah, Oct. 7, 1784.
Hannah White, d. William and Desire, Aug. 26, 1809.
Harriet Atwood, ch. William and Lydia, bp. Jan. 22, 1826. C.R.3.
Hart, s. Israel, bp. July 17, 1743. C.R.1.
Israel, s. William and Joan, May 27, 1705.
John Quincy, s. William and Lydia, Apr. 13, 1827.
John Quincy, ch. W[illia]m and Lidia, bp. July 13, 1828. C.R.3.
Lucy, d. Eleazer, bp. May 27, 1733. C.R.1.
Lydia Jacob, d. William and Lydia, June 26, 1824.
Lydia Jacob, ch. William and Lydia, bp. Jan. 22, 1826. C.R.3.
Martin Tuller, s. William and Desire, July 2, 1805.
Mary, ch. William and Lydia, bp. Jan. 22, 1826. C.R.3.
Philipe, d. Israel, bp. Sept. 2, 1739. C.R.1.
Philippe, d. William and Joan, Mar. 27, 1703.
Presella, d. Eleazer and Hannah, Mar. 20, 1786.
Priscilla, d. W[illia]m, bp. Dec. 1, 1745. C.R.1.
Prissilla, d. Will[ia]m (Peaks) and Prissilla, Sept. 17, 1759.
Rachel, ch. Eleazar and Rachel, bp. Aug. 22, 1725. C.R.1.
Rachel, d. W[illia]m and Priscilla, bp. Oct. 16, 1743. C.R.1.
Sarah, d. William and Joan, June 25, 1700.
Susanna, d. William and Joan, Dec. 27, 1708.
Thankefull, d. William (Peaks), Aug. 19, 1695.
Walter Scott, s. Martin T. and Abigail C., Feb. 16, 1830.
William, s. William, July 15, 1662.
William, s. Elezer and Hannah, Apr. 19, 1781.
William Pierce, s. William (Peaks) and Desire, Apr. 28, 1803.

PEAKS (see Peakes, Peek), Benjamin, s. Israel, bp. Mar. 26, 1748. C.R.1.
Eleazer, s. Israel and Lydia, Nov. 1, 1736. [Eleazar Peakes, C.R.1.]
Eleazer, s. W[illia]m, bp. May 20, 1753. C.R.1.
Elezar, s. Will[ia]m and Prissilla, Sept. 4, 1756. [Eleazar, C.R.1.]
Eliazer, s. William, Dec. 9, 1693.
Hanah, d. William, Apr. 18, 1692.
Harriot Atwood, d. W[illia]m and Lydia, May 5, 1818.
Iserell, s. William, Feb. 22, 1655.
Iserell, s. Iserell, Nov. 16, 1687.
Israel, s. Israel, bp. July 5, 1741. C.R.1.
Joseph, s. Israel, bp. Nov. 23, 1746. C.R.1.
Judith, d. William, May 20, 1698.
Leah, d. Eleazer and Rachel, Oct. 30, 1724. [Peakes, ch. Eleazar and Rachel, C.R.1.]
Lucy, d. Eleazer and Rachel, Oct. 12, 1731.
Lucy, d. Eleazer and Rachel, Dec. 15, 1733.
Lucy, d. Eleazar, bp. June 3, 1739. C.R.1.
Mary, d. William and Lydia, Mar. 1, 1815.
Priscilla, d. Wid. Peaks, bp. July 17, 1763. C.R.1.
Rachel, d. Eleazer and Rachel, Aug. 30, 1722.
Rachel, d. Will[ia]m and Prissilla, June 26, 1748. [Peakes, C.R.1.]
William, s. Eleazer and Rachel, Dec. 8, 1719.

PEARCE (see Peirce, Peirse, Perce, Pierce), Benjamen, s. Benjamen, Mar. 11, 1683-4.
David, s. John, June 1, 1695.
Ezra, s. Benja[min] (Peirce) Jr. and Eliza[beth], Feb. 1, 1752. [Peirce, C.R.1.]
Martha, d. Benjamen, Dec. 14, 1679.
Ruth, d. John, Sept. 6, 1689.

PEEK (see Peakes, Peaks), Betty, d. Mary, bp. Jan. 14, 1776. C.R.1.

PEIRCE (see Pearce, Peirse, Perce, Pierce), Abigail, d. Nathaniel and Nabby, Oct. 8, 1811.
Abner, s. Jeremiah, bp. June 2, 1751. C.R.1.
Adams, ch. Benjamin, June 11, 1695.
Alce, d. Calven Jr. and Alice, Feb. 10, 1808.
Anna Otis, d. Calvin Jr. and Alice, May 19, 1817.
Augustus, ch. Ezekiel and Martha, bp. May 29, 1757. C.R.1.
Bailey, s. Hayward and Judith, Aug. 29, 1787. [Pierce, ch. Howard, C.R.1.]
Becky, d. Hayward and Judith, Apr. 3, 1785. [Beckey Pierce, ch. Howard, C.R.1.]

PEIRCE, Benja[min], s. Benja[min] (Pierce) Jr. and Mary, Dec. 4, 1721. [Pierce, C.R.1.]
Benja[min], s. Benja[min] Jr. and Charrity, Mar. 1, 1746.
Betsey, d. Hayward and Judith, Nov. 25, 1795.
Caleb, s. Benjamin, June 12, 1690.
Caleb, s. Jeremiah, bp. May 5, 1734. C.R.1.
Caleb, s. Jeremiah, bp. Oct. 2, 1743. C.R.1.
Caleb, s. Benja[min] Jr. [Benja[min] 3d, C.R.1.] and Jane, Aug. 7, 1755.
Calvin, s. Calvin and Huldah, Mar. 16, 1782.
Calvin, s. Calvin Jr. and Alce, Mar. 6, 1812.
Charity, d. Benj[amin] Jr., bp. Dec. 24, 1769. C.R.1.
Clothyer, s. John, May 5, 1698.
Deborah, d. Thomas Jr., bp. Feb. 2, 1755. C.R.1.
Desire, d. Seth and Jemima, Mar. 6, 1779.
Ebenezer, s. Benjamin, Apr. 2, 1686.
Edwin Henry, s. Otis and Clarissa, Nov. 21, 1835.
Elijah, s. Capt. Hayward and Judith, July 30, 1789. [Pierce, s. Capt. Howard, C.R.1.]
Elijah Foster, s. Elijah and Lucy P., July 1, 1827.
Elisha, s. Benjamin, Nov. 24, 1699.
Elisha, s. Calvin and Huldah, Mar. 8, 1785.
Elisha, s. Calvin Jr. and Alice, Nov. 23, 1820.
Elizabeth Bourne, d. Elijah and Lucy P., May 9, 1833.
George Henry, s. Otis and Clarissa, bp. Oct. 5, 1845. C.R.1.
George Otis, s. Otis and Clarissa, Oct. 22, 1830.
Hannah, d. Calvin and Huldah, Sept. 15, 1779.
Hayward, s. Benja[min] Jr. and Jane, June 22, 1753. [Hayward Esq. [h. Judith (Bailey)], G.R.2.]
Hayward, s. Hayward and Judith, Mar. 24, 1782.
Hayward, s. Elijah and Rebecca, Sept. 6, 1817. [Pierce, C.R.1.] [Peirce, G.R.2.]
Henry, s. Otis and Clarissa, Oct. 27, 1841.
Henry Thomas, s. John and Mercy, Sept. 29, 1813.
Henry Thomas, ch. Mercy, wid., bp. July 4, 1819. C.R.1.
Howard, s. Benja[min] 3d, bp. July 1, 1753. C.R.1.
Hulda, d. Jerem[ia]h, bp. Oct. 6, 1734. C.R.1.
Huldah, d. Calvin and Huldah, Sept. 18, 1770.
James, s. Thom[a]s, bp. Apr. 28, 1771. C.R.1.
Jeremiah, s. Benjamin, Sept. 17, 1697.
John, s. Seth and Jamima, Oct. 29, 1776.
John B., s. Nathaniel and Sophia, July 22, 1832.
John Cushing, s. Matthew and w., bp. Dec. 20, 1778. C.R.1.
John Whitney, s. John and Marcy, Dec. 4, 1811.

PEIRCE, John Whitney, ch. Mercy, wid., bp. July 4, 1819. C.R.1.
Jonathan, s. Benja[min] Jr. and Charrity, Feb. 18, 1748.
Joseph, s. Seth and Jemima, Apr. —, 1769.
Joseph, s. Joseph and Sally, May 27, 1809.
Joseph Dexter, s. John and Mercy, Nov. 15, 1815.
Joseph Dexter, ch. Mercy, wid., bp. July 4, 1819. C.R.1.
Lidia, ch. Ezekiel and Martha, bp. May 29, 1757. C.R.1.
Louisa, d. Nathaniel and Nabby, July 23, 1816.
Lucy P. [———], w. Elijah [Oct. —, 1799]. G.R.2.
Luther, s. Benja[min] Jr., bp. Feb. 9, 1745. C.R.1.
Lydia, d. Benja[min] Jr. and Eliza[beth], Dec. 18, 1753. [Lidia, C.R.1.]
Lydia, d. Benja[min] Jr., bp. Oct. 17, 1756. C.R.1.
Lydia (see Lidia).
Marcy Little, d. Calvin Jr. and Alice, Aug. 13, 1814.
Martha, d. Jeremiah, bp. June 24, 1739. C.R.1.
Martin Bailey, s. Nath[anie]ll and Nabby, July 17, 1807.
Mary, d. Robart and Marcy, Sept. 2, 1757.
Mary, d. Robart and Marcy, Aug. 11, 1759.
Mary, d. Calvin and Huldah, Oct. 15, 1768.
Mary, d. Calvin Jr. and Alce, Apr. 2, 1810.
Matthew, ch. Thomas Jr. and Mary, bp. Nov. 4, 1753. C.R.1.
Mercy Little (see Marcy Little Peirce).
Nathaniel, s. Seth and Jemima, Feb. 7, 1773.
Nathaniel, s. Nathaniel and Nabby, Jan. 28, 1814.
Otis, s. Nathaniel and Winnet, July 27, 1801.
Persis, d. Benjamin, June 6, 1688.
Robart, s. Robart and Marcy, Oct. 17, 1761.
Roland, s. Ezekiel, bp. May 13, 1759. C.R.1.
Roland, [ch.] Caleb and w., bp. May 23, 1779. C.R.1.
Sally, d. Capt. Mathew dec'd, bp. Aug. 29, 1822. C.R.1.
Sally Ann, d. Joseph and Sally, Mar. 21, 1811.
Sarah, d. Elisha, bp. Apr. 8, 1733. C.R.1.
Sarah Bailey, d. Elijah and Lucy P., Jan. 10, 1829.
Silas, s. Hayward and Judith, Feb. 15, 1793. [Pierce, s. Capt. Hayward, C.R.1.]
Silas, s. Elijah and Lucy P., July 27, 1826.
Silvanus, s. Tho[mas] Jr., bp. July 13, 1761. C.R.1.
Sophia [? m.] [Apr. —, 1791]. G.R.2.
Thomas, s. Benjamin, Nov. 14, 1692.
Thomas, ch. Thomas Jr. and Mary, bp. Nov. 4, 1753. C.R.1.
Thomas, s. Thomas Jr., bp. May 29, 1757. C.R.1.
Thomas, s. Seth and Jemima, Aug. 26, 1767.
Thomas, s. Otis and Clarissa, Oct. 24, 1832.

PEIRCE, Waldo, s. Capt. Hayward and Judith, Feb. 21, 1778.
William, s. Seth and Jemima, ———— [rec. between ch. b. Apr. —, 1769, and ch. b. Feb. 7, 1773].
William, s. Nath[anie]ll and Winnit, Dec. 27, 1802.
Winnet Otis, d. Nath[anie]ll and Nabby, Apr. 18, 1809.
————, s. Elijah and Lucy P., May 28, 1831.

PEIRPOINT, Joseph, s. Ebnezer and Sarah, Mar. 13, 1754.
Nath[anie]ll, s. Ebenezer and Sarah, Dec. 10, 1751.

PEIRSE (see Pearce, Peirce, Perce, Pierce), Ezekell, s. Thomas, Nov. 13, 1718.

PENCHEN (see Pincen, Pincheon, Pinchion, Pinchon, Pincin, Pinison, Pinson), Thankfull, d. Ebenezer, Dec. 22, 1702.

PENNEY, John Baker, s. John and Temperence (Cushing), Feb. 12, 1809.

PENNIMAN, Henry Thomas, s. Silas and Cerene, Sept. 20, 1820.

PERCE (see Pearce, Peirce, Peirse, Pierce), Jaell, d. John, Feb. 24, 1692.
Jerusha, d. Benjamen, Feb. 13, 1681. [Pierce, d. Benjamin, C.R.2.]
John, s. John, Apr. 12, 1686.
Jonathan, s. John (Pearce), Feb. 24, 1688.
Michiell, s. John, Sept. 24, 1684.

PERKINS, Adeline O., ch. Thomas and Phebe, Sept. 13, 1843.
Delia Ann, ch. Thomas and Phebe, Nov. 6, 1834.
Sarah Thomas, ch. Thomas and Phebe, Aug. 5, 1829.

PERREY (see Perry, Pery), Simeon, s. Jo Jr. and Rachel, June 25, 1744.

PERRY (see Perrey, Pery), Abiel, s. Benja[min] and Ruth, Apr. 16, 1719.
Abigail, d. William, Mar. 22, 1692–3.
Abigail, d. Will[ia]m and Lydia, June 27, 1762.
Abner, s. Benja[min] and Ruth, Nov. 29, 1720.
Abner, s. Abner dec'd and Sarah, bp. Sept. 7, 1746. C.R.2.
Agatha, d. James, June 15, 1702.
Amos, s. William, Mar. 10, 1690–1.
Amos, s. Amos and Ruth, bp. Oct. 11, 1726. C.R.2.
Amos. s. Amos and Ruth, bp. Mar. 17, 1733–4. C.R.2.
Barnabas, s. Henry and w., bp. July 4, 1708. C.R.2.
Benjamin, s. William, Dec. 31, 1688. [Benjamen, C.R.2.]
Benjamin, s. Benjamin [s. Benjamin and Ruth, C.R.2.], Nov. 23, 1714.

PERRY, Benjamin, s. Benjamin and w., bp. Apr. 20, 1746. C.R.2.
Calvin, —— [1785]. C.R.3.
Calvin Willard, s. Calvin and Mercy, Jan. 8, 1821, in Hanover.
Charles [?], s. Amos and Sarah, Sept. 28, 1774.
Cushman, s. Amos and Sarah, May 17, 1771.
David, s. Thomas, Nov. 16, 1686.
Elizabeth, d. William, June 27, 1682. [Elizebeth, C.R.2.]
Elizabeth, ch. W[illia]m dec'd "Late" of Freetown, bp. June 11, 1732. C.R.2.
Elizabeth, d. Sam[ue]l and Eliz[abe]th, bp. July 4, 1736. C.R.2.
Elizbeth, d. Benj[a]m[in] and Ruth, bp. Sept. 10, 1731. C.R.2.
Elvira Jewett, d. Calvin and Mercy, Oct. 5, 1825. [w. Marsena Webb, C.R.3.]
Frances, d. Daniel, w. Henry Clapp [Apr. —, 1818]. G.R.2.
George Payson, s. Calvin and Mercy, Nov. 1, 1826.
George W., s. Sam[uel] N., housewright, and Eliza R. of Boston, Dec. 15, 1846.
Hannah, d. William, July 2, 1696.
Hannah, d. Joseph and Mercy, Apr. 23, 1722.
Hannah, d. Amos and Ruth, bp. May 31, 1731. C.R.2.
Harriet E. [————], w. Leonard L. [Apr. —, 1824]. C.R.3.
Huldah, d. Amos and Sarah, Oct. 4, 1767.
Isaac, s. William, Apr. 14, 1698.
Isaac, s. Benja[min] and Ruth, Feb. 5, 1725.
Isaac, s. Amos and Ruth, bp. Sept. 5, 1736. C.R.2.
Jemima, d. William, Aug. 28, 1701. [Jemimah, C.R.2.]
Jerusha, d. William, Feb. 11, 1699-[1]700.
John, s. Thomas, June 6, 1680.
Jonathan, s. Joseph and Mercy, July 10, 1716.
Jonathan, s. Amos and Ruth, bp. July 17, 1740. C.R.2.
Joseph, s. William, Apr. 9, 1684.
Joseph, s. Joseph and Mercy, May 28, 1719.
Joseph, s. Joseph, bp. June 14, 1724. C.R.2.
Joseph, ch. W[illia]m dec'd "Late" of Freetown, bp. June 11, 1732. C.R.2.
Kesiah, d. William. July 6, 1705. [Keziah, d. William and Elizabeth, C.R.2.]
Leonard Litchfield, s. Calvin and Mercy, Feb. 4, 1824.
Lucendy, d. Jo (Perrey) Jr. and Rachal, Nov. 16, 1746.
Lusanna, d. Sam[ue]l and Elizabeth, bp. Sept. 8, 1734. C.R.2.
Lusanna [or Lusanda], d. Joseph and w., bp. Apr. 26, 1747. C.R.2.
Lydia, d. William of Freetown, " & adopted by Elizabeth Tolman wife of Benj^m," bp. July 19, 1730. C.R.2.
Lydia, d. Will[ia]m and Lydia, Jan. 10, 1766.

PERRY, Mary, d. Thomas, Mar. 18, 1678.
Mary, d. James and Mary, bp. Dec. 1, 1706. C.R.2.
Mary, d. Amos and Ruth, bp. July 18, 1725. C.R.2.
Mary, d. Jo Jr. and Rachal, Mar. 31, 1749.
Mary, d. Amos and Sarah, Nov. 19, 1761.
Mary Franklin, d. Calvin and Mercy, Apr. 19, 1831.
Mercy [? m.], —— [1793]. C.R.3.
Mercy Aroline, d. Calvin and Mercy, Dec. 3, 1829.
Peleg, s. Benja[min] and Ruth, Feb. 22, 1717.
Priscilla, d. Amos and Ruth, bp. Oct. 13, 1723. C.R.2.
Rachel, d. Jo Jr. and Rachel, May 28, 1751.
Ruth, d. Amos and Ruth, bp. Sept. 10, 1721. C.R.2.
Ruth, d. Benja[min] and Ruth, Sept. 8, 1723.
Samuel, s. William, Sept. 6, 1685.
Samuel, s. Benjamin [s. Benjamin and Ruth, C.R.2.], Nov. 28, 1712.
Samuel Niles, s. Calvin and Mercy, Apr. 29, 1822, in Hanover.
Sarah Ann, d. Calvin and Mercy, Jan. 20, 1834.
Silence, d. Amos and Sarah, Feb. 9, 1764.
Simeon, s. Abner and Sarah, bp. Oct. 14, 1744. C.R.2.
Simeon, s. Joseph and Rachel, bp. Apr. 14, 1745. C.R.2.
Susanna, d. Thomas, Apr. 28, 1676. [Susana, C.R.2.]
Tabitha, d. Thomas, Apr. 12, 1684.
Tabitha, d. Thomas, bp. June 21, 1685. C.R.2.
Thomas, s. Thomas, Jan. 26, 1671.
William, s. William, bp. Dec. 29, 1678. C.R.2.
William, s. William, Dec. 25, 1694.
William, s. Amos and Ruth, bp. Aug. 30, 1729. C.R.2.
William, ch. Benj[a]m[in] (Pery) and Ruth, bp. Oct. 2, 1740. C.R.2.
William, s. Amos and Sarah, Sept. 30, 1757.
William, s. Will[ia]m and Lydia, Nov. 17, 1763.
Zillah, d. Benjamin and Ruth, bp. Nov. 10, 1728. C.R.2.
——, s. Calvin and Mercy, Nov. 16, 1840.

PERY (see Perrey, Perry), James, s. Thomas (Perry), Mar. 12, 1674. [Mar. 12, 1673, P.C.R.] [Perry, C.R.2.]

PETERSON, ——, d. Wid. Peterson, bp. Apr. 24, 1757. C.R.2.

PETTIS, Clarrissa, ch. David and Polly, Aug. 18, 1834. [Clarissa, G.R.2.]
Henry D., ch. David and Polly, June 22, 1828, in Provintstown.
Martha G., ch. David and Polly, June 30, 1839.
Mary A., ch. David and Polly, Aug. 3, 1836.
Naomi Downs, ch. David and Polly, May 15, 1831, in Provintstown.

PHILLIPS, Benjamin, s. John, bp. Aug. 15, 1658. C.R.2.
Grace, d. John, bp. Oct. 4, 1657. C.R.2.
Hannah, d. John, bp. Oct. 4, 1657. C.R.2.
Joseph, s. John, bp. Oct. 4, 1657. C.R.2.

PICHER (see Pitcher), Lydia, d. Joseph, May 4, 1717. [Lydiah Pitcher, d. Joseph and Mercy, C.R.2.]
Mary, d. Natho[nie]l, Jan. 21, 1716. [Pitcher, d. Nathaniel and Sarah, C.R.1.]
Sary, d. Nath[an]iell, Apr. 27, 1715. [Sarah Pitcher, d. Nathaniel, C.R.1.]

PICKLE (see Pickles), Jonah, s. Jonas, Feb. 5, 1658. [Pickles, s. Jonah, C.R.2.]

PICKLES (see Pickle), Alice, d. Nathan, May —, 1691. [Else, C.R.2.]
David (Pickells), s. Nathan, July 29, 1705. [Pickles, s. Nathan and Miriam, C.R.2.]
Else (see Alice).
Jonas, s. Jonas, Mar. 10, 1663.
Lydia, d. Jonas, Apr. 10, 1662 [*sic*, see Marcy and Nathan].
Lydia, d. Mr. [?] Pickles, bp. Apr. 30, 1665. C.R.2.
Marcy, d. Jonas, Dec. 28, 1660 [*sic*, see Lydia and Nathan]. [Mercy, C.R.2.]
Mercy, d. Nathan, May —, 1688. [Marcy, C.R.2.]
Miriam, d. Nathan and Miriam, Oct. —, 1697.
Nathan, s. Jonas, Jan. 28, 1661 [*sic*, see Lydia and Marcy].
Nathan, s. Nathan, Oct. —, 1693.
Nathan, s. Nathan and Miriam, July —, 1699.

PIERCE (see Pearce, Peirce, Peirse, Perce), Calvin, s. Elisha and Mary, Apr. 14, 1742.
Desire, d. Tho[ma]s and Mary, May 10, 1742. [Peirce, d. Dea. T., C.R.1.]
Elisha, s. Elisha and Mary, Apr. 9, 1739. [Peirce, C.R.1.]
Ezekiel, s. Thomas, bp. Dec. 4, 1720. C.R.1.
Ezekiel, s. Ezekiel, bp. Sept. 18, 1763. C.R.1.
Jane, d. Capt. Hayward and Judith, Dec. 14, 1780. [Peirce, C.R.1.] [Peirce, w. Nathaniel Cushing, G.R.14.]
Jemima, ch. Anna, wid., bp. Sept. 15, 1744. C.R.1.
Lidia, d. Thom[a]s, bp. Dec. 10, 1727. C.R.1.
Lucy, ch. Thomas, bp. May 20, 1770. C.R.1.
Lydia, d. Tho[ma]s and Mary, Aug. 16, 1726.
Martha, d. Benjamin, bp. June 25, 1682. C.R.2.

PIERCE, Martha, d. Benjamin Jr. and Mary, Jan. 5, 1712–13.
Mary, d. Benjamin Jr. and Mary, Feb. 4, 1717.
Mary, d. Tho[ma]s and Mary, Feb. 9, 1734.
Mary, d. Dea. Thomas, bp. Sept. 16, 1735. C.R.1.
Mary, d. Elisha and Mary, May 5, 1746. [Peirce, d. Dea. Elisha, C.R.1.]
Mary, d. Calvin, bp. July 26, 1789. C.R.1.
Meribah, ch. Thomas, bp. May 20, 1770. C.R.1.
Parmenus [h. Diana C. (Freeman)(Colored)], Nov. 12, 1828. G.R.14.
Persis, d. Elisha and Mary, July 2, 1748. [Peirce, d. Dea. Elisha, C.R.1.]
Sarah, d. Elisha and Sarah, Jan. 12, 1732.
Sarah [? m.], ——— [1828]. C.R.1.
Seth, s. Tho[ma]s and Mary, Sept. 7, 1728.
Solon, s. Ezekiel, bp. June 8, 1766. C.R.1.
Thomas, s. Thomas and Mary, Jan. 25, 1720.
——— [———], w. Otis, ——— [1800]. C.R.1.

PINCEN (see Penchen, Pincheon, Pinchion, Pinchon, Pincin, Pinison, Pinson), Bachsheba, d. Thomas, Nov. 15, 1673.
Betty, twin d. Thomas and Egatha, Apr. 12, 1736.
Deborah, d. Tho[ma]s and Egatha, May 3, 1741.
Ebenezer, s. Thomas, Apr. 30, 1677.
Elizabeth, d. Thomas Jr. [d. Thomas Jr. and Elizabeth, C.R.2.], Mar. 7, 1663–4.
Hannah, d. Thomas, Dec. 4, 1642.
Johanah, d. Thomas, Oct. 26, 1667. [Joanna Pinchen, d. Thomas Jr., C.R.2.]
Judeth, d. Tho[ma]s and Egatha, Jan. 5, 1743.
Mary, d. Thomas, Feb. 14, 1670.
Mary, d. Ebenezer, Sept. 16, 1704.
Mary, d. Tho[ma]s and Egatha, May 6, 1738.
Sarah, d. Thomas, Mar. 29, 1669. [Pinchon, d. Thomas Jr., C.R.2.]
Simion, s. Tho[ma]s and Egatha, Aug. 17, 1747.
Thomas, s. Thomas, May 15, 1640.
Thomas, s. Thomas Jr., Jan. 2, 1665. [Pinchen, C.R.2.]
Tho[ma]s, twin s. Thomas and Egatha, Apr. 12, 1736.
William, s. Tho[ma]s (Pincin) Jr. and Ann, Dec. 15, 1757.

PINCHEON (see Penchen, Pincen, Pinchion, Pinchon, Pincin, Pinison, Pinson), Merrel, d. Eben, bp. Oct. 5, 1766. C.R.1.

PINCHION (see Penchen, Pincen, Pincheon, Pinchon, Pincin, Pinison, Pinson), Abner, s. Tho[ma]s, bp. Sept. 4, 1748. C.R.1.

PINCHION, Deborah, d. Eben[e]zer, bp. Sept. 29, 1754. C.R.1.
John, s. Eben[ez]er and Eliz[a]beth, bp. Nov. 1, 1741. C.R.1.
Judeth, ch. Tho[ma]s Sr., bp. Oct. 29, 1752. C.R.2.
Mary, ch. Tho[ma]s Sr., bp. Oct. 29, 1752. C.R.2.
Simeon, s. Tho[ma]s and Agatha, bp. Oct. 10, 1752. C.R.2.

PINCHON (see Penchen, Pincen, Pincheon, Pinchion, Pincin, Pinison, Pinson), Ebenezer, s. Eben[e]z[er], bp. June 5, 1763. C.R.1.
Elizabeth, d. Ebenezar Jr., bp. Apr. 6, 1745. C.R.1.

PINCIN (see Penchen, Pincen, Pincheon, Pinchion, Pinchon, Pinison, Pinson), Agatha, d. Simeon and Sarah, Jan. 19, 1777.
Benja[min], s. Tho[ma]s Jr. and Ann, Apr. 15, 1760.
Elias, s. Simeon and Sarah, Dec. 24, 1788. [Pinson [h. Betsey C.], ———, 1789, G.R.14.]
Elias Parker, s. Elias and Betsey, Nov. 7, 1827.
Elizabeth, d. Tho[ma]s Jr. and Ann, Feb. 5, 1756.
Hannah, d. Abner and Han[na]h, Sept. 23, 1770.
Harriet Loring, d. Elias and Betsey, Feb. 23, 1819.
Lucy, d. Simeon and Sarah, Jan. 18, 1778.
Lucy, d. Perez and Sally [dup. Salley], July 1, 1809.
Perez, s. Simeon and Sarah, May 25, 1779. [Capt. Perez Pinson [h. Sally C.], G.R.14.]
Perez Alfred, s. Elias and Betsey, Aug. 31, 1830.
Polly, d. Perez and Sally [dup. Salley], July 7, 1811.
Sally [dup. Salley], d. Perez and Sally [dup. Salley], Sept. 3, 1807.
Simeon [Aug. —, 1753]. C.R.1. [Pincheon, s. Tho[ma]s and Agatha, C.R.2.]
Simeon, s. Simeon and Sarah, June 17, 1787.
Sophrona, d. Elias and Betsey, May 17, 1815.

PINISON (see Penchen, Pincen, Pincheon, Pinchion, Pinchon, Pincin, Pinson), Ebenezer, s. Eben[e]zer, bp. Oct. 27, 1751. C.R.1.

PINSON (see Penchen, Pincen, Pincheon, Pinchion, Pinchon, Pincin, Pinison), Addison F., ch. Elias and Betsey C., ———, 1843. G.R.14.
Betsey C. [———], w. Elias, ———, 1797. G.R.14.
Ebenezer, s. Ebenezer and Deborah, May 8, 1711.
Elias D., ch. Elias and Betsey C., ———, 1839. G.R.14.
Sally C. [———], w. Capt. Perez [Aug. —, 1789]. G.R.14.
Thomas, s. Ebenezer and Deborah, ———, 1707.

PITCHER (see Picher), Desire, d. Ezra and Zerviah, Sept. 25, 1733.
Desire, [ch.] Ezra Jr. and w., bp. Oct. 23, 1763. C.R.1.
Elisha, s. Ezra and Zerviah, Apr. 4, 1740.
Ezra, s. Ezra and Zerviah, June 2, 1735.
John, s. Ezra and Zerviah, Jan. 11, 1736.
Nathaniell, s. Nathaniell and Sarah, June 7, 1711. [Nathaniel, C.R.1.]
Nath[anie]ll, s. Ezra and Zerviah, Dec. 29, 1738.
Samuell, s. Nathaniell and Sarah, July 6, 1713.
Sarah, [ch.] Ezra Jr. and w., bp. Oct. 23, 1763. C.R.1.

POOLE, James H., ——, 1836. G.R.6.

PORTER (see Pourter), Alexander, s. Edward J. and Ruth, Oct. 16, 1836.
Charles, s. Edward J. and Ruth, July 28, 1829.
Edward F., s. Edward J. and Ruth, July 21, 1820.
Francis Edward, s. Edward, sailmaker, and Phebe, Aug. 28, 1844.
Laura M., d. Edward J. and Ruth, Sept. 24, 1839.
Lucy Gardner, d. Edward J. and Ruth, Feb. 9, 1822. [w. William H. Jenkins, G.R.6.]
Margaret Parker, d. Edward J. and Ruth, Apr. 20, 1824.
Molle, d. Nehemiah and Sarah, Nov. 3, 1766.
Nehemiah, s. Nehemiah, bp. Mar. 20, 1757. C.R.2.
Perez Gardner, s. Edward J. and Ruth, Nov. 28, 1831.
Sarah Ann, ch. Bengamin G. and Sarah, Jan. 27, 1829.
Sarah Jane, d. Edward J. and Ruth, Jan. 20, 1834.
William, s. Edward J. and Ruth, Jan. 22, 1827.
William Gardner, ch. Bengamin G. and Sarah, Nov. 4, 1831.

POTTER, Elizabeth F. [———], w. William E. [Feb. —, 1812]. G.R.14.
William E. [h. Elizabeth F.], —— [1807]. G.R.14.

POURTER (see Porter), Benjamin, s. Nehemiah (Porter) and Sarah, Mar. 10, 1763.
Lydia, d. Nehemiah and Sarah, Dec. 13, 1764.
Nehemiah, s. Nehemiah and Sarah, Dec. 14, 1756.
Sarah, d. Nehemiah (Porter) and Sarah, Oct. 14, 1760.
Silvenas, s. Nehemiah and Sarah, Dec. 29, 1758.

POWELL, —— [———], w. W. J., —— [1841]. C.R.1.

POWERS, Calvin, s. Walter, bp. Oct. 18, 1741. C.R.2.
Lydia, d. Nicalas and Bethiah, bp. May 5, 1736. C.R.2.

PRAT (see Pratt), Abigail, ch. Jonathan and Margarett, bp. Oct. 13, 1706. C.R.2.
Deborah, d. Jonathan, Apr. 3, 1700.
Margret, ch. Jonathan and Margarett, bp. Oct. 13, 1706. C.R.2.
Martha, d. Jonathan, Aug. 28, 1704.
Patience, d. Jonathan, Mar. 12, 1701-2.
Rachel, d. Jonathan and Margret, bp. July 16, 1710. C.R.2.

PRATT (see Prat), Abigail Wilder, d. Elias W. and Ruth, Aug. 2, 1826.
Abigaill, d. Jonathan, Nov. 5, 1692.
Allen, s. Thomas and Lucy, Sept. 7, 1814.
Belintha O. [———], w. Charles B. [Nov. —, 1847]. G.R.2.
Catharine Leavit, ch. Benj[amin] Jr. and Sarah, bp. July 5, 1835. C.R.3.
Charles Briggs, s. Elias W. and Ruth, Apr. 12, 1833.
Charles Copland, ch. Elias W. and Rachel, Jan. 6, 1842.
Deborah, ch. Jonathan and Margaret, bp. May 4, 1707. C.R.2.
Dolly S., w. William Young, ———, 1803. G.R.6.
Elias Edwards, s. Elias W. and Ruth, Apr. 16, 1829.
Elijah, Capt. [h. Polly E. (Marsh)], ———, 1808. G.R.2.
Elizabeth Briggs, d. Elias W. and Ruth, Nov. 28, 1824.
Emeline A. S., w. Cushing O. Litchfield, ———, 1836. G.R.7.
[E]meline Augusta, d. Elias W. and Ruth, Jan. 9, 1831.
Faustina D. [———], w. Charles B., ——— [1849]. G.R.2.
Jonathan, s. Jonathan, Oct. 6, 1697.
Margaret, d. Jonathan, Dec. 1, 1694.
Martha, ch. Jonathan (Prat) and Margarett, bp. Oct. 13, 1706. C.R.2.
Mary, d. Jabez and w. of Duxborough, bp. Sept. 3, 1710. C.R.2.
Othaniall, s. Jonathan, Jan. 25, 1708. [Othniel, s. Jonathan and Margaret, C.R.2.]
Patience, ch. Jonathan and Margaret, bp. May 4, 1707. C.R.2.
Ruth C., d. Elias W. and Rachel, Apr. 1, 1839.
Sophia, d. Thomas [Capt. Thomas, C.R.1.] and Lucy, Jan. 23, 1819.
Thomas, h. Lucy [Apr. —, 1773]. G.R.2.
Thomas, s. Thomas and Lucy, May 23, 1810, in Cohasset.
William, s. Thomas and Lucy, June 21, 1812, in Cohasset.
William Briggs, s. Elias W. and Ruth, Dec. 3, 1834.

PRAY, Grace, d. Ephram, June 11, 1707.

PREBBLE, Nathaniel, s. Abraham, bp. Apr. 9, 1648. C.R.2.

PRENTISS, George Henry [dup. omits Henry], ch. George and Henriette [dup. Henrietta], Feb. 10, 1836.

PRENTISS, Howard Malcom, ch. George and Henrietta [dup. Henriette], Aug. 19, 1834.
Nancy Henriette, ch. George and Henriette, July 11, 1832.
Ruth Boynton, ch. John F. and Leah, Sept. 24, 1838.
Sarah James, ch. John F. and Leah, Apr. 13, 1837.
William Henry, ch. John F. and Leah, Jan. 2, 1841.

PRESBY, George C. [Mar. —, 1833]. G.R.14.

PRINCE, Alce, d. Isaac, bp. Apr. 10, 1681. C.R.2.
Benjamin, s. Thomas, Feb. 28, 1693–4.
Job, s. Thomas, Apr. 14, 1695.
Thomas, s. Thomas, July 10, 1686.

PROUTTE (see Prouty), Abigail, d. Edward and Rebeccah, bp. June 12, 1737. C.R.2.

PROUTY (see Proutte), Adam, s. Isaac and Elizabeth, Dec. 14, 1721.
Adam, ch. Isaac and Elizabeth, bp. Apr. 21, 1723. C.R.2.
Alexander T. Lincoln, s. Caleb Jr. and Polly, July 15, 1814.
Almira, d. Jesse and Diadama, June 18, 1822.
Almira Hobart, [twin] d. Jesse and Diadama, May 3, 1827.
Ann Maria, d. Jesse and Diadama, Feb. 14, 1809.
Benjamin Williams, ch. William Jr. and Priscilla, July 23, 1828.
Caleb, s. Isaac and Elizabeth, Apr. 3, 1720.
Caleb, ch. Isaac and Elizabeth, bp. Apr. 21, 1723. C.R.2.
Caleb, s. Caleb and Martha, July 11, 1751.
Caleb, s. Caleb, bp. Sept. 19, 1779. C.R.1.
Caleb, s. Caleb and Sarah, July 22, 1783.
Caleb, s. Caleb, bp. Oct. 8, 1786. C.R.1.
Caleb Lincoln, s. Caleb Jr. and Polly, Oct. 20, 1819.
Caleb William, s. John and Joanna, June 27, 1810.
Caroline, d. Jesse and Diadama, Mar. 27, 1819.
Charles, s. Caleb and Sarah, Oct. 4, 1796.
Charles, s. Caleb, bp. Aug. 31, 1800. C.R.1.
Charles, s. Jesse and Diadama, Jan. 30, 1813.
Charles Turner, s. John and Joanna, Sept. 18, 1805.
Charles Turner, ch. John L. and Sarah C., Aug. 4, 1829.
Damrus, d. Nehem[ia]h and Lettes, Aug. 21, 1757. [Damaris, C.R.2.]
Damurs, d. Nehemiah and Lettes, June 18, 1753. [Damaris, d. Nehemiah and Lettice, C.R.2.]
David, s. Isaac, Aug. 15, 1716.
David, ch. Isaac and Elizabeth, bp. Apr. 21, 1723. C.R.2.

PROUTY, David, s. William and Jemima, Feb. 23, 1753.
Deborah, d. William and Jemima, Apr. 13, 1736.
Deborah, ch. W[illia]m and Elizabeth, bp. Oct. 12, 1740. C.R.2.
Edward, s. Richard, Sept. 30, 1679.
Edward, s. Edward, Oct. 6, 1702. [Proutey, C.R.2.]
Edward, s. Edward and Rebecca, bp. Oct. 26, 1740. C.R.2.
Edward, s. Edward and Rebecca, bp. May 16, 1742. C.R.2.
Eleanar, d. Elizabeth dec'd, grand d. Elizsabeth, bp. June 20, 1731. C.R.2.
Elijah, ch. Elijah D. and Mary, Nov. 26, 1836.
Elijah D., s. William and Hannah, Apr. 19, 1798.
Elisha, s. Edward, Mar. 19, 1715.
Elisha, s. Edward and Elizabeth, bp. June 24, 1716. C.R.2.
Elisabath, d. Edward, May 30, 1704. [Elizabeth Proutey, C.R.2.]
Elisabeth, d. William and Rachel, Dec. 21, 1770.
Eliza L., d. Jesse and Diadama, Jan. 10, 1815.
Elizabeth, d. Isaac and Elizabeth, Oct. 4, 1713.
Elizabeth, d. Isaac and Elizabeth, Dec. 27, 1724.
Elizabeth, d. William and Elizabeth, Feb. 27, 1728.
Elizabeth, ch. W[illia]m and Elizabeth, bp. Oct. 12, 1740. C.R.2.
Elizabeth, d. William and Hannah, Aug. 10, 1800.
Esther A. [――――], w. Bardin H., Nov. 6, 1825. G.R.2.
Eunice, d. Edward and Elizabeth, Mar. 1, 1711–12. [Proutie, C.R.2.]
Galen, s. William and Rachel, Apr. 22, 1774.
Hannah, d. Edward and Elizabeth, May 15, 1714. [Proute, C.R.2.]
Hannah, d. Caleb and Martha, Mar. 18, 1748.
Hannah E., ch. Elijah D. and Mary, July 1, 1840.
Hannah G., d. William and Hannah, May 10, 1809.
Harris Gilman, s. Jesse and Diadama, Apr. 4, 1807.
Henrietta, d. Isaac, shoemaker, and Matilda, July 7, 1847.
Henry Clay, s. Luther and Thankful, May 5, 1832.
Henry H., s. Jesse and Diadama, Sept. 23, 1803.
Isaac, s. Isaac and Elizabeth, Mar. 30, 1711–12.
Isaac, ch. Isaac and Elizabeth, bp. Apr. 21, 1723. C.R.2.
Isaac, s. Isaac and Elizabeth, Dec. 17, 1732.
Isabelle, ch. Elijah D. and Mary, July 4, 1833.
Isack, s. Richard, Nov. 18, 1689. [Isaac, C.R.2.]
Jacob, s. Isaace, Mar. 14, 1714.
Jacob, ch. Isaac and Elizabeth, bp. Apr. 21, 1723. C.R.2.
James, s. Richard, Oct. 30, 1677.
James, s. Edward, Oct. 16, 1706. [Proute, s. Edward (Prouty) and Elizabeth, C.R.2.]

PROUTY, James, s. Isaac and Eliz[abeth], bp. Sept. 6, 1730. C.R.2.
James Lincoln, ch. Lincoln and Rebekah, May 25, 1826.
James Little, s. John and Joanna, Feb. 20, 1813.
James Little, ch. Caleb W. and Abigail Y., June 20, 1843.
Jesse, s. William and Rachel, July 29, 1780.
Jesse, s. Jesse and Diadama, Oct. 13, 1817.
Joanna W. [———], w. ———, ——— [1776]. C.R.1.
Job, s. Isaac and Elizabeth, June 9, 1723.
John, s. Edward and Elizabeth, Oct. 17, 1710. [Proute, C.R.2.]
John, s. Isaac and Elizabeth, May 25, 1718.
John, ch. Isaac and Elizabeth, bp. Apr. 21, 1723. C.R.2.
John, s. Caleb and Sarah, Apr. 22, 1781.
John Ensign Otis, ch. Caleb W. and Abigail Y., Mar. 8, 1840.
John Hobart, ch. William Jr. and Priscilla, June 15, 1839.
John Lincoln, s. John and Joanna, June 22, 1804.
Jonathan, s. Richard, Sept. 1, 1682.
Jonathan, s. William and Jemima, Mar. 25, 1739.
Jonathan, s. Nehemiah and Lettes, Sept. 18, 1755.
Joseph Elbridge, s. Jesse and Diadama, June 17, 1823.
Juda C., d. Jesse and Diadama, July 27, 1820.
Julia Ann Sewell, [twin] d. Jesse and Diadama, May 3, 1827.
Lincoln, s. William and Rachel, Oct. 12, 1778.
Lincoln, s. William and Rachel, Feb. 25, 1782.
Lincoln, ch. William and Hannah, Sept. 2, 1804.
Lucy Lapham, ch. Lincoln and Rebekah, Jan. 4, 1829.
Lucy White, d. John and Joanna, Nov. 8, 1815.
Lusanna, d. William and Jemima, Apr. 18, 1734.
Lusanna, d. William and Jemima, June 15, 1748. [Lusannah, C.R.2.]
Lusannah, ch. W[illia]m and Elizabeth, bp. Oct. 12, 1740. C.R.2.
Luther, s. Caleb and Sarah, July 22, 1790.
Luther, ch. Caleb, bp. June 15, 1793. C.R.1.
Luther, s. Luther and Thankful, Feb. 22, 1825.
Luther Thomas, s. Luther and Thankful, Feb. 23, 1821.
Lydia, d. Jesse and Diadama, July 4, 1825.
Marcy, d. Caleb and w., bp. Aug. 19, 1750. C.R.1.
Margret, d. Nehem[ia]h and Lettes, Sept. 7, 1762.
Margret, d. Nehem[ia]h and Lettes, Jan. 3, 1765.
Margrett, d. Richard, Mar. 2, 1691–2.
Mary, d. Edward and Elizabeth, bp. Mar. 2, 1718. C.R.2.
Mary, d. Edward, Oct. 22, 1719.
Mary Ann, d. John and Joanna, Nov. 10, 1807. [w. Theodore Clement, G.R.6.]
Mary Ann, ch. Elijah D. and Mary, Nov. 16, 1845.

PROUTY, Mary Jane, d. Jesse and Diadama, June 22, 1805.
Matilda A., ch. Lincoln and Rebekah, Oct. 28, 1841.
Mercy (see Marcy).
Merrill, s. William and Rachel, June 7, 1784.
Molle, d. Nehem[ia]h and Lettes, Aug. 2, 1767.
Nathaniel, ch. Elijah D. and Mary, June 3, 1830.
Nathaniel L., s. William and Hannah, Jan. 25, 1812.
Nehemiah, s. Margret [dup. Mergret], Feb. 7, 1724 [dup. 1722].
Nehemiah, s. Margret, bp. June 24, 1739. C.R.2.
Olover B., ch. Isaac and Matilda P., July 11, 1841.
Orlander C., ch. Isaac and Matilda P., Aug. 24, 1843.
Philenia Paine, d. Caleb Jr. and Polly, June 26, 1816.
Prisce [Priscilla], d. Isaac, bp. May 29, 1757. C.R.2.
Rachel, d. Nehem[ia]h and Lettes, Aug. 28, 1760.
Rachel, d. William and Rachel, Oct. 16, 1769.
Rebecca, d. Edward and Rebeccah, bp. Aug. 31, 1735. C.R.2.
Rebekah Hobart, ch. Lincoln and Rebekah, Oct. 13, 1831.
Richard, s. Edward [s. Edward and Eliz[abeth], C.R.2.], Jan. 8, 1708–9.
Richard, s. William and Elizabeth, June 14, 1732.
Richard, ch. W[illia]m and Elizabeth, bp. Oct. 12, 1740. C.R.2.
Richard, s. William and Rachel, Nov. 3, 1775.
Ruth, d. Isaac and Elizabeth, Sept. 7, 1728.
Sally, d. Caleb and Sarah, Feb. 8, 1787.
Sally, ch. Caleb, bp. June 15, 1794. C.R.1.
Sally D., d. Jesse and Diadama, Feb. 25, 1811.
Sarah, d. Edward and Rebecca, bp. Jan. 29, 1743–4. C.R.2.
Sarah, ch. Caleb and w., bp. June 18, 1775. C.R.1.
Sarah, d. William and Rachel, June 24, 1777.
Sarah Lincoln, ch. John L. and Sarah C., Aug. 15, 1827.
Sarah Wilson, d. Luther and Thankful, Oct. 22, 1818.
Silas, s. Sarah, July —, 1799.
Susan Maria, d. Caleb Jr. and Polly, Aug. 23, 1824.
Susan Paine, d. Caleb Jr. and Polly, May 8, 1822.
Susannah, [ch.] Edward and Rebecca, bp. Aug. 24, 1746. C.R.2.
Sybil Hubbard, ch. Elijah D. and Mary, Jan. 23, 1828.
Thomas, s. Caleb and Sarah, Oct. 6, 1793. [Tho[ma]s Lincoln, C.R.1.]
Thomas Lincoln, s. Luther and Thankful, May 22, 1827.
William, s. Richard, Jan. 30, 1694–5.
William, s. William and Elizabeth, July 25, 1730.
William, ch. W[illia]m and Elizabeth, bp. Oct. 12, 1740. C.R.2.
William, s. William and Rachel, Apr. 23, 1772.
William, s. William and Hannah, Aug. 18, 1802.

PROUTY, William, ch. William Jr. and Priscilla, Dec. 23, 1833.
William Warren, ch. John L. and Sarah C., June 8, 1832.
———, s. Caleb W. and Abigail Y., Sept. —, 1838.
———, ch. Caleb W. and Abigail Y., May 31, 1842.
———, s. Caleb W., trader [dup. merchant], and Abby Y., Jan. [11], 1845 [dup. 1844].

PRYOR, Daniel, s. Daniel, grandchild of "sister Spring," bp. July 6, 1856. C.R.2.

RAINSFORD, Sarah A. [w. William H. Tilden], Aug. 6, 1808, in Abinton.

RAMSDEL, Benjamin, s. Joseph and Mary of Pembroke, bp. May 20, 1722. C.R.2.
Content, d. Samuel and Martha, bp. Apr. 3, 1720. C.R.2.
Gidion, ch. Thomas and Sarah, bp. May 15, 1715. C.R.2.
Jemimah, ch. Thomas and Sarah, bp. May 15, 1715. C.R.2.
Joseph, ch. Thomas and Sarah, bp. May 15, 1715. C.R.2.
Joseph, s. Joseph and Mary of Pembroke, bp. Nov. 1, 1719. C.R.1.
Mary, ch. Thomas and Sarah, bp. May 15, 1715. C.R.2.
Mary, ch. Sam[ue]ll and Mary of Pembroke, bp. Sept. 2, 1716. C.R.2.
Samuel, ch. Sam[ue]ll and Mary of Pembroke, bp. Sept. 2, 1716. C.R.2.
Sarah, d. Thomas and Sarah, bp. Aug. 14, 1715. C.R.2.

RAMSDIN (see Rumsdin), Giddion, s. Tho[mas], Sept. 13, 1712.
Lydia, d. Tho[ma]s, Sept. 5, 1719.
Mercy, d. Tho[ma]s, Nov. 5, 1717.

RANDAL (see Randall, Randull), Caleb, s. Isaac, bp. Aug. 20, 1704. C.R.2.
Caleb, s. Caleb and Hannah of Hanover, bp. Jan. 10, 1741–2. C.R.2.
Deborah, ch. Isaac, bp. ———, 1697. C.R.2.
Deborah, d. Gershom, bp. Dec. 1, 1751. C.R.2.
Elijah, s. Nehemiah and Ruth, bp. May 23, 1731. C.R.2.
Elisabeth, d. Gershom, bp. Mar. 23, 1755. C.R.2.
Elisha, s. Nehemiah and Ruth of Pembroke, bp. June 3, 1720. C.R.2.
Elisha, ch. Mary, bp. July 8, 1739. C.R.2.
Elizabeth, d. Capt. Nehemiah and Ruth, bp. Apr. 14, 1734. C.R.2.
Elizabeth, ch. Gershom and Elizabeth, bp. May 3, 1745. C.R.2.
Elizabeth (see Elisabeth).
Ezra, ch. Benj[a]m[in] and Sarah, bp. Apr. 4, 1731. C.R.2.

RANDAL, Gershom, s. Nehemiah and Ruth of Pembrok, bp. Oct. 1, 1721. C.R.2.
Gidion, s. Caleb and Hannah, bp. May 14, 1738. C.R.2.
Hannah, d. Caleb and Hannah, bp. Dec. 9, 1733. C.R.2.
James, s. Nehemiah and Mercy of Pembrooke, bp. Aug. 23, 1713. C.R.2.
Jane, ch. John and Jane, bp. July 28, 1723. C.R.2.
Job, ch. Job Jr. and Ursellah, bp. June 4, 1721. C.R.2.
Lydia, d. Elisha and Zeporah, bp. Oct. 11, 1747. C.R.2.
Margret, d. John and Jane, bp. Jan. 12, 1723–4. C.R.2.
Mary, ch. Job Jr. and Ursellah, bp. June 4, 1721. C.R.2.
Nehemiah, s. Nehemiah and Mercy, bp. Apr. 13, 1712. C.R.2.
Nehemiah, s. Elisha and Zeporah, bp. Dec. 13, 1741. C.R.2.
Nehemiah, s. Gershom and Elisabeth, bp. Sept. 6, 1747. C.R.2.
Robert, ch. Isaac, bp. ——, 1697. C.R.2.
Robert, s. Robert and Dorcass, bp. Aug. 12, 1733. C.R.2.
Robert, s. Perez and Sarah, bp. Apr. 9, 1749. C.R.2.
Ruth, ch. Isaac, bp. ——, 1699. C.R.2.
Ruth, d. Nehem[iah] and Ruth of Pembroke, bp. July 10, 1720. C.R.2.
Ruth, d. Samuel Jr. and Sally, May 31, 1822.
Sage, [ch.] Caleb and Hannah, bp. Sept. 12, 1736. C.R.2.
Samuel, s. Nehemiah and Ruth, bp. Mar. 30, 1729. C.R.2.
Sarah, ch. Job Jr. and Ursellah, bp. June 4, 1721. C.R.2.
Sarah, ch. John and Jane, bp. July 28, 1723. C.R.2.
Sarah, ch. Benj[a]m[in] and Sarah, bp. Apr. 4, 1731. C.R.2.
Susannah, d. Perez and Sarah, bp. Sept. 27, 1747. C.R.2.
Zepparah, d. Elisha and Zeporah, bp. Sept. 16, 1744. C.R.2.

RANDALL (see Randal, Randull), Abigail, d. Isaac and Deborah, Nov. —, 1709.
Abigail, d. Benja[min] and Hannah, June 13, 1760.
Abigal, d. Ezra and Margret, Dec. 13, 1757. [Abigail Randal, C.R.2.]
Achsah, d. Elijah and Hannah, Oct. 21, 1787.
Allin, s. Elijah and Hannah, Feb. 15, 1793.
Bailey, s. Perez and Sarah, bp. Oct. 14, 1750. C.R.2.
Benjamin, s. William, bp. Nov. 8, 1657. C.R.2.
Benjamin, s. Joseph, Jan. 11, 1688–9.
Benja[min], s. Benja[min] and Sarah, Nov. 20, 1725.
Benjamin, ch. Benj[a]m[in] (Randal) and Sarah, bp. Apr. 4, 1731. C.R.2.
Benjamin, s. Benja[min] and Hannah, Mar. 4, 1752. [Randal, s. Benja[min] Jr., C.R.2.]

RANDALL, Benjamin, s. Benja[min] and Hannah, Jan. 27, 1778.
Betsey, d. Benja[min] and Hannah, Apr. 6, 1765.
Calib, s. Isaac, July 29, 1703.
Charles, s. Joshua and Mercy, Sept. 30, 1738.
Daniel, s. Benja[min] and Sarah, Dec. 3, 1744. [Randal, C.R.2.]
Deborah, d. Isack, Aug. 23, 1693.
Elijah, s. Sam[ue]ll and Sarah, Dec. 21, 1758.
Elijah, s. Elijah and Hannah, Mar. 26, 1789.
Elisbeth, d. Isaac, Aug. 27, 1705. [Elizabeth Randal, d. Isaac and Deborah, C.R.2.]
Eliza A., d. Allen Jr., shoemaker, and Eliza (b. Charlestown), Aug. 28, 1849, in S. Scituate.
Elizabeth, d. William, Oct. —, 1652.
Elizabeth, twin d. Joseph, July 3, 1673.
Elizabeth (see Elisbeth).
Elizabeth, d. Joseph Jr. and Elizabeth, Apr. 22, 1712.
Elizabeth, d. John, Sept. 27, 1718.
Elizabeth, d. Jerusha, wid., bp. Oct. 5, 1718. C.R.1.
Elizabeth, d. Job Jr. and Mary, Jan. 22, 1736.
Elizabeth, d. Benja[min] and Sarah, Feb. 13, 1738.
Esther, d. Elijah and Hannah, Dec. 12, 1785.
Experence, d. Sam[ue]ll and w., bp. June 10, 1792. C.R.2.
Ezra, s. Benja[min] and Sarah, Apr. 9, 1729.
Ezra, s. Ezra and Margret, Nov. 30, 1758.
Gideon, s. Isaac, Sept. 13, 1699. [Gidion, C.R.2.]
Grace, d. Isaac and Deborah, Jan. 12, 1711–12.
Grace, d. Isaac and Deborah, bp. Apr. 12, 1713. C.R.2.
Hanna, ch. W[i]ll, bp. Nov. 23, 1645. C.R.1.
Hannah, d. Will[iam], Mar. —, 1644.
Hannah, d. Joseph, Mar. 7, 1677–8.
Hannah, d. Joshua, and Mercy, Feb. 2, 1740.
Hannah, d. Benja[min] and Hannah, Nov. 30, 1753. [Randal, C.R.2.]
Hannah Stetson, d. Elijah and Hannah, Apr. 30, 1791.
Hulda, d. Benja[min] and Sarah, Feb. 10, 1734. [Huldah Randal, C.R.2.]
Isaack, s. William, bp. Jan. 9, 1658. C.R.2.
Isack, s. Isack, Aug. 11, 1685. [Isaac, s. Isaac, C.R.2.]
Isaiah, s. Benja[min] and Sarah, Sept. 6, 1731. [Randal, C.R.2.]
Jacob, s. Isack, Mar. 19, 1690.
James, s. Job, Jan. 28, 1685–6.
Job, s. Will[iam], Feb. 8, 1654.
Job, s. Job, Dec. 4, 1683.
Job, s. Job Jr. and Ursula, June 8, 1710.

RANDALL, Joeph, s. Will, Mar. —, 1642.
John, s. William, Apr. —, 1650.
John, s. John, bp. June 16, 1678. C.R.2.
Joseph (see Joeph).
Joseph, ch. W[i]ll, bp. Nov. 23, 1645. C.R.1.
Joseph, s. Joseph, July 7, 1675.
Joseph, s. Benja[min], [illegible]3, 1723.
Joseph, ch. Benj[a]m[in] (Randal) and Sarah, bp. Apr. 4, 1731.
    C.R.2.
Joseph, s. Ezra and Margret, Mar. 24, 1755. [Randal, C.R.2.]
Joshua, s. Joseph Jr. and Elizabeth, Apr. 24, 1710.
Joshua, s. Joshua (Randal) and Mercy, Aug. 5, 1737.
Lusanna, d. Capt. Nehemiah (Randal), bp. Aug. 13, 1738. C.R.2.
Lydia, d. Job, Oct. 24, 1690.
Lydia, d. Benja[min] and Hannah, Sept. 14, 1767.
Margaret, d. Joseph, Dec. 18, 1683.
Margret, d. John and Jane, Sept. 5, 1726. [Margaret Randal,
    C.R.2.]
Mary, d. Job, Oct. 29, 1680.
Mary, d. Isaac and Deborah, July 31, 1707. [Randal, C.R.2.]
Mary, d. Job Jr. and Ursula, Feb. 11, 1717.
Mary, ch. John (Randal) and Jane, bp. July 28, 1723. C.R.2.
Mary, d. Sam[ue]ll and Sarah, May 6, 1753. [Randal, C.R.2.]
Mercy, d. Joseph, Mar. 10, 1684–5.
Mercy, d. Joshua and Mercy, Oct. 8, 1739.
Mercy Ann, w. David Sanford Jenkins Jr., May 12, 1838 [? in
    Pembroke]. P.R.17.
Molly, d. Benja[min] and Hannah, Sept. 26, 1757.
Nehemiah, s. Job, July 1, 1688.
Patience, d. John, bp. Aug. 3[worn], 1679. C.R.2.
Paul, s. Benja[min] and Sarah, Sept. 11, 1736.
Rachell (Randull), d. Izaac, Aug. 13, 1701. [Rachel Randal,
    C.R.2.]
Robert, s. Isaac, Sept. 7, 1695.
Ruth, d. Isaac, Sept. 27, 1697.
Ruth, d. Caleb and Hannah, bp. Oct. 11, 1730. C.R.2.
Ruth, ch. Mary (Randal), bp. July 8, 1739. C.R.2.
Ruth [———] [w. Capt. Nehemiah], ——, 1770. G.R.14.
Sally, d. Samuel Jr. and Sally, Oct. 29, 1814.
Samuel, s. Job, Mar. 10, 1694–5.
Samuel, s. Sam[ue]ll and Sarah, Sept. 22, 1754. [Randal, s. Sam-
    uel, C.R.2.]
Sarah, ch. W[i]ll, bp. Nov. 23, 1645. C.R.2.
Sarah, d. Joseph, Sept. 16, 1680.

RANDALL, Sarah, d. Job Jr. and Ursula, Apr. 11, 1713.
Sarah, d. Benja[min] and Sarah, Feb. 24, 1727.
Sarah, d. Sam[ue]ll and Sarah, Oct. 10, 1755. [Randal, C.R.2.]
Sarah, d. Benja[min] and Hannah, Nov. 22, 1755. [Randal, d. Benja[min] Jr., C.R.2.] [Randall, d. Capt. Benjamin, w. Lemuel Jacobs (s. Col. John), G.R.14.]
Stephen, s. Caled [? Caleb] and Hannah, bp. Nov. 30, 1729. C.R.2.
Susanah, d. Isack, Nov. 15, 1687. [Susannah, d. Isaace, C.R.2.]
Susanna, d. Benjamin and Hannah, Mar. 29, 1750. [Susannah Randal, d. Benjam[in] Jr. and Hannah, C.R.2.]
Thomas, s. Job Jr. and Ursula, Jan. 26, 1708.
Thomas, ch. Job (Randal) Jr. and Ursellah, bp. June 4, 1721. C.R.2.
Ursula, twin d. Joseph, July 3, 1673.
Ursula, d. Job Jr. and Ursula, Sept. 19, 1722. [Ursella Randal, d. Job and Ursella, C.R.2.]
William, s. William, Dec. —, 1647.
William, s. Benja[min] and Sarah, Jan. 20, 1741. [Randal, C.R.2.]

RANDULL (see Randal, Randall), Peraz, s. Isaace, Dec. 2, 1716. [Perez Randal, s. Isaac and Deborah, C.R.2.]

RAWLINGS (see Rawlins, Rollins), Ruth, d. Nathanael, Sept. 27, 1655. [Rawlins, d. Nathaniel, grand ch. Rich Sylvester, C.R.2.]

RAWLINS (see Rawlings, Rollins), Elizabeth, d. Nathanael, Mar. 1, 1653.
Elizabeth, d. Nathaniel, grand ch. Rich Sylvester, bp. Feb. 24, 1655. C.R.2.
Lydia, d. Nathaniel, bp. Nov. 23, 1656. C.R.2.
Nathainell, s. Nathaniell, Sept. 7, 1662. [Nathaniel, s. Nathaniel, C.R.2.]
Nathaniel, s. Nathaniel, bp. Dec. 11, 1659. C.R.2.
Patience, d. Nathaniell, bp. July 4, 1658. C.R.2.

RAY, Abigail, d. Caleb and Abigail, May 11, 1803.
Charles Morton, s. Caleb and Abigail, Aug. 2, 1803.
Sibil, d. Mary, bp. May 28, 1665. C.R.2.

RAYMOND, Calvin Harrison, ch. Lewis and Joanne, Apr. 5, 1840.
Fanny Margaret, ch. Lewis and Joanne, Apr. 9, 1830.
Joanna [———], w. Lewis, Nov. 27, 1809. G.R.14.
Joanne, ch. Lewis and Joanne, Oct. 19, 1834. [Joanna V., d. Lewis and Joanna, G.R.14.]
Lewis Harlow, ch. Lewis and Joanne, Nov. 29, 1832.

READ (see Reed), Joshua Bryant, ch. Jacob, bp. Aug. 6, 1820. c.r.2.

REED (see Read), Belinda [———], w. Joshua B., Feb. 15, 1825. g.r.14.
Ellen L., d. Horatio G., tack maker (b. N. Bridgewater), and Wealthy W. (b. Marshfield), June 15, 1839, in Marshfield.
Horatio G. H., s. Horatio G., tack maker (b. N. Bridgewater), and Wealthy W. (b. Marshfield), Apr. 12, 1828, in Marshfield.
Joshua B., s. Jacob and Thirza, June 28, 1818. [[h. Belinda] g.r.14.]
Joshua N., s. Joshua B., and Belenda, Aug. 8, 1846.
Maria W., d. Horatio G., tack maker (b. N. Bridgewater), and Wealthy W. (b. Marshfield), Feb. 25, 1833.
Mary Forbes, d. Horatio G., tack maker (b. N. Bridgewater), and Wealthy W. (b. Marshfield), Jan. 5, 1841, in Marshfield.
——— [———], wid. ———, ——— [1799]. c.r.1.

REYNOLDS, Lucy Jane, d. Philip, miller (b. Stoughton), and Lucy (b. Stoughton), July 13, 1848.

RICH, Caroline, w. Alfred James [Aug. —, 1828]. g.r.14.
Catharine S., d. Moses and Catharine, Oct. 9, 1809.
Catharine Scarboro, d. Capt. Moses, bp. Oct. 6, 1816. c.r.1.
George W., ch. Moses P. and Mary, Feb. 5, 1837.
Laura, ch. Moses P. and Mary, Jan. 26, 1839. [Laura Young, c.r.1.]
Lydia Waterman, ch. Moses P. and Mary, ———, 1840.
Lydia Waterman, ch. Mary, wid., bp. Apr. 1, 1849, a. 7. c.r.1.
Mary Parker, ch. Moses P. and Mary, Feb. 21, 1833.
Moses, ch. Moses P. and Mary, Oct. 29, 1834.
Moses Parker, s. Moses and Catharine, July 11, 1808.
Perry Parker, s. Mary, bp. May 7, 1809. c.r.1.
William H., ch. Moses P. and Mary, Nov. 19, 1843. [William Henry, c.r.1.]
———, ch. Moses P. and Mary, Jan. 31, 1842.

RICHARDSON, Andrew S., ch. Thomas and Judith A., May 2, 1838.
Elvira Cushing, d. Alvah and Betsey, Nov. 27, 1833.
George L., ch. Thomas and Judith A., July 2, 1840.
George W., s. Thom[as], shipjoiner, and Mary, Dec. 18, 1846.
Henry Jackson, s. Alvah and Betsey, Aug. 26, 1831.
James Barrell, s. Alvah and Betsey, Mar. 3, 1826.
Joseph Winslow, s. Alvah and Betsey, Dec. 2, 1823.
Leonard T., ch. Thomas and Judith A., Feb. 27, 1835, in Boston.

RICHARDSON, Ruth Elizabeth, d. Alvah and Betsey, Dec. 15, 1821.
Sarah Cole, d. Alvah and Betsey, Oct. 4, 1828.
Sarah E., ch. Thomas and Judith A., Oct. 14, 1836.
William H., s. Thomas, shipjoiner, and Mary W., Feb. 18, 1848.
Zimrai Carty, ch. Thomas and Mary, Feb. 19, 1844.
——, ch. Thomas and Judith A., Dec. 22, 1841.

RICKER, Belindia C., ch. William G. and Rebecca, Oct. 12, 1833, in Provintston.
George T., s. W[illia]m, sailor, and Rebecka, Feb. 28, 1845.
James Perry, ch. William G. and Rebecca, Feb. 13, 1843.
Lydia A., ch. William G. and Rebecca, Oct. 11, 1832, in Provintston.
Mary B., ch. William G. and Rebecca, Nov. 29, 1835.
Rebbecca F., d. William, mariner (b. Boston), and Rebbecca (b. Provincetown), June 28, 1849.
William R., ch. William G. and Rebecca, Feb. 20, 1839.

RIDER, Nero, negro, s. Nero and Sarah, Dec. 6, 1774.

RIGHT (see Wright, Wrighte, Write), Elizabeth, d. Thomas, June 2, 1683.
Janie, d. Thomas, Apr. —, 1685.
John, s. Thomas, Oct. —, 1688.
John, s. Mercy, Mar. 19, 1745.
John, s. Mercy, bp. June 21, 1747. C.R.2.
Mary, d. Thomas, Aug. 31, 1691.
Mercy, d. John [d. John and Lydia, C.R.2.], May 7, 1713.

RIPLEY (see Riply), George, ch. Hezekiah and Hannah, Mar. 2, 1794, in Kingston. P.R.20.
Harvey, ch. Hezekiah and Hannah, Feb. 15, 1807, in Kingston. P.R.20.
Hezekiah "from Kingston" [h. Hannah (Tilden)], Nov. 29, 1751. P.R.20.
Joseph Tilden, ch. Hezekiah and Hannah, Oct. 9, 1785, in Kingston. P.R.20.
Kenelm [Capt.], ch. Hezekiah and Hannah, Feb. 28, 1792, in Kingston. P.R.20.
Lucia, ch. Hezekiah and Hannah, Nov. 4, 1800, in Kingston. P.R.20.
Marcia, ch. Hezekiah and Hannah, w. Charles Tilden Otis, Jan. 10, 1816, in Kingston. P.R.20.
Rufus, ch. Hezekiah and Hannah, Aug. 9, 1787, in Kingston. P.R.20.
William, ch. Hezekiah and Hannah, Apr. 21, 1803, in Kingston. P.R.20.

RIPLY (see Ripley), Deborah, d. John, bp. June 8, 1712. C.R.2.
Sarah, d. Joshua and w., bp. Feb. 22, 1746-7. C.R.2.

ROBBINS, Charles, s. Anson and Rachel, June 29, 1817.
Clarisa, d. Anson and Rachel, June 20, 1813.
Elizabeth Turner, ch. George A. and Almira, Oct. 29, 1833.
George Anson, s. Anson and Rachel, July 20, 1807.
George W., s. Geo[rge] A., ship joiner, and Almira, May 13, 1849, in S. Scituate.
Horace, s. Anson and Rachel, Apr. 20, 1816.
Matilda, d. Anson and Rachel, Feb. 16, 1811. [Robins, C.R.2.]
Matilda L., ch. George A. and Almira, Feb. 6, 1844.
Rachel, d. Anson and Rachel, Apr. 13, 1820.
Walter, s. Anson and Rachel, Jan. 31, 1809. [Rollins [? Robbins], C.R.2.] [Robbins [h. Mary Otis (Torrey)], G.R.14.]

ROBBINSON (see Robinson, Robinsonn), William F., s. Azel, blacksmith, and Catharine, Dec. 25, 1844.

ROBERTSON, George Washington, s. John C. and Eleanor, Aug. 13, 1833.
John Curtis, s. Peter and Sally, June 17, 1801.
John Quincy, s. John C. and Eleanor, Sept. 13, 1831.
Nancy Curtis, d. John C. and Eleanor, Apr. 1, 1830.
Sarah Ann, d. Peter and Sally, Aug. 11, 1804.

ROBINSON (see Robbinson, Robinsonn), David W., s. David P., houswright, and Lucy L., Sept. 17, 1846.
Elmer A., s. David T., shoemaker (b. Hingham), and Lucy L., Feb. 27, 1849, in S. Scituate.
Harriet A., d. Wilbert, cooper (b. Union, Me.), and Harriet A. (b. Edgecombe, Me.), Dec. 8, 1849, in S. Scituate.
Joseph, s. Thomas, bp. Mar. 8, 1656. C.R.2.
Mary, d. Thomas, bp. Feb. 28, 1657. C.R.2.
Mary, d. Thomas, bp. Nov. 6, 1659. C.R.2.
Thomas, s. Thomas, bp. Mar. 5, 1653. C.R.2.
William, "servant Child to Col^a Cushing," bp. Aug. 2, 1724. C.R.2.
———, s. Asel, blacksmith, and Caroline, Mar. 16, 1847.

ROBINSONN (see Robbinson, Robinson), Susannah, d. Isaac, bp. Jan. 21, 1637. C.R.1.

ROGAN, Patrick [h. ———], —— [1807], in Co. Down, Parish Loughsland, Ire. G.R.10.

ROGERS (see Roggers), Abigail, d. Elizab[eth], bp. Apr. 24, 1664. C.R.2.
Alice, d. John, Mar. 26, 1685.
Caleb, s. John Sr. and Hannah, Apr. 14, 1718.
Daniel, s. John, Mar. 31, 1688.
Daniel, ch. John Jr. and Deborah, bp. July 20, 1712. C.R.2.
Daniell, s. John Jr. and Deborah, Oct. 17, 1708.
Deborah, d. John Jr. [d. John and Deborah, C.R.2.], Feb. 14, 1713-14.
Ebenezar, s. Samuel and Jael of Marshfield, bp. Oct. 24, 1714. C.R.2.
Elisha, s. Joshua and Mehitable, May 3, 1751.
Elisha, s. Joshua and Mehitable, Dec. 16, 1752.
Elizabeth, d. John, Oct. —, 1691.
Elizabeth, d. Sam[ue]ll and Jael of Marshfield, bp. ——, 1701. C.R.2.
Elizabeth, d. John Jr. and Deborah, Jan. 5, 1709-10.
Elizabeth, ch. John Jr. and Deborah, bp. July 20, 1712. C.R.2.
Eunice, d. Timothy, bp. Oct. 2[worn], 1677. C.R.2.
Eunice [? m.], June 13, 1804. G.R.6.
Gennet, d. William and Gennet, bp. May 29, 1720. C.R.2.
Hannah, d. John, May 26, 1704.
Hannah, d. Joshua and Mehitable, June 10, 1730.
Hannah, d. Joshua, bp. Aug. 15, 1736. C.R.1.
Jael, d. Sam[ue]ll and Jael of Marshfield, bp. Aug. 8, 1708. C.R.2.
James, ch. John and Deborah, bp. Feb. 19, 1726-7. C.R.2.
Janet (see Gennet).
Jeremiah, ch. John and Deborah, bp. Feb. 19, 1726-7. C.R.2.
Joannah, d. John of Marshfield, bp. Apr. 12, 1668. C.R.2.
John, s. John Jr., bp. Aug. 23, 1657. C.R.2.
John, s. John, Mar. 14, 1682-3.
John, s. John Jr. [ch. John Jr. and Deborah, C.R.2.], Feb. 29, 1711-12.
John, s. Joshua and Mehitable, Feb. 2, 1740.
John, s. Joshua and Mehitable, Apr. 15, 1748.
Joshua, s. John Sr. and Hannah, Apr. 22, 1708.
Joshua, s. Joshua and Mehitable, Mar. 31, 1737.
Joshua, s. Joshua and Sarah, bp. May 11, 1766. C.R.1.
Lois, d. Timothy, bp. Aug. 27, 1671. C.R.2.
Mary, d. Elizabeth, bp. Apr. 16, 1665. C.R.2.
Mary, ch. Samuel and Jael of Marshfield, bp. June 23, 1706. C.R.2.
Mary, d. John Sr. and Hannah, Apr. 15, 1712.
Mehetable, d. Joshua, bp. July 4, 1736. C.R.1.

ROGERS, Rhoda, d. Rhoda, bp. Aug. 3, 1662. C.R.2.
Ruth, d. Samuel and Jael of Marshfield, bp. ———, 1699.
Samuel, s. Timothy, bp. Sept. 18, 1670. C.R.2.
Samuel, ch. Samuel and Jael of Marshfield, bp. June 23, 1706. C.R.2.
Sarah, d. Sam[ue]ll and Jael, bp. June 16, 1717. C.R.2.
Sarah, d. Joshua and Sarah, bp. May 11, 1766. C.R.1.
Simeon, s. Sam[ue]ll Jr. of Marshfield, bp. Feb. 12, 1737–8. C.R.2.
Susannah, d. Samuel and Jael, bp. Oct. 8, 1710. C.R.2.
Thomas, s. Goodman of Duxberry, bp. May 6, 1638. C.R.1.
Thomas, s. Rhoda, bp. Mar. 25, 1660. C.R.2.
Thomas, s. John Sr., Aug. 15, 1695.
Thomas, s. Joshua and Mehitable, May 14, 1738.
Tho[ma]s, s. Joshua and Mehitable, July 26, 1745.
Timothy, s. Timothy, bp. Mar. 31, 1674. C.R.2.

ROGGERS (see Rogers), Joshua, s. Jos[hu]a and Sarah, Dec. 10, 1764.

ROLLINS (see Rawlings, Rawlins), Elizabeth, d. Nathanaell, June ———, 1661. [Elizeb[eth] Rawlings, d. Nathaniell, C.R.2.]

ROOSE (see Rose), Hanah, d. Thomas, May 23, 1669 [*sic*, see Patient].
Patient, d. Thomas, Mar. 31, 1668–9 [*sic*, see Hanah].
Thomas, s. Thomas, Sept. 10, 1666.

ROSE (see Roose), Asa, s. Gidion and Lydia, bp. July 4, 1742. C.R.2.
Asahel, s. Gidion and Lydia, bp. Apr. 27, 1740. C.R.2.
Bethiah, d. Joshua and Elizabeth of Marshfield, bp. Feb. 16, 1734–5. C.R.2.
Charles, s. Laban and Mabel, Apr. 20, 1789.
Elisabeth, d. Jeremiah, Sept. 13, 1703.
Elisabeth, d. Gidion and Lydia, bp. May 11, 1746. C.R.2.
Elisabeth, d. Laban and Mabel, July 8, 1783.
Elisha, s. Joseph and Elizabeth of Marshfield, bp. May 1, 1726. C.R.2.
Elizabeth (see Elisabeth).
Elizabeth, ch. Jeremiah, bp. Oct. 1, 1704. C.R.2.
Gedion, s. Laban and Mabel, June 27, 1786.
Gideon, s. Jeremiah, May 8, 1701.
Gideon, s. Gideon and Lydia, bp. June 16, 1734. C.R.2.
Gidion, ch. Jeremiah, bp. Oct. 1, 1704. C.R.2.
Gidion, s. Gidion Jr., bp. Nov. 6, 1757. C.R.2.

ROSE, Hannah, d. Joseph and Elizabeth of Marshfield, bp. July 25, 1725. C.R.2.
Hannah [――――], w. ―――― [Feb. ―, 1763]. C.R.3. G.R.2.
Jabez, "Reputed" s. Jabez Rose and Abigail Stanley, ――, 1700.
Jeremiah, s. Giddeon [Gidion, C.R.2.] and Lydia, Sept. 13, 1724.
John, s. Joshua and Elizabeth of Marshfield, bp. June 27, 1736. C.R.2.
Joseph, s. Joshua and Eliz[abeth] of Marshfield, bp. June 6, 1731. C.R.2.
Joseph, s. Laban and Mabel, Dec. 27, 1790.
Joshua, s. Joshua and w. of Marshfield, bp. Sept. 24, 1732. C.R.2.
Laban, s. Laban and Mabel, May 16, 1796.
Lydia, d. Gidion and Lydia, bp. Apr. 30, 1732. C.R.2.
Mary, d. Jabish (Rosse) [d. Jabez [dec'd] and Mary, C.R.2.], Feb. 7, 170[7–8].
Nathanael, [ch.] Gidion and Elizabeth, bp. May 9, 1736. C.R.2.
Prince, s. Gidion and Lydia, bp. Oct. 29, 1727. C.R.2.
Reuben (see Ruben).
Roland, s. Laban and Mabel, Jan. 7, 1792.
Ruben, s. Gidion and Elizabeth, bp. Oct. 30, 1743. C.R.2.
Ruth, d. Joshua of Marshfield, bp. Jan. 12, 1728–9. C.R.2.
Sarah, d. Laban and Hannah, Dec. 19, 1806.
Simeon, s. Gideon and Lydia, bp. Apr. 26, 1741. C.R.2.
Thomas, s. Jeremiah, Aug. 23, 1699.
Thomas, s. Jeremiah, Mar. 10, 1706–7.
Thomas, s. Jeremiah an[d] Elizabeth, bp. June 27, 1708. C.R.2.
Thomas, s. Gidion and Lydia, bp. Dec. 14, 1729. C.R.2.

ROSS, Mary E., d. Lucy A. (b. Weymouth), June 28, 1849, in S. Scituate.

RUGGLES, Betsey, d. Tho[ma]s and Eunice, Jan. 24, 1791.
Betsey, d. Tho[ma]s and Eunice, May 9, 1794.
Eunice, d. Tho[ma]s and Eunice, Sept. 20, 1783. [[w. Charles Foster] Sept. 28, P.R.5.]
George Thomas, ch. Samuel O. and Mary, Dec. 3, 1835.
George Thomas, ch. Samuel O. and Mary, Apr. 9, 1838.
Grace, d. John and Joanna, Sept. 11, 1725. [Mary "Alias Grace," C.R.2.]
Hannah, d. Jo[h]n and Joanna, June 22, 1723.
Hannah, d. John and Lusanna, Aug. 16, 1762.
Harriet, ch. Samuel O. and Harriet, Jan. 21, 1821.
Henry Turner, s. Tho[ma]s and w., bp. June 30, 1805. C.R.2.
John, s. John (Rugles) and Joanna, bp. Sept. 10, 1727. C.R.2.
John, s. John and Joanna, June 13, 1729.

RUGGLES, John, s. Thomas and Eunice, Dec. 14, 1781.
John, s. Tho[ma]s and Eunice, July 24, 1785.
Lusanna, d. John and Lusanna, Apr. 4, 1760.
Lusanna, d. Tho[ma]s and Eunice, June 24, 1787.
Mary (see Grace).
Mary Elizabeth, ch. Samuel O. and Mary, Jan. 1, 1828.
Samuel, ch. Samuel O. and Mary, Oct. 16, 1826.
Samuel, ch. Samuel O. and Mary, Feb. 5, 1830.
Samuel Oakman, s. Tho[ma]s and Eunice, May 29, 1797.
Sarah, d. Jo[h]n and Joanna, May 22, 1731.
Sarah, d. Tho[ma]s and Eunice, Oct. 19, 1789.
Sarah Lake, ch. Samuel O. and Mary, June 2, 1833.
Thomas, s. Jo[h]n and Joanna, July 31, 1721.
Thomas, s. John and Lusanna, Mar. 22, 1757.
Thomas, s. Tho[ma]s and Eunice, Mar. 24, 1792.

RUMSDIN (see Ramsdin), Sarah, d. Tho[mas] (Ramsdin), July 12, 1715.

RUSSEL, Georg, s. Deborah, Feb. 18, 1776, in Wolderbourgh.
John, s. Deborah, Jan. 31, 1763.
Mary, "Servt child to John Ruggles," bp. June 4, 1727. c.r.2.

SALMOND, Agnes, w. Zephaniah Talbot [Oct. —, 1796]. g.r.15.

SAMPSON (see Samson), Abby A., ch. John and Deborah R. (Wiswell), ———, 1831. g.r.14.
Abigail Ellis, d. John and Deborah, Oct. 24, 1830.
Ann Marie [? m.], Sept. 29, 1830. g.r.2.
Deborah Jacobs, d. John and Deborah [Deborah R. (Wiswell), g.r.14.], Jan. 9, 1826.
Gamaliel D. (see ——— Sampson).
Gamaliel Daman, s. John and Deborah [Deborah R. (Wiswell), g.r.14.], June 12, 1833.
James Wiswell, s. John and Deborah [Deborah R. (Wiswell), g.r.14.], Feb. 18, 1828.
John [h. Deborah R. (Wiswell)], ———, 1793. g.r.14.
John Briggs, s. John and Deborah, May 24, 1823.
Lois [———], w. Clark, ———, 1797. g.r.15.
Mary, ch. Charles, bp. Nov. 17, 1751. c.r.2.
Melzar, ch. Charles, bp. Nov. 17, 1751. c.r.2.
Sophia Simmons, d. John and Deborah, Oct. 10, 1834.
William G., s. John and Deborah [Deborah R. (Wiswell), g.r.14.], Sep[t]. 24, 1837.
———, ch. John and Deborah, Oct. 1, 1840. [Gamaliel D., ch. John and Deborah R. (Wiswell), g.r.14.]

SAMSON (see Sampson), ———, ch. Charls, bp. Aug. 9, 1747. c.r.2.

SANBORN, Andrew F., s. Levi, farmer, and Sarah F., Sept. 30, 1846.

SANDERS, Edward, s. John, Dec. 29, 1692–3 [*sic*].

SARJANT (see Searjeant), Mary, d. Thomas, Jan. 28, 1702–3.

SAWYER, Aaron [h. Lucy P.], Oct. 21, 1825. g.r.19.
Jerome H. [h. Sarah A.], Mar. 18, 1832. g.r.19.
Lucy P. [———], w. Aaron, July 29, 1805. g.r.19.
Sarah A. [———], w. Jerome H., May 18, 1829. g.r.19.

SCHULTZ, Matilda [? m.], Feb. 12, 1815. g.r.6.

SEAGRAVE, Harriet Edwards, ch. Rev. Edward and Harriet, May 7, 1833.
Mary Walker, ch. Rev. Edward and Harriet, Mar. 31, 1831.

SEARJEANT (see Sarjant), Elizabeth, d. Thomas, May 6, 1690.
Thaddeus, s. Thomas, Aug. 25, 1700.
Thomas, s. Thomas, Sept. 6 [? 3], 1692.
William, s. Thomas, Apr. 7, 1696.

SEARS, Caroline, ch. Isaac and Sarah S., Apr. 5, 1831.
Dolly, d. Peter and Susa, Mar. 1, 1780.
George A., ch. Isaac and Sarah S., May 27, 1836.
Isaac, s. Peter and Susa, Dec. 11, 1793.
James Isaac, ch. Isaac and Sarah S., June 29, 1829.
Julia [———], w. ———, —— [1811]. c.r.3.
Lucy, d. Peter and Susa, Mar. 3, 1791.
Peter, Capt. [h. Susa] ("Rev. soldeir"), Nov. 29, 1753. g.r.14.
Peter, s. Peter and Susa, Oct. 1, 1782.
Polly, d. Peter and Susa, Dec. 29, 1786.
Sally, d. Peter and Susa, Aug. 21, 1784.

SEAVERNS, Charles H. [h. Sarah L.] [Sept. —, 1807]. g.r.2.
Henry A., "A Soldier," Apr. 21, 1842. g.r.2.
Sarah L. [———], w. Charles H. [Feb. —, 1808]. g.r.2.

SEWALL, Edmund Quincy, ch. Rev. Edmund Q. and Caroline, Feb. 29, 1828, in Newburyport.
Ellen Devereux, ch. Rev. Edmund Q. and Caroline, Mar. 10, 1822, in Barnstable.
George Ward, ch. Rev. Edmund Q. and Caroline [Caroline W., c.r.1.], Feb. 7, 1834.

SHARP, Benoni, s. Deborah (w. Joseph Gannett), June —, 1682.

SHAW, George, s. John and Abigail of Plympton, bp. Dec. 29, 1723. C.R.2.
Isaac, s. John and Abigail of Plympton, bp. June 27, 1725. C.R.2.
Lydia, d. John and Abigail of Plympton, bp. July 31, 1726. C.R.2.

SHEAFE, Charles Cushing, s. Henry [Henry Esq., C.R.2.] and Lucy, Dec. 30, 1818.
Lucy Cushing, d. Henry and Lucy, July 29, 1814.

SHELLEY, Hannah, d. Robert, bp. July 2, 1637. C.R.1.

SHERMAN, Clara, ch. Israiel H. and Clarissa, —— [rec. after ch. b. Feb. 27, 1841].
Clarissa [————], w. Israel H. [July —, 1812]. G.R.2.
Israel H. [h. Clarissa] [Nov. —, 1802]. G.R.2.
Jane H., ch. Israiel H. and Clarissa, Aug. 31, 1838.
Lucy Jane, d. Otis Jr. and Angeline, Aug. 17, 1829.
Mary, w. George W. Brown, May 12, 1816. G.R.6.
Otis [h. Jennie (Howard)] [Sept. —, 1768]. G.R.2.
Otis Williams, s. Otis Jr. and Angeline, Aug. 2, 1831.
Warren Hobart, ch. Israiel H. and Clarissa, Feb. 27, 1841.
Warren S., ch. Israiel H. and Clarissa, ——, 1836.

SHIN, Samuel, "A Soldier," —— [1847]. G.R.2.

SHOFE, Gorge, twin s. Edward, June 2, 1705. [Shove, C.R.2.]
Mary, twin d. Edward, June 2, 1705. [Shove, C.R.2.]

SILLVERSTER (see Silverster, Silvester, Sylvester), Martha, d. Iserell (Silverster), Sept. 22, 1682. [Silvester, d. Israell, C.R.2.]

SILVER, Roza L., ——, 1823. G.R.10.

SILVERSTER (see Sillverster, Silvester, Sylvester), Bershewa, d. Iserell, Oct. 11, 1692.
Elisha, s. Iserell, Jan. 3, 1685. [Silvester, s. Israell, C.R.2.]
Iserell, s. Iserell, Sept. 23, 1674 [dup. 1675]. [Israell Silvister, s. Israell, bp. Sept. 19, 1675, C.R.2.]
Lois, d. Iserell, Jan. 27, 1680. [Silvester, d. Israell, C.R.2.]
Mary, d. Iserell, Mar. 10, 1683.
Petter, s. Iserell, Apr. 15, 1687.
Zebolon, s. Iserell, Jan. 25, 1689.

SILVESTER, (see Sillverster, Silverster, Sylvester), Abel, s. Abel and Lillis, Aug. 4, 181[worn] [1810]. [Sylvester [h. Arabella] [h. Deborah], ——, 1810, G.R.2.]

SILVESTER, Abigail, d. Benjamin, Nov. 12, 1695.
Abigail Lincoln, d. John and Bathsheba, Sept. 25, 1786.
Amos, s. Joseph, Nov. 15, 1685.
Amos, s. Amos [s. Amos and Elizabeth, C.R.2.], Sept. 14, 1707.
Anna, d. Joseph, May 5, 1669. [Sylvester, C.R.2.]
Barshua, ch. Israel, bp. ――, 1695. C.R.2.
Bathsheba, d. John and Bathsheba, Oct. 1, 1784.
Benjamin, s. Joseph, Dec. 11, 1680.
Benjamin, s. Benjamin, Dec. 26, 1687.
Benjamin, s. Benjamin, Feb. 17, 1698–9.
Benjamin, s. Benjamin Jr. and Jerusha, Nov. 5, 1711.
Benjamin, s. Benj[a]m[in] and Jerusha, bp. May 8, 1720. C.R.2.
Caleb, s. Amos [s. Amoss and Elizabeth, C.R.2.], Dec. 14, 1719.
Charles, s. Will[ia]m and Mary, Apr. 20, 1739.
Charles, s. Thomas Jr. and Releaf, Dec. 20, 1787.
Charles S., s. Abel and Lillis, Aug. 3, 1825. [Sylvester, G.R.18.]
Cloe, d. Elisha and Grace, July 23, 1765.
Danforth Newcomb, s. Abel and Lillis, Feb. 8, 1813.
David, s. Joseph, Apr. 20, 1683.
Deborah, d. Israell [d. Israel, C.R.2.], Apr. 18, 1696.
Deborah, d. Peter and Mary, Oct. 3, 1726.
Deborah, [ch.] Joseph and Lydia, bp. Aug. 5, 1739. C.R.2.
Deborah, d. Jacob and Deborah, July 17, 1753.
Deborah Bryant, d. John and Bathsheba, Mar. 9, 1793.
Desire, d. Richard and Desire, Dec. 8, 1706.
Desire, ch. Nehemiah, bp. Aug. 20, 1738. C.R.2.
Desire, d. Nehemiah, bp. June 2, 1754. C.R.2.
Edmond, s. Amos, June 23, 1721. [Edmund, s. Amos and Eliz[abeth], C.R.2.]
Elijah, s. Will[ia]m and Mary, July 13, 1744.
Elijah, s. William and Mary, bp. Apr. 20, 1746. C.R.2.
Elisha, ch. Zebulun and Mary, bp. Apr. 24, 1720. C.R.2.
Elisha, s. Elisha and Eunice, bp. Nov. 30, 1735. C.R.2.
Elisha, s. Elisha and Eunice, bp. June 4, 1738. C.R.2.
Elisha, s. Elisha and Grace, Nov. 28, 1752.
Elisha, ch. Zebulon and Mary, father of Thomas and Elisha, ――.
Elizabeth, d. Samuel and w. of Marshfield, bp. June 18, 1710. C.R.2.
Elizabeth, d. Amos and Elizabeth, bp. Apr. 24, 1726. C.R.2.
Elizabeth, d. John and Elizabeth of Marshfield, bp. Nov. 28, 1734. C.R.2.
Faith, d. Richard and Desire, May 13, 1708.
Hannah, d. John, bp. Oct. 16, 1681. C.R.2.

SILVESTER, Hannah, d. Peter [d. Peter and Mary, C.R.2.], Apr. 2, 1716.
Hannah, d. Joseph of Marshfield, bp. Mar. 19, 1720-21. C.R.2.
Hannah, d. Will[ia]m and Mary, Nov. 11, 1748.
Hannah, d. Elisha and Grace, Nov. 29, 1758.
Henry Hayden, s. Abel and Lillis, July 13, 180[worn] [1808]. [Sylvester, July 13, 1808, P.R.22.]
Hervey, s. Elisha Jr. and Abigail, June 12, 1779.
Hinksmen, s. Amos, Dec. 20, 1713. [Hincksman, s. Amos and Elizabeth, C.R.2.]
Isaac, s. Will[ia]m and Mary, June 27, 1746.
Israel, ch. Zebulon and Mary, ———, 1717.
Israel, ch. Zebulun and Mary, bp. Apr. 24, 1720. C.R.2.
Israel, s. Israel and w., bp. May 8, 1748. C.R.2.
Isral, s. Isral and Deliverance, Mar. 4, 1747.
Jacob, s. Zeb[ulo]n and Mary, Aug. 17, 1722.
Jacob, s. Benj[a]m[in] and Ruth, bp. Oct. 4, 1724. C.R.2.
Jacob, ch. Zebulun and Mary, bp. Oct. 10, 1731. C.R.2.
Jael, d. Mary, bp. Dec. 6, 1730. C.R.2.
James, s. Benj[a]m[in] and Ruth, bp. June 17, 1722. C.R.2.
James, s. Elisha and Eunice, bp. Nov. 23, 1740. C.R.2.
John, ch. Samuel and Lucretious of Marshfield, bp. June 22, 1707. C.R.2.
John, s. John and Eliz[abeth] of Marshfield, bp. Oct. 12, 1735. C.R.2.
John, s. John and Bathsheba, Jan. 13, 1789.
Jonathan, s. Joseph and Mary of Marshfield, bp. Apr. 5, 1713. C.R.2.
Joseph, s. Joseph, Nov. 11, 1664. [Sylvester, C.R.2.]
Joseph, s. John, bp. Mar. 31, 1674. C.R.2.
Joseph, s. Benjamin, bp. July 1, 1688. C.R.2.
Joseph, s. Benjamin, May 4, 1689.
Joseph, s. Amos, Jan. 9, 1711. [s. Amos and Elizabeth, C.R.2.]
Joseph, s. Joseph and Mary of Marshfield, bp. Oct. 15, 1727. C.R.2.
Joseph, s. Joseph and Lydia, bp. May 16, 1742. C.R.2.
Joshua, s. Samuel of Marshfield, bp. June 27, 1708. C.R.2.
Joshua, s. Peter and Mary, Oct. 6, 1717.
Lemuel, s. Joseph and Lidia [Lydia, C.R.2.], Dec. 9, 1728.
Levi, s. Peter and Mary, Jan. 12, 1723.
Lidia, d. John, bp. July 6, 1679. C.R.2.
Lillis, d. Elisha and Lillis, Aug. 7, 1778.
Lucretia, twin ch. Joseph of Marshfield, bp. May 23, 1725. C.R.2.
Lucy, d. Isral and Diliverance, June 28, 1744. [Luce, d. Israel and w., C.R.2.]

SILVESTER, Lucy A., ch. Abel and Lillis, Apr. 17, 1828.
Lucy Walker, d. Thomas O. and Lucy, Feb. 10, 1814.
Luke, s. Luke, bp. June 3, 1753. C.R.2.
Luke, ch. Zebulon and Mary, ———. [ch. Zebulun and Mary, bp. Oct. 10, 1731. C.R.2.]
Lurana, d. Elisha Jr. [dup. omits Jr.] and Hannah, May 30, 1748. [Lurania, C.R.2.]
Luther, s. Samuel and Hannah, Oct. 20, 1770.
Lydia (see Lidia).
Lydia, d. Benjamin, Jan. 26, 1692–3.
Lydia, d. Joseph and Lydia, bp. Nov. 9, 1735. C.R.2.
Marcy, d. Thomas Jr. and Releaf, Mar. 14, 1778.
Marcy, d. Elisha Jr. and Abigil, Aug. 3, 1781.
Margret, d. Joseph and Mary of Marshfield, bp. June 5, 1709. C.R.2.
Marlborough, s. W[illia]m, bp. May 27, 1753. C.R.2.
Martha, d. Zebulon and Mary, Mar. 30, 1716.
Martha, d. Zebulun and Mary, bp. Aug. 11, 1717. C.R.2.
Mary, d. Joseph, Dec. 24, 1666. [Sylvester, C.R.2.]
Mary, d. Israell, bp. May 17, 1685. C.R.2.
Mary, d. Benjamin, June 4, 1691.
Mary, d. Joseph and Mary of Marshfield, bp. Mar. 18, 1711. C.R.2.
Mary, d. Amos [d. Amoss and Elizabeth, C.R.2.], Dec. 29, 1716.
Mary, d. Peter and Mary, Nov. 7, 1721.
Mary, d. Amos [d. Amos and Elizabeth, C.R.2.], Oct. 19, 1723.
Mary, d. Zebulun and Mary, bp. Aug. 13, 1732. C.R.2.
Mary, d. Will[ia]m and Mary, July 30, 1741.
Mary Ann, ch. Abel and Lillis, Sept. 16, 1819.
Mercy, d. Sam[ue]ll of Marshfield, bp. Sept. 28, 1712. C.R.2.
Mercy (see Marcy).
Michael, s. Amos [s. Amos and Elizabeth, C.R.2.], Oct. 27, 1714.
Naomi, d. Joseph, Mar. 5, 1677–8. [Naomy, C.R.2.]
Nathanael, ch. Zebulun and Mary, bp. Oct. 10, 1731. C.R.2.
Nathanael, s. Nehemiah and Mehitabel, bp. July 29, 1750. C.R.2.
Nathaniel, s. Amos, Apr. 29, 1718. [Nathanaell, s. Amos and Elizabeth, C.R.2.]
Nathaniel, ch. Zebulon and Mary, ———.
Nathaniel S., s. Abel and Lillis, Sept. 24, 1822.
Nathaniell, s. Richard, Oct. 31, 1704.
Nehemiah, s. Richard, Jan. 24, 1714.
Nehemiah, ch. Richard and Desire, bp. Sept. 8, 1723. C.R.2.
Nehemiah, s. Nehemiah and Mehitabel, bp. May 16, 1742. C.R.2.
Nehemiah, s. Nehemiah and Mehitabel, bp. May 25, 1746. C.R.2.
Oakes, s. Samuel and Hannah, Feb. 11, 1774.

SILVESTER, Oliffe, d. Zabulon and Mary, Jan. 7, 1713-14. [Olieff, d. Zebulun and Mary, C.R.2.]
Peter, s. Israell, bp. Sept. 30, 1688. C.R.2.
Peter, s. Peter and Mary, Jan. 12, 1713.
Peter, s. Peter and Mary, bp. Feb. 28, 1714. C.R.2.
Polly, d. Samuel and Desire, June 21, 1788.
Rachel, ch. Samuel and Lucretious of Marshfield, bp. June 22, 1707. C.R.2.
Rachel, d. Thomas and Releaf, Mar. 16, 1782.
Releaf, d. Thomas Jr. and Releaf, July 25, 1773.
Richard [dup. Silverster], s. Iserell, Mar. 2, 1678-9. [Silvester, s. Israel, C.R.2.]
Richard, s. Benjamin and Mary, Sept. 19, 1702.
Richard, s. Benjamin, bp. July 16, 1704. C.R.2.
Richard, s. Nehemiah, bp. Oct. 30, 1743. C.R.2.
Ruggles, s. Elisha Jr. and Abigail, Dec. 27, 1776.
Ruth, d. Israell Jr., June 26, 1702.
Ruth, d. Richard, Aug. 6, 1717.
Ruth, d. Benj[a]m[in] and Ruth, bp. May 8, 1720. C.R.2.
Ruth, d. Richard and Desire, bp. Aug. 22, 1723. C.R.2.
Ruth, d. Joseph and Lydia, bp. May 9, 1731. C.R.2.
Samuel, ch. Samuel and Lucretious of Marshfield, bp. June 22, 1707. C.R.2.
Samuell, s. John, bp. Oct. 3[worn], 1676. C.R.2.
Seth, s. Richard and Desire, Apr. 10, 1711.
Seth, ch. Richard and Desire, bp. Sept. 8, 1723. C.R.2.
Seth, s. Nehemiah, bp. May 18, 1740. C.R.2.
Silience [dup. Silance Silverster], d. Iserell, Aug. 30 [dup. Aug. 31], 1677. [Silence Silvester, d. Israell, C.R.2.]
Simeon, s. Elisha and Eunice, bp. June 5, 1743. C.R.2.
Stafford, s. John and Bathsheba, Jan. 1, 1799.
Standly, s. Benjamin, Dec. 4, 1705.
Stephen, s. Nehemiah and w., bp. May 8, 1748. C.R.2.
Thomas, s. Sam[ue]ll of Marshfield, bp. Aug. 4, 1717. C.R.2.
Thomas, s. Elisha and Grace, Nov. 26, 1754. [Sylvester, C.R.2.]
Thomas 3d, s. Thomas Jr. and Releaf, Oct. 1, 1784.
Timothy, s. Joseph of Marshfield, bp. July 20, 1718. C.R.2.
Tryphena, d. Thomas Jr. and Releaf, Sept. 25, 1790. [Tryphine Sylvester, C.R.2.] [Tryphena Sylvester, w. Homer Bowker, G.R.14.]
Tryphosa, d. Thomas Jr. and Releaf, May 19, 1793.
Warren, s. Thomas Jr. and Releaf, Sept. 24, 1775.
William, s. Amos [s. Amos and Elisabeth, C.R.2.], Feb. 22, 1709.
William, s. John and Bathsheba, Mar. 21, 1791.
William Brown, s. Abel and Lillis, May 22, 1816.

SILVESTER, Zebulun, ch. Israel, bp. ——, 1695. C.R.2.
Zebulun, ch. Zebulun and Mary, bp. Oct. 10, 1731. C.R.2.

SIMMONS (see Simonds, Simons, Symmons, Symons), Aaron, s. Moses, bp. Aug. 4, 1672. C.R.2.
Aaron (see Aron).
Abigall, d. Ebenezer, Feb. 8, 1715.
Aron [dup. Simons], s. Moses and Rachell [dup. Rachel], Oct. 2 [dup. Oct. 7], 1720. [Aaron Symons, C.R.1.]
Benjamin, s. Silvanus and Elizabeth, Apr. 13, 180[worn].
Charles, s. Silvanus and Elizabeth, Dec. 8, 1825.
Charles Whiting, s. Cha[rle]s and Tamsin, Jan. 11, 1796.
Deborah, d. Aaron, bp. June 6, 1779. C.R.1.
Ebenezar, s. Ebenezar and Lydia, bp. June 28, 1724. C.R.2.
Ebinezar, s. Charles and Tamsin, Mar. 25, 1797.
Eliza Ellen, ch. Charles and Eliza, ——, 183[ ].
Elizabeth, d. Aaron, bp. July 1, 1753. C.R.1.
Elizabeth, d. Silvanus and Elizabe[t]h, Apr. 17, 1810.
Emely, d. Peleg and Lucy, Dec. 2, 1825.
Gridley, s. Silvanus and Elizabeth, Mar. 15, 1812.
Hiram, s. Silvanus and Elizabeth, Dec. 8, 1820.
John Dammon, s. Silvanus and Elizabeth, Mar. 4, 1803.
Joseph, [ch.] Aaron Jr. and w., bp. Sept. 21, 1777. C.R.1.
Joseph, s. Samuel [Sam[ue]ll, C.R.2.] and Thankful, Aug. 8, 1792.
Joseph, s. Silvanus and Elizabeth, May 18, 1808.
Joseph, s. Peleg and Lucy, Apr. 11, 1829.
Joseph H., ch. William and Sally A., Apr. 19, 1844.
Joshua, s. Ebenezer, Oct. 25, 1717. [Symons, C.R.1.]
Lettice, d. Moses Jr., bp. July 1, 1753. C.R.1.
Lydia, d. Samuel and Thankful, Sept. 13, 1796.
Margaret Damon, d. Peleg and Lucy, Apr. 13, 1818.
Mary, d. Peleg and Lucy, Jan. 29, 1827.
Melissa A. P., ch. William and Sally A., Feb. 15, 1827, in Boston.
Moses, s. Moses, bp. June 10, 1666. C.R.2.
Nabbe, d. Barnabas, bp. June 6, 1779. C.R.1.
Peleg, s. Ebenezer, bp. Sept. 1, 1728. C.R.2.
Peleg, s. Samuel and Thankful, Apr. 17, 1788.
Rebecka, ch. Aaron, bp. July 16, 1682. C.R.2.
Samuel (Simmon), s. Ebenezer, bp. July 18, 1725. C.R.2.
Samuel, s. Samuel and Thankful, Apr. 26, 1790.
Samuel J., ch. William and Sally A., Feb. 2, 1838, in Boston.
Sarah A. [? m.], July 15, 1812. G.R.6.
Sarah E. Damon, d. Silvanus and Elizabeth, Jan. 20, 1823.

SIMMONS, Silvanus, s. Silvanus and Elizabeth, Aug. 21, 1816.
Thomas, s. Samuel and Thankful, Aug. 18, 1794.
Thomas, s. Sam[ue]ll and w., bp. May 29, 1796. C.R.2.
Warren, s. Molly, June 30, 1780.
Warren, s. Samuel and Thankful, Jan. 23, 1799.
William A., ch. William and Sally A., Jan. 20, 1830, in Boston.
William Henry, s. Silvanus and Elizabeth, Mar. 19, 1814.
—— [———], w. S. A., —— [1825]. C.R.1.

SIMONDS (see Simmons, Simons, Symmons, Symons), Amelia, w. Rev. W[illia]m H. Kelton, July 17, 1837. G.R.2.
Damson, d. —— and w., bp. May 2, 1802. C.R.2.

SIMONS (see Simmons, Simonds, Symmons, Symons), Leah, d. Moses and Rachel, Feb. 12, 1725. [Symmons, C.R.1.]
Lydia, d. Ebenezer, Sept. 10, 1719. [Symmons, C.R.1.]
Mary, d. Sam[ue]ll and w., bp. June 3, 1804. C.R.2.
Moses, s. Moses and Rachel, Sept. 7, 1718. [Symons, C.R.1.]
Patience, d. Patience (wid. Moses), bp. Mar. 18, 1676. C.R.2.
Peleg, s. Sam[ue]ll and w., bp. Dec. —, 1792. C.R.2.
Rachel, d. Moses and Rachel, Apr. 20, 1723.
Ruth, d. Peleg and Ruth, Feb. 8, 176[0].
Sam[ue]ll, s. Sam[ue]ll and w., bp. Dec. —, 1792. C.R.2.
Sarah, d. Moses, bp. July 3, 1670. C.R.2.
Sarah, d. Ebenezer and Leah, Oct. 14, 1766.

SKIFF, John, s. Samuel and Eliza[beth], Apr. 3, 1745. [Skiffe, s. Samuel and Elisabeth, C.R.2.]

SLACK, Thomas, s. Thomas and Ruth of Plymton, bp. July 12, 1719. C.R.2.

SLOANE (see Sloene), Ann H., d. John, farmer (b. Ireland), and Christiana (b. Ireland), Dec. 24, 1840.
Robert G., s. John, farmer (b. Ireland), and Christiana (b. Ireland), Jan. 29, 1844.
William T., s. John, farmer (b. Ireland), and Christiana (b. Ireland), July 30, 1845.

SLOENE (see Sloane), Margaret E., d. John B., wood turner, and Christinia B., July 29, 1847.

SMITH, Abial, ch. Joseph and Rachel "formerly" of Hanover, bp. Nov. 3, 1734. C.R.2.
Abigail, ch. Israel, bp. July 12, 1752. C.R.2.
Abigail, d. Wid. Rachel Spooner, bp. May 13, 1753. C.R.2.
Abigal, d. Israel and Abigal, Apr. 7, 1750.

SMITH, Adelaide L. Torsleff, d. J[ohn] A[lbert] and A[ngeline] J.,
———, 1843. G.R.14.
Alice, d. Israel and Abigal, June 14, 1757. [Allice, C.R.2.]
Angeline J. [———], w. John Albert, ———, 1826. G.R.14.
Aphia [———], w. Caleb, ———, 1800. G.R.14.
Caleb [h. Aphia], ———, 1798. G.R.14.
Charls, s. Israel and Abigal, Oct. 29, 1755. [Charles, C.R.2.]
Fany Elizabeth, ch. Caleb and Affa, Aug. 9, 1828.
Isaac, ch. Joseph and Rachel "formerly" of Hanover, bp. Nov. 3, 1734. C.R.2.
Israel, ch. Joseph and Rachel "formerly" of Hanover, bp. Nov. 3, 1734. C.R.2.
Jerome V. C., [s.] John H., ship carpenter (b. Provincetown), and Mary, July 7, 1849.
John Albert [h. Angeline J.], ———, 1820. G.R.14.
John H. Jr., s. John H., shipwright, and Mary H., Oct. 10, 1846.
Joseph "brought to baptism by his uncle Israel And aunt Elizabeth Hatch," bp. June 8, 1712. C.R.2.
Joseph, s. Israel and Abigal, Apr. 21, 1747.
Joseph, ch. Israel, bp. July 12, 1752. C.R.2.
Joshua, ch. Joseph and Rachel "formerly" of Hanover, bp. Nov. 3, 1734. C.R.2.
Levi, ch. Joseph and Rachel "formerly" of Hanover, bp. Nov. 3, 1734. C.R.2.
Lucy, d. Israel and Abigal, Apr. 9, 1754.
Mary, d. Deborah, bp. Mar. 25, 1705. C.R.2.
Patrick, Nov. 21, 1831. G.R.10.
Peleg, ch. Joseph and Rachel "formerly" of Hanover, bp. Nov. 3, 1734. C.R.2.
Peleg, s. Israel and Abigal, May 6, 1752.
Rachel, ch. Joseph and Rachel "formerly" of Hanover, bp. Nov. 3, 1734. C.R.2.
Zachary Taylor, s. John H., ship carpenter (b. Provincetown), and Mary, July 7, 1849.
———, d. John H., shipwright, and Mary, Sept. 6, 1844.

SNOW, Elbridge T., Oct. 2, 1836. G.R.2.
Lettie A. [? m.], Nov. 29, 1836. G.R.2.

SOMERBY, Frederic T., Jan. 4, 1814. G.R.6.

SOPAR (see Soper), Abigail, d. Thomas, May 15, 1699.
David, s. Thomas, Nov. 22, 1709.
Elizabeth, d. Thomas, Nov. 13, 1695.
John, s. Thomas, July 24, 1714. [Soper, C.R.1.]

SOPAR, Joseph, s. Thomas, Jan. —, 1703.
Mary, d. Thomas, Apr. 23, 1697.
Sarah, d. Thomas, Jan. 24, 1708. [Soper, C.R.1.]
Thomas, s. Thomas, Feb. 2, 1706.

SOPER (see Sopar), Abigal, d. Joseph and Lydia, Jan. 18, 1734. [Abigail Soaper, C.R.1.]
Anna, d. John and Anna, July 14, 1746. [Ann, d. Ann,wid., C.R.1.]
David, s. Thomas, bp. Sept. 2, 1711. C.R.1.
Joseph, s. Joseph and Lydia, "Jane" 26, 1737.
Lydia, d. Joseph and Lydia, Dec. 18, 1732.
Mary, d. Joseph and Lydia, Mar. 18, 1742.
Mary, d. Joseph, bp. July 3, 1743. C.R.1.
Mary, d. Joseph, bp. July 10, 1747. C.R.1.
Persis, d. Joseph and Lydia, Dec. 13, 1740.
Seth, s. Joseph and Lydia, Sept. 11, 1730.

SOUL, Abigail, ch. Ichabod dec'd and w., bp. Mar. 6, 1742–3. C.R.2.
Sylla [?], ch. Ichabod dec'd and w., bp. Mar. 6, 1742–3. C.R.2.

SOUTHWORTH, Abigail, w. John Foster, June 7, 1769. G.R.13.
Catharine Wild, ch. James and Julia, May 31, 1842.
Edward, ch. James and Julia, Apr. 26, 1838.
George, s. Thomas [Cap[t]. Tho[ma]s, C.R.2.] and Sarah, May 23, 1815.
James, s. Thomas and Sarah, Dec. 11, 1798. [Southward, C.R.2.] [Southworth, G.R.14.]
John, s. Thomas [Cap[t]. Tho[ma]s, C.R.2.] and Sarah, Apr. 5, 1814.
Julia T., Dec. —, 1806. G.R.14.
Lucy J., d. Thomas and Sarah, May 30, 1802.
Nathan, s. Thomas [Capt. Thomas, C.R.2.] and Sarah, Jan. 8, 1806.
Sarah, d. Thomas and Sarah, June 16, 1809. [Southward, d. Capt. Southward and w., C.R.2.]
Sarah, ch. James and Julia, Aug. 18, 1840.
Temperance J., d. Thomas and Sarah, Sept. 29, 1810. [Temperance James, ch. Cap[t]. Tho[ma]s, C.R.2.]
Thomus, s. Thomas and Sarah, Oct. 20, 1807. [Thomas Southward, C.R.2.]

SPALDING (see Spaulding), Edwin James, ch. Edwin and Almeda, Sept. 26, 1837. [Spaulding, C.R.1.]
George Webster, ch. Edwin and Almeda, Aug. 26, 1842.
Henry Otis, ch. Edwin and Almeda, Apr. 1, 1840.
Maria, ch. Edwin and Almeda, Jan. 3, 1835. [Spaulding, C.R.1.]

SPARREL (see Sparrell, Sparriell), Elizabeth, d. James Nuton and Ruth, Sept. 2, 1767.
Elizabeth, ch. Wid. Sparrel, bp. June 4, 1775. C.R.1.
Hannah, d. James Nuten and Ruth, June 18, 1772.
Hannah, ch. Wid. Sparrel, bp. June 4, 1775. C.R.1.
James, s. James Nuton and Ruth, Apr. 7, 1770.
James, ch. Wid. Sparrel, bp. June 4, 1775. C.R.1.

SPARRELL (see Sparrel, Sparriell), Betsey, d. James and Rachel, July 9, 1808. [Sparrel, C.R.2.]
Charles Warren, s. James N. and Desire, Dec. 30, 1835.
Debby Cushing Nash, d. James N. and Desire, May 11, 1829.
Desire, d. James N. and Desire, Oct. 11, 1837. [Desire L., d. J. N. and D. B., G.R.14.]
Desire B. [———], w. James N. [Sept. —, 1798]. G.R.14.
George Henry, s. James N. and Desire, May 10, 1831.
George Partridge, s. James and Rachel, June 7, 1812.
Geo[rge] Partridge, ch. Cap[t]. Ja[me]s, bp. July 11, 1813. C.R.2.
James Newton, s. James N. and Desire, Feb. 19, 1825. [James N. Jr., "1st Lieut. Co. G. 18th Reg. M. V. M.," G.R.14.]
James Newton, ch. James N., bp. Nov. 16, 1828. C.R.2.
John, s. Betsey, Sept. 26, 1793.
Martha James, d. James N. and Desire, Feb. 16, 1823.
Martha James, ch. James N., bp. Nov. 16, 1828. C.R.2.
Mary Turner, d. James N. and Desire, Jan. 29, 1827.
Mary Turner, ch. James N., bp. Nov. 16, 1828. C.R.2.
Rachel, d. James [Cap[t]. Ja[me]s, C.R.2.] and Rachel, Oct. 12, 1815.
Rachel T., Apr. 18, 1776. G.R.14.

SPARRIELL (see Sparrel, Sparrell), James Newton, s. James and Rachel, May 8, 1798. [Sparrell, C.R.2.] [Sparrell [h. Desire B.], G.R.14.]
John Turner, s. James and Rachel, Jan. 9, 1803. [Sparrell, C.R.2.]
Mary, d. James and Rachel, Feb. 21, 1805.
William, s. James and Rachel, June 27, 1800.

SPAULDING (see Spalding), Charles A. [dup. Spalding], s. Edwin, yeoman (b. Plainfield, N.H.), and Almeda, Sept. 7, 1848.
Edwin, ——— [1807]. C.R.1.
George Webster, s. Edwin and Almeda, bp. July 5, 1846. C.R.1.
Henry Otis, s. Edwin and Almeda, bp. July 5, 1846. C.R.1.

SPENCER, Jane E., ch. John and Mary, Aug. 1, 1828, [in] Wenstminster, Eng.
Jeremiah, ch. John and Mary, Oct. 7, 1841, [in] Hingham.
John, Nov. 1, 1802, in Holy-Well, N. Wales.
John, —— [1811]. G.R.14.
John H., ch. John and Mary, Feb. 8, 1831, [in] Brookline, N.Y.
Mary [? m.], Nov. 17, 1803. G.R.14.
Mary A., ch. John and Mary, June 1, 1833, [in] Portland, Me.
Samuel, ch. John and Mary, Sept. 29, 1840, [in] Hingham.
Sarah T. [dup. omits T.], d. John, rope maker, and Mary, Sept. 15, 1845.
William R., ch. John and Mary, June 10, 1844, [in] Cohassett.

SPOONER, Bethia, d. John of Marshfield, bp. Jan. 15, 1737–8. C.R.2.

SPRAGUE, Abigail, d. Ezek[iel], bp. Feb. 1, 1756. C.R.2.
Abigail, d. Ezekel and Prissilla, Feb. 1, 1757.
Amos Washburn, s. L[aban] and Wealthy, Mar. 17, 1829.
Benjamin, s. Laban and Wealthty, Apr. 16, 1819.
Daniel Damon, s. Laban and Wealthy, Mar. 7, 1823.
Ezekel, s. Ezekiel and Prissilla, May 16, 1755.
Ezekiel, s. Ezekiel and Priscilla, bp. Sept. 29, 1754. C.R.2.
Franklin, ch. Jacob and Bathsheba, June 20, 1833.
Jacob, ch. Jacob and Bathsheba, July 24, 1830.
Joshua Columbia, s. L[aban] and Wealthy, Dec. 22, 1820.
Laban, s. Laban and Wealthy, Apr. 29, 1817, in Hingham.
Rebeca Prouty, d. Ezekel and Prissilla, Oct. 6, 1760.
Samuel, s. Ezekel and Prissilla, June 22, 1763.
William, s. Laban and Wealthy, Feb. 20, 1826.

SPROUT, Abigail, d. Ebenezer and Experience, Sept. 15, 1709.
Abigail, ch. Ebenezar and w., bp. July 22, 1711. C.R.2.
Anna, d. Robert, Mar. —, 1671–2.
Ebenezer, s. Robert, May —, 1676.
Elizabeth, d. Robert, July —, 1664.
Hannah, d. Robert, Aug. —, 1680. [Sprut, d. Robirt, C.R.2.]
James, s. Robert, Feb. —, 1673–4.
Mary, d. Robert, May 1, 1666.
Mary, d. Ebenezar, bp. Aug. 14, 1716 [*sic*, 1715]. C.R.2.
Mercy, d. Robert, July 15, 1662.
Robert, s. Robert, Apr. —, 1669.
Robert, s. James, May 3, 1713. [Sproute, s. James and Elizabeth, C.R.2.]
Robert, s. James, Jan. 1, 1715.

SPROUT, Thankfull, d. Ebenezer, Nov. 28, 1705.
Thankfull, ch. Ebenezar and w., bp. July 22, 1711. C.R.2.

STANDISH, ———, d. Shadrach Jr. and Mehetabel, Nov. 28, 1808. G.R.6.

STANDLACK (see Standley, Standlick, Standly, Stanley), Abigall, d. Richard, Sept. 21, 1671.
Daniell, s. Richard, Sept. 10, 1669.
Lida, d. Richard, Apr. 7, 1664.
Mary, d. Richard, Mar. 24, 1665.

STANDLEY, see Standlack, Standlick, Standly, Stanley), Jabez, s. Jabez and Deborah, Dec. 10, 1743. [Standly, C.R.2.]
Mary, d. Richard, bp. May 20, 1683. C.R.2.

STANDLICK (see Standlack, Standley, Standly, Stanley), Abigall, d. Richard, bp. June 25, 1682. C.R.2.
Lydiah, d. Richard, bp. June 25, 1682, a. 18. C.R.2.

STANDLY (see Standlack, Standley, Standlick, Stanley), Abigail, d. Abigail, Jan. 14, 1770.
Abigal, d. Jabez and Deborah, Nov. 1, 1747. [Abigail, d. Jabez and Abigail, C.R.2.]
Calven, s. Jabez Jr. and Mary (Thrift), Feb. 9, 1769.
Eliza[beth], d. Jabez Jr. and Mary (Thrift), Sept. 30, 1767.
Mary Thrift, d. Jabez Jr. and Mary (Thrift), Dec. 28, 1765.
Meek, s. Jabez and Deborah, Dec. 13, 1740. [Stanley, C.R.1.]
Sarah, d. Jabez Jr. and Mary (Thrift), Nov. 10, 1770.

STANLEY (see Standlack, Standley, Standlick, Standly), Calvin, ch. Jabez and Mary, bp. Mar. 16, 1777. C.R.1.
Daniel, s. Richard, bp. May 28, 1671. C.R.2.
Joanna, d. Richard, bp. Sept. 29, 1661. C.R.2.
Julia [———], w. Frederic [May —, 1844]. G.R.10.
Luther, ch. Jabez and Mary, bp. Mar. 16, 1777. C.R.1.
Mary Thrift, ch. Jabez and Mary, bp. Mar. 16, 1777. C.R.1.
Sarah, ch. Jabez and Mary, bp. Mar. 16, 1777. C.R.1.

STAPLES (see Steaples, Steples), Elizabeth, d. Sam[ue]ll and Elizabeth, bp. Sept. 30, 1711. C.R.2.
Samuel, s. Sam[ue]ll and Elizabeth, bp. Apr. 2, 1710. C.R.2.

STARR, Comfort, s. Thomas, bp. June 7, 1646. C.R.2.
Elizabeth, d. Thomas, bp. June 7, 1646. C.R.2.

STARSE, Sarah (Starse [?]), d. Samuel, bp. Nov. 18, 1683. C.R.2.

STEADMAN, Elizabeth, d. Goodman, bp. Nov. 24, 1637. C.R.1.

STEAPLES (see Staples, Steples), Joshua, s. Samuell and Elizabeth, bp. July 14, 1706. C.R.2.

STEPHENS (see Stevens), Charles Henry, ch. Luther (Stevens) and Ruth, May 7, 1826.
Cordelia, ch. Luther (Stevens) and Ruth, May 2, 1834.
Horace I. [? J.], s. Rev. Horace P. and Merriel, Nov. 20, 1847.
Lewis, ch. Luther (Stevens) and Ruth, July 30, 1821, in Plainfield.
Lucia Day, ch. Luther (Stevens) and Ruth, Dec. 15, 1840.
Samuel, ch. Luther (Stevens) and Ruth, Feb. 11, 1824, in Plainfield.

STEPHENSON (see Stepheson), Benja[min], s. Bryant and Deborah, Nov. 14, 1788.
Lusstanos, s. Bryant and w., bp. Jan. 9, 1792. C.R.2.
Reuben, s. Bryant and Deborah, Sept. 5, 1786.

STEPHESON (see Stephenson), Briant Parratt, s. Bryant and Deborah, Nov. 25, 1784.

STEPLES (see Staples, Steaples), Sarah, d. Samuel and Elizabeth, bp. Oct. 3, 1708. C.R.2.

STERER, Susanna, d. Benj[a]m[in] and Ruth, bp. Jan. 23, 1742–3. C.R.2.

STETSON (see Stetsun, Studson, Sturtson, Stutson), Abby F., d. Luther, boot maker, and Caroline, Feb. 26, 1848.
Abby L., "former" w. Geo[rge] O. Knapp [May —, 1830]. G.R.15.
Abiga, s. Benjamin Jr., July 4, 1704. [Abijah, C.R.2.]
Abigail, d. John, May —, 1677.
Abigail, d. Joseph Jr., Jan. 17, 1707–8.
Abigail, d. Abijah and Deborah, bp. Sept. 28, 1735. C.R.2.
[A]bigail, d. Isaac and Ruth, Dec. 26, 1762.
Abijah (see Abiga).
Abisha [h. Betsey L.], ——, 1793. G.R.14.
Abner, s. Samuell (s. Joseph) [s. Sam[ue]ll and Elizabeth, C.R.2.], Nov. 3, 1712.
Abner, s. Joshua and Lydia, Feb. 26, 1808.
Abner L., s. Abner, shipwright, and Julia, Dec. 6, 1845.
Abthiah, d. Joseph Jr., Apr. 24, 1706.
Alexander, ch. Thomas and Lydia, July 25, 1810.
Alice, ch. Samuel and Elizabeth, bp. Sept. 30, 1722. C.R.2.
Almira, d. Benja[min] 3d and Mary, July 29, 1806.

STETSON, Alpheus, s. Micah and Sarah, Apr. 9, 1793.
Alpheus, s. Micah and w., bp. June 29, 1794. C.R.2.
Amos, s. Robert, June 18, 1703.
Amos, ch. Robert, bp. Nov. 5, 1704. C.R.2.
Ann Maria, ch. Peleg and Rachel, Feb. 28, 1834.
Anna, d. W[illia]m and Hannah, bp. Sept. 24, 1732. C.R.2.
Anne, d. John, Dec. —, 1690.
Anthony, s. Robert, Sept. 12, 1693.
Anthony, ch. Robert, bp. ———, 1695. C.R.2.
Barnabas, s. John, July —, 1688.
Barshaba, d. John Jr. and Barshaba, Dec. 20, 1764.
Bathshua, d. Joseph, Sept. 29, 1693.
Benjamin, s. Robert, Aug. —, 1641.
Benjamin, s. Benjamin, Feb. 16, 1666–7. [Studson, C.R.2.]
Benjamin, s. Benjamin, July 1, 1696.
Benjamin, twin s. Benjamin and Mercy, Jan. 8, 1771.
Benjamin, s. George and Betsey, Dec. 20, 1785.
Benjamin, s. Benjamin Jr. and Lucy, Mar. 6, 1799.
Benjamin, s. Peleg, shoemaker, and Rachel (b. Weymouth), May 17, 1846.
Benjamin Elbridge, ch. Peleg and Rachel, Apr. 28, 1844.
Betsey, d. George and Betsey, Dec. 24, 1795.
Betsey B., ch. Elisha C. and Betsey, ——— [rec. between ch. b. Jan. 3, 1834, and ch. b. ———, 1840], in Leeds, Me.
Betsey L. [———], w. Abisha, ———, 1786. G.R.14.
Betsy, [twin] d. Silas and Martha, May 1, 1787.
Bithia, d. Benjamin, May 4, 1699.
Bithiah, d. Benjamin, May 14, 1675.
Caleb, s. Thomas, Mar. —, 1682–3. [Sturtson, C.R.2.]
Caleb, ch. W[illia]m and Hannah, bp. June 2, 1728. C.R.2.
Caleb, s. John Jr. and Barshaba, Sept. 22, 1769.
Caroline, ch. Thomas and Lydia, Mar. 15, 1812.
Caroline, d. Peleg, shoemaker, and Rachel (b. Weymouth), Apr. 22, 1842.
Charles, s. Charles and Lois, June 22, 1824.
Charles Cole, ch. Peleg and Rachel, May 17, 1846.
Charles Henry, ch. Thomas and Lydia, Nov. 27, 1818.
Charlotte, d. Joshua and Lydia, Jan. 9, 1813.
[C]hloe, d. Isaac and Ruth, Aug. 21, 1767.
Christopher, s. George and Betsey, Oct. 20, 1781. [[h. Mary] G.R.14.]
Clarissa, d. Mathew and Mary, Aug. 2, 1778.
Clarissa, d. Melzar and Clarissa, July 17, 1812.
Daniel K., ch. Samuel and Mary, Nov. 5, 1833.
David, s. Isaac and Ruth, July 7, 1769.

STETSON, Deborah, d. Benjamin, Dec. 3, 1682. [Sturtson, C.R.2.]
Deborah, d. Samwill, Oct. —, 1704.
Deborah, d. John Jr. and Barshaba, May 20, 1762.
Deborah, d. Melzar and Clarissa, Mar. 1, 1810.
Deborah Adams, d. Silas and Martha, Aug. 24, 1783.
Desire, d. Joseph Sr., Sept. —, 1676.
Ebenezar, s. Micah and Sarah, Oct. 14, 1787. [Ebenezer, G.R.14.]
Ebenezer, s. Thomas, July 22, 1693.
Elenor, d. Christopher and Mary, Jan. 8, 1813.
Elijah, s. Thomas, Mar. —, 1686-7. [Sturtson, C.R.2.]
Elijah, s. Elijah and Ruth, June 15, 1711.
Elijah, s. Elijah and Ruth, bp. Apr. 7, 1723. C.R.2.
Elisabeth, d. Samuell (s. Jos [*sic*, Joseph]), Mar. 27, 1717. [Elizabeth, d. Sam[ue]ll and Elizabeth, C.R.2.]
Elisabeth, ch. Elijah and Ruth, bp. Mar. 31, 1723. C.R.2.
Elisabeth, d. Jonah Jr., bp. May 13, 1753. C.R.2.
Elisha, s. Thomas, Mar. —, 1684-5.
Elisha, ch. Anthony and Anna, bp. Aug. 4, 1734. C.R.2.
Elisha, s. Micah and Sarah, May 8, 1799.
Elisha, ch. Elisha C. and Betsey, Nov. 19, 1817, in Pembrok [*sic*, see Hannah].
Elisha 2d, ch. Elisha C. and Betsey, Oct. 18, 1829, in Leeds, Me.
Eliza, d. Benja[min] 3d and Mary, Jan. 30, 1796, in Boston.
Eliza, d. Joshua and Lydia, May 3, 1810.
Elizabeth, d. Samuel, Apr. 1, 1682. [Sturtson, C.R.2.]
Elizabeth (see Elisabeth).
Ella C., d. Luther, shoemaker, and Caroline, Mar. 28, 1845.
Ephraim, s. Matthew and Hannah, bp. Nov. 17, 1745. C.R.2.
[E]phraim Arnold, s. Silas and Martha, Feb. 21, 1791.
Esther, d. Micah and Sarah, Nov. 24, 1785.
Eunice, d. Robert, Apr. 28, 1650. [Studson, C.R.2.]
Eunice, d. Benjamin, Mar. —, 1683-4.
Eunice, d. Jonah and Mercy, bp. Nov. 29, 1724. C.R.2.
Eunice, d. George and Eunice, bp. Oct. 25, 1747. C.R.2.
[E]unice, d. Isaac and Ruth, Jan. 2, 1761.
Fanny, d. Benja[min] 3d and Mary, Dec. 9, 1804.
George, s. Samuell (s. Joes [*sic*, Joseph]) [s. Sam[ue]ll and Elizabeth, C.R.2.], Nov. 6, 1714.
George, s. George and Unice, bp. June 2, 1751. C.R.2.
George, s. Christopher and Mary, Aug. 21, 1805. [George W. [h. Susan S.], Aug. 21, 1804, G.R.14.]
George F., ch. Roger and Susan, Feb. 24, 1837.
George Henry, ch. Peleg and Rachel, Sept. 14, 1839.
George W., s. George and Betsey, Apr. 10, 177[worn] [1778].

STETSON, George Washington, s. M[elzar] and Clarissa, Feb. 6, 1815.
George Washington, s. George W. and Sybel, June 30, 1821.
Gershom, s. Thomas, Jan. —, 1676-7. [Studson, C.R.2.]
Gershom, s. Mathew and Mary, July 27, 1765.
Gideon, s. Robert, July 19, 1709. [Gidion, s. Robert and Mary, C.R.2.]
Grace, d. Matthew and Hannah, bp. Oct. 10, 1742. C.R.2.
Grace, d. Mathew and Mary, Feb. 26, 1775.
Hannah, d. Thomas, Nov. —, 1671. [Studson, C.R.2.]
Hannah, d. Benjamin, June 1, 1679. [Hanah Sturtson, C.R.2.]
Hannah, d. Joseph Sr., June —, 1682.
Hannah, d. Joseph, Aug. 1, 1700.
Hannah, d. John and Bashaba, Mar. 4, 1776.
Hannah, ch. Elisha C. and Betsey, Apr. 25, 1818, in Pembrok [*sic*, see Elisha].
Hannah, d. Joshua and Lydia, May 13, 1826.
Hannah F., ch. Roger and Susan, Feb. 15, 1841.
Hannah M. [———], w. Samuel D., ——, 1820. G.R.15.
Hannah Milton, d. Silas and Martha, Apr. 29, 1797.
Harriet, d. Joshua and Lydia, Sept. 21, 1803.
Helen Thomas, d. George W. and Sybel, July 18, 1818.
Hesaciah, s. Joseph Jr., Aug. 29, 1703.
Honour, d. John, Mar. —, 1684.
Isaac, s. Robert, Mar. 15, 1696-7.
Isaac, ch. Robert, bp. ——, 1700. C.R.2.
Isaac, s. Anthony [s. Anthony and Anna, C.R.2.], Oct. 19, 1719.
Jacob, s. Matthew and Hannah, bp. Sept. 27, 1747. C.R.2.
James, s. Benjamin, Mar. 1, 1670-1. [Studson, C.R.2.]
James Elexander, s. Benja[min] 3d and Mary, Sept. 28, 1801.
James Hervy, ch. Thomas and Lydia, Nov. 26, 1805.
Jemima, d. Robert, Mar. 13, 1694-5.
Jeremiah, ch. Robert, bp. ——, 1695. C.R.2.
Joatham, s. Silas and Martha, Nov. 17, 1794.
Job, ch. W[illia]m and Hannah, bp. June 2, 1728. C.R.2.
John, s. Robert, Apr. —, 1648. [Studson, C.R.2.]
John, s. Samuel, Mar. —, 1694.
John, s. Abijah and Deborah, bp. July 9, 1732. C.R.2.
John, s. John Jr. and Barshaba, July 11, 1763.
John, s. John Jr. and Barshaba, Apr. 23, 1774.
John Randal, s. Peleg, shoemaker, and Rachael T. [dup. Rachel, omits T.] (b. Weymouth), Aug. 31, 1848.
Jonah, s. Samuel, Apr. —, 1691.
Jonah, s. Jonah and Mercy, bp. Feb. 25, 1721-2. C.R.2.

STETSON, Jonathan [h. Hulda (Magoun)] [h. Sally (Curtis)], ——, 1768. G.R.14.
Joseph, s. Robert, June —, 1639.
Joseph [Stetson], eldest s. Joseph, ——, 1667. [Studson, C.R.2.]
Joseph, s. Joseph Jr., May 23, 1698.
Joseph, s. Anthony and Anna, Feb. 24, 1722.
Joseph, ch. Samuel and Elizabeth, bp. Sept. 30, 1722. C.R.2.
Joseph, ch. Jos[eph] and w., bp. Jan. 19, 1744–5. C.R.2.
Joseph, twin s. Benjamin and Mercy, Jan. 8, 1771.
Joseph, s. Micah and Sarah, Jan. 15, 1791.
Joseph, s. Benja[min] 3d and Mary, Aug. 28, 1797, in Boston.
Joshua, s. Thomas, Jan. —, 1680–1. [Sturtson, C.R.2.]
Joshua, s. Elijah and Ruth, May 12, 1713.
Joshua, s. Sam[ue]ll (s. Jo), June 26, 1719.
Joshua, s. Elijah and Ruth, bp. July 28, 1728. C.R.2.
Joshua, s. George and Betsey, Aug. 10, 1788.
Joshua, s. Joshua and Lydia, Nov. 21, 1805.
Leah, ch. Benjamin Jr., bp. Sept. 24, 1704. C.R.2.
Leonora, ch. Elisha C. and Betsey, Jan. 9, 1826, in Leeds, Me.
Lois, d. Robert, Feb. —, 1652. [Studson, C.R.2.]
Lois, d. Joseph Sr., Mar. —, 1672.
Lois, d. Joseph, Aug. 10, 1692.
Lois, d. Joshua and Lydia, Aug. 19, 1822.
Louisa E., d. Geo[rge] W., shipwright, and Elizabeth B., Sept. 12, 1849, in S. Scituate.
Lucanna, d. John and Bashaba, June 4, 1779.
Lucindia C., ch. Elisha C. and Betsey, May 11, 1823, in Pembrok.
Lucy, d. Benja[min] and Mercy, Apr. 26, 1766.
Lucy, d. Benjamin Jr. and Lucy, Mar. 13, 1804.
Lucy Clapp, ch. Peleg and Rachel, May 11, 1837.
Luke, s. Elijah and Ruth, bp. May 15, 1726. C.R.2.
Lusanna, [twin] d. Micah and Sarah, Nov. 9, 1789.
Luscenda, [ch.] Joshua and Lillis, bp. Apr. 29, 1750. C.R.2.
Luther, s. Job and Mary, bp. May 6, 1750. C.R.2.
Luther, s. Melzar and Clarissa, Jan. 28, 1821.
Lydia, d. Samuel, July —, 1683.
Lydia, ch. Samuel and Rebecca, bp. Feb. 19, 1726–7. C.R.2.
Lydia, d. Jonah, bp. Oct. 26, 1755. C.R.2.
Lydia, d. Joshua and Lydia, July 19, 1816.
Lydia Drew, ch. Thomas and Lydia, Oct. 18, 1820.
Lydia Ford, d. Micah and Sarah, Sept. 25, 1796.
Malachi, [ch.] Job and Mary, bp. June 26, 1743. C.R.2.
Marcy, [twin] d. Micah and Sarah, Nov. 9, 1789. [Mercy, G.R.14.]
Margaret, d. Benjamin, Mar. 30, 1694.

STETSON, Margaret, d. Thomas, Aug. 4, 1698.
Margarett, d. Benjamin, Sept. —, 1685.
Martha, d. Robert [d. Robert and Mary, C.R.2.], Sept. 3, 1706.
Mary, d. Benjamin, Apr. 21, 1678. [Studson, C.R.2.]
Mary, d. Thomas, Mar. 3, 1691.
Mary, d. Joseph Jr., Feb. 1, 1713-14.
Mary, d. Anthony [d. Anthony and Anna, C.R.2.], Dec. 9, 1717.
Mary, d. John and Ruth, Jan. 22, 1747.
Mary, d. Gideon, bp. June 2, 1751. C.R.2.
Mary, d. Math[ew], bp. Nov. 6, 1757. C.R.2.
[M]ary, d. Isaac and Ruth, Jan. 1, 1765.
Mary, d. Mathew and Mary, Jan. 31, 1773.
Mary [———], w. Christopher, Apr. 10, 1785. G.R.14.
Mary [———], w. Samuel, —— [1793]. G.R.15.
Mary, d. Benja[min] 3d and Mary, Nov. 6, 1794.
Mary, d. Christopher and Mary, Nov. 23, 1807.
Mary, ch. Thomas and Lydia, Apr. 9, 1808.
Mary Ann, d. Benj[ami]n Jr. and Deborah, Sept. 14, 1831.
Mary Bracket, d. Silas and Martha, Nov. 12, 1781.
Mary Hannah, d. Benj[ami]n Jr. and Deborah, Nov. 18, 1828.
Mary J., ch. Samuel and Mary, Mar. 11, 1826, in Boston.
Mathew, s. Benjamen (Stetsun), Nov. 5, 1690.
Mathew, s. Mathew and Mary, Mar. 3, 1763.
Matthew, s. Benjamin, Jan. 12, 1668-9. [Mathew Studson, C.R.2.]
Matthew, s. Melzar and Clarissa, July 1, 1817.
Melinda, w. Waterman Josselin, ——, 1802. G.R.14.
Melvina W., d. Mathew, shipwright, and Sylvany B., Nov. 15, 1847. [Melvin W., G.R.15.]
Melzar, s. Melzar and Clarissa, Sept. 30, 1805.
Mercy, d. Samuel, June —, 1692.
Mercy, d. Benja[min] and Mercy, Mar. 30, 1768.
Mercy (see Marcy).
Mercy Turner, d. Benja[min] 3d and Mary, Apr. 30, 1803.
Micah, s. Jonah and Mercy, bp. July 4, 1729. C.R.2.
Morgan B., ch. Elisha C. and Betsey, Nov. 24, 1820, in Pembrok.
Moses W., s. Zilpah, Feb. 19, 1820.
Nancy, d. Benja[min] 3d and Mary, Dec. 31, 1799, in Boston.
Nathan, s. Silas and Martha, May 10, 1789.
Nathanael, ch. Elijah and Ruth, bp. Mar. 31, 1723. C.R.2.
Nath[anie]ll, s. Sam[ue]ll (Stutson) and Lydia, June —, 1700.
Nehemiah, s. Joseph, June 25, 1696.
Nelson, ch. Thomas and Lydia, Oct. 25, 1814.
Patience, d. Samuel, Dec. —, 1687.
Peleg, s. Benjamin Jr. and Lucy, Nov. 18, 1808.

STETSON, Prudence, d. Joseph Sr., Sept. —, 1678.
Rachel, [twin] d. Silas and Martha, May 1, 1787.
Rachel [? m.], Apr. 12, 1797. G.R.14.
Rebecca, ch. Samuel and Rebecca, bp. Feb. 19, 1726-7. C.R.2.
Rhoda, d. Job and Mary, bp. Feb. 10, 1744-5. C.R.2.
Robert, s. Robert, Jan. 29, 1653. [Studson, C.R.2.]
Robert, s. Joseph Sr., Dec. 9, 1670.
Robert, s. Robert and Mary, Sept. 3, 1710.
Robert, s. Robert, bp. May 18, 1740. C.R.2.
Rogers, s. Melzar and Clarissa, Dec. 19, 1803. [[h. Susan B.] G.R.14.]
Ruth, d. Joseph Jr., Sept. 11, 1689.
Ruth, d. Thomas, Dec. 11, 1695.
Ruth, d. Elijah and Ruth, bp. May 10, 1730. C.R.2.
Samuel, s. Samuel, June —, 1679. [Samuell Sturtson, C.R.2.]
Samuel, ch. Samuel and Rebecca, bp. Feb. 19, 1726-7. C.R.2.
Samuel, s. George, bp. Oct. 20, 1754. C.R.2.
Samuel, s. Silas and Martha, Apr. 28, 1793.
Samuel Dexter, ch. Thomas and Lydia, Dec. 2, 1816. [[h. Hannah M.] G.R.15.]
Samuel O., ch. Samuel and Mary, Jan. 27, 1823, in Boston.
Samuell, s. Robert, June —, 1646. [Samuel Studson, C.R.2.]
Samuell, s. Benjamin, Oct. —, 1673.
Samuell, s. Joseph Sr., Dec. —, 1679.
Sarah, d. Thomas, Jan. —, 1678-9. [Sturtson, C.R.2.]
Sarah, d. John Jr. and Barshaba, Apr. 12, 1772.
Sarah, d. Micah and Sarah, Nov. 23, 1783.
Sarah, d. George and Betsey, Sept. 16, 1791.
Sarah M., ch. Elisha C. and Betsey, ———, 1840.
Seth, s. Sam[ue]ll (Stutson) and Lydia, June —, 1698.
Silas, s. Sam[ue]ll (Stutson) and Lydia, June —, 1696.
Silas, s. Silas and Martha, June 25, 1785.
Silvina H., ch. Elisha C. and Betsey, Jan. 3, 1834, in Leeds, Me.
Simeon, ch. Elijah and Ruth, bp. Mar. 31, 1723. C.R.2.
Stephen, ch. W[illia]m and Hannah, bp. Sept. 28, 1738. C.R.2.
Susan, d. Joshua and Lydia, Aug. 23, 1819.
Susan B. [———], w. Rogers, Nov. 24, 1816. G.R.15.
Susan R., ch. Roger and Susan, July 27, 1838.
Susan S. [———], w. George W., Nov. 2, 1808. G.R.14.
Susana, d. Nathanaell and Susana, June 9, 1712.
Sybel Tilden, d. George W. and Sybel, Feb. 23, 1812.
Thomas, s. Robert, Dec. 11, 1643. [Dec. 11, 1641, P.C.R.]
Thomas, s. Thomas, Sept. —, 1674.
Thomas, s. John Jr. and Barshaba, Mar. 17, 1768.

STETSON, Thomas, s. Mathew and Mary, Nov. 6, 1769.
Thomas, ch. Thomas and Lydia, Jan. 18, 1804.
Warren, s. Melzar and Clarissa, Dec. 7, 1807.
Warren M., s. Matthew, shipwright, and Sylvana B. (b. Marshfield), Aug. 14, 1849, in S. Scituate.
William, s. Joseph Sr., Dec. —, 1673.
William, s. Robert, June 26, 1700.
William, ch. Robert, bp. Nov. 5, 1704. C.R.2.
William, ch. W[illia]m and Hannah, bp. Sept. 28, 1738. C.R.2.
William, s. Silas and Martha, May 6, 1799.
William F., ch. Elisha C. and Betsey, Oct. 3, 1831, in Leeds, Me.
William H., ch. Samuel and Mary, Nov. 14, 1820, in Boston.
Winslow, s. Mathew and Mary, Aug. 12, 1767.
Zilphia, d. Benjamin Jr. and Lucy, Oct. 28, 1795.
———, [ch.] Jonah Jr., bp. Apr. 3, 1757. C.R.2.

STETSUN (see Stetson, Studson, Sturtson, Stutson), Grace, d. Benjamen, Apr. 29, 1692.

STEVENS (see Stephens), Herbert R. [dup. Stephens], s. Lewis, mariner (b. Plainfield, N.H.), and Jane B. [dup. omits B.] (b. England), Feb. 23, 1848.
Lewis R., s. Lewis, sailor, and Jane, May 29, 1845.

STEWARD (see Stewart), Celia Ann, d. John E., farmer, and Ellen L., May 11, 1846.

STEWART (see Steward), George F. [Dec. —, 1846]. G.R.14.
John E., s. John E., farmer, and Ellen N., Apr. 24, 1848.
Mary Catharine, d. John E., yeoman, and Mary, May 10, 1844.

STOCKBRIDG (see Stockbridge, Stockbrige, Stockebridge), Abigall, d. Charles, Feb. 24, 1660, in Charlestowne.
Abigall, d. Charles (Stockbridge), Mar. 22, 1694–5.
Charles, s. Benjamin and Mary, Sept. 25, 1711. [Stockbridge, C.R.1.]
Elizabeth, d. Charles, Aug. 13, 1670.
Joseph, s. Charles (Stockbridge), June 28, 1672.
Mercy, d. Charles (Stockbridge), Aug. 11, 1692.
Rachell, d. Charles (Stockbridge), Apr. 9, 1690.
Samuell, s. Charles, July 9, 1679.
Sarah, d. Charles, May 30, 1665.
Thomas, s. Charles, Apr. 6, 1667.

STOCKBRIDGE (see Stockbridg, Stockbrige, Stockebridge), Abiel, d. Sam[ue]ll and Lydia, Feb. 14, 1720.
Abiel, d. Sam[ue]ll [Sam[ue]l, C.R.2.] Jr. and Sarah, Aug. 10, 1752.

STOCKBRIDGE, Abigal, d. Sam[ue]ll and Lidia, June 3, 1719. [Abigail, C.R.1.]
Alexander, s. Samuel and Sarah, Mar. 10, 1785.
Andrew, ch. David [dup. yeoman] and Sarah H., Aug. 2, 1844 [second dup. crossed out, 1843].
Anna M. [———] [w. Andrew], —— [1845]. G.R.16.
Anne, d. Thomas, May 31, 1710. [Ann, d. Thomas and Sarah, C.R.2.]
Asenath, d. Sam[ue]ll and Sarah, Apr. 12, 1758.
Barshubah, d. Joseph and Margret, bp. Dec. 1, 1706. C.R.2.
Benjamin, s. Benjamin, Aug. 30, 1704. [[h. Ruth (Otis)] G.R.6.]
Benja[min], s. Benja[min] and Ruth, Jan. 17, 1731.
Benjamin, s. Dr. Benja[min], bp. Feb. 20, 1732. C.R.1.
Benja[min], s. Benja[min] and Ruth, June 15, 1742.
Benja[min], s. Benja[min] and Ruth, Oct. 19, 1744.
Benjamin, s. Benja[min] (Stobridge) and Besheba, Feb. 16, 1790.
Betty, d. Samuel and Sarah, July 24, 1771.
Cassandra (see Kassandra).
Charles, s. Charles and Abigail, Oct. 13, 1709. [Charls, s. Charls and Abigail, C.R.2.]
Charles, s. Benja[min] and Ruth, Mar. 23, 1734.
Charles, s. Dr. Charles and Elenor, Jan. 9, 1790.
Charles [h. Mercy B.], ——, 1824. G.R.16.
Charls, s. Charles, Feb. 4, 1663.
Dama, d. John and Dama, Aug. 30, 1810.
David, s. Joseph and Dolly, Nov. 8, 1815.
David Henry, ch. David and Sarah H., May 21, 1842.
Deborah, d. Thomas, June 21, 1705.
Deborah [———], w. Joseph [Dec. —, 1807]. G.R.16.
Dolly (see Mary).
Ealonor Stetson, d. Dr. Charles and Eleonor, Nov. 29, 1787.
Elisabath, d. Benjamin, Aug. 19, 1702.
Elizabeth, d. Benja[min] and Ruth, Mar. 6, 1737.
Experience, d. Charles and Abigail, Jan. 1, 1703-4.
Hannah, d. ———, bp. Sept. 24, 1637. C.R.1.
Hannah, d. Charles, Jan. 30, 1697-8.
Hector, s. Samuel and Sarah, Nov. 22, 1782.
Hesther, d. John, bp. July 11, 1647. C.R.2.
Jacob, —— [1781]. G.R.16.
James, s. Samuel and Lydia, Apr. 4, 1714.
James, s. Sam[ue]ll Jr. and Sarah, July 27, 1739.
James, s. John and Dama, Sept. 6, 1812.
John, s. Joseph, bp. July 2, 1704. C.R.2.
[Jo]hn, s. Michael [Micael, C.R.2.] and Mary, Sept. 20, 1739.

STOCKBRIDGE, John, s. Samuel and Sarah, June 19, 1768.
John, s. John and Dama, Dec. 22, 181[worn] [1818]. [[h. Mary L.] G.R.16.]
Joseph, s. Joseph (Stockebridge), Oct. 1, 1698.
Joseph, s. Joseph and Dolly, Mar. 30, 180[6].
Josiah, s. Samuel and Sarah, Aug. 13, 1773.
Judith, d. Charles and Abigail, July 19, 1706.
Kassandra, d. Samuel and Sarah, May 19, 1775.
[K]eziah, d. Michael [Mical (Stochbridge), C.R.2.] and Mary, Nov. 23, 1741.
Liddiah, d. Samuell, Jan. 7, 1704-5.
Lucy, d. Joseph and Dolly, Oct. 20, 1809.
Lusannah, d. Joseph and Margred of Duxborough, bp. Nov. 25, 1711. C.R.2.
Lydia (see Liddiah).
Lydia, d. Sam[ue]ll Jr. and Sarah, Dec. 18, 1749.
Magaret, d. Joseph and Margaret, bp. Oct. 31, 1708. C.R.2.
Martha, d. Joseph and Dolly, Sept. 3, 1817.
Mary, d. John, bp. Apr. 29, 1655. C.R.2.
Mary, d. Dr. Charles and Elenor, Mar. 6, 1793.
Mary, d. Joseph and Dolly, Mar. 11, 1804. [Dolly [over "Mary," crossed out], C.R.2.]
Mary L. [———], w. John [Mar. —, 1831]. G.R.16.
Mercy, d. Benjamin and Mercy, May 6, 1707.
Mercy, d. Charls and Anna, bp. June 27, 1725. C.R.2.
Mercy, d. Benja[min] and Ruth, Oct. 1, 1736.
Mercy B. [———], w. Charles, ——, 1821. G.R.16.
Micah, s. Thomas [s. Thomas and Sarah, C.R.2.], Nov. 22, 1714.
Nancy Litchfield, d. Joseph and Dolly, Apr. 27, 1820.
Penelope, d. Samuel and Sarah, Oct. 25, 1780.
Persis, d. Samuel and Lydia, Jan. 22, 1707-8.
Polly, d. Benja[min] and Ruth, Jan. 17, 1740.
Polly, d. Samuel and Sarah, Mar. 30, 1777. [h. Joseph Wade, P.R.27.]
Ruth, d. Charles and Abigail, July 30, 1700.
Ruth, d. Benja[min] [Dr. Benja[min], C.R.1.] and Ruth, Nov. 18, 1733.
Ruth Otis, d. Dr. Charles and Elenor, May 27, 1785.
Sally, d. Joseph and Dolly, Oct. 2, 1812.
Samuel, s. Samuel and Lydia, May 13, 1711.
Samuel, s. Samuel and Sarah, July 26, 1769.
Sam[ue]ll, s. Sam[ue]ll Jr. and Sarah, Mar. 28, 1748. [Samuel, C.R.2.]
Sarah, d. John, bp. Mar. 15, 1645. C.R.2.

STOCKBRIDGE, Sarah, d. Thomas, Apr. 25, 1699.
Sarah, d. Thomas [d. Thomas and Sarah, C.R.2.], Oct. 26, 1718.
Sarah, d. Sam[ue]l Jr. and Sarah, Nov. 25, 1744.
Sarah B. [———], w. David [Nov. —, 1794]. G.R.15.
Susanah Stowell, d. John and Dama, Mar. 26, 1806.
Thomas, s. Thomas, Feb. 13, 1702–3.
Tho[ma]s, s. Tho[ma]s and Hannah, May 2, 1725.
Thomas, s. Benja[min] and Barthsheba, Aug. 5, 1792.

STOCKBRIGE (see Stockbridg, Stockbridge, Stockebridge), Benjamen, s. Charles, Oct. 9, 1677.

STOCKEBRIDGE (see Stockbridg, Stockbridge, Stockbrige), Mary, d. Thomas, Mar. 31, 1701.

STODARD (see Stoddard, Stodder, Stoder), Hannah Elizabeth, d. Josiah and Hannah, Oct. 9, 1807.
Josiah, s. Josiah and Hannah, Feb. 6, 1810. [Stoddard [h. Mary Ann], G.R.15.]
Rhoda, d. Josiah and Hannah, Jan. 9, 1815. [Stodart, C.R.2.]

STODDARD (see Stodard, Stodder, Stoder), Abigail, d. Hez[ekia]h Jr. and Lydia, June 14, 1784.
Benjamin, ch. Seth Jr. and w., bp. Nov. 1, 1795. C.R.2.
Charles H., ch. Francis and Hannah, Nov. 7, 1837.
Charles Lowell, s. Thomas and Matilda B., Sep[t]. 25, 1836.
Christopher, ch. Francis and Hannah, Jan. 1, 1844.
Cyrus, s. Obadiah and Celie, Apr. 7, 1797.
Cyrus, s. Cyrus and Lucy, June 14, 1820.
Daniel, s. Hez[ekia]h Jr. and Lydia, Sept. 26, 1773.
David, s. Hez[ekia]h Jr. and Jane, Sept. 27, 1795.
David T., s. David T. and Maria H., June 22, 1844.
David Turner, s. David and Elizabeth, Aug. 13, 1820.
Ebed L., ch. Samuel Jr. and Mary F., June 18, 1839. [Ebed F., G.R.8.]
Edmund S. [dup. Sewall], [twin] s. Thomas Jr. and Sally, Nov. 5, 1843.
Edwin, —— [1823]. G.R.2.
Edwin Q. [dup. Quincy], [twin] s. Thomas Jr. and Sally, Nov. 5, 1843.
Eliza, d. Josiah and Lydia, Nov. 15, 1827.
Eliza A., ch. Francis and Hannah, Sept. 25, 1839.
Elizabeth Jane, d. David and Elizabeth, Feb. 20, 1822.
Emma, d. Joseph, farmer, and Morgianna, Sept. 12, 1845.
Ezekiel, s. Isai[ah], bp. May 8, 1757. C.R.2.
Frances N., ch. Francis and Hannah, Dec. 10, 1834.

STODDARD, Francis A., ch. Francis and Hannah, Nov. 20, 1841.
Franklin, ch. Samuel Jr. and Mary F., Apr. 30, 1844.
Franklin, s. David T., shoemaker, and Marie, Feb. 26, 1847.
George W., ch. Francis and Hannah, Aug. 12, 1847.
Hannah, d. Josiah and w., bp. July 3, 1808. C.R.2.
Hannah C., d. Francis, shoemaker, and Hannah, Nov. 26, 1845.
Hannah E., ch. Francis and Hannah, Nov. 26, 1845.
Hannah Lapham, d. David and Elizabeth, Sept. 26, 1824.
Henry, ——, 1823. G.R.14.
Henry, s. Josiah and Lydia, Sept. 24, 1830.
Hezekiah, s. Hez[ekia]h Jr. and Lydia, Aug. 25, 1775.
Jane, d. Hez[ekia]h Jr. and Jane, Sept. 12, 1793.
Joanne, d. Hez[ekia]h and Jane, Oct. 11, 1803.
Joanne, d. Thomas Jr. and Sally, Sept. 11, 1831.
John, s. Cyrus and Lucy, Aug. 14, 1835.
John Ewell, s. Josiah and Lydia, Apr. 17, 1835.
Joseph C., ch. Thomas Jr. and w., Jan. 25, 1836, in Cohasset.
Joseph Edwin, s. Thomas and Matilda B., Nov. 6, 1839.
Joseph O., s. Thomas Jr. and Sally, Jan. 25, 1836, in Cohasset.
Joshua, s. Hez[ekia]h Jr. and Lydia, July 30, 1789.
Josiah [h. Hannah R. (Orcutt)] [h. Lydia (Ewell)], July 26, 1781.
    G.R.14.
Josiah, ch. Josiah and Mary A., Mar. 30, 1839. [Josiah Jr., "member of Co. K 38th Regt. M. V.," G.R.15.]
Josiah, ch. Josiah and ——, bp. May 14, 1843. C.R.3.
Julia Turner, d. Josiah and Lydia, Mar. 8, 1826.
Lucy [———], w. Melzar, —— [1762]. G.R.15.
Lucy, d. Hez[ekia]h Jr. and Lydia, July 31, 1786.
Lucy, d. Josiah and Lydia, Sep[t]. 26, 1832.
Lydia, d. Hez[ekia]h Jr. and Lydia, Oct. 22, 1777.
Mary [———], w. Seth, —— [1776]. G.R.16.
Mary, d. Hez[ekia]h and Jane, Oct. 7, 1805.
Mary A., ch. Josiah and Mary A., Nov. 21, 1837.
Mary Ann [———], w. Josiah, May 4, 1817. G.R.15.
Mary Ann, ch. Josiah and ——, bp. May 14, 1843. C.R.3.
Mary Emma, d. Samuel [dup. Jr.], shoemaker, and Mary F., Sept. 19, 1848.
Mary F. [———], w. Sam[ue]l, —— [1819]. C.R.3. [Mary F. L., Apr. 16, 1818, G.R.8.]
Melvin, d. Hez[ekia]h and Jane, Oct. 7, 1807.
Michael, s. Hez[ekia]h and Jane, —— [rec. between ch. b. Sept. 27, 1795, and ch. b. Oct. 11, 1803].
Nancy, d. Hez[ekia]h Jr. and Lydia, Dec. 10, 1779.
Noah James, s. Thomas 2d and Matilda, Apr. 14, 1834.

STODDARD, Salome Abigail, ch. W[illia]m and Sarah A., bp. May 23, 1847. C.R.3.
Sam[ue]l, father of W[illia]m, —— [1785]. C.R.3.
Samuel [h. Mary F. L.], July 8, 1810. G.R.8.
Samuel, s. Cyrus and Lucy, Feb. 1, 1824.
Samuel, s. Cyrus and Lucy, Jan. 29, 1834.
Samuel L., ch. Samuel Jr. and Mary F., June 30, 1841. [Samuel Jr., G.R.8.]
Sarah Waters, ch. W[illia]m and Sarah A., bp. May 19, 1844. C.R.3.
Seth [June —, 1821]. G.R.16.
Soloman A., s. W[illia]m, cordwainer, and Sarah A., Aug. 23, 1846.
Temperance, ch. Seth Jr. and w., bp. Nov. 1, 1795. C.R.2.
Thomas, s. Thomas Jr. and Sally, Sept. 6, 1841, in Cohasset.
William, s. Josiah and Hannah, Aug. 23, 1818.
William, s. Cyrus and Lucy, Apr. 15, 1828.
William Thomas, s. Thomas 2d and Matilda, Oct. 31, 1832.
Zenas, s. Hez[ekia]h Jr. and Lydia, Jan. 23, 1782.

STODDER (see Stodard, Stoddard, Stoder), Abigal, d. Joseph and Zibbiah, Mar. 13, 1721.
Bela, youngest s. [Hezekiah and Abigal], ——, 1763.
Betty, d. Benja[min] Jr. and Ruth, July 29, 1752.
Betty, d. Benja[min] Jr., bp. May 19, 1754. C.R.2.
Deran, s. Hez[ekia]h and Abigal, Dec. 13, 1761.
Desier, d. Benja[min] Jr. and Ruth, June 30, 1748. [Desire Stoddard, C.R.2.]
Desire, d. Hezekiah and Abigal, Nov. 14, 1745.
Elijah, s. Benja[min] (Stoder), Nov. 13, 1719. [Stoddard, s. Benj[a]m[in] and Mary, C.R.2.]
Elijah, s. Benja[min] Jr. and Ruth, Oct. 16, 1738. [Stoddard, C.R.2.]
Elijah, s. Elijah and Thank[fu]ll, May 26, 1777.
Elisha, s. Benjamin, July 12, 1715. [Stoddard, s. Benjamin and Mary, C.R.2.]
Eunice, d. Hezekiah and Lois, Apr. 16, 1715.
Hezekiah, s. Hezekiah and Lois, Aug. 28, 1722.
Hezekiah, s. Hezekiah and Abigal, May 20, 1747.
Isaiah, s. Benja[min] and Mary, June 6, 1723. [Stoddard, C.R.2.]
Joshua, s. Hezekiah and Lois, June 7, 1713. [Stoddard, C.R.2.]
Judith, d. Hezekiah and Abigal, Oct. 26, 1754.
Laban, s. Hezekiah and Abigal, July 16, 1744.
Lois, d. Hezekiah and Abigal, July 18, 1749.
Lucy, d. Benja[min] Jr. and Ruth, Aug. 19, 1750.

STODDER, Lucy, d. Melzar and Lucy, Aug. 28, 1785.
[M]argret, d. Hez[ekia]h and Abigal, Dec. 5, 1757.
Mary, d. Samwell, Sept. 30, 1705.
Mary, d. Benjamin, Apr. 4, 1711. [Stoddard, d. Benj[a]m[in] and Mary, c.r.2.]
Mary, d. Samuel, bp. Aug. 19, 1711. c.r.1.
Melzer, s. Isaiah and Mary, Oct. 5, 1756.
Nathan, s. Hezekiah Jr. and Lydia, Feb. 17, 1772.
[O]bediah, s. Hez[ekia]h and Abigal, July 4, 1760.
Olive, d. Hezekiah and Abigal, Apr. 21, 1751.
Perez, s. Elijah (Stoder) and Thank[fu]ll, May 21, 1773.
Polly, d. Melzar and Lucy, Oct. 23, 1787.
Rebecca, d. Hezekiah and Abigal, Feb. 25, 1753.
Ruth, d. Benja[min] Jr. and Ruth, Sept. 13, 1745. [Stoddard, c.r.2.]
Sally, d. Elijah and Thank[fu]l, Sept. 6, 1770.
Samuel, s. Hezekiah and Abigal, Apr. 15, 1756.
Sarah, d. Samuel, bp. Aug. 19, 1711. c.r.1.
Seth, s. Benja[min] Jr. and Ruth, Apr. 18, 1741. [Stoddard, c.r.2.]
Seth, s. Benja[min] (Stodde), ———. [This entry crossed out.]
Thankful [———] [mother of Rebecca Bates (w. Abial Turner)] [July —, 1785]. p.r. 25.
Thankfull, d. Elijah and Thank[fu]l, Aug. 18, 1768.

STODER (see Stodard, Stoddard, Stodder), Bathshua, d. Hezekiah and Lois, Feb. 10, 1711-12.
Benjamin, s. Benjamin (Stodder), Nov. 18, 1708. [Stoddard, s. Benjamin and Mary, c.r.2.]
Elisabath, d. Samwell, Oct. 25, 1702.
Leah, d. Samuel, Apr. 10, 1696.
Rachell, d. Samuel, Dec. 26, 1698.
Sarah, d. Samuel and Elizabeth, Mar. 19, 1709-10.
Seth, s. Samwell, Feb. 26, 1700.

STONE, Abigail K. [———], w. Rev. Cyrus, Aug. 28, 1812, in Waterford, Me. g.r.2.
Cyrus, Rev., June 9, 1793, in Marlboro, N.H. "He graduated at Dartmouth, 1822. Was 14 years a Missionary in India. Closing his life in establishing a Church and erecting a church Edifice in Beechwood." g.r.2.
Cyrus, s. Rev. Cyrus and Abigail, June 2, 1846, in Harwich. g.r.2.
Lizzie, d. Cyrus and Abigail K., Oct. 22, 1842, in Bingham, Me. g.r.2.

STORER, Sam[ue]l Stetson, ch. Capt. Storer of Portl[an]d, bp. Oct. 1, 1812. C.R.2.

STRAFFIN, David Franklin, s. David and Hannah, Oct. 20, 1823.
David Franklin, ch. David, bp. July 30, 1826. C.R.1.
Hannah Otis, d. David and Hannah, Jan. 7, 1826.
———, ch. David and Hannah, Jan. 18, 1828.

STRAW, Eliza [———], w. ———, —— [1806]. C.R.1.

STUDLEY (see Studlie, Studly), Abby, d. Solon, sailor, and Eunice W., May 4, 1848.
Abigail, d. Eliab, bp. July 21, 1747. C.R.1.
[Ab]igail Billings, d. Ammiel and Celia, Oct. 9, 1825.
Adeline, d. Allen and Mary, Dec. 26, 1813.
Alfred Homer, ch. Homer and Lydia, Jan. 22, 1842.
Allen, s. Susannah, Oct. 23, 1788.
Alson, s. John and Sarah, Nov. 16, 1795.
Alson, ch. John, bp. Oct. 14, 1798. C.R.1.
Amasa, s. David and Susannah, Jan. 4, 1722.
Amelia [———], w. Lewis, —— [1794]. G.R.2.
Amelia, ch. Lewis Jr. and w., bp. Oct. 7, 1832. C.R.1.
Amelia P. [———], w. William, ———, 1812. G.R.14.
Ammiel, s. William (Stedley) and Ruth, Apr. 9, 1783 [dup. crossed out in pencil, 1786].
Ammiel, ch. Charles A. and Amelia S., Nov. 9, 1832.
Benjamin, s. John and Sarah, Oct. 27, 1786.
Benjamin, ch. John, bp. Oct. 14, 1798. C.R.1.
Bennet Dunbar, s. Lewis and Lucy, May 15, 1796. [Studly, C.R.1.] [Studley [h. Deborah], G.R.2.] [Bennett Dunbar Studley, P.R.21.]
Bennett Dunbar, s. Bennett Dunbar and Deborah, Sept. 10, 1824. [Bennett Dunbar Jr., P.R.21.]
Benony, s. Benony and Abigal, July 25, 1723.
Bethana Eaton, d. Lewis Jr. and Emily, ——— [rec. after ch. b. May 7, 1835].
Betsey, d. John and Sarah, Jan. 30, 1798. [Betsy, C.R.1.]
Cassendana Ballou, d. Bennett D. and Deborah, July 18, 1833. [Cassie B., G.R.2.] [Cassendana Ballou, P.R.21.]
Celia [? m.], June 19, 1783. G.R.11.
Celia Elizabeth, ch. Charles A. and Amelia S., Feb. 26, 1838.
Charles, s. Lewis Jr. and Emely, Aug. 17, 1819.
Charles Amiel, twin s. Amiel and Celia, Feb. 24, 1809.
Cordelia, w. Samuel Litchfield, ———, 1817. G.R.2.
Cordelia M., ch. James and Martha, Apr. 16, 1839.

STUDLEY, Cushing O., ch. David W. and Eleanor T., Sept. 11, 1837.
Daniel, s. David and Susannah, Apr. 28, 1725.
David, s. David and Susannah, Nov. 12, 1720.
David Will[ia]m, s. Amiel and Celia, Aug. 16, 1807. [Studly, c.r.2.]
Daws, s. Lewis and Lucy, Feb. 16, 1794.
Deborah, d. Amasa, bp. July 21, 1754. c.r.1.
Deborah [———], w. Bennett D., ———, 1797. G.R.2. [[June —, 1797] P.R.21.]
Deborah, d. Amasa and Lydia, ———.
Deborah Nash, d. Bennett D. and Deborah, July 31, 1827.
[D]eborah Phillbrick, d. Amiel and Celia, Mar. 14, 1822.
Deborah Randol [dup. crossed out in pencil, Randall], d. Will[ia]m and Ruth, Dec. 27, 1780 [dup. crossed out in pencil, 1786].
Delilah, d. Lewis and Lucy, Sept. 3, 1804.
Edwin, ch. Charles A. and Amelia S., Nov. 29, 1834.
Edwin, s. Lewis Jr. and Emily, May 7, 1835.
Edwin B[ennett] [s. James Hervey], Oct. 18, 1848. P.R.21.
Edwin R., ch. David W. and Eleanor T., Jan. 22, 1835.
Elisabeth, d. Will[ia]m and Ruth, Feb. 2, 1785. [Elizabeth, G.R.14.]
Elizabeth, d. James and Sarah, May 6, 1725.
Ellen M., ch. David W. and Eleanor T., Nov. 2, 1839.
Emelia, d. Lewis Jr. and Emely, Sept. 9, 1826.
Eunice [w. Simeon Wade], Aug. 18, 1731. P.R.27.
Eunice T. [———], w. Liba, ——— [1804]. C.R.3. G.R.2.
Eunice Thomas, ch. Liba and Eunice T., Feb. 16, 1835.
Fanny, d. Lewis and Lucy, Mar. 16, 1800.
George W., ch. William Jr. and Amelia, June 16, 1833.
Hamen (S[t]udley), s. John and Sarah, Feb. 24, 1809.
Hannah, d. John and Sarah, Aug. 16, 1802.
Hannah, d. Amasa and Lydia, ———.
Henry L., ch. David W. and Eleanor T., Mar. 24, 1831, in Marshfield.
Henry Lincoln, s. Amiel and Celia, Sept. 30, 1810.
Henry O., ch. William Jr. and Amelia, Nov. 9, 1838.
Henry Solon, twin s. Amiel and Celia, Feb. 24, 1809.
Homer, s. John, bp. Sept. 3, 1809. C.R.1.
Horace Lincoln, ch. Homer and Lydia, Sept. 14, 1837.
Howland L. [h. Mary] [Oct. —, 1820]. G.R.2.
James, s. James and Sarah, Aug. 26, 1720. [Studly, C.R.1.]
James Harvey, s. Bennett D. and Deborah, Dec. 14, 1825. [James Hervey, P.R.21.]

SCITUATE BIRTHS 345

STUDLEY, James Ludlow, s. Amiel and Celia, Mar. 16, 1813.
Joa, d. Lewis and Lucy, Aug. 5, 1802.
John, s. John and Sarah, Feb. 25, 1790.
John, ch. John, bp. Oct. 14, 1798. C.R.1.
John, ch. Homer and Lydia, Jan. 31, 1840.
Joseph, s. Elihab, bp. June 7, 1741. C.R.1.
Joseph, s. Allen and Mary, Mar. 1, 1820.
Julia Ann, d. Lewis Jr. and Emely, Apr. 25, 1816.
Julia Anne, ch. Lewis Jr. and w., bp. Oct. 7, 1832. C.R.1.
Lewis, s. Lewis and Lucy, Oct. 20, 1791. [[h. Amelia] G.R.2.]
Lewis Jr., s. Lewis, —— [1822]. C.R.3.
Lewis, s. Lewis Jr. and Emely, July 26, 1824. [Lewis Jr., C.R.1.]
Lewis, ch. Lewis Jr. and w., bp. Oct. 7, 1832. C.R.1.
Lewis, d. [*sic*] Amasa and Lydia, ——.
Liba, s. Luis, bp. Aug. 21, 1808. C.R.1. [[h. Eunice T.] G.R.2.]
Liba, s. [L., written in pencil] Howland [L., written in pencil], seaman, and Mary (b. Springfield [dup. adds Vt.]), July 15, 1848.
Liba Howland Lewis, s. Amial and Celia, Oct. 31, 1820.
Libia, s. Lewis and Lucy, Oct. 29, 1807.
Lucy, d. Eliab, bp. Oct. 20, 1745. C.R.1.
Lucy [——], w. Lewis, —— [1769]. G.R.2.
Lucy [——], w. William, ——, 1785. G.R.14.
Lucy [dup. Studly], d. Lewis and Lucy, July 16, 1789.
Lucy, d. William Jr. and Lucy, Dec. 17, 1810.
Lucy, d. Allen and Mary, Jan. 28, 1818.
Lucy Dunbar, d. Lewis Jr. and Emely, Oct. 4, 1821.
Lucy Dunbar, ch. Lewis Jr. and w., bp. Oct. 7, 1832. C.R.1.
Lydia, d. Allen and Mary, Jan. 30, 1816.
Lydia, d. Amasa and Lydia, ——.
Margaret Bennett, d. Lewis Jr. and Emely, Aug. 2, 1831.
Margarett Bennett, d. Lewis Jr. and Emely, Nov. 5, 1832. [w. William P. Veale, G.R.2.]
Maria, d. David William and Eleanor T., Nov. 2, 1839.
Mary [——], w. Howland L. [Sept. —, 1821]. G.R.2.
Mary, w. A[lanson] A. C. Gilbert [Oct. —, 1828]. G.R.2.
Mary A. [——], w. James W., Nov. 21, 1837. G.R.15.
Mary Ann, d. David W., shipwright, and Elenor [dup. Eleanor, adds T.], Sept. 20, 1846.
Mary E., ch. James and Martha, May 11, 1838.
Mary Elizabeth, d. Amial and Cilea, July 8, 1815.
Mercy [dup. Marcy Studly], d. David [dup. Jr.] and Eliza[beth], May 4, 1745. [Mercy Studley, d. David Jr. and w., C.R.1.]

STUDLEY, Mercy, d. Amasa and Lydia, Sept. 15, 1763.
Mercy Peirce, d. Bennett D. and Deborah, Apr. 2, 1831. [Mercy Pierce, P.R.21.]
Mercy Thomas, ch. David W. and Eleanor T., Jan. 16, 1842.
Nancy, d. John and Sarah, Sept. 13, 1789.
Nancy, ch. John, bp. Oct. 14, 1798. C.R.1.
Nancy, d. Homer, yeoman, and Lydia, July 30, 1844.
Noah, s. David and Anna, bp. Apr. 23, 1758. C.R.1.
Olive, d. Daniel, bp. June 22, 1760. C.R.1.
Priscilla, d. Amasa, bp. June 21, 1752. C.R.1.
Priscilla, d. Amasa and Lydia, ———.
Rachel White, d. John and Sarah, Apr. 2, 1800.
Ruth [dup. crossed out in pencil, Studly], d. Will[ia]m and Ruth, Jan. 28 [dup. crossed out in pencil, Jan. 23], 1779.
Sarah, d. Benony, Mar. 31, 1716.
Sarah, d. James and Sarah, Jan. 18, 1718.
Sarah, d. Amasa, bp. May 15, 1763. C.R.1.
Sarah, d. Amasa and Lydia, ———.
Sarah Cole, d. John and Sarah, Aug. 4, 1792.
Sarah Cole, ch. John, bp. Oct. 14, 1798. C.R.1.
Silas, s. Allen and Mary, Sept. 27, 1821.
Solon Nash, s. Amial and Cilia, May 9, 1818.
Susanna, d. Amasa, bp. Sept. 12, 1756. C.R.1.
Susanna, d. Amasa and Lydia, ———.
Susannah, d. David and Susannah, Jan. 26, 1718.
Warren, ch. William Jr. and Amelia, Nov. 30, 1835.
Will[ia]m [dup. Studly], s. Will[ia]m and Ruth, Mar. 31, 1777. [Studley [h. Lucy], G.R.14.]
William, s. William Jr. and Lucy, July 14, 1809. [[h. Amelia P.] G.R.14.]
William W., ch. David W. and Eleanor T., Apr. 16, 1833.
Zebulon, s. Abigail, bp. Nov. 19, 1752. C.R.1.
Zoa (see Joa).
Zoe, d. John and Sarah, Apr. 2, 1805. [Zoa, C.R.1.]
[torn]g Otis, s. David W. and Eleaner T., Sept. 11, 1837.
[torn]m Wallace, s. David W. and Eleanor T., Apr. 16, 1833.
[torn] Lincoln, s. David W. and Eleanor T., Mar. 24, 1831.
[torn] Ruthven, s. David W. and Eleanor T., Jan. 22, 1835.
——— [———], wid. Lewis, ——— [1770]. C.R.1.
——— [———], w. Lewis Jr., ——— [1828]. C.R.1.
———, ch. Charles and Olive, May 1, 1843.
———, ch. William Jr. and Amelia, Jan. 9, 1844.
———, s. W. W., farmer, and Amelia, Feb. 17, 1848.
———, s. W[illia]m, housewright, and Amelia, Sept. 7 [184-].

SCITUATE BIRTHS 347

STUDLIE (see Studley, Studly), John, s. Benjamen, Dec. 11, 1684.

STUDLY (see Studley, Studlie), Abigall, d. Benony, Aug. 13, 1702.
Ammiel, s. David Jr. and Eliza[beth], July 18, 1757.
Benjamin, s. Benjamin, Dec. 7, 1687.
David, s. Benjamin, Jan. 19, 1696–7.
David, s. David Jr. and Eliza[beth], Oct. 13, 1748. [Studley, C.R.1.]
Dawes, ch. Luis and Lucy, bp. Sept. 20, 1795. C.R.1.
Deborah, d. Benjamin and Mary, Dec. 19, 1703.
Eliab, s. Benjamin and Mary, Sept. 10, 1706.
Eliab, s. Eliab, bp. May 19, 1751. C.R.1.
Elizabeth, d. Benjamin and Mary, June 8, 1701.
Elizabeth, d. David Jr. and Eliza[beth], Oct. 13, 1754. [Studley, C.R.1.]
Gideon, s. Benoni, May 15, 1710.
Hannah, d. Amasa, bp. June 15, 1760. C.R.1.
James, s. Benjamin, July 15, 1690.
James, s. Eliab, bp. June 24, 1739. C.R.1.
John, s. Benony, Feb. 25, 1704–5.
John, s. David and Eliza[beth], Feb. 20, 1760.
Jonathan, s. Benjamin, June 19, 1693.
Joshua, s. Benoni, Aug. —, 1707.
Lewis, ch. Amasa, bp. Oct. 12, 1766. C.R.1.
Lewis, ch. Luis and Lucy, bp. Sept. 20, 1795. C.R.1.
Lucy, ch. Luis and Lucy, bp. Sept. 20, 1795. C.R.1.
Lydia, d. Amasa and Lydia, bp. May 20, 1750. C.R.1.
Martha, ch. Thomas and Mary, bp. July 8, 1759. C.R.1.
Mary, d. Benjamin, Sept. 23, 1698.
Mary, d. Eliab, bp. June 26, 1743. C.R.1.
Mary, ch. Thomas and Mary, bp. July 8, 1759. C.R.1.
Mercy, ch. Amasa, bp. Oct. 12, 1766. C.R.1.
Thomas, ch. Thomas and Mary, bp. July 8, 1759. C.R.1.
Will[ia]m, s. David Jr. and Eliza[beth], Feb. 6, 1752. [Studley, C.R.1.]

STUDSON (see Stetson, Stetsun, Sturtson, Stutson), Benjamin, s. Rob[er]t, bp. Oct. 5, 1645. C.R.2.
Joseph, s. Rob[er]t, bp. Oct. 5, 1645. C.R.2.
Leah, d. Benjamin, May 6, 1702.
Samuel, s. Benjamin, bp. May 11, 1673. C.R.2.
Thomas, s. Rob[er]t, bp. Oct. 5, 1645. C.R.2.
Thomas, s. Thomas, bp. Mar. 31, 1674. C.R.2.
Timothy, s. Rob[er]t, bp. Oct. 11, 1657. C.R.2.

STURTSON (see Stetson, Stetsun, Studson, Stutson), Abigail, d. John, bp. July 14, 1678. C.R.2.
Barnabas, s. John, bp. July 16, 1682. C.R.2.
Elisha, s. Benjamin, bp. Apr. 25, 1686. C.R.2.
Eunice, d. Benjamin, bp. May 27, 1683. C.R.2.
John, s. John, bp. May 4, 1679. C.R.2.
Judah, s. Samuel, bp. May 14, 1682. C.R.2.

STUTSON (see Stetson, Stetsun, Studson, Sturtson), Abiel, s. Antho[ny] and Anna, Oct. 23, 1738.
Abigal, d. Abijah and Deborah, Nov. 4, 1733.
Adam, s. Abijah and Deborah, Mar. 12, 1729. [Stetson, C.R.2.]
Alice, d. Sam[ue]ll (s. Jo), Mar. 20, 1720.
Amos, s. Gideon and Mary, Jan. 9, 1741. [Stetson, s. Gidion, C.R.2.]
Anna, d. Antho[ny] (Stetson) and Anna, June 2, 1724. [Stetson, C.R.2.]
[A]nna, d. Isaac and Ruth, Sept. 22, 1755.
Benja[min], s. Antho[ny] and Anna, July 7, 1736.
Caleb, s. William and Hannah, May 31, 1726.
Charles, s. Antho[ny] (Stetson) and Anna, Oct. 17, 1726. [Charls Stetson, C.R.2.]
Deborah, d. Abijah and Deborah, Apr. 26, 1737. [Stetson, C.R.2.]
Elisha, s. Antho[ny] and Anna, Jan. 28, 1731.
[E]lisha, s. Isaac and Ruth, Apr. 8, 1759.
[E]lizabeth, d. Isaac and Ruth, Jan. 7, 1754. [Elisabeth Stetson, C.R.2.]
Eunice (see Unice).
Ezra, s. Antho[ny] and Anna, Sept. 22, 1729. [Stetson, C.R.2.]
Gideon, s. Gideon and Mary, May 6, 1737. [Gidion Stetson, s. Gidion and Lydia, C.R.2.]
Hannah, d. W[illia]m and Hannah, Jan. 18, 1731.
Hannah, d. Gidion and Mary, Nov. 23, 1747. [Stetson, C.R.2.]
Isaac, s. Isaac and Ruth, Nov. 30, 1750.
Job, s. William and Hannah, June 3, 1724.
John, s. Abijah and Deborah, Apr. 17, 1731.
Joseph, s. Sam[ue]ll (s. Jo), Mar. 25, 1724.
Lillis, d. Benja[min] Jr. and Lillis, July 25, 1726.
Lusanna, d. Joseph and Mary, Feb. 28, 1745. [Stetson, C.R.2.]
Lydia, d. Gidion and Mary, Nov. 28, 1745. [Stetson, C.R.2.]
Margreat, d. John (Stitson) Jr. and Barshaba, Aug. 9, 1766.
Martha, d. Anthony and Anna, Aug. 18, 1741. [Stetson, d. Anthony and Ann, C.R.2.]
Mary, d. Gidion and Mary, May 11, 1750.

SCITUATE BIRTHS 349

STUTSON, Molle, d. Joseph and Mary, Aug. 15, 1748. [Molly Stetson, C.R.2.]
Prudence, d. Joseph and Mary, Mar. 19, 1750. [Stetson, C.R.2.]
[R]uth, d. Isaac and Ruth, Mar. 27, 1752. [Stetson, C.R.2.]
Tho[ma]s, s. Antho[ny] and Anna, Apr. 22, 1734. [Stetson, C.R.2.]
[U]nice, d. Isaac and Ruth, May 31, 1757. [Stetson, C.R.2.]
Zenas, s. Gideon and Mary, Dec. 28, 1743. [Zenos Stetson, s. Gidion, C.R.2.]

SUPPLE, Edward [h. Ann], —— [1824], in Killmoo, Co. Cork, Ire. G.R.10.
Richard, —— [1806], in Co. Cork, Ire. G.R.10.

SUTTEN (see Sutton), Anna, d. John, Apr. 30, 1709. [Sutton, C.R.1.]
Benjamin, s. John, bp. July 21, 1678. C.R.2.
Benjemen, s. John, Mar. 22, 1674–5.
Elizabeth, d. John, Oct. 20, 1662. [Sutton, d. Elizab[eth], C.R.2.]
Elizabeth, d. Nathaniel and Margaret, Mar. 8, 1711–12.
Hanah, d. John, Nov. 3, 1669.
Hester, d. John, Oct. 25, 1671.
John, s. John, Feb. 28, 1663.
John, s. John, Sept. 19, 1695.
Mary, d. John, Jan. 22, 1665.
Nancy, d. Abner, bp. Mar. 18, 1804. C.R.1.
Nathan, s. John, Aug. 6, 1679.
Nathan, s. John, bp. Nov. 12, 1682. C.R.2.
Nathanell, s. John, July 31, 1676.
Nathaniell, s. John, bp. July 21, 1678. C.R.2.
Nathaniell, s. John, May 28, 1711.
Ray, s. Nathanael and Margaret, Feb. 27, 1709–10.
Sarah, d. John, Nov. 3, 1667.
Seth, s. John, Apr. 3, 1706.
——, s. John, May 15, 1705.

SUTTON (see Sutten), Abigail, d. Abner and Anna, June 6, 1784.
Abner, s. Jo[h]n, bp. May 31, 1730. C.R.1.
Abner, grand s. Jo[h]n and Ann, bp. Aug. 20, 1758. C.R.1.
Abner, s. Abner and Anna, Feb. 6, 1782.
Andrew, grand s. Jo[h]n and Ann, bp. Aug. 20, 1758. C.R.1.
Anna, d. John, bp. July 4, 1725. C.R.1.
Deborah, d. Ira and Betsey, May 1, 1801.
Dianna, d. Ira and Betsey, Aug. 28, 1803.
Elizabeth, d. Geo[rge], bp. Aug. 28, 1653. C.R.2.
Elizabeth, w. Joseph Ellms, ——, 1710. G.R.8.

SUTTON, Hannah, d. Jesse and Elizabeth, bp. June 22, 1760. c.r.1.
Jesse, s. Jesse, bp. Oct. 30, 1763. c.r.1.
Joanna [? m.], —— [1787]. g.r.2.
Joanna, d. Reuben and Sarah, Aug. 27, 1811.
Joe, d. Abner and Anna, Apr. 6, 1787.
John, s. Jo[h]n, Nov. 27, 1720.
John, grand s. Jo[h]n and Ann, bp. Aug. 20, 1758. c.r.1.
Lydia, d. George, bp. Sept. 13, 1646. c.r.2.
Mary, d. Jo[h]n, bp. June 25, 1727. c.r.1.
Molley, d. Abner and Anna, Nov. 25, 1779.
Nancy, d. Abner and Anna, Dec. 12, 1778.
Nathan, s. John, bp. Sept. 28, 1712. c.r.1.
Nathaneel, s. Jesse, bp. May 28, 1769. c.r.1.
Nath[anie]l, ch. Jesse and w., bp. Aug. 9, 1759. c.r.1.
Ray, s. Jesse, bp. Sept. 25, 1774. c.r.1.
Reuben, s. Abner and Anna, Oct. 9, 1777.
Reubin, s. Jo[h]n, bp. Mar. 31, 1732. c.r.1.
Sarah, d. George, bp. Dec. 3, 1648. c.r.2.
Sarah, d. George, bp. Sept. 15, 1650. c.r.2.
Sarah, d. Reuben and Sarah, Mar. 30, 1810.
Seth, s. John, bp. Nov. 16, 1707. c.r.1.
Seth, s. Jesse, bp. Sept. 2, 1770. c.r.1.
Seth, s. Abner and Anna, Mar. 26, 1790.
Seth, s. Reuben and Sarah, Mar. 29, 1813.
Tamor Lincoln, d. John and w., bp. July 28, 1776. c.r.1.
Thankful, d. Jesse, bp. June 8, 1766. c.r.1.

SWEETLAND, Lucy, d. —— and Ruth (d. Jacob Wade), bp. Aug. 11, 1776. c.r.1.

SWIFFT, Thomas, s. Thomas and Rachell, Mar. 29, 1712. [Swift, s. Thomas and Rachel, c.r.2.]

SYLVESTER (see Sillverster, Silverster, Silvester), Abigail V. [——], w. William [Aug. —, 1821]. g.r.14.
Adeline Eliza, ch. Nathaniel B. and Adeline, Sept. 21, 1839.
Almira, d. Warren and Hannah, Nov. 18, 1805.
Amelia W. [——], w. Edmond H. [Apr. —, 1840]. g.r.2.
Anny, w. Elijah Bowker, Apr. 1, 1768. g.r.17.
Anthony, —— [1787]. g.r.15.
Arabella [——], w. Abel, ——, 1813. g.r.2.
Ariannah G. [——], w. Henry H. [Nov. —, 1823]. g.r.2.
Austin Turner, ch. Jotham T. and Mary, Aug. 10, 1840.
Barstow, s. Capt. W[illia]m, bp. July 10, 1757. c.r.2.

SYLVESTER, Belintha Orine, d. Henry H., sailor, and Ariannah, Nov. 10, 1847. [Belintha Olive, P.R.22.]
Benjamin, s. Richard, bp. May 17, 1657. C.R.2.
Betsey W. [———], w. William T., ———, 1827. G.R.15.
Bristol, s. Fruitful and Patty, Aug. 7, 1799.
Celia, d. Israel, bp. Oct. 22, 1752. C.R.2.
Celia, d. Israel, bp. Aug. 3, 1755. C.R.2.
Charles Franklin, ch. Abel Jr. and Arabella, July 22, 1843.
Charles T., s. Peter and Emma, Dec. 19, 1846. [———, 1847, G.R. 14.]
Charles Thomas, s. Thomas Jr. and Nabby, May 4, 1821.
Charles Warren, s. Warren and Hannah, Mar. 31, 1807.
Charlotte U., ch. Peter and Emma, June 24, 1837.
Danforth Perry, s. Henry H., fisherman, and Arianna (Glines), Aug. 9, 1849.
Deborah Walker, d. T[homas] and Lucy, May 19, 1822.
Ebenezar, twin ch. Joseph of Marshfield, bp. May 23, 1725. C.R.2.
Edmand Howard, ch. Abel Jr. and Arabella, Oct. 25, 1834, in Hingham. [Edmund H. [h. Amelia W.], G.R.2.]
Elisabeth [———], w. Jos. ——— [1777]. G.R.15.
Elisha, s. Lemuel, bp. May 8, 1757. C.R.2.
Eliza J., ch. Peter and Emma, May 18, 1840.
Elizabeth (see Elisabeth).
Elizabeth Stetson, d. Tho[ma]s Jr. and Nabby, Jan. 31, 1827.
Ella A., d. Nath[aniel] B., cordwainer, and Adaline [dup. Adeline], Aug. 28, 1846.
Francis Marion, s. James and Elizabeth, June 21, 1822.
Fruitful, colored, May 6, 1765. G.R.14.
George, s. Thomas Jr. and Nabby, May 3, 1824. [Silvester [h. Nancy W. (Bowker)], G.R.14.]
George Henry, ch. Abel Jr. and Arabella, Apr. 27, 1833, in Hingham. [[h. Sarah M.] G.R.2.]
George W., ch. Nathaniel B. and Adeline, Feb. 5, 1844.
Gershom, s. Nehemiah, bp. Nov. 20, 1757. C.R.2.
Gideon Young, s. James and Elizabeth, Apr. —, 1826.
Harvy, s. Warren and Hannah, Feb. 19, 1810. [Hervey Turner, C.R.2.]
Helen Lois, Dec. 10, 1837. P.R.22.
Henrietta, d. Jotham and Mary, May 13, 1846.
Hesther, d. Richard, bp. Mar. 26, 1654. C.R.1.
Hittie, colored, Jan. 17, 1771. G.R.14.
Howard, s. Elisha Jr. and Abagil, June 4, 1784.
Ichabod, s. Fruitful and Patty, Nov. 5, 1795.
James, s. Fruitful and Patty, May 1, 1802.

SYLVESTER, James Little, [twin]s. James and Elizabeth, Jan. 1, 1819.
Jane Lewis, d. Thomas O. and Lucy, Nov. 9, 1818.
John, s. John, bp. Sept. 29, 1672. C.R.2.
John Otis, [twin] s. James and Elizabeth, Jan. 1, 1819.
John Otis, s. James and Elizabeth, Sept. 22, 1820.
Josephine Arabella, ch. Abel Jr. and Arabella, Nov. 8, 1836.
Jotham Turner, s. Jotham and Lydia, Feb. 10, 1817.
Katy, d. Fruitful and Patty, Jan. 28, 1807.
Laura Ann, d. James and Elizabeth, July 27, 1828. [w. Edward James, G.R.5.]
Lilles H. [———], w. Abel, —— [1786]. G.R.18.
Lydia, d. Fruitful and Patty, July 19, 1809.
Lydia, d. Jotham and Lydia, May 11, 1819.
Marcia Ann, d. Thomas O. and Lucy, Feb. 14, 1824.
Mary Augusta, Aug. 9, 1839. P.R.22.
Mary Elizabeth, d. James and Elizabeth, Apr. 2, 1824.
Mary L., d. Peter, shoemaker, and Anna [dup. Emma], June 21, 1844.
Mary W., Nov. 5, 1842. P.R.22.
Matilda T., d. Nathaniel B., shoemaker, and Adeline, Mar. 19, 1849, in S. Scituate.
Naomi, d. Richard, bp. Apr. 14, 1650. C.R.2.
Naomi, d. Joseph, bp. Nov. 19, 1671. C.R.2.
Nathan, s. Thomas Jr. and Nabby, June 4, 1816.
Nathaniel, s. Thomas Jr. and Nabby, Sept. 17, 1813.
Patty, d. Fruitful and Patty, Sept. 10, 1797.
Peter, s. Fruitful and Patty, Nov. 8, 1812.
Philo, s. Fruitful and Patty, Feb. 2, 1805.
Rachel Amelia, ch. Nathaniel B. and Adeline, Sept. 28, 1841.
Rhoda, colored, —— [1778]. G.R.14.
Roxana Thomas, d. Thomas O. and Lucy, Feb. 13, 1816.
Sarah, d. John, bp. Apr. 16, 1671. C.R.2.
Sarah Elizabeth, ch. Abel Jr. and Arabella, Dec. 22, 1838.
Sarah M. [———], w. George H. [Nov. —, 1836]. G.R.2.
Sela, d. Israel and Deliverance, June 5, 1756.
Solomon, s. Joseph, bp. Mar. 31, 1674. C.R.2.
Thomas, s. Fruitful and Patty, July 30, 1815.
Tryphosy, d. Tho[ma]s and w., bp. Nov. 2, 1794. C.R.2.
William, s. Thomas Jr. and Nabby, Sept. 12, 1818.
William Henry, Sept. 15, 1840. P.R.22.
William T. "Co. G. 18 Reg. Mass. Vol." [h. Betsey W.], ——, 1816. G.R.15.
———, s. Thomas O. and Lucy, Apr. 25, 1821.
———, ch. Abel Jr. and Arabella, Dec. 8, 1840.

SYMMES (see Symms), Hannah, d. Timothy and E[l]izabeth, May 12, 1712. [Symms, C.R.2.]

SYMMONS (see Simmons, Simonds, Simons, Symons), Aaron, s. Aaron and Eliz[abeth], bp. Oct. 28, 1750. C.R.1.
Barnabas, s. Moses Jr., bp. June 20, 1756. C.R.1.
Betty, d. Moses, bp. Aug. 4, 1728. C.R.1.
John, s. Moses, bp. Mar. 15, 1667. C.R.2.
Lydia, d. Aron, bp. Sept. 23, 1759. C.R.1.
Mary, d. Ebenezer, bp. Nov. 19, 1721. C.R.1.
Mary, d. Aaron, bp. Oct. 17, 1756. C.R.1.
Rachel, d. Aaron, bp. June 30, 1765. C.R.1.
Rhoda, d. Aron, bp. Sept. 23, 1759. C.R.1.
Ruben, s. Ebenezar, bp. Aug. 28, 1726. C.R.2.
Samuel, s. Moses Jr., bp. Apr. 22, 1750. C.R.1.
Sarah, d. Moses, bp. Oct. 5, 1735. C.R.1.
Sarah, d. Moses Jr., bp. June 5, 1748. C.R.1.

SYMMS (see Symmes), Anthony, s. Timothy [s. Timothy and Elizabeth, C.R.2.], Sept. 22, 1716.
Anthony, s. Timothy and Eliz[abeth], bp. July 15, 1722. C.R.2.
Timothy, s. Timothy and Elizabeth, May 27, 1714.

SYMONS (see Simmons, Simonds, Simons, Symmons), Abigail, d. Ebenez[e]r, bp. Apr. 14, 1717. C.R.1.
Ebenezer, s. Aaron, June 10, 1689.
Elizabeth, d. Aaron, Aug. 27, 1686.
Job, s. Moses, bp. Oct. 4, 1674. C.R.2.
Lydia, d. Aaron, Mar. 27, 1693.
Mary, d. Aaron, Mar. 11, 1683–4.
Moses, s. Aaron, Feb. 24, 1681–2. [Simmons, C.R.2.]
Moses, s. Moses, bp. Apr. 14, 1717. C.R.1.
Rebekah, d. Aaron, Dec. 2, 1679.

TAILER (see Tailor, Taylor), Isaac, s. Isaac and Ruth, bp. Sept. 3, 1721. C.R.2.
Lettice, d. Rachel, wid., bp. Apr. 20, 1740. C.R.2.

TAILOR (see Tailer, Taylor), Isaac, s. Isaac and Ruth, bp. June 27, 1725. C.R.2.
Ruben, s. David and Elizabeth, bp. Mar. 19, 1731–2. C.R.2.
Ruth, d. Isaac and Ruth, bp. Aug. 11, 1723. C.R.2.

TALBOT, Eliza S., ch. Zepheniah and Agnes, June 26, 1829, in Hanover. [w. Edward Southworth, G.R.15.]
Hannah R., ch. Zepheniah and Agnes, Apr. 28, 1833, in Hanover.

TALBOT, Mary [——], w. Capt. W[illia]m H., —— [1821]. G.R.14.
Mary B., ch. Zepheniah and Agnes, Apr. 25, 1827, in Hanover.
Robert S., ch. Zepheniah and Agnes, Oct. 15, 1838.
William F., s. W[illia]m H., mariner, and Mary, July 1, 1845.
William H., ch. Zepheniah and Agnes, Jan. 26, 1819, in R.I.
    [Capt. William H. [h. Mary], G.R.14.]
Zephaniah, Capt. [h. Agnes (Salmond)], Nov. 8, 1793. G.R.15.
Zepheniah, ch. Zepheniah and Agnes, June 22, 1834, in Hanover.

TAYLOR (see Tailer, Tailor), David, s. Isaac, Mar. 15, 1700–1.
Delight, d. David and Elizabeth, Mar. 7, 1732.
Elizabeth, d. William, July 5, 1692.
Isaac, s. Isaac, Feb. 20, 1693.
John, s. Isaac and Ruth, bp. May 31, 1719. C.R.2.
Jonathan, s. Isaac, Jan. 15, 1698–9.
Lydia, d. William, Mar. 20, 1688–9.
Martha Paine, d. John S. [dup. omits S.], farmer [dup. shoemaker] (b. Quincy), and Cordelia (b. Provincetown) [dup. b. Boston], Nov. 17, 1849.
Mary, d. Isaac, June 10, 1696.
Mary, d. William, July 13, 1696.
Rachiel, d. Isaac and Sarah, bp. June 1, 1707. C.R.2.
Sarah, d. David and Eliz[abe]th, bp. Apr. 1, 1736. C.R.2.
Stephen Snow, s. John S., trader, and Cordelia A., July 26, 1845.
William T., s. William, farmer, and Betsey, Aug. 28, 1847.

TEWELL (see Tuell), Castell, s. Benjamin, June 1, 1716.
    [Castle Tuell, s. Benjamin and Joanna, C.R.2.]

TEWSBURY, —— [——], w. ——, —— [1803]. C.R.1.

THOMAS, Abiah [——], w. N. Esq. of Marshfield, Dec. —, 1721. C.R.1.
Abigail, ch. N. Esq. and Abiah, Mar. 12, 1744. C.R.1.
Allathea, ch. N. Esq. and Abiah, May 1, 1742. C.R.1.
Charles, ch. N. Esq. and Abiah, Feb. 6, 1768. C.R.1.
Francis, s. Rev. Nehemiah and Hannah, Apr. 13, 1804.
Frank, —— [1824]. G.R.10.
Hannah, ch. N. Esq. and Abiah, July 22 [? 21], 1760. C.R.1.
Hannah Cushing, d. Seth and Ruth, June 24, 18[torn].
Harriet, d. Rev. Nehemiah and Hannah, Sept. 1, 1798.
Henry, s. Rev. Nehemiah and Hannah, Dec. 14, 179[6].
Lucy, ch. N. Esq. and Abiah, Nov. 27, 1757. C.R.1.
Lucy Otis, d. Rev. Nehemiah and Hannah, Aug. 30, 1800.
N. Esq. of Marshfield [h. Abiah], July 26, 1712. C.R.1.

THOMAS, Nathaniel, ch. N. Esq. and Abiah, Oct. 1, 1750. c.r.1.
Nehemiah, ch. N. Esq. and Abiah, June 3, 1748. c.r.1.
Nehemiah, ch. N. Esq. and Abiah, Feb. 3, 1766. c.r.1.
Olive, ch. N. Esq. and Abiah, Dec. 28, 1752. c.r.1.
Ruth, ch. N. Esq. and Abiah, Aug. 3, 1746. c.r.1.
Ruth, ch. N. Esq. and Abiah, June 14, 1755. c.r.1.
Ruth, d. Seth and Ruth, June 23, 182[torn].
Sarah Helen, d. Francis and Sarah [Aug. —, 1834]. g.r.6.
Seth [July —, 1829]. g.r.14.
Seth, s. Seth and Ruth, May 20, 18[torn].
William, s. Seth and Ruth, Apr. 11, 182[torn].
Winslow, ch. N. Esq. and Abiah, July 21, 1763. c.r.1.

THOMSON (see Tomson), Ann, d. Robert, Oct. 18, 1718. [Tomson, d. Robert and Ann, c.r.2.]
Barnabas, s. Robert [s. Robert and Anne, c.r.2.], Apr. 18, 1717.
John, s. Robert and Anna, Apr. 8, 1720. [Tomson, s. Robert and Anne, c.r.2.]
Robert, s. Robert [s. Robert and Ann, c.r.2.], June 26, 1715.
Thomas, s. Robert and Ann, Oct. 26, 1721.

THORNDIKE, Arabella, d. Israel and Mercy, July 30, 1831.
Artemas, s. Theophilus, —— [1812]. c.r.3.
Artemus, [twin] s. Israel and Mercy, Apr. 2, 1812, in Camden.
Clarissa, d. Israel and Mercy, Oct. 18, 1820, in Cohassett.
Clementina, d. Israel and Mercy, July 13, 1826.
Juliettee, d. Israel and Mercy, Nov. 13, 1814, in Camden. [Julietta, d. Theophilus, c.r.3.]
Mary Jane, d. Israel and Mercy, Oct. 13, 1827.
Mercy, d. Israel and Mercy, June 19, 1817, in Cohassett.
Septimus, [twin] s. Israel and Mercy, Apr. 2, 1812, in Camden.
Theophilus W., s. Israel and Mercy, Feb. 19, 1810, in Camden.
Thomas J., s. Israel and Mercy, Aug. 5, 1822.

THORNE, Mary, "adopted" d. Thomas Pincheon and Sarah, bp. Oct. 19, 1712. c.r.2.

THORTING, Margaret A., d. Philip, boat builder, and Christiana, Feb. 14, 1845.

THRIFT, Hannah, d. Will[ia]m and Han[na]h, Sept. 27, 1732.

THURSTON, William, s. Elnathan Jr. and Louiza M., Aug. 12, 1829.

TICKNER, Hannah, d. William, Oct. 17, 1697.
John, s. William, bp. May 15, 1659. c.r.2.

TICKNER, John, s. William, June 24, 1699.
Lydia, d. William, June 24, 1702.
William, s. William, bp. June 26, 1664. C.R.2.
William, s. William, Dec. 2, 1700.

TILDEN (see Tildin, Tillden), Aamos, s. Thomas and Abigail, Mar. 22, 1774. [Amos, C.R.1.]
Abigail, ch. Samuel, bp. ——, 1699. C.R.2.
Abigail, d. David and Abigail, Sept. 14, 1713.
Abigail, d. Sam[ue]ll and Desire of Marshfield, bp. Aug. 23, 1719. C.R.2.
Abigail, d. Thomas and Abigail, Nov. 6, 1767.
Abigail Bailey, d. Christopher and Aseneth, Aug. 26, 1825. [Abby B., G.R.6.]
Abigail Bailey, ch. Christopher and Asenath, bp. Oct. 6, 1833. C.R.1.
Alice M., ch. William H. and Sarah A., Sept. 14, 1843. [Alice C., G.R.14.]
Alonzo, ch. Amos H. and Martha, Apr. 11, 1838.
Amos H., Feb. 27, 1812. G.R.14.
Asenath, ——, 1803. G.R.6.
Atherton Wales, s. Thatcher and Lucy, Aug. 28, 1796.
Atherton Wales, s. Thatcher, bp. Oct. 3, 1802. C.R.2.
Benjamin, s. Joseph, bp. Feb. 20, 1668. C.R.2.
Benjamin, s. Nathaniell Jr., May 18, 1705.
Bethiah, d. Jo[h]n, bp. June 2, 1746. C.R.1.
Betsey, d. Thatcher and Lucy, June 21, 1803. [Betsy, C.R.2.]
Caroline, d. Luther [Cap[t]. Luther, C.R.2.] and Philenda, Sept. 4, 1820.
Catharine [————], w. George [Apr. —, 1807]. G.R.2.
Catharine Hall, ch. Colman and Harriet, Feb. 4, 1838.
Charles, s. Thatcher and Lucy, May 30, 1815.
Charles, ch. Luther A. and Sarah S., Mar. 23, 1835.
Charles W., ch. William H. and Sarah A., Oct. 25, 1835, in Marshfield.
Christopher, s. Joseph of Marshfield, bp. May 4, 1712. C.R.1.
Christopher, s. John and Marcy, Sept. 14, 1800.
Christopher, ch. John, bp. Sept. 1, 1805. C.R.1.
Christopher, s. Christopher and Aseneth [Asenath, C.R.1.], Sept. 11, 1833.
Colman, s. John and Marcy, Mar. 29, 1810.
David, s. Stephen [Steven Sr., C.R.2.], Nov. 6, 1685.
David, s. David and Abigail, Nov. 22, 1711.
David, s. David, Jan. 27, 1717.

TILDEN, David, s. John and Marcy, Sept. 27, 1804.
Deborah, d. Thomas and Abigail, Feb. 22, 1770. [first w. Joseph Bailey, P.R.9.]
Deborah, d. John and Marcy, Oct. 7, 1802.
Deborah, ch. John, bp. Sept. 1, 1805. C.R.1.
Desire, d. Sam[ue]ll and Desire of Marshfield, bp. Sept. 18, 1720. C.R.2.
Ebenezer, s. Stephen, June 16, 1682.
Ebenezer, s. Steven, bp. Sept. 9, 1683. C.R.2.
Ebenezer, s. Ebenez[e]r of Marshfield, bp. July 7, 1717. C.R.1.
Edward Bartlet, s. Thatcher and Lucy, Oct. 24, 1806. [Edward Bartlett, s. Thacher and w., C.R.2.]
Elijah, s. David and Abigal, Mar. 18, 1719.
Elisha, s. Nath[anie]ll [Nathaniel, C.R.1.] Jr., June 14, 1720.
Elizabeth, d. Nathanael, July 6, 1681. [Elizebeth, d. Nathaniell, C.R.2.]
Elizabeth Colman, d. John and Marcy, July 1, 1808. [Elizebeth Colman, C.R.1.] [Elizabeth C., w. Charles Chipman, G.R.7.]
Ephraim, s. Stephen, Nov. 20, 1680.
Ephraim, s. Steven, bp. June 25, 1682. C.R.2.
Evelina, ch. Samuel Jr. and Peggy, Mar. 19, 1796. P.R.5.
Ezra, s. David and Abigal, July 10, 1724.
Freeman F., ch. Samuel Jr. and Peggy, Mar. 29, 1804. P.R.5.
Hannah [dup. Hanah Tillden], d. Steven, Oct. 14, 1662.
Hannah, d. Stephen, bp. July 31, 1664.
Hannah, d. Stephen Jr., Apr. 25, 1696.
Hannah (Tiden), d. David, Jan. 11, 1715–16.
Hannah, d. Joseph and Sarah, May 27, 1766.
Hannah [———], w. Coleman, —— [1810]. C.R.1.
Harriet F., ch. William H. and Sarah A., Oct. 15, 1837, in Marshfield.
Henry, s. Thatcher and Lucy, June 9, 1800.
Henry, s. Thatcher and w., bp. Oct. 3, 1802. C.R.2.
Isaac, s. Stephen, Aug. 28, 1678. [Isaace, C.R.2.]
James Otis, s. Christopher and Aseneth, May 4, 1832.
James Otis, ch. Christopher and Asenath, bp. Oct. 6, 1833. C.R.1. [b. ——, 1832, G.R.6.]
James W., s. John Jr. and Sally, July 17, 1835.
Job, s. Joseph and Sarah, Oct. 17, 1725.
John, s. Joseph, Dec. —, 1652.
John, s. Joseph, Oct. 1, 1715.
John, s. Thomas and Abigail, Apr. 30, 1772. [Capt. John, G.R.6.]
John Jr., s. John and Mercy, July 26, 1797.
John, s. John Jr. and Sally, Feb. 12, 1830.

TILDEN, Joseph, s. Joseph, Feb. 12, 1656.
Joseph, s. Nathanael [Nathaniell, C.R.2.], abt. Apr. 10, 1685.
Joseph, s. Joseph, Sept. 20, 1711.
Joseph, s. Joseph, bp. Mar. 13, 1768. C.R.1.
Joseph, d. Tho[ma]s and Abigail, Sept. 4, 1785.
Joseph, ch. William P. and Mary J., May 26, 1839.
Joseph, ch. William H. and Sarah A., July 14, 1842.
Josephine, ch. Amos H. and Martha, Apr. 24, 1840.
Josephine, d. Amos H., housewright, and Martha, Sept. 6, 1846.
Josiah R., ch. William H. and Sarah A., Apr. 22, 1834, in Marshfield.
Julia, d. Luther and Philenda, Dec. 30, 1806.
Julia Maria, ch. Luther A. and Sarah S., Sept. 7, 1829.
Laura, ch. William P. and Mary J., June 30, 1837.
Lucy Brooks, d. Luther [Cap[t]. Luther, C.R.2.] and Philenda, Aug. 16, 1818.
Lucy Turner, d. Thatcher and Lucy, July 27, 1794.
Lucy Turner, d. Thatcher and w., bp. Oct. 3, 1802. C.R.2.
Luther [h. Philenda (Brooks)] [h. Sarah (Benson)], —— [1777]. G.R.14.
Luther Albert, s. Luther and Philenda, June 24, 1804. [[h. Sarah F.] G.R.14.]
Lydia, ch. Samuel, bp. ——, 1701. C.R.2.
Lydia, d. Tho[ma]s and Abigail, June 22, 1779. [w. Joseph Bailey, second w. John Otis, P.R.10.]
M. Louisa, ch. William H. and Sarah A., ——, 1845. G.R.14.
Marcy [——], w. ——, —— [1771]. C.R.1. [w. Capt. John, G.R.6.]
Marcy, d. John and Marcy, Aug. 26, 1795.
Margaret, d. Nathanael, July 6, 1696.
Margaret, d. Joseph, bp. Apr. 12, 1772. C.R.1.
Maria, d. Jotham and Betsey [w. Elijah Brooks], Apr. 21, 1802. G.R.14.
Martha [? m.], Sept. 23, 1814. G.R.14.
Mary, d. Nathanael [Nathaniell, C.R.2.], Dec. 11, 1674.
Mary, d. Nathanael, Oct. 11, 1694.
Mary, d. Stephen Jr., Oct. 3, 1698.
Mary, d. Ebenezer of Marshfield, bp. July 3, 1715. C.R.1.
Mary, d. David and Abigal, Mar. 31, 1722.
Mary, d. John and Sibel, Sept. 11, 1750.
Mary, d. Tho[ma]s and Abigail, June 10, 1777.
Mary, ch. Samuel Jr. and Peggy, Apr. 5, 1802. P.R.5.
Mary, d. Luther and w., bp. Sept. 5, 1809. C.R.2.
Mary L., ch. William H. and Sarah A., Feb. 8, 1841.

TILDEN, Mercy, d. Sam[ue]ll Jr. and Desire of Marshfield, bp. Sept. 9, 1722. C.R.2.
Mercy (see Marcy).
Mercy, ch. Samuel Jr. and Peggy, Jan. 19, 1799. P.R.5.
Mercy Colman, d. John Jr. and Sally, Jan. 27, 1833.
Nabby [――――], wid. Amos [Dec. —, 1785]. C.R.1.
Nathanael, s. Joseph, Sept. —, 1650. [Nathaniel, C.R.2.]
Nathanael, s. Nathanael, Mar. 27, 1678. [Nathaniell, s. Nathaniell, C.R.2.]
Nathaniell, s. Nathaniell Jr., Aug. 6, 1701.
Patience, d. Tho[ma]s and Abigail, Mar. 7, 1781.
Peggy, ch. Samuel Jr. and Peggy, Aug. 23, 1791. P.R.5.
Peter Thatcher, s. Thatcher and Lucy, Nov. 2, 1792.
Peter Thatcher, s. Thatcher and w., bp. Oct. 3, 1802. C.R.2.
Philenda, d. Luther and Philenda, Mar. 2, 1802, in Boston.
Phillippa [――――], w. Christopher, —— [1809]. C.R.1. [Philippa, G.R.6.]
Rachel, d. Benj[a]m[in] and Grace, bp. Oct. 8, 1732. C.R.2.
Rebeccah, d. Samuel of Marshfield, bp. June 17, 1705. C.R.2.
Rebekah, d. Joseph, Feb. —, 1654. [Rebecca, C.R.2.]
Ruth, d. Stephen, June 1, 1676.
Ruth, d. Nath[anie]ll Jr., May 20, 1716.
Ruth, d. Sam[ue]ll and Desire of Marshfield, bp. Oct. 4, 1724. C.R.2.
Samuel, s. Joseph, Sept. 12, 1660.
Samuel, ch. Samuel, bp. ――――, 1699. C.R.2.
Samuel Jr. [h. Peggy Foster], Apr. 15, 1765. P.R.5.
Samuel 3d, ch. Samuel Jr. and Peggy, Aug. 28, 1794. P.R.5.
Samuel 4th, ch. Samuel Jr. and Peggy, Jan. 4, 1814. P.R.5.
Sarah, ch. Samuel, bp. ――――, 1703. C.R.2.
Sarah, d. Joseph, May 23, 1718.
Sarah, d. John and Sibel, Mar. 15, 1756.
Sarah, d. Joseph and Sarah, Oct. 9, 1763.
Sarah, d. Luther and Philenda, Apr. 24, 1809.
Sarah A. [――――], w. William H., ——, 1807. G.R.14.
Sarah A., ch. William H. and Sarah A., Apr. 3, 1831, in Marshfield.
Sarah F. [――――], w. L. Albert, —— [1803]. G.R.14.
Sarah Maria, d. John Jr. and Sally, Sept. 29, 1826.
Sereno, s. Amos H., housewright, and Martha, Oct. 29, 1844.
Sibbel, d. Tho[ma]s and Abigail, May 10, 1783.
Steven, s. Joseph, May 14, 1649 [*sic*].
Steven, s. Joseph, May 14, 1659. P.C.R. [Stephen, C.R.2.]
Tho[ma]s, s. John and Sibel, Sept. 18, 1743.
Thomas, s. Tho[ma]s and Abigail, June 18, 1775.

TILDEN, Thomas, s. John and Marcy, Feb. 9, 1799.
Thomas, ch. John, bp. Sept. 1, 1805. C.R.1.
Thomas, s. Christopher and Aseneth, Apr. 1, 1827.
Thomas, ch. Christopher and Asenath, bp. Oct. 6, 1833. C.R.1.
William Augustus White, s. Amos and Lydia, Nov. 28, 1813.
William H. [h. Sarah A. (Rainsford)], Aug. 18, 1804, in Marshfield.
William H. [h. Sarah A.], ———, 1807. G.R.14.
William H., ch. William H. and Sarah A., Sept. 11, 1832, in Marshfield.
William Phillips, s. Luther [Cap[t]. Luther, C.R.2.] and Philenda, May 9, 1811.
———, ch. Amos H. and Martha, Jan. 27, 1842.

TILDIN (see Tilden, Tillden), Adaline, [twin] d. Amos and Lydia, Sept. 25, 1808.
Amos, s. Amos and Lydia, Oct. 25, 1806.
Benjamin, s. Sam[ue]ll and Sarah of Marshfield, bp. Oct. 5, 1712. C.R.2.
Eleza, d. Amos and Lydia, May 7, 1800.
Elijah, s. Amos and Lydia, Apr. 20, 1802.
Emaline, [twin] d. Amos and Lydia, Sept. 25, 1808.
Lendal, s. Amos and Lydia, Sept. 4, 1796.
Lydia, d. Amos and Lydia, June 4, 1798.
Margaret, w. Jotham Wade, Mar. 28, 1772. [Tilden, P.R.27.]
Martha, twin d. John and Marcy, Sept. 26, 1812. [Tilden, C.R.1.]
Mary, d. Amos and Lydia, May 11, 1804. [Tilden, G.R.2.]
Mary, twin d. John and Marcy, Sept. 26, 1812. [Tilden, C.R.1.]

TILLDEN (see Tilden, Tildin), Abigall, d. Steven, July 11, 1666. [Abigail Tilden, d. Stephen, C.R.2.]
Elizabeth, d. Joseph, May 1, 1665. [Tilden, C.R.2.]
Joseph, s. Steven, May 13, 1672.
Joshua, s. Steven Jr., Mar. 25, 1693-4.
Judeth, d. Steven, June 1, 1670. [Judith Tilden, d. Stephin, C.R.2.]
Lidia, d. Joseph, June 9, 1666. [Lydia Tilden, C.R.2.]
Marcy, d. Steven, May 1, 1674.
Mary, d. Steven, Apr. 7, 1668. [Tilden, d. Stephen, C.R.2.]
Steven, s. Steven, Feb. 5, 1663. [Stephen Tilden, s. Stephen, C.R.2.]
Steven, s. Steven Jr., Jan. 18, 1690.

TIRRELL, Polly [———], w. ———, "formerly" w. David Pettis, ——— [1800]. G.R.2.

TOBIE (see Toby), Thomas, s. Thomas and Mary, bp. Mar. 23, 1724-5. C.R.2.

TOBIN, Edward, —— [1831]. G.R.10.

TOBY (see Tobie), Anna, d. Thomas and Mary, bp. Oct. 26, 1729. C.R.2.
Elisha, ch. Thomas and Mary, bp. Oct. 2, 1720. C.R.2.
Jane, ch. Thomas and Mary, bp. Oct. 2, 1720. C.R.2.
Luke, s. Thomas and Mary, bp. July 2, 1727. C.R.2.
Martha, d. Thomas and Mary, bp. Aug. 13, 1721. C.R.2.
Mary, ch. Thomas and Mary, bp. Oct. 2, 1720. C.R.2.
Mercy, d. Elisha and w., bp. Mar. 1, 1740-1. C.R.2.

TOLLMAN (see Tolman, Toolman), Benjamin, s. Benjamin and Elizabeth, Mar. 28, 1710. [Tolman, C.R.2.]
Joseph, s. Benjamin, Sept. 6, 1715. [Tolman, s. Benjamin and Elizabeth, C.R.2.]
Samuel, s. Benjamin and Elizabeth, Oct. 22, 1711. [Tolman, C.R.2.]
William, s. Benj[amin], Jan. 12, 1716. [Tolman, s. Benjamin and Elizabeth, C.R.2.]

TOLMAN (see Tollman, Toolman), Abigail F. [——], w. Samuel, wid. Israel Hatch, —— [1819]. G.R.15.
Arrithusa, d. Joseph and Bethiah, June 5, 1777.
Bethiah, d. Joseph and Bethiah, Feb. 20, 1785.
Betsey B. [? m.], —— [1809]. G.R.15.
Charles, s. Elishua and Meriam [s. Elisha and Miriam, C.R.2.], Dec. 4, 1749.
Charles, s. Charles and Mary, Apr. 17, 1781.
Charles, s. Charles Jr. and Betsey, Mar. 3, 1815. [[h. Sarah W.] G.R.15.]
Charles, ch. Charles and Sarah W., Apr. 10, 1841.
Charles, ——, 1843. G.R.15.
Charles, ch. Charles and Sarah W., Mar. 10, 1844.
Deborah A., "adopted" d. Joseph C. and Betsey, —— [1842]. G.R.15.
Ebenezar, s. Benjamin and Elisabeth, bp. Nov. 21, 1723. C.R.2.
Elisha, s. Benja[min] and Eliza[beth], Nov. 20, 1718. [Tollman, C.R.2.]
Elisha, s. Charles and Mary, Oct. 10, 1777.
Elisha, s. Elisha and Judith, Jan. 5, 1813.
Elishua, s. Elisha and Meriam, June 19, 1744. [Elisha, s. Elishah and Miriam, C.R.2.]
Eliza C., ch. W[illia]m and Susan C., May 1, ——.

TOLMAN, Elizabeth, d. Joseph and Mary, bp. Nov. 8, 1747. C.R.2.
Elizabeth, d. Sam[ue]ll and w., bp. Jan. 5, 1800. C.R.2.
Elizabeth T. [? m.], ———, 1844. G.R.15.
Ezra, s. Elkenah [Elkana, C.R.2.] and Elizabeth, Nov. 16, 1739.
George Bardin, s. Elisha and Judith, Oct. 29, 1817.
Hannah, d. Benj[a]m[in] and Mary, bp. Oct. 29, 1722. C.R.2.
Hannah, d. Joseph and Hannah, bp. Sept. 29, 1740. C.R.2.
Hannah, d. Joseph and Bethiah, Mar. 8, 1779.
Harriet T. [? m.] [July —, 1829]. G.R.14.
James Turner, s. Sam[ue]l Jr. and Judith H., Aug. 22, 1825.
John, s. Benj[a]m[in] and Elizabeth, bp. July 10, 1726. C.R.2.
Joseph, s. Joseph and Mary, bp. Oct. 28, 1750. C.R.2.
Joseph Copeland, s. Samuel [Sam[ue]ll, C.R.2.] and Rebecca, Feb. 6, 1795.
Joseph Roberson, s. Joseph and Bethiah, Feb. 10, 1787.
Judith Winslow, d. Elisha and Judith, June 18, 1815.
Marcus, s. Samuel [Sam[ue]ll, C.R.2.] and Rebecca, Nov. 9, 1792.
Mary, d. Joseph and Mary, bp. Nov. 3, 1745. C.R.2.
Mary C., d. Charles Jr. and Betsey, Dec. 27, 1811.
Mary Turner, d. Joseph Jr. and w., bp. Nov. 4, 1792. C.R.2.
Mary Turner, d. Joseph and Bethiah, Aug. 17, 1793.
Mercy, d. Elishua and Merian [d. Elisha and Miriam, C.R.2.], Oct. 7, 1746.
Mercy, d. Elisha and Miriam, bp. Aug. 2, 1747. C.R.2.
Michal, d. Cha[rle]s and Mary, Mar. 14, 1785.
Miriam, d. Elisha and Meriam, June 2, 1742.
Nabby Turner, d. Joseph and Bethiah, Aug. 21, 1772.
Nathaniel Winslow, s. Elisha and Judith, Nov. 25, 1823.
Polley, d. Elisha and Judith, Nov. 12, 1808. [Polly, C.R.2.]
Polly, d. Charles and Mary, May 7, 1783.
Rebecca, d. Samuel and Rebecca, May 12, 1788.
Roxana, d. Joseph and Bethiah, May 5, 1775.
Ruth, d. Benjamin and Elizabeth, bp. Mar. 27, 1721. C.R.2.
Samuel, s. Joseph and Mary, bp. Jan. 29, 1743-4. C.R.2.
Samuel, s. Elisha and Merian, Apr. 25, 1756. [Sam[ue]ll, C.R.2.]
Samuel, s. Samuel and Rebecca, Aug. 8, 1785. [[h. Judith (Hatch)] G.R.15.]
Samuel, s. Samuel Jr. [and] Judeth H., Feb. 28, 1820.
Sarah, d. Elishua and Meriam, Aug. 17, 1753. [Toleman, d. Elisha and Mer[ia]m, C.R.2.]
Sarah Hatch, d. Elisha and Judith, Sept. 10, 1810.
Sarah Hatch, ch. Elisha, bp. Sept. 29, 1811. C.R.2.
Sarah W. [———], w. Charles, w. Samuel Tolman, May 26, 1820. G.R.15.

TOLMAN, Silvester, d. Cha[rle]s and Mary, Jan. 11, 1791. [Sylvester, C.R.2.]
Susan, d. Joseph R. and Susan B., July 25, 1825.
Thomas, s. Joseph R. and Susan B., Oct. 10, 1819, in Boston. [Thomas J., G.R.14.]
Turner, s. Sam[ue]ll and w., bp. Apr. 28, 1798. C.R.2.
William, s. William C., farmer, and Susan, Apr. 1, 1844.
William C., s. Charles Jr. and Betsey, Sept. 11, 1818.

TOMSON (see Thomson), Robert, s. Robert and Ann, bp. June 2, 1723. C.R.2.

TOOLMAN (see Tollman, Tolman), Elizabeth, d. Benjamin (Toollman) and Elizabeth, Nov. 5, 1713. [Tolman, C.R.2.]

TORE (see Torrey, Torry), Abigail, d. ———, bp. Nov. 6, 1757. C.R.2.
Betsy, d. Mathew and w., bp. July 1, 1792. C.R.2.

TORREY (see Tore, Torry), Abigail Waters, d. George and Eliza, June 22, 1834.
Abigaill, d. William and Margarett, Feb. 23, 1708-9. [Abigail Torry, d. William and Margaret, C.R.2.]
Adeline M., d. John D., shipwright, and Mary Ann, Mar. 19, 1844.
Albert, [twin] s. George and Eliza, Mar. 17, 1837.
Alfred, [twin] s. George and Eliza, Mar. 17, 1837.
Betsey, d. George and Thankful, July 6, 1789.
Betsey Capen [ch. John S. and Mary Ann], bp. Nov. 6, 1842. C.R.3.
Bithiah, d. James, July 19, 1665. [Bethaia Torry, d. Anne, C.R.2.]
Caleb, s. Josiah, Oct. 4, 1695.
Caleb, s. Caleb and Mary, June 24, 1738. [Torry, C.R.2.]
Caleb, s. Caleb and Hannah, June 23, 1784.
Calvin, s. Joseph, bp. Aug. 7, 1737. C.R.1.
Charles, s. James and Eunice, June 25, 1791.
Charles, s. Charles and Hannah, Nov. 21, 1813.
Charles, s. Charles dec'd, bp. June 2, 1816. C.R.1.
Charles, s. David and Vesta, Dec. 15, 1825.
Damaris, d. James, Oct. 26, 1651. [Torry, C.R.2.]
Daniel, s. Caleb and Hannah, May 11, 1782.
David, s. George and Thankful, Jan. 18, 1787.
David [h. Vesta] [Feb. —, 1797]. G.R.14.
David, s. David and Vesta, June 27, 1821. [David Jr., G.R.14.]
Deborah, d. Joseph and Deborah, Oct. 29, 1724. [Torry, C.R.2.]

Torrey, Deborah, d. Caleb and Mary, May 9, 1747. [Torry, d. Dea. Caleb and Mary, c.r.2.]
Elioenar S., d. George O., carpenter, and Martha S. (b. Saco, Me.), Sept. 6, 1848. [Elioenar S[tephens], ch. George O[tis] and Martha S., p.r.24.]
Elizabeth Joice, d. George and Eliza, Sept. 27, 1822.
Eunice, d. James, Aug. 8, 1702. [Torry, c.r.2.]
Eunice (see Unice).
Eunice, d. James and Eunice, Oct. 11, 1787.
Eveline [? m.] [June —, 1821]. g.r.14.
Everett, s. David and Vesta, May 27, 1828.
Frances, d. George and Eliza, Mar. 21, 1832.
Franklin, s. David and Vesta, Oct. 25, 1830.
George, s. Caleb and Mary, Jan. 19, 1758.
George, s. George and Thankful, Oct. 8, 1785.
George Howard, s. David and Vesta, Mar. 29, 1819.
George Otis, s. George and Eliza, Aug. 27, 1820.
Gracey, d. James and Eunice, May 24, 1798. [Gracy Torry, c.r.2.]
Hannah, d. William and Honour, Sept. 25, 1715.
Hannah, d. Caleb and Mary, May 19, 1752. [Torey, d. Cap[t]. Caleb, c.r.2.]
Hannah, ch. Hannah, wid., bp. Mar. 22, 1816. c.r.1.
Harriot, d. James and Eunice, Apr. 1, 1795.
Henry, s. George and Eliza, Sept. 9, 1824.
Henry O., s. George O., shipwright, and Martha, Nov. 18 [184–]. [Henry O[tis], ch. George O[tis] and Martha S., Nov. 18, 1845, p.r.24.]
Honour, d. William and Honor, Dec. 18, 1711.
Isaac, s. Caleb and Mary, May 27, 1740. [Torry, c.r.2.]
Isaac, s. George and Thankful, June 14, 1791.
James, s. James, Sept. 3, 1644.
James, s. Caleb and Mary, Jan. 15, 1755. [Tory, c.r.2.]
James, s. James and Eunice, Apr. 18, 1783.
Jane, d. Samuel and Barsheba, Feb. 15, 1723. [Torry, d. Sam[ue]l and Barshua, c.r.2.]
Jemima, d. Josiah, Feb. 27, 1696–7.
Joana, d. James, May 4, 1663. [Joanna Torry, c.r.2.]
John Day, s. George and Eliza, Oct. 14, 1816.
Joseph, s. James, Mar. 18, 1648.
Joseph, s. James, Sept. 13, 1694. [Torry, c.r.2.]
Joseph, s. Joseph and Deborah, Oct. 28, 1722.
Joseph, s. Joseph and Deborah, bp. July 5, 1724. c.r.2.
Josiah, s. James, Jan. 28, 1658. [Torry, c.r.2.]
Josiah, s. George and Eliza, Dec. 1, 1829.

TORREY, Kezia, d. Josiah and Sarah, May 1, 1702. [Torry, C.R.2.]
Lucy, d. George and Thankful, Apr. 9, 1793.
Lucy, d. George and Eliza, Jan. 2, 1841.
Lydia, d. James, June 14, 1698. [Torry, C.R.2.]
Margaret, d. William and Margaret, Apr. 29, 1707. [Torry, C.R.2.]
Mary, d. James, Feb. 14, 1656. [Torry, C.R.2.]
Mary, d. Caleb and Mary, Feb. 11, 1742. [Torry, C.R.2.]
Mary, d. George and Thankful, Sept. 23, 1797.
Mary A. [―――], w. John D., ―― [1802]. C.R.3.
Mary Ann, ch. John D. and Mary, bp. Nov. 6, 1842. C.R.3.
Mary Emmons, w. Rev. Albert Bryant, ――, 1840. G.R.7.
Mary Otis, d. David and Vesta, Apr. 17, 1817. [w. Walter Robbins, G.R.14.]
Mercy, d. William and Honour, Aug. 4, 1722.
Mercy, d. John D., ―― [1843]. C.R.3.
Mercy Vinal, ch. John D. and Mary A., bp. June 7, 1844. C.R.3.
Otis, s. George and Thankful, July 4, 1799.
Otis, s. George and Eliza, Oct. 10, 1825.
Otis, s. George and Eliza, June 2, 1827.
Rachell, d. David and Hope, Mar. 7, 1712-13. [Rachel Torry, C.R.2.]
Ruth, d. Caleb and Mary, Sept. 10, 1736.
Sally Rand, d. James and Eunice, Apr. 16, 1793.
Samuel, s. William and Honour, June 2, 1720.
Samuel, s. Samuel and Polly, Mar. 24, 1783, in Middleboroug[h].
Sarah, d. James, Feb. 9, 1660. [Torry, C.R.2.]
Sarah, d. George and Thankful, Mar. 2, 1783.
Stephen, s. James, June 2, 1696. [Torry, C.R.2.]
Stephen, s. David and Hope, Jan. ―, 1710-11.
Thankful Otis, d. George and Eliza, Sept. 21, 1818.
Unice, d. Will[ia]m and Honour, Mar. 31, 1725.
Vesta [―――], w. David [Apr. ―, 1790]. G.R.14.
Vesta H., d. David and Vesta, Aug. 25, 1823.
Walter Scott, s. John D., shipwright, and Mary A., Apr. 6, 1845.
Walter Scott, ch. John D. and Mary A., bp. Nov. 22, 1846. C.R.3.
Willard, s. David and Vesta, Sep[t]. 25, 1833.
William, s. James, Mar. 15, 1646. [Torry, C.R.2.]
William, s. William and Honour, Dec. 22, 1713.
William, s. William and Honour, Apr. 17, 1718.
William Turner, s. James and Eunice, Feb. 5, 1786.
―――, ch. James and Elizabeth, Apr. 7, 1700.

TORRY (see Tore, Torrey), Abel, s. Sam[ue]l and Barshua, bp. Aug. 18, 1728. C.R.2.
Abigail, d. Joseph and Bathsheba, bp. June 8, 1729. C.R.2.

TORRY, Ann, d. James, Sept. 16, 1680.
Benjamin, s. Keziah, bp. Aug. 19, 1722. C.R.2.
Caleb, ch. Josiah, bp. ———, 1700. C.R.2.
David, s. James, Jan. 4, 1687–8. [Torey, C.R.2.]
Elizabeth, d. James, Sept. 7, 1689.
Elizabeth, ch. Dea. James, bp. ———, 1692. C.R.2.
Elizabeth, d. David and Hope, bp. Aug. 11, 1717. C.R.2.
James, s. James, Apr. 5, 1682. [Tore, C.R.2.]
James, ch. James and Sarah of Marshfield, bp. July 2, 1721. C.R.2.
Jeremiah, ch. Josiah, bp. ———, 1700. C.R.2.
Jonathan, s. James, Sept. 20, 1654.
Joseph, s. James, bp. Mar. 25, 1649. C.R.1.
Josiah, s. Josiah, July 23, 1687.
Luther, s. Joseph, bp. Oct. 7, 1733. C.R.1.
Mary, d. Josiah, Sept. 24, 1685.
Mary Ann, d. John D. and Mary Ann, July 28, 1841. [Torrey, C.R.3.]
Mary Turner, d. James Jr. and w., bp. Sept. 23, 1804. C.R.2.
Mercy Vinal, d. John D. and Mary Ann, Apr. 19, 1843.
Nathanell, s. James, Mar. 29, 1686. [Nathaniel Torey, C.R.2.]
Noah, s. Joseph and Deborah, bp. June 4, 1727. C.R.2.
Paul, s. Joseph and Barsheba, bp. Aug. 24 [?], 1731. C.R.2.
Rachell, d. James, Feb. 5, 1692–3. [Rachel, C.R.2.]
Ruth, d. Josiah, Jan. 20, 1694.
Ruth, ch. Josiah, bp. ———, 1700. C.R.2.
Sammuell, s. James, May 20, 1691. [Samuel, C.R.2.]
Sarah, ch. James and Sarah of Marshfield, bp. July 2, 1721. C.R.2.
Stephen, ch. David and Hope, bp. June 21, 1713. C.R.2.
William, s. James, Sept. 14, 1683. [Torey, C.R.2.]

TOTMAN (see Totmon, Tottman), Alexander, s. Benjamin and Eunice, Jan. 1, 1826.
Benjamin Cushing, ch. Thomas and Ruth, Nov. 24, 1821, in Hingham.
Benj[ami]n O., s. Benj[ami]n and Eunice, Aug. 12, 1821.
Benjamin Turner, s. Stephen and Hannah, Feb. 12, 1795.
Betsey Ann, d. Benjamin and Eunice, July 25, 1823.
Caroline L., d. Stephen Jr. and Lydia, Oct. 18, 1817.
Charles, s. Stephen and Hannah, Feb. 26, 1787.
Charles, s. Stephen and w., bp. May 20, 1796. C.R.2.
Charles, s. Charles and Sophia, May 7, 1813.
Charles Henry, ch. Thomas and Ruth, Jan. 11, 1833.
Christian, d. Stephen, Jan. 17, 1699.
David Otis, s. Benj[ami]n and Eunice, Sep[t]. 20, 1832.

TOTMAN, David Wade, ch. Thomas and Ruth, May 5, 1827.
Dorcassina, d. Charles and Sophia, Dec. 11, 1820.
Ebenezer, s. Stephen and Hannah, Sept. 2, 1783.
Fanny, d. Stephen and Hannah, June 26, 1785.
Francis, s. Alexander, farmer, and Lucy K. (b. Medford), May 6, 1849.
George, s. Charles and Sophia, Jan. 25, 1815.
Gridley, s. Stephen Jr. and Lydia, May 18, 1810.
Gustavus, ch. Thomas and Ruth, May 13, 1835.
Hannah, d. Stephen and Hannah, Dec. 26, 1779.
Harris Miner, s. Stephen and Hannah, Oct. 19, 1793.
Horrace C., s. Charles and Sophia, Nov. 21, 1818.
Isaac, s. Stephen and Hannah, Sept. 7, 1781. [[h. Mary] G.R.14.]
Isaac, s. Isaac and Mary, May 23, 1811.
Isaac R., s. Stephen Jr. and Lydia, Feb. 7, 1812.
James, ch. Ebenez[e]r, bp. May 10, 1812. C.R.2.
James Bartlett, s. Benj[amin] and Eunice, Ap[r]. 23, 1834.
Jesse Lee, s. Benj[amin] and Eunice, Aug. 11, 1839.
John C., ch. Thomas and Ruth, June 23, 1842.
Joseph, ch. Ebenezer, bp. May 10, 1812. C.R.2.
Lucinda T., d. Stephen Jr. and Lydia, July 7, 1816.
Lydia, d. Stephen and Hannah, Sept. 26, 1791.
Lydia, d. Stephen Jr. and Lydia, Apr. 15, 1800.
Lydia, d. Stephen Jr. and Lydia, Oct. 7, 1814.
Lydia Brooks, d. Isaac and Mary, Apr. 13, 1815.
Mary, d. Stephen, Nov. 6, 1696.
Mary [————], w. Isaac [Sept. —, 1781]. G.R.14.
Mary, d. Isaac and Mary, Sept. 12, 1808.
Nancy, d. Stephen Jr. and Lydia, Feb. 21, 1802.
Polly, d. Stephen and Hannah, Feb. 16, 1789.
Salley, d. Stephen and Hannah, Nov. 25, 1798.
Sarah Bowker, ch. Thomas and Ruth, Jan. 12, 1831.
Sophia Davis, d. Charles and Sophia, Dec. 23, 1816.
Stephen, s. Stephen, Oct. 11, 1691.
Stephen, s. Stephen, May 27, 1695.
Stephen, ch. Ebenezer and Grace, bp. Dec. 4, 1757. C.R.2.
Stephen, s. Stephen and Hannah, Jan. 13, 1778.
Stephen, s. Stephen Jr. and Lydia, Mar. 20, 1798.
Susannah, d. Stephen Jr. and Lydia, Apr. 18, 1804.
Thomas, ch. Ebenezer and Grace, bp. Dec. 4, 1757. C.R.2.
Thomas, s. Stephen and Hannah, July 7, 1797. [[h. Ruth (Cushing)] G.R.14.]
Thomas Cushing, ch. Thomas and Ruth, Dec. 25, 1828, in Hingham.

TOTMAN, William, s. Stephen Jr. and Lydia, Mar. 24, 1807.
William Warren, s. Benj[ami]n and Eunice, Dec. 2, 1829.

TOTMON (see Totman, Tottman), Hannah, d. Ebenez[e]r and Grace, May 10, 1773.
Lucy, d. Ebenezer and Grace, Dec. 19, 1758.
Lydia, d. Ebenez[e]r and Grace, July 29, 1761.
Stephen, s. Ebenezer and Grace, Apr. 1, 1756.
Thomus, s. Ebenezer and Grace, Nov. 20, 1753.

TOTTMAN (see Totman, Totmon), Samuell, s. Steven, July 20, 1693.

TOWER, Abigail, d. Benj[a]min Jr. and w., bp. May 4, 1746. C.R.2.
Benjamin H., Mar. —, 1783. G.R.15.
Bethiah, d. Benja[min] and Bethiah, Jan. 10, 1720.
Chloe, d. Abigail, May 15, 1782.
David, s. Benj[a]m[in] Jr., bp. July 10, 1743. C.R.2.
David, s. James and Lucy, July 6, 1788.
Deborah, d. Benjamin [d. Benjamin and Bethiah, C.R.2.], Feb. 16, 1718.
Ester, d. Benj[a]m[in] and w. of Abbinton, bp. Aug. 6, 1743. C.R.2.
Horace, s. Solomon and Sarah, Apr. 10, 1810.
James, s. Benja[min] and Bethiah, Feb. 16, 1722.
James A., ch. John S. and Jane, Apr. 21, 1838.
John, s. James and Lucy, Oct. 19, 1781.
John, s. Solomon and Sarah, Mar. 27, 1814.
Jonathan, s. Benj[a]m[in] and Bethiah, bp. Nov. 3, 1724. C.R.2.
Jonathan, s. Jona[than] and Lydia, bp. Aug. 26, 1753. C.R.2.
Lucy, d. James and Lucy, Oct. 14, 1791.
Lucy, d. Solomon and Sarah, Mar. 20, 1812.
Lydiah, [ch.] Jonathan and Lydia, bp. Apr. 17, 1748. C.R.2.
Mary, d. Solomon and Sarah, Jan. 9, 1817. [Mary W., P.R.22.]
Matthew, s. James, Dec. 1, 1755.
Nancy, May —, 1788. G.R.15.
Polly, d. James and Lucy, Oct. 11, 1783.
Rachel, d. James and Lucy, May 20, 1794.
Sarah, d. Solomon and Sarah, Oct. 13, 1808.
Solomon, s. James and Lucy, Oct. 25, 1785.

TRUANT, Mary, d. John [?] of Marshfield, bp. Feb. 12, 1737-8. C.R.2.

TRUMBULL, William of Charlestown, —— [1782]. G.R.14.

TUE, Amy, d. David and Alice, Aug. 11, 1825.
Hamilton, s. David and Alice, Oct. 29, 1822.
Harriot Williams, d. David and Alice, Mar. 23, 1821.

TUELL (see Tewell), Mehettabell, d. Samewell, Oct. 4, 1703.
Thankfull, d. Samuel, Sept. 15, 1701.

TURNER, Abbigal, d. Sam[ue]ll and Abigal, Sept. 26, 1720. [Abigail, d. Lt. Sam[ue]l, C.R.1.] [Abigail, d. Capt. Samuel and Abigail, G.R.1.]
Abby H., ch. Perez and Sarah, Jan. 10, 1837.
Abel, s. William and Abigail, bp. June 8, 1729. C.R.2.
Abial, s. Abial Jr. and Lurana, Jan. 11, 1779.
Abial, s. Rowland and Hannah, Feb. 1, 1799. [Abiel, s. Roland and w., C.R.2.] [Abiel [h. Rebecca], G.R.14.] [Abial [h. Rebecca (Bates)], P.R.25.]
Abiel, d. [*sic*] Abiel and Eliza[beth], May 3, 1741.
Abiell, s. John and Abigail, Oct. 4, 1706. [Abiel, s. John [dec'd] and Abigail, C.R.2.]
Abiezer, s. Josiah, June 17, 1703.
Abiezer, s. Abiezer and Grace, Oct. 19, 1727.
Abiezer, ch. Abiezer, bp. July 13, 1729. C.R.1.
Abigail [———], w. Capt. Samuel, ———, 1686. G.R.1.
Abigail, d. John, June 29, 1690.
Abigail (see Abbigal).
Abigail, d. W[illia]m and Abigail, bp. May 23, 1731. C.R.2.
Abigail, d. Asa and Abigail, Dec. 14, 1771.
Abigail, d. Elisha and Prudence, Jan. 20, 1773.
Abigail, d. Elisha and Prudence, Jan. 12, 1779. [w. John James, G.R.5.]
Abigail, d. Samuel Adams and Lydia, Sept. 23, 1819.
Abigal, d. Sam[ue]ll and Abigal, May 30, 1725. [Abigail, d. Lt. Sam[ue]ll, C.R.1.]
Abigal, d. Abiel and Eliza[beth], Sept. 24, 1743. [Abigail, C.R.2.]
Abigal, d. Jesse and Lydia, Oct. 19, 1744. [Abigail, C.R.2.]
Abigall, d. Thomas, Feb. 10, 1665. [This entry crossed out.]
Abigall, d. Nathanell, Feb. 10, 1666.
Abigall, d. Thomas (grand s. Hum[phrey]), Aug. 15, 1714. [Abigail, d. "M^r: Lawyer Turner," C.R.1.]
Abner, s. Daniell, July —, 1672.
Abner, s. Abner and Naomy, May 11, 1714.
Abner, s. Abner and Aimy, bp. Sept. 11, 1720. C.R.2.
Abner, s. Caleb and Rachel, bp. Sept. 1, 1734. C.R.2.
Affee, d. Col. Will[ia]m and w., bp. Aug. 23, 1795. C.R.2.

TURNER, Albion, s. Lemuel and Lusanna, Oct. 1, 1814.
Almira [———], w. Job A., —— [1814]. G.R.2.
Amasa, s. Daniell, Dec. 10, 1674.
Amasa, s. Amasa and Anna, Aug. 20, 1705.
Amasa, s. Amasa and Anna, bp. May 18, 1718. C.R.2.
Amasa, s. Harris and w., bp. May 3, 1801. C.R.2.
Amos, s. John Sr., bp. June 4, 1671. C.R.2. [Col. Amos, G.R.1.]
Amos, s. Amos, Nov. 16, 1695.
Amos, ch. Capt. Amos, bp. July 10, 1709. C.R.1.
Amos, s. Amos Jr., bp. July 4, 1731. C.R.1.
An, d. Japhet, bp. June 24, 1683. C.R.2.
Andrew, s. Barker and Polly, Aug. 13, 1812.
Ann, d. John Jr., Feb. 23, 1662. [Anne, C.R.2.]
Ann, d. Amos Jr., bp. Apr. 13, 1729. C.R.1.
Ann, ch. Benjamin and Sarah, bp. Nov. 2, 1735. C.R.2.
Ann, d. John B. and Hannah, Dec. 4, 1831.
Anna, ch. Amasa dec'd and Anna, bp. July 20, 1712. C.R.2.
Anna, d. Abiezer, bp. Nov. 17, 1734. C.R.1.
Anna Eliza, d. —— and w., bp. Oct. —, 1808. C.R.2.
Annah, twin d. Abiel and Eliza[beth], June 29, 1747. [Anna, twin ch. Abial and Elisabeth, C.R.2.]
Anne, d. Amos, Apr. 7, 1699.
Anne, d. Philip and Elizabeth, Aug. 11, 1702.
Anne, ch. Capt. Amos, bp. July 10, 1709. C.R.1.
Annie Maria, w. Peleg Ford, ——, 1843. G.R.14.
Aphia, d. Willi[a]m and Eunice, Oct. 9, 1791.
Arabella, ch. William and Sarah, May 9, 1837.
Arvilla H. [? m.], ——, 1783. G.R.14.
Asa, s. Jonathan and Abigal [Abigail, C.R.2.], Feb. 20, 1743.
Asa, s. Asa and Abigail, Nov. 6, 1773.
Avis, d. Luther and Grace, June 12, 1794.
Barker [h. Polly] [Sept. —, 1785]. G.R.15.
Barker, s. Barker and Polly, Feb. 16, 1808.
Bartlet, s. John and Mercy, bp. Oct. 12, 1718. C.R.2.
Bathshua, d. Joseph, Dec. 30, 1679. [Barshua, C.R.2.]
Benjamin, s. John Sr., Mar. 5, 1660.
Benjamin, twin s. Benjamin, Aug. 5, 1698.
Benjamin, s. Thomas Sr., June 23, 1704.
Benjamin, ch. Amasa dec'd and Anna, bp. July 20, 1712. C.R.2.
Benja[min], s. Benja[min] Jr. and Mercy, June 25, 1724.
Benja[min], s. Benja[min] Jr. and Mercy, June 1, 1733.
Ben[ja]min, s. Israel and Deborah, Sept. 6, 1760.
Benjamin, d. [sic] Elisha and Prudence, Oct. 31, 1769.
Benjamin, s. Elisha and Prudence, Mar. 19, 1777.

TURNER, Benjamin, s. Rowland and Hannah, June 15, 179[4].
    [s. Roland, C.R.2.] [[h. Hannah C.] G.R.14.]
Benjamin, s. Nath[anie]ll Jr. and Sally, June 11, 1806.
Benjamin Thomas, ch. Samuel H. and Mary E., Jan. 24, 1837.
Bethiah, d. Abiel and Eliza[beth], May 4, 1751.
Bethiah, d. Abiel and Eliza[beth], Jan. 4, 1753.
Bethie, d. Daniell, Dec. 18, 1680.
Betsey, d. Job and Abiel, Mar. 6, 1784.
Betsy, d. James, bp. Sept. 8, 1782. C.R.1.
Bettey, d. Roland and Hannah, Feb. 22, 1778.
Bettey, d. James and Deborah, Apr. 21, 1782.
Betty, d. Hawkins and Lusanna, bp. Sept. 2, 1739. C.R.2.
Betty, d. William and Betty, Aug. 14, 1771.
Betty, d. Israel and Mercy, Aug. 12, 1792. [Bettsy, C.R.2.]
Caleb, s. Thomas Sr., Aug. 16, 1691.
Caleb, ch. Caleb and Rachel, bp. Mar. 24, 1722–3. C.R.2.
Calven, s. Jonathan and Abigal, Dec. 18, 1748. [Calvin, s.
    Jonathan and Abigail, C.R.2.]
Caroline Cushing, d. Samuel and Lydia, May 31, 1835.
Catherine, [ch.] Hawkins and Lusanna, bp. Oct. 5, 1735. C.R.2.
Catherine S., ch. Francis and Temperance F., ——, 1842. G.R.14.
Charles, s. Thomas, May 3, 1675.
Charles [dup. adds H.], Capt., "Master of the Brig Fanny of
    Boston," Nov. 21, 1790. G.R.14.
Charles, s. Samuel A. and Lydia, Sept. 3, 1826.
Charles, ch. Sam[uel] A., bp. Oct. 14, 1827. C.R.2.
Charles Lee, s. William and Eunice, Apr. 14, 1777.
Charles Nichols, s. John B. and Hannah, June 12, 1818.
Charlotte, d. Seth and Mary, Nov. 17, 1793.
Charls, s. Charls, Sept. 30, 1705. [Charles, s. Charles and w.,
    C.R.2.]
Charls, s. Charles and Eunice, bp. Aug. 5, 1733. C.R.2.
Chloe Stowers, d. John and Chloe, Apr. 27, 1796. [Cloe Stowers,
    C.R.2.]
Clara, d. John B. and Hannah, July 2, 1814.
Clarrissa, d. Abiel Jr. and w., bp. June 5, 1791. C.R.2.
Cleressa, d. Abial Jr. and Lurana, Dec. 14, —— [rec. after ch. b.
    June 3, 1790].
Consider, ch. Richard, bp. [Dec.] 20, 1751. C.R.2.
Content, ch. Caleb and Rachel, bp. Mar. 24, 1722–3. C.R.2.
David, s. John Jr., Nov. 5, 1670.
David, ——, 1671. G.R.1.
David, s. John Jr., bp. Apr. 20, 1673. C.R.2.
David, s. Thomas Sr., Oct. 22, 1693.

TURNER, David, s. Thomas (grand s. Hum[phrey]), May 5, 1695.
David, s. Philip and Elizabeth, Dec. 17, 1701.
David, ch. Benjamin and Sarah, bp. Nov. 2, 1735. C.R.2.
[D]avid, s. Israel and Deborah, Aug. 16, 1753.
David, s. Jesse and Lydia, Dec. 4, 1754.
David, s. Jonathan and Sarah, Oct. 13, 1781.
David, s. Samuel and Lydia, Mar. 9, 1833. [David W. [h. Mary Ann (Hatch)], G.R.14.]
David S., s. Benjamin and Hannah C., July 19, 1828. [David Shiverick, C.R.2.]
Debe, d. James and Deborah, July 28, 1763. [Deborah, d. James Jr., C.R.1.]
Deborah, d. Jonathan, Dec. 2, 1678.
Deborah, d. John, Sept. 14, 1704.
Deborah, d. Ruth, wid., bp. June 21, 1752. C.R.2.
Deb[o]rah, d. Israel and Deborah, Oct. 26, 1756.
Deborah, d. Israel and Mercy, May 2, 1790.
Deborah, ch. Deb[o]r[ah], wid., bp. July 4, 1824. C.R.2.
Delia, d. Barker and Polly, Nov. 26, 1813.
Desier, d. Abiezer and Grace, Feb. 22, 1728.
Desier, d. Abiezer and Han[na]h, July 9, 1768.
Desire, ch. Abiezer, bp. July 13, 1729. C.R.1.
Desire, d. Ja[me]s and Mary, Apr. 4, 1735.
Desire, ch. Abiezer, bp. Apr. 29, 1770. C.R.1.
Desire, d. James and Deborah, Aug. 26, 1773.
Dorothy, d. Hawkins and Lusanna, bp. Dec. 6, 1730. C.R.2.
Edward, s. Charls and Eunice, bp. Sept. 3, 1739. C.R.2.
Edwin A., ch. William 2d and Lucy, Aug. 26, 1843.
Elemina, ch. Barker and Polly, Nov. 16, 1810.
Eliab, s. Daniell, Feb. 14, 1669–70.
Eliab, s. Amasa and Anna, Dec. 17, 1706.
Eliab, ch. Amasa dec'd and Anna, bp. July 20, 1712. C.R.2.
Elijah, s. Nath[anie]ll and Mary, Mar. 13, 1749.
Elijah Bailey, s. Elijah and Mary, Sept. 19, 1794. [Elija Bailey, s. Elijah Jr. and w., C.R.2.] [Elijah B., G.R.14.]
Elisha, s. John Sr., Mar. 8, 1656.
Elisha, s. Elisha, Mar. 11, 1688.
Elisha, s. Elisha, July 24, 1700.
Elisha, s. Josiah, Mar. —, 1702.
Elisha, s. Benja[min] Jr. and Mercy, Feb. 24, 1729.
Elisha, s. Elisha and Prudence, Aug. 25, 1771.
Elisha, s. Elisha and Prudence, Mar. 5, 1784.
Eliza, d. Abiezer and Han[na]h, Sept. 9, 1771.
Eliza, d. Perez and Hannah, Mar. 25, 1806.

TURNER, Elizabeth, d. Thomas, July —, 1656.
Elizabeth, d. Nathan, Jan. —, 1684-5.
Elizabeth, d. Elisha, Apr. 3, 1692.
Elizabeth, d. Philip and Elizabeth, June 22, 1705.
Elizabeth, ch. Philip and Eliz[abeth], bp. Oct. 23, 1709. C.R.2.
Elizabeth, d. Joshua and Elizabeth, Mar. 27, 1712.
Elizabeth, ch. Japhet and Hannah, bp. Aug. 8, 1714, in Pembroke. C.R.2.
Elizabeth, ch. Joshua and Elizabeth, bp. Feb. 26, 1726-7. C.R.2.
Elizabeth, d. W[illia]m and Abigail, bp. Apr. 1, 1733. C.R.2.
Elizabeth, d. Hawkins and Lusanna, bp. Oct. 23, 1737. C.R.2.
Elizabeth, d. Abiel and Eliza[beth], Nov. 15, 1739.
[E]liza[beth], d. Benja[min] and Marcy, Apr. 5, 1747. [Elisabeth, [ch.] Benj[a]m[in] and Mercy, C.R.2.]
Elizabeth, d. Samuel A. and Lydia, June 18, 1837.
Elizabeth R., d. Benjamin and Hannah C., Nov. 2, 1821.
Eliz[abe]th Robinson, ch. Benja[min], bp. Oct. 5, 1828. C.R.2.
Ellen, ch. Samuel H. and Mary E., ——— [rec. after ch. b. Sept. 20, 1838].
Epherim [dup. Ephreiem], s. Thomas, June —, 1667 [dup. 1668].
Ephraim, s. Thomas (grand s. Hum[phrey]), Feb. 9, 1693-4.
Ephraim, s. Charles, Nov. 26, 1701 [*sic*, see Thomas].
Ephraim, s. Thomas (grand s. Hum[phrey]), Mar. 17, 1708-9. [s. "M⁀ Lawyer Turner," C.R.1.]
Ephraim, s. Charles [Charls, C.R.2.] and Mercy, Aug. 15, 1709.
Esther, d. Seth and Mary, July 20, 1778.
Eudora, ch. William and Sarah, June 19, 1840.
Eunice, d. Thomas, Apr. 10, 1661.
Eunice, d. Charls and Eunice, bp. May 3, 1730. C.R.2.
Eunice, d. Will[ia]m and Eunice, Feb. 6, 1782.
Eunice (see Unice Whiting Turner).
Ezekiel, ch. Capt. Amos, bp. July 10, 1709. C.R.1.
Ezekiel, s. Isaac and Ruth, bp. Sept. 23, 1722. C.R.2.
Ezekiell, s. John Sr., Jan. 7, 1650.
Ezekiell, s. Amos, Mar. 23, 1700-1.
Ezra, s. Asa and Abigail, July 21, 1782.
Fanny, d. Elijah and Mary, Mar. 11, 1783.
Frances, d. Will[ia]m and Eunice, May 20, 1784.
Frances, ch. Nathaniel 2d and Lusanna, May 17, 1837.
Francis, s. Cha[rle]s Jr. and Hannah, Oct. 6, 1799. [s. Col. Charles, C.R.2.] [[h. Temperance (Foster)] G.R.14.]
George, s. Charls and Eunice, bp. May 26, 1738. C.R.2.
George, s. Sarah, wid., bp. Sept. 30, 1770. C.R.1.
George, s. Will[ia]m and Eunice, Nov. 28, 1793.

TURNER, George Robinson, s. Abiel and Rebecca, Oct. 7, 1829. [[h. Emeline I. Merritt] G.R.14.] [ch. Abial and Rebecca, P.R.25.]
George W., ch. Melzer S. and Sarah, ———, 1832, in Pembroke.
Grace, d. Thomas, ———, 1665.
Grace, d. John Sr., bp. Aug. 2, 1668. C.R.2.
Grace, d. Benjamin, Dec. 17, 1695.
Grace, d. Philip and Elizabeth, Feb. 9, 1711–12.
Grace, d. John and w., bp. Oct. 9 [1715]. C.R.2.
Grace, ch. Caleb and Rachel, bp. Mar. 24, 1722–3. C.R.2.
Grace, d. Abiezer and Grace, Dec. 1, 1730.
Grace, d. Abiezer, bp. June 3, 1733. C.R.1.
Grace, d. Hawkins and Lusanna, bp. July 1, 1733. C.R.2.
Grace, d. Luther and Grace, Mar. 24, 1784.
Gustavus, s. Samuel and Lydia, Dec. 11, 1839.
H. Elizabeth [? m.], ———, 1845. G.R.19.
Hannah, d. Daniell, Aug. 14, 1668.
Hannah, d. Thomas (grand s. Hum[phrey]), June 15, 1697.
Hannah, d. Eliab, Feb. —, 1699–[1]700.
Hannah, d. Japhet and Hannah, bp. Apr. 28, 1706. C.R.2.
Hannah, d. Amasa and Anna, Oct. 26, 1708.
Hannah, ch. Amasa dec'd and Anna, bp. July 20, 1712. C.R.2.
Hannah, d. Abiezer and Grace, July 24, 1734.
Hannah, ch. Benjamin and Sarah, bp. Nov. 2, 1735. C.R.2.
Hannah [————], w. Col. Cha[rle]s, ——— [dup. [Apr. —]] [1763]. C.R.3.
Hannah, d. Abiezer and Han[na]h, Apr. 3, 1767.
Hannah, ch. Abiezer, bp. Apr. 29, 1770. C.R.1.
Hannah, d. Seth and Mary, Aug. 6, 1780.
Hannah, d. John B. and Hannah, Apr. 7, 1826.
Hannah C. [————], w. Benjamin, ——— [1800]. G.R.14.
Hannah C., ch. Perez and Sarah, Nov. 4, 1843.
Hannah Cushing, d. Perez and Hannah, Nov. 1, 1799.
Hannah Jacob, ch. Deb[o]r[ah], wid., bp. July 4, 1824. C.R.2.
Hannah Tolman, d. Charles Jr. and Hannah, Jan. 28, 1794. [Hannah Tolmon, C.R.2.]
Harriet T. [————], w. Melzar S. [Nov. —, 1830]. G.R.6.
Harriet Torrey, d. Samuel and Lydia, June 18, 1829.
Harvey, s. Seth and Mary, Aug. 16, 1787.
Haukings, s. Benjamin, Aug. 27, 1704. [Hawkins, C.R.2.]
Hawkins, s. Hawkins and Lusanna, bp. Nov. 1, 1741. C.R.2.
Henry, ch. Francis and Temperance F., ———, 1830. G.R.14.
Henry Abiel, s. Abiel and Rebecca, Nov. 21, 1827. [Henry A[bial], ch. Abial and Rebecca, P.R.25.]
Henry J. [h. Mary T.], Apr. 22, 1818. G.R.14.

TURNER, Henry Job, s. Job and Abiel, Aug. 15, 1793.
Huldah L., ch. Barker and Polly, Nov. 20, 1815.
Humphrey, ——, 1594, in Kent, Eng. G.R.1.
Humphrey, s. Thomas, Sept. —, 1663.
Humphrey, ch. William and Sarah, Sept. 28, 1831.
Humphry [dup. Humphery], s. Seth and Mary, July 13, 1790.
Icabud, s. John Jr., Apr. 9, 1676.
Ignatius, s. Jonathan, Mar. 15, 1697-8.
Isaac, s. Jonathan, Feb. 27, 1682.
Isaac, s. Isaack and Ruth, bp. Apr. 5, 1719. C.R.2.
Isaac, s. Jonathan and Abigal, May 22, 1754.
Isaack, s. John Sr., bp. Apr. 30, 1665. C.R.2.
Israel, s. Philip and Elizabeth, Feb. 17, 1707.
Israel, ch. Japhet and Hannah, bp. Aug. 8, 1714, in Pembroke. C.R.2.
[I]srael, s. Israel and Deborah, June 17, 1745.
Israel, s. Israel and Mercy, Nov. 2, 1784.
Israell, s. John Jr., Feb. 14, 1654. [grand ch. Humfry Turner, C.R.2.]
Jacob, s. John Jr., Mar. 10, 1667.
Jacob, s. John Jr., bp. Apr. 20, 1673. C.R.2.
Jacob, ch. Elisha, bp. ——, 1695. C.R.2.
[J]acob, s. Israel and Deborah, Nov. 26, 1749.
Jael, d. Elisha, Apr. 5, 1694.
Jael, d. Elisha, Aug. 17, 1696.
Jael, ch. Joshua and Elizabeth, bp. Feb. 26, 1726-7. C.R.2.
James, s. Samuell, Dec. 18, 1706. [Capt. James [h. Mary], G.R.1.]
James, ch. Sam[ue]l, bp. Apr. 24, 1715. C.R.1.
James, s. Ja[me]s and Mary, July 13, 1733.
James, s. James and Deborah, Jan. 23, 1778.
James, ch. Samuel, bp. Oct. 20, 1820. C.R.2.
Jane, d. Amos, May 4, 1697.
Jane, ch. Capt. Amos, bp. July 10, 1709. C.R.1.
Jane, d. Amos, bp. Dec. 29, 1727. C.R.1.
Japhet, s. Japhet, bp. Sept. 17, 1704. C.R.2.
Japheth, s. John Jr., Feb. 9, 1650.
Japheth, s. Japheth, Jan. 4, 1682.
Jemima, d. Jonathan, Oct. 9, 1680. [Jemymah, C.R.2.]
Jemima, d. Thomas (grand s. Hum[phrey]) [d. Thomas and Hannah, C.R.2.], Jan. 7, 1706-7.
Jenny, d. Luther and Grace, Dec. 14, 1791.
Jesse, s. Jonathan, bp. July 2, 1704. C.R.2.
Jesse, s. Jonathan and Mercy, Dec. 24, 1704.
Jesse, s. Seth and Mary, Jan. 29, 1784.

TURNER, Job, s. Samuell, May 9, 1709.
Job, s. Samuel, bp. Feb. 22, 1713–14. C.R.1.
Job, s. Philip and Elizabeth, bp. Dec. 26, 1714. C.R.2.
Job, s. Nath[anie]ll [Nath[anie]l, C.R.2.] and Mary, July 2, 1755.
Job Abiel, s. John B. and Hannah, Apr. 7, 1816.
John, s. John Sr., Oct. 30, 1654. [bp. Oct. 29 [*sic*], C.R.2.]
John, s. Benjamin, Jan. 1, 1692–3.
John, s. John, Apr. 23, 1695.
John, ch. Richard, bp. [Dec.] 20, 1751. C.R.2.
John, s. Abiel Jr. and Lurana, Apr. 19, 1769.
John, s. John and Chloe, July 12, 1798.
John, s. Samuel A. [Samuel A. Esq., C.R.2.] and Lydia, Nov. 1, 1829.
John Bryant, s. Job and Abiel, Dec. 8, 1786.
John Bryant, s. Job, bp. Oct. 5, 1788. C.R.1.
John Bryant, s. John B. and Hannah, June 29, 1823. [[h. Maria P.] G.R.2.]
John Deane, s. Abiel [Abial, P.R.25.] and Rebecca, May 8, 1835.
John Henry, ch. Perez and Sarah, Feb. 7, 1835. ["Co. F. 43 Mass. Reg't" [h. Sarah E.], G.R.14.]
Jonathan, s. John Sr., Sept. 20, 1646.
Jonathan, s. John Sr., bp. May [worn], 1649. C.R.2.
Jonathan, s. Jonathan, Mar. 13, 1687.
Jonathan, s. Isaac and Ruth, May 27, 1714.
Jonathan, s. Jesse and Lydia, Dec. 27, 1742.
Jonatha[n] Star, s. Hawkins, bp. June 10, 1744. C.R.2.
Joseph, s. Humfery, bp. Jan. 1, 1636. C.R.1.
Joseph, s. Jo[h]n Sr., Jan. 12, 1647 [dup. 1648]. [Josepth, Jan. 12, 1647, P.C.R.]
Joseph, s. Joseph, bp. June 11, 1682. C.R.2.
Joseph, s. Benjamin, Apr. 18, 1694.
Joseph, s. Thomas Sr., Apr. 3, 1696.
Joseph, s. Charles [s. Charls and Joanna, C.R.2.], Oct. 28, 1718.
Joseph, s. Joseph and Elizabeth, Jan. 17, 1727.
Joseph, s. Benja[min] Jr. and Mercy, Feb. 27, 1735.
Joseph, ch. Richard, bp. [Dec.] 20, 1751. C.R.2.
Joseph, s. Roland and w., bp. Aug. 27, 1791. C.R.2.
Josepth, s. John Sr., Jan. 12, 1649. P.C.R. [Joseph, C.R.2.]
Joshua, s. Japhet, bp. June 24, 1683. C.R.2.
Joshua, s. Thomas Sr., July 7, 1689.
Joshua, s. Joshua and Elizabeth, Feb. 5, 1713–14.
[J]oshua, s. Israel and Deborah, Aug. 31, 1747.
Joshua Davis, s. Harris and w., bp. May 8, 1796. C.R.2.
Josiah, s. Thomas, Jan. —, 1672.
Josiah, s. Josiah, Nov. 15, 1700.

TURNER, Juda Hatch, d. Harris and w., bp. Oct. 7, 1798. C.R.2.
Julia, d. Charl[es] Jr. [Col. Charles, C.R.2.] and Hannah, Oct. 13, 1803.
Julia, ch. Theodore and Hannah, Mar. 17, 1828.
Julia A., ch. Melzer S. and Sarah, Apr. 28, 1830, in Duxbury.
Kezia, d. Jonathan, May 3, 1685. [Keziah, C.R.2.]
Lamuel, s. Elijah and Mary, Aug. 28, 1776.
Laura M., d. Melza [dup. Melzer] S. and Emeline, Aug. 23, 1848.
Lazarus, s. Eliab, Aug. 14, 1695.
Lemuel, s. Isaac and Ruth, bp. Aug. 14, 1720. C.R.2.
Lettis, d. Thomas (grand s. Hum[phrey]), Apr. 17, 1711. [d. "M⁽ʳ⁾ Lawyer Turner," C.R.1.]
Liddiah, d. Tho[mas], carpenter, Apr. 26, 1704.
Lillis, d. Samewell, Apr. 27, 1701.
Lilly, ch. Sam[ue]l, bp. Apr. 24, 1715. C.R.1.
[L]ucanna, d. Benja[min] and Marcy, Sept. 12, 1744. [Lusanna, d. Benj[a]m[in] and Mercy, C.R.2.]
Luce, d. Hawkins and ———, bp. Oct. 11, 1747. C.R.2.
Lucelia, ——— [1847]. C.R.1.
Lucelia Maria, d. Melzar [dup. Melzer] S., mechanic, and Emeline, Dec. 16, 1849.
Lucinda, d. Elijah and Mary, May 15, 1791.
Lucretia, d. Hawkins, bp. Aug. 18, 1728. C.R.2.
Lucy, d. Benja[min] Jr. and Mercy, Jan. 17, 1726.
Lucy, d. John and Mary, Jan. 2, 1772.
Lucy, d. Job and Abiel, Feb. 18, 1777.
Lucy, d. Elisha and Prudence, Feb. 23, 1781.
Lucy, ch. Luther, bp. Aug. 4, 1805. C.R.2.
Lucy, ch. Perez and Sarah, Jan. 27, 1832.
Lucy, ch. Nathaniel 2d and Lusanna, Mar. 7, 1834.
Lucy B. [? m.] [Aug. —, 1809]. G.R.14.
Lucy Cole, d. Shiverick and Arvilla, Apr. 11, 1814.
Lurana, ch. Joshua and Elizabeth, bp. Feb. 26, 1726-7. C.R.2.
Lusanna, ch. Caleb and Rachel, bp. Mar. 12, 1732-3. C.R.2.
Lusanna (see Lucanna).
Luther, s. Jona[than] and Abigal, Mar. 14, 1760.
Lydia, d. John Sr., Jan. 24, 1652.
Lydia, d. Nathnael, Aug. —, 1675.
Lydia, d. John and Abigail, July 5, 1699.
Lydia (see Liddiah).
Lydia, d. Thomas and Martha, bp. June 17, 1705. C.R.2.
Lydia, d. Amos, May 26, 1707.
Lydia, ch. Capt. Amos, bp. July 10, 1709. C.R.1.
Lydia, ch. Caleb and Rachel, bp. Dec. 9, 1734. C.R.2.

TURNER, Lydia, d. Ja[me]s [Capt. James, G.R.1.] and Mary, Feb. 16, 1736.
Lydia, [ch.] W[illia]m and Abigail, bp. June 13, 1736. C.R.2.
Lydia, d. Jona[than] and Abigail, Sept. 9, 1746.
Lydia, d. Jesse and Lydia, Feb. 3, 1753.
Lydia, d. James and Deborah, Oct. 28, 1767.
Lydia, d. Elisha and Lydia, Sept. 11, 1793.
Lydia [———], w. Samuel, Sept. 13, 1796. G.R.14.
Lydia, d. Nath[anie]ll Jr. and Sally, Sept. 10, 1798. [w. Capt. Francis G. Chubuck, G.R.6.]
Malborough, s. Caleb and Rachel, bp. Sept. 5, 1731. C.R.2.
Marcy, d. Charls, Sept. 24, 1703.
Marcy, d. Nath[anie]ll Jr. and Sally, Apr. 13, 1808.
Margaret, d. Joseph, Sept. 20, 1677. [Margeret, C.R.2.]
Margaret, d. John, Jan. —, 1696-7.
Margret, s. Abiel and Eliza[beth] [Elisabeth, C.R.2.], June 27, 1745.
Maria Frances, d. John B. and Hannah, Feb. 23, 1829.
Maria P. [———], w. John B. [Nov. —, 1822]. G.R.2.
Maria Wade, d. Samuel and Lydia, Sept. 20, 1837.
Martha, d. Jonathan and Mercy, Apr. 24, 1700.
Martha, d. Abiel and Eliza[beth], Feb. 8, 1755.
Martha, d. Roland and Hannah, May 31, 1783.
Martha, d. Benjamin and Hannah C., Apr. 9, 1826.
Martha, ch. Benja[min], bp. Oct. 5, 1828. C.R.2.
Mary, d. Humfery, bp. Jan. 25, 1634. C.R.1.
Mary, d. Thomas, Sept. 15, 1658.
Mary, d. John Sr., Dec. 10, 1658.
Mary [———], w. Col. Amos, ———, 1667. G.R.1.
Mary, d. Daniell, Apr. 13, 1679.
Mary, d. Elisha, June 10, 1690.
Mary, d. Amose, June —, 1702.
Mary, d. Amose, Apr. 23, 1704.
Mary, d. Jonathan and Mercy, July 28, 1706.
Mary, ch. Capt. Amos, bp. July 10, 1709. C.R.1.
Mary, d. Thomas (grand s. Hum[phrey]), July 2, 1717. [d. "M' Lawyer Turner," C.R.1.]
Mary, ch. Nathan and Fear, bp. July 19, 1724. C.R.2.
Mary, [ch.] Joshua and Elizabeth, bp. Nov. 12, 1732. C.R.2.
Mary, d. Thomas and Mary, bp. July 7, 1734. C.R.2.
Mary, d. Ja[me]s and Mary, Feb. 12, 1739.
Mary, d. John and Mary, June 23, 1769.
Mary, d. James [James Jr., C.R.1.] and Deborah, Nov. 20, 1775.
Mary, d. Elijah and Mary, Oct. 18, 1779.

TURNER, Mary, d. Nath[anie]ll Jr. and Sally, June 2, 1796. [w. Capt. Tho[ma]s L. Manson, June 2, 1797, G.R.6.]
Mary, d. Nath[anie]ll and Rachel, Sept. 10, 1798.
Mary, d. Barker and Polly, June 23, 1809.
Mary [? m.], —— [1820]. G.R.2.
Mary, d. Nathaniel 3d and Mary, Aug. 10, 1828.
Mary B., d. Elijah B. and Lucy B., July 30, 1847.
Mary Clapp, d. John B. and Hannah, Nov. 29, 1820.
Mary Eliza [————], w. Samuel H., ——, 1819. G.R.6.
Mary Rand, d. Cha[rle]s Jr. [Charles Esq., C.R.2.] and Hannah, Dec. 22, 1796.
Mary Rand, ch. Theodore and Hannah, July 17, 1833.
Mary T. [————], w. Henry J., ——, 1827. G.R.14.
Matilda, d. Cha[rle]s Jr. and Hannah, Jan. 25, 1801.
Matilda, d. Samuel A. and Lydia, Oct. 24, 1824.
Mehetabell, d. Nathaell, Mar. 29, 1673.
Mehetable, d. James, bp. Apr. 8, 1744. C.R.1.
Mehetible, d. Ja[me]s and Mary, Jan. 1, 1743.
Melzar S., —— [1808]. G.R.6.
Melzar Stoddard, s. Luther "formerly" of Pembroke, bp. Oct. 5, 1806. C.R.2.
Mercy, d. Jonathan, Oct. 27, 1690.
Mercy (see Marcy).
Mercy, d. Benja[min] and Mercy, May 28, 1738.
Mercy, d. Jesse and Lydia, Dec. 9, 1741.
Mercy, d. Israel and Mercy, Mar. 5, 1786.
Mercy Dwelly, d. James [James Jr., C.R.1.] and Deb[o]r[ah], Jan. 3, 1770.
Meriam, d. John Jr., Apr. 8, 1658.
Miriam, d. John Jr., bp. May 15, 1659. C.R.2.
Miriam, d. Charles [Charls, C.R.2.] and Mercy, Oct. 31, 1707.
Miriam, d. Charles and Mercy, Feb. 3, 1713–14.
Nabby, d. Jonathan and Sarah, Jan. 27, 1771.
Nabby, d. Roland and Hannah, June 15, 1779.
Nancy, d. Jonathan and Sarah, Nov. 15, 1778.
Nancy, d. Will[ia]m and Eunice, May 8, 1789.
Nathan, s. Thomas, Mar. 1, 1654.
Nathan, s. Thomas, bp. Mar. 25, 1655. C.R.2.
Nathan, s. Nathan, Apr. —, 1689.
Nathan, s. Nathan and Leah, bp. July 14, 1723. C.R.2.
Nathan, s. Simeon and w., bp. Dec. 4, 1757. C.R.1.
Nathanael, s. Nathanael, Dec. 24, 1678.
Nathanael, ch. W[illia]m and Abigail, bp. Feb. 10, 1739–40. C.R.2.
Nathanael, s. Jam[e]s and Mary, Apr. 12 1741. [Nathaniel, C.R.1.]

TURNER, Nathaniel, s. Umphrey, bp. Mar. 10, 1638. C.R.1.
Nathaniel, ch. Sam[ue]l, bp. Apr. 24, 1715. C.R.1.
Nathaniel, s. Nath[anie]ll [Nath[anie]l, C.R.2.] and Mary, Mar. 21, 1752.
Nathaniel, s. Nath[anie]ll and Rachel, Jan. 27, 1800.
Nathaniel, s. Nath[anie]ll Jr. and Sally, June 25, 1802.
Nathaniel James, s. Nath[anie]l 3d and Mary, May 27, 1834.
Nathaniell, s. Thomas, Mar. 1, 1654. P.C.R.
Nathaniell, s. Samewell, Dec. 20, 1702. [Nathaniel, s. Capt. Samuel and Abigail, ———, 1703, G.R.1.]
Nath[anie]ll, s. Philip and Eliza[beth], Aug. 5, 1717. [Nathanael, C.R.2.]
Nath[anie]ll, s. James and Deborah, Sept. 28, 1765. [Nathaneel, C.R.1.]
Nehemiah, s. Abner and Naomy, Nov. 18, 1711.
Nehemiah, s. Abner and Aimy, bp. Sept. 11, 1720. C.R.2.
Olive, d. Asa and Abigail, Apr. 12, 1785.
Oriense, d. Will[ia]m and Eunice, Aug. 28, 1786.
Pegge, d. Abial Jr. and Lurana, June 3, 1790.
Peleg, s. Benja[min] and Mercy, Apr. 13, 1741.
Percis, d. Jonathan and Abigal, Sept. 25, 1752. [Persis, C.R.2.]
Peres, ch. Benja[min], bp. Oct. 5, 1828. C.R.2.
Perez, s. Jonathan and Sarah, Dec. 8, 1772.
Perez, s. Perez and Hannah, June 12, 1804. [[h. Sally G.] G.R.14.]
Perez, s. Benjamin and Hannah C., Mar. 9, 1824.
Philip, s. John Jr., Aug. 18, 1673.
Philip, s. John Jr., bp. Aug. 15, 1675. C.R.2.
Philip, s. Philip and Elizabeth, Feb. 2, 1709-10.
Philip, s. Philip and Elizabeth, bp. July 12, 1713. C.R.2.
Philip, s. Philip [s. Philip and Elizabeth, C.R.2.], June 29, 1716.
Phillip, s. Israel and Deborah, Feb. 9, 1741. [Philip, C.R.2.]
Polly, d. Seth and Mary, Apr. 20, 1775.
Princes, ch. Joshua and Elizabeth, bp. Feb. 26, 1726-7. C.R.2.
Priscilla, d. Caleb and Rachel, bp. May 15, 1726. C.R.2.
Priscilla, d. Amos, bp. Dec. 29, 1727. C.R.1.
Prudence, d. Elisha and Prudence, Mar. 25, 1768.
Quintus Carolus, s. Charles Jr. Esq. and Hannah, Nov. 21, 1790.
Rachel, ch. Caleb and Rachel, bp. Mar. 24, 1722-3. C.R.2.
Rachel, d. John and Mary, Apr. 18, 1776.
Rachel, d. Nath[anie]ll and Rachel, Apr. 12, 1797.
Rachell, d. Daniell, Apr. 9, 1687.
Rebecca [———], w. Abiel [Mar. —, 1802]. G.R.14.
Rebekah, d. Thomas Sr., Apr. 17, 1687.
Releaf, d. Thomas (grand s. Hum[phrey]), June 8, 1701.

TURNER, Reuben (see Ruben).
Reuben, s. Asa and Abigail, Oct. 21, 1777.
Rhoda, d. Elisha and Prudence, Mar. 5, 1775.
Richard, s. John, June 5, 1702.
Robart C., s. Perez and Hannah, Jan. 22, 181[worn] [1810]. [Robert V. C., ——, 1810, G.R.14.]
Robinson, s. Abiel [Abiell, C.R.2.] and Eliza[beth], Feb. 17, 1737.
Robinson, s. Abiel Jr. and Lurana, Sept. 12, 1767.
Roland, s. Benjamin and Hannah C., Sept. 29, 1820.
Roland, ch. Benja[min], bp. Oct. 5, 1828. C.R.2.
Rowland, twin s. Abiel and Eliza[beth], June 29, 1747. [Roland, twin ch. Abial and Elisabeth, C.R.2.]
Rowland, s. Roland and Hannah, Sept. 2, 1786.
Ruben, s. Jona[than] and Abigal [Abigail, C.R.2.], Jan. 23, 1739.
Ruth, d. John Sr., bp. May 17, 1662. C.R.2.
Ruth, d. Jonathan, Mar. 6, 1693–4.
Ruth, ch. Jonathan, bp. ——, 1695. C.R.2.
Ruth, d. Thomas (grand s. Hum[phrey]), Mar. 26, 1703.
Ruth, d. Thomas and Martha, bp. May 11, 1707. C.R.2.
Ruth, ch. Richard, bp. [Dec.] 20, 1751. C.R.2.
Ruth, d. Jona[than] and Abigal, Dec. 10, 1755.
Ruth, d. John and Mary, Jan. 19, 1774.
Sally, d. Jonathan and Sarah, July 17, 1775.
Sally, w. Elisha Foster, Mar. 7, 1785. P.R.5.
Sally, d. David and Lydia, Nov. 8, 1819.
Sally G. [———], w. Perez [Aug. —, 1807]. G.R.14.
Sally Hatch, d. Shiverick and Arvilla, Oct. 28, 1817.
Sally Jones, d. Nath[anie]ll Jr. and Sally, July 26, 1792.
Samewell, s. Samewell, Feb. 16, 1704–5.
Sammuell, s. Nathanell, Feb. 25, 1671.
Samuel, ch. Sam[ue]l, bp. Apr. 24, 1715. C.R.1.
Samuel, ch. Nathan and Fear, bp. July 19, 1724. C.R.2.
Samuel, s. Israel and Mercy, Feb. 22, 1788. [[h. Lydia] G.R.14.]
Samuel, s. Charles Esq. and w., bp. Aug. 19, 1792. C.R.2.
Samuel, s. Samuel and Lydia, May 2, 1831.
Samuel A., s. Charles Jr. and Hannah, Mar. 22, 1792.
Samuel Humphery, s. James, bp. June 15, 1788. C.R.1.
Samuel Humphrey, s. James and Deborah, Sept. 15, 1784.
Samuel Humphry, s. Nath[anie]ll Jr. and Sally, Aug. 13, 1811. [h. Mary Eliza, ——, 1812, G.R.6.]
Samuel Humphry, ch. Samuel H. and Mary E., Sept. 20, 1838.
Samuell, s. John Jr., bp. Aug. 4, 1661. C.R.2.
Samuell, s. Thomas, Feb. 25, 1670. [This entry crossed out.] [Capt. Samuel [h. Abigail], G.R.1.]

TURNER, Sam[ue]ll, s. James and Mary, Mar. 12, 1746. [Samuel, c.r.1.]
Sam[ue]ll, s. Charls Esq. and w., bp. July 22, 1792. C.R.2.
Sarah, d. John Jr., July 25, 1665.
Sarah, d. Eliab, Aug. 2, 1697.
Sarah, d. Tho[ma]s (grand s. Hum[phrey]), Jan. 19, 1704–5.
Sarah, d. Charls and Mercy, bp. Dec. 2, 1715. C.R.2.
Sarah, ch. Benjamin and Sarah, bp. Nov. 2, 1735. C.R.2.
Sarah, d. Simeon, bp. Apr. 22, 1759. C.R.1.
Sarah E. [———], w. John H., ———, 1834. G.R.14.
Sarah Jane, ch. Perez and Sarah, Sept. 2, 1830.
Sarah S., d. Perez and Hannah, Mar. 16, 1816.
Sarah Stockbridge, d. Perez and w., bp. Sept. 1, 1799. C.R.2.
Sarah Whitcomb, d. Abiel and Rebecca, Oct. 2, 1832. [w. Charles H. Merritt, G.R.14.] [ch. Abial and Rebecca, P.R.25.]
Seth, s. Amose, Nov. 28, 1705. [Lt. Seth, G.R.1.]
Seth, ch. Capt. Amos, bp. July 10, 1709. C.R.1.
Seth, s. Jesse and Lydia, Dec. 19, 1746.
Seth, s. Jesse and Lydia, Nov. 29, 1748.
Seth, s. Jonathan and Abigal [Abigail, C.R.2.], Mar. 31, 1751.
Seth, s. Seth and Mary, Mar. 30, 1782.
Shiverick, s. Rowland and Hannah, Nov. 21, 1788.
Siles, s. Asa and Abigail, Apr. 24, 1790.
Simeon, s. Caleb and Rachel, bp. July 19, 1724. C.R.2.
Simeon, s. Nathan dec'd, bp. Nov. 29, 1724. C.R.2.
Sophia, d. Elisha and Prudence, July 29, 1786.
Sophia, d. Job and Abiel, May 9, 1789.
Star, s. Joseph and Elizabeth, bp. Mar. 6, 1725–6. C.R.2.
Star, s. Joseph and Eliz[abe]th, bp. Dec. 6, 1730. C.R.2.
Stephen, s. William and Eunice, May 4, 1779.
Susanna, d. Isaac and Ruth, Aug. 12, 1712.
Susannah, d. Jona[than] and Abigal, Dec. 28, 1741.
Susea, d. Asa and Abigail, Sept. 14, 1779.
Temprence, d. Elijah and Mary, Mar. 17, 1789.
Theodore, s. Charles Jr. and Hannah, Sept. 13, 1795. [Theadore, s. Charles Esq. and w., C.R.2.]
Theodore, ch. Theodore and Hannah, Oct. 14, 1831.
Theodore, ch. Theodore and Hannah, Mar. 15, 1835.
Thomas, s. Thomas, Dec. —, 1670.
Thomas, s. Nathan, July 15, 1680.
Thomas, s. Thomas Sr., Sept. 18, 1682.
Thomas, s. Thomas (grand s. Hum[phrey]), Mar. 31, 1699.
Thomas, s. Charles and Mercy, Mar. 9, 1701 [*sic*, see Ephraim].
Thomas, s. Charls and Mercy, bp. Mar. 11, 1710–11. C.R.2.

TURNER, Thomas, s. Thom[a]s and Mary, bp. May 15, 1737. C.R.2.
Thomas, ch. Theodore and Hannah, Feb. 27, 1827.
Thyne "alias" Vine, s. Joseph and Eliz[abeth], bp. Apr. 1, 1733. C.R.2.
Unice Whiting, d. Harris, bp. Oct. 30, 1803. C.R.2.
Vine (see Thyne).
Vine, ch. Richard, bp. [Dec.] 20, 1751. C.R.2.
Waitstill, s. Isaac and Ruth, bp. Nov. 29, 1724. C.R.2.
Waldo, ch. William and Sarah, Aug. 22, 1842.
William, s. Thomas Sr., Jan. 13, 1683.
William, twin s. Benjamin, Aug. 5, 1698.
William, s. W[illia]m and Abigail, bp. Nov. 26, 1727. C.R.2.
William, s. Charls and Unice, bp. Jan. 25, 1746–7. C.R.2.
Will[ia]m, s. Will[ia]m and Bety, Sept. 22, 1769.
William, s. Charles Jr. [Col. Charles, C.R.2.] and Hannah, Mar. 16, 1805.
William, s. Harris and w. "lately moved to Townsend," bp. May 10, 1807. C.R.2.
William [Mar. —, 1813]. G.R.14.
William, s. Perez and Hannah, Mar. 3, 181[worn].
William Francis, ch. William and Sarah, Mar. 29, 1834.
Will[ia]m Thrift, s. Abiezer and Han[na]h, Sept. 15, 1764.
Xoa, d. William and Eunice, Feb. 12, 1775.
Zilpha, d. Roland and Hannah, Apr. 7, 1781.
———, s. Nathanael and Mehetabell, "about two weeks before" Mar. 22, 1680.
———, ch. Charls and Eunice, bp. May 6, 1741. C.R.2.
———, fourth ch. Elijah and Mary, May 28, 1786.
———, d. Melzar S., ship wright, and Emeline, Dec. 16, 1849.

TUTTLE, Catharine E. [———], w. ———, ——— 1805]. C.R.1.

UPHAM, Charles Thomas, ch. Artemus and Abigail, Jan. 16, 1839.

UTLEY, Lydia, d. Samuel, Dec. 28, 1659.

VANDURA, Manuel F., ——— [1828]. G.R.10.

VARNEY, Fenton Watson, s. Nathaniel, shoemaker, and Sophronia, Nov. 1, 1844.

VAUGHAN, Daniell, ch. George and Elizabeth, bp. May 31, 1657. C.R.2.
Elizabeth, ch. George and Elizabeth, bp. May 31, 1657. C.R.2.
John, s. Geo[rge] and Elizab[eth], bp. Nov. 7, 1658. C.R.2.
Joseph, ch. George and Elizabeth, bp. May 31, 1657. C.R.2.
Mary, d. Geo[rge] and Elizab[eth], bp. July 1, 1660. C.R.2.

VEALE, William P. [h. Margaret B. (Studley)], Mar. 7, 1828. G.R.2.

VILA, James F., June 27, 1838. G.R.14.

VINAL (see Vinall), Abby M., d. Abel A., yeoman, and Merrial (b. Springfield, Vt.), Apr. 25, 1849, in S. Scituate.
Abby S., d. Seth S., shoemaker, and Harriet, June 27, 1844.
Abby Turner, d. Alvyen and Eliza, Mar. 16, 1838. [Abbie T., ch. Alvin and Eliza, ——, 1837, G.R.7.]
Abby Turner, ch. Alvyen and Eliza, bp. July 5, 1840. C.R.3.
Abel, s. William and Lucy, Apr. 30, 1791.
Abel Augustine, s. Abel and Julette, Feb. 4, 1814.
Abigail, d. Stephen Jr., bp. July 25, 1731. C.R.1.
Abigail [——], w. John, —— [1800]. G.R.2.
Abigail, d. Hayward and Beckey, Mar. 31, 1817.
Abigail, d. John and Abigail, Aug. 12, 1821.
Adeline, d. John S. and Mary Ann, July 1, 1825.
Adeline Matilda, d. John S. and Mary Ann, Nov. 7, 1826.
Albert, s. Paul and Maria, ——.
Alice, ch. Lemuel, bp. Dec. 14, 1812. C.R.1.
Alice, d. Lemuel and Polly, Nov. 2, 1818. [w. John E. Dinnin, G.R.6.]
Allen L., s. John and Abigail, July 21, 1831.
Almira, d. Lemuel and Polly, Nov. 12, 1802.
Alvin Damon, ch. Abel A. and Joan, July 20, 1837.
Alvyen, s. Levi and Patience, July 4, 1797. [Alvin [h. Eliza], G.R.7.]
Alvyen, s. Paul and Maria, Aug. 14, 1819.
Alvyen, ch. Paul and Maria, bp. July 2, 1826. C.R.3.
Amos, ch. Seth H. and Harriet L., Mar. 26, 1840.
Ann E., d. John and Abigail, Mar. 27, 1838. [Anna E., G.R.2.]
Anna, d. Jacob 3d and Anna, Feb. 10, 1732.
Anna, ch. Jacob (s. Jacob) and Anna, bp. Nov. 3, 1734. C.R.1.
Anna, d. Issachor, bp. July 3, 1768. C.R.1.
Anna Eldora [dup. Eldorah], d. Thomas [dup. bricklayor] and Chloe, July 30, 1844.
Anne, d. Elijah, bp. Aug. 7, 1720. G.R.1.
Arabella, d. Hayward and Beckey, Sept. 11, 1813.
Asa, s. Joseph, bp. Aug. 26, 1753. C.R.1.
Asa, s. Joseph [Josep, C.R.1.] and Thankfull, Sept. 15, 1766.
Asa, s. Asa and Thankful, Feb. 22, 1790.
Asa, s. Asa Jr. and Sally, Aug. 20, 1821.
Bailey, [twin] s. Stephen and Charlotte, Apr. 23, 1795.
Benjamin, s. Jo[h]n 3d, bp. Oct. 27, 1745. C.R.1.

VINAL, Benjamin, s. Benja[min] and Sarah, Jan. 7, 1776.
Betsey, d. Nath[anie]l and Prissilla, Dec. 5, 1797.
Betsey Capen, d. John S. and Mary Ann, June 8, 1829.
Betsey White, d. Asa Jr. and Sally, Aug. 20, 1817. [w. Capt. Thomas J. Burrows, G.R.6.]
Betty, d. Ezekel and Molley, Aug. 27, 1769. [Betsy, d. Ezekiel, C.R.1.]
Caroline Augusta, d. Gideon and Sarah, June 10, 1816.
Catharine Green, d. Lot and Eleanor, Sept. 4, 1828.
Catharine Green, ch. Lot and Eleanor, bp. May 23, 1830. C.R.3.
Charles, s. William and Lucy, July 3, 1796.
Charles, s. John and Abigail, Mar. 1, 1823.
Charles, s. Paul and Maria, ——— [rec. after ch. b. Dec. 13, 1832].
Charles Augustus, ch. Freeman and Sarah A. M., Mar. 23, 1843.
Charles Carroll, ch. Charles and Elizabeth K., Sept. 17, 1831. [Rev. Charles C., G.R.6.]
Charles Thomas, ch. Paul and Maria, bp. May 3, 1835. C.R.3.
Charlotte, [twin] d. Stephen and Charlotte, Apr. 23, 1795.
Clarisa, d. Nath[anie]l and Prissilla, Feb. 16, 1800.
Clarissa [———], w. Jacob, ——— [1791]. C.R.3.
Clarissa [———], w. Jacob, ——— [1796]. C.R.3.
Clarissa, d. Levi and Sally, July 2, 1830.
Clodius, s. Jacob Jr., bp. Oct. 9, 1743. C.R.1.
Cordelia Turner, d. Thomas and Chloe, July 23, 1842.
Cushing, s. Lemuel and Polly, Oct. 16, 1800.
Cushing, ch. Lemuel, bp. Oct. 3, 1802. C.R.1.
Cynthia (see Zinthia).
David, s. Stephen, Feb. 17, 1716.
David, s. Issachar and Mary, Mar. 12, 1742.
David Henry, s. Abel and Julette, Dec. 26, 1816.
Debbe, d. Capt. Israel, bp. Sept. 5, 1773. C.R.1.
Deborah, d. Stephen, July 12, 1714.
Deborah, d. Stephen, bp. Oct. 9, 1715. C.R.1.
Deborah, d. Issacher [Isachar, C.R.1.] and Judeth, Mar. 31, 1758.
Delight, d. Ezra, bp. Apr. 14, 1771. C.R.1.
Desire, d. Joshua, bp. June 14, 1761. C.R.1.
Dexter, s. Nath[anie]ll Jr. and Deborah, Nov. 14, 1798. [[h. Eliza L.] G.R.11.]
Drusilla, d. Jonathan and Drusilla, Oct. 23, 1807.
Eaton, s. Hayward and Beckey, Feb. 5, 1811.
Eaton Webster, s. Nathaniel J., shoemaker, and Abagail J., Oct. 12, 1848.
Edmond Ramond, s. Abel and Julette, Apr. 18, 1818.
Egeatous, s. Jobe and Sarah, Aug. 28, 1797.

VINAL, Eleanor, d. Job and Sarah, Mar. 14, 1801.
Eleanor, d. Stephen and Charlotte, Feb. 14, 1803.
Elijah J., ch. Charles and Elizabeth K., May 17, 1837.
Elijah Pope, s. Jonathan and Drucilla, Feb. 19, 1803.
Elisabeth, d. Jacob (Vinall), Nov. 1, 1715.
Eliza, d. Stephen and Charlotte, Nov. 13, 1800.
Eliza [———], w. Alvyen [dup. Alvin], —— [1802]. C.R.3. [w. Alvin, G.R.7.]
Eliza, d. Asa and Thankful, Sept. 7, 1803.
Eliza, d. Joseph and Mercy, Aug. 8, 1832.
Eliza L. [———], w. Dexter, Apr. 20, 1802. G.R.11.
Elizabeth (see Elisabeth).
Elizabeth, d. Jacob Jr., Aug. 8, 1717.
Elizabeth, d. Jo[h]n Jr. and Mary, Sept. 12, 1744. [Elisabeth, C.R.2.]
Elizabeth, d. Capt. Israel Jr., bp. July 8, 1770. C.R.1.
Elizabeth Rose, d. Alvyen and Eliza, Sept. 12, 1832. [eldest d. Alvin and Eliza, G.R.7.]
Ella, d. Howard and Clarrissa (b. Danvers), Mar. 8, 1848.
Ellen Thomas, d. Lot and Eleanor, Oct. 27, 1824. [Ellen V., w. Lewis Studley Jr., C.R.3.]
Ellen Thomas, ch. Lot and Eleanor, bp. Aug. 6, 1826. C.R.3.
Elsa W., d. Howard and Clara (b. Quincy), Mar. 10, 1848.
Eunice O., w. Allen Bowker (s. Edward and Lydia), Oct. 20, 1777. G.R.14.
Eunice Thomas, d. Levi and Patience, Nov. 5, 1803.
Evelina, d. Hayward and Beckey, Nov. 23, 1807.
Ezekiel, s. John Jr. and Mary, May 13, 1742.
Ezekiel Turner, ch. Seth H. and Harriet L., Feb. 25, 1835.
Ezra, s. "J^{no}" Jr., bp. Apr. 17, 1743. C.R.1.
Ezra, s. Joseph and Thankfull, Jan. 20, 1774.
Ezra, s. Ezra and Polly, June 16, 1812.
Ezra, s. John S. and Mary Ann, Oct. 2, 1831.
Ezra, s. Levi Jr. and Judith, Sept. 25, 1832.
Ezra, ch. Levi and Judith, bp. July 5, 1840. C.R.3.
Ezra, "Formerly of Co. K. 29 Mass. Vols.," Dec. 27, 1840. G.R.7.
Francis, s. Ezekel and Molley, Mar. 9, 1761.
Francis, ch. Ezekiel and Molly, bp. Dec. 6, 1767. C.R.1.
Francis Hatch, [twin] s. Abel and Julette, Oct. 28, 1821.
Frank Thomas, ch. Charles and Elizabeth K., Apr. 11, 1845.
Frederick Hammond, s. J[oseph] and Mercy, Nov. 26, 1826.
Freeman, s. Levi and Sally, Dec. 22, 1815. [[h. Sarah A. M.] G.R.7.]

VINAL, Freeman, ch. Capt. Levi, bp. Aug. 1, 1824. C.R.1.
Galen Lincoln, s. Nath[anie]l Jr. and Deborah, Dec. 7, 1802.
Gedion, s. Capt. William and Lucy, Mar. 12, 1789.
George Eaton, s. Eaton and Maria, bp. Apr. 12, 1848. C.R.1.
George Eton, ch. Eaton and Maria, Feb. 7, 1843.
George Galiton, s. Lot and Eleanor, Nov. 8, 1830. [George Gallaton, C.R.3.]
George Galiton, s. Lot and Eleanor, Feb. 9, 1833.
George Gallatin, ch. Lot, bp. Mar. 27, 1842. C.R.3.
George H., ch. Abel A. and Joan, Sept. 23, 1841.
George O., s. Paul and Maria, Dec. 13, 1832.
George Otis, ch. Paul and Maria, bp. July 6, 1834. C.R.3.
George Washington, ch. Stephen and w., bp. Nov. 2, 1794. C.R.1.
George Whitefield, s. Abel and Julette, July 3, 1815.
Gideon, s. Stephen (Vinall), bp. Sept. 6, 1709. C.R.1.
Gideon (see Gedion).
Gideon, s. Gideon and Sarah, Apr. 19, 1826.
Hannah, d. John, bp. June 5, 1709. C.R.1.
Hannah, d. Seth, bp. May 26, 1754. C.R.1.
Hannah Bailey, ch. Seth H. and Harriet L., Feb. 19, 1822, in Marshfield.
Hannah Crehore, d. Thomas and Chloe, Jan. 7, 1830.
Hannah Litchfield, d. Nath[anie]l Jr. and Deborah, June 5, 1795.
Harriet Jewett, d. Levi and Sally, Dec. 12, 1825.
Harriot, d. Levi and Patience, Aug. 8, 1799.
Hayward, s. Nathaniel and Priscilla, Nov. 4, 1785.
Hayward, s. Hayward and Beckey, May 18, 1820.
Henery Frances, s. Will[ia]m Jr. and Sally, Feb. 17, 1805. [Capt. Henry F., h. Lydia J., G.R.6.]
Henry A., s. Eaton, sailor, and Maria, July 14, 1845.
Henry Augustus, s. Eaton and Maria, bp. Apr. 12, 1848. C.R.1.
Henry Glover, s. Thomas and Chloe, Mar. 10, 1839.
Henry L., s. John and Abigail, Jan. 22, 1829.
Henry Monroe, s. Levi Jr. and Judith, Dec. 15, 1814.
Henry Monroe, ch. Levi Jr. and Judith, bp. May 7, 1826. C.R.3.
Howard, —— [1785]. C.R.1.
Ignatius, s. Ignat[i]us, bp. June 30, 1745. C.R.1.
Ignatius, s. Ignatius, bp. Mar. 29, 1747. C.R.1.
Ignatius, s. Ignatius, bp. May 27, 1764. C.R.1.
Ignatius, s. Ignatius Jr. and w., bp. Jan. 2, 1794. C.R.1.
Ignatius, —— [1798]. C.R.1.
Isabella Thomas, d. Asa, ship joiner, and Sarah (b. Lowell), June 12, 1849.
Isaiah, s. Stephen and Charlotte, Nov. 17, 1808.

VINAL, Israel, s. Capt. Israel, bp. Jan. 13, 1744. C.R.1.
Israel, s. Capt. Israel Jr., bp. Oct. 5, 1766. C.R.1.
Israel Cook, s. Levi Jr. and Judith, Sept. 19, 1829. [[h. Sarah C. (Vinal)] G.R.7.]
Issachar, s. Stephen, Mar. 27, 1718.
Jacob, s. Jacob Jr., Apr. 15, 1719.
Jacob, s. Jacob Jr., bp. June 5, 1737. C.R.1.
Jacob, s. Levi and Patience, July 7, 1792.
James, ch. Capt. Levi, bp. Aug. 1, 1824. C.R.1.
James, s. Joseph and Mercy, —— [rec. after ch. b. Aug. 8, 1832]. [James B[ontecou], Sept. 7, 1834, P.R.26.]
James Bingham, s. Thomas and Chloe, Jan. 7, 1824.
James B[ontecou], Oct. 29, 1836. P.R.26.
James C., s. John and Abigail, Sept. 28, 1834.
James Monroe, s. Levi and Patience, June 3, 1809.
James Monroe, ch. Lot, bp. Mar. 27, 1842. C.R.3.
James Monrow, s. Lot and Eleanor, July 25, 1835.
Jane, d. Jacob 3d, bp. May 18, 1755. C.R.1.
Jane Crawford, ch. Henry F. and Lydia, Nov. 8, 1837.
Jefferson, s. Levi and Patience, Feb. 16, 1807.
Jemima, d. Jacob Jr., bp. July 7, 1751. C.R.1.
Joanna, d. Jacob (Vinall) and Mary, Jan. 15, 1711.
Joanna, d. Jacob, bp. Oct. 29, 1730. C.R.1.
Job, s. Ignatious, bp. June 5, 1763. C.R.1.
Job, s. Job and Sarah, Feb. 2, 1787.
Job [h. Betsey B.] [Feb. —, 1817]. G.R.2.
Job, s. Robert and Polly, Apr. 15, 1819.
Job Howard, s. Job and Betsey B., May 23, 1848.
Jo[h]n, s. Jo[h]n Jr. and Mary, Dec. 10, 1737.
John [h. Abigail], —— [1798]. G.R.2.
John, s. John and Abigail, June 2, 1825, in Cohasset. [John Jr., G.R.2.]
John, —— [1827]. C.R.1.
John Frederick, s. Gideon and Sarah, Jan. 28, 1820.
John Spurr, s. Job and Sarah, Mar. 9, 1793.
John T., Aug. 10, 1823. G.R.7.
John Thomas, s. John S. and Mary Ann, Aug. 9, 1822.
Jonathan, s. Jacob (Vinall) and Mary, Feb. "ye last," 1707.
Jonathan, s. Capt. Israel, bp. Apr. 17, 1743. C.R.1.
Joseph, s. Jacob Jr. and Eliza[beth], June 21, 1721.
Joseph, s. Joseph, bp. June 25, 1749. C.R.1.
Joseph, s. Joseph, bp. May 15, 1757. C.R.1.
Joseph, s. Asa and Thankful, Sept. 5, 1798 [dup. 1797]. [Sept. 5, 1797, P.R.26.]

VINAL, Joseph, s. Joseph and Mercy, July 7, 1820. [Joseph Jr., P.R.26.]
Joseph, ch. Seth H. and Harriet L., Nov. 18, 1824, in Marshfield.
Joseph Hammond, s. Gideon and Sarah, Sept. 6, 1829.
Joseph Perkins, s. Lot and Eleanor, Oct. 3, 1837.
Joseph Perkins, ch. Lot, bp. Mar. 27, 1842. C.R.3.
Joshua, s. Ezekiel, bp. July 30, 1732. C.R.1.
Joshua, s. Seth, bp. Apr. 5, 1752. C.R.1.
Joshua, ch. Seth H. and Harriet L., Nov. 7, 1829.
Judith, d. Issachar, bp. July 7, 1765. C.R.1.
Judith [———], w. Levi 2d, —— [1772]. C.R.3.
Judith [———], w. Levi, —— [1792]. C.R.3.
Judith, d. Levi Jr. and Judith, Dec. 15, 1813.
Judith Ann, d. Will[ia]m Jr. and Sally, Aug. 30, 1813.
Judith Annis, d. Levi Jr. and Judith, Feb. 1, 1817.
Judith Annis, ch. Levi Jr. and Judith, bp. May 7, 1826. C.R.3.
Julia Elizabeth, ch. Charles and Elizabeth K., July 15, 1839.
Julia Matilda, [twin] d. Abel and Julette, Oct. 28, 1821.
Lemuel, s. Capt. Israel Jr., bp. June 1, 1777. C.R.1.
Lemuel, s. Lemuel and Sally, Apr. 18, 1823. [Lemuel Jr., G.R.6.]
Lendal, s. Simeon and Sarah, Mar. 9, 1797.
Lendall, s. Simeon, bp. Oct. 13, 1805. C.R.1.
Leroy (see Looroy).
Lettice, d. Joseph, bp. July 7, 1751. C.R.1.
Lettis, d. Joseph and Thankfull, Nov. 18, 1768. [Lettice, C.R.1.]
Levi, s. Jacob 3d, bp. June 28, 1754. C.R.1.
Levi, s. Levi and Patiance [Patience, C.R.3.], Mar. 9, 1788.
Levi, s. Levi Jr. and Judith, Sept. 24, 1823.
Levi, ch. Levi Jr. and Judith, bp. May 7, 1826. C.R.3.
Looroy, s. Levi Jr. and Judith, Sept. 4, 1819.
Looroy, ch. Levi Jr. and Judith, bp. May 7, 1826. C.R.3.
Lot, s. Jacob, bp. May 22, 1768. C.R.1.
Lot, s. Levi and Patience, Sept. 15, 1801. [[h. Eleanor] G.R.7.]
Louiza, d. Levi Jr. and Judith, Sept. 29, 1825. [Louisa, C.R.3.]
Lucius Henry, ch. Charles and Elizabeth K., Feb. 23, 1833.
Lucy, d. Will[ia]m and Lucy, Oct. 12, 1784.
Lucy, d. Simeon and Sarah, Sept. 15, 1793.
Lucy, d. Asa and Thankful, Dec. 3, 1805.
Lucy, ch. Simeon, bp. July 6, 1806. C.R.1.
Lucy, d. Levi Jr. and Judith, Oct. 19, 1826.
Lucy, ch. Seth H. and Harriet L., Jan. 23, 1832.
Lucy Cole, d. Jonathan and Drucilla, Apr. 9, 1805.
Lucy Otis, ch. Henry F. and Lydia, Jan. 25, 1841.
Lucy Otis, d. Henry F. and Lydia, bp. June 1, 1845. C.R.1.

VINAL, Lusanna, ch. John (s. Jacob) and Sarah, bp. July 11, 1731. C.R.1.
Lydia, d. Israel 3d and Rebekah, Sept. 5, 1786.
Lydia, d. Levi and Patiance, Dec. 11, 1789.
Lydia, d. Lemuel and Polly, Dec. 10, 1806.
Lydia, d. Levi Jr. and Judith, Mar. 14, 1822.
Lydia, ch. Levi Jr. and Judith, bp. May 7, 1826. C.R.3.
Lydia Frances, ch. Henry F. and Lydia [Lydia J., G.R.6.], Apr. 23, 1835.
Lydia Frances, d. Henry F. and Lydia, bp. June 19, 1836. C.R.1.
Lydia J. [———], w. Capt. Henry F., Feb. 5, 1809. G.R.6.
Mabel, d. Job and Sarah, July 18, 1790. [w. Thomas Litchfield, G.R.7.]
Mahala Thomas, d. Asa Jr. and Sally, Sept. 26, 1823.
Marcy, d. Issacher and Judeth, Apr. 22, 1755.
Marcy, d. Israel Jr., bp. June 5, 1768. C.R.1.
Marcy, ch. Paul and Maria, bp. July 2, 1826. C.R.3.
Marcy Waterman, d. Lemuel and Polly, Jan. 27, 1799.
Maria [———], w. Eaton, ——— [1812]. G.R.6.
Maria, d. Paul and Maria, Oct. 29, 1823.
Maria, ch. Paul and Maria, bp. July 2, 1826. C.R.3.
Maria [? m.] [Mar. —, 1830]. G.R.2.
Maria Eaton, ch. Eaton and Maria, Jan. 13, 1835. [w. George H. Webb, G.R.6.]
Maria Eaton, d. Eaton and Maria, bp. July 5, 1840. C.R.1.
Maria Howard, d. Hayward and Beckey, Jan. 5, 1824.
Mariah Frances, d. Alvyen and Eliza, Oct. 20, 1839. [Mariah [dup. Maria Frances, second dup. Maria], d. Alvin, w. Ward Hayward, C.R.3.]
Martha, d. Joseph, bp. Mar. 16, 1748. C.R.1.
Martha, d. Joseph, bp. Aug. 15, 1756. C.R.1.
Martha A., w. Jairus Litchfield, Sept. 7, 1785. G.R.2.
Martha Ann, d. Nath[anie]ll Jr. and Deborah, June 20, 1804.
Martha Ann, d. Abel, farmer, and Merriel, Nov. 17, 1846.
Martha Woodbury, d. Robert and Polly, Apr. 27, 1822.
Mary, d. Stephen, bp. Aug. 14, 1720. G.R.1.
Mary, d. Jacob Jr. and Elizabeth, Jan. 10, 1725.
Mary, d. Jacob Jr., bp. Oct. 22, 1727. C.R.1.
Mary, d. Jo[h]n Jr. and Mary, Dec. 20, 1739.
Mary, d. Issachar and Judeth, Dec. 2, 1752.
Mary, d. Jacob 3d, bp. June 28, 1754. C.R.1.
Mary, ch. Issacar and Judith, bp. July 11, 1756. C.R.1.
Mary, d. Stephen, bp. Sept. 18, 1757. C.R.1.
Mary, d. Joshua, bp. May 29, 1763. C.R.1.

VINAL, Mary Ann, d. John S. and Mary Ann, Oct. 8, 1823.
Mary E., d. Job and Betsey B. [Mar. —, 1849]. G.R.2.
Mary Elizabeth, ch. Eaton and Maria, Mar. 20, 1840.
Mary Elizebeth, d. Job, shoemaker, and Betsey B., Mar. 29, 1849.
Mary Emeline, d. Alvin, shoemaker, and Eliza, Apr. 20, 1844. [——, 1845, G.R.7.]
Mary Emeline, ch. Alvyen and Eliza, bp. July 5, 1846. C.R.3.
Mary Jane, d. Paul and Maria, Oct. 1, 1830.
Mary Lincoln, d. Lemuel and Polly, May 4, 1804.
Mary Thomas, d. Thomas and Chloe, Mar. 3, 1826.
Mary Tilden, ch. Stephen and w., bp. Nov. 2, 1794. C.R.1.
Mary Williams, d. Will[ia]m Jr. and Sally, Sept. 8, 1820.
Melinda, d. Gideon and Sarah, Nov. 22, 1833.
Melzar, s. John and Abigail, Sept. 29, 1836.
Melzer, s. John and Abigail, Aug. 13, 1840.
Mercy (see Marcy).
Mercy, ch. Issacar and Judith, bp. July 11, 1756. C.R.1.
Mercy, d. William and Lucy, Apr. 21, 1787.
Mercy [———] [w. Joseph], July 22, 1800. P.R.26.
Mercy, d. Paul and Maria, Apr. 27, 1816.
Mercy, d. Joseph and Mercy, Dec. 15, 1821.
Mercy Waterman, ch. Lemuel, bp. Oct. 3, 1802. C.R.1.
Meriel [———], w. Abel A. [Apr. —, 1808]. G.R.14.
Molly, d. Jacob Jr., bp. Oct. 16, 1748. C.R.1.
Moses, s. Joseph and Mercy, Oct. 4, 1828.
Nahum, s. Simeon and Sarah, Feb. 6, 1801.
Nahum, s. Simeon, bp. Oct. 28, 1805. C.R.1.
Nancy, ch. Stephen and w., bp. Nov. 2, 1794. C.R.1.
Nancy, d. Levi and Sally, Jan. 18, 1818.
Nancy, ch. Capt. Levi, bp. Aug. 1, 1824. C.R.1.
Nancy Jenkins, ch. Henry F. and Lydia, Mar. 19, 1840.
Nancy Odel, d. Alvyan, farmer, and Eliza, July 8, 1848.
Nathaneel, s. Capt. Israel Jr., bp. Oct. 5, 1766. C.R.1.
Nath[anie]l, s. John (s. Jacob), bp. Oct. 20, 1734. C.R.1.
Nath[anie]l, —— [1764]. C.R.1.
Nathaniel, s. Nath[anie]l and Priscilla, Dec. 29, 1787.
Nathaniel, s. Dexter and Eliza L., Mar. 21, 1826. [[h. Maria W. Bailey] G.R.8.]
Nathaniel James, s. Hayward and Beckey, Mar. 3, 1827.
Nath[anie]ll, s. Joseph and Thankfull, Feb. 22, 1771. [Nath[anie]l C.R.1.]
Nelson, s. Levi and Sally, Dec. 13, 1820.
Nelson, ch. Levi, bp. May 7, 1826. C.R.3.
Nicholas, s. Jacob 3d and Anna, Apr. 4, 1731.

VINAL, Nicolas, ch. Jacob (s. Jacob) and Anna, bp. Nov. 3, 1734. C.R.I.
Olive, d. Asa and Thankful, Oct. 14, 1791. [w. Atwood Litchfield, P.R.6.]
Olive H., d. Ezra of E. Boston [Aug. —, 1849]. C.R.3.
Orphan, d. Joshua, bp. Aug. 13, 1769. C.R.I.
Otis, s. Lemuel and Polly, June 28, 1810.
Otis Bailey, s. Simeon, Jan. 12, 1839.
Owen T., s. Isreal and Bethiah M., Apr. 2 [1845?].
Patience, d. Ignatius, bp. July 3, 1766. C.R.I.
Patience, d. Ignatius, bp. Nov. 20, 1768. C.R.I.
Patience, d. Levi and Patience, Feb. 21, 1812.
Patience, ch. Capt. Levi, bp. Aug. 1, 1824. C.R.I.
Patience, ch. Alvyen and Eliza, bp. Nov. 3, 1844. C.R.3.
Patience G. [G., written in pencil], d. Alvyen and Eliza, Aug. 25, 1841. [Patience, ch. Alvin and Eliza, ——, 1842, G.R.7.]
Paul, s. Levi and Patience, Oct. 31, 1794.
Paul Jewett, s. Paul and Maria, Nov. 26, 1825.
Phebe, d. Ezekiel, bp. Nov. 24, 1771. C.R.I.
Polley, d. Nathaniel and Priscilla, Mar. 20, 1784.
Polly, d. Lemuel and Polly, Dec. 10, 1801.
Polly, d. Joseph and Mercy, Sept. 18, 1824.
Priscilla, d. Jacob Jr., bp. Oct. 22, 1727. C.R.I.
Priscilla, d. Nath[anie]l and Priscilla, Mar. 10, 1795.
Priscilla, d. Dexter and Eliza L., Apr. 14, 1824.
Prisilla, d. Jacob Jr. and Elizabeth, May 18, 1723.
Rachel, d. Stephen Jr., bp. Aug. 5, 1733. C.R.I.
Rachel, ch. Stephen and w., bp. Nov. 2, 1794. C.R.I.
Rebeccah, d. Joshua, bp. Sept. 28, 1766. C.R.I.
Rebeckkah, d. Joshua, bp. July 8, 1764. C.R.I.
Rebekah, d. Israel 3d and Lydia, ——.
Rhoda, d. Stephen Jr., bp. June 5, 1748. C.R.I.
Robert, s. Capt. Israel Jr., bp. Oct. 5, 1766. C.R.I.
Robert, s. Job and Sarah, May 12, 1789.
Robert, s. Nath[anie]l and Priscilla, Mar. 11, 1792.
Roscoe, ch. Freeman and Sarah A. M., —— [rec. after ch. b. Mar. 23, 1843].
Roxana, d. Robert and Polly, July 6, 1817.
Ruth, d. John Jr. and Mary, Apr. 23, 1746.
Ruth, d. Joshua and Ruth, bp. Mar. 11, 1759. C.R.I.
Salley, d. Nath[anie]l and Priscilla, Mar. 13, 1790.
Sally, d. Benja[min] and Sarah, Mar. 7, 1785. [Sarah, w. Lemuel G.R.6.]
Sally, d. Israel 3d and Sally, —— [rec. after ch. b. June 30, 1788].

VINAL, Sally, d. Asa and Thankful, Feb. 7, 1800.
Sally Eveleth, d. Will[ia]m Jr. and Sally, Sept. 14, 1806.
Sally Hatch, d. Jonathan and Drucilla, Nov. 25, 1800.
Sally Hatch, d. Jonathan, bp. Nov. 21, 1802. C.R.1.
Salmon, s. Simeon and Sarah, Aug. 17, 1804.
Samuel, s. Isachor, bp. Feb. 16, 1773. C.R.1.
Sarah, d. Stephen Jr., bp. Oct. 12, 1735. C.R.1.
Sarah, d. Jo[h]n (s. Jacob), bp. Oct. 31, 1736. C.R.1.
Sarah, d. Ezra and w., bp. July 5, 1767. C.R.1.
Sarah, d. Benjamin, bp. Oct. 31, 1773. C.R.1.
Sarah (see Sally).
Sarah, d. Job and Sarah, Feb. 24, 1788.
Sarah, ch. Seth H. and Harriet L., Oct. 25, 1836.
Sarah A. M. (see ——— Vinal).
Sarah Ann, d. Gideon and Sarah, Mar. 27, 1818.
Sarah Curtis, d. John S. and Mary Ann, May 13, 1833. [w. Israel C. Vinal, G.R.7.]
Sarah Curtis [ch. John S. and Mary Ann], bp. Nov. 6, 1842. C.R.3.
Sarah Ellms, d. Thomas and Chloe, May 31, 1828.
Sarah Eveleth [dup. Eveloth], d. Hervy [dup. Henry] F. and Lydia J. [dup. omits J.], Dec. 19, 1845.
Sarah H. [———], w. ——— [Jan. —, 1821]. C.R.3.
Sarah Hall, d. Alvyen and Eliza, Nov. 1, 1843.
Sarah Hall, ch. Alvyen and Eliza, bp. Nov. 3, 1844. C.R.3.
Sarah Jane, d. Lemuel and Sally, May 15, 1825.
Sarah Lincoln, d. Asa Jr. and Sally, July 26, 1814.
Sarah Little, d. Levi and Sally, Apr. 28, 1823.
Sarah Little, ch. Levi, bp. May 7, 1826. C.R.3.
Sedocia, ch. Ezekiel and Molly, bp. Dec. 6, 1767. C.R.1.
Sedoshe, d. Ezekel and Molley, Sept. 19, 1764.
Seth, s. Jacob, Mar. 11, 1719.
Seth, s. Seth, bp. Sept. 10, 1749. C.R.1.
Seth, s. Seth, bp. July 18, 1756. C.R.1.
Seth Hatch, ch. Seth H. and Harriet L., Dec. 27, 1818, in Marshfield.
Simeon, s. Jo[h]n Jr., bp. May 13, 1739. C.R.1.
Simeon, s. Ezra, bp. Dec. 4, 1768. C.R.1.
Simeon, s. Simeon and Sarah, Mar. 4, 1795.
Simeon, ch. Simeon, bp. July 6, 1806. C.R.1.
Sophia, d. Israel 3d and Rebekah, June 30, 1788.
Sophrona, d. Hayward and Beckey, Feb. 4, 1809.
Stephen, s. Stephen (Vinall), bp. Sept. 6, 1709. C.R.1.
Stephen, s. Ignatius, bp. Apr. 2, 1749. C.R.1.
Stephen, s. Issacher and Judeth, Sept. 23, 1760.

VINAL, Stephen, s. Issachar, bp. July 7, 1765. C.R.1.
Stephen, s. Stephen and Charlotte, Nov. 1, 1792.
Stephen [Aug. —, 1810]. C.R.1.
Stephen Bailey, ch. Charles and Elizabeth K., Aug. 20, 1842.
Temperance, d. Stephen Jr., bp. June 5, 1748. C.R.1.
Thankful, d. Asa and Thankful, Sept. 24, 1795.
Thankfull, d. Jo[h]n (s. Jacob), bp. Oct. 20, 1734. C.R.1.
Thomas, s. Ignatius Jr., bp. Aug. 16, 1794. C.R.1.
Thomas, s. Job and Sarah, Nov. 9, 1794.
Thomas, s. Job and Sarah, Mar. 17, 1799.
Thomas H., s. Thomas, —— [1837]. C.R.1.
Thomas Hobert, s. Lemuel and Polly, Nov. 19, 1808. [Thomas Hobart, C.R.1.]
Thomas May, s. Thomas and Chloe, Sept. 25, 1837.
Thomas Whittemore, s. Abel and Julitte, Dec. 8, 1830.
Turner Wade, s. Abel and Julette, July 7, 1820.
Warren, ch. Paul and Maria, bp. July 2, 1826. C.R.3.
Warren Dexter, s. Warren J. and Martha (b. Hingham), July 31, 1848.
Warren James, s. Paul and Maria, Oct. 2, 1817.
Warren Joy, s. Dexter and Eliza L., Dec. 2, 1821.
Whitman Bailey, s. Abel and Julittee, June 3, 1824.
Whitney, s. Jonathan and Drucilla, Jan. 14, 1799.
Whitney, s. Jonathan, bp. Oct. 27, 1802. C.R.1.
William, s. Issachar and Judeth, July 25, 1751,
William, ch. Issacar and Judith, bp. July 11, 1756. C.R.1.
William, s. Capt. Israel Jr., bp. Oct. 5, 1766. C.R.1.
William, s. Capt. Will[ia]m and Lucy, Aug. 26, 1782.
William, s. Gideon and Sarah, Dec. 12, 1822.
William, s. William Jr. and Sally, Apr. 23, 1825.
William Howard, s. Paul and Maria, Jan. 15, 1822.
William Howard, s. Paul and Maria, Sept. 17, 1828.
William Howard, ch. Paul and Maria, bp. May 15, 1831. C.R.3.
William Jenks, s. Lot and Eleanor, Sept. 10, 1826.
William L., s. William and Sally, Apr. 23, 1825. G.R.6.
William Lanord, s. Will[ia]m Jr. and Sally, Dec. 20, 1802.
William R., ch. Abel A. and Joan, Oct. 24, 1843.
Zerviah, d. Seth and Hannah, bp. May 10, 1747. C.R.1.
Zinthia, d. Job and Sarah, Nov. 21, 1791.
—— [——], w. Lemuel, —— [1786]. C.R.1.
—— [——], w. Freeman [Jan. —, 1821]. C.R.3. [Sarah A. M., Dec. 15, 1820, G.R.7.]
—— [——], w. James (s. Tho[ma]s), —— [1823]. C.R.3.
——, d. Abel A. and Merriel, Apr. 9, 1848.
——, d. Nathaniel 2d, shoemaker, and Maria W., Nov. 29, 1849.

VINALL (see Vinal), Abigail Cariell, d. Ezra and Polly, Feb. 17, 1805. [Abigail Carrel Vinal, C.R.1.]
Adeline, d. Ezra and Polly, Aug. 20, 1808. [Vinal, d. Ezry, C.R.1.]
Elijah, s. John, Feb. 19, 1694-5.
Elizabeth, d. John, Nov. 30, 1667.
Elizabeth, d. John, Apr. 26, 1697.
Ezekell, s. John, June 4, 1704.
Gideon, s. Steven [Stephen, C.R.2.], Aug. 17, 1678.
Gideon, s. Stephen Jr., Dec. 29, 1706.
Hannah, d. John, Sept. 30, 1669.
Hannah, d. Steven, July 10, 1671.
Hannah, d. John and Mary, June 11, 1707.
Hannah, d. Stephen Jr. and Mary, Mar. 12, 1711-12.
Ignatious, s. Jacob, Oct. 30, 1717.
Israell, s. Jacob, Sept. 21, 1698.
Jacob, s. John, Sept. 2, 1670.
Jacob, s. John, Dec. 19, 1691.
Jacob, s. Jacob and Mary, Sept. —, 1700.
Job, s. Jacob and Mary, Apr. 6, 1713.
John, s. Steven, Sept. 20, 1667.
John, s. John, Sept. 8, 1699.
John, s. Jacob and Mary, Sept. —, 1705.
John, s. John, Oct. 7, —— [rec. before ch. b. Nov. 30, 1667].
Jonathan, s. Jonathan and Cloea, Dec. 9, 1766. [Vinal, C.R.1.]
Mary, d. Steven, Nov. 29, 1662.
Mary, d. Jacob, Jan. 3, 1696-7.
Mary, d. John, Nov. 13, 1701.
Mary Ann, d. Ezra and Polly, Aug. 2, 1802.
Nicholas, s. Jacob and Mary, Feb. 28, 1703.
Olive Hammon, d. Ezra and Polly, July 8, 1810. [Vinal, C.R.1.]
Samuell, s. Steven, July 4, 1681.
Sarah, d. John and Mary, Apr. 28, 1711. [Vinal, C.R.1.]
Stephen, s. Stephen Jr., Apr. 24, 1705.
Steven, s. Steven, Jan. 1, 1664.
Steven, s. Steven, May 9, 1670.
Steven, s. Steven, Mar. 11, 1674-5.

VINING, Floretta, d. Alexander, trader (b. Abington), and Fanny M. (b. Middleboro), May 21, 1849, in S. Scituate.

WADE (see Waid, Waide, Wead), Abednego, s. Nath[anie]ll and Hannah, Oct. 22, 1750. [Abednigo Waid, s. Nath[anie]l, C.R.1.]
Abednego, s. Stephen and Mercy, June 22, 1783.
Abednego, ch. Mercy, wid., bp. Sept. 11, 1796. C.R.1.

WADE, Abner, s. Joseph and Rachel, bp. Nov. 23, 1746. C.R.2.
Anna, d. Zebulon and w., bp. Aug. 5, 1750. C.R.2.
Anthony, ch. Joseph and Polly, June 20, 1808 [? in Boston]. P.R.27.
Arethusa Mansfield, d. Nath[anie]l and Betsey, May 7, 1823.
Barne, ch. Zebulon and w., bp. July 19 [?], 1749. C.R.2.
Betsey, d. Snell and Charlotte, Mar. 11, 1793.
Betsy, d. Stephen and Mercy, Aug. 11, 1789.
Betsy, ch. Charlotte, wid., bp. July 3, 1796. C.R.1.
Betsy, ch. Mercy, wid., bp. Sept. 11, 1796. C.R.1.
Caleb, s. Joseph, bp. [Apr.] 12, 1752. C.R.2.
Calvin, s. Joseph and Rachel, bp. Aug. 19, 1744. C.R.2.
Caroline, d. Shadrach and Mable [Mabel, P.R.28.], Oct. 14, 1814.
Celia (see Sela).
Charles, ch. Joseph and Polly, Sept. 14, 1817 [? in Boston]. P.R.27.
Charles L[owell], ch. Joseph and Polly, July 25, 1819 [? in Boston]. P.R.27.
Claracy, d. Nath[anie]l Jr. and Deborah, Dec. 8, 1793.
Clarissa Faustina, ch. Henry and Rachel T., July 20, 1835.
Cornelius (see Cornelius Briggs).
David, s. Nath[anie]ll, bp. Sept. 18, 1737. C.R.1.
David, s. Nath[anie]ll and Hannah, July 21, 1738.
David, s. Nath[anie]l Jr. and Deborah, Sept. 12, 1795.
Deborah, d. Nath[anie]ll Jr. and Patience, Sept. 26, 1771. [Waade, C.R.1.]
Deborah, d. Nath[anie]l Jr. and Deborah, Sept. 11, 1787.
Deborah Otis, d. Snell and Charlottee, May 25, 1786.
Deborah Otis, ch. Charlotte, wid., bp. July 3, 1796. C.R.1.
Edward, ch. Joseph and Polly, July 7, 1807 [? in Boston]. P.R.27.
Edward P[reble], ch. Joseph and Polly, Sept. 14, 1809 [? in Boston]. P.R.27.
Elisabeth, d. Isacher and Thankfull, Apr. 21, 1765.
Elizabeth, d. Joseph, Jan. 1, 1708–9.
Elizabeth, ch. Joseph, bp. Aug. 24, 1712. C.R.1.
Elizabeth, [ch.] Joseph and Rachel, bp. Oct. 24, 1736. C.R.2.
Elizabeth, ch. Isachor, bp. Nov. 23, 1766. C.R.1. [w. Nathaniel Ellms, G.R.8.]
Elizabeth, d. Nathaniel and Betsey, Oct. 7, 1817.
Eunice, ch. Simeon and Eunice, Jan. 13, 1754. P.R.27.
Eunice, ch. Simeon and Eunice [w. —— Bryant], Aug. 27, 1761. P.R.27.
Eunice (see Unice).
George, ch. Simeon and Eunice, Oct. 21, 1765. P.R.27.
George W. P., s. Nath[aniel] Jr., marriner, and Lettis C., Sept. 28, 1846.

WADE, Hannah, d. Nicholas, bp. Aug. 3, 1656. C.R.2.
Hannah, d. Isacher and Thankfull, Nov. 27, 1751. [Waid, d. Isachar and Thankfull, C.R.1.]
Hannah, d. Nath[anie]ll Jr. [Nathaneel, C.R.1.] and Patience, Oct. 14, 1766.
Hannah (Wadde), d. Stephen and Mary, Nov. 15, 1791.
Hannah, ch. Mercy, wid., bp. Sept. 11, 1796. C.R.1.
Hannah, d. Jotham and Margaret, Dec. 23, 1798. [w. Thomas T[ilden] Bailey, P.R.11.]
Hannah, ch. Jothom, bp. June 4, 1804. C.R.1.
Hannah, d. Shadrach and Mabel, July 5, 1823.
Henry, s. Nath[anie]ll Jr. and Deborah, Jan. 29, 1799.
Henry Otis, s. Henry and Rachel T., Feb. 24, 1829.
Henry S., ch. Joseph and Polly, Jan. 17, 1804 [? in Boston]. P.R.27.
Issachar, s. Joseph, Dec. 14, 1714. [Issacher, C.R.1.]
Issacher, s. Issacher and Thankfull, Oct. 22, 1758. [Issachar Waid, s. Issachar, C.R.1.]
Jacob, s. Joseph and Ruth, Oct. 9, 1712.
James Hervey, s. Shadrach Jr., Nov. 9, 1839. P.R.28.
James Merritt, s. Shadrach and Mabel, Nov. 5, 1816. [James Merrit, C.R.1.] [James Merritt, P.R.28.]
James Merritt, s. Shadrach and Mabel, Mar. 1, 1819.
Jetson, s. Shadrach and Mabel, Apr. 2, 1826. [Judson, C.R.1.] [Jetson, P.R.28.]
Jetson, s. Shadrach, —— [1829]. C.R.1.
John, s. Issacher and Thankfull, Sept. 10, 1755. [Waid, s. Issachar, C.R.1.]
John Richard, s. Henry and Rachel T., Oct. 18, 1832.
Joseph, s. Joseph, Nov. 24, 1710.
Joseph, ch. Joseph, bp. Aug. 24, 1712. C.R.1.
Joseph, ch. Simeon and Eunice, Oct. 25, 1767. P.R.27.
Joseph, ch. Joseph and Polly, Dec. 9, 1801 [? in Boston]. P.R.27.
Jotham, ch. Simeon and Eunice, Aug. 7, 1758 [*sic* see death]. P.R.27.
Jotham, ch. Simeon and Eunice, Aug. 12, 1759. P.R.27.
Jotham, s. Simeon and Eunice, Apr. 21, 1763. [h. Margaret (Tilden), P.R.27.]
Jotham, ch. Simeon and Unice, bp. Apr. 14, 1765. C.R.1.
Juliettee, d. Nath[anie]ll Jr. and Deborah, Aug. 19, 1791.
Laura, ch. Joseph and Polly, Feb. 22, 1811 [? in Boston]. P.R.27.
Laura, ch. Joseph and Polly, July 24, 1814 [? in Boston]. P.R.27.
Levi, s. Nath[anie]ll and Hannah, Jan. 21, 1732.
Levi, s. Nath[anie]ll, bp. June 24, 1733. C.R.1.

WADE, Lucy, d. Issacher and Thankfull, Aug. 25, 1768. [d. Issachor, bp. July 31 [*sic*], C.R.1.]
Lydia Foster, d. Jotham and Margaret, Apr. 11, 1795. [w. Job Bailey, G.R.2. P.R.27.]
Mabel, d. Stephen and Mercy, Jan. 9, 1787.
Mabel, d. Shadrach and Mabel, Dec. 15, 1828.
Mabil, d. Mercy, wid., bp. Mar. 2, 1796. C.R.1.
Margaret, d. Nicholas, Apr. 7, 1690.
Margaret, d. Jotham and Margaret, Aug. 27, 1802.
Margarett, ch. Jothom, bp. June 4, 1804. C.R.1.
Maria, ch. Joseph and Polly, Dec. 24, 1811 [? in Boston]. P.R.27.
Maria, ch. Joseph and Polly, July 19, 1815 [? in Boston]. P.R.27.
Mary, d. Nicholas, Dec. 3, 1688.
Mary, d. Jotham and Margaret, July 23, 1800. [w. Stephen Litchfield, P.R.27.]
Mary, ch. Jothom, bp. June 4, 1804. C.R.1.
Mary Ellen, d. Henry and Rachel T., June 10, 1840.
Matilda, d. Nath[anie]l Jr. and Deborah, Aug. 8, 1789.
Myra L. [————], w. ————, ———— [1832]. C.R.3.
Nancy, d. Issacher and Thankfull, Feb. 14, 1774.
Nancy, ————, 1776. G.R.8.
Nancy, d. Issachor, bp. Oct. 18, 1778. C.R.1.
Nathanael, s. Nicholas, Oct. 11, 1694.
Nathaniel, s. Nath[anie]l Jr. and Deborah, Sept. 28, 1785.
Nathaniel, s. Nathaniel and Betsey, July 22, 1820.
Nathaniel James Clapp, s. Nathaniel, mariner, and Lilias C., Apr. 17, 1849.
Nath[anie]ll, s. Nath[anie]ll and Hannah, Dec. 29, 1730. [Nathaniel, s. Nathaniel and Hannah, C.R.1.]
Nath[anie]ll, s. Nath[anie]ll Jr. and Patiance, Feb. 9, 1763. [Nathaneel, s. Nathaneel, C.R.1.]
Nicholas, s. Nicholas, bp. July 1, 1660. C.R.2.
Olive, d. Jotham and Margaret, Oct. 14, 1804.
Olive, d. Jotham, bp. July 6, 1806. C.R.1.
Otis, s. Snell and Charlottee, Apr. 22, 1784.
Otis, ch. Charlotte, wid., bp. July 3, 1796. C.R.1.
Patiance Hatch, d. Nath[anie]ll Jr. and Deborah, July 14, 1801.
Patience, d. Nath[anie]ll Jr. [Nathaniel Jr., C.R.1.] and Patience, Feb. 6, 1760.
Polly, ch. Joseph and Polly, Apr. 14, 1800 [? in Boston]. P.R.27.
Polly, ch. Joseph and Polly, May 6, 1806 [? in Boston]. P.R.27.
Rachel, d. Joseph and Rachel, bp. Apr. 9, 1749. C.R.2.
Rachel Turner, d. Henry and Rachel T., Dec. 11, 1830.
Ruth, d. Nicholas, Aug. 3, 1692.

WADE, Ruth, d. Joseph, Nov. 23, 1706.
Ruth, ch. Joseph, bp. Aug. 24, 1712. C.R.1.
Sally, d. Jotham and Margaret, Aug. 23, 1796.
Sally Coal, d. Snell and Charlottee, Mar. 17, 1789.
Sally Cole, ch. Charlotte, wid., bp. July 3, 1796. C.R.1.
Sarah, d. Joseph, May 2, 1719.
Sarah, ch. Jothom, bp. June 4, 1804. C.R.1.
Sela, d. Simeon, bp. Apr. 8, 1770. C.R.1. [Celia, ch. Simeon and Eunice [w. Eleazer Peakes], b. Jan. 2, P.R.27.]
Shadrach, s. Stephen and Mercy, Dec. 17, 1784. [h. Mabel (Merritt), P.R.28.]
Shadrach, ch. Mercy, wid., bp. Sept. 11, 1796. C.R.1.
Shadrach, —— [1805]. C.R.1.
Shadrach, s. Shadrach and Mable [Mabel, P.R.28], Jan. 11, 1813.
Shadrack, s. Nath[anie]ll and Hannah, Mar: 13, 1734.
Simeon [h. Eunice (Studley)], Nov. 7, 1722. P.R.27.
Simeon, ch. Simeon and Eunice, May 25, 1750. P.R.27.
Simeon, ch. Simeon and Eunice, father of Eliza, July 29, 1756. P.R.27.
Simeon, ch. Simeon and Unice, bp. Apr. 14, 1765. C.R.1.
Snell, s. Issacher and Thankfull, Mar. 25, 1762.
Snell, ch. Isachor, bp. Nov. 23, 1766. C.R.1.
Snell, s. Snell and Charlottee, Mar. 24, 1795.
Snell, ch. Charlotte, wid., bp. July 3, 1796. C.R.1.
Stephen, s. Nath[anie]ll and Hannah, Apr. 17, 1755.
Stephen, s. Nath[anie]l, bp. Dec. 12, 1756. C.R.1.
Stephen, s. Shadrach and Mabel, Jan. 18, 1821.
Stephen, s. Shadrach Jr., Sept. 25, 1841. P.R.28.
Thankfull, d. Issacher [Issachar, C.R.1,] and Thankfull, Aug. 8, 1753.
Unice, ch. Simeon and Unice, bp. Apr. 14, 1765. C.R.1.
William, ch. Simeon and Eunice, June 14, 1752. P.R.27.
William Warren, s. Shadrach and Mabel, Jan. 27, 1831.
Zebulan, ch. Simeon and Eunice, June 27, 1775. P.R.27.
Zebulon, s. Joseph, Mar. 3, 1716.
Zebulon, ch. Zebulon and w., bp. July 19 [?], 1749. C.R.2.
Zebulun, s. Joseph, bp. June 23, 1717. C.R.1.
Zebulun, s. Wid. Wade (w. Simeon), bp. Aug. 6, 1775. C.R.1.

WAID (see Wade, Waide, Wead), Charles, s. Joseph Jr., bp. May 4, 1760. C.R.1.
Joseph, s. Joseph Jr., bp. Dec. 4, 1737. C.R.1.
Lucy, d. Joseph Jr., bp. Nov. 14, 1756. C.R.1.
Luther, s. Joseph Jr., bp. Apr. 5, 1741. C.R.1.

WAID, Meshach, s. Nath[anie]ll, bp. July 6, 1740. C.R.1.
Nicolas, s. Nath[anie]l, bp. Feb. 15, 1746. C.R.1.
Peggy, d. Cornelius, bp. Mar. 15, 1747. C.R.1.
Shadrach, s. Nat[hanie]l, bp. June 8, 1735. C.R.1.
Simeon, s. Joseph and Ruth, bp. June 27, 1725. C.R.1.
Zebulon, s. Joseph Jr., bp. Nov. 14, 1756. C.R.1.

WAIDE (see Wade, Waid, Wead), Cornelius, s. Cornelius, bp. Apr. 1, 1750. C.R.1.

WALCOT, Anna M., ch. Dexter and Harriet A., Feb. 24, 1844.

WALKER, Sarah A., d. Asa, tack maker, and Hulda B., Aug. 31, 1846.

WALL, Mary [———], w. ———, —— [1781]. C.R.3.

WANTON, Edward, s. Edward [s. Edward and Elizabeth, C.R.4.], Sept. 13, 1658, in Boston.
Elizabeth, d. Edward [s. Edward and Elizabeth, C.R.4.], Sept. 16, 1668.
George, s. Edward, Aug. 25, 1666. [Georg, s. Edward and Elizabeth, C.R.4.]
Hanah, d. Ed[ward], July 25, 1677. [Hannah, d. Edward and Mary, C.R.4.]
Hannah, d. Michael and Abigal [Abigail, C.R.4.], Jan. 17, 1721.
Joseph, s. Edward [s. Edward and Elizabeth, C.R.4.], May 1, 1664, in Boston.
John, s. Edward [s. Edward and Elizabeth, C.R.4.], Dec. 24, 1672.
Lidy, d. Stephen and Hannah, Oct. 31, 1708 [? in Scituate]. C.R.4.
Lusanna, d. Michael, Nov. 11, 1717. [Luccanna [dup. Lusanna], d. Michael and Abigal, Jan. 17, C.R.4.]
Margret, [twin] d. Edward, Sept. 22, 1674. [Margeat, d. Edward and Elizebeth, C.R.4.]
Mary, d. Stephen and Hannah, May 31, 1707 [? in Scituate]. C.R.4.
Mary, d. Mikell [d. Michael and Mary, C.R.4.], Oct. 4, 1707.
Michael, s. Michael and Abigal [Abigail, C.R.4.], Aug. 14, 1724.
Mikell, s. Edward, Apr. 9, 1679. [Micah, s. Edward and Mary, C.R.2.]
Philip, s. Edward, May 9, 1686. [Phillip, s. Edward and Mary, C.R.4.]
Ruth, d. Mikell [d. Michael and Mary, C.R.4.], Oct. 30, 1705.
Sarah, [twin] d. Edward [d. Edward and Elizebeth, C.R.4.], Sept. 22, 1674.

WANTON, Stephen, s. Michael and Mary, Nov. 18, 1709.
Steven, s Edward, Mar. 5, 1682. [s. Edward and Mary, Mar. 1, C.R.4.]
William, s. Edward [s. Edward and Elizabeth, C.R.4.], Sept. 15, 1670.

WARD, Catherine [———], w. Edward, —— [1820]. G.R.10.
Catherine, d. Daniel, fisherman (b. Ireland), and Charlotte (b. Ireland), May 9, 1836, in Boston.
Catherine, d. Daniel, fisherman (b. Ireland), and Charlotte (b. Ireland), Nov. 4, 1844, in Boston.
Celia [? m.], —— [1802]. G.R.10.
Charlotte [———], w. Daniel, —— [1810], in Ballymena, Co. Antrim, Ire. G.R.10.
Charlotte, d. Daniel, fisherman (b. Ireland), and Charlotte (b. Ireland), Oct. 9, 1845, in Boston.
Daniel, —— [1809], in Colerain, Co. Derry, Ire. G.R.10.
Daniel, s. Daniel, fisherman (b. Ireland), and Charlotte (b. Ireland), Feb. 4, 1843, in Boston.
George, s. Daniel, fisherman (b. Ireland), and Charlotte (b. Ireland), July 1, 1848, in Boston.
John, s. Daniel, fisherman (b. Ireland), and Charlotte (b. Ireland), Nov. 9, 1838 [*sic*, see Mary], in Boston.
Mary, d. Daniel, fisherman (b. Ireland), and Charlotte (b. Ireland), Oct. 4, 1838 [*sic*, see John], in Boston.
Mary, d. Daniel, fisherman (b. Ireland), and Charlotte (b. Ireland), Nov. 8, 1847, in Boston.
William, s. Daniel, fisherman (b. Ireland), and Charlotte (b. Ireland), Jan. 5, 1841, in Boston.

WARDEN, Elizabeth, d. Thomas, Mar. 5, 1692-3.
Francis, s. Thomas, Sept. 22, 1695.
Samuel, s. Thomas, May 28, 1698.
Thomas, s. Thomas, Jan. 11, 1690-1.

WARNER, Hannah [———], w. James W., Aug. 5, 1805. G.R.19.
James W. [h. Hannah], July 1, 1820. G.R.19.

WARREN, Anna, d. John and Naomi, bp. July 28, 1728. C.R.2.
James, s. John and Naomi, Dec. 4, 1714.
James, ch. John and Naomy, bp. Sept. 8, 1717. C.R.2.
James, s. John and Naomy, bp. Aug. 3, 1718. C.R.2.
John, s. John and Aimy, bp. Sept. 11, 1720. C.R.2.
Naomy, ch. John and Naomy, bp. Sept. 8, 1717. C.R.2.
Nathanael, s. John and Naomi of Pembroke, bp. Sept. 30, 1722. C.R.2.

WARTERS (see Waters), Charles I. [?] B. [h. Marry (Bixby)], Nov. 22, 1814, in Thompson, Conn.

WARWICK, Ann, d. Mary "lately Fettindgo," bp. Nov. 17, 1754. C.R.1.

WASON, Robert, s. Thom[a]s and Ann, bp. July 7, 1734. C.R.2.

WATERMAN, Andrew Jenkins, s. Anthony and Lydia, Nov. 19, 1833.
Antho[n]y, s. Antho[n]y and Deborah, Feb. 3, 1763.
Anthony, s. Anthony Jr. and Deborah, Mar. 22, 1792. [Capt. Anthoney [w. Lydia], G.R.6.] [Anthony, P.R.2.]
Anthony, s. Anthony Jr. and Lydia, Jan. 8, 1818.
Asa Delano, s. Asa and w., bp. Sept. 5, 1802. C.R.2.
Betsey, d. Anthony Jr. and Deborah, Aug. 21, 1789. [w. Braddock Cole, P.R.2.]
Charlotte, d. Samuel and Sarah, Sept. 27, 1804. [Charlotte Cushing, d. Sam[ue]ll and w., C.R.2.]
Clarissa, d. Anthony and Deborah, July 13, 1802. [Clanse, P.R.2.]
Clarissa Curtis, d. George and Maria, Jan. 26, 1830.
Deborah, d. Nath[anie]ll and Mercy, Jan. 9, 1768.
Deborah, d. Antho[ny] and Deborah, Apr. 4, 1779.
Deborah Foster, d. Anthoney and Deborah, Nov. 24, 1795.
Ebenezer Copland, ch. James and Huldah, Mar. 1, 1840.
Elizabeth Turner, ch. James and Huldah, July 2, 1833.
Foster, s. Antho[n]y and Deborah, Mar. 13, 1768.
Frances, d. Samuel and Sarah, June 8, 1807. [Francis [*sic*], d. Sam[ue]ll and w., C.R.2.]
Frederick, s. Anthony and Lydia, Feb. 26, 1825.
George, s. Anthony and Deborah, Feb. 12, 1800. [Feb. 20, P.R.2.]
Hannah, d. Nath[anie]ll and w., bp. June 24, 1792. C.R.2.
Helen Otis, d. George and Maria, July 16, 1828.
Henry, s. Anthony and Deborah, Feb. 11, 1797.
James, s. Antho[n]y and Deborah, Apr. 22, 1770.
James, s. Anthony and Deborah, Feb. 19, 1798.
Jotham, s. Anth[on]y and Deborah, Aug. 21, 1774.
Lemuel C., s. Samuel and Sarah, July 14, 1814. [Lem[ue]l Cushing, C.R.2.]
Louisa J. [J., written in pencil], ch. Samuel Jr. and Louisa H., Mar. 27, 1840.
Lydia [————], w. Capt. Anthony [Aug. —, 1794.] G.R.6.
Lydia, d. Anthony Jr. and Lydia, Jan. 27, 1820.
Lydia Copeland, ch. James and Huldah, Feb. 8, 1831.

WATERMAN, Marcy, d. Anthony and Deborah, Dec. 15, 1804.
Maria Ann, d. George and Maria, Aug. 21, 1826.
Mary Elizabeth, d. George and Maria, Sept. 7, 1832.
Mercy, d. Nath[anie]ll and Mercy, Nov. 17, 1770.
Mercy (see Marcy).
Mercy, ch. Anthony and Deborah, Dec. 7, 1807. P.R.2.
Nancy, d. Anthony Jr. and Deborah, Mar. 20, 1788. [ch. Anthoney and w., C.R.1.] [ch. Anthony and Deborah, P.R.2.]
Nath[anie]ll, s. Antho[n]y and Deborah, Jan. 29, 1761.
Nath[anie]ll, s. Nath[anie]ll and Mercy, Dec. 22, 1772.
Olive S. [———], w. Tho[ma]s, ——, 1795. G.R.15.
Otis, s. Anthony Jr. and Deborah, Jan. 17, 1794.
Otis, s. Anthony Jr. and Lydia, Jan. 14, 1822.
Polly, d. Nath[anie]ll [Nathaneel, C.R.1.] and Mercy, Sept. 12, 1778.
Polly, d. Anthony Jr. and Deborah, Apr. 12, 1791.
Polly, d. Anthony and Lydia, Aug. 23, 1829.
Rodolfus C., ch. Lemuel C. and Elizabeth B., Jan. 16, 1840.
Samuel, s. Antho[n]y and Deborah, Aug. 13, 1772.
Samuel, s. Samuel and Sarah, Oct. 31, 1810.
Samuel [dup. Warterman], ch. Samuel Jr. [dup. taner, omits Jr.] and Louisa H., Oct. 29, 1846.
Samuel K., ch. Samuel Jr. and Louisa H., Mar. 5, 1844.
Sarah C., d. Samuel and Sarah, May 25, 1800. [Sarah Cushing, d. Sam[ue]ll and w., C.R.2.]
Silvia, d. Thomas and Olive S., May 16, 1821. [Sylvia B., G.R.15.]
Thomas, s. Antho[n]y and Deborah, Oct. 17, 1765.
Thomas, s. Tho[ma]s and Sarah, Mar. 20, 1791. [[h. Olive S.] G.R.15.]
Thomas Barstow, s. Thomas and Olive S., Jan. 9, 1830. [[h. Clara C.] G.R.15.]

WATERS (see Warters), John W., ch. Charles I. [?] [dup. J.] B. and Mary [dup. adds B.], July 28, 1836 [dup. 1835], in Holden.
Mary E., ch. Charles I. [?] [dup. J.] B. and Mary [dup. adds B.], Nov. 24, 1840, in Middlebourth.

WEAD (see Wade, Waid, Waide), Deborah, d. Thomas, May 10, 1691.
Jacob, s. Thomas, Nov. 13, 1673.
Joseph, s. Thomas, Feb. 2, 1675.
Rachell, d. Thomas, Jan. 29, 1692.
Sarah, d. Thomas, Sept. 22, 1678. [Waide, C.R.2.]

WEATHERAL (see Wetheral, Wetherall, Wetherel, Wetherell, Wethrell, Witheral, Witherall, Witherel, Witherell, Witherle, Witherlee), Hannah, d. Semion (Weth[ere]ll) and Mary, Aug. 22, 178[worn, ? 1788].

WEATHERBEE, ―――― [――――], w. S. B., ―――― [1805]. C.R.1.

WEBB, Barnabas, s. Barnabas and Nanne, June 27, 1784.
Barnabas, s. Barnabas Jr. and Betsey, Oct. 16, 1810.
Barnabus, s. Thomas and Margrett, Aug. 20, 1753.
Benjamin F., s. Marsena and Martha, Feb. 8, 1836.
Catharine Stevens, d. Stephen and Patience H., Jan. 7, 1824.
Charles D., s. Seth and Eliza, Nov. 15, 1840.
Charles Stockbridge, s. Stephen and Patience H., Sept. 26, 1828.
Clarissa Wade, d. Stephen and Patience H., Jan. 12, 1835.
Deborah Silvester, d. Barnabas and Nanne, Nov. 6, 1799.
Deborah Turner, d. Stephen and Patience H., Oct. 12, 1833.
Desire, d. Samuel, bp. May 22, 1757. C.R.1.
Elijah Sylvester, s. Marsena and Martha, Oct. 17, 1829.
Eliza, d. Barnabas and Nanne, Sept. 30, 1797.
Eliza, d. Seth Jr. and Eliza, Mar. 14, 1822.
Eliza D., d. Seth Jr. and Eliza, May 23, 1825.
Eliza Ellen, [twin] d. Marsena and Martha, Dec. ―, 1838.
Ellen Maria, d. Seth and Eliza, Sept. 13, 1834.
George Hughes, s. Seth and Eliza, Mar. 16, 1833. [[h. Maria E. (Vinal)] G.R.6.]
Hannah, d. Marsena and Martha, Dec. 20, 1833.
Henry, s. Seth and Eliza, July 6, 1838. [――, 1839, G.R.6.]
Henry Francis, ch. Barnabus and Sarah, Jan. 12, 1838.
Jesse Dunbar, s. Seth Jr. and Eliza, Mar. 7, 1824.
Jesse Dunbar, s. Seth [Capt. Seth, C.R.1.] and Eliza, June 25, 1831.
John Lawrence, s. Stephen and Patience H., Oct. 12, 1830.
John W. Dunbar, s. Seth and Eliza, ―――― [rec. between ch. b. May 23, 1825, and ch. b. Mar. 29, 1828].
Laura, d. Lemuel C. [dup. omits C.], sailor, and Lucy V., Oct. 11, 1847.
Leander, ch. Lemuel and Lucy V., May 30, 1843.
Lemuel, s. Samuel, bp. Aug. 28, 1763. C.R.1.
Lemuel, s. Samuel [and] Mercy, Oct. 2, 1764.
Lemuel, s. Lemuel and Lear, Sept. 18, 1798.
Lemuel, ch. Lemuel and Lucy V., Feb. 25, 1830.
Louisa, ch. Lemuel and Lucy V., May 23, 1833.
Louiza, d. Marsena and Martha, Sept. 5, 1831.
Lucretia, [twin] ch. Lemuel and Lucy V., Mar. 1, 1839.
Lucy, d. Barnabas and Nanne, Dec. 7, 1792.

WEBB, Lucy, ch. Lemuel and Lucy V., July 29, 1831.
Lucy Ellen, d. Stephen and Patience H., Dec. 31, 1842.
Luther, [twin] ch. Lemuel and Lucy V., Mar. 1, 1839.
Lydia, d. Thomas, bp. Apr. 25, 1756. C.R.1.
Margarette, d. Seth and Eliza, May 10, 1836.
Marsena, s. Barnabas and Nanne [Anna, C.R.3.], Sept. 11, 1789.
Marsena, s. Marsena and Martha, May 30, 1826. [[h. Elvira J. (Perry)] G.R.7.]
Martha Jane, [twin] d. Marsena and Martha, Dec. —, 1838.
Mary, d. T[homas] and Margarett, bp. May 6, 1750. C.R.1.
Mary Baker, d. Seth and Eliza, Apr. 14, 1830.
Mary Thomas, ch. Barnabus and Sarah, July 13, 1840.
Mercy, ch. Wid. Webb, bp. June 11, 1775. C.R.1.
Nancy (Weebb), d. Barnabas and Nanne, Jan. 29, 1782.
Otis, s. Sam[ue]l, bp. June 25, 1761. C.R.1.
Patience Hatch, d. Stephen and Patience H., Jan. 16, 1826.
Paul, s. Thomas, bp. Sept. 24, 1758. C.R.1.
Paul, s. Thomas and Margrett, Sept. 15, 1759.
Paul, s. Barnabas and Nanne, Feb. 27, 1802.
Polly, d. Barnabas and Nanne, Sept. 10, 1786.
Samuel, s. Sam[ue]l, bp. Sept. 22, 1754. C.R.1.
Sarah Dunbar, d. Seth and Eliza, Mar. 29, 1828.
Sarah Elizabeth, ch. Barnabus and Sarah, Jan. 28, 1834.
Seth, s. Samuel and Mercy, bp. Apr. 29, 1753. C.R.1.
Seth Jr., s. Lemuel and Lear, Oct. 15, 1796.
Seth, Capt. [h. Eliza (Dunbar)], ——, 1797. G.R.6.
Seth, s. Seth Jr. and Eliza, Feb. 14, 1823. [[h. Helen (Gibbons)] G.R.6.]
Stephen, s. Barnabas and Nanne, July 4, 1795.
Stephen D., s. Stephen and Patience H., Aug. 4, 1827.
Thomas, s. Thomas, bp. Mar. 24, 1750. C.R.1.
Thomas, s. Barnabas and Nancy [dup. Nanne], Oct. 5, 1779.
Thomas Richmond, s. Marsena and Martha, May 3, 1828.
———, w. Everett Torrey, —— [1808]. C.R.1.
———, s. Barnabus, sailor, and Sarah W., Nov. 29 [? 1845].

WEBSTER, Eliza A., ch. William R. and Eliza, Sept. 30, 1843.

WELCH (see Welsh), Edmond Parker, ch. Michael and Sarah, Nov. 5, 1833.
Sarah Ellen, ch. Michael and Sarah, Feb. 14, 1836.
Susan Augusta, ch. Michael and Sarah, Oct. 30, 1840.

WELSH (see Welch), Mary, w. Patrick Dunn, —— [1833]. G.R.10.

WETHERAL (see Weatheral, Wetherall, Wetherel, Wetherell, Wethrell, Witheral, Witherall, Witherel, Witherell, Witherle, Witherlee), Charles, s. Semion and Mary, May 14, 178[6]. [Whitheral, s. Simeon, C.R.1.]
Eunice, d. Semion and Mary, May 29, 1793.

WETHERALL (see Weatheral, Wetheral, Wetherel, Wetherell, Wethrell, Witheral, Witherall, Witherel, Witherell, Witherle, Witherlee), Polly, d. Semion (Wetherell) and Mary, Dec. 28, 1779.
Sally, d. Semion (Wetherell) and Mary, May 27, 178[4]. [Salla Whitheral, d. Simeon, C.R.1.]

WETHEREL (see Weatheral, Wetheral, Wetherall, Wetherell, Wethrell, Witheral, Witherall, Witherel, Witherell, Witherle, Witherlee), Anne, d. Semion (Wethrell) and Mary, Aug. 22, 1777.

WETHERELL (see Weatheral, Wetheral, Wetherall, Wetherel, Wethrell, Witheral, Witherall, Witherel, Witherell, Witherle, Witherlee), Daniell, s. Samuell, Mar. 20, 1706–7.
Eunice, d. Samuel and Eunice, June 1, 1713.
Hannah, d. Daniell, bp. June 24, 1660. C.R.2.
Hannah, d. Samuell, Apr. 29, 1680. [Hanna, C.R.2.]
Hannah, d. William, May 7, 1705. [Witherel, d. William and Sarah, C.R.2.]
Isabell, d. Samuell, Feb. 20, 1704–5.
Joseph, s. Samuel and Eunice, June 5, 1709.
Joshua, s. Samewell [Samuell, C.R.2.], June 6, 1683.
Mary, d. William, Apr. 12, 1707. [Witherell, C.R.2.]
Mary, d. Samuell, Nov. 29, 1716.
Samuel, s. Samuel, Jan. 10, 1699–1700.
Samuel, s. Samuel and Eunice, Jan. 25, 1710–11.
Samuell, s. Samuell, Oct. 10, 1678. [Witherell, s. Samuel, C.R.2.]
Sarah, d. Will, bp. Sept. 7, 1645. C.R.2.
Sarah, d. Samuell, bp. Dec. 4, 1681. C.R.2.
Sarah, d. William, Apr. 28, 1703. [Witherill, d. Willim (Whitheril), C.R.2.]
Theophilus, s. Samuell, Mar. 31, 1703.
Theop[hi]lus, s. Semion and Mary, Feb. 26, 1782.
Timothy, s. Samuel, Aug. 10, 1715.
William, s. William (Witherell), Mar. 27, 1702.

WETHRELL (see Weatheral, Wetheral, Wetherall, Wetherel, Wetherell, Witheral, Witherall, Witherel, Witherell, Witherle, Witherlee), Lydia, d. Josiah and Lydia, Sept. 13[torn].

WEYBORN (see Wiborne).

WHEATON (see Wheton).

WHEELDEN, Benjamin, s. Henry and Lisabeth, bp. Jan. 9, 1728. C.R.1.
Susanna, d. Henry and Elizb[eth], bp. July 30, 1727. C.R.1.

WHEELWRIGHT, Sarah, d. John and Sarah, Dec. 1, 1747.

WHERITY, Eliza [———], w. Nicholas, Sept. 13, 1831. G.R.10.

WHETCOM (see Whetcomb, Whetcombe, Whitcom, Whitcomb), Nathanaell, twin s. James (Whetcomb), Aug. 19, 1697.

WHETCOMB (see Whetcom, Whetcombe, Whitcom, Whitcomb), Elizabeth, d. Israell and Mary, May —, 1709.
Hannah, d. Israell and Mary, Sept. —, 1706.
Israell, s. Israell and Mary, Mar. 20, 1700-1.
John, s. Israell [Israel, C.R.1.] and Mary, Jan. 18, 1711-12.
Mary, d. Israell and Mary, Mar. 9, 1703.
Noah, s. Israel, bp. Oct. 7, 1716. C.R.1.

WHETCOMBE (see Whetcom, Whetcomb, Whitcom, Whitcomb), Content, d. Robert, Aug. 4, 1695.
Elizabeth, d. Robert (Whetcomb), Feb. 13, 170[4].
James, s. James (Whetcomb), Aug. 31, 1695.
James, twin s. James (Whetcomb), Aug. 21, 1697.
Joanna, twin d. James, Mar. 22, 1699-1700.
Mary, twin d. James, Mar. 22, 1699-1700.
Melea, d. Robert, May 8, 1699.

WHETESTON (see Whetston, Whetstone, Whiston), Bathsheba, d. John, bp. Sept. 18, 1681. C.R.2.
John, s. John, bp. May 1, 1687. C.R.2.

WHETON, Alis, d. Obadiah, Mar. 4, 1683-4.
Lidiah, d. Obadiah, Dec. 22, 1704.

WHETSTON (see Wheteston, Whetstone, Whiston), Joseph, s. John, bp. May 27, 1683. C.R.2.
Mercy, d. John, bp. May 26, 1678. C.R.2.
Susanna, d. John, bp. June 10, 1688. C.R.2.

WHETSTONE (see Wheteston, Whetston, Whiston), Abigall, d. John, bp. May 16, 1680. C.R.2.
Bathsheba, d. John, bp. July 1, 1660. C.R.2.
Increase, s. John, bp. Aug. 10, 1656. C.R.2.

WHETSTONE, Increase, ch. John and w., bp. May 4, 1718. C.R.2.
John, ch. John and w., bp. May 4, 1718. C.R.2.

WHISTON (see Wheteston, Whetson, Whetstone), Increse, s. John, Apr. 9, 1713.
Joseph, s. John, Oct. 26, 1716.

WHITAKER (see Whittaker), George Henry, ch. John L. and Betsey, Aug. 27, 1842.
Jane Elizabeth, ch. John L. and Betsey, Aug. 13, 1840.
John Lawrence, ch. John L. and Betsey, Jan. 26, 1835.
John Lawrence, s. John, shipwright, and Betsey, Apr. 1, 1844.
Warren Streeter, ch. John L. and Betsey, July 11, 1838.

WHITCOM (see Whetcom, Whetcomb, Whetcombe, Whitcomb), Jacob, s. John and Patty, Apr. 12, 1798. [Whitcomb [h. Jane S.], G.R.8.]

WHITCOMB (see Whetcom, Whetcomb, Whetcombe, Whitcom), Betty, d. Jo[h]n and Sarah, Feb. 2, 1737.
Charles, s. John Jr. and Hannah, Jan. 23, 1766.
Charles, s. Jacob and Jane, Sept. 18, 1822.
Charles, s. Jacob and Jane, Oct. 4, 1828.
Charles, ch. Jacob and Jane, bp. May 15, 1831. C.R.3.
Cynthia [———], w. Noah [Aug. —, 1782]. G.R.8.
Esther Willard, d. Jacob and Jane, Sept. 15, 1820.
Esther Willard, ch. Jacob and Jane, bp. May 15, 1831. C.R.3.
George W., s. Jacob and Jane, Feb. 23, 1833.
Hannah, d. Israel, bp. Aug. 7, 1709. C.R.1.
Hannah [? m.], ——— [1779]. G.R.8.
Hannah, d. Noah and Cynthia, Dec. 13, 1810.
Harvey, ——— [1809]. C.R.1.
Hervey, s. Noah and Cynthia, Dec. 3, 1814.
Jane, d. Noah and Cynthia, Mar. 12, 1812.
Jane S. [———], w. Jacob [June —, 1796]. G.R.8.
John, s. Jo[h]n and Sarah, Jan. 4, 1735.
John, s. John Jr. and Hannah, Apr. 24, 1759.
Joseph, ——— [1773]. G.R.8.
Julia T., d. Noah and Cynthia, Feb. 26, 1829.
Martha Ainslie, d. Jacob and Jane, Dec. 22, 1818.
Martha Ainslie, ch. Jacob and Jane, bp. May 15, 1831. C.R.3.
Mary, d. Noah and Mary, Apr. 22, 1744. [Whitcom, C.R.1.]
Mary, d. John and Sarah, Apr. 18, 1752.
Mercy, d. Jacob and Jane, Mar. 1, 1831. [Marcy, C.R.3.]
Noah [Nov. —, 1782]. G.R.8.
Rebecca, ch. Jacob and Jane, bp. May 15, 1831. C.R.3.

WHITCOMB, Rebekah, d. Jacob and Jane, July 7, 1826.
Reuben (see Ruben).
Rosilla Howard, d. Jacob and Jane, Sept. 3, 1824.
Rosilla Howard, ch. Jacob and Jane, bp. May 15, 1831. C.R.3.
Ruben, s. John and Sarah, Dec. 24, 1740.
Samuel, s. John Jr. and Hannah, Dec. 11, 1769.
Sarah, d. Jo[h]n and Sarah, Jan. 28, 1744.
Sarah, d. Noah and Cynthia, Nov. 27, 1822.
Simion, s. John and Sarah, May 5, 1762.
Thankful, d. John and Sarah, June 10, 1746.
Thankful, d. Noah and Mary, June 10, 1746.
Willard, s. Noah and Cynthia, June 21, 1809.
Will[ia]m, s. John Jr. and Hannah, May 10, 1763.
William, s. John Jr., bp. May 20, 1764. C.R.1.
William, s. Noah and Cynthia, Apr. 16, 1821.

WHITE, Abigail, d. Timothy, Oct. 31, 1682.
Abigail, d. Timothy and Rebecah, June 29, 1712.
Abigail, d. Tim[othy] Jr., bp. May 29, 1737. C.R.1.
Alice Maria, d. Timothy and Alice B., Apr. 27, 1828.
Almira, d. Timothy and Tempe, Aug. 8, 1803.
Anna, d. Resolved, June 5, 1649. [June 4, P.C.R.]
Betty, d. Timothy Jr., bp. July 7, 1765. C.R.1.
Catharina, d. Timothy and Tempe, June 28, 1795.
Catharine, d. Tim[oth]y Jr., bp. Mar. 26, 1769. C.R.1.
Catharine, d. Timothy Jr., bp. Jan. 12, 1772. C.R.1.
Catharine, ch. Timothy, bp. Aug. 8, 1802. C.R.1.
Deborah, d. Joseph and Elizabeth of Marshfield, bp. Aug. 23, 1713. C.R.2.
Desier, d. Timo[thy], Jan. 13, 1719.
Edwin, [? twin] ch. Timothy and Alice B., Mar. 22, ——.
Elizabeth, d. Resolved, June 4, 1652.
Elizabeth, d. Timothy, Oct. 9, 1688.
Elizabeth, d. Timothy and Rebecah, July 18, 1710.
Elizabeth, [? twin] ch. Timothy and Alice B., Mar. 22, ——.
George, s. Timothy and Alice B., Apr. 17, 1834.
George Howard, s. Timothy and Alice B., Mar. 3, 1840.
Howard, s. Timothy and Tempe, May 28, 1799. [Dea. Howard [h. Rachel], G.R.6.]
Howard, s. Timothy, bp. Mar. 9, 1802. C.R.1.
Howard, s. Timothy and Alice B., Sept. 29, 1836.
John, s. Resolved, Mar. 11, 1644.
Joseph, s. Joseph, May 1, 1674.
Joseph, s. Timothy Jr., bp. Nov. 11, 1770. C.R.1.

WHITE, Joseph, s. Tim[othy] Jr. dec'd, bp. July 14, 1774. C.R.1.
Joseph, s. Timothy and Tempe, May 15, 1808.
Joseph, s. Timothy and Alice B., Feb. 28, 1826.
Josiah, s. Resolved, Sept. 29, 1654.
Mary, d. Joseph, May 25, 1671.
Mary, d. Joseph, Aug. 7, 1697.
Mary, d. Timothy, Sept. 9, 1714.
Patience, d. Timothy, bp. May 2, 1773. C.R.1.
Rachel [——], "former" w. Dea. Howard [Dec. —, 1792]. G.R.6.
Rebecca, d. Timo[thy], Oct. 29, 1717.
Resolved, s. Resolved, bp. Nov. 14, 1647. C.R.2.
Resolved, s. Resolved, Nov. 12, 1648.
Samuel, s. Resolved, bp. Mar. 15, 1645. C.R.2.
Samuell, s. Resolved, Mar. 13, 1646.
Sarah, d. Timothy, Apr. 26, 1685.
Sarah, d. Timo[thy], —— [rec. after ch. b. Jan. 13, 1719].
Sarah, d. Tim[othy], bp. Oct. 30, 1743. C.R.1.
Sarah, d. Timothy and Tempe, Aug. 15, 1801.
Susanna, d. Resolved, Aug. —, 1656.
Timothy, s. Timothy, Nov. 17, 1679.
Timothy, s. Timothy, Oct. 4, 1708.
Timothy, s. Timothy Jr., bp. May 10, 1741. C.R.1.
Timothy, s. Timothy Jr., bp. June 1, 1766. C.R.1.
Timothy, s. Timothy and w., bp. June 20, 1790. C.R.1.
Timothy, s. Timothy and Tempe, Mar. 28, 1797.
Timothy, ch. Timothy, bp. Aug. 8, 1802. C.R.1.
Timothy, s. Timothy and Alice B., Jan. 28, 1824.
Warren Fay, s. Timothy and Alice B., Mar. 23, 1830.
William, s. Resolved, Apr. 18, 1642.

WHITING, Aurelia, ch. Moody B. and Aurelia (Jenkins), Oct. 28, 1841.
Aurelia, ch. Moody B. and Aurelia, bp. June 4, 1849. C.R.1.
Elizabeth, ch. Benjamin and Lydia, Oct. 19, 1821.
Jared, ch. Benjamin and Lydia, May 26, 1798.
Jared, ch. Benjamin and Lydia, Mar. 31, 1819.
Joanne, ch. Benjamin and Lydia, Mar. 16, 1807.
Joel, ch. Benjamin and Lydia, May 19, 1809.
Lydia, ch. Benjamin and Lydia, Jan. 3, 1803.
Maria, ch. Benjamin and Lydia, Dec. 7, 1804.
Mary, d. W[illia]m of Hanover, bp. Nov. 3, 1805. C.R.2.
Mary, ch. Benjamin and Lydia, Apr. 15, 1812.
Mary, ch. Moody B. and Aurelia, bp. June 4, 1849. C.R.1.

WHITING, Mary A., ch. Moody B. and Aurelia (Jenkins), Apr. 5, 1844.
Oliver T., ch. Moody B. and Aurelia (Jenkins), Aug. 12, 1839.
Pemelia, ch. Benjamin and Lydia, Oct. 27, 1815.
Richard, ch. Benjamin and Lydia, Apr. 19, 1800.

WHITTAKER (see Whitaker), Charles Henry, ch. James (Whitaker) and Hannah W., Mar. 20, 1838.
Willis Franklin, s. John L. and Betsey, Oct. 2, 1847.

WHITTEMORE, Charlotte, d. Joseph and Sarah, June 12, 1795.
Joseph James Lloyd, s. Capt. Isaac and Betsey, Oct. 15, 1811.
Jos[eph] James Lloyd, ch. Cap[t]. Isaac dec'd, bp. Oct. 7, 1821. C.R.2.

WHITTEN, Anna, d. Jacob and Anna, Feb. 12, 1757.

WIBORNE, Elizabeth, d. John, Feb. 3, 1694–5.
John, s. John, Aug. 31, 1698.

WIGHT, Lucy Ellen, ch. Rev. Daniel and Lucy (Flint), July 25, 1843.
Mary Anna P. [dup. Perkins] [———], w. Rev. Daniel [Apr. —, 1816]. C.R.3.

WILCUT, Hannah, d. Philip, bp. July 24, 1720. C.R.1.

WILDER, Alfred, ch. Charles and Mary Ann, June 27, 1836.
Charles Henry, ch. Charles and Mary Ann, Jan. 19, 1834.
Ellen, d. Charles, shoemaker, and Mary A., Nov. 27, 1846.
George A., s. John, farmer, and Lydia (b. Hanover), July 25, 1849, in S. Scituate.
George W., s. Harrison, farmer, and Lucy, Aug. 23, 1846.
Harriet M., d. Laban, cordwainer, and Harriet, July 20, 1845.
Harrison [h. Lucy], July 13, 1813. G.R.14.
Harritt M., d. Laban, shoemaker, and Harriett, July 18, 1847.
Lucy [———], w. Harrison, Dec. 17, 1810. G.R.14.
Mary A. [———], w. Charles [July —, 1811]. G.R.14.
———, ch. Harrison and Lucy, Apr. 21, 1844.

WILLARD, Daniel, s. George, bp. Sept. 14, 1645. C.R.2.
Deborah, d. George, bp. Sept. 14, 1645. C.R.2.
Joshua, s. Geo[rge], bp. Nov. 2, 1645. C.R.2.

WILLIAMSON, Abigail B., ch. Joshua and Abigail, Nov. —, 1834, in Marshfield.
Caroline, ch. Joshua and Abigail, Apr. 29, 1840.
Harriet, ch. Timothy and Polly, May 16, 1825.

WILLIAMSON, James E., ch. Timothy and Polly, Dec. 1, 1809.
Joan, ch. Timothy and Polly, Jan. 8, 1800, in Marshfield.
Joel B., ch. Timothy and Polly, June 16, 1821.
Lewis B., ch. Timothy and Polly, Mar. 6, 1822.
Lucy Hyland, d. James and Lucy, May 15, 1831.
Mary E., ch. Timothy and Polly, Jan. 15, 1814, in Marchfield.
Phineas Nichols, s. James and Lucy, Jan. 12, 1829.
Rebbecca P., ch. Timothy and Polly, Dec. 24, 1807, in Marchfield.
Reuben, ch. Timothy and Polly, Mar. 31, 1798, in Marchfield.
Sally, ch. Timothy and Polly, July 22, 1818, in Marchfield.
Seth, ch. Timothy and Polly, June 17, 1812, in Marchfield.
Simeon, ch. Timothy and Polly, Aug. 8, 1802, in Marchfield.
Timothy, ch. Timothy and Polly, Sept. 17, 1805, in Marchfield.

WILLIS, Sarah A. [? m.], —— [1819]. G.R.15.

WILLS, Lydia, d. Will[iam], Apr. —, 1645.
Lydia, d. Samuel, Nov. 26, 1676.
Samuell, s. Will, May —, 1640.

WILLSON (see Wilson), Abigal, d. Will[ia]m and Hannah, May 27, 1748.
Hannah, d. Will[ia]m and Hannah, Mar. 24, 1744.
William, s. Will[ia]m and Hannah, June 7, 1742. [Wilson, C.R.2.]

WILSON (see Willson), Abigail, d. W[illia]m and Mary, bp. June 21, 1747. C.R.2.

WING, John, s. Ebenezer and Betsey, Nov. 1, 1779.
Mary, d. Bachelor, Oct. 16, 1704.

WINSLOE (see Winslow), Elizabeth, d. Maj. Winsloe, bp. Oct. 2, 1664. C.R.2.
Thomas, s. Kenelm, bp. Mar. 3, 1672. C.R.2.

WINSLOW (see Winsloe), Adaline, ch. Harvey and Clarissa, May 19, 1842.
Adeline Francis, d. William and Sarah, Oct. —, 1823.
Albert, [twin] ch. Harvey and Clarissa, Nov. 11, 1840.
Alfred, [twin] ch. Harvey and Clarissa, Nov. 11, 1840.
Anna, d. Nath[aniel] and Sarah, May 21, 1776.
Charlotte Ann, d. William and Sarah, July —, 1826.
Charlotte Curtis, d. Nath[anie]ll and w., bp. Nov. 1, 1801. C.R.2.
Clarissa C., d. Nath[anie]ll and Clarissa, June 15, 1802.
Clarrissa, ch. Harvey and Clarissa, Apr. 25, 1829, in Hingham.
Elizabeth, d. Dr. Isaac and Elizabeth, Nov. 14, 1769.
Elizabeth R., ch. Harvey and Clarissa, Aug. 8, 1824, in Hingham.

WINSLOW, Ellen C., d. William and Sarah, Mar. 19, 1830.
Faith, d. Nathaniel, bp. Sept. 3, 1665. C.R.2.
Harriot, [twin] d. Nath[anie]ll and Clarissa, Feb. 9, 1804.
Harvey [h. Clarissa (Humphrey)], July 4, 1800, in Marshfield [Marshfield, written in pencil].
Harvey, ch. Harvey and Clarissa, Feb. 22, 1822, in Hingham.
Henry T., s. Harvey Jr., laborer, and Rhoda V., June 7, 1846.
Joseph, s. Oliver, bp. Oct. 28, 1753. C.R.2.
Josiah, s. Kenelm of Yarmouth, bp. July 31, 1670. C.R.2.
Josiah, s. Nath[anie]ll and Sarah, Apr. 12, 1774.
Josiah, [twin] s. Nath[anie]ll and Clarissa, Feb. 9, 1804.
Judith, d. Nath[anie]l and Sarah, Sept. 18, 1780.
Kenelm, s. Kenelm of Yarmouth, bp. Aug. 9, 1668. C.R.2.
Levi, s. Louisa, Mar. 27, 1847.
Louisa, ch. Harvey and Clarissa, Nov. 26, 1826, in Hingham.
Lucy, d. Nath[anie]ll Jr. and w., bp. Nov. 12, 1797. C.R.2.
Lydia, d. Nath[anie]l and Sarah, Oct. 15, 1786.
Mary, d. Samuell, bp. Mar. 30, 1679. C.R.2.
Mary, d. Nath[anie]ll [Nath[anie]ll Jr., C.R.2.] and Clarissa, Feb. 22, 179[9].
Mary L., d. Louisa, Dec. 13, 1844.
Matilda Esther, d. Hervey, farmer, and Rhoda I. [? J.], Mar. 28, 1848.
Nathaniel, s. Nathaniel of Marishfield, bp. July 31, 1670. C.R.2.
Nath[anie]l W., s. William and Sarah, Mar. 10, 1840.
Nath[anie]ll, s. Nath[anie]ll and Sarah, Aug. 3, 1767.
Oliver, s. Oliver, bp. Sept. —, 1757. C.R.2.
Oliver, —— [1788]. G.R.15.
Rhoda V., d. Henry Jr., laborer, and Rhoda, Dec. 23, 1844..
Richard, s. Samuell, bp. Mar. 30, 1679. C.R.2.
Richard S., ch. Harvey and Clarissa, July 9, 1831, in Hingham.
Richard W., Apr. 30, 1824, in Marchfield [Marchfield, written in pencil].
Rufus, ch. Harvey and Clarissa, Jan. 6, 1836.
Ruth, d. Oliver and Agatha, July 11, 1739.
Ruth, d. Nath[anie]ll and Clarissa, July 13, 179[7].
Sarah, d. Nath[anie]ll and Sarah, Aug. 29, 1769.
Sarah, d. Nath[anie]ll and Clarissa, Oct. 22, 180[worn].
Sarah Waterman, d. William and Sarah, Aug. 26, 1820.
Thirza, w. Dennis Curtis Jr., Mar. 4, 1807, in Marshfield.
Walter Hatch, s. Nath[anie]ll and Sarah, July 17, 1772.
William, s. Nath[anie]l and Sarah, Jan. 28, 1788.
William, s. William and Sarah, Sept. 28, 1834.
——, ch. Clarissa, Sept. 19, 1840.

WINSOR, Emor Jenks, ch. Amasa and Angeline, Aug. 15, 1830.
Fanny, ———— [1782]. C.R.1.
Jacob Barstow, ch. Amasa and Angeline, Apr. 15, 1833.
Sarah Almira, ch. Amasa and Angeline, Sept. 15, 1843.
Silas Smith, ch. Amasa and Angeline, Sept. 28, 1828, in Wellfleet.

WINTER, John, s. John, bp. Apr. 1, 1638. C.R.1.

WISE, Abby S., d. John W., shoemaker, and Lear A., Aug. 11, 1845.
Abigail, d. William and Sally, May 27, 1818.
Adeline, d. William and Sally, Oct. 31, 1824.
Elen A., ch. William Jr. and w., Apr. 2, 1844.
Elizabeth, d. William and Sally, June 29, 1817.
George Henry, s. William and Sally, June 24, 1828.
John William, s. William and Sally, July 30, 1823.
Sally [————], w. William [Oct. —, 1791]. G.R.14.
William [h. Sally], ———— [1782]. G.R.14.
————, d. John W., cordwainer, and Leah A., Jan. 1, 1847.

WISWELL, Deborah R., w. John Sampson, ————, 1798. G.R.14.

WITHERAL (see Weatheral, Wetheral, Wetherall, Wetherel, Wetherell, Wethrell, Witherall, Witherel, Witherell, Witherle, Witherlee), Mercy, d. Simion and Mary, Nov. 2, 179[1].

WITHERALL (see Weatheral, Wetheral, Wetherall, Wetherel, Wetherell, Wethrell, Witheral, Witherel, Witherell, Witherle, Witherlee), Anson, s. Simeon and Mary, Mar. 6, 1802. [Witherell [h. Joan M.], G.R.6.]

WITHEREL (see Weatheral, Wetheral, Wetherall, Wetherel, Wetherell, Wethrell, Witheral, Witherall, Witherell, Witherle, Witherlee), Hannah, d. Samuel, July 19, 1720.

WITHERELL (see Weatheral, Wetheral, Wetherall, Wetherel, Wetherell, Wethrell, Witheral, Witherall, Witherel, Witherle, Witherlee), Anson Decatur, s. Anson and Joanne M., Nov. 13, 1829.
Charles Anson, s. Theophilus and Deborah, Dec. 27, 1819.
Clarissa, d. Simeon and Mary, Feb. 25, 1796.
Deborah, d. Theophilus and Deborah, Jan. 2, 1823.
Elizabeth, d. Theophilus and Deborah, Oct. 15, 1821.
George Otis, s. Anson and Joanne M., Aug. 15, 1831.
George Otis, s. Anson and Joanne M., July 6, 1833.
Hannah, d. William, Feb. 20, 1646. [Hanna Wetherell, C.R.2.]
Hannah, d. Simeon, bp. Feb. 19, 1794. C.R.1.
Joan M. [————], w. Anson, Sept. 20, 1806. G.R.6.

WITHERELL, Joanna, d. Anson and Joanna M., ——— [rec. after ch. b. Jan. 14, 1837].
John, s. John, bp. Oct. 3 [worn], 1676. C.R.2.
Joshua Jenkins, ch. Anson and Joanna M., Jan. 14, 1837.
Mary Ann, d. Theophilus and Deborah, Sept. 12, 1818.
Mary Lincoln, d. Charles and Polly, Aug. 17, 1809.
Mary P., d. Anson, shipwright, and Joan M., Mar. 31, 1845.
Sally, d. Theophilus and Deborah, Nov. 26, 1824.
Sarah, d. Will[iam], Feb. 10, 1644.
Sarah, w. Jesse Dunbar, ———, 1760. G.R.6.

WITHERLE (see Weatheral, Wetheral, Wetherall, Wetherel, Wetherell, Wethrell, Witheral, Witherall, Witherel, Witherell, Witherlee), Judife, d. Theophilus (Witherlee), July 28, 1689.
Lydia, d. Theophelus, Mar. 14, 1683. [Lidia Wetherell, d. Theophilus, C.R.2.]

WITHERLEE (see Weatheral, Wetheral, Wetherall, Wetherel, Wetherell, Wethrell, Witheral, Witherall, Witherel, Witherell, Witherle), Elizabeth, d. Theopelus, Aug. 22, 1679. [Wetherel, d. Theophelus, C.R.2.]
John, s. John, July 25, 1675.
Joshuah, s. John, July 5, 1683. [Joshua Wetherell, C.R.2.]
Mary, d. Theophelus, Jan. 12, 1677. [Wetherel, C.R.2.]
Mary, d. Theophelus, Mar. 23, 1681. [Wetherell, C.R.2.]
Ruth, d. Theophelus, June 19, 1687.
Thomas, s. John, Mar. 3, 1681. [Wetherell, C.R.2.]
William, s. John, May 25, 1678. [Witherell, C.R.2.]

WITHINGTON, Mary, d. Henry and Mary of Kingston, bp. Sept. 13, 1730. C.R.2.

WOODARD (see Woodart, Woodward, Woodwart, Woodword, Woodworth, Woothworth), Amy, d. Joseph, bp. Aug. 18, 1751. C.R.1.
Benjamin, s. Robert, May 31, 1690.
Benjamin, s. Benjamin and Mary, Dec. 18, 1713.
Benjamin, s. James and Mary, Oct. 7, 1758.
Bethia, d. Robert, Dec. 5, 1685. [Bethiah Woodward, C.R.2.]
Bethiah, d. James and Sarah, Jan. 23, 1737. [Woodart, C.R.2.]
Deborah, d. Robert, May 11, 1701.
Elisha, s. James and Mary, Sept. 27, 1756.
Elizabeth, d. Robert, Aug. 23, 1692.
George, s. John, farmer, and Sarah, May 7 [? 1845].
James, s. Robert, Jan. 25, 1687-8. [Woodward, C.R.2.]
James, s. Robert, Aug. 9, 1709.

WOODARD, James, s. James and Sarah, Sept. 17, 1732.
James, s. James and Mary, Aug. 12, 1754.
Joanna, d. Robert, Feb. 20, 1694-5.
Joseph, s. James and Sarah, June 6, 1744.
Lydia, d. Robert, Sept. 3, 1706.
Lydia, d. James and Sarah, Aug. 31, 1734. [Woodart, C.R.2.]
Mary, d. Robert, Apr. 27, 1699. [Woodward, C.R.2.]
Mary, d. James and Sarah, May 14, 1742. [Woodart, C.R.2.]
Robert, s. Robert, Apr. 15, 1697.
Ruth, d. Benja[min], bp. Sept. 15, 1754. C.R.1.
Sam[ue]ll, s. James and Mary, Oct. 9, 1750.
Sarah, d. James and Sarah, Mar. 27, 1736. [Woodart, C.R.2.]
Sarah, d. James and Sarah, Apr. 14, 1740. [Woodart, C.R.2.]
Sarah, d. Joseph, bp. May 21, 1749. C.R.1.
Will[ia]m, s. James and Mary, July 12, 1752.

WOODART (see Woodard, Woodward, Woodwart, Woodword, Woodworth, Woothworth), Bethiah, d. Eben[ezer] and Bethiah, bp. July 19, 1730. C.R.2.
Betty, d. James, bp. July 23, 1749. C.R.2.
Deborah, d. Benjamin and Deborah of Leister, bp. Sept. 17, 1738. C.R.2.
Hannah, d. Robert Jr., bp. May 26, 1722. C.R.2.
Jesse, s. Benjamin and Mary, bp. Aug. 3, 1729. C.R.2.
John, s. James and Sarah, bp. June 28, 1747. C.R.2.
Joseph, s. James and Mary, bp. Oct. 28, 1744. C.R.2.
Mary, ch. Benj[a]m[in] and Mary, bp. Sept. 24, 1721. C.R.2.
Right, ch. Benj[a]m[in] and Mary, bp. Sept. 24, 1721. C.R.2.
Simeon, s. Benj[a]m[in] and Mary, bp. May 17, 1724. C.R.2.
Wright (see Right).

WOODFALL, Catherine G. [———], w. Ja[me]s [Oct. —, 1828]. C.R.3.
W[illia]m, s. Tho[ma]s, ——— [1827]. C.R.3. [William T., July 28, 1826, in N. Y. City, G.R.7.]

WOODMAN, Barnabas James, s. Barnabas and Ann, Feb. 7, 1828.
Barnabas Man, s. James and Leah, Apr. 10, 1803, in Freeport.
Barnabas Mann, ch. Lear, wid., bp. June 30, 1805. C.R.1.
James, s. James and Leah, Feb. 22, 1805.
Lucy, d. Barnabas and Ann, Aug. 11, 1833.
Mary, d. James and Leah, Aug. 17, 1801, in Freeport.
Mary, ch. Lear, wid., bp. June 30, 1805. C.R.1.
Mary Ann, d. Barnabas and Ann, Dec. 20, 1828.
Rebekah Allen, d. Barnabas and Ann, Jan. 5, 1831.

WOODWARD (see Woodard, Woodart, Woodwart, Woodword, Woodworth, Woothworth), Aaron (see Aren).
Ann, d. Robert (Woodarrd), May 4, 1704.
Ann Sanders, d. John and Mary, Apr. 9, 1795.
Aren, ch. Robert, bp. Sept. 10, 1704. C.R.2.
Benjamin, ch. Robert, bp. ——, 1695 or 96. C.R.2.
Benjamin, ch. Benj[a]m[in] and Mary, bp. June 3, 1716. C.R.2.
Deborah, ch. Benjamin and Deborah, bp. July 16, 1682. C.R.2.
Deborah, ch. Robert, bp. Sept. 10, 1704. C.R.2.
Desire Turner, d. John and Mary, Oct. 18, 1803.
Elizabeth, ch. Benjamin and Deborah, bp. July 16, 1682. C.R.2.
Elizabeth, ch. Robert, bp. ——, 1695 or 96. C.R.2.
Elizabeth Pedley, d. John and Mary, Nov. 13, 1799.
Hannah Church, d. John and Mary, July 25, 1801.
Joanna, ch. Robert, bp. ——, 1696. C.R.2.
John, s. Benj[a]m[in] and Mary, bp. Feb. 23, 1717–18. C.R.2.
John, s. John and Mary, bp. Nov. 29, 1719. C.R.2.
John Pedley, s. John and Mary, Feb. 28, 1797.
Lydia, d. Robert and Bethia, bp. Sept. 12, 1708. C.R.2.
Mary [dup. Polly], d. John and Mary, Mar. 25, 1786.
Mary Allen, d. Mary, Dec. 28, 1812.
Nancy, d. John and Mary, Apr. 9, 1795.
Polly (see Mary).
Thomas, ch. Benj[a]m[in] and Mary, bp. June 3, 1716. C.R.2.

WOODWART (see Woodard, Woodart, Woodward, Woodword, Woodworth, Woothworth), Abel, s. Benjamin and Mary, bp. Apr. 2, 1727. C.R.2.

WOODWORD (see Woodard, Woodart, Woodward, Woodwart, Woodworth, Woothworth), Elizabeth M., ch. John and Sarah, June 17, 1836.
Margaret, ch. Eb[e]n[eze]r (Woodard), bp. Sept. 26, 1725. C.R.1.
Mary L., ch. John and Sarah, July 19, 1841.
Sarah J. [dup. Sarah Jane Woodward], ch. John and Sarah, Oct. 7, 1838.

WOODWORTH (see Woodard, Woodart, Woodward, Woodwart, Woodword, Woothworth), Abigail, d. Joseph, Apr. —, 1685.
[A]ma, d. Joseph and Sarah, June 17, 1751.
Ann, d. Ebenezar and Joanna, bp. Apr. 2, 1727. C.R.2.
Anna, d. Benja[min] and Anna, Apr. 7, 1723. [Anne, C.R.1.]
Anna, d. Benjamin, bp. Oct. 23, 1743. C.R.1.
Anna, d. Benjamin and Abigail, Oct. 29, 1781.

WOODWORTH, Benjamin, s. Benjamin and Ann, Feb. 20, 1717.
Benjamin, s. Benja[min], bp. June 17, 1750. C.R.1.
Benjamin, s. Benjamin and Abigail, Dec. 29, 1782.
Benjamun, s. Joseph, Aug. —, 1676.
Cattern, d. Thomas, Oct. 5, 1673.
Deborah, d. Thomas, Jan. 2, 1667.
Ebenezer, s. Thomas and Deborah, Aug. 10, 1690.
Ebenezer, s. Marth Woodwarth "Alies martha Right," Apr. 19, 1700.
Ebinessar, s. Thomas, May 25, 1676.
Elenor, d. Ebenezer and Mary, Jan. 24, 1712–13.
Elineor, ch. Ebenezer, bp. Sept. 9, 1722. C.R.1.
Elizabeth, d. Joseph, Aug. —, 1680.
Esakiah, s. Thomas, Feb. 5, 1670.
Eunice, d. Joseph, Jan. —, 1682-3.
Hannah, d. Thomas and Deborah, Sept. 7, 1685.
Hannah, d. Ebenez[e]r and Mary, May 7, 1725. [Woodword, ch. Eb[e]n[eze]r (Woodard), C.R.1.]
Hannah, d. Benja[min], bp. June 28, 1747. C.R.1.
[H]annah, d. Joseph and Sarah, Sept. 6, 1757.
Hezekiah (see Esakiah).
James, s. Robert (Wodworth), bp. Oct. 2, 1709. C.R.2.
[J]ames, s. Joseph and Sarah, June 17, 1754.
James, s. Joseph, bp. Oct. 17, 1756. C.R.1.
Jerusha, d. Thomas and Deborah, Dec. 1, 1688.
John, s. Thomas and Deborah, Aug. 31, 1683.
John, s. Jo[h]n and Mary, Sept. 7, 1720.
Joseph, s. Benja[min] and Anna, July 20, 1720.
[Jo]seph, s. Joseph and Sarah, June 14, 1746.
Margret, d. Joseph, July 19, 1673.
Margret, d. Eben[eze]r and Mary, May 14, 1723.
Mary, d. Walter, Mar. 10, 1650–1.
Mary, d. Thomas, July 8, 1678.
Mary, ch. Ebenezer, bp. Sept. 9, 1722. C.R.1.
Mehetable, d. Walter, Aug. 15, 1662.
Nabby, d. Benja[min] and Abigail, Jan. 30, 1780. [Nabbe, C.R.1.]
Ruth, d. Joseph, May —, 1687.
Samuel, s. Benja[min] and Abigail, Jan. 13, 1784.
Samuel, s. Benja[min], bp. July 16, 1786. C.R.1.
Sarah, d. Joseph, Aug. —, 1678.
[S]arah, d. Joseph and Sarah, May 12, 1749.

WOOLSON, Jonah, s. —— and w. "Sometime" of Watertown, bp. July 3, 1715. C.R.2.

WOOTHWORTH (see Woodard, Woodart, Woodward, Woodwart, Woodword, Woodworth), Joseph, s. Joseph, Mar. 19, 1670–1.

WORMWOOL, Elizabeth, "adopted" ch. Johanna Turner of Marshfield, bp. May 5, 1728. C.R.2.

WORTHELIKE, Alce, [twin] d. Petter, Aug. 18, 1676.
Hanah, [twin] d. Petter, Aug. 18, 1676.
Mary, d. Peter, Sept. 10, 1678.
Sarah, d. Petter, Apr. 26, 1682.

WRIGHT (see Right, Wrighte, Write), David, s. Edward, bp. July 3, 1670. C.R.2.
Deborah R. [———], w. Jonathan, ——— [1781]. G.R.2.
Edward, s. Edward, bp. Nov. 19, 1671. C.R.2.
Eleanor Northey, d. James and Lucy, Jan. 4, 1793.
Elisha Bass, s. Thomas and Mercy T., Nov. 15, 1835.
George, s. Thomas and Mercy T., Aug. 19, 1832.
Grace, d. Edward, bp. June 20, 1669. C.R.2.
Hannah, d. Edward, bp. Aug. 4, 1667. C.R.2.
Hannah, d. Thomas and Mercy T., Aug. 26, 1824.
James, s. Jesse and w., bp. Oct. 7, 1792. C.R.2.
James, s. Thomas and Mercy T., Apr. 12, 1829.
James W., ch. James and Charlotte, Oct. 18, 1843.
Jonathan [Mar. —, 1766]. C.R.1. [[h. Deborah R.] G.R.2.]
Joseph, d. Edward, bp. June 29, 1673. C.R.2.
Lucenda Bass, d. Thomas and Mercy T., Mar. 13, 1822.
Lucy, d. James and Lucy, Sept. 23, 1794.
Margaret, d. Edward, bp. June 11, 1665. C.R.2.
Mary Woodward, d. James and Lucy, Apr. 17, 1799.
Mercy, d. Edw[ar]d, bp. June 10, 1666. C.R.2.
Mercy Tolman, d. Thomas and Mercy, July 24, 1819.
Salley, d. James and Lucy, Aug. 9, 1797.
Thomas, s. John, Sept. 20, 1709.
Thomas, s. Thomas and Mercy T., Apr. 24, 1826.
Thomas B., ch. James and Charlotte, June 25, 1845.
Thomas B., s. James and Charlotte, May 25, 1846.

WRIGHTE (see Right, Wright, Write), James [dup. Right], s. John (Write) and Mary, Aug. 10, 1769.
Mary [dup. Right], d. John and Mary, July 8, 1785 [dup. 1786].

WRITE (see Right, Wright, Wrighte), John [dup. Right], s. John and Mary, Oct. 20, 1772.

YOUNG (see Younge), Abigail Bates, d. Reuben and Abigail, May 1, 1791.
Almira Little, d. Ephraim L. and Rebecca L., Sept. 21, 1821. [Elmira, C.R.3.]
Alvira C., d. Ephraim Jr. [Aug. —, 1849]. C.R.1. [Elvira, Apr. 2, G.R.6.]
Andrew, s. Ezekiel Jr. and Elizabeth, May 25, 1802.
Andrew P., s. Joseph C. and Lydia, Aug. 11, 1827.
Andrew Power, ch. Ezekiel and Elizabeth, bp. Sept. 3, 1815. C.R.1.
Angalina, d. Stephen Fullerton and Lucy, Oct. 16, 1806.
Anna Morton, d. Joseph and Disire, Dec. 4, 1793.
Benja[min], s. Joseph and Desire, July 21, 1787 [*sic*, see Joseph].
Betsey, d. Joshua and Celia, Jan. 3, 1780.
Caleb Bates, s. Reuben and Abigail, Apr. 2, 1793.
Carlos Loring, ch. W[illia]m and Dolly, bp. Nov. 5, 1847. C.R.3.
Celia, d. Joshua and Celia, July 14, 1777.
Celie, d. Ephraim L. and Rebecca L., Aug. 28, 1813.
Charles, [twin] s. Gideon W. and Nancy, Mar. 31, 1831.
Christofer, s. Ezekel and Lusanna, Mar. 3, 1764. [Christopher, s. Ezekiel, C.R.1.]
Clarissa Gardner, d. Ezekiel and Elizabeth, July 18, 1809.
Clarissa Gardner, ch. Ezekiel and Elizabeth, bp. Sept. 3, 1815. C.R.1.
Cynthia (see Zinthia).
Deborah, d. Joseph and Desire, Apr. 7, 1789.
Deborah, d. Joshua and Celia, July 21, 1789. [This entry crossed out.]
Desire, d. Joseph, bp. —— 1, 1796. C.R.1.
Dolly [——], w. W[illia]m [Nov. —, 1803]. C.R.3.
Ebenezer, s. Thomas, Apr. 1, 1703.
Ebenezer Scott, s. Ezekel [Ezekiel, C.R.1.] and Lucanna, July 26, 1772.
Edmond [Edward, written above in pencil], [twin] ch. Erastus A. and Mary, May 19, 1834.
Edmund, s. James K., shoemaker, and Mary, Jan. 23, 1846.
Edward (see Edmond).
Edward Irving, s. Ephraim L. and Rebecca L., July 4, 1832.
Edwin, s. Gideon W. and Nancy, Aug. 4, 1819, in Charlestown.
Edwin, [twin] ch. Erastus A. and Mary, May 19, 1834.
Elcia Baker, d. Joshua and Celia, Dec. 23, 1772.
Elesebath Cudworth, d. Joshua and Celia, May 31, 1775.
Elisha, s. Elisha and w., bp. June 3, 1792. C.R.2.
Eliza, d. Gideon W. and Nancy, Sept. 15, 1828.
Elizabeth, d. George, Nov. 17, 1671.
Elizabeth (see Elesebath Cudworth Young).

SCITUATE BIRTHS 421

YOUNG, Elizabeth, d. Gedion and Elizabeth, Sept. 26, 1798.
Elizabeth, ch. Gideon, bp. Oct. 12, 1800. C.R.1.
Elvira (see Alvira C.).
Emely, d. Joshua and Celia, Feb. 23, 1795.
Ephraim, s. Joshua and Celia, Sept. 4, 1787.
Ephraim, s. Ephraim L. and Rebecca L., Jan. 2, 1824. [[h. Mary A. (Clements)] G.R.6.]
Erastus Henry, ch. Erastus A. and Mary, Oct. 1, 1826, in Boston.
Erastus Uddear, s. Stephen Fullerton and Lucy, Aug. 17, 1796.
Ezekiel, s. Joseph (Younge) and Lydia, June 22, 1731. [Ezekel, C.R.1.] [Ezekiel, C.R.2.]
Ezekiel, s. Joseph and Desire, Apr. 19, 1779.
Ezekiel James, s. Ezekiel and Elizabeth, Dec. 5, 1810.
Ezekiel James, ch. Ezekiel and Elizabeth, bp. Sept. 3, 1815. C.R.1.
Fidelia, w. Robert F. Foster, May 20, 1831. G.R.6.
Frederick, s. Gideon W. and Nancy, Jan. 22, 1833.
Gedion White, s. Gedion and Elizabeth, May 25, 1796.
George, s. Thomas, Nov. 30, 1689.
George Little, s. Gideon W. and Nancy, June 26, 1822.
George Martin, s. Ephraim L. and Rebecca L., Feb. 10, 1828.
Georgiana Winsor, ch. Erastus A. and Mary, Oct. 17, 1831.
Gideon, s. Ezekiel, bp. Sept. 12, 1763. C.R.1.
Gideon W., s. Gideon W. and Nancy, Mar. 7, 1836.
Gideon White (see Gedion White Young).
Gidion, s. Ezekel and Lusanna, Mar. 9, 1761.
Gidion White, ch. Gideon, bp. Oct. 12, 1800. C.R.1.
Hannah, d. Joshua, bp. Sept. 23, 1733. C.R.1.
Henry, [twin] s. Gideon W. and Nancy, Mar. 31, 1831.
Isaac, s. Thomas, Sept. 20, 1706.
Isaac, s. Joseph and Anña of Truro, bp. Aug. 7, 1720. C.R.2.
James, s. Reuben and Abigail, May 10, 1786.
James Otis, s. Gideon W. and Nancy, Apr. 14, 1826.
Jane Bates, d. Reuben and Abigail, Oct. 14, 1788.
Janes [sic] W., s. James H., shoemaker, and Mary, Dec. 23, 1847.
Jeny, d. George and Mary, Mar. 15, 1742.
Joanna White, d. Ezekel [Ezekiel, C.R.1.] and Lucanna, Jan. 23, 1776.
Joannah, d. Elisha and w., bp. Sept. 14, 1794. C.R.2.
Job, s. George and Mary, Mar. 25, 1731.
John Henry, s. Ephraim L. and Rebecca L., Jan. 25, 1826. [[dup. Dea. John H.] [h. Susan Maria] C.R.3.]
Joseph, s. Thomas, Oct. 3, 1692.
Joseph, s. Thomas, Oct. 10, 1701.
Joseph, s. Joseph and Anna of Truroe, bp. Aug. 4, 1723. C.R.2.

YOUNG, Joseph, s. Ezekiel and Lussanna, Dec. 20, 1755.
Joseph, s. Joseph and Desire, Nov. 30, 1786 [*sic*, see Benja[min]].
Joseph Chester, s. Ezekiel Jr. and Elizabeth, July 18, 1804.
Joseph Chester, ch. Ezekiel and Elizabeth, bp. Sept. 3, 1815. C.R.1.
Joshua, s. Thomas, Sept. 27, 1704.
Joshua, s. Joshua and Celia, June 25, 1782.
Larae [Laura], d. Gedion and Elizabeth, July 18, 1802. [Laura, d. Gideon, C.R.1.]
Lillis, d. George and Mary, Nov. 5, 1736.
Lillis, d. George, bp. Dec. 23, 1737. C.R.1.
Louiza Emeline, d. Eph[rai]m L. and Rebecca L., June 13, 1830.
Lucy, d. George and Mary, Mar. 31, 1740.
Lucy Hatch, d. Stephen Fullerton and Lucy, June 23, 1799.
Lusanna, d. George, bp. Dec. 23, 1737. C.R.1.
Lusanna White, d. Joseph and Desire, Aug. 19, 1791. [Lusannah White, C.R.1.]
Lusannah, d. George and Mary, Dec. 22, 1734.
Lydia, d. Ezekiel and Lusanna, Nov. 7, 1758.
Lydia, d. Ezekiel, bp. June 15, 1760. C.R.1.
Lydia, d. Gideon [dup. Gedion] and Elizabeth, Jan. 15, 1791.
Malvina, d. Ephraim L. and Rebecca L., Aug. 31, 1815.
Marcy, d. Ezekiel Jr. and Elizabeth, Jan. 31, 1807.
Mary, d. Gedion and Elizabeth, Aug. 6, 1806.
Mary, d. Gideon, bp. Oct. 2, 1808. C.R.1.
Mary Louisa, w. Fred S. Pratt, Oct. 13, 1848. G.R.6.
Mary Maria, d. Ephraim L. and Rebecca L., Sept. 16, 1819.
Mary Power, ch. Ezekiel and Elizabeth, bp. Sept. 3, 1815. C.R.1.
Mary Thomas, d. Reuben and Abigail, Sept. 19, 1784.
Mehetable, d. Reuben and Abigail, Apr. 25, 1781.
Mercy (see Marcy).
Noah Hatch, s. Stephen Fullerton and Lucy, Nov. 16, 1802.
Patience, d. Joshua and Celia, Aug. 15, 1785.
Pebody, s. Joshua and Celia, July 21, 1789.
Pebody, s. Joshua and Celia, July 9, 1798.
Priscilla, d. George and Mary, Feb. 23, 1732.
Priscilla, d. George, bp. Sept. 2, 1733. C.R.1.
Rebecca Hatch, d. Ephraim L. and Rebecca L., Dec. 27, 1817.
Reuben Bates, s. Reuben and Abigail, Oct. 28, 1782.
Sarah, d. Thomas, Sept. 12, 1695.
Sarah, d. Joseph (Younge) and Lydia, June 10, 1733.
Sarah, d. Thomas, bp. July 31, 1757. C.R.1.
Sarah, d. Tho[ma]s and Jaell, Dec. 2, 1757.
Sarah Farnam, ch. Erastus A. and Mary, Feb. 8, 1829, in Boston.
Sarah Loring, ch. William and Dolly, bp. Nov. 5, 1847. C.R.3.

SCITUATE BIRTHS

YOUNG, Silvenas, s. George and Mary, Apr. 2, 1739. [Silvanus, C.R.1.]
Stephen, s. Stephen Fullerton and Lucy, May 9, 1809.
Stephen Fulerton, s. Ezekel and Lusanna, Dec. 6, 1769.
Stephen Fullington, s. Ezekiel, bp. Sept. 15, 1771. C.R.1.
Susan Maria [———], w. John Henry, —— [1828]. C.R.3.
Thomas, s. Georg, Nov. 5, 1663.
Thomas, s. Thomas, Sept. 29, 1698.
Thomas, s. Thomas, May 18, 1700.
Thomas, s. Tho[ma]s and Jaell, Sept. 20, 1758.
Wales, s. Lucy, Sept. 10, 1765.
William, s. Ezekiel and Lusanna, Feb. 23, 1779.
William, s. Gidion and Elizabeth, Aug. 10, 1800. [ch. Gideon, C.R.1.] [[h. Dolly S. (Pratt)] G.R.6.]
William, s. Gideon W. and Nancy, Mar. 31, 1817, in Charlestown.
Zinthia, d. Joshua and Celia, Nov. 12, 1793.
———, ch. Erastus A. and Mary, June 10, 1835.
———, ch. Erastus A. and Mary, May 4, 1836.

YOUNGE (see Young), Deborah, d. George and Mary, Oct. 6, 1727. [Young, C.R.1.]
Hanah, d. George, May 7, 1666. [Hannah Young, C.R.2.]
Isaac, s. George and Mary, Mar. 15, 1722. [Young, C.R.1.]
James, s. George and Mary, May 22, 1724.
Margrid, d. George, May 17, 1669.
Mary, d. George (Young) and Mary, Jan. 10, 1725. [Young, C.R.1.]
Patience, d. George, Mar. 3, 1673.
Ruben, s. George and Mary, June 17, 1729. [Reuben Young, C.R.1.]
Ruth, d. Joseph and Lydia, Nov. 24, 1729. [Young, C.R.1.]

UNIDENTIFIED.

———, Abagail C., w. —— Barge [July —, 1769]. C.R.1. [Abigail, w. Henry Barge, G.R.2.]
———, Abbie, d. Alvin [Mar. —, 1838]. C.R.3.
———, Abbie W., w. James Damon, ——, 1818. G.R.2.
———, Abiah, w. N. Thomas Esq. of Marshfield, Dec. —, 1721. C.R.1.
———, Abigail, w. Capt. Samuel Turner, ——, 1686. G.R.1.
———, Abigail, w. Israel Bailey, —— [1767]. G.R.6.
———, Abigail (see Abagail C.).
———, Abigail, w. Charles Curtis, —— [1775]. C.R.3.
———, Abigail, w. Hon. Cushing Otis, M.D., —— [1775]. G.R.14.

——, Abigail, w. William Elliot [June —, 1783]. G.R.2.
——, Abigail, w. Elisha Briggs, —— [1786]. G.R.14.
——, Abigail, w. John Vinal, —— [1800]. G.R.2.
——, Abigail F., w. Samuel Tolman, wid. Israel Hatch, —— [1819]. G.R.15.
——, Abigail K., w. Rev. Cyrus Stone, Aug. 28, 1812, in Waterford, Me.
——, Abigail V., w. William Sylvester [Aug. —, 1821]. G.R.14.
——, Alice M., w. George H. Clapp, ——, 1830. G.R.14.
——, Almira, w. Job A. Turner, —— [1814]. G.R.2.
——, Almira, w. Samuel S. Cudworth, July 25, 1820. G.R.2.
——, Amelia, w. Lewis Studley, —— [1794]. G.R.2.
——, Amelia P., w. William Studley, ——, 1812. G.R.14.
——, Angeline J., w. John Albert Smith, ——, 1826. G.R.14.
——, Ann, w. Geo[rge] P. Clapp [May —, 1819]. G.R.15.
——, Anna M. [w. Andrew Stockbridge], —— [1845]. G.R.16.
——, Anna W., w. Charles Clapp, —— [1818]. C.R.3.
——, Anne E., w. Rev. W. H. Fish, ——, 1815. G.R.14.
——, Annie E., w. Franklin Litchfield, ——, 1842. G.R.8.
——, Aphia, w. Caleb Smith, ——, 1800. G.R.14.
——, Arabella, w. Abel Sylvester, ——, 1813. G.R.2.
——, Ariannah G., w. Henry H. Sylvester [Nov. —, 1823]. G.R.2.
——, Arvilla H., w. Shadrach B. Merritt, —— [1800]. G.R.2.
——, Augusta C., w. Philip Foster [Oct. —, 1830]. G.R.14.
——, Barbara, w. John Curran, —— [1842], in Co. Galway, Ire. G.R.10.
——, Belinda, w. Joshua B. Reed, Feb. 15, 1825. G.R.14.
——, Belintha O., w. Charles B. Pratt [Nov. —, 1847]. G.R.2.
——, Benjamin, "a Boy whom Jemima the wife of Capt Israel Vinal brot . . . before the Chh to train up in the nurtured & fear of God," bp. Oct. 14, 1753. C.R.1.
——, Bethia, ——, 1675.
——, Betsey, w. Walter Jacobs [Feb. —, 1778]. G.R.14.
——, Betsey, w. Ebenezer T. Fogg, ——, 1791. G.R.14.
——, Betsey, w. Walter Foster [Dec. —, 1795]. G.R.14.
——, Betsey, w. Zeba Cushing [Mar. —, 1802]. G.R.9.
——, Betsey C., w. Elias Pinson, ——, 1797. G.R.14.
——, Betsey C., w. Harvey Litchfield [Apr. —, 1817]. G.R.9.
——, Betsey G., w. Henry Jackson, —— [1824]. C.R.3.
——, Betsey L., w. Abisha Stetson, ——, 1793. G.R.14.
——, Betsey W., w. William T. Sylvester, ——, 1827. G.R.15.
——, Betsy, w. —— Clapp, —— [1773]. C.R.1. [Betsey w. Leonard, G.R.12.]

―――, Betsy C., w. James Barrell, ――― [1784]. G.R.2.
―――, Caroline, w. Amos W. Merritt, ――― [1836]. G.R.2.
―――, Caroline J., w. George W. Litchfield, Aug. 11, 1845. G.R.8.
―――, Catharine, w. George Tilden [Apr. ―, 1807]. G.R.2.
―――, Catharine, w. William E. Hunt, ―――, 1831. G.R.8.
―――, Catharine, w. Martin Burke, ――― [1834]. G.R.10.
―――, Catharine E., w. ――― Tuttle, ――― [1805]. C.R.1.
―――, Catharine M., w. Asahel F. Nott, ―――, 1833. G.R.2.
―――, Catherine, w. Robert Hall, Oct. 3, 1810. G.R.6.
―――, Catherine, w. Edward Ward, ――― [1820]. G.R.10.
―――, Catherine G., w. Ja[me]s Woodfall [Oct. ―, 1828]. C.R.3.
―――, Catherine H., w. Benjamin Brown Jr., ―――[1831]. C.R.3. [Catharine H., Mar. 3, 1831, G.R.7.]
―――, Celia, w. Eleazar Peakes, ――― [1771]. C.R.3.
―――, Celinda, w. John Lewis, ――― [1812]. G.R.14.
―――, Charlotte, w. Chandler Curtis, ――― [1795]. C.R.1.
―――, Charlotte, w. Harvey Hall, ――― [1805]. C.R.1.
―――, Charlotte, w. Daniel Ward, ――― [1810], in Ballymena, Co. Antrim, Ire. G.R.10.
―――, Charlotte, w. Elias Carr, Oct. 16, 1813. G.R.6.
―――, Charlotte E., wid. Geo[rge] O. Leonard, ――― [1806]. C.R.1.
―――, Clara M., w. Job E. Curtis, June 5, 1849. G.R.2.
―――, Clarissa, w. Jacob Vinal, ――― [1791]. C.R.3.
―――, Clarissa, w. Jacob Vinal, ――― [1796]. C.R.3.
―――, Clarissa, w. John Brown [Oct. ―, 1799]. G.R.2.
―――, Clarissa, w. Francis Merritt, ―――, 1806. G.R.14.
―――, Clarissa, w. Israel H. Sherman [July ―, 1812]. G.R.2.
―――, Cynthia, w. Capt. Daniel Ellms, ――― [1776]. G.R.6.
―――, Cynthia, w. Noah Whitcomb [Aug. ―, 1782]. G.R.8.
―――, Cynthia, w. Anthony Chubuck [Oct. ―, 1798]. G.R.6.
―――, Cynthia B., w. John Dalby [June ―, 1816]. G.R.2.
―――, Debby, w. Martin Merritt, ――― [1797]. C.R.1. [w. Martin D., G.R.11.]
―――, Deborah, w. Caleb Bailey [Nov. ―, 1773]. C.R.1.
―――, Deborah, w. Bartlett Briggs [Oct. ―, 1777]. G.R.6.
―――, Deborah, w. Bennett D. Studley, ―――, 1797. G.R.2.
―――, Deborah, w. Joseph Colman Jr. [Nov. ―, 1802]. C.R.3.
―――, Deborah, w. Nymphas Litchfield, ――― [1805]. G.R.2.
―――, Deborah, w. Joseph Stockbridge [Dec. ―, 1807]. G.R.16.
―――, Deborah, w. Isaiah Hyland, ―――, 1810. G.R.6.
―――, Deborah, w. George Curtis, ――― [1814]. C.R.1.
―――, Deborah, w. Hosea V. Orcutt, ―――, 1817. G.R.2.

―――, Deborah, w. Kilburn D. Merritt, ―――, 1829. G.R.11.
―――, Deborah B., w. Ira [Apr. ―, 1793]. G.R.15.
―――, Deborah C., w. Nath[anie]l Litchfield, ―――, 1786. G.R.6.
―――, Deborah R., w. Jonathan Wright, ――― [1781]. G.R.2.
―――, Deborah T., w. Thomas Gannett, ――― [1796]. G.R.6.
―――, Desire B., w. James N. Sparrell [Sept. ―, 1798]. G.R.14.
―――, Diana, w. Rufus Curtis, ――― [1779]. G.R.6.
―――, Dolly, w. W[illia]m Young [Nov. ―, 1803]. C.R.3.
―――, Electa W., second w. Howard Litchfield [Mar. ―, 1817]. G.R.6.
―――, Elisabeth, w. Jos. Sylvester, ――― [1777]. G.R.15.
―――, Eliza, w. Bernard Litchfield, ――― [1799]. G.R.14.
―――, Eliza, w. Enoch Litchfield, Apr. 29, 1801. G.R.8.
―――, Eliza, w. Alvyen [dup. Alvin] Vinal, ――― [1802]. C.R.3. [w. Alvin, G.R.7.]
―――, Eliza, w. ――― Straw, ――― [1806]. C.R.1.
―――, Eliza, w. Robert Cook, ――― [1817]. G.R.6.
―――, Eliza, w. Nicholas Wherity, Sept. 13, 1831. G.R.10.
―――, Eliza C., w. David S. Jenkins, ――― [1804]. C.R.3.
―――, Eliza J., w. John McKee, ――― [1827]. G.R.15.
―――, Eliza L., w. Dexter Vinal, Apr. 20, 1802. G.R.11.
―――, Eliza L., w. Samuel C. Cudworth, ―――, 1819. G.R.14.
―――, Elizabeth, w. David Little, Sept. 29, 1686. P.R.1.
―――, Elizabeth, w. Caleb Jenkins, ――― [1763]. G.R.6.
―――, Elizabeth (see Elisabeth).
―――, Elizabeth, w. Ebenezer Osborne, ――― [1781]. G.R.2.
―――, Elizabeth, w. Samuel Hyland, ――― [1807]. G.R.8.
―――, Elizabeth, w. John Gardner Jr. [Aug. ―, 1824]. G.R.15.
―――, Elizabeth, w. Liba Litchfield, ―――, 1824. G.R.14.
―――, Elizabeth F., w. William E. Potter [Feb. ―, 1812]. G.R.14.
―――, Elizabeth R., w. William H. Merritt, ―――, 1822. G.R.14.
―――, Elizabeth W., w. ――― Osborn, ――― [1782]. C.R.1.
―――, Elizabeth W., w. Reuben Griggs, Mar. 22, 1819. G.R.14.
―――, Ellen M., w. John A. Merritt [Sept. ―, 1831]. G.R.11.
―――, Ellen M., w. John F. Otis, ―――, 1832. G.R.14.
―――, Emily, w. Dea. James L. Merritt [Apr. ―, 1795]. G.R.2.
―――, Emily S., w. Joseph Brown, Jan. 31, 1819. G.R.2.
―――, Esther [w. Capt. John Mack], ―――, 1769. G.R.6.
―――, Esther A., w. Bardin H. Prouty, Nov. 6, 1825. G.R.2.
―――, Eunice A., w. Samuel Loring, Aug. 8, 1841. G.R.19.
―――, Eunice T., w. Liba Studley, ――― [1804]. C.R.3. G.R.2.
―――, Fanny, w. Dennis McCarthy, ―――, 1832. G.R.10.
―――, Fanny E., w. James Merritt, ―――, 1828. G.R.14.

SCITUATE BIRTHS

———, Faustina D., w. Charles B. Pratt, ——— [1849]. G.R.2.
———, Francis M., w. M. H. Litchfield, ——— [1811]. C.R.1.
———, Georgia W., w. B. T. Manson [Oct. —, 1832]. G.R.6.
———, Georgianna, w. Benj[amin] Manson, ——— [1832]. C.R.1.
———, Hannah, w. ——— Rose [Feb. —, 1763]. C.R.3. G.R.2.
———, Hannah, w. Col. Cha[rle]s Turner, ——— [dup. [Apr. —]] [1763]. C.R.3.
———, Hannah, w. Capt. Nathaniel, ——— [1769]. G.R.2.
———, Hannah, w. Daniel Litchfield [Feb. —, 1785]. G.R.8.
———, Hannah, w. Col. John Jacobs, Dec. 18, 1788. G.R.14.
———, Hannah, w. James W. Warner, Aug. 5, 1805. G.R.19.
———, Hannah, w. Theodore Clement, ——— [1807]. C.R.1.
———, Hannah, w. Coleman Tilden, ——— [1810]. C.R.1.
———, Hannah, w. Sumner F. Barrett, ——— [1811]. C.R.1.
———, Hannah, w. Capt. Chandler Clapp, ———, 1817. G.R.6.
———, Hannah B., w. Eleazer Hatch, ——— [1794]. G.R.14.
———, Hannah B., w. Timothy B. Chapman, ———, 1835. G.R.19.
———, Hannah C., w. Benjamin Turner, ——— [1800]. G.R.14.
———, Hannah C., w. Chandler Clapp, ——— [1818]. C.R.1.
———, Hannah C., w. Benjamin P. Nichols, Nov. 4, 1844. G.R.19.
———, Hannah E., w. Geo[rge] M. Allen, ———, 1807. G.R.6.
———, Hannah M., w. Samuel D. Stetson, ———, 1820. G.R.15.
———, Hannah S., w. John Damon, ——— [1816]. G.R.2.
———, Hannah W., w. Thomas Tilden Bailey, ———, 1798. G.R.2.
———, Harriet, w. ——— Clapp [Aug. —, 1801]. C.R.3.
———, Harriet, w. Monro Merritt, ——— [1824]. C.R.3.
———, Harriet C., w. Elijah Clapp, ——— [1802]. C.R.3.
———, Harriet E., w. Leonard L. Perry [Apr. —, 1824]. C.R.3.
———, Harriet T., w. Lewis N. Curtis, ——— [1822]. C.R.3.
———, Harriet T., w. Melzar S. Turner [Nov. —, 1830]. G.R.6.
———, Henrietta E., w. Amos Litchfield [Aug. —, 1846]. G.R.14.
———, Huldah, w. Gad Leavitt, ——— [1767]. G.R.15.
———, Jane H., w. Peleg T. Brown [Sept. —, 1838]. G.R.2.
———, Jane S., w. Jacob Whitcomb [June —, 1796]. G.R.8.
———, Jane T., w. John Beal [Nov. —, 1794]. G.R.6.
———, Jerusha, w. Franklin Damon, ———, 1820. G.R.6.
———, Joan, w. Levi Newcomb, [Mar. —, 1802]. G.R.2.
———, Joan M., w. Anson Witherell, Sept. 20, 1806. G.R.6.
———, Joanna, w. Abiel Cudworth [Oct. —, 1784]. G.R.2.
———, Joanna, w. Lewis Raymond, Nov. 27, 1809. G.R.14.
———, Joanna W., w. ——— Prouty, ——— [1779]. C.R.1.
———, Joseph, s. Joseph, ——— [1799]. C.R.3.
———, Judith, w. John Briggs Jr., May 4, 1754.

——, Judith, w. Levi Vinal 2d, —— [1772]. C.R.3.
——, Judith, w. Levi Vinal, —— [1792]. C.R.3.
——, Judith A., w. Hatherly Merritt, —— [? 1837]. C.R.3.
——, Judith C., w. Amos Albee, —— [1784]. G.R.2.
——, Julia, w. —— Sears, —— [1811]. C.R.3.
——, Julia, w. Frederic Stanley [May —, 1844]. G.R.10.
——, Julia Ann, w. George B. Litchfield, —— [1842]. G.R.2.
——, Julia F., w. William Brown [Jan. —, 1804]. G.R.8.
——, Laura, w. John —— [Nov. —, 1812]. C.R.3.
——, Laura, d. John, —— [1844]. C.R.3.
——, Lilles H., w. Abel Sylvester, —— [1786]. G.R.18.
——, Lois L., w. Samuel Ellms, —— [1775]. G.R.8.
——, Louisa J., w. George B. Hayden, ——, 1835. G.R.14.
——, Louisa P., w. —— Hobart, —— [1822]. C.R.3.
——, Lucinda, w. Daniel T. Hunt, —— [1823]. G.R.15.
——, Lucretia, w. George K. Cushing, —— [1769]. G.R.14.
——, Lucy, w. Melzar Stoddard, —— [1762]. G.R.15.
——, Lucy, w. Lewis Studley, —— [1769]. G.R.2.
——, Lucy, w. Ensign Otis Jr., ——, 1782. G.R.6.
——, Lucy, w. William Studley, ——, 1785. G.R.14.
——, Lucy, w. John Briggs, —— [1787]. G.R.2.
——, Lucy, w. Elijah Cudworth [May —, 1792]. G.R.14.
——, Lucy, w. Charles Brown [Mar. —, 1793]. G.R.8.
——, Lucy, w. Charles Brown, —— [1802]. C.R.3.
——, Lucy, w. Freeman Litchfield, —— [1805]. C.R.3. [—— [1803], G.R.8.]
——, Lucy, w. Bailey Merritt [Feb. —, 1807]. G.R.2.
——, Lucy, w. —— Merritt, —— [1808]. C.R.1.
——, Lucy, w. Luther Damon [July —, 1809]. G.R.14.
——, Lucy, w. Harrison Wilder, Dec. 17, 1810. G.R.14.
——, Lucy, w. —— Nutter, —— [1820]. C.R.1.
——, Lucy, w. Allen Merritt [Sept. —, 1828]. C.R.1.
——, Lucy E., w. William Dorr [May —, 1848]. G.R.14.
——, Lucy P., w. Elijah Peirce [Oct. —, 1799]. G.R.2.
——, Lucy P., w. Aaron Sawyer, July 29, 1805. G.R.19.
——, Lucy S., w. Waters B. Barker [Oct. —, 1820]. G.R.15.
——, Lucy S., w. George P. Fogg, ——, 1828. G.R.14.
——, Lucy V., w. Ozias Clapp [July —, 1832]. G.R.6.
——, Lucy W., w. Capt. Ezekiel Jones, —— [1789]. G.R.6.
——, Lydia, w. James Little, ——, 1756. G.R.6.
——, Lydia, w. Tho[ma]s Barstow, ——, 1757. G.R.15.
——, Lydia, w. Amos Merritt [Aug. —, 1762]. C.R.1.
——, Lydia, w. Dea. Amos Merritt, —— [1767]. G.R.2.
——, Lydia, w. Abner Litchfield, —— [1773]. G.R.8.

——, Lydia, w. Capt. Anthony Waterman [Aug. —, 1794]. G.R.6.
——, Lydia, w. Samuel Turner, Sept. 13, 1796. G.R.14.
——, Lydia, w. ——— Chubbuck, —— [1800]. C.R.1.
——, Lydia, w. Job Otis, ——, 1808. G.R.6.
——, Lydia A., w. Austin Damon [Mar. —, 1825]. G.R.15.
——, Lydia B., w. Lewis Brown, ——, 1819. G.R.2.
——, Lydia Frances, w. Albert S. Greene, Mar. 8, 1841. G.R.15.
——, Lydia J., w. Capt. Henry F. Vinal, Feb. 5, 1809. G.R.6.
——, Lydia Y., w. Dr. Elisha James, —— [1790]. C.R.3.
——, Mabel, w. [dup. adds Dea.] Israel Cudworth, —— [1795]. C.R.3.
——, Marcy, w. ——— Tilden, —— [1771]. C.R.1. [w. Capt. John, G.R.6.]
——, Margaret, w. Capt. Benjamin Brown, Feb. 25, 1805. G.R.9.
——, Margarette P., second w. Capt. Perez Jenkins, Apr. 20, 1824. G.R.6.
——, Maria, w. Eaton Vinal, —— [1812]. G.R.6.
——, Maria F., w. Ward L. Hayward, ——, 1839. G.R.7.
——, Maria P., w. John B. Turner [Nov. —, 1822]. G.R.2.
——, Maria W., w. Gridley Bryant, Dec. 15, 1794. G.R.2.
——, Marion L., w. Tho[ma]s F. Bailey [Nov. —, 1840]. C.R.3.
——, Martha, w. ——— Litchfield, —— [1804]. C.R.1. [w. William, G.R.2.]
——, Martha, w. ——— Merritt, —— [1807]. C.R.1.
——, Martha, w. G. H. Damon, —— [1827]. C.R.1.
——, Martha Ann, w. John P. Cushing, —— [1848]. G.R.2.
——, Martha H., w. Dr. W[illia]m Gordak [Aug. —, 1805]. G.R.11.
——, Martha J., w. Hosea Damon, ——, 1823. G.R.14.
——, Mary, w. Col. Amos Turner, ——, 1667. G.R.1.
——, Mary, w. Samuel Gannett, —— [1770]. G.R.2.
——, Mary, w. Seth Stoddard, —— [1776]. G.R.16.
——, Mary, w. Heman Holmes, —— [1777]. C.R.3.
——, Mary, w. Ichabod Cook [Nov. —, 1779]. G.R.2.
——, Mary, w. ——— Wall, —— [1781]. C.R.3.
——, Mary, w. Ambrose Cole, —— [1782]. C.R.1.
——, Mary, w. Christopher Stetson, Apr. 10, 1785. G.R.14.
——, Mary, w. Daniel Otis, Feb. —, 1787, in New Bedford. C.R.4.
——, Mary, w. Abraham Harris, —— [1788]. G.R.14.
——, Mary, w. Samuel Stetson, —— [1793]. G.R.15.
——, Mary, w. Daniel Noonan, —— [1796], in Killeen, Co. Galway, Ire. G.R.10.

——, Mary, w. Amasa Palmer, —— [1804]. G.R.15.
——, Mary, w. Jeremiah L. Emerson, Jan. 23, 1808. G.R.2.
——, Mary, w. Thomas Flynn, —— [1817]. G.R.10.
——, Mary, w. Howland L. Studley [Sept. —, 1821]. G.R.2.
——, Mary, w. Capt. W[illia]m H. Talbot, —— [1821]. G.R.14.
——, Mary, w. O. Merritt, July 30, 1828. G.R.6.
——, Mary, w. Henry Mott, —— [1837]. G.R.2.
——, Mary, w. Daniel Broughton, —— [1842]. G.R.10.
——, Mary, w. Daniel Doherty [Nov. —, 1846]. G.R.10.
——, Mary A., w. John D. Torrey, —— [1802]. C.R.3.
——, Mary A., w. Peleg Ford [Jan. —, 1809]. G.R.5.
——, Mary A., w. Charles Wilder [July —, 1811]. G.R.14.
——, Mary A., w. Caleb Osborne, —— [1821]. C.R.3.
——, Mary A., w. James W. Studley, Nov. 21, 1837. G.R.15.
——, Mary Ann, w. Noah C. Bailey, ——, 1808. G.R.2.
——, Mary Ann, w. Josiah Stoddard, May 4, 1817. G.R.15.
——, Mary Ann, w. William Hatch [May —, 1817]. G.R.14.
——, Mary Anna P. [dup. Perkins], w. Rev. Daniel Wight [Apr. —, 1816]. C.R.3.
——, Mary C., w. Job E. Curtis, Nov. 23, 1845. G.R.2.
——, Mary E., w. Bartlett Hayden, —— [1833]. G.R.14.
——, Mary E., w. J. S. Barker [Jan. —, 1839]. G.R.15.
——, Mary E., w. Edw[ard] F. Freeman, ——, 1841. G.R.14.
——, Mary Eliza, w. Samuel H. Turner, ——, 1819. G.R.6.
——, Mary F., w. Sam[ue]l Stoddard, —— [1819]. C.R.3. [Mary F. L., Apr. 16, 1818, G.R.8.]
——, Mary Frances, w. A[lanson] A. C. Gilbert [May —, 1841]. G.R.2.
——, Mary H., w. Milo Kellogg, —— [1800]. G.R.14.
——, Mary J., w. Peleg Hyland, ——, 1820. G.R.8.
——, Mary L., w. Perez Litchfield [Aug. —, 1796]. G.R.6.
——, Mary L., w. John Stockbridge [Mar. —, 1831]. G.R.16.
——, Mary M., w. W[illia]m E. Hunt, —— [1819]. G.R.11.
——, Mary P., w. Norton Curtis [Sept.—,1813]. C.R.3.
——, Mary P., w. Stephen Benson, —— [1827]. G.R.14.
——, Mary S., w. C. L. Litchfield, ——, 1818. G.R.6.
——, Mary S., w. A. A. C. Gilbert [Oct. —, 1828]. C.R.1.
——, Mary T., w. —— Baker, —— [1776]. C.R.1.
——, Mary T., w. E. R. Mungo [May —, 1798]. G.R.2.
——, Mary T., w. Oliver P. Hayes, May 23, 1825. G.R.2.
——, Mary T., w. Henry J. Turner, ——, 1827. G.R.14.
——, Mary V., w. Russel [dup. Dea. Russell] Cook [Sept. —, 1807 [dup. 1806]]. C.R.3.
——, Mary W., w. Stephen Litchfield [July —, 1800]. G.R.2.

——, Matilda F., w. Darius Harrub [Feb. —, 1815]. C.R.3.
——, Matty [Matthew], s. Winsor and Content, bp. Aug. 24, 1746. C.R.1.
——, Mehitable, w. Samuel Hyland, —— [1788]. G.R.8.
——, Mercey, w. Joseph Brown, —— [1777]. G.R.8.
——, Mercie, w. Samuel Hatch [Mar. —, 1786]. G.R.4.
——, Mercy (see Marcy).
——, Mercy, w. Stephen Mott [Sept. —, 1779]. G.R.11.
——, Mercy [w. Joseph Vinal], July 22, 1800. P.R.26.
——, Mercy A., w. David S. Jenkins [May —, 1838]. G.R.6.
——, Mercy B., w. Charles Stockbridge, ——, 1821. G.R.16.
——, Mercy G., w. Allen Clapp [Mar. —, 1800]. G.R.8.
——, Mercy J., w. Joseph Gannett Jr., —— [1814]. G.R.2.
——, Mercy V., w. Joseph Bates, Feb. 10, 1811. G.R.6.
——, Mercy W., w. Isaiah Alden [Jan. —, 1799]. G.R.6.
——, Meriel, w. Abel A. Vinal [Apr. —, 1808]. G.R.14.
——, Myra L., w. —— Wade, —— [1832]. C.R.3.
——, Nabby, wid. Amos Tilden [Dec. —, 1785]. C.R.1.
——, Nancy, w. Daniel Hatch, —— [1777]. G.R.2.
——, Nancy, w. Geo[rge] Cushing, —— [1782]. C.R.3. [[June —, 1782] G.R.14.]
——, Nancy, w. Nathaniel Ellms, Sept. 18, 1800. G.R.14.
——, Nancy, w. Thomas O. Hayden, July 30, 1845. G.R.7.
——, Nancy L., w. George H. Briggs [Apr. —, 1820]. G.R.14.
——, Nancy O., w. Joseph H. Brown [July —, 1849]. G.R.2.
——, Olive L., w. Israel M. Barnes, Dec. 31, 1820. G.R.8.
——, Olive S., w. Tho[ma]s Waterman, ——, 1795. G.R.15.
——, Patience V., w. Jesse D. Hutchinson, ——, 1812. G.R.7.
——, Patience Vinal, w. Edward Brown, —— [1841]. C.R.3.
——, Penelope, w. Tilden L. Clapp, —— [1805]. G.R.14.
——, Phebe, w. Stephen Bartlett, Feb. 21, 1802.
——, Philenda D., w. Gera J. Ford [May —, 1819]. G.R.14.
——, Phillippa, w. Christopher Tilden, —— [1809]. C.R.1.
——, Polly, w. Elisha Coleman, —— [1783]. C.R.1.
——, Polly, w. —— Tirrell, "formerly" w. David Pettis, —— [1800]. G.R.2.
——, Priscilla, w. —— Hayes, —— [1793]. C.R.1. [Pricilla, w. Jonathan, G.R.2.]
——, Rachel, w. Lawrence Litchfield, Sept. 5, 1758. P.R.19.
——, Rachel, w. Capt. Simeon Bates, —— [1765]. G.R.6.
——, Rachel, w. Perkins Clapp, —— [1783]. G.R.14.
——, Rachel, w. Bailey Jenkins, ——, 1787. G.R.14.
——, Rachel, "former" w. Dea. Howard White [Dec. —, 1792]. G.R.6.

——, Rebecca, w. John Mann [Oct. —, 1769]. G.R.6.
——, Rebecca, w. Lawrence Litchfield, —— [1775]. C.R.1.
——, Rebecca, w. Rufus Litchfield, —— [1779]. C.R.3.
——, Rebecca, w. Waterman Bailey [Mar. —, 1796]. G.R.2.
——, Rebecca, w. Abiel Turner [Mar. —, 1802]. G.R.14.
——, Rhoda, w. Archibald Mitchell, —— [1775]. G.R.2.
——, Ruth [w. Capt. Nehemiah Randall], ——, 1770. G.R.14.
——, Ruth, w. John Gardner, Dec. 7, 1801. G.R.15.
——, Ruth, w. Israel Nichols, June —, 1809. G.R.6.
——, Ruth T., w. Harris Damon [Dec. —, 1794]. G.R.14.
——, Sally, w. Ensign Merritt, —— [1783]. G.R.6.
——, Sally, w. Elijah Damon, ——, 1784. G.R.14.
——, Sally, w. —— James, —— [1786]. G.R.6. [w. Dea. Joshua, G.R.14.]
——, Sally, w. William Wise [Oct. —, 1791]. G.R.14.
——, Sally, w. Augustus Cole, —— [1791]. C.R.3.
——, Sally, w. Capt. John C. Jones [Oct. —, 1802]. G.R.6.
——, Sally C., w. Capt. Perez Pinson [Aug. —, 1789]. G.R.14.
——, Sally F., w. Isaac H. Haskins [Mar. —, 1816]. G.R.15.
——, Sally G., w. Perez Turner [Aug. —, 1807]. G.R.14.
——, Sarah, d. Henry and Marget, bp. Apr. 3, 1743. C.R.1.
——, Sarah, w. Lemuel Vinal [Oct. —, 1785]. G.R.6.
——, Sarah, w. Consider Glass, ——, 1795. G.R.6.
——, Sarah, w. Luther Curtis, ——, 1806. G.R.6.
——, Sarah A., w. William H. Tilden, ——, 1807. G.R.14.
——, Sarah A., w. George W. Leavitt [Jan. —, 1828]. G.R.14.
——, Sarah A., w. Jerome H. Sawyer, May 18, 1829. G.R.19.
——, Sarah A. M. (see ——, ——).
——, Sarah B., w. David Stockbridge [Nov. —, 1794]. G.R.15.
——, Sarah B., w. Philip D. Minot, —— [1812]. G.R.2.
——, Sarah B., w. William Mayo, —— [1816]. G.R.8.
——, Sarah E., w. William H. Litchfield, May 31, 1828. G.R.8.
——, Sarah E., w. John H. Turner, ——, 1834. G.R.14.
——, Sarah F., w. L. Albert Tilden, —— [1803]. G.R.14.
——, Sarah H., w. Washington Lee [Oct. —, 1782]. G.R.2.
——, Sarah H., w. —— Vinal [Jan. —, 1821]. C.R.3.
——, Sarah L., w. Charles H. Seaverns [Feb. —, 1808]. G.R.2.
——, Sarah L., w. Jesse D. Hutchinson, —— [1822]. C.R.3. [——, 1823, G.R.7.]
——, Sarah L., w. Samuel W. Cook, —— [1823]. G.R.2.
——, Sarah M., w. Joseph H. Harvey, Jan. 24, 1833. G.R.2.
——, Sarah M., w. George H. Sylvester [Nov. —, 1836]. G.R.2.
——, Sarah V., w. James T. Bailey, Apr. 30, 1835. G.R.2.
——, Sarah W., w. Capt. John Otis [Dec. —, 1799]. G.R.6.

——, Sarah W., w. Charles Tolman, w. Samuel Tolman, May 26, 1820. G.R.15.
——, Sebre, w. Elisha Merritt, —— [1782]. C.R.1.
——, Selina C., w. Perry L. Parker [Nov. —, 1824]. G.R.9.
——, Sophia, w. Tho[ma]s Litchfield, —— [1787]. C.R.3.
——, Sophia, w. Nathaniel Mayo, —— [1795]. G.R.2.
——, Sophia, w. [dup. adds Dea.] Marshall Litchfield, —— [1798]. C.R.3.
——, Sophia J., w. William Damon, May 5, 1821. G.R.2.
——, Sophia L., w. Howard L. Litchfield, —— [1810]. C.R.1.
——, Stella, w. Rev. Samuel Deane, —— [1787]. G.R.14.
——, Susan, w. James T. Barce, ——, 1848. G.R.7.
——, Susan B., w. Rogers Stetson, Nov. 24, 1816. G.R.15.
——, Susan M., w. Caleb Bailey [Apr. —, 1806]. G.R.2.
——, Susan Maria, w. John Henry Young, —— [1828]. C.R.3.
——, Susan N., w. Caleb Bailey [Apr. —, 1806]. G.R.2.
——, Susan S., w. George W. Stetson, Nov. 2, 1808. G.R.14.
——, Susan W., w. Joseph E. Corlew, M.D., ——, 1823. G.R.14.
——, Temprance, w. Meshach Litchfield, —— [1794]. G.R.16.
——, Thankful [w. —— Stodder] [mother of Rebecca Bates (w. Abial Turner)] [July —, 1785]. P.R.25.
——, Tryphosa, w. Benj[amin] R. Jacobs, —— [1792]. G.R.14.
——, Vesta, w. David Torrey [Apr. —, 1790]. G.R.14.
——, Welthea, w. William James [Aug. —, 1792]. G.R.14.
——, ——, w. —— Briggs, —— [1753]. C.R.1.
——, ——, wid. —— Jenkins, —— [1761]. C.R.1.
——, ——, w. Joab Litchfield, —— [1761]. C.R.1.
——, ——, wid. Cornelius Bates, —— [1765]. C.R.1.
——, ——, w. —— Mann, —— [1770]. C.R.1.
——, ——, wid. Lewis Studley, —— [1770]. C.R.1.
——, ——, mother of Israel Nichols, —— [1775]. C.R.3.
——, ——, w. Samuel Holbrook, —— [1783]. C.R.1.
——, ——, w. Lemuel Vinal, —— [1786]. C.R.1.
——, ——, w. Harvey Litchfield, —— [1795]. C.R.3.
——, ——, w. —— Nash, ——, 1797. G.R.6.
——, ——, w. Tilden Ames, —— [1798]. C.R.1.
——, ——, w. Otis Ellms, —— [1798]. C.R.1.
——, ——, wid. —— Reed, —— [1799]. C.R.1.
——, ——, w. Otis Pierce, —— [1800]. C.R.1.
——, ——, w. Lincoln Litchfield [Apr. —, 1803]. C.R.1.
——, ——, w. —— Tewsbury, —— [1803]. C.R.1.
——, ——, w. —— Jordan, —— [1804]. C.R.1.
——, ——, w. S. B. Weatherbee, —— [1805]. C.R.1.
——, ——, ch. Prince and w., bp. June 4, 1808. C.R.2.

——, ——, w. Geo[rge] W. Brown, —— [1815]. C.R.1.
——, ——, w. —— Chubuck, —— [1816]. C.R.1.
——, ——, w. Freeman Vinal [Jan. —, 1821]. C.R.3. [Sarah A. M., Dec. 15, 1820, G.R.7.]
——, ——, w. Nichols Curtis, —— [1822]. C.R.3.
——, ——, w. James Vinal (s. Tho[ma]s), —— [1823]. C.R.3.
——, ——, w. S. A. Simmons, —— [1825]. C.R.1.
——, ——, w. Lewis Studley Jr., —— [1828]. C.R.1.
——, ——, w. —— Nash, ——, 1832. G.R.6.
——, ——, w. W. J. Powell, —— [1841]. C.R.1.

NEGROES, ETC.

Abel, s. Henry "Serv* to M* Jacob Lyncoln" and Margaret "Serv* to M* Edward Jenkins," bp. Apr. 25, 1742. C.R.1.
Absolom, s. Cesar "Serv* to Cap* Torry," bp. Oct. 22, 1738. C.R.2.
Andrew, s. Jesse, bp. May 30, 1756. C.R.1.
Asher, s. Philis "Slave to Doc* Otis," bp. June 2, 1754. C.R.2.
Betty, ch. Philis "Negro Slave to Dr. Otis," bp. Sept. 3, 1749. C.R.2.
Bristol, s. Bristol "Serv* to Cap* Barker" and Judith, bp. Nov. 22, 1741. C.R.1.
Bristol, s. Chess, bp. Sept. 9, 1750. C.R.1.
Britain, s. Winser and Jenny "Serv* to Cap* Barker," bp. Oct. 7, 1739. C.R.1.
Candice, "Serv* to Ebenezer Baily," bp. Nov. 19, 1752. C.R.1.
Cesar, "negro Serv* Child of Joshua Young Baptized in S*, youngs House being dangerously Sick & S*, youngs wife promising to Educated in y* Fear & ways of y* D——," bp. Jan. 15, 1739. C.R.1.
Charles, s. Cuffee and Flora, bp. Mar. 24, 1744. C.R.1.
Chloe, d. Windsor "Servant to Job Otis," bp. Sept. 4, 1768. C.R.1.
Coffee, "Serv* child of Job Cowing," bp. Apr. 9, 1753. C.R.1.
Cuffee, s. Cuffee and Flora, negroes, bp. Mar. 27, 1743. C.R.1.
Dinah, d. Coffee and Flora, bp. Aug. 26, 1753. C.R.1.
Elisabeth, d. Cesar "negro Servant . . . , to Capt Torry" and Sarah "free Indian woman," bp. Aug. 28, 1748. C.R.2.
Friday, negro, s. Trany "Negro Woman," Mar. 4, 1796.
Grace, negro, d. Meriah, Mar. 20, 1712–13.
Henery, s. Henry "Serv* to Jacob Lincoln," bp. June 1, 1746, C.R.1.
Hittee, ch. "M*: Bar: Littles Negro Woman," bp. June 19, 1774. C.R.1.

Issachar, s. "Cesar Negro and Sarah; Indn," bp. Sept. 28, 1746. c.r.2.
Jane, d. Jesse, bp. May 30, 1756. c.r.1.
Jenny, d. Winser, bp. Oct. 14, 1753. c.r.1.
Jess, s. Jess and Priscilla, bp. Aug. 23, 1752. c.r.1.
Judith, d. Chess "Servt to M.^r Js: Baily" and Priscilla "[Servant] to Mr Joshua Otis," bp. July 22, 1744. c.r.1.
Katherine, ch. Cuba "Negro Slave to Mr Isaac Turner," bp. May 26, 1745. c.r.2.
Katy, d. Delly "Servt to Capt David Clap," bp. Oct. 10, 1742. c.r.1.
Lebeus, s. Sambo "free Negro," bp. Apr. 26, 1752. c.r.2.
Luke, s. Winser, bp. June 3, 1759. c.r.1.
Lusanna, negro, d. Cesar "Slave to Capt Caleb Torry," bp. Dec. 11, 1743. c.r.2.
Mark, s. Philis "Negro Servant of Deacon Joseph Cushing Junr," bp. [July] 16, 1753. c.r.2.
Mary, negro, d. Meriah, May 4, 1708.
Mercy, d. "to a negro of Dr Otis," bp. May 23, 1756. c.r.2.
Olive, ch. Philis "Negro Slave to Dr. Otis," bp. Sept. 3, 1749. c.r.2.
Patience, d. Winser, bp. Sept. 9, 1750. c.r.1.
Patience, d. Winsor "Servant of Job Otis," bp. May 15, 1763. c.r.1.
Patte, d. Ann "negro Servant to Galen Clap," Mar. 18, 1772.
Peggy, d. Delly "Servt to Capt David Clap," bp. Oct. 10, 1742. c.r.1.
Peggy, d. Winser, bp. May 23, 1756. c.r.1.
Phebe, d. Ann "negro Servant to Galen Clap," Nov. 20, 1769.
Phillis, "negro Servt child of Col.^o Turner," bp. June 8, 1735. c.r.1.
Prudence, d. Chess "Servt to Israel Baily," bp. June 26, 1743. c.r.1.
Reubin, s. Coffe and Flora, bp. Nov. 20, 1748. c.r.1.
Richard, ch. Cuba "Negro Slave to m.^r Isaac Turner," bp. May 5, 1745. c.r.2.
Robert, s. Winser, bp. July 15, 1744. c.r.1.
Robert, s. Winser, bp. May 14, 1749. c.r.1.
Ruben, ch. Philis "Negro Slave to Dr. Otis," bp. Sept. 3, 1749. c.r.2.
Ruth, d. Anthony and Phebie, bp. June 28, 1724. c.r.2.
Simeon, s. Coffy, bp. June 23, 1751. c.r.1.
Susanna, d. Henry and Margaret, bp. July 1, 1744. c.r.1.
Susanna, d. Chess, bp. Oct. 30, 1748. c.r.1.
Tamar, d. Cesar and Sarah, bp. Sept. 23, 1744. c.r.2.

Tamar, d. Henery, bp. Sept. 2, 1753. c.r.1.
Thomas, ch. Cuba "Negro Slave to m⁣ʳ Isaac Turner," bp. May 5 1745. c.r.2.
William, s. Sambo "free Negro" and Martha "Indian," bp. Oct. 14, 1750. c.r.2.
Windsor, s. Windsor "Servant to Job Otis," bp. Oct. 7, 1764. c.r.1.
Winser, s. Winser and Jenny "Servᵗ to Capᵗ Barker," bp. Oct. 7, 1739. c.r.1.
Winser, s. Winser "Servᵗ to Mʳ Job Otis," bp. Mar. 28, 1741. c.r.1.
Winsor, s. Winsor and Jenny, bp. May 1, 1743. c.r.1.
Zilpah, d. Phillis, bp. July 19, 1752. c.r.1.
Zilpah, d. Chess, bp. June 1, 1760. c.r.1.

www.ingramcontent.com/pod-product-compliance
Lightning Source LLC
Chambersburg PA
CBHW030540080526
44585CB00012B/210